TAKING SIDES

Clashing Views in

Constitutional Law

FIRST EDITION

D0032395

TAKING SIDES

Clashing Views in
Constitutional Law

FIRST EDITION

Selected, Edited, and with Introductions by

Thomas J. Hickey
State University of New York (SUNY Cobleskill)

Connect
Learn
Succeed™

TAKING SIDES: CLASHING VIEWS IN CONSTITUTIONAL LAW, FIRST EDITION

Taking Sides is published by the **Contemporary Learning Series** group within the McGraw-Hill Higher Education division.

1 2 3 4 5 6 7 8 9 0 DOC/DOC 1 0 9 8 7 6 5 4 3 2 1 0

MHID: 0-07-805079-0
ISBN: 978-0-07-805079-4
ISSN: 1098-5395

Managing Editor: *Larry Loeppke*
Senior Developmental Editor: *Jade Benedict*
Permissions Coordinator: *DeAnna Dausener*
Senior Marketing Communications Specialist: *Mary Klein*
Marketing Coordinator: *Alice Link*
Project Manager: *Erin Melloy*
Design Coordinator: *Brenda A. Rolwes*
Cover Graphics: *Rick D. Noel*

Compositor: MPS Limited, a Macmillan Company
Cover Image: © Getty Images/RF

Editors/Academic Advisory Board

Members of the Academic Advisory Board are instrumental in the final selection of articles for each edition of *TAKING SIDES*. Their review of articles for content, level, and appropriateness provides critical direction to the editors and staff. We think that you will find their careful consideration well reflected in this volume.

TAKING SIDES: Clashing Views in Constitutional Law

First Edition

EDITOR

Thomas J. Hickey
State University of New York (SUNY Cobleskill)

ACADEMIC ADVISORY BOARD MEMBERS

Editors/Academic Advisory Board continued

Preface

> *But the peculiar evil of silencing the expression of an opinion is that it is rob-*
> *bing the human race, posterity as well as the existing generation—those who*
> *dissent from the opinion, still more than those who hold it. If the opinion is*
> *right, they are deprived of the opportunity of exchanging error for truth; if*
> *wrong, they lose, what is almost as great a benefit, the clearer perception and*
> *livelier impression of truth produced by its collision with error.*

—John Stuart Mill, *On Liberty,* 1859

Discussion and debate are essential components of the learning process. To have confidence in our viewpoints, we must expose them to others and learn from others' ideas in a constant process of reformulation and refinement. As J.S. Mill teaches, only rarely does any point of view present a complete version of the truth; however, we move closer to the truth when we are willing to exchange our opinions with others, defend our positions, and refine our ideas by what we learn from an intellectual opponent.

This book presents students and teachers with an opportunity to exchange viewpoints by focusing on a series of controversial issues in constitutional law. Few issues in modern society generate more substantial disagreement in our morning newspapers or around the dinner table. The issues focus on an important aspect of life in the United States and were selected in an effort to engage students. Hopefully, they will also generate classroom discussion and debate and provide a vehicle for interactive learning.

Many of the topics presented in this volume are hotly contested. Few reflective people will find themselves adopting truly neutral positions on these issues, and there may be a tendency to embrace one side of a debate without fully considering the opposing arguments. As you read these materials, try to resist that temptation and keep an open mind. For example, if you are an advocate for a woman's right to obtain a lawful abortion, think about how you would develop an argument if you were an abortion opponent. Even though such an exercise may not change your views, it will provide you with greater insight into the abortion debate.

Organization of the book This book considers 20 issues in constitutional law and includes 40 articles presented in a pro and con format. The Introduction to each issue presents a synopsis and sets the stage for the Yes and No debate between the authors. All issues conclude with a Postscript that considers some of the more important points in the debate and includes up-to-date suggestions for further reading on the topics. In addition, the *Internet References* page that accompanies each unit provides a list of Internet site addresses (URLs) that will serve as a guide for additional research.

A word to the instructor An *Instructor's Resource Guide with Test Questions* (multiple-choice and essay) is available from the publisher for instructors using *Taking Sides* in their courses. A guidebook, *Using Taking Sides in the Classroom,* which considers methods and techniques for integrating the pro-con format into a classroom setting is available as well. An online version of *Using Taking Sides in the Classroom* and a correspondence service for adopters can be found at http://www.mhcls.com/takingsides/.

Acknowledgements I would like to thank several of my friends and colleagues for their help and support: Rolando V. del Carmen, Sue Titus Reid, Alisa Smith, Dick Ayre, John P. Matthews, Bob Whorf, Tom Kane, and Fred Kowal.

Thomas J. Hickey
State University of New York (SUNY Cobleskill)

This book is dedicated to Nancy, Michael, Megan, Tom Sr., and Bailey.

Contents In Brief

UNIT 1 Judicial Authority and the Separation of Powers 1

Issue 1. Is Judicial Review a Legitimate Power of U.S. Courts? 2

Issue 2. Do U.S. Supreme Court Decisions Become the Supreme Law of the Land and Binding Precedents for Future Cases? 24

Issue 3. Does the U.S. Supreme Court Have the Power to Determine the Constitutionality of Presidential Actions during Wartime? 44

Issue 4. Should Noncitizens Accused of Terrorism Have the Right to a Writ of Habeas Corpus in U.S. Courts? 67

UNIT 2 State and Federal Relations in the U.S. Constitutional System 97

Issue 5. Is Congress Given a Broad Grant of Implied Powers by the Constitution? 98

Issue 6. Should Congress Have Broad Constitutional Power to Regulate the States Under the Interstate Commerce Clause? 119

Issue 7. Should the Bill of Rights be Fully Binding on State Proceedings? 141

Issue 8. Should the States be Permitted to Abolish the Exclusionary Rule of Evidence in Criminal Cases? 159

UNIT 3 Privacy and Civil Liberties 193

Issue 9. Does the Bill of Rights to the U.S. Constitution Guarantee a Right to Privacy? 194

Issue 10. Does a Constitutional Right to Privacy Protect a Woman's Right to Obtain a Lawful Abortion? 210

Issue 11. Does a Constitutional Right to Privacy Protect the Rights of Homosexual Couples to Engage in Intimate Personal Relationships? 238

Issue 12. Does the Constitution Protect the Right to Possess a Firearm Unconnected With Service in a Militia? 268

Issue 13. Does Confining Sex Offenders Indefinitely in Mental Hospitals After They Have Served Their Prison Sentences Violate the Constitution? 298

Issue 14. Is the Death Penalty an Unconstitutional Punishment for Juvenile Offenders? 321

UNIT 4 Equal Protection of Law 345

Issue 15. Does the U.S. Constitution Require that Public Institutions and Facilities be Racially Integrated? 346

Issue 16. Are "Affirmative Action" Admissions Policies at Public Universities Permitted by the Constitution?   371

Issue 17. Does the Fourteenth Amendment Require the States to Use a "One Person, One Vote" Standard for Apportioning Legislative Districts?   401

UNIT 5   Religious Liberty, Free Speech, and Association   429

Issue 18. Does a State Law That Requires Public School Teachers to Teach "Creation Science" Whenever They Teach the Theory of Evolution Violate the First Amendment?   430

Issue 19. Should Burning an American Flag Be a Form of Expression Protected by the First Amendment?   464

Issue 20. Does the First Amendment Permit the Government to Censure the Media?   495

Contents

Preface   vii

Correlation Guide   xix

Introduction   xxii

UNIT 1   JUDICIAL AUTHORITY AND THE SEPARATION OF POWERS   1

Issue 1.   Is Judicial Review a Legitimate Power of U.S. Courts?   2

YES: John Marshall, from *Marbury v. Madison*, 5 U.S. 137 (1803)   5

NO: John B. Gibson, from *Eakin v. Raub*, 12 Sergeant & Rawle 330 (1825)   16

Chief Justice John Marshall asserts that judicial review is a legitimate and indispensable power of the courts in the U.S. constitutional system. Pennsylvania Supreme Court Justice John B. Gibson argues, in response to Marshall, that the U.S. Constitution itself provides no textual basis for the power of judicial review.

Issue 2.   Do U.S. Supreme Court Decisions Become the Supreme Law of the Land and Binding Precedents for Future Cases?   24

YES: Earl Warren, from *Cooper v. Aaron*, 358 U.S. 1 (1958)   27

NO: Edwin Meese III, from "The Law of the Constitution: A Bicentennial Lecture," a paper presented at the Citizen's Forum on the Bicentennial of the Constitution, New Orleans, LA (October 21, 1986)   34

Chief Justice Earl Warren asserts that the interpretation of the Constitution set forth in a particular decision is the supreme law of the land and it is binding on the states. Former U.S. Attorney General Edwin Meese III argues that a decision by the Supreme Court does not establish a supreme law of the land that is binding on all persons and parts of the government.

Issue 3.   Does the U.S. Supreme Court Have the Power to Determine the Constitutionality of Presidential Actions during Wartime?   44

YES: Hugo L. Black, from *Youngstown Sheet & Tube Co. v. Sawyer*, 343 U.S. 579 (1942)   47

NO: Fred M. Vinson, Dissenting, in *Youngstown Sheet & Tube Co. v. Sawyer*, 343 U.S. 579 (1942)   52

Justice Hugo L. Black, writing for the Supreme Court in *Youngstown Sheet & Tube Co. v. Sawyer*, held that President Truman's order seizing the nation's steel mills during the Korean War infringed upon the lawmaking powers of Congress and was not justified by his role as Commander in Chief of the armed forces. Justice Fred M. Vinson's dissenting opinion in *Youngstown Sheet & Tube Co. v. Sawyer* asserted that President Truman's seizure of the steel mills was proper because it was a temporary measure justified by the emergency nature of the situation as an effort to preserve the status quo, until the Congress could take action.

Issue 4.   Should Noncitizens Accused of Terrorism Have the Right to a Writ of Habeas Corpus in U.S. Courts?   67

YES: **Anthony M. Kennedy,** from *Boumediene v. Bush,* U.S. Supreme Court (2008)   *71*

NO: **Antonin E. Scalia,** Dissenting, in *Boumediene v. Bush,* U.S. Supreme Court (2008)   *85*

Justice Anthony M. Kennedy, in *Boumediene v. Bush* (2008), asserted that the constitutional right to a writ of habeas corpus applies to all accused terrorists, including those designated as enemy combatants. Justice Antonin E. Scalia, dissenting, asserted that the Constitution does not ensure habeas corpus for aliens held by the United States in areas over which our government is not sovereign.

UNIT 2   STATE AND FEDERAL RELATIONS IN THE U.S. CONSTITUTIONAL SYSTEM   97

Issue 5.   Is Congress Given a Broad Grant of Implied Powers by the Constitution?   98

YES: **John Marshall,** from *McCulloch v. Maryland,* 17 U.S. 316 (1819)   *102*

NO: **Thomas Jefferson,** "Opinion on the Constitutionality of the Bill for Establishing a National Bank," in Julian P. Boyd (ed.), *The Papers of Thomas Jefferson,* 31 vols. vol. 19, 1950, pp. 275–282   *109*

Chief Justice John Marshall, writing for the Supreme Court in 1819, asserted that congressional powers may be implied in the Constitution, if they are "necessary and proper" for carrying out an express power, such as establishing a national bank in order to raise revenue; in addition, a state may not tax such an entity because "the power to tax is the power to destroy." Thomas Jefferson, widely recognized as one of the most influential U.S. "founding fathers," asserts that the powers of Congress should be limited and not include the authority to establish a national bank. The authority to incorporate a bank is not included in the Constitution as an enumerated power of Congress.

Issue 6.   Should Congress Have Broad Constitutional Power to Regulate the States Under the Interstate Commerce Clause?   119

YES: **Robert H. Jackson,** from *Wickard v. Filburn,* 317 U.S. 111 (1942)   *123*

NO: **William H. Rehnquist,** from *United States v. Lopez,* 541 U.S. 549 (1995)   *129*

Justice Robert H. Jackson, writing for the Supreme Court in 1942, in the aftermath of the New Deal, asserted that the "power of Congress over interstate commerce is plenary and complete in itself, may be exercised to its utmost extent, and acknowledges no limitations other than are prescribed in the Constitution." Moreover, "no form of state activity can constitutionally thwart the regulatory power granted by the commerce clause to Congress." Chief Justice William H. Rehnquist, writing for the Supreme Court in 2000, asserted that congressional power to pass laws under the Constitution's Interstate Commerce Clause is limited to cases that demonstrate a direct link to "instrumentalities, channels, or goods involved in interstate commerce." Thus, the passage of laws designed to regulate the possession of guns in school zones should be left to the discretion of the states.

Issue 7.   Should the Bill of Rights be Fully Binding on State Proceedings?   141

YES: **Hugo L. Black,** from *Adamson v. California,* 322 U.S. 46 (1947)   *145*

NO: **Benjamin N. Cardozo,** from *Palko v. Connecticut,* 302 U.S. 319 (1937)   *151*

Justice Hugo L. Black, in a dissenting opinion in *Adamson v. California* (1947), asserted that the Supreme Court's "selective incorporation" approach to the constitutional protections in the Bill of Rights "degrades" those safeguards. Moreover, the Fifth, Sixth, and Eighth Amendments were specifically designed to confine the exercise of power by judges, particularly in criminal cases. Justice Benjamin N. Cardozo, writing for the Supreme Court in *Palko v. Connecticut* (1937), asserted that only those Bill of Rights protections that are "implicit in a concept of ordered liberty" are binding on state proceedings through the Due Process Clause of the Fourteenth Amendment.

Issue 8.   Should the States be Permitted to Abolish the Exclusionary Rule of Evidence in Criminal Cases?   159

YES: **Akhil Reed Amar,** from "Against Exclusion (Except to Protect Truth or Prevent Privacy Violations)," *Harvard Journal of Law and Public Policy* (Winter 1997)   *161*

NO: **Yale Kamisar,** from "In Defense of the Search and Seizure Exclusionary Rule," *Harvard Journal of Law and Public Policy* (Winter 2003)   *169*

Yale law professor Akhil Reed Amar argues that if reliable evidence is excluded from trials, wrongful acquittals and erroneous convictions will result. Moreover, he believes that the exclusionary rule of evidence hurts innocent defendants while helping the guilty ones. University of Michigan law professor Yale Kamisar contends that the exclusionary rule is the sole effective remedy to secure compliance with the Constitution by the police and that admitting evidence obtained illegally requires courts to condone lawless activities of law enforcement officers.

UNIT 3 PRIVACY AND CIVIL LIBERTIES   193

Issue 9. Does the Bill of Rights to the U.S. Constitution Guarantee a Right to Privacy?   194

YES: **William O. Douglas,** from *Griswold v. Connecticut*, 381 U.S. 479 (1965) *198*

NO: **Hugo L. Black,** from *Griswold v. Connecticut*, 381 U.S. 479 (1965) *202*

Justice William O. Douglas asserted that the Constitution has rights that emanate from certain Amendments that form a "penumbra," which provides a right to privacy protected from governmental interference. Justice Hugo L. Black, in contrast, asserted that a constitutional right to privacy is not found in any explicit provision in the Bill of Rights. Therefore, he would vote to uphold the Connecticut law prohibiting contraceptives.

Issue 10. Does a Constitutional Right to Privacy Protect a Woman's Right to Obtain a Lawful Abortion?   210

YES: **Harry A. Blackmun,** from *Roe v. Wade*, 410 U.S. 113 (1973) *214*

NO: **William H. Rehnquist,** from *Roe v. Wade*, 410 U.S. 113 (1973) *231*

Justice Harry A. Blackmun, writing for the U.S. Supreme Court in *Roe v. Wade* (1973), asserted that the constitutional right to privacy, established in *Griswold v. Connecticut* (1965), is sufficiently broad to protect a woman's right to terminate her pregnancy. Justice William H. Rehnquist, dissenting in *Roe v. Wade* (1973), asserted that although privacy may be a form of liberty protected by the Fourteenth Amendment, such an interest is protected only against state actions without due process of law. Moreover, the right to an abortion is not "so rooted in the traditions and conscience of our people as to be ranked as fundamental."

Issue 11. Does a Constitutional Right to Privacy Protect the Rights of Homosexual Couples to Engage in Intimate Personal Relationships?   238

YES: **Anthony M. Kennedy,** from Majority Opinion, *Lawrence v. Texas*, 539 U.S. 558 (2003) *242*

NO: **Antonin E. Scalia,** from Dissenting Opinion, *Lawrence v. Texas*, 539 U.S. 558 (2003) *253*

Justice Anthony M. Kennedy, writing for the U.S. Supreme Court in *Lawrence v. Texas* (2003), held that a Texas law making it a crime for two persons of the same sex to engage in intimate sexual conduct violates the Fourteenth Amendment's Due Process Clause. Justice Antonin E. Scalia, dissenting in *Lawrence v. Texas* (2003), asserted that the Texas law does not infringe a "fundamental right." Moreover, it bears a rational relationship to what the Constitution considers a legitimate state interest and does not deny the equal protection of the laws.

Issue 12.   Does the Constitution Protect the Right to Possess a Firearm Unconnected With Service in a Militia?   268

YES: Antonin E. Scalia, from Majority Opinion, *District of Columbia v. Heller*, 554 U.S.__ (2008).   *272*

NO: John Paul Stevens, from Dissenting Opinion, *District of Columbia v. Heller*, 554 U.S.__ (2008).   *286*

Justice Antonin E. Scalia, writing for the U.S. Supreme Court in *District of Columbia v. Heller* (2008), held that a District of Columbia law making it a crime to carry an unregistered handgun and prohibiting the registration of handguns, but that authorizes the police chief to issue one-year licenses and requires residents to keep lawfully owned handgun unloaded and dissembled or bound by a trigger lock or similar device, violates the Second Amendment. Justice John Paul Stevens, dissenting in *District of Columbia v. Heller* (2008), argued that neither the text of the Second Amendment nor the arguments advanced by its proponents evidenced the slightest interest in limiting any legislature's authority to regulate private civilian uses of firearms. Moreover, there is no indication that the framers intended to enshrine the common-law right of self-defense in the Constitution.

Issue 13.   Does Confining Sex Offenders Indefinitely in Mental Hospitals After They Have Served Their Prison Sentences Violate the Constitution?   298

YES: Stephen Breyer, from Dissenting Opinion, *Kansas v. Hendricks*, 521 U.S. 346 (1997)   *300*

NO: Clarence Thomas, from Majority Opinion, *Kansas v. Hendricks*, 521 U.S. 346 (1997)   *309*

Associate Justice Stephen Breyer asserts that if a state's law attempts to inflict additional punishment on an offender after he has served a prison sentence, it will violate the U.S. Constitution. Justice Clarence Thomas, in contrast, contends that post-imprisonment civil confinement laws do not violate the Constitution.

Issue 14.   Is the Death Penalty an Unconstitutional Punishment for Juvenile Offenders?   321

YES: Anthony M. Kennedy, from Majority Opinion, *Roper v. Simmons*, U.S. Supreme Court (2005)   *323*

NO: Antonin E. Scalia, from Dissenting Opinion, *Roper v. Simmons*, U.S. Supreme Court (2005)   *331*

Associate Justice Anthony M. Kennedy, writing for the Court, asserts that the death penalty is an unacceptable punishment for juveniles who commit murder because it constitutes cruel and unusual punishment in violation of the Eighth and Fourteenth Amendments. Associate Justice Antonin E. Scalia, dissenting in the same case, argues that there is no clear social consensus that would favor abolishing the death penalty in these cases and that in doing so the Court's majority is usurping the powers of state legislatures.

UNIT 4   EQUAL PROTECTION OF LAW   345

Issue 15.   Does the U.S. Constitution Require that Public Institutions and Facilities be Racially Integrated?   346

YES: **Earl Warren**, from Majority Opinion, *Brown v. Board of Education of Topeka, Kansas*, 347 U.S. 483 (1954)   *351*

NO: **Henry B. Brown**, from Majority Opinion, *Plessy v. Ferguson*, 163 U.S. 537 (1896)   *359*

Chief Justice Earl Warren, writing for the U.S. Supreme Court in *Brown v. Board of Education of Topeka*, held that state laws that segregate white and black children solely on the basis of race deny to African American children their Fourteenth Amendment right to the equal protection of law. Warren also expressly rejected the "separate but equal" doctrine developed in *Plessy v. Ferguson* (1896). In contrast, Justice Henry B. Brown, writing for the Court in *Plessy v. Ferguson*, held that Louisiana's law providing for "separate but equal" accommodations for persons of different races on passenger trains does not violate the Thirteenth or Fourteenth Amendment to the U.S. Constitution.

Issue 16.   Are "Affirmative Action" Admissions Policies at Public Universities Permitted by the Constitution?   371

YES: **Sandra D. O'Connor**, from Majority Opinion, *Grutter v. Bollinger*, 539 U.S. 306 (2003)   *375*

NO: **William H. Rehnquist**, from Dissenting Opinion, *Grutter v. Bollinger*, 539 U.S. 306 (2003)   *392*

Associate Justice Sandra D. O'Connor, writing for the U.S. Supreme Court in *Grutter v. Bollinger* (2003), held that a state law school's narrowly tailored use of race in admissions decision to further a compelling state interest in obtaining the educational benefits that flow from a diverse student body is not prohibited by the Equal Protection Clause of the Fourteenth Amendment or federal statutes. Chief Justice William H. Rehnquist, dissenting in *Grutter v. Bollinger* (2003), asserted that when it comes to the use of race, the connection between a state's interest and the means used to attain them must be precise. In this case, it is not; therefore, the use of race as an admissions criterion violates the Equal Protection Clause.

Issue 17.   Does the Fourteenth Amendment Require the States to Use a "One Person, One Vote" Standard for Apportioning Legislative Districts?   401

YES: **Earl H. Warren**, from Majority Opinion, *Reynolds v. Sims*, 377 U.S. 533 (1963)   *405*

NO: **John M. Harlan**, from Dessenting Opinion, *Reynolds v. Sims*, 377 U.S. 533 (1963)   *417*

Chief Justice Earl H. Warren, writing for the U.S. Supreme Court in *Reynolds v. Sims* (1963), held that both houses of a state's legislature must be apportioned on an equal population basis. The Equal Protection Clause requires an honest and good-faith effort by the states to do so.

Justice John M. Harlan, in contrast, believes that *Reynolds v. Sims*, which involved congressional districting by the states, has the effect of placing basic aspects of state political systems under "the pervasive overlordship of the federal judiciary."

UNIT 5 RELIGIOUS LIBERTY, FREE SPEECH, AND ASSOCIATION   429

Issue 18. Does a State Law That Requires Public School Teachers to Teach "Creation Science" Whenever They Teach the Theory of Evolution Violate the First Amendment?   430

YES: **William J. Brennan**, from Majority Opinion, *Edwards v. Aguillard*, 482 U.S. 578 (1987)   *434*

NO: **Antonin E. Scalia**, from Dissenting Opinion, *Edwards v. Aguillard*, 482 U.S. 578 (1987)   *443*

Justice William J. Brennan, writing for the U.S. Supreme Court in *Edwards v. Aguillard* (1987), held that the Louisiana law that required public school teachers to teach "creation science" whenever they taught the theory of evolution was a violation of the First Amendment's Establishment Clause because the law lacked a clear secular purpose. Justice Antonin E. Scalia, dissenting in *Edwards v. Aguillard* (1987), asserted that the Louisiana law had a valid secular purpose—protecting academic freedom and that the statute should therefore be upheld.

Issue 19. Should Burning an American Flag Be a Form of Expression Protected by the First Amendment?   464

YES: **William J. Brennan**, from Majority Opinion, *Texas v. Johnson*, 491 U.S. 397 (1989)   *468*

NO: **William H. Rehnquist**, from Dissenting Opinion, *Texas v. Johnson*, 491 U.S. 397 (1989)   *481*

Justice William J. Brennan, writing for the U.S. Supreme Court in *Texas v. Johnson* (1989), held that the defendant's act of burning an American flag at the Republican National Convention was expressive conduct, protected by the First Amendment. Moreover, the state of Texas could not lawfully prohibit flag desecration as a means of preserving the flag as a symbol of national unity. Furthermore, the statute was not sufficiently narrow to prohibit only those acts that were likely to result in a serious disturbance. Chief Justice William H. Rehnquist, dissenting in *Texas v. Johnson* (1989), asserted that because the American flag occupies a unique position as the symbol of our nation, the state of Texas is justified in prohibiting flag burning in a case such as this.

Issue 20. Does the First Amendment Permit the Government to Censure the Media?   495

YES: **Pierce Butler**, from Dissenting Opinion, *Near v. Minnesota*, 283 U.S. 697 (1931)   *499*

NO: **Charles E. Hughes**, from Majority Opinion, *Near v. Minnesota*, 283 U.S. 697 (1931)   *506*

Justice Pierce Butler, dissenting in *Near v. Minnesota* (1931), asserted that the Court's decision to prevent states from stopping the publication of malicious, scandalous, and defamatory periodicals gives to freedom of the press a meaning and a scope not previously recognized, and construes "liberty" in the Due Process Clause of the Fourteenth Amendment to restrict the states in a way that is unprecedented. Chief Justice Charles E. Hughes, writing for the Court in *Near v. Minnesota* (1931), held that the Minnesota law, which allowed the newspaper to be shut down, was the essence of censorship and a violation of the First Amendment.

Contributors   522

Correlation Guide

The *Taking Sides* series presents current issues in a debate-style format designed to stimulate student interest and develop critical thinking skills. Each issue is thoughtfully framed with an issue summary, an issue introduction, and a post-script. The pro and con essays—selected for their liveliness and substance—represent the arguments of leading scholars and commentators in their fields.

Taking Sides: Clashing Views in Constitutional Law, is an easy-to-use reader that presents issues on important topics such as *Judicial Authority, Exclusionary Rule of Evidence,* and the *Death Penalty for Juvenile Offenders.* For more information on *Taking Sides* and other *McGraw-Hill Contemporary Learning Series* titles, visit www.mhhe.com/cls.

This convenient guide matches the issues in **Taking Sides: Constitutional Law,** with the corresponding chapters in three of our best-selling McGraw-Hill Criminal Justice textbooks by Bohm/Haley, Inciardi and Masters et al.

Taking Sides: Constitutional Law	Introduction to Criminal Justice, 6/e by Bohm/Haley	CJ: Realities and Challenges, by Masters et al.	Criminal Justice, 9/e by Inciardi
Issue 1: Is Judicial Review a Legitimate Power of U.S. Courts?	**Chapter 8:** The Administration of Justice	**Chapter 8:** The Courts	**Chapter 10:** The Structure of American Courts
Issue 2: Do U.S. Supreme Court Decisions Become the Supreme Law of the Land and Binding Precedents for Future Cases?	**Chapter 4:** The Rule of Law	**Chapter 8:** The Courts	**Chapter 10:** The Structure of American Courts
Issue 3: Does the U.S. Supreme Court have the Power to Determine the Constitutionality of Presidential Actions during Wartime?		**Chapter 8:** The Courts	
Issue 4: Should Non-Citizens Accused of Terrorism Have the Right to a Writ of Habeas Corpus in U.S. Courts?	**Chapter 8:** The Administration of Justice	**Chapter 10:** Sentencing	**Chapter 16:** Prison Conditions and Inmate Rights
Issue 5: Is Congress Given a Broad Grant of Implied Powers by the Constitution?	**Chapter 4:** The Rule of Law		

(continued)

Taking Sides: Constitutional Law	Introduction to Criminal Justice, 6/e by Bohm/Haley	CJ: Realities and Challenges, by Masters et al.	Criminal Justice, 9/e by Inciardi
Issue 6: Should Congress have the Constitutional Power to Regulate the States Under the Interstate Commerce Clause?	**Chapter 4:** The Rule of Law		
Issue 7: Should the Bill of Rights be Fully Binding on State Proceedings?	**Chapter 4:** The Rule of Law		**Chapter 5:** The Process of Justice: An Overview
Issue 8: Should the States be Permitted to Abolish the Exclusionary Rule of Evidence in Criminal Cases?	**Chapter 4:** The Rule of Law	**Chapter 7:** Legal and Special Issues in Policing	**Chapter 5:** The Process of Justice: An Overview
Issue 9: Does the Bill of Rights to the U.S. Constitution Guarantee a Right to Privacy?	**Chapter 5:** History and Structure of American Law Enforcement	**Chapter 7:** Legal and Special Issues in Policing	**Chapter 5:** The Process of Justice: An Overview
Issue 10: Does a Constitutional Right to Privacy Protect a Woman's Right to Obtain a Lawful Abortion?	**Chapter 4:** The Rule of Law	**Chapter 7:** Legal and Special Issues in Policing	**Chapter 5:** The Process of Justice: An Overview
Issue 11: Does a Constitutional Right to Privacy Protect the Rights of Homosexual Couples to have Intimate Personal Relationships?	**Chapter 5:** History and Structure of American Law Enforcement	**Chapter 7:** Legal and Special Issues in Policing	**Chapter 5:** The Process of Justice: An Overview
Issue 12: Does the Constitution Protect the Right to Possess a Firearm Unconnected With Service in a Militia?	**Chapter 4:** The Rule of Law		
Issue 13: Does Confining Sex Offenders Indefinitely in Mental Hospitals After They Have Served Their Prison Sentences Violate the Constitution?	**Chapter 9:** Sentencing, Appeals, and the Death Penalty	**Chapter 10:** Sentencing	**Chapter 13:** Sentencing, Appeal, and the Judgment of Death
Issue 14: Is the Death Penalty an Unconstitutional Punishment for Juvenile Offenders?	**Chapter 9:** Sentencing, Appeals, and the Death Penalty	**Chapter 15:** Juvenile Justice	**Chapter 18:** Juvenile Justice: An Overview

Taking Sides: Constitutional Law	Introduction to Criminal Justice, 6/e by Bohm/Haley	CJ: Realities and Challenges, by Masters et al.	Criminal Justice, 9/e by Inciardi
Issue 15: Does the U.S. Constitution Require that Public Institutions and Facilities be Racially Integrated?	**Chapter 10:** Institutional Corrections	**Chapter 12:** Jails and Prisons	
Issue 16: Are "Affirmative Action" Admissions Policies at Public Universities Permitted by the U.S. Constitution?			
Issue 17: Does the Fourteenth Amendment Require the States to Use a "One Person, One Vote" Standard for Apportioning Legislative Districts?			
Issue 18: Does a State Law that Requires Public School Teachers to Teach "Creation Science" Whenever They Teach the Theory of Evolution Violate the First Amendment?			
Issue 19: Should Burning an American Flag be a Form of Expression Protected by the First Amendment?	**Chapter 3:** Explaining Crime	**Chapter 2:** Types of Crime	**Chapter 2:** Crime and the Nature of Law
Issue 20: Does the First Amendment Permit the Government to Censure the Media?			

Introduction

Thomas J. Hickey

"The life of the law has not been logic: it has been experience. The felt necessities of the time, the prevalent moral and political theories, institutions of public policy, avowed or unconscious, even the prejudices which judges share with their fellow-men, have a good deal more to do than the syllogism in determining the rules by which men should be governed. The law embodies the story of a nation's development through many centuries, and it cannot be dealt with as if it contained only the axioms and corollaries of a book of mathematics. In order to know what it is, we must know what it has been, and what it tends to become."

—Oliver Wendell Holmes, *The Common Law*, 1881:1

The study of the law is a fascinating enterprise. It is the study of our history as a people. It is the study of our cultural values and social priorities. Some of our country's greatest minds have engaged in this undertaking and we have all benefited greatly as a result of their wisdom. Justice Oliver Wendell Holmes, quoted above, is widely considered one of the most prominent figures in United States Supreme Court history. His observations about the development of the common law suggest that as students of the law we must also become students of society. Our body of law is a dynamic and evolving enterprise that both determines and is determined by the practical necessities of everyday life in our democratic republic. It is a direct result of "people who have gotten their hands dirty" by taking strong positions on matters having a significant influence on the quality of life in this country. Moreover, the development of law does not occur in a vacuum—it is the result of the clash of competing philosophical viewpoints that determine the nature of what our society is and what it will be in the future.

This volume presents competing viewpoints in the context of *constitutional law,* which is defined as the body of precedents developed primarily by the Supreme Court interpreting the Constitution of the United States. As Professors Sullivan and Gunther have observed, United States Supreme Court decisions "are no doubt the richest source of constitutional law." Thus, most of the readings presented in this volume have been excerpted directly from opinions of the Court, most often in highly controversial cases.

Although a comprehensive treatment of constitutional law is beyond the scope of the present initiative, the topics presented in this edition were selected in order to provide a broad range of exposure to important constitutional issues. We endeavored to provide a sample of topics that would be amenable to consideration during a single-semester constitutional law/issues course.

Moreover, we hope to promote classroom discussion of many of these very important issues in constitutional law and encourage students to think critically about the decisions the Supreme Court has made. The topics selected for this first edition are, stated broadly, the doctrine of judicial review and the scope of judicial power, the nature of state and federal relations in our democratic republic, civil rights and liberties, the nature of due process, and the equal protection of law.

In a very real and compelling way constitutional law does constitute, to use Justice Holmes's words, "the story of our nation's development." This volume attempts to document that story by considering some of the most classic precedents in U.S. history. For example, in Unit 1 we discuss what is perhaps the most famous case in U.S. history, *Marbury v. Madison* (1803), authored by Chief Justice John Marshall. We then attempt to illustrate how the doctrine of judicial review has evolved throughout our history by focusing on such noteworthy cases as *Cooper v. Aaron* (1958), which addressed whether U.S. Supreme Court decisions become binding precedents for future cases and litigants. Next, we consider the nature of relations between the executive and judicial branches by analyzing *Youngstown Sheet & Tube Co. v. Sawyer* (1952), a Korean War era case. The final case discussed in this section is a relatively recent one, *Boumediene v. Bush* (2008), which considers judicial power to issue "the great writ," Habeas Corpus. By approaching our analysis of judicial power in this fashion, we hope to have given students an overview of constitutional law in this area that demonstrates, to paraphrase Holmes, "what the law has been, and what it will become."

We have also tried to present a combination of cases that would be found in any traditional constitutional law treatise, as well as more current decisions that have had a significant impact on our lives. Hopefully, students will learn that constitutional law is a vital, evolving, and dynamic area of study that has serious implications for the quality of life in the United States. For example, Issue 12 considers whether there is a constitutional right under the Second Amendment to possess a firearm unconnected with service in a militia, and to use that weapon for traditionally lawful purposes such as self-defense. The case presented in that section, in which the Supreme Court first recognized these rights, is *District of Columbia v. Heller* (2008). As this book goes to press, the Supreme Court has heard oral arguments in another highly significant gun control case that has challenged the city of Chicago's restrictive firearms law, *McDonald v. City of Chicago*. The Introduction to Issue 12 and Postscript in this section discusses Second Amendment law in considerable detail and analyzes it in the context of American society. All of the issues presented in this volume utilize a similar approach and it is strongly recommended that students be asked to read the Introductions and Postscripts to each issue.

We have also attempted to demonstrate the evolution of important legal doctrines by focusing on several recurrent themes that have developed in constitutional law throughout our nation's history. To modify Justice Holmes's observation slightly, if we are to know what the law will become, we must know what it has been. These themes include issues involving the distribution of state and federal power in our democratic republic, privacy and civil liberties, the equal protection of law, and finally religious liberty, free speech, and association.

The cases selected to illustrate these recurrent themes are often classic and famous ones that have had a significant impact on U.S. history. For example, we begin our discussion of the distribution of state and federal power by considering another important case authored by Chief Justice John Marshall, *McCulloch v. Maryland* (1819) (establishing, inter alia, that Congress has implied powers under the Constitution). Other classic Supreme Court cases include *Griswold v. Connecticut* (1965) (establishing a constitutional right to privacy), *Roe v. Wade* (1973) (establishing that the right to privacy protects a woman's right to obtain an abortion), *Brown v. Board of Education of Topeka* (1954) (establishing that the Equal Protection Clause requires integrated public school systems), and *Reynolds v. Sims* (1963) (establishing that the federal Constitution requires the states to use a "one person, one vote" standard for apportioning legislative districts).

Precedents such as the ones discussed above illustrate another important legal principle that is consistent with Justice Holmes's earlier observations: "The law is a seamless web." As a first year law student, I recall hearing my professors make this statement and thinking, "What does that mean?" Based upon reflection and some years of both academic and professional legal experience, it appears to mean a few different things. First, it is associated with the doctrine of *legal holism,* which emphasizes that the study of law should not be conducted in a fragmented or piecemeal way. Rather, the study of law should be conducted by recognizing that the body of a society's law is interrelated and systemic—a holistic enterprise.

Another way to consider the idea that "the law is a seamless web" is to view it in the context of society as a systemic and organic whole. The study of constitutional law illustrates this principle vividly. For example, Issue 4 considers whether noncitizens accused of terrorism have the right to a writ of habeas corpus in U.S. courts. In *Boumediene v. Bush* (2008), the Supreme Court held that they have this most basic right. This important decision may well have a "ripple effect" throughout American society. First, it has already impacted our collective notion of due process. In addition, it has influenced our perspective on the limits of governmental authority and the proper enforcement mechanisms in terrorism cases. Finally, it has reaffirmed our commitment to the rule of law as a guiding principle for our legal system. Thus, it is true that the decisions that form the body of U.S. constitutional law cannot be considered in isolation. They both shape our society and are shaped by society. Justice Holmes was right: In order to know what the law is, "we must know what it has been, and what it tends to become."

Another matter we confronted in developing this volume was the sheer magnitude of the choices available to anyone attempting to present an overview of constitutional law. Even a cursory look at the classic constitutional law treatises, including those by Sullivan and Gunther, Tribe, and many others that exceed 1500 pages of text, indicates the incredible scope and diversity of this field of study. Selecting precisely which issues would be presented in this volume, therefore, was a considerable challenge. Fortunately, the editors of this series had the foresight to seek the advice of approximately 200 professors from across the United States. Their suggestions for potential topics and perspectives on the study of constitutional law were invaluable and have influenced this work greatly.

One of those cogent suggestions was to include a copy of the U.S. Constitution as an appendix at the end of this volume, which is provided in Appendix A. Another useful suggestion was to highlight where to find additional legal resources for pursing more intensive study of these issues. An excellent and free reference Web site provided by Cornell University is: www.law.cornell.edu. Another noteworthy resource is www.findlaw.com. From these Web sites students will be able to gain access to virtually all of the full Supreme Court decisions excerpted in this volume, including dissenting and concurring opinions.

In conclusion, the opinions that you will form about the issues presented in this volume are important ones that, to paraphrase Justice Holmes, may someday influence "what the law is to become." We hope that you will enjoy your study of constitutional law and will debate the issues presented in this volume with energy and passion. In later editions, we will make every effort to keep the topics included current, interesting, and challenging. We will also welcome any suggestions for improvements to this work that you may have as well as for additional topics to be considered in future editions. My e-mail address is hickeytj@cobleskill.edu.

Internet References . . .

Cornell University Law School's Legal Information Institute

Not-for-profit group that believes everyone should be able to read and understand the laws that govern them.

www.law.cornell.edu

Findlaw

The world's leading provider of online legal information and Internet marketing solutions for law firms.

www.findlaw.com

National Institute of Justice (NIJ)

The NIJ sponsors projects and disseminates research about justice system. This site provides links to NIJ research, programs, publications, and initiatives.

http://www.ojp.usdoj.gov/nij/

Judicial Authority and the Separation of Powers

*T*he U.S. Constitution is a document that specifies the powers of the different branches of government. There are gray areas, however, and questions sometimes arise about the legitimacy of powers being exercised by the different branches. Moreover, even though the Constitution embodies the separation of powers doctrine, there are times when due to practical necessities, the powers of one branch may be delegated to another. This section focuses primarily on the Article III powers and the roles that courts may legitimately exercise.

- Is Judicial Review a Legitimate Power of U.S. Courts?
- Do U.S. Supreme Court Decisions Become the Supreme Law of the Land and Binding Precedents for Future Cases?
- Does the U.S. Supreme Court Have the Power to Determine the Constitutionality of Presidential Actions during Wartime?
- Should Noncitizens Accused of Terrorism Have the Right to a Writ of Habeas Corpus in U.S. Courts?

ISSUE 1

Is Judicial Review a Legitimate Power of U.S. Courts?

YES: John Marshall, from *Marbury v. Madison,* 5 U.S. 137 (1803)

NO: John B. Gibson, from *Eakin v. Raub*, 12 Sergeant & Rawle 330 (1825)

ISSUE SUMMARY

YES: Chief Justice John Marshall asserts that judicial review is a legitimate and indispensable power of the courts in the U.S. constitutional system.

NO: Pennsylvania Supreme Court Justice John B. Gibson argues, in response to Marshall, that the U.S. Constitution itself provides no textual basis for the power of judicial review.

There has been a long debate over the proper role of the judiciary in the U.S. governmental system. At the core of the debate rests the concept of judicial review, which may be defined as the power of courts to pass judgment on laws passed by legislatures and actions of executive branch authorities to determine if they are consistent with the Constitution. If the law or executive branch action is found to violate a particular constitutional directive, it may be declared void or "unconstitutional."

Judicial review gives judges an awesome power—the final word on matters implicating or interpreting the Constitution. In modern American society, it is difficult to imagine an issue that does not in some way implicate a constitutional provision, including, among other things, highly personal decisions such as the right to intimate associations and sexual freedom, to end one's life in the event of a terminal illness, to own and possess firearms, and to terminate an unwanted pregnancy.

The power of judicial review has allowed the U.S. courts on many occasions to strike down laws passed by both the federal and state legislatures. For example, in the last few years the Supreme Court has held unconstitutional the state of Oregon's law against physician-assisted suicide. The Court has also used the power of judicial review to scrutinize executive branch officials and ordered former president Richard M. Nixon to surrender tape recordings made in his office as a part of the Watergate scandal during the 1970s. But, should courts have this awesome power?

Early in our nation's history, Alexander Hamilton asserted in *The Federalist, no. 78*, that judicial review did not elevate the courts to a position superior to the other branches of government; rather, the doctrine "supposes that the power of the people" enshrined in the Constitution is paramount. It is worth noting that Hamilton's position was strenuously opposed by Robert Yates and other delegates to the Constitutional Convention, who embraced a more restrictive view of judicial authority.

The federal government has been described as one of "enumerated powers." This restriction means that its powers are limited solely to those stated expressly in the United States Constitution. Article I outlines the powers of the legislative branch. These include, among other things, the power to elect representatives and senators, establish taxes, make laws, to regulate commerce among the states, coin money, and many others. Article II establishes the powers of the executive branch. Among other things, it establishes the President as Commander in Chief of the armed forces and provides for impeachment and removal from office for "Treason, Bribery, or other high Crimes and Misdemeanors." Article III establishes the U.S. Supreme Court and expressly permits Congress to establish inferior federal courts. In addition, it outlines the powers of the Supreme Court and gives it *original jurisdiction* in several different types of cases, including, among other things, cases arising under the Constitution, laws of the United States, those involving U.S. treaties, cases involving ambassadors, controversies between two or more states, and cases in which a state is a party.

Black's Law Dictionary (5th ed., 1979, p. 991) defines *original jurisdiction* as the power "to take cognizance of a cause at its inception, try it, and pass judgment upon the law and facts." This exists in contrast to *appellate jurisdiction*, which is defined as "[T]he power vested in an appellate court to review and revise the judicial action of an inferior court." The distinction between these two types of jurisdiction was crucial in *Marbury v. Madison* (1803).

It is worth noting that nothing in Article III or any other portion of the Constitution grants the power of judicial review to the courts or makes the Supreme Court the final arbiter of disputes among the different branches of government. How, then, did the power of judicial review come to be a cornerstone of the U.S. legal system? The answer to this important question lies in Chief Justice John Marshall's seminal opinion in *Marbury v. Madison* (1803), a case many legal scholars regard as the most important in U.S. legal history. It involved a dispute between President John Adams who was about to leave office and the newly elected president, Thomas Jefferson. The two presidents had major philosophical differences. Adams was an ardent "federalist," which meant that he believed in a strong federal government, sometimes at the expense of strong state and local governments. Jefferson, in contrast, is sometimes described as an "antifederalist," because he felt that federal governmental power should be limited and that the state and local governments should retain most of the power in the new republic.

Just before John Adams left office, he appointed several new judges to positions as justices of the peace in the District of Columbia. These individuals have been widely described in the legal literature as "midnight appointees." The documents that had created these appointments were signed by Adams, but had not yet been delivered by the time he left office. When Thomas Jefferson took office, he refused to honor the appointments. William Marbury and several of the other midnight appointees then asked the Supreme Court to issue a *writ of mandamus,* to compel Jefferson's Secretary of State, James Madison, to deliver the appointments. A writ of mandamus is an order of a court to a named governmental official commanding him or her to perform a duty imposed by law. The U.S. Congress had previously passed a new federal law, the Judiciary Act of 1789, which had created the justice of the peace positions and expressly permitted the Supreme Court to issue writs of mandamus.

Earlier we mentioned the doctrine of *original jurisdiction* and observed that Article III expressly gives it to the Supreme Court only in several specific types of cases. This may be contrasted with the Court's *appellate jurisdiction,* which the Congress may change by passing a traditional law.

In *Marbury,* Chief Justice Marshall held that Congress could not expand the *original jurisdiction* of the Supreme Court by passing a traditional statute, although it may have been able to do so by following the proper procedures for a constitutional amendment, which is by design a much more difficult and cumbersome process. Because the Judiciary Act of 1789 had expanded the Court's original jurisdiction, it was unconstitutional and the portion that allowed the Supreme Court to issue writs of mandamus was unenforceable.

The key to *Marbury v. Madison,* then, is what gave the Supreme Court the power to declare that the portion of the Judiciary Act of 1789 that allowed it to issue writs of mandamus was unconstitutional. In the excerpt from *Marbury v. Madison* that follows, try to determine precisely what Chief Justice Marshall says to support this enormous "power grab" by the Court. Does he find any support in the text of the Constitution for the power of judicial review? Does Marshall give any other reasonable justification for judicial review?

Marbury v. Madison was decided in 1803. In later years, the implications of the power of judicial review had become more widely apparent. Justice John B. Gibson, of the Pennsylvania Supreme Court, in *Eakin v. Raub* (1825) took issue with Chief Justice Marshall's expansive view of the power of U.S. courts in our governmental system. Stated Gibson: "I am aware, that a right to declare all constitutional acts void . . . is generally held as a professional dogma; but I apprehend, rather as a matter of faith than of reason." In the excerpt from *Eakin v. Raub* that follows try to identify the specific reasons for Justice Gibson's reservations about the power of judicial review.

In Your Opinion . . .

- Who makes the better case about the proper role of the judiciary in the U.S. governmental system, Chief Justice Marshall or Justice Gibson?
- Are there any good alternatives to judical review?
- Could abolition of judicial review lead to a breakdown in our government?
- Why have commentators described the Supreme Court's decision in *Marbury v. Madison* as the greatest "power grab" in U.S. governmental history?
- What issues did the Supreme Court decide in *Marbury v. Madison*?
- Is the power of judicial review "built on a foundation of sand?"

Marbury v. Madison

Mr. Chief Justice Marshall delivered the opinion of the Court.

At the last term, on the affidavits then read and filed with the clerk, a rule was granted in this case requiring the Secretary of State to show cause why a mandamus should not issue directing him to deliver to William Marbury his commission as a justice of the peace for the county of Washington, in the District of Columbia.

No cause has been shown, and the present motion is for a mandamus. The peculiar delicacy of this case, the novelty of some of its circumstances, and the real difficulty attending the points which occur in it require a complete exposition of the principles on which the opinion to be given by the Court is founded.

These principles have been, on the side of the applicant, very ably argued at the bar. In rendering the opinion of the Court, there will be some departure in form, though not in substance, from the points stated in that argument.

In the order in which the Court has viewed this subject, the following questions have been considered and decided.

1. Has the applicant a right to the commission he demands?
2. If he has a right, and that right has been violated, do the laws of his country afford him a remedy?
3. If they do afford him a remedy, is it a mandamus issuing from this court?

The first object of inquiry is:

1. Has the applicant a right to the commission he demands?

His right originates in an act of Congress passed in February, 1801, concerning the District of Columbia. . . .

[The Constitution seems] to contemplate three distinct operations:

1. The nomination. This is the sole act of the President, and is completely voluntary.
2. The appointment. This is also the act of the President, and is also a voluntary act, though it can only be performed by and with the advice and consent of the Senate.

Supreme Court of the United States, 1803.

3. The commission. To grant a commission to a person appointed might perhaps be deemed a duty enjoined by the Constitution. "He shall," says that instrument, "commission all the officers of the United States." . . .

The [President's] signature is a warrant for affixing the great seal to the commission, and the great seal is only to be affixed to an instrument which is complete. It attests, by an act supposed to be of public notoriety, the verity of the Presidential signature.

It is never to be affixed till the commission is signed, because the signature, which gives force and effect to the commission, is conclusive evidence that the appointment is made.

The commission being signed, the subsequent duty of the Secretary of State is prescribed by law, and not to be guided by the will of the President. He is to affix the seal of the United States to the commission, and is to record it.

This is not a proceeding which may be varied if the judgment of the Executive shall suggest one more eligible, but is a precise course accurately marked out by law, and is to be strictly pursued. It is the duty of the Secretary of State to conform to the law, and in this he is an officer of the United States, bound to obey the laws. He acts, in this respect, as has been very properly stated at the bar, under the authority of law, and not by the instructions of the President. It is a ministerial act which the law enjoins on a particular officer for a particular purpose. . . .

It has also occurred as possible, and barely possible, that the transmission of the commission and the acceptance thereof might be deemed necessary to complete the right of the plaintiff.

The transmission of the commission is a practice directed by convenience, but not by law. It cannot therefore be necessary to constitute the appointment, which must precede it and which is the mere act of the President. If the Executive required that every person appointed to an office should himself take means to procure his commission, the appointment would not be the less valid on that account. The appointment is the sole act of the President; the transmission of the commission is the sole act of the officer to whom that duty is assigned, and may be accelerated or retarded by circumstances which can have no influence on the appointment. A commission is transmitted to a person already appointed, not to a person to be appointed or not, as the letter enclosing the commission should happen to get into the post office and reach him in safety, or to miscarry. . . .

It is therefore decidedly the opinion of the Court that, when a commission has been signed by the President, the appointment is made, and that the commission is complete when the seal of the United States has been affixed to it by the Secretary of State. . . .

Mr. Marbury, then, since his commission was signed by the President and sealed by the Secretary of State, was appointed, and as the law creating the office gave the officer a right to hold for five years independent of the Executive, the appointment was not revocable, but vested in the officer legal rights which are protected by the laws of his country.

To withhold the commission, therefore, is an act deemed by the Court not warranted by law, but violative of a vested legal right.

This brings us to the second inquiry, which is:

1. If he has a right, and that right has been violated, do the laws of his country afford him a remedy?

The very essence of civil liberty certainly consists in the right of every individual to claim the protection of the laws whenever he receives an injury. One of the first duties of government is to afford that protection. In Great Britain, the King himself is sued in the respectful form of a petition, and he never fails to comply with the judgment of his court.

In the third volume of his *Commentaries,* page 23, Blackstone states two cases in which a remedy is afforded by mere operation of law.

"In all other cases," he says,

> it is a general and indisputable rule that where there is a legal right, there is also a legal remedy by suit or action at law whenever that right is invaded. . . .

The Government of the United States has been emphatically termed a government of laws, and not of men. It will certainly cease to deserve this high appellation if the laws furnish no remedy for the violation of a vested legal right. . . .

By the Constitution of the United States, the President is invested with certain important political powers, in the exercise of which he is to use his own discretion, and is accountable only to his country in his political character and to his own conscience. To aid him in the performance of these duties, he is authorized to appoint certain officers, who act by his authority and in conformity with his orders.

In such cases, their acts are his acts; and whatever opinion may be entertained of the manner in which executive discretion may be used, still there exists, and can exist, no power to control that discretion. The subjects are political. They respect the nation, not individual rights, and, being entrusted to the Executive, the decision of the Executive is conclusive. The application of this remark will be perceived by adverting to the act of Congress for establishing the Department of Foreign Affairs. This officer, as his duties were prescribed by that act, is to conform precisely to the will of the President. He is the mere organ by whom that will is communicated. The acts of such an officer, as an officer, can never be examinable by the Courts.

But when the Legislature proceeds to impose on that officer other duties; when he is directed peremptorily to perform certain acts; when the rights of individuals are dependent on the performance of those acts; he is so far the officer of the law, is amenable to the laws for his conduct, and cannot at his discretion, sport away the vested rights of others.

The conclusion from this reasoning is that, where the heads of departments are the political or confidential agents of the Executive, merely to execute the will of the President, or rather to act in cases in which the Executive possesses a constitutional or legal discretion, nothing can be more perfectly clear than that their acts are only politically examinable. But where a specific duty is assigned by law, and individual rights depend upon the performance of that duty, it seems equally clear that the individual who considers himself injured has a right to resort to the laws of his country for a remedy.

If this be the rule, let us inquire how it applies to the case under the consideration of the Court.

The power of nominating to the Senate, and the power of appointing the person nominated, are political powers, to be exercised by the President according to his own discretion. When he has made an appointment, he has exercised his whole power, and his discretion has been completely applied to the case. If, by law, the officer be removable at the will of the President, then a new appointment may be immediately made, and the rights of the officer are terminated. But as a fact which has existed cannot be made never to have existed, the appointment cannot be annihilated, and consequently, if the officer is by law not removable at the will of the President, the rights he has acquired are protected by the law, and are not resumable by the President. They cannot be extinguished by Executive authority, and he has the privilege of asserting them in like manner as if they had been derived from any other source.

The question whether a right has vested or not is, in its nature, judicial, and must be tried by the judicial authority. If, for example, Mr. Marbury had taken the oaths of a magistrate and proceeded to act as one, in consequence of which a suit had been instituted against him in which his defence had depended on his being a magistrate; the validity of his appointment must have been determined by judicial authority.

So, if he conceives that, by virtue of his appointment, he has a legal right either to the commission which has been made out for him or to a copy of that commission, it is equally a question examinable in a court, and the decision of the Court upon it must depend on the opinion entertained of his appointment.

That question has been discussed, and the opinion is that the latest point of time which can be taken as that at which the appointment was complete and evidenced was when, after the signature of the President, the seal of the United States was affixed to the commission.

It is then the opinion of the Court:

1. That, by signing the commission of Mr. Marbury, the President of the United States appointed him a justice of peace for the County of Washington in the District of Columbia, and that the seal of the United States, affixed thereto by the Secretary of State, is conclusive testimony of the verity of the signature, and of the completion of the appointment, and that the appointment conferred on him a legal right to the office for the space of five years.
2. That, having this legal title to the office, he has a consequent right to the commission, a refusal to deliver which is a plain violation of that right, for which the laws of his country afford him a remedy.

It remains to be inquired whether,

3. He is entitled to the remedy for which he applies. This depends on:
1. The nature of the writ applied for, and
2. The power of this court.

1. The Nature of the Writ

Blackstone, in the third volume of his *Commentaries,* page 110, defines a mandamus to be

> a command issuing in the King's name from the Court of King's Bench, and directed to any person, corporation, or inferior court of judicature within the King's dominions requiring them to do some particular thing therein specified which appertains to their office and duty, and which the Court of King's Bench has previously determined, or at least supposes, to be consonant to right and justice.

Lord Mansfield, in 3 Burrows, 1266, in the case of *The King v. Baker et al.,* states with much precision and explicitness the cases in which this writ may be used.
"Whenever," says that very able judge,

> there is a right to execute an office, perform a service, or exercise a franchise (more especially if it be in a matter of public concern or attended with profit), and a person is kept out of possession, or dispossessed of such right, and has no other specific legal remedy, this court ought to assist by mandamus, upon reasons of justice, as the writ expresses, and upon reasons of public policy, to preserve peace, order and good government. . . .

Or, in the words of Lord Mansfield, the applicant, in this case, has a right to execute an office of public concern, and is kept out of possession of that right.
These circumstances certainly concur in this case.
Still, to render the mandamus a proper remedy, the officer to whom it is to be directed must be one to whom, on legal principles, such writ may be directed, and the person applying for it must be without any other specific and legal remedy. . . .
If one of the heads of departments commits any illegal act under colour of his office by which an individual sustains an injury, it cannot be pretended that his office alone exempts him from being sued in the ordinary mode of proceeding, and being compelled to obey the judgment of the law. How then can his office exempt him from this particular mode of deciding on the legality of his conduct if the case be such a case as would, were any other individual the party complained of, authorize the process?
It is not by the office of the person to whom the writ is directed, but the nature of the thing to be done, that the propriety or impropriety of issuing a mandamus is to be determined. Where the head of a department acts in a case

in which Executive discretion is to be exercised, in which he is the mere organ of Executive will, it is again repeated, that any application to a court to control, in any respect, his conduct, would be rejected without hesitation.

But where he is directed by law to do a certain act affecting the absolute rights of individuals, in the performance of which he is not placed under the particular direction of the President, and the performance of which the President cannot lawfully forbid, and therefore is never presumed to have forbidden—as for example, to record a commission, or a patent for land, which has received all the legal solemnities; or to give a copy of such record—in such cases, it is not perceived on what ground the Courts of the country are further excused from the duty of giving judgment that right to be done to an injured individual than if the same services were to be performed by a person not the head of a department.

This opinion seems not now for the first time to be taken up in this country. . . .

It is true that the mandamus now moved for is not for the performance of an act expressly enjoined by statute. . . .

This, then, is a plain case of a mandamus, either to deliver the commission or a copy of it from the record, and it only remains to be inquired:

Whether it can issue from this Court.

The act to establish the judicial courts of the United States authorizes the Supreme Court

> to issue writs of mandamus, in cases warranted by the principles and usages of law, to any courts appointed, or persons holding office, under the authority of the United States.

The Secretary of State, being a person, holding an office under the authority of the United States, is precisely within the letter of the description, and if this Court is not authorized to issue a writ of mandamus to such an officer, it must be because the law is unconstitutional, and therefore absolutely incapable of conferring the authority and assigning the duties which its words purport to confer and assign.

The Constitution vests the whole judicial power of the United States in one Supreme Court, and such inferior courts as Congress shall, from time to time, ordain and establish. This power is expressly extended to all cases arising under the laws of the United States; and consequently, in some form, may be exercised over the present case, because the right claimed is given by a law of the United States.

In the distribution of this power, it is declared that

> The Supreme Court shall have original jurisdiction in all cases affecting ambassadors, other public ministers and consuls, and those in which a state shall be a party. In all other cases, the Supreme Court shall have appellate jurisdiction.

It has been insisted at the bar, that, as the original grant of jurisdiction to the Supreme and inferior courts is general, and the clause assigning original jurisdiction to the Supreme Court contains no negative or restrictive words, the power remains to the Legislature to assign original jurisdiction to that Court in other cases than those specified in the article which has been recited, provided those cases belong to the judicial power of the United States.

If it had been intended to leave it in the discretion of the Legislature to apportion the judicial power between the Supreme and inferior courts according to the will of that body, it would certainly have been useless to have proceeded further than to have defined the judicial power and the tribunals in which it should be vested. The subsequent part of the section is mere surplusage—is entirely without meaning—if such is to be the construction. If Congress remains at liberty to give this court appellate jurisdiction where the Constitution has declared their jurisdiction shall be original, and original jurisdiction where the Constitution has declared it shall be appellate, the distribution of jurisdiction made in the Constitution, is form without substance.

Affirmative words are often, in their operation, negative of other objects than those affirmed, and, in this case, a negative or exclusive sense must be given to them or they have no operation at all.

It cannot be presumed that any clause in the Constitution is intended to be without effect, and therefore such construction is inadmissible unless the words require it.

If the solicitude of the Convention respecting our peace with foreign powers induced a provision that the Supreme Court should take original jurisdiction in cases which might be supposed to affect them, yet the clause would have proceeded no further than to provide for such cases if no further restriction on the powers of Congress had been intended. That they should have appellate jurisdiction in all other cases, with such exceptions as Congress might make, is no restriction unless the words be deemed exclusive of original jurisdiction.

When an instrument organizing fundamentally a judicial system divides it into one Supreme and so many inferior courts as the Legislature may ordain and establish, then enumerates its powers, and proceeds so far to distribute them as to define the jurisdiction of the Supreme Court by declaring the cases in which it shall take original jurisdiction, and that in others it shall take appellate jurisdiction, the plain import of the words seems to be that, in one class of cases, its jurisdiction is original, and not appellate; in the other, it is appellate, and not original. If any other construction would render the clause inoperative, that is an additional reason for rejecting such other construction, and for adhering to the obvious meaning.

To enable this court then to issue a mandamus, it must be shown to be an exercise of appellate jurisdiction, or to be necessary to enable them to exercise appellate jurisdiction.

It has been stated at the bar that the appellate jurisdiction may be exercised in a variety of forms, and that, if it be the will of the Legislature that a mandamus should be used for that purpose, that will must be obeyed. This is true; yet the jurisdiction must be appellate, not original.

It is the essential criterion of appellate jurisdiction that it revises and corrects the proceedings in a cause already instituted, and does not create that case. Although, therefore, a mandamus may be directed to courts, yet to issue such a writ to an officer for the delivery of a paper is, in effect, the same as to sustain an original action for that paper, and therefore seems not to belong to appellate, but to original jurisdiction. Neither is it necessary in such a case as this to enable the Court to exercise its appellate jurisdiction.

The authority, therefore, given to the Supreme Court by the act establishing the judicial courts of the United States to issue writs of mandamus to public officers appears not to be warranted by the Constitution, and it becomes necessary to inquire whether a jurisdiction so conferred can be exercised.

The question whether an act repugnant to the Constitution can become the law of the land is a question deeply interesting to the United States, but, happily, not of an intricacy proportioned to its interest. It seems only necessary to recognise certain principles, supposed to have been long and well established, to decide it.

That the people have an original right to establish for their future government such principles as, in their opinion, shall most conduce to their own happiness is the basis on which the whole American fabric has been erected. The exercise of this original right is a very great exertion; nor can it nor ought it to be frequently repeated. The principles, therefore, so established are deemed fundamental. And as the authority from which they proceed, is supreme, and can seldom act, they are designed to be permanent.

This original and supreme will organizes the government and assigns to different departments their respective powers. It may either stop here or establish certain limits not to be transcended by those departments.

The Government of the United States is of the latter description. The powers of the Legislature are defined and limited; and that those limits may not be mistaken or forgotten, the Constitution is written. To what purpose are powers limited, and to what purpose is that limitation committed to writing, if these limits may at any time be passed by those intended to be restrained? The distinction between a government with limited and unlimited powers is abolished if those limits do not confine the persons on whom they are imposed, and if acts prohibited and acts allowed are of equal obligation. It is a proposition too plain to be contested that the Constitution controls any legislative act repugnant to it, or that the Legislature may alter the Constitution by an ordinary act.

Between these alternatives there is no middle ground. The Constitution is either a superior, paramount law, unchangeable by ordinary means, or it is on a level with ordinary legislative acts, and, like other acts, is alterable when the legislature shall please to alter it.

If the former part of the alternative be true, then a legislative act contrary to the Constitution is not law; if the latter part be true, then written Constitutions are absurd attempts on the part of the people to limit a power in its own nature illimitable.

Certainly all those who have framed written Constitutions contemplate them as forming the fundamental and paramount law of the nation, and consequently the theory of every such government must be that an act of the Legislature repugnant to the Constitution is void.

This theory is essentially attached to a written Constitution, and is consequently to be considered by this Court as one of the fundamental principles of our society. It is not, therefore, to be lost sight of in the further consideration of this subject.

If an act of the Legislature repugnant to the Constitution is void, does it, notwithstanding its invalidity, bind the Courts and oblige them to give it effect? Or, in other words, though it be not law, does it constitute a rule as operative as if it was a law? This would be to overthrow in fact what was established in theory, and would seem, at first view, an absurdity too gross to be insisted on. It shall, however, receive a more attentive consideration.

It is emphatically the province and duty of the Judicial Department to say what the law is. Those who apply the rule to particular cases must, of necessity, expound and interpret that rule. If two laws conflict with each other, the Courts must decide on the operation of each.

So, if a law be in opposition to the Constitution, if both the law and the Constitution apply to a particular case, so that the Court must either decide that case conformably to the law, disregarding the Constitution, or conformably to the Constitution, disregarding the law, the Court must determine which of these conflicting rules governs the case. This is of the very essence of judicial duty.

If, then, the Courts are to regard the Constitution, and the Constitution is superior to any ordinary act of the Legislature, the Constitution, and not such ordinary act, must govern the case to which they both apply.

Those, then, who controvert the principle that the Constitution is to be considered in court as a paramount law are reduced to the necessity of maintaining that courts must close their eyes on the Constitution, and see only the law.

This doctrine would subvert the very foundation of all written Constitutions. It would declare that an act which, according to the principles and theory of our government, is entirely void, is yet, in practice, completely obligatory. It would declare that, if the Legislature shall do what is expressly forbidden, such act, notwithstanding the express prohibition, is in reality effectual. It would be giving to the Legislature a practical and real omnipotence with the same breath which professes to restrict their powers within narrow limits. It is prescribing limits, and declaring that those limits may be passed at pleasure.

That it thus reduces to nothing what we have deemed the greatest improvement on political institutions—a written Constitution, would of itself be sufficient, in America where written Constitutions have been viewed with so much reverence, for rejecting the construction. But the peculiar expressions of the Constitution of the United States furnish additional arguments in favour of its rejection.

The judicial power of the United States is extended to all cases arising under the Constitution.

Could it be the intention of those who gave this power to say that, in using it, the Constitution should not be looked into? That a case arising under the Constitution should be decided without examining the instrument under which it arises?

This is too extravagant to be maintained.

In some cases then, the Constitution must be looked into by the judges. And if they can open it at all, what part of it are they forbidden to read or to obey?

There are many other parts of the Constitution which serve to illustrate this subject.

It is declared that "no tax or duty shall be laid on articles exported from any State." Suppose a duty on the export of cotton, of tobacco, or of flour, and a suit instituted to recover it. Ought judgment to be rendered in such a case? ought the judges to close their eyes on the Constitution, and only see the law?

The Constitution declares that "no bill of attainder or *ex post facto* law shall be passed."

If, however, such a bill should be passed and a person should be prosecuted under it, must the Court condemn to death those victims whom the Constitution endeavours to preserve?

"No person," says the Constitution, "shall be convicted of treason unless on the testimony of two witnesses to the same overt act, or on confession in open court."

Here, the language of the Constitution is addressed especially to the Courts. It prescribes, directly for them, a rule of evidence not to be departed from. If the Legislature should change that rule, and declare one witness, or a confession out of court, sufficient for conviction, must the constitutional principle yield to the legislative act?

From these and many other selections which might be made, it is apparent that the framers of the Constitution contemplated that instrument as a rule for the government of courts, as well as of the Legislature.

Why otherwise does it direct the judges to take an oath to support it? This oath certainly applies in an especial manner to their conduct in their official character. How immoral to impose it on them if they were to be used as the instruments, and the knowing instruments, for violating what they swear to support!

The oath of office, too, imposed by the Legislature, is completely demonstrative of the legislative opinion on this subject. It is in these words:

> I do solemnly swear that I will administer justice without respect to persons, and do equal right to the poor and to the rich; and that I will faithfully and impartially discharge all the duties incumbent on me as according to the best of my abilities and understanding, agreeably to the Constitution and laws of the United States.

Why does a judge swear to discharge his duties agreeably to the Constitution of the United States if that Constitution forms no rule for his government? if it is closed upon him and cannot be inspected by him?

If such be the real state of things, this is worse than solemn mockery. To prescribe or to take this oath becomes equally a crime.

It is also not entirely unworthy of observation that, in declaring what shall be the supreme law of the land, the Constitution itself is first mentioned, and not the laws of the United States generally, but those only which shall be made in pursuance of the Constitution, have that rank.

Thus, the particular phraseology of the Constitution of the United States confirms and strengthens the principle, supposed to be essential to all written Constitutions, that a law repugnant to the Constitution is void, and that courts, as well as other departments, are bound by that instrument.

The rule must be discharged.

John B. Gibson

 **NO**

Eakin v. Raub

12 Sergeant & Rawle (Pennsylvania Supreme Court), 330 (1825)

GIBSON, J-, dissenting

13* . . .

It seems to me, there is a plain difference, hitherto unnoticed, between acts that are repugnant to the constitution of the particular state, and acts that are repugnant to the constitution of the United States; my opinion being, that the judiciary is bound to execute the former, but not the latter. I shall hereafter attempt to explain this difference, by pointing out the particular provisions in the constitution of the United States, on which it depends. **I am aware, that a right to declare all constitutional acts void, without distinction as to either constitution, is generally held as a professional dogma; but I apprehend, rather as a matter of faith than of reason.** I admit, that I once embraced the same doctrine, but without examination, and I shall, therefore, state the arguments that impelled me to abandon it, with great respect for those by whom it is still maintained. But I may premise, that it is not a little remarkable, that although the right in question has all along been claimed by the judiciary, no judge has ventured to discuss it, except Chief Justice MARSHALL (in Marbury) and if the argument of a jurist so distinguished for the strength of his ratiocinative powers be found inconclusive, it may fairly be set down to the weakness of the position which he attempts to defend. . . . Now, in questions of this sort, precedents ought to go for absolutely nothing. The constitution is a collection of fundamental laws, not to be departed from in practice, nor altered by judicial decision, and in the construction of it, nothing would be so alarming as the doctrine of *communis error,* which affords a ready justification for every usurpation that has not been resisted *in limine.* Instead, therefore, of resting on the fact, that the right in question has universally been assumed by the American courts, the judge who asserts it ought to be prepared to maintain it on the principles of the constitution.

*14 I begin, then, by observing, that in this country, the powers of the judiciary are divisible into those that are POLITICAL, and those that are purely CIVIL. Every power by which one organ of the government is enabled to control another, or to exert an influence over its acts, is a political power. The

Pennsylvania Supreme Court, 1825.

political powers of the judiciary are *extraordinary* and *adventitious;* such, for instance, as are derived from certain peculiar provisions in the constitution of the United States, of which hereafter: and they are derived, by direct grant, from the common fountain of all political power. On the other hand, its civil, are its *ordinary* and *appropriate* powers; being part ot its essence, and existing independently of any supposed grant in the constitution. But where the government exists by virtue of a *written* constitution, the judiciary does not necessarily derive from that circumstance, any other than its ordinary and appropriate powers. **Our judiciary is constructed on the principles of the common law, which enters so essentially into the composition of our social institutions as to be inseparable from them, and to be, in fact, the basis of the whole scheme of our civil and political liberty.**

*15 . . .

The constitution and the *right* of the legislature to pass the act, may be in collision; but is that a legitimate subject for judicial determination? If it be, the judiciary must be a peculiar organ, to revise the proceedings of the legislature, and to correct its mistakes; and in what part of the constitution are we to look for this proud preeminence? Viewing the manner in the opposite direction, what would be thought of an act of assembly in which it should be declared that the supreme court had, in a particular case, put a wrong construction on the constitution of the United States, and that the judgment should therefore be reversed? It would doubtless be thought a usurpation of judicial power. But it is by no means clear, that to declare a law void which has been enacted according to the forms prescribed in the constitution, is not a usurpation of legislative power. It is an act of sovereignty; and sovereignty and legislative power are said by Sir WILLIAM BLACKSTONE to be convertible terms. It is the business of the judiciary to interpret the laws, not scan the authority of the lawgiver; and without the latter, it cannot take cognizance of a collision between a law and the constitution. So that to affirm that the judiciary has a right to judge of the existence of such collision, is to take for granted the very thing to be proved. . . .

*16 But it has been said to be emphatically the business of the judiciary, to ascertain and pronounce what the law is; and that this necessarily involves a consideration of the constitution. It does so: but how far? [If the judiciary will inquire into anything beside the form of enactment, where shall it stop? There must be some point of limitation to such an inquiry]; for no one will pretend, that a judge would be justifiable in calling for the election returns, or scrutinizing the qualifications of those who composed the legislature.

*17 Now, as the judiciary is not expressly constituted for [the purpose of determining constitutionality], it must derive whatever authority of the sort it may possess, from the reasonableness and fitness of the thing. . . . But, in theory, all the organs of the government are of equal capacity; or, if not equal, each must be supposed to have superior capacity only for those things which peculiarly belong to it; and as legislation peculiarly involves the consideration of those limitations which are put on the law-making power, and the interpretation of the laws when made, involves only the construction of the laws themselves, it follows, that the construction of the constitution, in this particular, belongs to the legislature, which ought, therefore, to be taken to have superior capacity to judge of the constitutionality of its own acts. *But suppose all to be of equal capacity, in every respect, why should one exercise a controlling power over the rest? That the judiciary is of superior rank, has never been pretended, although it has been said to be co-ordinate. . . .*

It may be alleged that no such power is claimed, and that the judiciary does no positive act, but merely refuses to be instrumental in giving effect to an unconstitutional law. This is nothing more than a repetition, in a different form of the argument—that an unconstitutional law is *ipso facto* void; for a refusal to act under the law must be founded on a right in each branch to judge of the acts of all the others, before it is bound to exercise its functions to give those acts effect. No such right is recognised in the different branches of the national government, except the judiciary (and that, too, on account of the peculiar provisions of the constitution). . . .

*18 Every one knows how seldom men think exactly alike on ordinary subjects; and a government constructed on the principle of assent by all its parts, would be inadequate to the most simple operations. The notion of a complication of counter-checks has been carried to an extent in theory, of which the framers of the constitution never dreamt. When the entire sovereignty was separated into its elementary parts, and distributed to the appropriate branches, all things incident to the exercise of its powers were committed to each branch exclusively. The negative which each part of the legislature may exercise, in regard to the acts of the other, was thought sufficient to prevent material infractions of the restraints which were put on the power of the whole; for, had it been intended to interpose the judiciary as an additional barrier, the matter would surely not have been left in doubt. The judges would not have been left to stand on the insecure and ever-shifting ground of public opinion, as to constructive power; they would have been placed on the impregnable ground of an express grant; they would not have been compelled to resort to the debates in the convention, or the opinion that was generally entertained at the time. A constitution, or a statute, is supposed to contain the whole will of the body from which it emanated; and I would just as soon resort to the debates in the legislature, for the construction of an act of assembly, as to the debates in the convention, for the construction of the constitution.

The power is said to be restricted to cases that are free from doubt or difficulty. But the abstract existence of a power cannot depend on the clearness or obscurity of the case in which it is to be exercised; for that is a, consideration that cannot present itself, before the question of the existence of the power shall have been determined; and if its existence be conceded, no considerations of policy, arising from the obscurity of the particular case, ought to influence the exercise of it. . . . To say, therefore, that the power is to be exercised but in perfectly clear cases, is to betray a doubt of the propriety of exercising it at all. Were the same caution used in judging of the existence of the power, that is inculcated as to the exercise of it, the profession would, perhaps, arrive at a different conclusion. The grant of a power so extraordinary, ought to appear so plain, that he who should run might read. . . .

*19 . . . But what I have in view in this inquiry, is, the supposed right of the judiciary to interfere in cases where the constitution is to be carried into effect through the instrumentality of the legislature, and where that organ must necessarily first decide on the constitutionality of its own act. The oath to support the constitution is not peculiar to the judges, but is taken indiscriminately by every officer of the government, and is designed rather as a test of the political principles of the man, than to bind the officer in the discharge of his duty; otherwise it were difficult to determine what operation it is to have in the case of a recorder of deeds, for instance, who in the execution of his office has nothing to do with the constitution. But granting it to relate to the official conduct of the judge, as well as every other officer, and not to his political principles, still it must be understood in reference to supporting the constitution, *only as far as that may be involved in his official duty;* and consequently if his official duty does not comprehend an inquiry into the authority of the legislature, neither does his oath. . . .

*20 But do not the judges do a *positive* act in violation of the constitution when they give effect to an unconstitutional law? Not if the law has been passed according to the forms established in the constitution. The fallacy of the question is in supposing that the judiciary adopts the acts of the legislature as its own; . . . [T]he fault is imputable to the legislature, and on it the responsibility exclusively rests. In this respect the judges are in the predicament of jurors, who are bound to serve in capital cases although unable, under any circumstances, to reconcile it to their duty to deprive a human being of life. To one of these, who applied to be discharged from the panel, I once heard it remarked, by an eminent and humane judge, "*You* do not deprive a prisoner of life, by finding him guilty of a capital crime; you but pronounce his case to be within the law, and it is, therefore, those who declare the law, and not you, who deprive him of life." . . .

But it has been said that this construction would deprive the citizen of the advantages which are peculiar to a written constitution, by at once declaring the power of the legislature, in practice, to be illimitable. I ask, what are those advantages? The principles of a written constitution are more fixed and certain, and more apparent to the apprehension of the people than principles which depend on tradition and the vague comprehension of the individuals who compose the nation, and who cannot all be expected to receive the same impressions or entertain the same notions on any given subject. But there is no magic or inherent power in parchment and ink, to command respect and protect principles from violation. In the business of government, a recurrence to first principles answers the end of an observation at sea, with a view to correct the dead-reckoning; and for this purpose a written constitution is an instrument of inestimable value. It is of inestimable value also, in rendering its principles familiar to the mass of the people; for, after all, there is no effectual guard against legislative usurpation, but public opinion, the force of which, in this country, is inconceivably great. . . . Once let public opinion be so corrupt as to sanction every misconstruction of the constitution, and abuse of power, which the temptation of the moment may dictate, and the party which may happen to be predominant, will laugh at the puny efforts of a dependent power to arrest it in its course.

*21 For these reasons, I am of opinion, that it rests with the people, in whom full and absolute sovereign power resides, to correct abuses in legislation, by instructing their representatives to repeal the obnoxious act. What is wanting to plenary power in the government, is reserved by the people, for their own immediate use; and to redress an infringement of their rights in this respect, would seem to be an accessory of the power thus reserved. It might, perhaps, have been better to vest the power in the judiciary; as it might be expected, that its habits of deliberation, and the aid derived from the arguments of counsel, would more frequently lead to accurate conclusions. On the other hand, the judiciary is not infallible; and an error by it would admit of no remedy but a more distinct expression of the public will, through the extraordinary medium of a convention; whereas, an error by the legislature admits of a remedy by an exertion of the same will, in the ordinary exercise of the right of suffrage—a mode better calculated to attain the end, without popular excitement. It may be said, the people would probably not notice an error of their representatives. But they would as probably do so, as notice an error of the judiciary; and beside, it is a *postulate* in the theory of our government, and the very basis of the superstructure, that the people are wise, virtuous, and competent to manage their own affairs; and if they are not so, in fact, still, every question of this sort must be determined according to the principles of the constitution, as it came from the hands of its framers, and the existence of a defect which was not foreseen, would not justify those who administer the government, in applying a corrective in practice, which can be provided only by a convention.

Long and uninterrupted usage is entitled to respect; and although it cannot change an admitted principle of the constitution, it will go far to settle a question of doubtful right. But although this power has all along been claimed by the state judiciary, it has never been exercised. . . .

*22 But in regard to an act of assembly, which is found to be in collision with the constitution, laws or treaties of the United States, I take the duty of the judiciary to be exactly the reverse. By becoming parties to the federal constitution the states have agreed to several limitations of their individual sovereignty, to enforce which, it was thought to be absolutely necessary, to prevent them from giving effect to laws in violation of those limitations, through the instrumentality of their own judges. Accordingly, it is declared in the fifth article and second section of the federal constitution, that "This constitution, and the laws of the United States which shall be made in pursuance thereof, and all treaties made, or which shall be made under the authority of the United States, shall be the *supreme* law of the land; and the *judges* in every *state* shall be BOUND thereby; anything in the *laws* or *constitution* of any *state* to the contrary notwithstanding."

POSTSCRIPT

Is Judicial Review a Legitimate Power of U.S. Courts?

*M*arbury v. Madison has been described accurately as a "watershed" case in U.S. legal history. A close reading of *Marbury v. Madison* indicates that Chief Justice Marshall analyzed three essential issues:

1. Did William Marbury and the other "midnight appointees" have a right to the commissions as justices of the peace? Marshall's answer was "yes."
2. Did the failure to deliver the commissions entitle Marbury and the others to a remedy under the law? Once again, Marshall's answer was "yes."
3. Was the proper remedy a writ of mandamus issued by the Supreme Court? Marshall's answer to this essential question was "no."

The answer to the third question is the key to understanding *Marbury v. Madison.* Because the U.S. Congress had passed an ordinary statute, the Judiciary Act of 1789, which expanded the original jurisdiction of the Supreme Court to include issuing writs of mandamus, the part of the law that permitted it to do so, Section 13, was "unconstitutional." Marshall asserted that if the Supreme Court is faced with a conflict between a law passed by the Congress and a provision of the Constitution, it has the power to declare the law unconstitutional and refuse to enforce it. This is because the Constitution is the most fundamental source of law in our nation. A traditional statute cannot override the more fundamental provisions of the Constitution.

The more controversial aspect of *Marbury v. Madison* is, however, Marshall's assertion that the courts should be the branch of government to decide if a legislative act is in conflict with the Constitution. Stated Marshall in a now very famous passage from *Marbury v. Madison:* "[i]t is emphatically the province and duty of the judicial department to say what the law is." The critical question is why do the courts have this power, instead, for example, the Congress? Renowned constitutional scholar Laurence Tribe asserts that the Congress could have just as easily be given the final word on the constitutionality of a statute.

Pennsylvania Supreme Court Justice John B. Gibson's dissenting opinion in *Eakin v. Raub* demonstrates an acute awareness of *Marbury's* limitations. Stated Gibson: "I am aware, that a right to declare all constitutional acts void . . . is generally held as a professional dogma; but I apprehend, rather as a matter of faith than of reason." (13). Gibson continues: "The constitution and the *right* of the legislature to pass [a law] may be in collision; but is that a legitimate subject for *judicial determination* [emphasis added]. If it be, the judiciary must be a peculiar organ to revise the proceedings of the legislature and to correct its mistakes; and in what part of the constitution are we to look for this proud preeminence?" (15).

Who, then, states the more defensible position, Chief Justice Marshall or Justice Gibson? Should the courts have the power of judicial review, or do the legislative and executive branches have an equally strong argument for retaining the power to review the constitutionality of statutes or executive directives?

Before you answer these important questions, you may wish to consider that there may be significant practical reasons for giving the courts, rather than the Congress or the executive branch, the final say on constitutional matters. First, the judges of the federal courts are lifetime appointees, who are, at least in theory, less sensitive to political pressures than members of Congress or the president, who must run for re-election. Second, members of Congress and the president are, again in theory, more sensitive to the desires of the social majority, who have elected them to office. The courts therefore are theoretically in a better position to defend the rights of minorities, an essential purpose of the Constitution.

Moreover, in the years since *Marbury v. Madison* was decided, the Courts have demonstrated a genuine sensitivity to the prerogatives of the executive and legislative branches by developing a set of legal doctrines designed to restrict the exercise of judicial review. Although a detailed discussion of these doctrines is beyond the scope of the present initiative, they include, among others, the *case or controversy* requirement—courts will not decide hypothetical disputes, a real case or controversy must be presented. *Standing*—courts will not decide a case unless a party can demonstrate an actual and personal injury. *Ripeness*—courts will not decide a case that is premature, or in which the issues have not yet developed fully. *Mootness*—courts will not decide a case in which the essential issues have been already resolved. *Political questions*—courts will not decide a case where the issues are better left for decision by a coequal branch of government. These self-imposed restriction doctrines have evolved to specifically limit the exercise of judicial review by the courts.

As you consider the issues posed in *Marbury v. Madison,* and Justice Gibson's response in *Eakin v. Raub,* always bear in mind that *Marbury* involved review by the courts of a law passed by the U.S. Congress. It did not consider the issue of the review of a state court decision by the U.S. Supreme Court. Such cases fall within the Supreme Court's appellate jurisdiction and, if they involve federal constitutional claims or issues, clearly fall within the Court's purview. This principle, which has been established in a multitude of famous precedents such as *Martin v. Hunter's Lessee* (1816), and *McCulloch v. Maryland* (1819), will be considered in much greater detail in Issue 5.

In conclusion, *Marbury v. Madison* continues to be a cornerstone of U.S. legal history. According to Kathleen M. Sullivan and Gerald Gunther, the case is "very much alive [today and] rests on reasoning significant for the contemporary exercise of judicial power." Therefore, understanding its central reasoning "is essential to thinking about Court power today." (2).

For additional reading on the courts and the principle of judicial review, see: Kathleen M. Sullivan and Gerald Gunther, *Constitutional Law* (Foundation Press, 15th ed., 2004); Laurence H. Tribe, *American Constitutional Law* (Foundation Press, 2nd ed., 1988); Cliff Sloan and David McKean, *The Great Decision: Jefferson, Adams, Marshall, and the Battle for the Supreme Court* (Public Affairs, 2009); Alpheus Thomas Mason and Donald Grier Stephenson, Jr., *American Constitutional Law* (Pearson Prentice Hall, 15th ed., 2009); Bernard Schwartz, *A History of the Supreme Court* (Oxford University Press, 1993); Kermit L. Hall, Paul Finkelman, and James Ely, Jr., *American Legal History: Cases and Materials* (Oxford University Press, 3rd ed., 2005); Kermit L. Hall, *The Oxford Companion to the Supreme Court of the United States* (Oxford University Press, 1992); Walter F. Murphy, James E. Fleming, Sotirios A. Barber, and Stephen Macedo, *American Constitutional Interpretation* (Foundation Press, 3rd ed., 2003); David M. O'Brien, *Constitutional Law and Politics: Struggles for Power and Government Accountability* (W.W. Norton, 6th ed., 2005); Craig R. Ducat, *Constitutional Interpretation* (Wadsworth, 9th ed., 2009); John H. Garvey, T. Alexander Aleinikoff, and Daniel A. Farber, *Modern Constitutional Theory: A Reader* (Thompson West, 5th ed., 2004).

ISSUE 2

Do U.S. Supreme Court Decisions Become the Supreme Law of the Land and Binding Precedents for Future Cases?

YES: Earl Warren, from *Cooper v. Aaron*, 358 U.S. 1 (1958)

NO: Edwin Meese III, from "The Law of the Constitution: A Bicentennial Lecture," a paper presented at the Citizen's Forum on the Bicentennial of the Constitution, New Orleans, LA (October 21, 1986)

ISSUE SUMMARY

YES: Chief Justice Earl Warren asserts that the interpretation of the Constitution set forth in a particular decision is the supreme law of the land and it is binding on the states.

NO: Former U.S. Attorney General Edwin Meese III argues that a decision by the Supreme Court does not establish a supreme law of the land that is binding on all persons and parts of the government.

Issue 1 considered the power of judicial review. We observed that this doctrine has become a cornerstone of U.S. constitutional law that has withstood a variety of challenges throughout our nation's history.

You should note that constitutional scholars have distinguished between two different "types" of judicial review that federal courts may exercise: *horizontal* and *vertical*. The latter refers to a case such as *Marbury v. Madison* in which the Supreme Court held unconstitutional a statute passed by a coequal branch of government, the U.S. Congress. Thus, it is viewed as a horizontal type of review:

Legislative branch—Executive branch—Judicial branch

The constitutional legitimacy of the doctrine of judicial review is at its weakest point in these cases because, as Pennsylvania Supreme Court Justice John B. Gibson had observed in *Eakin v. Raub*, nowhere the Constitution states that the Supreme Court has any more power to interpret the document than the other branches of government.

Vertical judicial review refers to the power of the Supreme Court to review a decision of a state's highest court when it interprets a federal law or a provision of the U.S. Constitution:

U.S. Supreme Court

↑

State's Highest Court

As noted constitutional scholars Kathleen M. Sullivan and Gerald Gunther have observed, the textual and historical support for the Supreme Court's authority in such cases is significantly stronger than in those involving horizontal judicial review. Moreover, particularly during the formative years of the new nation, the power to direct states' interpretations of federal law and the Constitution was crucial. To paraphrase the late Justice Oliver Wendell Holmes, one of the greatest figures in U.S. Supreme Court history, it is likely that the new nation would have been able to survive without the power of horizontal judicial review. It may not have survived without the power to direct states' interpretations of federal law and the U.S. Constitution.

A related issue is presented in this issue: whether U.S. Supreme Court decisions become the supreme law of the land and are binding precedents for future cases. This issue is a highly significant one for a number of reasons. First, if Supreme Court decisions were binding solely on the parties before the court and had no status as a precedent for future similar cases, a veritable avalanche of litigation could result that would swamp our court systems. Litigants would be forced to retry every case, even if a highly similar one had been decided previous day by the courts. Moreover, governmental officials could feel free to disregard any Supreme Court decision, at odds with their own views, simply because they were not a party in the previous case.

This issue is presented squarely in *Cooper v. Aaron,* 358 U.S. 1 (1958). In the aftermath of the Supreme Court's historic public school desegregation decision in *Brown v. Board of Education,* 347 U.S. 483 (1954), Arkansas Governor Faubus and other state officials were highly resistant to desegregating Little Rock's public school system. *Brown* had originated in Topeka, Kansas; the state of Arkansas was not a party in that case. Based on the *Brown* decision, however, a U.S. District Court in Arkansas had commanded the public schools in Little Rock to adopt a desegregation policy. Faubus then refused to permit African American students to attend Little Rock public schools and used the Arkansas National Guard to stop the desegregation efforts. The U.S. District Court then issued an injunction against Faubus, and the African American students were permitted to attend the public schools, despite strong public resistance.

Arkansas public officials argued that they were not bound by the precedent set in *Brown v. Board of Education.* In response, a unanimous Supreme Court stated in *Cooper v. Aaron:*

> [T]he Governor and [Arkansas] legislature [argue] that they are not bound by our holding in *Brown.* It is necessary only to recall some basic constitutional propositions which are settled doctrine. Article VI of the Constitution makes the Constitution the 'supreme law of the land.' In 1803, Chief Justice Marshall, speaking for a unanimous Court, referring to the Constitution as 'the fundamental and paramount law of the nation,' declared in the notable case of *Marbury v. Madison* that 'it is emphatically the province and duty of the judicial department to say what the

law is.' This decision declared the basic principle that the federal judiciary is supreme in the exposition of the law of the Constitution, and that principle has ever since been respected by this Court and the Country as a permanent and indispensable feature of our Constitutional system.

On relatively rare occasions in our nation's legal history, however, another viewpoint has emerged, which emphasizes that Supreme Court decisions do not establish a supreme law of the land that is binding on all persons and parts of the government. The dissension is often accompanied by arguments that a U.S. Supreme Court decision has infringed on state sovereignty, executive branch prerogatives, that the Court "is making law," or has exceeded its constitutional authority in some other manner, this perspective has had relatively few proponents throughout U.S. history.

One advocate of this proposition, however, is former U.S. Attorney General Edwin Meese III. Meese was Attorney General during the Reagan administration, which had found itself at odds with U.S. Supreme Court decisions on any number of occasions. In a speech given at the Citizen's Forum on the Bicentennial of the Constitution in 1986, Meese opined: "[A Supreme Court decision] binds the parties in a case and also the executive branch for whatever enforcement is necessary. But such a decision does not establish a 'supreme law of the land' that is binding on all persons and parts of the government, henceforth and forevermore."

The implications of Meese's position are significant indeed. His views on this issue were first published in a *Tulane Law Journal* article in 1987 (*Tulane Law Journal*, vol. 61, p. 987). In that same journal issue, former U.S. Attorney General Ramsey Clark challenged Meese's views and illustrated one of the fundamental flaws in his argument. Stated Clark: "If the same desegregation orders had to be litigated to the Supreme Court for every school district [in the United States], [segregation] would have prevailed outright." (*Tulane Law Journal*, vol. 61, pp. 1093, 1094).

It is quite possible that the continuation of segregation was what some officials in the state of Arkansas had in mind. Resistance to the Supreme Court's decision in *Brown v. Board of Education* was relatively widespread, particularly in the South. Few rational persons would argue, however, that postponing desegregation would have been a positive development. In fact, *Brown v. Board of Education* has been described by Professor Bernard Schwartz as one of only a handful of "watershed" cases in U.S. Supreme Court history. To have permitted state officials opposed to desegregation to derail the incipient efforts to establish a more integrated society would have been completely unconscionable.

In Your Opinion . . .

- Who states the better position on this issue?
- The Supreme Court held in *Cooper v. Aaron* that the interpretation of the Constitution, set forth in its decisions, is the supreme law of the land. Do you agree?
- What are the implications of this decision for the U.S. court systems and the administration of justice?

YES

Earl Warren

Cooper v. Aaron

. . . Opinion of the Court by THE CHIEF JUSTICE, MR. JUSTICE BLACK, MR. JUSTICE FRANKFURTER, MR. JUSTICE DOUGLAS, MR. JUSTICE BURTON, MR. JUSTICE CLARK, MR. JUSTICE HARLAN, MR. JUSTICE BRENNAN, and MR. JUSTICE WHITTAKER.

As this case reaches us it raises questions of the highest importance to the maintenance of our federal system of government. It necessarily involves a claim by the Governor and Legislature of a State that there is no duty on state officials to obey federal court orders resting on this Court's considered interpretation of the United States Constitution. Specifically it involves actions by the Governor and Legislature of Arkansas upon the premise that they are not bound by our holding in *Brown v. Board of Education*, 347 U.S. 483. That holding was that the Fourteenth Amendment forbids States to use their governmental powers to bar children on racial grounds from attending schools where there is state participation through any arrangement, management, funds or property. We are urged to uphold a suspension of the Little Rock School Board's plan to do away with segregated public schools in Little Rock until state laws and efforts to upset and nullify our holding in *Brown v. Board of Education* have been further challenged and tested in the courts. We reject these contentions. . . .

The following are the facts and circumstances so far as necessary to show how the legal questions are presented.

On May 17, 1954, this Court decided that enforced racial segregation in the public schools of a State is a denial of the equal protection of the laws enjoined by the Fourteenth Amendment. *Brown v. Board of Education*, [358 U.S. 1, 6] 347 U.S. 483. The Court postponed, pending further argument, formulation of a decree to effectuate this decision. That decree was rendered May 31, 1955. *Brown v. Board of Education*, 349 U.S. 294. In the formulation of that decree the Court recognized that good faith compliance with the principles declared in *Brown* might in some situations "call for elimination of a variety of obstacles in making the transition to school systems operated in accordance with the constitutional principles set forth in our May 17, 1954, decision." Id., at 300. The Court went on to state:

> "Courts of equity may properly take into account the public interest in the elimination of such obstacles in a systematic and effective manner. But it should go without saying that the vitality of these constitutional principles cannot be allowed to yield simply because of disagreement with them."

Supreme Court of the United States, 1958.

"While giving weight to these public and private considerations, the courts will require that the defendants make a prompt and reasonable start toward full compliance with our May 17, 1954, ruling. Once such a start has been made, the courts may find that additional time is necessary to carry out the ruling in an effective manner. The burden rests upon the defendants to establish that such time is necessary in the public interest and is consistent with good faith compliance at the earliest practicable date. To that end, the courts may consider problems related to administration, arising from the physical condition of the school plant, the school transportation system, personnel, revision of school districts and attendance areas into compact units to achieve a system of determining admission to the public schools on a nonracial basis, and revision of local laws and regulations which may be necessary in solving the foregoing problems." 349 U.S., at 300–301. [358 U.S. 1, 7]

Under such circumstances, the District Courts were directed to require "a prompt and reasonable start toward full compliance," and to take such action as was necessary to bring about the end of racial segregation in the public schools "with all deliberate speed." Ibid. Of course, in many locations, obedience to the duty of desegregation would require the immediate general admission of Negro children, otherwise qualified as students for their appropriate classes, at particular schools. On the other hand, a District Court, after analysis of the relevant factors (which, of course, excludes hostility to racial desegregation), might conclude that justification existed for not requiring the present non-segregated admission of all qualified Negro children. In such circumstances, however, the courts should scrutinize the program of the school authorities to make sure that they had developed arrangements pointed toward the earliest practicable completion of desegregation, and had taken appropriate steps to put their program into effective operation. It was made plain that delay in any guise in order to deny the constitutional rights of Negro children could not be countenanced, and that only a prompt start, diligently and earnestly pursued, to eliminate racial segregation from the public schools could constitute good faith compliance. State authorities were thus duty bound to devote every effort toward initiating desegregation and bringing about the elimination of racial discrimination in the public school system.

On May 20, 1954, three days after the first *Brown* opinion, the Little Rock District School Board adopted, and on May 23, 1954, made public, a statement of policy entitled "Supreme Court Decision—Segregation in Public Schools." In this statement the Board recognized that

> It is our responsibility to comply with Federal Constitutional Requirements and we intend to do so when the Supreme Court of the United States outlines the method to be followed. [358 U.S. 1, 8] . . .

[On] September 4, 1957, the United States Attorney for the Eastern District of Arkansas was requested by the District Court to begin an immediate investigation in order to fix responsibility for the interference with the orderly implementation of the District Court's direction to carry out the desegregation program. Three days later, September 7, the District Court denied a petition of the School Board and the Superintendent of Schools for an order temporarily suspending continuance of the program.

Upon completion of the United States Attorney's investigation, he and the Attorney General of the United States, at the District Court's request, entered the proceedings and filed a petition on behalf of the United States, as amicus curiae, to enjoin the Governor of Arkansas and officers of the Arkansas National Guard from further attempts to prevent obedience to the court's order. After hearings on the petition, the District Court found that the School Board's plan had been obstructed by the Governor through the use of National Guard troops, and granted a preliminary injunction on September [358 U.S. 1, 12] 20, 1957, enjoining the Governor and the officers of the Guard from preventing the attendance of Negro children at Central High School, and from otherwise obstructing or interfering with the orders of the court in connection with the plan. 156 F. Supp. 220, affirmed, *Faubus v. United States*, 254 F.2d 797. The National Guard was then withdrawn from the school.

The next school day was Monday, September 23, 1957. The Negro children entered the high school that morning under the protection of the Little Rock Police Department and members of the Arkansas State Police. But the officers caused the children to be removed from the school during the morning because they had difficulty controlling a large and demonstrating crowd which had gathered at the high school. 163 F. Supp., at 16. On September 25, however, the President of the United States dispatched federal troops to Central High School and admission of the Negro students to the school was thereby effected. Regular army troops continued at the high school until November 27, 1957. They were then replaced by federalized National Guardsmen who remained throughout the balance of the school year. Eight of the Negro students remained in attendance at the school throughout the school year.

We come now to the aspect of the proceedings presently before us. On February 20, 1958, the School Board and the Superintendent of Schools filed a petition in the District Court seeking a postponement of their program for desegregation. Their position in essence was that because of extreme public hostility, which they stated had been engendered largely by the official attitudes and actions of the Governor and the Legislature, the maintenance of a sound educational program at Central High School, with the Negro students in attendance, would be impossible. The Board therefore proposed that the Negro students already admitted to the school be withdrawn [358 U.S. 1, 13] and sent to segregated schools, and that all further steps to carry out the Board's desegregation program be postponed for a period later suggested by the Board to be two and one-half years.

After a hearing the District Court granted the relief requested by the Board. Among other things the court found that the past year at Central High School had been attended by conditions of "chaos, bedlam and turmoil"; that there were "repeated incidents of more or less serious violence directed against the Negro students and their property"; that there was "tension and unrest among the school administrators, the classroom teachers, the pupils, and the latters' parents, which inevitably had an adverse effect upon the educational program": that a school official was threatened with violence: that a "serious financial burden" had been cast on the School District; that the education of the students had suffered "and under existing conditions will continue to suffer"; that the Board would continue to need "military assistance or its equivalent"; that the local police department would not be able "to detail enough men to afford the necessary protection"; and that the situation was "intolerable." 163 F. Supp., at 20–26. . . .

The significance of these findings, however, is to be considered in light of the fact, indisputably revealed by the record before us, that the conditions they depict are directly traceable to the actions of legislators and executive officials of the State of Arkansas, taken in their official capacities, which reflect their own determination to resist this Court's decision in the *Brown* case and which have brought about violent resistance to that decision in Arkansas. In its petition for certiorari filed in this Court, the School Board itself describes the situation in this language: "The legislative, executive, and judicial departments of the state government opposed the desegregation of Little Rock schools by enacting laws, calling out troops, making statements villifying federal law and federal courts, and failing to utilize state law enforcement agencies and judicial processes to maintain public peace."

One may well sympathize with the position of the Board in the face of the frustrating conditions which have confronted it, but, regardless of the Board's good faith, the actions of the other state agencies responsible for those conditions compel us to reject the Board's legal position. Had Central High School been under the direct management of the State itself, it could hardly be suggested [358 U.S. 1, 16] that those immediately in charge of the school should be heard to assert their own good faith as a legal excuse for delay in implementing the constitutional rights of these respondents, when vindication of those rights was rendered difficult or impossible by the actions of other state officials. The situation here is in no different posture because the members of the School Board and the Superintendent of Schools are local officials, from the point of view of the Fourteenth Amendment, they stand in this litigation as the agents of the State.

The constitutional rights of respondents are not to be sacrificed or yielded to the violence and disorder which have followed upon the actions of the Governor and Legislature. As this Court said some 41 years ago in a unanimous opinion in a case involving another aspect of racial segregation: "It is urged that this proposed segregation will promote the public peace by preventing race conflicts. Desirable as this is, and important as is the preservation of the public peace, this aim cannot be accomplished by laws or ordinances which deny rights created or protected by the Federal Constitution." *Buchanan v. Warley*, 245 U.S. 60, 80. Thus law and order are not here to be preserved by depriving the Negro children of their constitutional rights. The record before us clearly establishes that the growth of the Board's difficulties to a magnitude beyond its unaided power to control is the product of state action. Those difficulties, as counsel for the Board forthrightly conceded on the oral argument in this Court, can also be brought under control by state action.

The controlling legal principles are plain. The command of the Fourteenth Amendment is that no "State" shall deny to any person within its jurisdiction the equal protection of the laws. "A State acts by its legislative, its executive, or its judicial authorities. It can act in no [358 U.S. 1, 17] other way. The constitutional provision, therefore, must mean that no agency of the State, or of the officers or agents by whom its powers are exerted, shall deny to any person within its jurisdiction the equal protection of the laws. Whoever, by virtue of public position under a State government, . . . denies or takes away the equal protection of the laws, violates the constitutional inhibition; and as he acts in the name and for the State, and is clothed with the State's power, his act is that of the State. This must be so, or the constitutional prohibition has no meaning." Ex parte Virginia, 100 U.S. 339, 347. Thus the prohibitions of the Fourteenth Amendment extend to all action of the State denying equal protection of the laws; whatever the agency of the State taking the action, see *Virginia v. Rives*, 100 U.S. 313; *Pennsylvania v. Board of Directors of City Trusts of Philadelphia*, 353 U.S. 230; *Shelley v. Kraemer*, 334 U.S. 1; or whatever the guise in which it is taken, see *Derrington v. Plummer*, 240 F.2d 922; *Department of Conservation and Development v. Tate*, 231 F.2d 615. In short, the constitutional rights of children not to be discriminated against in school admission on grounds of race or color declared by this Court in the *Brown* case can neither be nullified openly and directly by state legislators or state executive or judicial officers, nor nullified indirectly by them through evasive schemes for segregation whether attempted "ingeniously or ingenuously." *Smith v. Texas*, 311 U.S. 128, 132.

What has been said, in the light of the facts developed, is enough to dispose of the case. However, we should answer the premise of the actions of the Governor and Legislature that they are not bound by our holding in the *Brown* case. It is necessary only to recall some basic constitutional propositions which are settled doctrine. [358 U.S. 1, 18]

Article VI of the Constitution makes the Constitution the "supreme Law of the Land." In 1803, Chief Justice Marshall, speaking for a unanimous Court, referring to the Constitution as "the fundamental and paramount law of the nation," declared in the notable case of *Marbury v. Madison*, 1 Cranch 137, 177, that "It is emphatically the province and duty of the judicial department to say what the law is." This decision declared the basic principle that the federal judiciary is supreme in the exposition of the law of the Constitution, and that principle has ever since been respected by this Court and the Country as a permanent and indispensable feature of our constitutional system. It follows that the interpretation of the Fourteenth Amendment enunciated by this Court in the *Brown* case is the supreme law of the land, and Art. VI of the Constitution makes it of binding effect on the States "any Thing in the Constitution or Laws of any State to the Contrary notwithstanding." Every state legislator and executive and judicial officer is solemnly committed by oath taken pursuant to Art. VI, cl. 3, "to support this Constitution." Chief Justice Taney, speaking for a unanimous Court in 1859, said that this requirement reflected the framers' "anxiety to preserve it [the Constitution] in full force, in all its powers, and to guard against resistance to or evasion of its authority, on the part of a State. . . ." *Ableman v. Booth*, 21 How. 506, 524.

No state legislator or executive or judicial officer can war against the Constitution without violating his undertaking to support it. Chief Justice

Marshall spoke for a unanimous Court in saying that: "If the legislatures of the several states may, at will, annul the judgments of the courts of the United States, and destroy the rights acquired under those judgments, the constitution itself becomes a solemn mockery. . . ." *United States v. Peters*, 5 Cranch 115, 136. A Governor who asserts a [358 U.S. 1, 19] power to nullify a federal court order is similarly restrained. If he had such power, said Chief Justice Hughes, in 1932, also for a unanimous Court, "it is manifest that the fiat of a state Governor, and not the Constitution of the United States, would be the supreme law of the land; that the restrictions of the Federal Constitution upon the exercise of state power would be but impotent phrases. . . ." *Sterling v. Constantin*, 287 U.S. 378, 397–398.

It is, of course, quite true that the responsibility for public education is primarily the concern of the States, but it is equally true that such responsibilities, like all other state activity, must be exercised consistently with federal constitutional requirements as they apply to state action. The Constitution created a government dedicated to equal justice under law. The Fourteenth Amendment embodied and emphasized that ideal. State support of segregated schools through any arrangement, management, funds, or property cannot be squared with the Amendment's command that no State shall deny to any person within its jurisdiction the equal protection of the laws. The right of a student not to be segregated on racial grounds in schools so maintained is indeed so fundamental and pervasive that it is embraced in the concept of due process of law. *Bolling v. Sharpe*, 347 U.S. 497. The basic decision in *Brown* was unanimously reached by this Court only after the case had been briefed and twice argued and the issues had been given the most serious consideration. Since the first *Brown* opinion three new Justices have come to the Court. They are at one with the Justices still on the Court who participated in that basic decision as to its correctness, and that decision is now unanimously reaffirmed. The principles announced in that decision and the obedience of the States to them, according to the command of the Constitution, [358 U.S. 1, 20] are indispensable for the protection of the freedoms guaranteed by our fundamental charter for all of us. Our constitutional ideal of equal justice under law is thus made a living truth. . . .

"Per Curiam.

"The Court, having fully deliberated upon the oral arguments had on August 28, 1958, as supplemented by the arguments presented on September 11, 1958, and all the briefs on file, is unanimously of the opinion that the judgment of the Court of Appeals for the Eighth Circuit of August 18, 1958, 257 F.2d 33, must be affirmed. In view of the imminent commencement of the new school year at the Central High School of Little Rock, Arkansas, we deem it important to make prompt announcement of our judgment affirming the Court of Appeals. The expression of the views supporting our judgment will be prepared and announced in due course."

"It is accordingly ordered that the judgment of the Court of Appeals for the Eighth Circuit, dated August 18, 1958, 257 F.2d 33, reversing the judgment of the District Court for the Eastern District of Arkansas, dated June 20,

1958, 163 F. Supp. 13, be affirmed, and that the judgments of the District Court for the Eastern District of Arkansas, dated August 28, 1956, see 143 F. Supp. 855, and September 3, 1957, enforcing the School Board's plan for desegregation in compliance with the decision of this Court in *Brown v. Board of Education*, 347 U.S. 483, 349 U.S. 294, be reinstated. It follows that the order of the Court of Appeals dated August 21,1958, staying its own mandate is of no further effect.

"The judgment of this Court shall be effective immediately, and shall be communicated forthwith to the District Court for the Eastern District of Arkansas.". . .

Edwin Meese III  **NO**

The Law of the Constitution: A Bicentennial Lecture

. . . Perhaps no country in history has been blessed with liberty and prosperity more than our own. And while our Founding Fathers were careful to give thanks to divine Providence, they also knew much effort and sacrifice would be due from them if their good fortune was to continue.

As you know, less than a month ago, in the East Room of the White House, a new Chief Justice and a new Justice of the Supreme Court were sworn in— William Rehnquist and Antonin Scalia, respectively. After both men had taken their oaths to support the Constitution, President Reagan reflected on what he called the "inspired wisdom" of our Constitution. "Hamilton, Jefferson and all the Founding Fathers," he said,

> recognized that the Constitution is the supreme and ultimate expression of the will of the American people. They saw that no one in office could remain above it, if freedom were to survive through the ages. They understood that, in the words of James Madison, if 'the sense in which the Constitution was accepted and ratified by the nation is not the guide to expounding it, there can be no security for a faithful exercise of its powers.'

In concluding, the President repeated a warning given by Daniel Webster more than a century ago. It is a thought especially worth remembering as we approach the bicentennial anniversary of our Constitution. "Miracles do not cluster," Webster said. "Hold on to the Constitution of the United States of America and to the Republic for which it stands—what has happened once in 6,000 years may never happen again. Hold on to your Constitution, for if the American Constitution shall fall there will be anarchy throughout the world."

During its nearly two hundred years, the Constitution, which Gladstone pronounced "the most wonderful work ever struck off at a given time by the brain and purpose of man," has been reflected upon and argued about from many perspectives by great men and lesser ones. The scrutiny has not always been friendly. The debates over ratification, for example, were often rancorous, and scorn was poured on many of the constitutional provisions devised by the Federal Convention in 1787. The Federalists and the Anti-Federalists were, to

From a paper presented at the Citizen's Forum on the Bicentennial of the Constitution (New Orleans, LA, October, 21, 1986).

say the very least, in notable disagreement. Richard Henry Lee of Virginia, a leading Anti-Federalist, was convinced, for example, that the new Constitution was "in its first principles, most highly and dangerously oligarchic." He feared, as did a good many others, for the fate of democratic government under so powerful an instrument. Still others thought it unlikely so large a nation could survive without explicit provision for cultivating civic virtue among the citizens. The critics of the proposed Constitution had serious reservations about this new enterprise in popular government, an effort even the friends of the Constitution conceded was a "novel experiment."

But no sooner was the Constitution adopted than it became an object of astonishing reverence. The losers in the great ratification debates pitched in to make the new government work. Indeed, so vast was the public enthusiasm that one Senator complained that, in praising the new government, "declamatory gentlemen" were painting "the state of the country under the old Congress"—that is, under the Articles of Confederation—"as if neither wood grew nor water ran in America before the happy adoption of the Constitution."

It has not all been easy going, of course. There has been some pretty rough sailing during the nearly 200 years under the Constitution. In fact, the greatest political tragedy in American history was played out in terms of the principles of the Constitution. You see, the debate over nationalism versus confederalism that had first so divided the Federal Convention, and later had inflamed the animosities of Federalists and Anti-Federalists, lingered on. Its final resolution was a terrible and bloody one—the War Between the States. And in the War's wake, the once giddy, almost unqualified adoration of the Constitution subsided into realism.

Today our great charter is once again under close scrutiny. Once again it is grist for the editorial mills of our nation's newspapers and news magazines. And while the attention is generally respectful, it is, to be sure, not uncritical. This attitude, I think, befits both the subject and our times. It shows better than anything else the continuing health of our republic and the vigor of our politics.

Since becoming Attorney General, I have had the pleasure to speak about the Constitution on several occasions. I have tried to examine it from many angles. I have discussed its moral foundations. I have also addressed on separate occasions its great structural principles—federalism and separation of powers. Tonight I would like to look at it from yet another perspective and try to develop further some of the views that I have already expressed. Specifically, I would like to consider a distinction that is essential to maintaining our limited form of government. [That is the necessary distinction between the Constitution and constitutional law.] The two are not synonymous.

What, then, is this distinction?

The Constitution is—to put it simply but, one hopes, not simplistically—the Constitution. [It is a document of our most fundamental law.] It begins "We the People of the United States, in Order to form a more perfect Union . . ." and ends up, some 6,000 words later, with the 26th Amendment. It creates the institutions of our government, it enumerates the powers those institutions may wield, and it cordons off certain areas into which government may not enter. It prohibits the national authority, for example, from passing *ex post facto* laws while it prohibits the states from violating the obligations of contracts.

The Constitution is, in brief, the instrument by which the consent of the governed—the fundamental requirement of any legitimate government—is transformed into a government complete with "the powers to act and a structure designed to make it act wisely or responsibly." Among its various "internal contrivances" (as James Madison called them) we find federalism, separation of powers, bicameralism, representation, an extended commercial republic, an energetic executive, and an independent judiciary. Together, these devices form the machinery of our popular form of government and secure the rights of the people. [The Constitution, then, is the Constitution, and as such it is, in its own words, "the supreme Law of the Land."]

Constitutional law, on the other hand, is that body of law which has resulted from the Supreme Court's adjudications involving disputes over constitutional provisions or doctrines. [To put it a bit more simply, constitutional law is what the Supreme Court says about the Constitution in its decisions resolving the cases and controversies that come before it.]

And in its limited role of offering judgment, the Court has had a great deal to say. In almost two hundred years, it has produced nearly 500 volumes of *Reports* of cases. While not all these opinions deal with constitutional questions, of course, a good many do. This stands in marked contrast to the few, slim paragraphs that have been added to the original Constitution as amendments. So, in terms of sheer bulk, constitutional law greatly overwhelms the Constitution. But in substance, it is meant to support and not overwhelm the Constitution whence it is derived.

And this body of law, this judicial handiwork, is, in a fundamental way, unique in our scheme. For the Court is the only branch of our government that routinely, day in and day out, is charged with the awesome task of addressing the most basic, the most enduring political questions: What *is* due process of law? How *does* the idea of separation of powers affect the Congress in certain circumstances? And so forth. The answers the Court gives are very important to the stability of the law so necessary for good government. But as constitutional historian Charles Warren once noted, what's most important to remember is that "however the Court may interpret the provisions of the Constitution, [it is still the Constitution which is the law, not the decisions of the Court]."

By this, of course, Charles Warren did not mean that a constitutional decision by the Supreme Court lacks the character of law. Obviously, it does have binding quality: [It binds the parties in a case and also the executive branch for whatever enforcement is necessary. But such a decision does not establish a "supreme Law of the Land" that is binding on all persons and parts of government, henceforth and forevermore].

This point should seem so obvious as not to need elaboration. Consider its necessity in particular reference to the Court's own work. The Supreme Court would face quite a dilemma if its own constitutional decisions really were "the supreme Law of the Land" binding on all persons and governmental entities, including the Court itself, for then the Court would not be able to change its mind. It could not overrule itself in a constitutional case. Yet we know that the Court has done so on numerous occasions. I do not have to remind a New Orleans audience of the fate of *Plessy v. Ferguson*, the infamous case involving a Louisiana railcar law, which in 1896 established the legal doctrine of "separate but equal." It finally and fortunately was struck down in 1954, in *Brown v. Board of Education*. Just this past term, the Court overruled itself in *Batson v. Kentucky* by reversing a 1965 decision that had made preemptory challenges to persons on the basis of race virtually unreviewable under the Constitution.

These and other examples teach effectively the point that constitutional law and the Constitution are not the same. Even so, although the point may seem obvious, there have been those down through our history—and especially, it seems, in our own time—who have denied the distinction between the Constitution and constitutional law. Such denial usually has gone hand in hand with an affirmation—that constitutional decisions are on a par with the Constitution in the sense that they, too, are "the supreme Law of the Land," from which there is no appeal.

Perhaps the most well-known instance of this denial occurred during the most important crisis in our political history. In 1857, in *The Dred Scott* case, the Supreme Court struck down the Missouri Compromise by declaring that Congress could not prevent the extension of slavery into the teritories and that blacks could not be citizens and thus eligible to enjoy the constitutional privileges of citizenship. This was a constitutional decision, for the Court said that the right of whites to possess slaves was a property right affirmed in the Constitution.

This decision sparked the greatest political debate in our history. In the 1858 Senate campaign in Illinois, Stephen Douglas went so far in his defense of *Dred Scott* as to equate the decision with the Constitution. "It is the fundamental principle of the judiciary," he said in his third debate with his opponent, Abraham Lincoln, "that its decisions are final. It is created for that purpose so that when you cannot agree among yourselves on a disputed point you appeal to the judicial tribunal which steps in and decides for you, and that decision is binding on every good citizen." Furthermore, he said, "The Constitution has created that Court to decide all Constitutional questions in the last resort, and when such decisions have been made, they become the law of the land." It plainly was Douglas's view that constitutional decisions by the Court were authoritative, controlling and final, binding on all persons and parts of government the instant they are made—from then on.

Lincoln, of course, disagreed. And in his response to Douglas we can see the nuances and subtleties, and the correctness, of the position that makes most sense in a constitutional democracy like ours—a position that seeks to maintain the important function of judicial review while at the same time upholding the right of the people to govern themselves through the democratic branches of government.

Lincoln said that insofar as the Court "decided in favor of Dred Scott's master and against Dred Scott and his family"—the actual parties in the case—he did not propose to resist the decision. But Lincoln went on to say: "We nevertheless do oppose [*Dred Scott*] . . . as a political rule which shall be binding on the voter, to vote for nobody who thinks it wrong, which shall be binding on the members of Congress or the President to favor no measure that does not actually concur with the principles of that decision."

I have provided this example, not only because it comes from a well-known episode in our history, but also because it helps us understand the implications of this important distinction. If a constitutional decision is not the same as the Constitution itself, if it is not binding in the same way that the Constitution is, we as citizens may respond to a decision disagree with. As Lincoln in effect pointed out, we can make our responses through the presidents, the senators, and the representatives we elect at the national level. We can also make them through those we elect at the state and local levels.

Thus, not only can the Supreme Court respond to its previous constitutional decisions and change them, as it did in *Brown* and has done on many other occasions. So can the other branches of government, and, through them, the American people.

As we know, Lincoln himself worked to overturn *Dred Scott* through the executive branch. The Congress joined him in this effort. Fortunately, *Dred Scott*—the case—lived a very short life.

Once we understand the distinction between constitutional law and the Constitution, once we see that constitutional decisions need not be seen as the last words in constitutional construction, once we comprehend that these decisions do not necessarily determine future public policy—once we see all of this, we can grasp a correlative point: that constitutional interpretation is not the business of the Court only, but also, and properly, the business of all branches of government.

The Supreme Court, then, is not the only interpreter of the Constitution. Each of the three coordinate branches of government created and empowered by the Constitution—the executive and legislative no less than the judicial—has a duty to interpret the Constitution in the performance of its official functions. In fact, every official takes an oath precisely to that effect.

For the same reason that the Constitution cannot be reduced to constitutional law, the Constitution cannot simply be reduced to what Congress or the President say it is either. Quite the contrary. The Constitution, the original document of 1787 plus its amendments, is and must be understood to be the standard against which all laws, policies and interpretations must be measured. It is the consent of the governed with which the actions of the governors must be squared.

And this also applies to the power of judicial review. For as Justice Felix Frankfurter once said, "The ultimate touchstone of constitutionality is the Constitution itself and not what we have said about it."

Judicial review of Congressional and executive actions for their constitutionality has played a major role throughout our political history. The exercise of this power produces constitutional law. And in this task even the courts themselves have on occasion been tempted to think that the law of their decisions is on a par with the Constitution.

Some thirty years ago, in the midst of great racial turmoil, our highest Court seemed to succumb to this very temptation. By a flawed reading of our

Constitution and *Marbury v. Madison*, and an even more faulty syllogism of legal reasoning, the Court in a 1958 case called *Cooper v. Aaron* appeared to arrive at conclusions about its own power that would have shocked men like John Marshall and Joseph Story.

In this case the Court proclaimed that the constitutional decision it had reached that day was nothing less than "the supreme law of the land." Obviously the decision was binding on the parties in the case; but the implication that everyone would have to accept its judgments uncritically, that it was a decision from which there could be no appeal, was astonishing; the language recalled what Stephen Douglas said about *Dred Scott*. In one fell swoop, the Court seemed to reduce the Constitution to the status of ordinary constitutional law, and to equate the judge with the lawgiver. Such logic assumes, as Charles Evans Hughes once quipped, that the Constitution is "what the judges say it is." The logic of *Cooper v. Aaron* was, and is, at war with the Constitution, at war with the basic principles of democratic government, and at war with the very meaning of the rule of law.

Just as *Dred Scott* had its partisans a century ago, so does *Cooper v. Aaron* today. For example, a U.S. Senator criticized a recent nominee of the President's to the bench for his sponsorship while a state legislator of a bill that responded to a Supreme Court decision with which he disagreed. The decision was *Stone v. Graham*, a 1980 case in which the Court held unconstitutional a Kentucky statute that required the posting of the Ten Commandments in the schools of that state. The bill co-sponsored by the judicial nominee—which, by the way, passed his state's Senate by a vote of 39 to 9—would have permitted the posting of the Ten Commandments in the schools of his state. In this, the nominee was acting on the principle Lincoln well understood—that legislators have an independent duty to consider the constitutionality of proposed legislation. Nonetheless, the nominee was faulted for not appreciating that under *Cooper v. Aaron*, Supreme Court decisions are the law of the land—just like the Constitution. He was faulted, in other words, for failing to agree with an idea that would put the Court's constitutional interpretations in the unique position of meaning the same as the Constitution itself.

My message today is that such interpretations are not and must not be placed in such a position. To understand the distinction between the Constitution and constitutional law is to grasp, as John Marshall observed in *Marbury*, "that the framers of the Constitution contemplated that instrument as a *rule for the government of courts, as well as of the legislature*." This was the reason, in Marshall's view, that a "written Constitution is one of the greatest improvements on political institutions."

Likewise, James Madison, expressing his mature view of the subject, wrote that as the three branches of government are coordinate and equally bound to support the Constitution, "each must in the exercise of its functions be guided by the text of the Constitution according to its own interpretation of it." And, as his lifelong friend and collaborator, Jefferson, once said, the written Constitution is "our peculiar security."

But perhaps no one has ever put it better than did Abraham Lincoln, seeking to keep the lamp of freedom burning bright in the dark moral shadows cast by the Court in the *Dred Scott* case. Recognizing that Justice Taney in his opinion in that case had done great violence not only to the text of the Constitution but to the intentions of those who had written, proposed, and ratified it, Lincoln argued that,

> if the policy of government, upon vital questions affecting the whole people, is to be irrevocably fixed by decisions of the Supreme Court, the instant they are made, in ordinary litigation between parties, in personal actions, the people will have ceased to be their own rulers, having, to that extent, practically resigned their government into the hands of that imminent tribunal.

Once again, we must understand that the Constitution is, and must be understood to be, superior to ordinary constitutional law. This distinction must be respected. To confuse the Constitution with judicial pronouncements allows no standard by which to criticize and to seek the overruling of what University of Chicago Law Professor Philip Kurland once called the "derelicts of constitutional law"—cases such as *Dred Scott* and *Plessy v. Ferguson*. To do otherwise, as Lincoln said, is to submit to government by judiciary. But such a state could never be consistent with the principles of our Constitution. Indeed, it would be utterly inconsistent with the very idea of the rule of law to which we, as a people, have always subscribed.

We are the heirs to a long Western tradition of the rule of law. Some 2,000 years ago, for example, the great statesman of the ancient Roman Republic, Cicero, observed, "We are in bondage to the law in order that we may be free." Today, the rule of law is still the very fundament of our civilization, and the American Constitution remains its crowning glory.

But if law, as Thomas Paine once said, is to remain "King" in America we must insist that every department of our government, every official, and every citizen be bound by the Constitution. That's what it means to be "a nation of laws, not of men." As Jefferson once said:

> It is jealousy and not confidence which prescribes limited constitutions to brad down those whom we are obliged to trust with power . . . In questions of power, then, let no more be heard of confidence in man, but bind him down from mischief by the chains of the Constitution.

Again, thank all of you for the honor of addressing you this evening. In closing, let me urge you again to consider Daniel Webster's words: "Hold on to the Constitution . . . and the Republic for which it stands—what has happened once in 6,000 years may never happen again. Hold on to your Constitution."

POSTSCRIPT

Do U.S. Supreme Court Decisions Become the Supreme Law of the Land and Binding Precedents for Future Cases?

The readings in this section present very different views of the proper role of the U.S. Supreme Court in our governmental system. The Court in *Cooper v. Aaron* presented the ultimate issue as follows: "As this case reaches us, it raises questions of the highest importance to the maintenance of our federal system of government. It necessarily involves a claim by the Governor and Legislature of a State that there is no duty on state officials to obey federal court orders resting on this Court's interpretation of the United States Constitution."

This case had reached the Supreme Court after it had become clear that some governmental authorities in the state of Arkansas were attempting to thwart implementation of desegregation plans for public school systems in the aftermath of *Brown v. Board of Education*. First, in November 1956, the state had adopted a constitutional amendment commanding the Arkansas General Assembly to oppose "in every Constitutional manner the Unconstitutional desegregation decisions [*Brown v. Board of Education* (1954), and *Brown v. Board of Education II* (1955)—the decision commanding the United States District Courts to supervise and implement the first *Brown* decision 'with all deliberate speed']." In addition, the state adopted a "pupil assignment law," relieving children from mandatory attendance at racially mixed schools.

In 1957, the day before the African American students were to enter the main high school in Little Rock, Governor Faubus sent units of the Arkansas National Guard to the high school grounds and asserted that the school was "off limits" to African Americans. Although the Little Rock School Board had made a good faith effort to comply with the *Brown* desegregation mandate, and the African American students had entered the high school under the protection of the Little Rock Police Department and the Arkansas State Police, the officers later caused the students to be removed from school because they had difficulty controlling a large and unruly crowd that had gathered. The officers were later replaced by federal National Guardsmen who remained at the school for the rest of the year. Eight very brave African American students attended the school for the remainder of the year.

When confronted with this situation, the U.S. Supreme Court took a highly principled stand: "The constitutional rights of [the African American students] are not be sacrificed or yielded to the violence and disorder which have followed upon the actions of the Governor and Legislature." The Court continued:

> [T]he constitutional rights of children not to be discriminated against in school admission on grounds of race or color declared by this Court in the *Brown* case can neither be nullified openly and directly by state legislators or state executive or judicial officers, nor nullified indirectly by them through evasive schemes for segregation whether attempted 'ingeniously or ingenuously.' [Citation omitted].

Can you imagine what the implications would have been if the Supreme Court had allowed the government of the state of Arkansas to ignore its holding in *Brown v. Board of Education?* It seems highly plausible that in some regions of this country, schools and other public institutions would have remained segregated well into the latter portion of the twentieth century.

Furthermore, it is hard to imagine how much courage it must have taken for the African American students in this case to remain in school and confront the hatred and racism that were directed toward them. Their commitment, in addition to the conviction of others, including Dr. Martin Luther King, to reject racism during the Civil Rights movement is what finally caused the mantle of segregation to crack.

In fairness to Edwin Meese, who served in the administration of former president Ronald Reagan, the issues that appeared to cause the most concern for the Reagan administration did not present civil rights issues in the same sense that *Brown* and *Cooper* did. Although Meese's speech and law review article implicitly rejected *Cooper v. Aaron's* basic constitutional premise, the Reagan administration appeared to be focused more specifically on issues surrounding the administration of justice in society. These included disagreements with the Supreme Court on matters pertaining to the constitutional rights of criminal suspects, capital punishment, and the proper application of prophylactic rules of evidence. For example, in several different cases, the U.S. Justice Department under Meese's direction challenged the constitutional basis of *Miranda v. Arizona*, 384 U.S. 436 (1966). As you are probably aware from watching a variety of police shows on television and in the movies, this seminal criminal law decision had held that suspects exposed to custodial interrogation by the police had to be advised of the following rights:

- You have the right to remain silent.
- Anything you say may be used against you.
- You have the right to the presence of an attorney.
- If you cannot afford an attorney, one will be provided for you.

Likewise, Meese and the Reagan Justice Department favored restricting the application of the exclusionary rule of evidence that provides generally that evidence obtained illegally may not be used against a suspect in a criminal trial to prove their guilt. Viewed cumulatively, Meese's approach to the administration of justice emphasized restricting the reach of earlier Warren Court precedents that expanded the rights of suspects in criminal proceedings.

What then would have happened to the rights of suspects in criminal proceedings, if, following the arguments presented in Meese's article, state governments and their agents were empowered to disregard Supreme Court precedents that had established the rights of the accused? It may be difficult to imagine the confusion, injustice, and disruption of the rule of law that could have resulted. It is little wonder, then, that former U.S. Attorney General Ramsey Clark, who had served as a member of the late president Lyndon B. Johnson's administration, described Meese's position as "a clumsy, vague assault on law."

For additional readings on these issues, see: Kathleen M. Sullivan and Gerald Gunther, *Constitutional Law* (Foundation Press, 15th ed., 2004); Laurence H. Tribe, *American Constitutional Law* (Foundation Press, 2nd ed., 1988); Alpheus Thomas Mason and Donald Grier Stephenson, Jr., *American Constitutional Law* (Pearson Prentice Hall, 15th ed., 2009); Bernard Schwartz, *A History of the Supreme Court* (Oxford University Press, 1993); Kermit L. Hall, Paul Finkelman, and James Ely, Jr., *American Legal History: Cases and Materials* (Oxford University Press, 3rd ed., 2005); Kermit L. Hall, *The Oxford Companion to the Supreme Court of the United States* (Oxford University Press, 1992); Walter F. Murphy, James E. Fleming, Sotirios A. Barber, and Stephen Macedo, *American Constitutional Interpretation* (Foundation Press, 3rd ed., 2003); David M. O'Brien, *Constitutional Law and Politics: Struggles for Power and Government Accountability* (W.W. Norton, 6th ed., 2005); Craig R. Ducat, *Constitutional Interpretation* (Wadsworth, 9th ed., 2009); John H. Garvey, T. Alexander Aleinikoff, and Daniel A. Farber, *Modern Constitutional Theory: A Reader* (Thompson West, 5th ed., 2004). See also: Gerald Gunther, "The Subtle Vices of the 'Passive Virtues': A Comment on Principle and Expediency in Judicial Review," *Columbia Law Review,* vol. 64, pp. 1–25 (1964); Ramsey Clark, "Enduring Constitutional Issues," *Tulane Law Journal,* vol. 61, pp. 1093–1095 (1987); Edwin Meese, "The Tulane Speech: What I Meant," *The Washington Post* (November 13, 1986, p. A21).

ISSUE 3

Does the U.S. Supreme Court Have the Power to Determine the Constitutionality of Presidential Actions during Wartime?

YES: Hugo L. Black, from *Youngstown Sheet & Tube Co. v. Sawyer,* 343 U.S. 579 (1942)

NO: Fred M. Vinson, Dissenting, in *Youngstown Sheet & Tube Co. v. Sawyer,* 343 U.S. 579 (1942)

ISSUE SUMMARY

Yes: Justice Hugo L. Black, writing for the Supreme Court in *Youngstown Sheet & Tube Co. v. Sawyer,* held that President Truman's order seizing the nation's steel mills during the Korean War infringed upon the lawmaking powers of Congress and was not justified by his role as Commander in Chief of the armed forces.

No: Justice Fred M. Vinson's dissenting opinion in *Youngstown Sheet & Tube Co. v. Sawyer* asserted that President Truman's seizure of the steel mills was proper because it was a temporary measure justified by the emergency nature of the situation as an effort to preserve the status quo, until the Congress could take action.

One of the more important constitutional principles designed to prevent abuses of governmental authority is the separation of powers doctrine. Articles I, II, and III of the U.S. Constitution outline the powers of each of the branches of government. Article I enumerates the powers of Congress. Article II outlines the powers of the executive branch. Article III, the Judicial Article, outlines the authority of the courts. In theory, the separation of powers doctrine asserts that each of the branches performs separate functions, which may not be infringed by another branch. In practice, however, governmental duties sometimes overlap. The grants of power contained in Articles I, II, and III will be discussed more fully in later sections of this volume.

For purposes of analyzing the issues presented in *Youngstown Sheet & Tube Co. v. Sawyer,* however, it is important to note that Article I enumerates the powers of Congress and expressly grants it the power to make laws. Article II, in contrast, lists the powers of the executive branch and provides that the President is the "Commander in Chief of the Army and Navy of the United States."

In *Youngstown Sheet & Tube Co. v. Sawyer*, 343 U.S. 579 (1952), a case that arose during the Korean War, a dispute had developed between the nation's steel companies and their workers over a new collective bargaining agreement. The employees' union gave notice of an intention to strike when their existing contract expired. Despite efforts to mediate the dispute by federal agencies, there was no settlement. Steel was an essential component of virtually all weapons and other war materials. President Truman, therefore, issued Executive Order 10340, directing the Secretary of Commerce to take possession of most of the steel mills and keep them running under federal direction. The Secretary issued orders to the presidents of these companies, ordering them to serve as operating managers for the United States. The next morning, President Truman sent a message to Congress reporting his action. The executives of the companies brought an action in federal court challenging President Truman's directive, asserting that the seizure of the steel mills was not authorized by an act of Congress or by any constitutional provision.

Justice Hugo Black identified two essential issues in this case: First—Should a final determination of the constitutional validity of the President's order be made by the Supreme Court at this stage of the proceedings? Second—If so, was the seizure order within the constitutional power of the President?

Justice Black held first that the issue was *ripe* for a judicial determination. *Black's Law Dictionary* (1973) defines *ripeness* as an Article III requirement, wherein "[T]he question . . . is whether there is a substantial controversy, between parties having adverse legal interests, of sufficient immediacy and reality to warrant the issuance of a . . . judgment." Ripeness, along with several additional doctrines that have been developed by the courts, is a self-imposed restriction of the scope of judicial review.

Second, Justice Black analyzed whether the seizure order for the steel mills was within the constitutional power of the President. He observed that "[T]he President's power, if any, to issue the order must stem either from an act of Congress or from the Constitution itself." There was no statute that expressly authorized the President to take possession of property as he did in this case. Therefore, he continued, if the President had the authority to seize the mills, it would have to be found in some provision of the Constitution.

The government had argued that presidential power to seize the steel mills should be implied from the aggregate of his powers under the Constitution. Stated Justice Black:

> The order cannot properly be sustained as an exercise of the President's military power as Commander in Chief of the Armed Forces. . . . Even though 'theater of war' be an expanding concept, we cannot with faithfulness to our constitutional system hold that the Commander in Chief of the Armed Forces has the ultimate power as such to take possession of private property in order to keep labor disputes from stopping production. This is a job for the Nation's lawmakers, not for its military authorities. . . . The Founders of this Nation entrusted the lawmaking

45

power to the Congress alone in both good and bad times. It would do no good to recall the historical events, the fears of power, and the hopes for freedom that lay behind their choice. Such a review would but confirm our holding that this seizure order cannot stand.

Chief Justice Fred Vinson, dissenting, observed that the President of the United States directed his cabinet member to take possession of the nation's steel mills because "a work stoppage would immediately jeopardize and imperil our national defense and the defense of those joined with us in resisting aggression, and would add to the continuing danger of our soldiers, sailors, and airmen engaged in combat in the field." He also asserted that the majority's decision in this case would imperil the ability of "future Presidents to act in time of crisis."

Questions on fundamental separation of powers that implicate the authority of the executive branch of government have surfaced on several different occasions in American history. Some commentators have also observed a strong tendency to permit the expansion of executive branch powers during times of national crisis. For example, in the aftermath of the invasion of Pearl Harbor during World War II, a presidential executive order permitted persons of Japanese ancestry to be detained in military internment camps. Likewise, on September 11, 2001, the World Trade Center in New York City was destroyed by fanatics who had declared war on the United States. In the immediate aftermath of that crisis, President George W. Bush issued an executive order that concluded a national emergency existed for defense purposes and gave the President the power to detain persons with a suspected connection to terrorism as "unlawful combatants." Moreover, such persons could be held indefinitely, and without charges, a court hearing, or the assistance of counsel.

As you read the excerpts from *Youngstown Sheet & Tube Co. v. Sawyer*, think about whether it would have made a difference if Congress had passed a statute before this case that authorized the President to seize factories or other instruments of commerce in the event of a national war effort. Would it have alleviated the separation of powers issue and resulted in a different outcome? A similar issue will be considered in Issue 4 of this volume as well.

In Your Opinion . . .

- Is it wise to permit the executive branch of government to exercise such expansive powers during times of national crisis?
- Should the President be given a broad scope of authority to deal with military issues or other threats to our nation?
- Faced with the closure of the nation's steel mills, would you have joined Justice Black's majority opinion in *Youngstown Sheet & Tube Co. v. Sawyer,* or would you have sided with Chief Justice Vinson's dissenting opinion.

YES

Hugo L. Black

Youngstown Sheet & Tube Co. v. Sawyer

Mr. Justice Black delivered the opinion of the Court.

We are asked to decide whether the President was acting within his constitutional power when he issued an order directing the Secretary of Commerce to take possession of and operate most of the Nation's steel mills. The mill owners argue that the President's order amounts to lawmaking, a legislative function which the Constitution has expressly confided to the Congress, and not to the President. The Government's position is that the order was made on findings of the President that his action was necessary to avert a national catastrophe which would inevitably result from a stoppage of steel production, and that, in meeting this grave emergency, the President was acting within the aggregate of his constitutional powers as the Nation's Chief Executive and the Commander in Chief of the Armed Forces of the United States. The issue emerges here from the following series of events:

In the latter part of 1951, a dispute arose between the steel companies and their employees over terms and conditions that should be included in new collective bargaining agreements. Long-continued conferences failed to resolve the dispute. On December 18, 1951, the employees' representative, United Steelworkers of America, CIO, gave notice of an intention to strike when the existing bargaining agreements expired on December 31. The Federal Mediation and Conciliation Service then intervened in an effort to get labor and management to agree. This failing, the President on December 22, 1951, referred the dispute to the Federal Wage Stabilization Board to investigate and make recommendations for fair and equitable terms of settlement. This Board's report resulted in no settlement. On April 4, 1952, the Union gave notice of a nationwide strike called to begin at 12:01 a.m. April 9. The indispensability of steel as a component of substantially all weapons and other war materials led the President to believe that the proposed work stoppage would immediately jeopardize our national defense and that governmental seizure of the steel mills was necessary in order to assure the continued availability of steel. Reciting these considerations for his action, the President, a few hours before the strike was to begin, issued Executive Order 10340, a copy of which is attached as an appendix, *post,* p. 589. The order directed the Secretary of Commerce to take possession of most of the steel mills and keep them running. The Secretary immediately issued his own possessory orders, calling upon the presidents of the various seized companies to serve as

Supreme Court of the United States, 1942.

operating managers for the United States. They were directed to carry on their activities in accordance with regulations and directions of the Secretary. The next morning the President sent a message to Congress reporting his action. Cong. Rec. April 9, 1952, p. 3962. Twelve days later, he sent a second message. Cong. Rec. April 21, 1952, p. 4192. Congress has taken no action.

Obeying the Secretary's orders under protest, the companies brought proceedings against him in the District Court. Their complaints charged that the seizure was not authorized by an act of Congress or by any constitutional provisions. The District Court was asked to declare the orders of the President and the Secretary invalid and to issue preliminary and permanent injunctions restraining their enforcement. Opposing the motion for preliminary injunction, the United States asserted that a strike disrupting steel production for even a brief period would so endanger the well-being and safety of the Nation that the President had "inherent power" to do what he had done—power "supported by the Constitution, by historical precedent, and by court decisions." The Government also contended that, in any event, no preliminary injunction should be issued, because the companies had made no showing that their available legal remedies were inadequate or that their injuries from seizure would be irreparable. Holding against the Government on all points, the District Court, on April 30, issued a preliminary injunction restraining the Secretary from "continuing the seizure and possession of the plants . . . and from acting under the purported authority of Executive Order No. 10340." 103 F.Supp. 569. On the same day, the Court of Appeals stayed the District Court's injunction. 90 U.S.App.D.C. _____, 197 F.2d 582. Deeming it best that the issues raised be promptly decided by this Court, we granted certiorari on May 3 and set the cause for argument on May 12. 343 U.S. 937.

Two crucial issues have developed: *First.* Should final determination of the constitutional validity of the President's order be made in this case which has proceeded no further than the preliminary injunction stage? *Second.* If so, is the seizure order within the constitutional power of the President?

I

It is urged that there were nonconstitutional grounds upon which the District Court could have denied the preliminary injunction, and thus have followed the customary judicial practice of declining to reach and decide constitutional questions until compelled to do so. On this basis, it is argued that equity's extraordinary injunctive relief should have been denied because (a) seizure of the companies' properties did not inflict irreparable damages, and (b) there were available legal remedies adequate to afford compensation for any possible damages which they might suffer. While separately argued by the Government, these two contentions are here closely related, if not identical. Arguments as to both rest in large part on the Government's claim that, should the seizure ultimately be held unlawful, the companies could recover full compensation in the Court of Claims for the unlawful taking. Prior cases in this Court have cast doubt on the right to recover in the Court of Claims on account of properties unlawfully taken by government officials for public use as these properties were alleged to have been. *See e.g., Hooe v. United States,* 218 U.S. 322, 335–336; *United States v. North American Co.,* 253 U.S. 330, 333. *But see Larson v. Domestic & Foreign Corp.,* 337 U.S. 682. 701–702. Moreover, seizure and governmental operation of these going businesses were bound to result in many present and future damages of such nature as to be difficult, if not incapable, of measurement. Viewing the case this way, and in the light of the facts presented, the District Court saw no reason for delaying decision of the constitutional validity of the orders. We agree with the District Court, and can see no reason why that question was not ripe for determination on the record presented. We shall therefore consider and determine that question now.

II

The President's power, if any, to issue the order must stem either from an act of Congress or from the Constitution itself. There is no statute that expressly authorizes the President to take possession of property as he did here. Nor is there any act of Congress to which our attention has been directed from which such a power can fairly be implied. Indeed, we do not understand the Government to rely on statutory authorization for this seizure. There are two statutes which do authorize the President to take both personal and real property under certain conditions. However, the Government admits that these conditions were not met, and that the President's order was not rooted in either of the statutes. The Government refers to the seizure provisions of one of these statutes (§ 201 (b) of the Defense Production Act) as "much too cumbersome, involved, and time-consuming for the crisis which was at hand."

Moreover, the use of the seizure technique to solve labor disputes in order to prevent work stoppages was not only unauthorized by any congressional enactment; prior to this controversy, Congress had refused to adopt that method of settling labor disputes. When the Taft-Hartley Act was under consideration in 1947, Congress rejected an amendment which would have authorized such governmental seizures in cases of emergency. Apparently, it was thought that the technique of seizure, like that of compulsory arbitration, would interfere with the process of collective bargaining. Consequently, the plan Congress adopted in that Act did not provide for seizure under any circumstances. Instead, the plan sought to bring about settlements by use of the customary devices of mediation, conciliation, investigation by boards of inquiry, and public reports. In some instances, temporary injunctions were authorized to provide cooling-off periods. All this failing, unions were left free to strike after a secret vote by employees as to whether they wished to accept their employers' final settlement offer.

It is clear that, if the President had authority to issue the order he did, it must be found in some provision of the Constitution. And it is not claimed that express constitutional language grants this power to the President. The contention is that presidential power should be implied from the aggregate of his powers under the Constitution. Particular reliance is placed on provisions in Article II which say that "The executive Power shall be vested in a President . . . ," that "he shall take Care that the Laws be faithfully executed," and that he "shall be Commander in Chief of the Army and Navy of the United States."

The order cannot properly be sustained as an exercise of the President's military power as Commander in Chief of the Armed Forces. The Government attempts to do so by citing a number of cases upholding broad powers in military commanders engaged in day-to-day fighting in a theater of war. Such cases need not concern us here. Even though "theater of war" be an expanding concept, we cannot with faithfulness to our constitutional system hold that the Commander in Chief of the Armed Forces has the ultimate power as such to take possession of private property in order to keep labor disputes from stopping production. This is a job for the Nation's lawmakers, not for its military authorities.

Nor can the seizure order be sustained because of the several constitutional provisions that grant executive power to the President. In the framework of our Constitution, the President's power to see that the laws are faithfully executed refutes the idea that he is to be a lawmaker. The Constitution limits his functions in the lawmaking process to the recommending of laws he thinks wise and the vetoing of laws he thinks bad. And the Constitution is neither silent nor equivocal about who shall make laws which the President is to execute. The first section of the first article says that "All legislative Powers herein granted shall be vested in a Congress of the United States. . . ." After granting many powers to the Congress, Article I goes on to provide that Congress may

> make all Laws which shall be necessary and proper for carrying into Execution the foregoing Powers, and all other Powers vested by this Constitution in the Government of the United States, or in any Department or Officer thereof.

The President's order does not direct that a congressional policy be executed in a manner prescribed by Congress—it directs that a presidential policy be executed in a manner prescribed by the President. The preamble of the order itself, like that of many statutes, sets out reasons why the President believes certain policies should be adopted, proclaims these policies as rules of conduct to be followed, and again, like a statute, authorizes a government official to promulgate additional rules and regulations consistent with the policy proclaimed and needed to carry that policy into execution. The power of Congress to adopt such public policies as those proclaimed by the order is beyond question. It can authorize the taking of private property for public use. It can make laws regulating the relationships between employers and employees, prescribing rules designed to settle labor disputes, and fixing wages and working conditions in certain fields of our economy. The Constitution does not subject this lawmaking power of Congress to presidential or military supervision or control.

It is said that other Presidents, without congressional authority, have taken possession of private business enterprises in order to settle labor disputes. But even if this be true, Congress has not thereby lost its exclusive constitutional authority to make laws necessary and proper to carry out the powers vested by the Constitution "in the Government of the United States, or any Department or Officer thereof."

The Founders of this Nation entrusted the lawmaking power to Congress alone in both good and bad times. It would do no good to recall the historical events, the fears of power, and the hopes for freedom that lay behind their choice. Such a review would but confirm our holding that this seizure order cannot stand.

The judgment of the District Court is *Affirmed.*

Fred M. Vinson  **NO**

Youngstown Sheet & Tube Co. v. Sawyer

Mr. Chief Justice Vinson, with whom Mr. Justice Reed and Mr. Justice Minton join, dissenting.

The President of the United States directed the Secretary of Commerce to take temporary possession of the Nation's steel mills during the existing emergency because

> a work stoppage would immediately jeopardize and imperil our national defense and the defense of those joined with us in resisting aggression, and would add to the continuing danger of our soldiers, sailors, and airmen engaged in combat in the field.

The District Court ordered the mills returned to their private owners on the ground that the President's action was beyond his powers under the Constitution.

This Court affirms. Some members of the Court are of the view that the President is without power to act in time of crisis in the absence of express statutory authorization. Other members of the Court affirm on the basis of their reading of certain statutes. Because we cannot agree that affirmance is proper on any ground, and because of the transcending importance of the questions presented not only in this critical litigation, but also to the powers of the President and of future Presidents to act in time of crisis, we are compelled to register this dissent.

I

In passing upon the question of presidential powers in this case, we must first consider the context in which those powers were exercised.

Those who suggest that this is a case involving extraordinary powers should be mindful that these are extraordinary times. A world not yet recovered from the devastation of World War II has been forced to face the threat of another and more terrifying global conflict. . . .

In 1950, when the United Nations called upon member nations "to render every assistance" to repel aggression in Korea, the United States furnished its vigorous support. For almost two full years, our armed forces have been fighting in Korea, suffering casualties of over 108,000 men. Hostilities have not abated. The "determination of the United Nations to continue its action in Korea to meet the

Supreme Court of the United States, 1942.

aggression" has been reaffirmed. Congressional support of the action in Korea has been manifested by provisions for increased military manpower and equipment and for economic stabilization, as hereinafter described. . . .

Our treaties represent not merely legal obligations, but show congressional recognition that mutual security for the free world is the best security against the threat of aggression on a global scale. The need for mutual security is shown by the very size of the armed forces outside the free world. Defendant's brief informs us that the Soviet Union maintains the largest air force in the world, and maintains ground forces much larger than those presently available to the United States and the countries joined with us in mutual security arrangements. Constant international tensions are cited to demonstrate how precarious is the peace.

Even this brief review of our responsibilities in the world community discloses the enormity of our undertaking. Success of these measures may, as has often been observed, dramatically influence the lives of many generations of the world's peoples yet unborn. Alert to our responsibilities, which coincide with our own self-preservation through mutual security, Congress has enacted a large body of implementing legislation. As an illustration of the magnitude of the over-all program, Congress has appropriated $130 billion for our own defense and for military assistance to our allies since the June 1950 attack in Korea. . . .

Congress recognized the impact of these defense programs upon the economy. Following the attack in Korea, the President asked for authority to requisition property and to allocate and fix priorities for scarce goods. In the Defense Production Act of 1950, Congress granted the powers requested and, *in addition,* granted power to stabilize prices and wages and to provide for settlement of labor disputes arising in the defense program. The Defense Production Act was extended in 1951, a Senate Committee noting that in the dislocation caused by the programs for purchase of military equipment "lies the seed of an economic disaster that might well destroy the military might we are straining to build." Significantly, the Committee examined the problem "in terms of just one commodity, steel," and found "a graphic picture of the overall inflationary danger growing out of reduced civilian supplies and rising incomes." Even before Korea, steel production at levels above theoretical 100% capacity was not capable of supplying civilian needs alone. Since Korea, the tremendous military demand for steel has far exceeded the increases in productive capacity. This Committee emphasized that the shortage of steel, even with the mills operating at full capacity, coupled with increased civilian purchasing power, presented grave danger of disastrous inflation.

The President has the duty to execute the foregoing legislative programs. Their successful execution depends upon continued production of steel and stabilized prices for steel. Accordingly, when the collective bargaining agreements between the Nations steel producers and their employees, represented by the United Steel Workers, were due to expire on December 31, 1951, and a strike shutting down the entire basic steel industry was threatened, the President acted to avert a complete shutdown of steel production. On December 22, 1951, he certified the dispute to the Wage Stabilization Board, requesting that the Board investigate the dispute and promptly report its recommendation as to fair and equitable terms of settlement. The Union complied with the President's request and delayed its threatened strike while the dispute was before the Board. After a special Board panel had conducted hearings and submitted a report, the full Wage Stabilization Board submitted its report and recommendations to the President on March 20, 1952.

The Board's report was acceptable to the Union, but was rejected by plaintiffs. The Union gave notice of its intention to strike as of 12:01 a.m., April 9, 1952, but bargaining between the parties continued with hope of settlement until the evening of April 8, 1952. After bargaining had failed to avert the threatened shutdown of steel production, the President issued [his] Executive Order. . . .

Twelve days passed without action by Congress. On April 21, 1952, the President sent a letter to the President of the Senate in which he again described the purpose and need for his action and again stated his position that "The Congress can, if it wishes, reject the course of action I have followed in this matter." Congress has not so acted to this date.

Meanwhile, plaintiffs instituted this action in the District Court to compel defendant to return possession of the steel mills seized under Executive Order 10340. In this litigation for return of plaintiffs' properties, we assume that defendant Charles Sawyer is not immune from judicial restraint, and that plaintiffs are entitled to equitable relief if we find that the Executive Order under which defendant acts is unconstitutional. We also assume without deciding that the courts may go behind a President's finding of fact that an emergency exists. But there is not the slightest basis for suggesting that the President's finding in this case can be undermined. Plaintiffs moved for a preliminary injunction before answer or hearing. Defendant opposed the motion, filing uncontroverted affidavits of Government officials describing the facts underlying the President's order.

Secretary of Defense Lovett swore that

> a work stoppage in the steel industry will result immediately in serious curtailment of production of essential weapons and munitions of all kinds.

He illustrated by showing that 84% of the national production of certain alloy steel is currently used for production of military-end items and that 35% of total production of another form of steel goes into ammunition, 80% of such ammunition now going to Korea. The Secretary of Defense stated that: "We are holding the line [in Korea] with ammunition, and not with the lives of our troops." . . .

One is not here called upon even to consider the possibility of executive seizure of a farm, a corner grocery store or even a single industrial plant. Such considerations arise only when one ignores the central fact of this case—that the Nation's entire basic steel production would have shut down completely if there had been no Government seizure. Even ignoring for the moment whatever confidential information the President may possess as "the Nation's organ for foreign affairs," the uncontroverted affidavits in this record amply support the finding that "a work stoppage would immediately jeopardize and imperil our national defense."

Plaintiffs do not remotely suggest any basis for rejecting the President's finding that any stoppage of steel production would immediately place the

Nation in peril. Moreover, even self-generated doubts that any stoppage of steel production constitutes an emergency are of little comfort here. The Union and the plaintiffs bargained for 6 months with over 100 issues in dispute—issues not limited to wage demands, but including the union shop and other matters of principle between the parties. At the time of seizure, there was not, and there is not now, the slightest evidence to justify the belief that any strike will be of short duration. The Union and the steel companies may well engage in a lengthy struggle. Plaintiffs' counsel tells us that "sooner or later" the mills will operate again. That may satisfy the steel companies and, perhaps, the Union. But our soldiers and our allies will hardly be cheered with the assurance that the ammunition upon which their lives depend will be forthcoming—"sooner or later," or, in other words, "too little and too late."

Accordingly, if the President has any power under the Constitution to meet a critical situation in the absence of express statutory authorization, there is no basis whatever for criticizing the exercise of such power in this case.

II

The steel mills were seized for a public use. The power of eminent domain, invoked in this case, is an essential attribute of sovereignty, and has long been recognized as a power of the Federal Government. *Kohl v. United States,* 91 U.S. 367 (1876). Plaintiffs cannot complain that any provision in the Constitution prohibits the exercise of the power of eminent domain in this case. The Fifth Amendment provides: "nor shall private property be taken for public use, without just compensation." It is no bar to this seizure for, if the taking is not otherwise unlawful, plaintiffs are assured of receiving the required just compensation. *United States v. Pewee Coal Co.,* 341 U.S. 114 (1951).

Admitting that the Government could seize the mills, plaintiffs claim that the implied power of eminent domain can be exercised only under an Act of Congress; under no circumstances, they say, can that power be exercised by the President unless he can point to an express provision in enabling legislation. This was the view adopted by the District Judge when he granted the preliminary injunction. Without an answer, without hearing evidence, he determined the issue on the basis of his "fixed conclusion . . . that defendant's acts are illegal" because the President's only course in the face of an emergency is to present the matter to Congress and await the final passage of legislation which will enable the Government to cope with threatened disaster.

Under this view, the President is left powerless at the very moment when the need for action may be most pressing and when no one, other than he, is immediately capable of action. Under this view, he is left powerless because a power not expressly given to Congress is nevertheless found to rest exclusively with Congress'.

Consideration of this view of executive impotence calls for further examination of the nature of the separation of powers under our tripartite system of Government.

The Constitution provides:

Art. I,

Section 1. "All legislative Powers herein granted shall be vested in a Congress of the United States. . . ."

Art. II,

Section 1. "The executive power shall be vested in a President of the United States of America. . . ."

Section 2. "The President shall be Commander in Chief of the Army and Navy of the United States. . . ."

"He shall have Power, by and with the Advice and Consent of the Senate, to make Treaties, provided two thirds of the Senators present concur; . . ."

Section 3. "He shall from time to time give to the Congress Information of the State of the Union, and recommend to their Consideration such Measures as he shall judge necessary and expedient; . . . He shall take Care that the Laws be faithfully executed. . . ."

Art. III,

Section 1. "The judicial power of the United States shall be vested in one supreme Court, and in such inferior Courts as the Congress may from time to time ordain and establish."

The whole of the "executive power" is vested in the President. Before entering office, the President swears that he "will faithfully execute the Office of President of the United States, and will to the best of [his] Ability, preserve, protect and defend the Constitution of the United States." Art. II, §1.

This comprehensive grant of the executive power to a single person was bestowed soon after the country had thrown the yoke of monarchy. Only by instilling initiative and vigor in all of the three departments of Government, declared Madison, could tyranny in any form be avoided.

Hamilton added:

> Energy in the Executive is a leading character in the definition of good government. It is essential to the protection of the community against foreign attacks; it is not less essential to the steady administration of the laws; to the protection of property against those irregular and high-handed combinations which sometimes interrupt the ordinary course of justice; to the security of liberty against the enterprises and assaults of ambition, of faction, and of anarchy.

It is thus apparent that the Presidency was deliberately fashioned as an office of power and independence. Of course, the Framers created no autocrat capable of arrogating any power unto himself at any time. But neither did they create an automaton impotent to exercise the powers of Government at a time when the survival of the Republic itself may be at stake.

In passing upon the grave constitutional question presented in this case, we must never forget, as Chief Justice Marshall admonished, that the Constitution is "intended to endure for ages to come, and, consequently, to be adapted to the various crises of human affairs," and that "[i]ts means are adequate to its ends." Cases do arise presenting questions which could not have been foreseen by the Framers. In such cases, the Constitution has been treated as a living document adaptable to new situations. But we are not called upon today to expand the Constitution to meet a new situation. For, in this case, we need only [to] look to history and time-honored principles of constitutional law—principles that have been applied consistently by all branches of the Government throughout our history. It is those who assert the invalidity of the Executive Order who seek to amend the Constitution in this case.

III

A review of executive action demonstrates that our Presidents have on many occasions exhibited the leadership contemplated by the Framers when they made the President, Commander in Chief and imposed upon him the trust to "take Care that the Laws be faithfully executed." With or without explicit statutory authorization, presidents have at such times dealt with national emergencies by acting promptly and resolutely to enforce legislative programs, at least to save those programs until Congress could act. Congress and the courts have responded to such executive initiative with consistent approval.

Our first President displayed at once the leadership contemplated by the Framers. When the national revenue laws were openly flouted in some sections of Pennsylvania, President Washington, without waiting for a call from the state government, summoned the militia and took decisive steps to secure the faithful execution of the laws. When international disputes engendered by the French revolution threatened to involve this country in war, and while congressional policy remained uncertain, Washington issued his Proclamation of Neutrality. Hamilton, whose defense of the Proclamation has endured the test of time, invoked the argument that the Executive has the duty to do that which will preserve peace until Congress acts and, in addition, pointed to the need for keeping the Nation informed of the requirements of existing laws and treaties as part of the faithful execution of the laws. . . .

Without declaration of war, President Lincoln took energetic action with the outbreak of the War Between the States. He summoned troops and paid them out of the Treasury without appropriation therefor. He proclaimed a naval blockade of the Confederacy and seized ships violating that blockade. Congress, far from denying the validity of these acts, gave them express approval. The most striking action of President Lincoln was the Emancipation Proclamation, issued in aid of the successful prosecution of the War Between the States, but wholly without statutory authority.

In an action furnishing a most apt precedent for this case, President Lincoln, without statutory authority, directed the seizure of rail and telegraph lines leading to Washington. Many months later, Congress recognized and confirmed the power of the President to seize railroads and telegraph lines and provided criminal penalties for interference with Government operation. This Act did not confer on the President any additional powers of seizure. Congress plainly rejected the view that the President's acts had been without legal sanction until ratified by the legislature. Sponsors of the bill declared that its purpose was only to confirm the power which the President already possessed. Opponents insisted a statute authorizing seizure was unnecessary, and might even be construed as limiting existing Presidential powers. . . .

In 1941, President Roosevelt acted to protect Iceland from attack by Axis powers, when British forces were withdrawn, by sending our forces to occupy Iceland. Congress was informed of this action on the same day that our forces reached Iceland. The occupation of Iceland was but one of "at least 125 incidents" in our history in which Presidents,

> without congressional authorization, and in the absence of a declaration of war, [have] ordered the Armed Forces to take action or maintain positions abroad.

Some six months before Pearl Harbor, a dispute at a single aviation plant at Inglewood, California, interrupted a segment of the production of military aircraft. In spite of the comparative insignificance of this work stoppage to total defense production, as contrasted with the complete paralysis now threatened by a shutdown of the entire basic steel industry, and even though our armed forces were not then engaged in combat, President Roosevelt ordered the seizure of the plant

> pursuant to the powers vested in [him] by the Constitution and laws of the United States as President of the United States of America and Commander in Chief of the Army and Navy of the United States.

The Attorney General (Jackson) vigorously proclaimed that the President had the moral duty to keep this Nation's defense effort a "going concern." His ringing moral justification was coupled with a legal justification equally well stated:

> The Presidential proclamation rests upon the aggregate of the Presidential powers derived from the Constitution itself and from statutes enacted by the Congress.
> The Constitution lays upon the President the duty "to take care that the laws be faithfully executed." Among the laws which he is required to find means to execute are those which direct him to equip an enlarged army, to provide for a strengthened navy, to protect Government property, to protect those who are engaged in carrying out the business of the Government, and to carry out the provisions of the Lend-Lease Act. For the faithful execution of such laws, the President has back of him not only each general law enforcement power conferred by the various acts of Congress, but the aggregate of all such laws plus that wide discretion as to method vested in him by the Constitution for the purpose of executing the laws.
> The Constitution also places on the President the responsibility and vests in him the powers of Commander in Chief of the Army and of the Navy. These weapons for the protection of the continued existence of the Nation are placed in his sole command and the implication is clear that he should not allow them to become paralyzed by failure to obtain supplies for which Congress has appropriated the money and which it has directed the President to obtain. . . .

More recently, President Truman acted to repel aggression by employing our armed forces in Korea. Upon the intervention of the Chinese Communists, the President proclaimed the existence of an unlimited national emergency requiring the speedy build-up of our defense establishment. Congress responded by providing for increased manpower and weapons for our own armed forces, by increasing military aid under the Mutual Security Program, and by enacting economic stabilization measures, as previously described.

This is but a cursory summary of executive leadership. But it amply demonstrates that Presidents have taken prompt action to enforce the laws and protect the country whether or not Congress happened to provide in advance for the particular method of execution. At the minimum, the executive actions reviewed herein sustain the action of the President in this case. And many of the cited examples of Presidential practice go far beyond the extent of power necessary to sustain the President's order to seize the steel mills. The fact that temporary executive seizures of industrial plants to meet an emergency has not been directly tested in this Court furnishes not the slightest suggestion that such actions have been illegal. Rather, the fact that Congress and the courts have consistently recognized and given their support to such executive action indicates that such a power of seizure has been accepted throughout our history.

History bears out the genius of the Founding Fathers, who created a Government subject to law but not left subject to inertia when vigor and initiative are required.

IV

Focusing now on the situation confronting the President on the night of April 8, 1952, we cannot but conclude that the President was performing his duty under the Constitution to "take Care that the Laws be faithfully executed"—a duty described by President Benjamin Harrison as "the central idea of the office."

The President reported to Congress the morning after the seizure that he acted because a work stoppage in steel production would immediately imperil the safety of the Nation by preventing execution of the legislative programs for procurement of military equipment. And, while a shutdown could be averted by granting the price concessions requested by plaintiffs, granting such concessions would disrupt the price stabilization program also enacted by Congress. Rather than fail to execute either legislative program, the President acted to execute both.

Much of the argument in this case has been directed at straw men. We do not now have before us the case of a President acting solely on the basis of his own notions of the public welfare. Nor is there any question of unlimited executive power in this case. The President himself closed the door to any such claim when he sent his Message to Congress stating his purpose to abide by any action of Congress, whether approving or disapproving his seizure action. Here, the President immediately made sure that Congress was fully informed of the temporary action he had taken only to preserve the legislative programs from destruction until Congress could act.

The absence of a specific statute authorizing seizure of the steel mills as a mode of executing the laws—both the military procurement program and the anti-inflation program—has not until today been thought to prevent the President from executing the laws. Unlike an administrative commission confined to the enforcement of the statute under which it was created, or the head of a department when administering a particular statute, the President is a constitutional officer charged with taking care that a "mass of legislation" be executed. Flexibility as to mode of execution to meet critical situations is a matter of practical necessity. This practical construction of the "Take Care" clause, advocated by John Marshall, was adopted by this Court in *In re Neagle, In re Debs* and other cases cited *supra. See also Ex parte Quirin,* 317 U.S. 1, 26 (1942). Although more restrictive views of executive power, advocated in dissenting opinions of Justices Holmes, McReynolds and Brandeis, were emphatically rejected by this Court in *Myers v. United States, supra,* members of today's majority treat these dissenting views as authoritative.

There is no statute prohibiting seizure as a method of enforcing legislative programs. Congress has in no wise indicated that its legislation is not to be executed by the taking of private property (subject, of course, to the payment of just compensation) if its legislation cannot otherwise be executed. Indeed, the Universal Military Training and Service Act authorizes the seizure of any plant that fails to fill a Government contract or the properties of any steel producer that fails to allocate steel as directed for defense production. And the Defense Production Act authorizes the President to requisition equipment and condemn real property needed without delay in the defense effort. Where Congress authorizes seizure in instances not necessarily crucial to the defense program, it can hardly be said to have disclosed an intention to prohibit seizures where essential to the execution of that legislative program.

Whatever the extent of Presidential power on more tranquil occasions, and whatever the right of the President to execute legislative programs as he sees fit without reporting the mode of execution to Congress, the single Presidential purpose disclosed on this record is to faithfully execute the laws by acting in an emergency to maintain the *status quo,* thereby preventing collapse of the legislative programs until Congress could act. The President's action served the same purposes as a judicial stay entered to maintain the *status quo* in order to preserve the jurisdiction of a court. In his Message to Congress immediately following the seizure, the President explained the necessity of his action in executing the military procurement and anti-inflation legislative programs and expressed his desire to cooperate with any legislative proposals approving, regulating or rejecting the seizure of the steel mills. Consequently, there is no evidence whatever of any Presidential purpose to defy Congress or act in any way inconsistent with the legislative will. . . .

The Framers knew, as we should know in these times of peril, that there is real danger in executive weakness. There is no cause to fear executive tyranny so long as the laws of Congress are being faithfully executed. Certainly there is no basis for fear of dictatorship when the executive acts, as he did in this case, only to save the situation until Congress could act. . . .

V

The diversity of views expressed in the six opinions of the majority, the lack of reference to authoritative precedent, the repeated reliance upon prior dissenting opinions, the complete disregard of the uncontroverted facts showing the gravity of the emergency, and the temporary nature of the taking all serve to demonstrate how far afield one must go to affirm the order of the District Court.

The broad executive power granted by Article II to an officer on duty 365 days a year cannot, it is said, be invoked to avert disaster. Instead, the President must confine himself to sending a message to Congress recommending action. Under this messenger-boy concept of the Office, the President cannot even act to preserve legislative programs from destruction so that Congress will have something left to act upon. There is no judicial finding that the executive action was unwarranted because there was, in fact, no basis for the President's finding of the existence of an emergency for, under this view, the gravity of the emergency and the immediacy of the threatened disaster are considered irrelevant as a matter of law.

Seizure of plaintiffs' property is not a pleasant undertaking. Similarly unpleasant to a free country are the draft which disrupts the home and military procurement which causes economic dislocation and compels adoption of price controls, wage stabilization and allocation of materials. The President informed Congress that even a temporary Government operation of plaintiffs' properties was "thoroughly distasteful" to him, but was necessary to prevent immediate paralysis of the mobilization program. Presidents have been in the past, and any man worthy of the Office should be in the future, free to take at least interim action necessary to execute legislative programs essential to survival of the Nation. A sturdy judiciary should not be swayed by the unpleasantness or unpopularity of necessary executive action, but must independently determine for itself whether the President was acting, as required by the Constitution, to "take Care that the Laws be faithfully executed."

As the District Judge stated, this is no time for "timorous" judicial action. But neither is this a time for timorous executive action. Faced with the duty of executing the defense programs which Congress had enacted and the disastrous effects that any stoppage in steel production would have on those programs, the President acted to preserve those programs by seizing the steel mills. There is no question that the possession was other than temporary in character, and subject to congressional direction—either approving, disapproving, or regulating the manner in which the mills were to be administered and returned to the owners. The President immediately informed Congress of his action, and clearly stated his intention to abide by the legislative will. No basis for claims of arbitrary action, unlimited powers, or dictatorial usurpation of congressional power appears from the facts of this case. On the contrary, judicial, legislative and executive precedents throughout our history demonstrate that, in this case, the President acted in full conformity with his duties under the Constitution. Accordingly, we would reverse the order of the District Court. . . .

POSTSCRIPT

Does the U.S. Supreme Court Have the Power to Determine the Constitutionality of Presidential Actions during Wartime?

The separation of powers doctrine has had a fascinating history. At its basis, it is designed to limit governmental power by assigning distinct powers to the different branches of government. *Youngstown Sheet & Tube Co. v. Sawyer* (1952) raises separation of powers issues on at least two different levels. First, there is the question of whether the Supreme Court should review the actions of a coequal branch of government, the executive branch. Second, there is the issue of Congressional lawmaking power versus the need for presidential flexibility to respond to a crisis facing our nation.

A more recent case that presented the first type of separation of powers question was *United States v. Nixon*, 418 U.S. 683 (1974). This case concerned a burglary that had been committed at the famous Watergate Hotel in Washington, D.C. A grand jury had indicted seven of President Richard M. Nixon's aides on felony charges including conspiracy and other Watergate-associated offenses. It had also named President Nixon as an unindicted coconspirator. A subpoena was issued by a U.S. District Court that directed President Nixon to produce certain tape recordings and documents relating to his conversations with aides and advisers. Nixon released transcripts of some of the tapes, but refused to release the tapes themselves. The court had rejected the President's claims of absolute executive privilege, lack of jurisdiction, and of failure to satisfy the requirements of a federal rule of civil procedure. It further held that the judiciary, not the President, was the final arbiter of a claim of executive privilege. The President filed an appeal in the U.S. Court of Appeals. Prior to a ruling by that court, however, the U.S. Supreme Court granted certiorari due to its importance to our governmental system.

The President's counsel argued that this dispute did not present a "case" or "controversy" that could properly be adjudicated by the federal courts and that they should not intrude into areas committed to other branches of government. The President also contended that the subpoena should be declared invalid, or "quashed," because it demanded "confidential conversations between a President and his close advisors that it would be inconsistent with the public interest to produce."

Writing for the Supreme Court, Chief Justice Burger quoted what is perhaps one of the most famous passages in U.S. Constitutional law from *Marbury v. Madison* (1803): "[i]t is emphatically the province and the duty of the judicial department to say what the law is." Chief Justice Burger continued:

> Notwithstanding the deference each branch must accord the others, the 'judicial power of the United States' vested in the federal courts by Art. III, Section 1, of the Constitution can no more be shared with the Executive Branch than the Chief Executive, for example, can share with the Judiciary the veto power, or the Congress share with the Judiciary the power to override a Presidential veto. Any other conclusion would be contrary to the basic concept of separation of powers and the checks and balances that flow from the scheme of a tripartite government.

Moreover, while the Supreme Court recognized a *qualified* presidential privilege to maintain the confidentiality of conversations with his aides, it was outweighed by the need for the evidence in a criminal trial. (A qualified privilege is one that may be overcome for a sufficiently compelling reason.) Thus, the Supreme Court ordered President Nixon to produce the tape recordings and documents, which led directly to his resignation from office shortly thereafter.

An even more recent case involving judicial review of presidential actions and a claim of executive privilege was asserted in *Clinton v. Jones*, 520 U.S. 681 (1997). Paula Jones sought to recover damages from President Bill Clinton based on sexual advances he had allegedly made toward her, while he was Governor of Arkansas, and before he had taken office as President of the United States. Clinton argued that "in all but the most exceptional cases," the Constitution "affords the president temporary immunity from civil damages litigation arising out of events that occurred before he took office." Writing for a unanimous Supreme Court, Justice John Paul Stevens disagreed:

> [Jones] is merely asking the courts to exercise their core Article III jurisdiction to decide cases and controversies. Whatever the outcome of this case, there is no possibility that the decision will curtail the scope of the official powers of the Executive Branch. The litigation of questions that relate entirely to the unofficial conduct of the individual who happens to be the President poses no perceptible risk of misallocation of either judicial power or executive power.

The Court therefore held that President Clinton was subject to the jurisdiction of the U.S. District Court. During a later *deposition* in this case, Monica Lewinsky, a witness and former White House intern, denied having engaged in sexual relations with President Clinton. A deposition is part of the discovery process in a civil lawsuit, wherein an actual or potential witness is questioned under oath by a party to the case. Linda Tripp, a Lewinsky friend, had tape-recorded conversations in which Lewinsky had discussed her sexual relationship with President Clinton. When President Clinton was deposed he had denied having a relationship with Lewinsky. This led to charges of perjury and obstruction of justice as well as impeachment proceedings against Clinton. Shortly thereafter, a U.S. District Court judge held President Clinton in contempt of court for giving false testimony during his deposition.

The Arkansas Supreme Court also suspended Clinton's license to practice law. Clinton agreed to a 5-year suspension and was fined $25,000 in order to avoid a disbarment proceeding and to preclude further investigation by an independent counsel. He was not, however, prosecuted in a criminal case for his false testimony.

An additional case that implicated the separation of powers doctrine and involved President Clinton occurred in 1998. *Clinton v. City of New York*, 524 U.S. 417 (1998), considered the constitutionality of the "Line Item Veto Act," which had been passed by Congress. It had given the President the power to "cancel" three types of budgetary provisions that had been signed into law: "(1) any dollar amount of discretionary budget authority, (2) any item of new direct spending, or (3) any limited tax benefit." President Clinton used this authority to cancel two provisions in two different statutes. The City of New York and others who were adversely impacted by these actions filed suit in U.S. District Court claiming that the "Line Item Veto Act," which had given the President the authority to cancel these provisions, was unconstitutional. On appeal, the U.S. Supreme Court held that the Act was unconstitutional. Stated Justice John Paul Stevens: "If the Line Item Veto Act were valid, it would authorize the President to create a different law—one whose text was not voted on by either House of Congress or presented to the President for his signature." It therefore violated the Constitution's "Presentment Clause" and was unconstitutional.

Cases such as *United States v. Nixon, Clinton v. Jones,* and *New York v. Clinton* are challenging ones for the U.S. Supreme Court because they raise the issue of whether it is overreaching its Constitutional authority. Issue 1 considered the development of the doctrine of judicial review in the context of Chief Justice John Marshall's seminal decision in *Marbury v. Madison* (1803). A fundamental question posed by that case was the issue of why the courts should have the authority to pass on the constitutionality of actions of the executive and legislative branches of government. The answer given to this question by Justice Marshall has not been entirely satisfactory to many students of the Constitution because nowhere does it state that the Courts have this awesome power. In any case, it is not difficult to imagine why courts are sometimes hesitant to decide such contentious issues.

Over time, the courts themselves have developed several discretionary doctrines to limit the exercise of judicial review that focus on *justiciability*, the issue of whether the case is ready to be decided on the merits. Although a detailed discussion of these doctrines is beyond the scope of the present initiative, brief consideration of them is warranted. Please note that each of these limitations on judicial review emerges directly from Article III's "case or controversy" requirement, which mandates that the courts decide only real cases between adverse parties. Hypothetical or theoretical disputes do not satisfy this important constitutional standard and the federal courts will never issue advisory opinions.

Our earlier discussion of *Youngstown Sheet & Tube Co. v. Sawyer* (1952) considered the *ripeness* doctrine. This means that courts will not consider a legal issue until it has matured into an actual case and controversy between adverse parties. For example, in *United Public Workers v. Mitchell*, 330 U.S. 75 (1947), Congress had passed a statute, the Hatch Act, which prohibited federal workers from involvement in political campaigns. Several workers filed suit to prevent the enforcement of the Act. The problem was, however, that they had not yet engaged in the prohibited political activities. Thus, the Supreme Court held that the case was not ripe for adjudication.

A related doctrine is *mootness*, which means that although a case may have at one time presented an issue that would be subject to a decision on the merits, it has been resolved and no longer presents an actual controversy. To cite an extreme example for illustration purposes, suppose a pregnant woman wanted to challenge a state's abortion laws in federal court. The normal human gestation process is invariably about nine months long. To gain a hearing on the merits in federal court would normally take significantly longer than nine months. If the court were so disposed, it could rule that the issue was moot by the time it came to trial. This issue was presented in one of the most contentious cases in U.S. Supreme Court history, *Roe v. Wade*, 410 U.S. 113 (1973). There the Court held that the mootness issue in this case "was capable of repetition," yet "would evade review," each time it was presented; therefore it allowed Roe's case to proceed.

Another doctrine that limits the exercise of judicial review is *standing*. According to the noted constitutional scholar Laurence Tribe, the standing inquiry consists of two parts: an injury in fact and the requirement that an injured party must be asserting his or her own legal rights. Speaking generally, one cannot assert the rights of another to gain legal standing. There are exceptions, however. For example, the laws of most states will give a parent or lawful guardian to sue on behalf of an injured minor.

A final doctrine that was asserted unsuccessfully by the executive branch in *Youngstown Sheet & Tube Co. v. Sawyer, United States v. Nixon*, and *Clinton v. Jones* is the *political question* doctrine. It asserts that courts should not decide cases that the Constitution allocates to a coequal branch of government. As you have already seen, invocation of this doctrine is rarely successful, and then, only in exceptional cases. The most noteworthy case to discuss this doctrine to this point in our legal history is *Baker v. Carr*, 369 U.S. 186 (1962), which concerned the apportionment of legislative voting districts in Tennessee. This case held that the apportionment of legislative districts was not a political question. Therefore, the Court did not defer to the legislature's judgment on this issue. The case is a significant one because it served as a foundation for the Supreme Court's conclusion 2 years later in *Reynolds v. Sims*, 377 U.S. 533 (1964) that the U.S. Constitution required the states to adopt a "one person, one vote" standard to apportion U.S. congressional districts.

After reviewing the readings in this section, do you feel that the separation of powers doctrine serves as an effective check on governmental power? Moreover, do you believe that the Supreme Court should have the power to review the constitutionality of presidential executive orders during wartime? These questions are highly important ones. We will continue to explore a similar issue in Issue 4 of this volume as well.

For additional readings on these issues, see: Kathleen M. Sullivan and Gerald Gunther, *Constitutional Law* (Foundation Press, 15th ed., 2004); Laurence H. Tribe,

American Constitutional Law (Foundation Press, 2nd ed., 1988); Alpheus Thomas Mason and Donald Grier Stephenson, Jr., *American Constitutional Law* (Pearson Prentice Hall, 15th ed., 2009); Bernard Schwartz, *A History of the Supreme Court* (Oxford University Press, 1993); Kermit L. Hall, Paul Finkelman, and James Ely, Jr., *American Legal History: Cases and Materials* (Oxford University Press, 3rd ed., 2005); Kermit L. Hall, *The Oxford Companion to the Supreme Court of the United States* (Oxford University Press, 1992); Walter F. Murphy, James E. Flemming, Sotirios A. Barber, and Stephen Macedo, *American Constitutional Interpretation* (Foundation Press, 3rd ed., 2003); David M. O'Brien, *Constitutional Law and Politics: Struggles for Power and Government Accountability* (W.W. Norton, 6th ed., 2005); Craig R. Ducat, *Constitutional Interpretation* (Wadsworth, 9th ed., 2009); John H. Garvey, T. Alexander Aleinikoff, and Daniel A. Farber, *Modern Constitutional Theory: A Reader* (Thompson West, 5th ed., (2004). See also: Louis J. Sirico, Jr., "How the Separation of Powers Doctrine Shaped the Executive," *The University of Toledo Law Review,* vol. 40, p. 617 (2009); Linda Jellum, 'Which is to be Master,' the Judiciary or the Legislature? When Statutory Directives Violate Separation of Powers," *UCLA Law Review,* vol. 56, p. 837 (2009); Ronald J. Krotoszynski, "The Shot (Not) Heard 'Round the World: Reconsidering the Perplexing U.S. Preoccupation with the Separation of Executive and Legislative Powers," *BCL Review,* vol. 31, p. 1 (2010)

ISSUE 4

Should Noncitizens Accused of Terrorism Have the Right to a Writ of Habeas Corpus in U.S. Courts?

YES: Anthony M. Kennedy, from *Boumediene v. Bush,* U.S. Supreme Court (2008)

NO: Antonin E. Scalia, Dissenting, in *Boumediene v. Bush*, U.S. Supreme Court (2008)

ISSUE SUMMARY

YES: Justice Anthony M. Kennedy, in *Boumediene v. Bush* (2008), asserted that the constitutional right to a writ of habeas corpus applies to all accused terrorists, including those designated as enemy combatants.

NO: Justice Antonin E. Scalia, dissenting, asserted that the Constitution does not ensure habeas corpus for aliens held by the United States in areas over which our government is not sovereign.

A *writ* is a court order requiring someone to perform some particular action. *Habeas corpus*, a Latin term, is translated as "you have the body." A *writ of habeas corpus* is an order from a court to a person who has custody of another, most often a prison or jail official, to produce the confined individual before a court for a determination of the legality of his or her detention. Sometimes termed "the great writ," it is a cornerstone of the rule of law in the United States. According to *Black's Law Dictionary* (1979), the writ's primary purpose is to release persons who are subjected to unlawful imprisonment.

That the founding fathers of this nation took the right to a writ of habeas corpus very seriously is evidenced by the fact that it is one of only a very few protections provided in the body of the original Constitution, and not the Bill of Rights. Article I, Section 9, states: "The privilege of the Writ of Habeas Corpus shall not be suspended [this is termed the "Suspension Clause"], unless when in Cases of Rebellion or Invasion the public Safety may require it."

(Other rights specified in Article I, Sections 9 and 10, are protections against a *bill of attainder*—a legislative action to punish someone without the benefit of a judicial trial, and ex post facto laws—a law that punishes conduct that was not a crime when the act was committed originally.)

The great writ prevents governmental authorities from detaining persons without charges for indefinite periods. Noted author and human rights activist Jacobo Timerman once described the horrors of indeterminate confinement and torture in the Argentinian prisons. Timerman, a newspaper editor in Buenos Aires, was imprisoned without charges or recourse to judicial process in 1977 by the Argentinian military dictatorship. In a book titled *Prisoner Without a Name, Cell Without a Number,* he described his experiences in prison. This work is excellent reading and illustrates why the writ of habeas corpus should never be suspended except under the most compelling circumstances.

The origin of the writ of habeas corpus in the English legal system is often traced to the Magna Carta in 1215. It was later embraced by the founding fathers in the United States and now has both a constitutional and statutory basis. Moreover, throughout the entire course of U.S. history, the right to a writ of habeas corpus has only been suspended on a few occasions. In 1862, President Abraham Lincoln suspended it in Maryland and some midwestern states in order to "suppress the insurrection [the Civil War] existing in the United States." Several years later, President Ulysses S. Grant suspended habeas corpus in parts of South Carolina, to enforce civil rights laws against the Ku Klux Klan. Moreover, the great writ was also suspended in Hawaii in 1942 in the aftermath of the attack on Pearl Harbor.

All states have provisions for a writ of habeas corpus in their legal codes. The U.S. Congress has codified the right in federal law as well in 28 U.S.C. Section 2241.

In a related military order dated November 13, 2001, and published in the *Federal Register,* former president George W. Bush concluded that a national emergency existed for defense purposes, which was caused by the terrorist attacks of September 11, 2001. The order provided that the President would have the power to detain persons with a suspected connection to terrorists as "unlawful combatants." Moreover, such persons could be held indefinitely, and without charges, a court hearing, or the assistance of counsel. Since this order was issued, several different cases have alleged that these provisions violate the U.S. Constitution.

In *Hamdi v. Rumsfeld*, 542 U.S. 507 (2004), a U.S. citizen was captured in Afghanistan and turned over to U.S. military authorities. The government alleged that Hamdi had been fighting for the Taliban. He was held initially at Guantanamo Bay, Cuba, and was later transferred to a naval brig in Norfolk, Virginia. The Bush administration asserted that because Hamdi was fighting against the United States, he could be held as an enemy combatant, without access to an attorney or U.S. courts.

In 2002, Hamdi's father filed a habeas corpus petition in the U.S. District Court. After reviewing the case, the Court ordered a federal public defender be granted access to *Hamdi*. This decision was overturned, however, by the Fourth Circuit Court of Appeals, which held that the U.S. District Court judge should have utilized a deferential standard of review. When the case was returned to the District Court, the judge ruled that the government's evidence to support holding *Hamdi* was highly inadequate. The court further ordered the government to produce documents for "meaningful judicial review" of the case. The government appealed and the Fourth Circuit again reversed, and ruled that because *Hamdi* was apprehended "in a combat zone in a foreign theater of conflict," it was not proper for any court to hear a challenge of his status. It further held that Article II's grant of war making powers to the President and the separation of powers principle prevented courts from interfering with the authority of the other branches of government in this integral area of national security.

The U.S. Supreme Court granted review, although no single opinion of a Justice commanded a majority. Eight of the nine justices held, however, that the President does not have the power to hold indefinitely a U.S. citizen without fundamental due process safeguards that are subject to judicial review by the courts.

Two years later, the Court considered *Hamdan v. Rumsfeld*, 548 U.S. 557 (2006). Hamdan, a citizen of Yemen, had been a chauffeur and bodyguard for Osama bin Laden and was captured during the invasion of Afghanistan. He was charged with conspiracy to commit terrorism and taken to Guantanamo Bay, Cuba, where he was to be tried by a military commission. Hamdan filed a petition for a writ of habeas corpus, asserting that the military commission was a violation of federal law and the Geneva Convention.

The central issues in this case were whether the U.S. Congress may limit the Supreme Court's jurisdiction to hear cases of accused combatants before a military commission takes place, whether the special military commissions that had been developed violated federal law, and whether U.S. courts can enforce the provisions of the Geneva Convention. The Supreme Court, in an opinion by Justice John Paul Stevens, held that President Bush did not have the power to develop the war crimes tribunals and found that they were illegal under both Military Justice Law and the Geneva Convention.

Even more recently, the Court decided *Boumediene v. Bush* (2008), the latest case to consider the status of alien enemy combatants detained at Guantanamo Bay. Individuals detained at this facility presented the Court with a question not decided by the earlier terrorism cases: whether they have a constitutional right to a writ of habeas corpus. The government argued that noncitizens designated as enemy combatants and detained in territory located outside U.S. borders have no privilege of habeas corpus or other constitutional rights.

Moreover, in 2006, the U.S. Congress had passed the Military Commissions Act, 28 U.S.C.A. Section 2241. Subsection (e) provided:

> (e) [N]o court, justice, or judge shall have jurisdiction to hear or consider—(1) an application for a writ of habeas corpus filed by or on behalf of an alien detained by the Department of Defense at Guantanamo Bay, Cuba, who—
> (A) is currently in military custody . . .

This effect of this statute, therefore, was to deny the courts jurisdiction to consider requests for habeas corpus relief filed by alien prisoners incarcerated at Guantanamo Bay.

Justice Anthony Kennedy, writing for the Court, held, however:

[T]he [Habeas Corpus] Suspension Clause protects the rights of the detained by a means consistent with the essential design of the Constitution. It ensures that, except during periods of formal suspension, the judiciary will have a time-tested device, the writ, to maintain 'the delicate balance of governance' that is itself the surest safeguard of liberty. The Clause protects the rights of the detained by affirming the duty and authority of the Judiciary to call the jailer to account.

Justice Kennedy further observed, "[T]he laws and Constitution are designed to survive, and remain in force, in extraordinary times. Liberty and security can be reconciled; and in our system, they are reconciled within the framework of the law. The Framers decided that habeas corpus, a right of first importance, must be a part of that framework, a part of that law. Therefore, the petitioners were entitled to invoke 'the fundamental protections of habeas corpus.'"

Justice Antonin Scalia, dissenting, had a very different perspective on the issues presented in this case. He stated:

[T]he procedures prescribed by Congress in the Detainee Treatment Act provide the essential protections that habeas corpus guarantees; there has thus been no suspension of the writ, and no basis exists for judicial intervention beyond what the Act allows. My problem with today's opinion is more fundamental still: The writ of habeas corpus does not, and never has, run in favor of aliens abroad; the Suspension Clause thus has no application, and the Court's intervention in this military matter is entirely ultra vires. [Justice Scalia means that the Supreme Court has taken an action beyond the scope of its legitimate powers.]

In Your Opinion . . .

- How would you decide this case if you were a member of the Supreme Court?
- Should accused noncitizen terrorists have a right to a hearing in U.S. courts?
- Should the right to a writ of habeas corpus in U.S. courts even apply to noncitizen suspected terrorists who are held by military authorities beyond the territorial jurisdiction of the United States?

Boumediene v. Bush

Justice Kennedy delivered the opinion of the Court.

Petitioners are aliens designated as enemy combatants and detained at the United States Naval Station at Guantanamo Bay, Cuba. There are others detained there, also aliens, who are not parties to this suit.

Petitioners present a question not resolved by our earlier cases relating to the detention of aliens at Guantanamo: whether they have the constitutional privilege of habeas corpus, a privilege not to be withdrawn except in conformance with the Suspension Clause, Art. I, §9, cl. 2. We hold these petitioners do have the habeas corpus privilege. Congress has enacted a statute, the Detainee Treatment Act of 2005 (DTA), 119 Stat. 2739, that provides certain procedures for review of the detainees' status. We hold that those procedures are not an adequate and effective substitute for habeas corpus. Therefore, §7 of the Military Commissions Act of 2006 (MCA), 28 U.S. C. A. §2241(e) (Supp. 2007), operates as an unconstitutional suspension of the writ. We do not address whether the President has authority to detain these petitioners nor do we hold that the writ must issue. These and other questions regarding the legality of the detention are to be resolved in the first instance by the District Court. . . .

III

In deciding the constitutional questions now presented we must determine whether petitioners are barred from seeking the writ or invoking the protections of the Suspension Clause either because of their status, i.e., petitioners' designation by the Executive Branch as enemy combatants, or their physical location, i.e., their presence at Guantanamo Bay. The Government contends that noncitizens designated as enemy combatants and detained in territory located outside our Nation's borders have no constitutional rights and no privilege of habeas corpus. Petitioners contend they do have cognizable constitutional rights and that Congress, in seeking to eliminate recourse to habeas corpus as a means to assert those rights, acted in violation of the Suspension Clause.

We begin with a brief account of the history and origins of the writ. Our account proceeds from two propositions. First, protection for the privilege of habeas corpus was one of the few safeguards of liberty specified in a Constitution that, at the outset, had no Bill of Rights. In the system conceived by the Framers the writ had a centrality that must inform proper interpretation of the Suspension Clause. Second, to the extent there were settled precedents

Supreme Court of the United States, 2008.

or legal commentaries in 1789 regarding the extraterritorial scope of the writ or its application to enemy aliens, those authorities can be instructive for the present cases.

A

The Framers viewed freedom from unlawful restraint as a fundamental precept of liberty, and they understood the writ of habeas corpus as a vital instrument to secure that freedom. Experience taught, however, that the common-law writ all too often had been insufficient to guard against the abuse of monarchial power. That history counseled the necessity for specific language in the Constitution to secure the writ and ensure its place in our legal system.

Magna Carta decreed that no man would be imprisoned contrary to the law of the land. Art. 39, in *Sources of Our Liberties* 17 (R. Perry & J. Cooper eds. 1959) ("No free man shall be taken or imprisoned or dispossessed, or outlawed, or banished, or in any way destroyed, nor will we go upon him, nor send upon him, except by the legal judgment of his peers or by the law of the land"). Important as the principle was, the Barons at Runnymede prescribed no specific legal process to enforce it. Holdsworth tells us, however, that gradually the writ of habeas corpus became the means by which the promise of Magna Carta was fulfilled. 9 W. Holdsworth, *A History of English Law* 112 (1926) (hereinafter Holdsworth). . . .

This history was known to the Framers. It no doubt confirmed their view that pendular swings to and away from individual liberty were endemic to undivided, uncontrolled power. The Framers' inherent distrust of governmental power was the driving force behind the constitutional plan that allocated powers among three independent branches. This design serves not only to make Government accountable but also to secure individual liberty. See *Loving v. United States,* 517 U.S. 748, 756 (1996) (noting that "[e]ven before the birth of this country, separation of powers was known to be a defense against tyranny"); cf. *Youngstown Sheet & Tube Co. v. Sawyer,* 343 U.S. 579, 635 (1952) (Jackson, J., concurring) ("[T]he Constitution diffuses power the better to secure liberty"); *Clinton v. City of New York,* 524 U.S. 417, 450 (1998) (Kennedy, J., concurring) ("Liberty is always at stake when one or more of the branches seek to transgress the separation of powers"). Because the Constitution's separation-of-powers structure, like the substantive guarantees of the Fifth and Fourteenth Amendments, see *Yick Wo v. Hopkins,* 118 U.S. 356, 374 (1886), protects persons as well as citizens, foreign nationals who have the privilege of litigating in our courts can seek to enforce separation-of-powers principles, see, *e.g., INS v. Chadha,* 462 U.S. 919, 958–959 (1983).

That the Framers considered the writ a vital instrument for the protection of individual liberty is evident from the care taken to specify the limited grounds for its suspension: "The Privilege of the Writ of Habeas Corpus shall not be suspended, unless when in Cases of Rebellion or Invasion the public Safety may require it." Art. I, §9, cl. 2; see Amar, Of Sovereignty and Federalism, 96 *Yale L. J.* 1425, 1509, n. 329 (1987) ("[T]he non-suspension clause is the original Constitution's most explicit reference to remedies"). The word "privilege" was used, perhaps, to avoid mentioning some rights to the exclusion of others. (Indeed, the only mention of the term "right" in the Constitution, as ratified, is in its clause giving Congress the power to protect the rights of authors and inventors. See Art. I, §8, cl. 8.) . . .

"[T]he practice of arbitrary imprisonments, have been, in all ages, the favorite and most formidable instruments of tyranny. The observations of the judicious Blackstone . . . are well worthy of recital: 'To bereave a man of life . . . or by violence to confiscate his estate, without accusation or trial, would be so gross and notorious an act of despotism as must at once convey the alarm of tyranny throughout the whole nation; but confinement of the person, by secretly hurrying him to jail, where his sufferings are unknown or forgotten, is a less public, a less striking, and therefore a *more dangerous engine* of arbitrary government.' And as a remedy for this fatal evil he is everywhere peculiarly emphatical in his encomiums on the *habeas corpus* act, which in one place he calls 'the BULWARK of the British Constitution.'" C. Rossiter ed., p. 512 (1961) (quoting 1 Blackstone *136, 4 *id.*, at *438). . . .

In our own system the Suspension Clause is designed to protect against these cyclical abuses. The Clause protects the rights of the detained by a means consistent with the essential design of the Constitution. It ensures that, except during periods of formal suspension, the Judiciary will have a time-tested device, the writ, to maintain the "delicate balance of governance" that is itself the surest safeguard of liberty. See *Hamdi*, 542 U.S., at 536 (plurality opinion). The Clause protects the rights of the detained by affirming the duty and authority of the Judiciary to call the jailer to account. See *Preiser v. Rodriguez*, 411 U.S. 475, 484 (1973) ("[T]he essence of habeas corpus is an attack by a person in custody upon the legality of that custody"); cf. *In re Jackson*, 15 Mich. 417, 439–440 (1867) (Cooley, J., concurring) ("The important fact to be observed in regard to the mode of procedure upon this [habeas] writ is, that it is directed to, and served upon, not the person confined, but his jailer"). The separation-of-powers doctrine, and the history that influenced its design, therefore must inform the reach and purpose of the Suspension Clause.

B

The broad historical narrative of the writ and its function is central to our analysis, but we seek guidance as well from founding-era authorities addressing the specific question before us: whether foreign nationals, apprehended and detained in distant countries during a time of serious threats to our Nation's security, may assert the privilege of the writ and seek its protection. The Court has been careful not to foreclose the possibility that the protections of the Suspension Clause have expanded along with post-1789 developments that define the present scope of the writ. See *INS v. St. Cyr*, 533 U.S. 289, 300–301 (2001). But the analysis may begin with precedents as of 1789, for the Court has said that "at the absolute minimum" the Clause protects the writ as it existed when the Constitution was drafted and ratified. *Id.*, at 301. . . .

We know that at common law a petitioner's status as an alien was not a categorical bar to habeas corpus relief. See, *e.g.*, *Sommersett's Case*, 20 *How.*

St. Tr. v. 1, 80–82 (1772) (ordering an African slave freed upon finding the custodian's return insufficient); see generally *Khera v. Secretary of State for the Home Dept.,* [1984] A. C. 74, 111 ("Habeas corpus protection is often expressed as limited to 'British subjects.' Is it really limited to British nationals? Suffice it to say that the case law has given an emphatic 'no' to the question"). We know as well that common-law courts entertained habeas petitions brought by enemy aliens detained in England—"entertained" at least in the sense that the courts held hearings to determine the threshold question of entitlement to the writ. See *Case of Three Spanish Sailors, 2 Black. W.* 1324, 96 *Eng. Rep.* 775 (C. P. 1779); *King v. Schiever, 2 Burr.* 765, 97 *Eng. Rep.* 551 (K. B. 1759); *Du Castro's Case,* Fort. 195, 92 *Eng. Rep.* 816 (K. B. 1697). . . .

IV

Were we to hold that the present cases turn on the political question doctrine, we would be required first to accept the Government's premise that *de jure* sovereignty is the touchstone of habeas corpus jurisdiction. This premise, however, is unfounded. For the reasons indicated above, the history of common-law habeas corpus provides scant support for this proposition; and, for the reasons indicated below, that position would be inconsistent with our precedents and contrary to fundamental separation-of-powers principles. . . .

B

The Government's formal sovereignty-based test raises troubling separation-of-powers concerns as well. The political history of Guantanamo illustrates the deficiencies of this approach. The United States has maintained complete and uninterrupted control of the bay for over 100 years. At the close of the Spanish–American War, Spain ceded control over the entire island of Cuba to the United States and specifically "relinquishe[d] all claim[s] of sovereignty . . . and title." See Treaty of Paris, Dec. 10, 1898, U.S.-Spain, Art. I, 30 Stat. 1755, T. S. No. 343. From the date the treaty with Spain was signed until the Cuban Republic was established on May 20, 1902, the United States governed the territory "in trust" for the benefit of the Cuban people. *Neely v. Henkel,* 180 U.S. 109, 120 (1901) ; H. Thomas, *Cuba or The Pursuit of Freedom* 436, 460 (1998). And although it recognized, by entering into the 1903 Lease Agreement, that Cuba retained "ultimate sovereignty" over Guantanamo, the United States continued to maintain the same plenary control it had enjoyed since 1898. Yet the Government's view is that the Constitution had no effect there, at least as to noncitizens, because the United States disclaimed sovereignty in the formal sense of the term. The necessary implication of the argument is that by surrendering formal sovereignty over any unincorporated territory to a third party, while at the same time entering into a lease that grants total control over the territory back to the United States, it would be possible for the political branches to govern without legal constraint.

Our basic charter cannot be contracted away like this. The Constitution grants Congress and the President the power to acquire, dispose of, and govern territory, not the power to decide when and where its terms apply. Even when the United States acts outside its borders, its powers are not "absolute and unlimited" but are subject "to such restrictions as are expressed in the Constitution." *Murphy v. Ramsey*, 114 U.S. 15, 44 (1885). Abstaining from questions involving formal sovereignty and territorial governance is one thing. To hold the political branches have the power to switch the Constitution on or off at will is quite another. The former position reflects this Court's recognition that certain matters requiring political judgments are best left to the political branches. The latter would permit a striking anomaly in our tripartite system of government, leading to a regime in which Congress and the President, not this Court, say "what the law is." *Marbury v. Madison,* 1 Cranch 137, 177 (1803).

These concerns have particular bearing upon the Suspension Clause question in the cases now before us, for the writ of habeas corpus is itself an indispensable mechanism for monitoring the separation of powers. The test for determining the scope of this provision must not be subject to manipulation by those whose power it is designed to restrain.

C

As we recognized in *Rasul,* 542 U.S., at 476; *id.,* at 487 (Kennedy, J., concurring in judgment), the outlines of a framework for determining the reach of the Suspension Clause are suggested by the factors the Court relied upon in *Eisentrager.* In addition to the practical concerns discussed above, the *Eisentrager* Court found relevant that each petitioner:

> "(a) is an enemy alien; (b) has never been or resided in the United States; (c) was captured outside of our territory and there held in military custody as a prisoner of war; (d) was tried and convicted by a Military Commission sitting outside the United States; (e) for offenses against laws of war committed outside the United States; (f) and is at all times imprisoned outside the United States." 339 U.S., at 777.

Based on this language from *Eisentrager,* and the reasoning in our other extraterritoriality opinions, we conclude that at least three factors are relevant in determining the reach of the Suspension Clause: (1) the citizenship and status of the detainee and the adequacy of the process through which that status determination was made; (2) the nature of the sites where apprehension and then detention took place; and (3) the practical obstacles inherent in resolving the prisoner's entitlement to the writ.

Applying this framework, we note at the onset that the status of these detainees is a matter of dispute. The petitioners, like those in *Eisentrager,* are not American citizens. But the petitioners in *Eisentrager* did not contest, it seems, the Court's assertion that they were "enemy alien[s]." *Ibid.* In the instant cases, by contrast, the detainees deny they are enemy combatants. They have been afforded some process in CSRT proceedings to determine their status; but, unlike in *Eisentrager, supra,* at 766, there has been no trial by military commission for violations of the laws of war. The difference is not trivial. The records from the *Eisentrager* trials suggest that, well before the petitioners brought their case to this Court, there had been a rigorous adversarial process to test the legality of their detention. The *Eisentrager* petitioners were charged by a bill of particulars that made detailed factual allegations against them. See 14 United Nations War Crimes Commission, Law Reports of Trials of War Criminals 8–10 (1949) (reprint 1997). To rebut the accusations, they were entitled to representation by counsel, allowed to introduce evidence on their own behalf, and permitted to cross-examine the prosecution's witnesses. See Memorandum by Command of Lt. Gen. Wedemeyer, Jan. 21, 1946 (establishing "Regulations Governing the Trial of War Criminals" in the China Theater), in Tr. of Record in *Johnson v. Eisentrager,* O. T. 1949, No. 306, pp. 34–40.

In comparison the procedural protections afforded to the detainees in the CSRT hearings are far more limited, and, we conclude, fall well short of the procedures and adversarial mechanisms that would eliminate the need for habeas corpus review. Although the detainee is assigned a "Personal Representative" to assist him during CSRT proceedings, the Secretary of the Navy's memorandum makes clear that person is not the detainee's lawyer or even his "advocate." See App. to Pet. for Cert. in No. 06-1196, at 155, 172. The Government's evidence is accorded a presumption of validity. *Id.,* at 159. The detainee is allowed to present "reasonably available" evidence, *id.,* at 155, but his ability to rebut the Government's evidence against him is limited by the circumstances of his confinement and his lack of counsel at this stage. And although the detainee can seek review of his status determination in the Court of Appeals, that review process cannot cure all defects in the earlier proceedings. See Part V, *infra.* . . .

It is true that before today the Court has never held that noncitizens detained by our Government in territory over which another country maintains *de jure* sovereignty have any rights under our Constitution. But the cases before us lack any precise historical parallel. They involve individuals detained by executive order for the duration of a conflict that, if measured from September 11, 2001, to the present, is already among the longest wars in American history. See *Oxford Companion to American Military History* 849 (1999). The detainees, moreover, are held in a territory that, while technically not part of the United States, is under the complete and total control of our Government. Under these circumstances the lack of a precedent on point is no barrier to our holding.

We hold that Art. I, §9, cl. 2, of the Constitution has full effect at Guantanamo Bay. If the privilege of habeas corpus is to be denied to the detainees now before us, Congress must act in accordance with the requirements of the Suspension Clause. Cf. *Hamdi,* 542 U.S., at 564 (Scalia, J., dissenting) ("[I]ndefinite imprisonment on reasonable suspicion is not an available option of treatment for those accused of aiding the enemy, absent a suspension of the writ"). This Court may not impose a *de facto* suspension by abstaining from these controversies. See Hamdan, 548 U.S., at 585, n. 16 {"[A]bstention is not appropriate in cases . . . in which the legal challenge 'turn[s] on the status of the persons as to whom the military asserted its power'" (quoting *Schlesinger v. Councilman,* 420 U.S. 738, 759 (1975))}. The MCA does not purport to be a formal suspension of the writ; and the Government, in its submissions to us, has not argued that it is. Petitioners, therefore, are entitled to the privilege of habeas corpus to challenge the legality of their detention.

V

In light of this holding the question becomes whether the statute stripping juris-diction to issue the writ avoids the Suspension Clause mandate because Congress has provided adequate substitute procedures for habeas corpus. The Govern-ment submits there has been compliance with the Suspension Clause because the DTA review process in the Court of Appeals, see DTA §1005(e), provides an adequate substitute. Congress has granted that court jurisdiction to consider

"(i) whether the status determination of the [CSRT] . . . was consistent with the standards and procedures specified by the Secretary of Defense . . . and (ii) to the extent the Constitution and laws of the United States are appli-cable, whether the use of such standards and procedures to make the determi-nation is consistent with the Constitution and laws of the United States." . . .

A

The two leading cases addressing habeas substitutes, *Swain v. Pressley*, 430 U.S. 372 (1977), and *United States v. Hayman*, 342 U.S. 205 (1952), . . . provide little guidance here. The statutes at issue were attempts to streamline habeas corpus relief, not to cut it back.

The statute discussed in *Hayman* was 28 U.S. C. §2255. It replaced tradi-tional habeas corpus for federal prisoners (at least in the first instance) with a process that allowed the prisoner to file a motion with the sentencing court on the ground that his sentence was, *inter alia,* "imposed in violation of the Constitution or laws of the United States." 342 U.S., at 207, n. 1. The purpose and effect of the statute was not to restrict access to the writ but to make post-conviction proceedings more efficient. It directed claims not to the court that had territorial jurisdiction over the place of the petitioner's confinement but to the sentencing court, a court already familiar with the facts of the case. As the *Hayman* Court explained

"Section 2255 . . . was passed at the instance of the Judicial Conference to meet practical difficulties that had arisen in administering the habeas cor-pus jurisdiction of the federal courts. Nowhere in the history of Section 2255 do we find any purpose to impinge upon prisoners' rights of collateral attack upon their convictions. On the contrary, the sole purpose was to minimize the difficulties encountered in habeas corpus hearings by affording the same rights in another and more convenient forum." *id.,* at 219.

See also *Hill v. United States,* 368 U.S. 424 , and n. 5 (1962) (noting that §2255 provides a remedy in the sentencing court that is "exactly commensu-rate" with the pre-existing federal habeas corpus remedy).

The statute in *Swain,* D.C. Code Ann. §23-110(g) (1973), applied to prison-ers in custody under sentence of the Superior Court of the District of Columbia. Before enactment of the District of Columbia Court Reform and Criminal Proce-dure Act of 1970 (D.C. Court Reform Act), 84 Stat. 473, those prisoners could file habeas petitions in the United States District Court for the District of Columbia. The Act, which was patterned on §2255, substituted a new collateral process in the Superior Court for the pre-existing habeas corpus procedure in the District

Court. See *Swain,* 430 U.S., at 374–378. But, again, the purpose and effect of the statute was to expedite consideration of the prisoner's claims, not to delay or frustrate it. See *id.,* at 375, n. 4 (noting that the purpose of the D.C. Court Reform Act was to "alleviate" administrative burdens on the District Court).

That the statutes in *Hayman* and *Swain* were designed to strengthen, rather than dilute, the writ's protections was evident, furthermore, from this significant fact: Neither statute eliminated traditional habeas corpus relief. In both cases the statute at issue had a saving clause, providing that a writ of habeas corpus would be available if the alternative process proved inadequate or ineffective. *Swain, supra,* at 381; *Hayman, supra,* at 223. The Court placed explicit reliance upon these provisions in upholding the statutes against constitutional challenges. See *Swain, supra,* at 381 (noting that the provision "avoid[ed] any serious question about the constitutionality of the statute"); *Hayman, supra,* at 223 (noting that, because habeas remained available as a last resort, it was unnecessary to "reach constitutional questions"). . . .

To the extent any doubt remains about Congress' intent, the legislative history confirms what the plain text strongly suggests: In passing the DTA Congress did not intend to create a process that differs from traditional habeas corpus process in name only. It intended to create a more limited procedure. See, e.g., 151 Cong. Rec. S14263 (Dec. 21, 2005) (statement of Sen. Graham) (noting that the DTA "extinguish[es] these habeas and other actions in order to effect a transfer of jurisdiction over these cases to the DC Circuit Court" and agreeing that the bill "create[s] in their place a very limited judicial review of certain military administrative decisions"); *id.,* at S14268 (statement of Sen. Kyl) ("It is important to note that the limited judicial review authorized by paragraphs 2 and 3 of subsection (e) [of DTA §1005] are not habeas-corpus review. It is a limited judicial review of its own nature").

It is against this background that we must interpret the DTA and assess its adequacy as a substitute for habeas corpus. The present cases thus test the limits of the Suspension Clause in ways that *Hayman* and *Swain* did not.

B

We do not endeavor to offer a comprehensive summary of the requisites for an adequate substitute for habeas corpus. We do consider it uncontroversial, however, that the privilege of habeas corpus entitles the prisoner to a meaningful opportunity to demonstrate that he is being held pursuant to "the erroneous application or interpretation" of relevant law. *St. Cyr,* 533 U.S., at 302. And the habeas court must have the power to order the conditional release of an individual unlawfully detained—though release need not be the exclusive remedy and is not the appropriate one in every case in which the writ is granted. See *Ex parte Bollman,* 4 *Cranch* 75, 136 (1807) (where imprisonment is unlawful, the court "can only direct [the prisoner] to be discharged"); R. Hurd, *Treatise on the Right of Personal Liberty,* and *On the Writ of Habeas Corpus and the Practice Connected with It: With a View of the Law of Extradition of Fugitives* 222 (2d ed. 1876) ("It cannot be denied where 'a probable ground is shown that the party is imprisoned without just cause, and therefore, hath a right to be delivered,' for the writ then becomes a 'writ of right, which may not be denied but ought to be granted to every man that is committed or detained in prison or otherwise restrained of his liberty'"). But see *Chessman v. Teets*, 354 U. S. 156,165–166 (1957) (remanding in a habeas case for retrial within a "reasonable time"). These are the easily identified attributes of any constitutionally adequate habeas corpus proceeding. But, depending on the circumstances, more may be required. . . .

The idea that the necessary scope of habeas review in part depends upon the rigor of any earlier proceedings accords with our test for procedural adequacy in the due process context. See *Mathews v. Eldridge*, 424 U.S. 319, 335 (1976) (noting that the Due Process Clause requires an assessment of, *inter alia*, "the risk of an erroneous deprivation of [a liberty interest;] and the probable value, if any, of additional or substitute procedural safeguards"). This principle has an established foundation in habeas corpus jurisprudence as well, as Chief Justice Marshall's opinion in *Ex parte Watkins*, 3 Pet. 193 (1830), demonstrates. Like the petitioner in *Swain*, Watkins sought a writ of habeas corpus after being imprisoned pursuant to a judgment of a District of Columbia court. In holding that the judgment stood on "high ground," 3 Pet., at 209, the Chief Justice emphasized the character of the court that rendered the original judgment, noting it was a "court of record, having general jurisdiction over criminal cases." *Id.*, at 203. In contrast to "inferior" tribunals of limited jurisdiction, *ibid.*, courts of record had broad remedial powers, which gave the habeas court greater confidence in the judgment's validity. See generally Neuman, Habeas Corpus, Executive Detention, and the Removal of Aliens, 98 *Colum. L. Rev.* 961, 982–983 (1998).

Accordingly, where relief is sought from a sentence that resulted from the judgment of a court of record, as was the case in *Watkins* and indeed in most federal habeas cases, considerable deference is owed to the court that ordered confinement. See *Brown v. Allen*, 344 U.S. 443, 506 (1953) (opinion of Frankfurter, J.) (noting that a federal habeas court should accept a state court's factual findings unless "a vital flaw be found in the process of ascertaining such facts in the State court"). Likewise in those cases the prisoner should exhaust adequate alternative remedies before filing for the writ in federal court. See *Ex parte Royall*, 117 U.S. 241, 251–252 (1886) (requiring exhaustion of state collateral processes). Both aspects of federal habeas corpus review are justified because it can be assumed that, in the usual course, a court of record provides defendants with a fair, adversary proceeding. In cases involving state convictions this framework also respects federalism; and in federal cases it has added justification because the prisoner already has had a chance to seek review of his conviction in a federal forum through a direct appeal. The present cases fall outside these categories, however; for here the detention is by executive order.

Where a person is detained by executive order, rather than, say, after being tried and convicted in a court, the need for collateral review is most pressing. A criminal conviction in the usual course occurs after a judicial hearing before a tribunal disinterested in the outcome and committed to procedures designed to ensure its own independence. These dynamics are not inherent in executive detention orders or executive review procedures. In this context the need for habeas corpus is more urgent. The intended duration of the detention and the reasons for it bear upon the precise scope of the inquiry. Habeas corpus proceedings need not resemble a criminal trial, even when the detention is by executive order. But the writ must be effective. The habeas court must have sufficient authority to conduct a meaningful review of both the cause for detention and the Executive's power to detain.

To determine the necessary scope of habeas corpus review, therefore, we must assess the CSRT process, the mechanism through which petitioners' designation as enemy combatants became final. Whether one characterizes the CSRT process as direct review of the Executive's battlefield determination that the detainee is an enemy combatant—as the parties have and as we do—or as the first step in the collateral review of a battlefield determination makes no difference in a proper analysis of whether the procedures Congress put in place are an adequate substitute for habeas corpus. What matters is the sum total of procedural protections afforded to the detainee at all stages, direct and collateral. . . .

For the writ of habeas corpus, or its substitute, to function as an effective and proper remedy in this context, the court that conducts the habeas proceeding must have the means to correct errors that occurred during the CSRT proceedings. This includes some authority to assess the sufficiency of the Government's evidence against the detainee. It also must have the authority to admit and consider relevant exculpatory evidence that was not introduced during the earlier proceeding. Federal habeas petitioners long have had the means to supplement the record on review, even in the postconviction habeas setting. See *Townsend v. Sain*, 372 U.S. 293, 313 (1963), overruled in part by *Keeney v. Tamayo-Reyes*, 504 U.S. 1, 5 (1992). Here that opportunity is constitutionally required.

Consistent with the historic function and province of the writ, habeas corpus review may be more circumscribed if the underlying detention proceedings are more thorough than they were here. In two habeas cases involving enemy aliens tried for war crimes, *In re Yamashita*, 327 U.S. 1 (1946), and *Ex parte Quirin*, 317 U.S. 1 (1942), for example, this Court limited its review to determining whether the Executive had legal authority to try the petitioners by military commission. See *Yamashita, supra,* at 8 ("[O]n application for habeas corpus we are not concerned with the guilt or innocence of the petitioners. We consider here only the lawful power of the commission to try the petitioner for the offense charged"); *Quirin, supra,* at 25 ("We are not here concerned with any question of the guilt or innocence of petitioners"). Military courts are not courts of record. See *Watkins*, 3 Pet., at 209; Church 513. And the procedures used to try General Yamashita have been sharply criticized by Members of this Court. See Hamdan, 548 U.S. at 617; *Yamashita, supra,* at 41–81 (Rutledge, J., dissenting). We need not revisit these cases, however. For on their own terms, the proceedings in *Yamashita* and *Quirin,* like those in *Eisentrager,* had an adversarial structure that is lacking here. See *Yamashita, supra,* at 5 (noting that General Yamashita was represented by six military lawyers and that "[t]hroughout the proceedings . . . defense counsel . . . demonstrated their professional skill and resourcefulness and their proper zeal for the defense with which they were charged"); *Quirin, supra,* at 23–24; Exec.

Order No. 9185, 7 *Fed. Reg.* 5103 (1942) (appointing counsel to represent the German saboteurs).

The extent of the showing required of the Government in these cases is a matter to be determined. We need not explore it further at this stage. We do hold that when the judicial power to issue habeas corpus properly is invoked the judicial officer must have adequate authority to make a determination in light of the relevant law and facts and to formulate and issue appropriate orders for relief, including, if necessary, an order directing the prisoner's release. . . .

A

In light of our conclusion that there is no jurisdictional bar to the District Court's entertaining petitioners' claims the question remains whether there are prudential barriers to habeas corpus review under these circumstances.

The Government argues petitioners must seek review of their CSRT determinations in the Court of Appeals before they can proceed with their habeas corpus actions in the District Court. As noted earlier, in other contexts and for prudential reasons this Court has required exhaustion of alternative remedies before a prisoner can seek federal habeas relief. Most of these cases were brought by prisoners in state custody, *e.g., Ex parte Royall*, 117 U.S. 241, and thus involved federalism concerns that are not relevant here. But we have extended this rule to require defendants in courts-martial to exhaust their military appeals before proceeding with a federal habeas corpus action. See *Schlesinger*, 420 U.S., at 758.

The real risks, the real threats, of terrorist attacks are constant and not likely soon to abate. The ways to disrupt our life and laws are so many and unforeseen that the Court should not attempt even some general catalogue of crises that might occur. Certain principles are apparent, however. Practical considerations and exigent circumstances inform the definition and reach of the law's writs, including habeas corpus. The cases and our tradition reflect this precept.

In cases involving foreign citizens detained abroad by the Executive, it likely would be both an impractical and unprecedented extension of judicial power to assume that habeas corpus would be available at the moment the prisoner is taken into custody. If and when habeas corpus jurisdiction applies, as it does in these cases, then proper deference can be accorded to reasonable procedures for screening and initial detention under lawful and proper conditions of confinement and treatment for a reasonable period of time. Domestic exigencies, furthermore, might also impose such onerous burdens on the Government that here, too, the Judicial Branch would be required to devise sensible rules for staying habeas corpus proceedings until the Government can comply with its requirements in a responsible way. Cf. *Ex parte Milligan*, 4 Wall., at 127 ("If, in foreign invasion or civil war, the courts are actually closed, and it is impossible to administer criminal justice according to law, *then,* on the theatre of active military operations, where war really prevails, there is a necessity to furnish a substitute for the civil authority, thus overthrown, to preserve the safety of the army and society; and as no power is left but the military, it is allowed to govern by martial rule until the laws can have their free course"). Here, as is true with detainees apprehended abroad, a relevant consideration in determining the courts' role is whether there are suitable alternative processes in place to protect against the arbitrary exercise of governmental power.

The cases before us, however, do not involve detainees who have been held for a short period of time while awaiting their CSRT determinations. Were that the case, or were it probable that the Court of Appeals could complete a prompt review of their applications, the case for requiring temporary abstention or exhaustion of alternative remedies would be much stronger. These qualifications no longer pertain here. In some of these cases six years have elapsed without the judicial oversight that habeas corpus or an adequate substitute demands. And there has been no showing that the Executive faces such onerous burdens that it cannot respond to habeas corpus actions. To require these detainees to complete DTA review before proceeding with their habeas corpus actions would be to require additional months, if not years, of delay. The first DTA review applications were filed over a year ago, but no decisions on the merits have been issued. While some delay in fashioning new procedures is unavoidable, the costs of delay can no longer be borne by those who are held in custody. The detainees in these cases are entitled to a prompt habeas corpus hearing.

Our decision today holds only that the petitioners before us are entitled to seek the writ; that the DTA review procedures are an inadequate substitute for habeas corpus; and that the petitioners in these cases need not exhaust the review procedures in the Court of Appeals before proceeding with their habeas actions in the District Court. The only law we identify as unconstitutional is MCA §7, 28 U.S. C. A. §2241(e) (Supp. 2007). Accordingly, both the DTA and the CSRT process remain intact. Our holding with regard to exhaustion should not be read to imply that a habeas court should intervene the moment an enemy combatant steps foot in a territory where the writ runs. The Executive is entitled to a reasonable period of time to determine a detainee's status before a court entertains that detainee's habeas corpus petition. The CSRT process is the mechanism Congress and the President set up to deal with these issues. Except in cases of undue delay, federal courts should refrain from entertaining an enemy combatant's habeas corpus petition at least until after the Department, acting via the CSRT, has had a chance to review his status.

B

Although we hold that the DTA is not an adequate and effective substitute for habeas corpus, it does not follow that a habeas corpus court may disregard the dangers the detention in these cases was intended to prevent. *Felker, Swain,* and *Hayman* stand for the proposition that the Suspension Clause does not resist innovation in the field of habeas corpus. Certain accommodations can be made to reduce the burden habeas corpus proceedings will place on the military without impermissibly diluting the protections of the writ.

In the DTA Congress sought to consolidate review of petitioners' claims in the Court of Appeals. Channeling future cases to one district court would no doubt reduce administrative burdens on the Government. This is a legitimate objective that might be advanced even without an amendment to §2241. If, in a future case, a detainee files a habeas petition in another judicial district in which a proper respondent can be served, see *Rumsfeld v. Padilla,* 542 U.S. 426, 435–436 (2004), the Government can move for change of venue to the court that will hear these petitioners' cases, the United States District Court for the District of Columbia. See 28 U.S. C. §1404(a); *Braden v. 30th Judicial Circuit Court of Ky.,* 410 U.S. 484, n. 15 (1973).

Another of Congress' reasons for vesting exclusive jurisdiction in the Court of Appeals, perhaps, was to avoid the widespread dissemination of classified information. The Government has raised similar concerns here and elsewhere. See Brief for Respondents 55–56; *Bismullah* Pet. 30. We make no attempt to anticipate all of the evidentiary and access-to-counsel issues that will arise during the course of the detainees' habeas corpus proceedings. We recognize, however, that the Government has a legitimate interest in protecting sources and methods of intelligence gathering; and we expect that the District Court will use its discretion to accommodate this interest to the greatest extent possible. Cf. *United States v. Reynolds,* 345 U.S. 1, 10 (1953) (recognizing an evidentiary privilege in a civil damages case where "there is a reasonable danger that compulsion of the evidence will expose military matters which, in the interest of national security, should not be divulged").

These and the other remaining questions are within the expertise and competence of the District Court to address in the first instance.

***

In considering both the procedural and substantive standards used to impose detention to prevent acts of terrorism, proper deference must be accorded to the political branches. See *United States v. Curtiss-Wright Export Corp.,* 299 U.S. 304, 320 (1936). Unlike the President and some designated Members of Congress, neither the Members of this Court nor most federal judges begin the day with briefings that may describe new and serious threats to our Nation and its people. The law must accord the Executive substantial authority to apprehend and detain those who pose a real danger to our security.

Officials charged with daily operational responsibility for our security may consider a judicial discourse on the history of the Habeas Corpus Act of 1679 and like matters to be far removed from the Nation's present, urgent concerns. Established legal doctrine, however, must be consulted for its teaching. Remote in time it may be; irrelevant to the present it is not. Security depends upon a sophisticated intelligence apparatus and the ability of our Armed Forces to act and to interdict. There are further considerations, however. Security subsists, too, in fidelity to freedom's first principles. Chief among these are freedom from arbitrary and unlawful restraint and the personal liberty that is secured by adherence to the separation of powers. It is from these principles that the judicial authority to consider petitions for habeas corpus relief derives.

Our opinion does not undermine the Executive's powers as Commander in Chief. On the contrary, the exercise of those powers is vindicated, not eroded, when confirmed by the Judicial Branch. Within the Constitution's separation-of-powers structure, few exercises of judicial power are as legitimate or as necessary as the responsibility to hear challenges to the authority of the Executive to imprison a person. Some of these petitioners have been in custody for six years with no definitive judicial determination as to the legality of their detention. Their access to the writ is a necessity to determine the lawfulness of their status, even if, in the end, they do not obtain the relief they seek.

Because our Nation's past military conflicts have been of limited duration, it has been possible to leave the outer boundaries of war powers undefined. If, as some fear, terrorism continues to pose dangerous threats to us for years to come, the Court might not have this luxury. This result is not inevitable, however. The political branches, consistent with their independent obligations to interpret and uphold the Constitution, can engage in a genuine debate about how best to preserve constitutional values while protecting the Nation from terrorism. Cf. Hamdan, 548 U.S., at 636 (Breyer, J., concurring) ("[J]udicial insistence upon that consultation does not weaken our Nation's ability to deal with danger. To the contrary, that insistence strengthens the Nation's ability to determine—through democratic means—how best to do so").

It bears repeating that our opinion does not address the content of the law that governs petitioners' detention. That is a matter yet to be determined. We hold that petitioners may invoke the fundamental procedural protections of habeas corpus. The laws and Constitution are designed to survive, and remain in force, in extraordinary times. Liberty and security can be reconciled; and in our system they are reconciled within the framework of the law. The Framers decided that habeas corpus, a right of first importance, must be a part of that framework, a part of that law.

The determination by the Court of Appeals that the Suspension Clause and its protections are inapplicable to petitioners was in error. The judgment of the Court of Appeals is reversed. The cases are remanded to the Court of Appeals with instructions that it remand the cases to the District Court for proceedings consistent with this opinion.

It is so ordered.

 **NO**

Dissenting, *Boumediene v. Bush*

Justice Scalia, with whom the Chief Justice Thomas and Justice Alito join, dissenting.

Today, for the first time in our Nation's history, the Court confers a constitutional right to habeas corpus on alien enemies detained abroad by our military forces in the course of an ongoing war. The Chief Justice's dissent, which I join, shows that the procedures prescribed by Congress in the Detainee Treatment Act provide the essential protections that habeas corpus guarantees; there has thus been no suspension of the writ, and no basis exists for judicial intervention beyond what the Act allows. My problem with today's opinion is more fundamental still: The writ of habeas corpus does not, and never has, run in favor of aliens abroad; the Suspension Clause thus has no application, and the Court's intervention in this military matter is entirely ultra vires.

I shall devote most of what will be a lengthy opinion to the legal errors contained in the opinion of the Court. Contrary to my usual practice, however, I think it appropriate to begin with a description of the disastrous consequences of what the Court has done today.

I

America is at war with radical Islamists. The enemy began by killing Americans and American allies abroad: 241 at the Marine barracks in Lebanon, 19 at the Khobar Towers in Dhahran, 224 at our embassies in Dar es Salaam and Nairobi, and 17 on the USS Cole in Yemen. See National Commission on Terrorist Attacks upon the United States, The 9/11 Commission Report, pp. 60–61, 70, 190 (2004). On September 11, 2001, the enemy brought the battle to American soil, killing 2,749 at the Twin Towers in New York City, 184 at the Pentagon in Washington, D.C., and 40 in Pennsylvania. See *id.*, at 552, n. 9. It has threatened further attacks against our homeland; one need only walk about buttressed and barricaded Washington, or board a plane anywhere in the country, to know that the threat is a serious one. Our Armed Forces are now in the field against the enemy, in Afghanistan and Iraq. Last week, 13 of our countrymen in arms were killed.

The game of bait-and-switch that today's opinion plays upon the Nation's Commander in Chief will make the war harder on us. It will almost certainly cause more Americans to be killed. That consequence would be tolerable if necessary to preserve a time-honored legal principle vital to our constitutional Republic. But it is this Court's blatant *abandonment* of such a principle that produces the decision today. The President relied on our settled precedent in

Supreme Court of the United States, June 12, 2008.

Johnson v. Eisentrager, 339 U.S. 763 (1950), when he established the prison at Guantanamo Bay for enemy aliens. Citing that case, the President's Office of Legal Counsel advised him "that the great weight of legal authority indicates that a federal district court could not properly exercise habeas jurisdiction over an alien detained at [Guantanamo Bay]." Memorandum from Patrick F. Philbin and John C. Yoo, Deputy Assistant Attorneys General, Office of Legal Counsel, to William J. Haynes II, General Counsel, Dept. of Defense (Dec. 28, 2001). Had the law been otherwise, the military surely would not have transported prisoners there, but would have kept them in Afghanistan, transferred them to another of our foreign military bases, or turned them over to allies for detention. Those other facilities might well have been worse for the detainees themselves.

In the long term, then, the Court's decision today accomplishes little, except perhaps to reduce the well-being of enemy combatants that the Court ostensibly seeks to protect. In the short term, however, the decision is devastating. At least 30 of those prisoners hitherto released from Guantanamo Bay have returned to the battlefield. . . . But others have succeeded in carrying on their atrocities against innocent civilians. In one case, a detainee released from Guantanamo Bay masterminded the kidnapping of two Chinese dam workers, one of whom was later shot to death when used as a human shield against Pakistani commandoes. . . . Another former detainee promptly resumed his post as a senior Taliban commander and murdered a United Nations engineer and three Afghan soldiers. . . . Still another murdered an Afghan judge. . . . It was reported only last month that a released detainee carried out a suicide bombing against Iraqi soldiers in Mosul, Iraq. . . .

These, mind you, were detainees whom *the military* had concluded were not enemy combatants. Their return to the kill illustrates the incredible difficulty of assessing who is and who is not an enemy combatant in a foreign theater of operations where the environment does not lend itself to rigorous evidence collection. Astoundingly, the Court today raises the bar, requiring military officials to appear before civilian courts and defend their decisions under procedural and evidentiary rules that go beyond what Congress has specified. As The Chief Justice's dissent makes clear, we have no idea what those procedural and evidentiary rules are, but they will be determined by civil courts and (in the Court's contemplation at least) will be more detainee-friendly than those now applied, since otherwise there would no reason to hold the congressionally prescribed procedures unconstitutional. If they impose a higher standard of proof (from foreign battlefields) than the current procedures require, the number of the enemy returned to combat will obviously increase.

But even when the military has evidence that it can bring forward, it is often foolhardy to release that evidence to the attorneys representing our enemies. And one escalation of procedures that the Court *is* clear about is affording the detainees increased access to witnesses (perhaps troops serving in Afghanistan?) and to classified information. See *ante,* at 54–55. During the 1995 prosecution of Omar Abdel Rahman, federal prosecutors gave the names of 200 unindicted co-conspirators to the "Blind Sheik's" defense lawyers; that information was in the hands of Osama Bin Laden within two weeks. . . . In another case, trial testimony revealed to the enemy that the United States had been monitoring their cellular network, whereupon they promptly stopped using it, enabling more of them to evade capture and continue their atrocities. . . .

And today it is not just the military that the Court elbows aside. A mere two terms ago in *Hamdan v. Rumsfeld*, 548 U.S. 557 (2006), when the Court held (quite amazingly) that the Detainee Treatment Act of 2005 had not stripped habeas jurisdiction over Guantanamo petitioners' claims, four Members of today's five-Justice majority joined an opinion saying the following:

> "Nothing prevents the President from returning to Congress to seek the authority [for trial by military commission] he believes necessary."
>
> "Where, as here, no emergency prevents consultation with Congress, judicial insistence upon that consultation does not weaken our Nation's ability to deal with danger. To the contrary, that insistence strengthens the Nation's ability to determine—through democratic means—how best to do so. The Constitution places its faith in those democratic means." . . .

Turns out they were just kidding. For in response, Congress, at the President's request, quickly enacted the Military Commissions Act, emphatically reasserting that it did not want these prisoners filing habeas petitions. It is therefore clear that Congress and the Executive—*both* political branches—have determined that limiting the role of civilian courts in adjudicating whether prisoners captured abroad are properly detained is important to success in the war that some 190,000 of our men and women are now fighting. As the Solicitor General argued, "the Military Commissions Act and the Detainee Treatment Act . . . represent an effort by the political branches to strike an appropriate balance between the need to preserve liberty and the need to accommodate the weighty and sensitive governmental interests in ensuring that those who have in fact fought with the enemy during a war do not return to battle against the United States." Brief for Respondents 10–11 (internal quotation marks omitted).

But it does not matter. The Court today decrees that no good reason to accept the judgment of the other two branches is "apparent." *Ante,* at 40. "The Government," it declares, "presents no credible arguments that the military mission at Guantanamo would be compromised if habeas corpus courts had jurisdiction to hear the detainees' claims." *Id.,* at 39. What competence does the Court have to second-guess the judgment of Congress and the President on such a point? None whatever. But the Court blunders in nonetheless. Henceforth, as today's opinion makes unnervingly clear, how to handle enemy prisoners in this war will ultimately lie with the branch that knows least about the national security concerns that the subject entails.

A

The Suspension Cause of the Constitution provides: "The Privilege of the Writ of Habeas Corpus shall not be suspended, unless when in Cases of Rebellion or Invasion the public Safety may require it." Art. I, §9, cl. 2. As a court of law operating under a written Constitution, our role is to determine whether there is a conflict between that Clause and the Military Commissions Act. A conflict arises only if the Suspension Clause preserves the privilege of the writ for aliens held by the United States military as enemy combatants at the base in Guantanamo Bay, located within the sovereign territory of Cuba.

We have frequently stated that we owe great deference to Congress's view that a law it has passed is constitutional. . . . That is especially so in the area of foreign and military affairs; "perhaps in no other area has the Courtaccorded Congress greater deference." . . . Indeed, we accord great deferenceeven when the President acts alone in this area. . . .

How, then, does the Court weave a clear constitutional prohibition out of pure interpretive equipoise? The Court resorts to "fundamental separation-of-powers principles" to interpret the Suspension Clause. . . . According to the Court, because "the writ of habeas corpus is itself an indispensable mechanism for monitoring the separation of powers," the test of its extraterritorial reach "must not be subject to manipulation by those whose power it is designed to restrain.". . .

That approach distorts the nature of the separation of powers and its role in the constitutional structure. The "fundamental separation-of-powers principles" that the Constitution embodies are to be derived not from some judicially imagined matrix, but from the sum total of the individual separation-of-powers provisions that the Constitution sets forth. Only by considering them one-by-one does the full shape of the Constitution's separation-of-powers principles emerge. It is nonsensical to interpret those provisions themselves in light of some general "separation-of-powers principles" dreamed up by the Court, Rather, they must be interpreted to mean what they were understood to mean when the people ratified them. And if the understood scope of the writ of habeas corpus was "designed to restrain" (as the Court says) the actions of the Executive, the understood *limits* upon that scope were (as the Court seems not to grasp) just as much "designed to restrain" the incursions of the Third Branch. "Manipulation" of the territorial reach of the writ by the Judiciary poses just as much a threat to the proper separation of powers as "manipulation" by the Executive. As I will show below, manipulation is what is afoot here. The understood limits upon the writ deny our jurisdiction over the habeas petitions brought by these enemy aliens, and entrust the President with the crucial wartime determinations about their status and continued confinement.

B

The Court purports to derive from our precedents a "functional" test for the extraterritorial reach of the writ, *ante,* at 34, which shows that the Military Commissions Act unconstitutionally restricts the scope of habeas. That is remarkable because the most pertinent of those precedents, *Johnson v. Eisentrager,* 339 U.S. 763, conclusively establishes the opposite. There we were confronted with the claims of 21 Germans held at Landsberg Prison, an American military facility located in the American Zone of occupation in postwar Germany. They had been captured in China, and an American military commission sitting there had convicted them of war crimes—collaborating with the Japanese after Germany's surrender. *Id.*, at 765–766. Like the petitioners here, the Germans claimed that their detentions violated the Constitution and international law, and sought a writ of habeas corpus. Writing for the Court, Justice Jackson held that American courts lacked habeas jurisdiction:

> "We are cited to [*sic*] no instance where a court, in this or any other country where the writ is known, has issued it on behalf of an alien enemy who, at no relevant time and in no stage of his captivity, has been within its territorial jurisdiction. Nothing in the text of the Constitution extends such a right, nor does anything in our statutes." *Id.,* at 768.

Justice Jackson then elaborated on the historical scope of the writ:

> "The alien, to whom the United States has been traditionally hospitable, has been accorded a generous and ascending scale of rights as he increases his identity with our society. . . ."
>
> "But, in extending constitutional protections beyond the citizenry, the Court has been at pains to point out that it was the alien's presence within its territorial jurisdiction that gave the Judiciary power to act." . . .

Eisentrager thus held—*held* beyond any doubt—that the Constitution does not ensure habeas for aliens held by the United States in areas over which our Government is not sovereign. . . .

There is simply no support for the Court's assertion that constitutional rights extend to aliens held outside U.S. sovereignterritory, see *Verdugo-Urquidez,* 494 U.S., at 271, and *Eisentrager* could not be clearer that the privilege of habeas corpusdoes not extend to aliens abroad. By blatantly distorting *Eisentrager,* the Court avoids the difficulty of explaining why itshould be overruled. . . . The rule that aliens abroad are not constitutionally entitled to habeas corpus has not proved unworkable in practice; if anything, it is the Court's "functional" test that does not (and never will) provide clear guidance for the future. *Eisentrager* forms a coherent whole with the accepted proposition that aliens abroad have no substantive rights under our Constitution. Since it was announced, no relevant factual premises have changed. It has engendered considerable reliance on the part of our military. And, as the Court acknowledges, text and history do not clearly compel a contrary ruling. It is a sad day for the rule of law when such an important constitutional precedent is discarded without an *apologia,* much less an apology.

C

What drives today's decision is neither the meaning of the Suspension Clause, nor the principles of our precedents, but rather an inflated notion of judicial supremacy. The Court says that if the extraterritorial applicability of the Suspension Clause turned on formal notions of sovereignty, "it would be possible for the political branches to govern without legal constraint" in areas beyond the sovereign territory of the United States. *Ante,* at 35. That cannot be, the Court says, because it is the duty of this Court to say what the law is. *Id.,* at 35–36. It would be difficult to imagine a more question-begging analysis. "The very foundation of the power of the federal courts to declare Acts of Congress unconstitutional lies in the power and duty of those courts to decide cases and controversies *properly before them."* . . . And that is precisely the question in these cases: whether the Constitution confers habeas jurisdiction on federal courts to decide petitioners' claims. It is both irrational and arrogant to say that the answer must be yes, because otherwise we would not be supreme.

But so long as there are *some* places to which habeas does not run—so long as the Court's new "functional" test will not be satisfied *in every case*—then there will be circumstances in which "it would be possible for the political branches to govern without legal constraint." Or, to put it more impartially, areas in which the legal determinations of the *other* branches will be (shudder!) *supreme.* In other words, judicial supremacy is not really assured by the constitutional rule that the Court creates. The gap between rationale and rule leads me to conclude that the Court's ultimate, unexpressed goal is to preserve the power to review the confinement of enemy prisoners held by the Executive anywhere in the world. The "functional" test usefully evades the precedential landmine of *Eisentrager* but is so inherently subjective that it clears a wide path for the Court to traverse in the years to come.

III

Putting aside the conclusive precedent of *Eisentrager,* it is clear that the original understanding of the Suspension Clause was that habeas corpus was not available to aliens abroad, as Judge Randolph's thorough opinion for the court below detailed See 476 F. 3d 981, 988–990 (CADC 2007).

The Suspension Clause reads: "The Privilege of the Writ of Habeas Corpus shall not be suspended, unless when in Cases of Rebellion or Invasion the public Safety may require it." U.S. Const., Art. I, §9, cl. 2. The proper course of constitutional interpretation is to give the text the meaning it was understood to have at the time of its adoption by the people. . . . That course is especially demanded when (as here) the Constitution limits the power of Congress to infringe upon a pre-existing common-law right. The nature of the writ of habeas corpus that cannot be suspended must be defined by the common-law writ that was available at the time of the founding. . . .

In sum, *all* available historical evidence points to the conclusion that the writ would not have been available at common law for aliens captured and held outside the sovereign territory of the Crown. Despite three opening briefs, three reply briefs, and support from a legion of *amici,* petitioners have failed to identify a single case in the history of Anglo-American law that supports their claim to jurisdiction. The Court finds it significant that there is no recorded case *denying* jurisdiction to such prisoners either. . . . But a case standing for the remarkable proposition that the writ could issue to a foreign land would surely have been reported, whereas a case denying such a writ for lack of jurisdiction would likely not. At a minimum, the absence of a reported case either way leaves unrefuted the voluminous commentary stating that habeas wasconfined to the dominions of the Crown.

What history teaches is confirmed by the nature of the limitations that the Constitution places upon suspension of the common-law writ. It can be suspended only "in Cases of Rebellion or Invasion." Art. I, §9, cl. 2. The latter case (invasion) is plainly limited to the territory of the United States; and while it is conceivable that a rebellion could be mounted by American citizens abroad, surely the overwhelming majority of its occurrences would be domestic. If the extraterritorial scope of habeas turned on flexible, "functional" considerations, as the Court holds, why would the Constitution limit its suspension almost entirely to instances of domestic crisis? Surely there is an even greater justification for suspension in foreign lands where theUnited States might hold prisoners of war during an ongoing conflict. And correspondingly, there is less threat to liberty whenthe Government suspends the writ's (supposed) application in foreign lands, where even on the most extreme view prisonersare entitled to fewer constitutional rights. It makes no sense, therefore, for the Constitution generally to forbid suspension ofthe writ abroad if indeed the writ has application there.

It may be objected that the foregoing analysis proves too much, since this Court has already suggested that the writ of habeas corpus *does* run abroad for the benefit of United States citizens. "[T]he position that United States citizens throughout the world may be entitled to habeas corpus rights . . . is precisely the position that this Court adopted in *Eisentrager*, . . . even while holding that aliens abroad did not have habeas corpus rights." . . . The reason for that divergence is not difficult to discern. The common-law writ, as received into the law of the new constitutional Republic, took on such changes as were demanded by a system in which rule is derived from the consent of the governed, and in which citizens (not "subjects") are afforded defined protections against the Government. As Justice Story wrote for the Court,

> "The common law of England is not to be taken in all respects to be that of America. Our ancestors brought with them its general principles, and claimed it as their birthright; but they brought with them and adopted only that portion which was applicable to their situation." . . .

In sum, because I conclude that the text and history of the Suspension Clause provide no basis for our jurisdiction, I would affirm the Court of Appeals even if *Eisentrager* did not govern these cases.

* * *

Today the Court warps our Constitution in a way that goes beyond the narrow issue of the reach of the Suspension Clause, invoking judicially brainstormed separation-of-powers principles to establish a manipulable "functional" test for the extraterritorial reach of habeas corpus (and, no doubt, for the extraterritorial reach of other constitutional protections as well). It blatantly misdescribes important precedents, most conspicuously Justice Jackson's opinion for the Court in *Johnson v. Eisentrager*. It breaks a chain of precedent as old as the common law that prohibits judicial inquiry into detentions of aliens abroad absent statutory authorization. And, most tragically, it sets our military commanders the impossible task of proving to a civilian court, under whatever standards this Court devises in the future, that evidence supports the confinement of each and every enemy prisoner.

The Nation will live to regret what the Court has done today. I dissent. . . .

POSTSCRIPT

Should Noncitizens Accused of Terrorism Have the Right to a Writ of Habeas Corpus in U.S. Courts?

The authors of the readings in this section have very different viewpoints on whether a writ of habeas corpus, a fundamental constitutional right, should be available to noncitizens accused of being terrorists, who are confined outside the United States.

Justice Anthony Kennedy is known to be a fairly conservative jurist. Confronted with this important question in *Boumediene v. Bush* (2008), Kennedy asserted that the power of the government to detain even noncitizens accused of being terrorists must be subject to judicial review. Stated Justice Kennedy: "Security subsists, too, in fidelity to freedom's first principles. Chief among these are freedom from arbitrary and unlawful restraint and the personal liberty that is secured by adherence to the separation of powers."

Justice Antonin Scalia, in contrast, believed that the Supreme Court should defer to the President's views on this crucial issue. Scalia stated: "The game of bait-and-switch that today's opinion plays upon the Nation's Commander in Chief will make the war [on terrorism] harder on us. It will almost certainly cause more Americans to be killed."

Slightly more than a year before *Boumediene* was decided, President George W. Bush had issued Executive Order 13440, titled "Interpretation of the Geneva Convention Common Article 3 as Applied to a Program of Detention and Interrogation Operated by the Central Intelligence Agency." Bush stated: "I hereby determine that a program of detention and interrogation approved by the Director of the Central Intelligence Agency fully complies with the obligations of the United States under Common Article 3. . . ." According to many commentators, however, the program of detention and interrogation sanctioned by Bush's Executive Order permitted inhumane practices, including "water-boarding," sleep deprivation, and a number of other interrogation techniques that straddled the limits of the definition of "torture."

Moreover, as Justice Scalia observed, President Bush had relied on the legal advice of Patrick F. Philbin and John C. Yoo, Deputy Assistant Attorneys General, Office of Legal Counsel of the United States Department of Justice, for the proposition that "the great weight of legal authority indicates that a federal district court could not properly exercise habeas jurisdiction over an alien detained at [Guantanamo Bay]." One of the problems, however, with the legal "advice" given by Yoo and other Justice Department attorneys that has been discussed extensively in the academic and popular literature is whether the opinions were so tainted by politics that they were essentially worthless. A simple Google search of "John Yoo Torture Memo" yields literally thousands of commentaries criticizing the role that he and others had played in supporting highly questionable Bush administration policies. It seems plausible that history's judgment of the Bush administration, and particularly the actions of U.S. Department of Justice during his Presidency, may well be a harsh one.

Following the Supreme Court's decision in *Boumediene,* President Barack Obama issued a new Executive Order titled "Ensuring Lawful Interrogations," which expressly revoked Bush's 2007 Executive Order. Issued on January 22, 2009, it states:

> Consistent with the requirements of the Federal torture statute, the Detainee Treatment Act of 2005 [citations omitted], the Convention Against Torture, Common Article 3, and other laws regulating the treatment and interrogation of individuals detained in any armed conflict, such persons shall in all circumstances be treated humanely and shall not be subjected to violence to life and person (including murder of all kinds, mutilation, cruel treatment, and torture), not to outrages upon personal dignity (including humiliating and degrading treatment), whenever such individuals are in the custody or under the effective control of an officer, employee, or other agent of the United States Government or detained within a facility owned, operated, or controlled by a department or agency of the United States.

On its face, President Obama's Executive Order would appear to signal an end to the use of torture or other questionable interrogation techniques by U.S. government. Moreover, in conjunction with the Supreme Court's decision in *Boumediene,* which extended the right to habeas corpus review to noncitizens held outside the territorial jurisdiction of the United States, it would seem that adequate due process safeguards consistent with American traditions and the rule of law are now in place to prevent abuses of governmental authority, even in terrorism cases.

Do you agree with the Court's decision in *Boumediene*? Or, is Justice Scalia correct in asserting that the Separation of Powers doctrine should require U.S. courts to defer to the executive branch's judgment of how to prosecute a war on terrorism? Which position would serve to better ensure Americans' safety? While the easy answer may be: "Let's throw them into a cell forever and toss away the key; they have been responsible for American deaths," is such a policy consistent with the philosophical foundations of a great nation?

The answer to this question may be found in the lessons of history. In the aftermath of the Japanese invasion of Pearl Harbor, a military order, issued under the authority of a law passed by the U.S. Congress, had banned all persons of Japanese ancestry, including U.S. citizens and noncitizens, from certain areas of the West Coast. Justified by the need to prevent espionage and sabotage, the order had effectively led to the exclusion of persons of Japanese heritage from their homes and their imprisonment in detention camps. In upholding the authority of the U.S. Congress and the executive branch to develop such policies, Justice Hugo Black stated: "But when, under conditions of modern warfare, our shores are threatened by hostile forces, the power to protect must be commensurate with the threatened danger."

Justice Black's admonition, made during World War II and following the Japanese attack on Pearl Harbor, seems remarkably similar to Bush administration justifications for the extreme measures taken against suspected terrorists during the War on Terrorism and in the aftermath of the September 11, 2001, attack on the World Trade Center. To paraphrase George Santayana, however, "those who fail to learn the lessons of history are doomed to repeat them."

The case described above that sanctioned detaining persons of Japanese ancestry, *Korematsu v. United States*, 323 U.S. 214 (1942), is commonly regarded as one of the darkest moments in U.S. Supreme Court history. Dissenting in *Korematsu*, Justice Robert Jackson commented astutely:

> [A] judicial construction of the due process clause that will sustain this order is a far more subtle blow to liberty than the promulgation of the order itself. A military order, however unconstitutional, is not apt to last longer than the military emergency. Even during that period, a succeeding commander may revoke it all. But once a judicial opinion rationalizes such an order to show that it conforms to the Constitution, or rather rationalizes the Constitution to show that the Constitution sanctions such an order, the Court for all time has validated the principle of racial discrimination in criminal procedure and of transplanting American citizens. The principle then lies about like a loaded weapon, ready for the hand of any authority that can bring forward a plausible claim of an urgent need. Every repetition imbeds that principle more deeply in our law and thinking and expands it to new purposes. All who observe the work of courts are familiar with what Judge Cardozo described as "the tendency of a principle to expand itself to the limit of its logic." But if we review and approve, that passing incident becomes the doctrine of the Constitution. There it has a generative power of its own, and all that it creates will be in its own image.

Do you believe that Justice Jackson's dissenting opinion in *Korematsu* would have applied with equal force to the Supreme Court in *Boumediene v. Bush* if it had sanctioned the arguments of the Bush administration, the U.S. Justice Department, and military authorities? Try to remember that *Boumediene* was decided by a bitterly divided U.S. Supreme Court on a five-to-four vote. Thus, the right to a writ of habeas corpus for suspected terrorists held outside the territorial jurisdiction of the United States now hangs by a one-vote thread in the U.S. Supreme Court.

For additional readings on these compelling issues, see: Amanda McRae, "*Boumediene v. Bush*: Another Chapter in the Court's Jurisprudence on Civil Liberties at Guantanamo Bay," *The Duke Journal of Constitutional Law & Public Policy Sidebar*, vol. 4 (2009); Riddhi Dasgupta, "Commentary: *Boumediene v. Bush* and Extraterritorial Habeas Corpus in Wartime," *The Hastings Constitutional Law Quarterly*, vol. 36, p. 425 (2008); Erwin Chemerinsky, "Twentieth Annual Supreme Court Review: The Constitutional and National Security," *The Touro Law Review*, vol. 25, p. 577 (2009); A. Hays Butler, "The Supreme

Court's Decision in *Boumediene v. Bush*: The Military Commissions Act of 2006 and Habeas Corpus Jurisdiction," *Rutgers Journal of Law & Public Policy*, vol. 6, p. 149 (2008); Megan Gaffney, *"Boumediene v. Bush*: Legal Realism and the War on Terror," *Harvard Civil Rights-Civil Liberties Law Review*, vol. 44, p. 197 (2009); Martin J. Katz, "Guantanamo, Boumediene, and Jurisdiction-Stripping: The Imperial President Meets the Imperial Court," *Constitutional Commentary*, vol. 25, p. 377 (2009); Norman L. Reimer, "Guantanamo: Peering Through the Keyhole At America's Soul," *Champion*, vol. 32, p. 7 (2008); and Gerald L. Neuman, "The Extraterritorial Constitution After *Boumediene v. Bush*," *Southern California Law Review*, vol. 82, p. 259 (2009).

Internet References . . .

Street Law, Inc.

Street Law, Inc. is a nonprofit organization dedicated to providing practical, participatory education about law, democracy, and human rights.

www.streetlaw.org

Justia: U.S. Supreme Court Center

Search engine catering to the legal environment.

www.supremejustia.com

SCOTUS Blog

Supreme Court of the United States blog.

www.scotusblog.com

LexisNexis

LexisNexis provides legal, news, public records information, including tax and regulatory publications in online ROM formats.

www.lexisnexis.com

State and Federal Relations in the U.S. Constitutional System

*O*ne of the major enduring controversies in U.S. constitutional law is the interaction of the states and the federal systems in our republican form of government. The relationship has been a fluid one throughout much of U.S. history; however, the principle of federalism and its emphasis on a strong federal government have been largely favored by the Supreme Court since the time of John Marshall, Jeffersonian arguments for less centralized governments and state powers have also been compelling ones.

- Is Congress Given a Broad Grant of Implied Powers by the Constitution?

- Should Congress have Broad Constitutional Power to Regulate the States Under the Interstate Commerce Clause?

- Should the Bill of Rights be Fully Binding on State Proceedings?

- Should the States be Permitted to Abolish the Exclusionary Rule of Evidence in Criminal Cases?

ISSUE 5

Is Congress Given a Broad Grant of Implied Powers by the Constitution?

YES: John Marshall, from *McCulloch v. Maryland*, 17 U.S. 316 (1819)

NO: Thomas Jefferson, "Opinion on the Constitutionality of the Bill for Establishing a National Bank," in Julian P. Boyd (ed.), *The Papers of Thomas Jefferson*, 31 vols. vol. 19, 1950, pp. 275–282

ISSUE SUMMARY

YES: Chief Justice John Marshall, writing for the Supreme Court in 1819, asserted that congressional powers may be implied in the Constitution, if they are "necessary and proper" for carrying out an express power, such as establishing a national bank in order to raise revenue; in addition, a state may not tax such an entity because "the power to tax is the power to destroy."

NO: Thomas Jefferson, widely recognized as one of the most influential U.S. founding fathers, asserts that the powers of Congress should be limited and not include the authority to establish a national bank. The authority to incorporate a bank is not included in the Constitution as an enumerated power of Congress.

$\mathbf{T}$he doctrine of *federalism* asserts that the U.S. governmental system is characterized by a power sharing arrangement between the states and the federal government. Accordingly, the federal government is described as one having *enumerated* powers, which are specified in the U.S. Constitution. For example, Article I, Section 8, specifies many of the powers of Congress, which include, among other things: providing for the national defense; developing and collecting taxes; borrowing money; regulating commerce with foreign countries, the states, and Indian Tribes; establishing uniform rules of naturalization and bankruptcies; coining money; establishing post offices; creating tribunals inferior to the Supreme Court; and "mak[ing] all Laws which shall be necessary and proper for carrying into execution" its constitutional powers.

Article II outlines the powers of the executive branch. These include acting as Commander in Chief of the armed forces, the power to grant reprieves and pardons for offenses against the United States, the power to make treaties with the advice and consent of the Senate, appoint ambassadors and judges of the Supreme Court, and ensure that the laws of the United States are faithfully executed.

Article III is the judicial article. It provides that the judicial power of the United States shall be "vested in one Supreme Court, and in such inferior courts as Congress may from time to time ordain and establish." It also extends the judicial power to "all Cases, in Law and Equity, arising under th[e] Constitution," and the laws of the United States and outlines the Supreme Court's original jurisdiction, to include, among other things, cases affecting ambassadors, cases of admiralty and maritime jurisdiction, to controversies in which the United States is a party, and to controversies between two or more states.

Moreover, the Tenth Amendment to the U.S. Constitution states: "The powers not delegated to the United States by the Constitution, nor prohibited by it to the States, are reserved to the States respectively, or to the people." Thus, in contrast to the enumerated powers of the federal government, state governments are sometimes described as having *plenary* powers. Often termed *police* powers, these include the authority to develop laws to promote public safety, health and morals, and welfare, and are as broad as necessary to accomplish legitimate state objectives.

One of the great historic controversies in U.S. Constitutional law has been the issue of the proper balance of powers in our federalist governmental system. States' rights advocates, or *anti-Federalists,* including Thomas Jefferson, Patrick Henry, and others, believed that a decentralized form of governmental power, vested principally in state governments, would help to ensure that the people retained control of the new republic. Perhaps as a consequence of their less-than-positive experiences with the British monarchy, these individuals shared a strong distrust of centralized governmental authority.

Noted *Federalists,* including Alexander Hamilton, James Madison, and John Marshall, believed, in contrast, that the lion's share of power in the new republic should reside in the federal government. Their reasons included, among other things, the proposition that a strong federal government would be better able to facilitate interstate and international commerce and provide for a strong national defense.

McCulloch v. Maryland (1819) presents a clear case of the struggle between congressional authority and the state power. The Congress had chartered the second Bank of the United States in an effort to promote national commerce. Shortly thereafter, the state of Maryland passed a law imposing a state tax on the national bank. The state then brought a lawsuit against the bank to enforce its tax.

Chief Justice John Marshall, an ardent federalist, wrote the opinion of the Court, which focused on two primary issues: whether chartering the bank was within the constitutional power of the U.S. Congress, and, if so, whether Maryland's tax on the bank was permissible. As you may have guessed by now, Marshall's opinion adopted a strong nationalist position. First, he held that even though the Constitution did not expressly authorize the Congress to charter a bank, that power was implied. Marshall then distinguished between a constitution and an ordinary law. He stated that a constitution should not be expected to specify "all the subdivisions of which its great powers will admit, and of all the means by which they may be carried into execution." To do so would cause it to "partake of the prolixity [complexity and detail] of a legal code." In a now-famous passage, Marshall stated: "[w]e must never forget that it is a constitution we are expounding." What Marshall is saying is that constitutions differ fundamentally from ordinary laws. Constitutions provide a grand outline for the structure of government, whereas statutes provide the details and mechanisms for carrying out that broad design. Therefore, because the power to incorporate a bank was implied by the Congress's authority to raise revenue, an enumerated power, it was authorized by the "Necessary and Proper Clause," in Article I, Section 8, which gives the Congress the power "[t]o make all laws which shall be necessary and proper for carrying into Execution . . . [its enumerated powers]."

Second, Marshall ruled that the state of Maryland did not have the power to tax the bank. If a law passed by the Congress is rationally related to a constitutionally defined power, the courts will give it great deference. Stated Marshall: "The great principle is that the Constitution and the laws made in pursuance thereof are supreme; that they control the Constitution and the laws of the respective States, and cannot be controlled by them." Marshall then asserted that if the state were allowed to tax one instrument of the federal government:

> [T]hey may tax any and every other instrument. They may tax the mail; they may tax the mint; they may tax patent right; they may tax the papers of the custom house; they may tax judicial process; they may tax all the means employed by the Government to an excess which would defeat all the ends of Government. This was not intended by the American people. They did not intend to make their Government dependent on the States.

McCulloch v. Maryland, then, presents a clear statement of a nationalist approach to the distribution of federal and state powers in the U.S. governmental system. Thomas Jefferson, in contrast, had a very different view of the proper relationship between the states and the federal government, which is reflected in his essay on the constitutionality of establishing a national bank.

Jefferson, an ardent anti-Federalist, believed that the new nation was best served by decentralizing power at the federal level and giving it to the states. Such a decentralized system would help to ensure that our government remained closer and more responsive to the people of this nation.

One way to ensure that the lion's share of powers remained at the state level was to adopt a restrictive view of the national government's authority under the federal Constitution. You may recall that the powers of the Congress are specified in Article I. Nowhere does it specify that the Congress has the power to incorporate a national bank. This is the linchpin of Jefferson's argument that establishing a national bank is unconstitutional. Stated Jefferson: "The incorporation of a bank, and other powers assumed by this [legislation] have not, in my opinion, been delegated to the United States by the Constitution." Moreover, Jefferson believed that the Congressional powers could be "carried into execution without a bank. A bank is therefore not *necessary*, and consequently not authorized by [the necessary and proper clause]."

In Your Opinion . . .

- Do you agree with Chief Justice Marshall or Thomas Jefferson?
- In stating the issue more broadly, was a powerful national government essential to the development of the United States?
- Would vesting more power in state governments have helped to ensure that our governments remained more responsive to "the people?"

McCulloch v. Maryland

Marshall, Chief Justice, delivered the opinion of the Court.

In the case now to be determined, the defendant, a sovereign State, denies the obligation of a law enacted by the legislature of the Union, and the plaintiff, on his part, contests the validity of an act which has been passed by the legislature of that State. The Constitution of our country, in its most interesting and vital parts, is to be considered, the conflicting powers of the Government of the Union and of its members, as marked in that Constitution, are to be discussed, and an opinion given which may essentially influence the great operations of the Government. No tribunal can approach such a question without a deep sense of its importance, and of the awful responsibility involved in its decision. But it must be decided peacefully, or remain a source of hostile legislation, perhaps, of hostility of a still more serious nature; and if it is to be so decided, by this tribunal alone can the decision be made. On the Supreme Court of the United States has the Constitution of our country devolved this important duty.

The first question made in the cause is—has Congress power to incorporate a bank? . . .

The power now contested was exercised by the first Congress elected under the present Constitution. The bill for incorporating the Bank of the United States did not steal upon an unsuspecting legislature and pass unobserved. Its principle was completely understood, and was opposed with equal zeal and ability. After being resisted first in the fair and open field of debate, and afterwards in the executive cabinet, with as much persevering talent as any measure has ever experienced, and being supported by arguments which convinced minds as pure and as intelligent as this country can boast, it became a law. The original act was permitted to expire, but a short experience of the embarrassments to which the refusal to revive it exposed the Government convinced those who were most prejudiced against the measure of its necessity, and induced the passage of the present law. . . .

In discussing this question, the counsel for the State of Maryland have deemed it of some importance, in the construction of the Constitution, to consider that instrument not as emanating from the people, but as the act of sovereign and independent States. The powers of the General Government, it has been said, are delegated by the States, who alone are truly sovereign, and must be exercised in subordination to the States, who alone possess supreme dominion. . . .

Supreme Court of the United States, 1819

From these conventions the Constitution derives its whole authority. The government proceeds directly from the people; is "ordained and established" in the name of the people, and is declared to be ordained,

> in order to form a more perfect union, establish justice, insure domestic tranquillity, and secure the blessings of liberty to themselves and to their posterity. . . .

This Government is acknowledged by all to be one of enumerated powers. The principle that it can exercise only the powers granted to it would seem too apparent to have required to be enforced by all those arguments which its enlightened friends, while it was depending before the people, found it necessary to urge; that principle is now universally admitted. But the question respecting the extent of the powers actually granted is perpetually arising, and will probably continue to arise so long as our system shall exist. In discussing these questions, the conflicting powers of the General and State Governments must be brought into view, and the supremacy of their respective laws, when they are in opposition, must be settled.

If any one proposition could command the universal assent of mankind, we might expect it would be this—that the Government of the Union, though limited in its powers, is supreme within its sphere of action. This would seem to result necessarily from its nature. It is the Government of all; its powers are delegated by all; it represents all, and acts for all. Though any one State may be willing to control its operations, no State is willing to allow others to control them. The nation, on those subjects on which it can act, must necessarily bind its component parts. But this question is not left to mere reason; the people have, in express terms, decided it by saying, "this Constitution, and the laws of the United States, which shall be made in pursuance thereof," "shall be the supreme law of the land," and by requiring that the members of the State legislatures and the officers of the executive and judicial departments of the States shall take the oath of fidelity to it. The Government of the United States, then, though limited in its powers, is supreme, and its laws, when made in pursuance of the Constitution, form the supreme law of the land, "anything in the Constitution or laws of any State to the contrary notwithstanding."

Among the enumerated powers, we do not find that of establishing a bank or creating a corporation. But there is no phrase in the instrument which, like the Articles of Confederation, excludes incidental or implied powers and which requires that everything granted shall be expressly and minutely described. Even the 10th Amendment, which was framed for the purpose of quieting the excessive jealousies which had been excited, omits the word "expressly," and declares only that the powers "not delegated to the United States, nor prohibited to the States, are reserved to the States or to the people," thus leaving the question whether the particular power which may become the subject of contest has been delegated to the one Government, or prohibited to the other, to depend on a fair construction of the whole instrument. The men who drew and adopted this amendment had experienced the embarrassments resulting from the insertion of this word in the Articles of Confederation, and probably omitted it to avoid those embarrassments. A Constitution, to contain an accurate detail of all the subdivisions of which its great powers will admit, and of all the means by which they may be carried into execution, would partake of the prolixity of a legal code, and could scarcely be embraced by the human mind. It would probably never be understood by the public. Its nature, therefore, requires that only its great outlines should be marked, its important objects designated, and the minor ingredients which compose those objects be deduced from the nature of the objects themselves. That this idea was entertained by the framers of the American Constitution is not only to be inferred from the nature of the instrument, but from the language. Why else were some of the limitations found in the 9th section of the 1st article introduced? It is also in some degree warranted by their having omitted to use any restrictive term which might prevent its receiving a fair and just interpretation. In considering this question, then, we must never forget that it is *a Constitution* we are expounding.

Although, among the enumerated powers of Government, we do not find the word "bank" or "incorporation," we find the great powers, to lay and collect taxes; to borrow money; to regulate commerce; to declare and conduct a war; and to raise and support armies and navies. The sword and the purse, all the external relations, and no inconsiderable portion of the industry of the nation are intrusted to its Government. It can never be pretended that these vast powers draw after them others of inferior importance merely because they are inferior. Such an idea can never be advanced. But it may with great reason be contended that a Government intrusted with such ample powers, on the due execution of which the happiness and prosperity of the Nation so vitally depends, must also be intrusted with ample means for their execution. The power being given, it is the interest of the Nation to facilitate its execution. It can never be their interest, and cannot be presumed to have been their intention, to clog and embarrass its execution by withholding the most appropriate means. Throughout this vast republic, from the St. Croix to the Gulf of Mexico, from the Atlantic to the Pacific, revenue is to be collected and expended, armies are to be marched and supported. The exigencies of the Nation may require that the treasure raised in the north should be transported to the south that raised in the east, conveyed to the west, or that this order should be reversed. Is that construction of the Constitution to be preferred which would render these operations difficult, hazardous, and expensive? Can we adopt that construction (unless the words imperiously require it) which would impute to the framers of that instrument, when granting these powers for the public good, the intention of impeding their exercise, by withholding a choice of means? If, indeed, such be the mandate of the Constitution, we have only to obey; but that instrument does not profess to enumerate the means by which the powers it confers may be executed; nor does it prohibit the creation of a corporation, if the existence of such a being be essential, to the beneficial exercise of those powers. . . .

[T]he Constitution of the United States has not left the right of Congress to employ the necessary means for the execution of the powers conferred on the Government to general reasoning. To its enumeration of powers is added that of making

> all laws which shall be necessary and proper for carrying into exe-
> cution the foregoing powers, and all other powers vested by this
> Constitution in the Government of the United States or in any depart-
> ment thereof. . . .

But the argument on which most reliance is placed [by the state of Maryland] is drawn from that peculiar language of this clause. Congress is not empowered by it to make all laws which may have relation to the powers conferred on the Government, but such only as may be "necessary and proper" for carrying them into execution. The word "necessary" is considered as controlling the whole sentence, and as limiting the right to pass laws for the execution of the granted powers to such as are indispensable, and without which the power would be nugatory. That it excludes the choice of means, and leaves to Congress in each case that only which is most direct and simple.

Is it true that this is the sense in which the word "necessary" is always used? Does it always import an absolute physical necessity so strong that one thing to which another may be termed necessary cannot exist without that other? We think it does not. If reference be had to its use in the common affairs of the world or in approved authors, we find that it frequently imports no more than that one thing is convenient, or useful, or essential to another. . . .

We think [that this is] so for the following reasons:

1st. The clause is placed among the powers of Congress, not among the limitations on those powers.

2nd. Its terms purport to enlarge, not to diminish, the powers vested in the Government. It purports to be an additional power, not a restriction on those already granted. No reason has been or can be assigned for thus concealing an intention to narrow the discretion of the National Legislature under words which purport to enlarge it. The framers of the Constitution wished its adoption, and well knew that it would be endangered by its strength, not by its weakness. Had they been capable of using language which would convey to the eye one idea and, after deep reflection, impress on the mind another, they would rather have disguised the grant of power than its limitation. If, then, their intention had been, by this clause, to restrain the free use of means which might otherwise have been implied, that intention would have been inserted in another place, and would have been expressed in terms resembling these. "In carrying into execution the foregoing powers, and all others," etc., "no laws shall be passed but such as are necessary and proper." Had the intention been to make this clause restrictive, it would unquestionably have been so in form, as well as in effect. . . .

We admit, as all must admit, that the powers of the Government are limited, and that its limits are not to be transcended. But we think the sound construction of the Constitution must allow to the national legislature that discretion with respect to the means by which the powers it confers are to be carried into execution which will enable that body to perform the high duties assigned to it in the manner most beneficial to the people. Let the end be legitimate, let it be within the scope of the Constitution, and all means which are appropriate, which are plainly adapted to that end, which are not prohibited, but consist with the letter and spirit of the Constitution, are Constitutional. . . .

After the most deliberate consideration, it is the unanimous and decided opinion of this Court that the act to incorporate the Bank of the United States is a law made in pursuance of the Constitution, and is a part of the supreme law of the land. . . .

It being the opinion of the Court that the act incorporating the bank is constitutional, and that the power of establishing a branch in the State of Maryland might be properly exercised by the bank itself, we proceed to inquire:

2. Whether the State of Maryland may, without violating the Constitution, tax that branch?

That the power of taxation is one of vital importance; that it is retained by the States; that it is not abridged by the grant of a similar power to the Government of the Union; that it is to be concurrently exercised by the two Governments are truths which have never been denied. But such is the paramount character of the Constitution that its capacity to withdraw any subject from the action of even this power is admitted. The States are expressly forbidden to lay any duties on imports or exports except what may be absolutely necessary for executing their inspection laws. If the obligation of this prohibition must be conceded—if it may restrain a State from the exercise of its taxing power on imports and exports—the same paramount character would seem to restrain, as it certainly may restrain, a State from such other exercise of this power as is in its nature incompatible with, and repugnant to, the constitutional laws of the Union. A law absolutely repugnant to another as entirely repeals that other as if express terms of repeal were used. . . .

This great principle is that the Constitution and the laws made in pursuance thereof are supreme; that they control the Constitution and laws of the respective States, and cannot be controlled by them. From this, which may be almost termed an axiom, other propositions are deduced as corollaries, on the truth or error of which, and on their application to this case, the cause has been supposed to depend. These are, 1st. That a power to create implies a power to preserve; 2nd. That a power to destroy, if wielded by a different hand, is hostile to, and incompatible with these powers to create and to preserve; 3d. That, where this repugnancy exists, that authority which is supreme must control, not yield to that over which it is supreme. . . .

That the power of taxing it by the States may be exercised so as to destroy it is too obvious to be denied. But taxation is said to be an absolute power which acknowledges no other limits than those expressly prescribed in the Constitution, and, like sovereign power of every other description, is intrusted to the discretion of those who use it. But the very terms of this argument admit that the sovereignty of the State, in the article of taxation itself, is subordinate to, and may be controlled by, the Constitution of the United States. How far it has been controlled by that instrument must be a question of construction. In making this construction, no principle, not declared, can be admissible which would defeat the legitimate operations of a supreme Government. It is of the very essence of supremacy to remove all obstacles to its action within its own sphere, and so to modify every power vested in subordinate governments as to exempt its own operations from their own influence. This effect need not be stated in terms. It is so involved in the declaration of supremacy, so necessarily implied in it, that the expression of it could not make it more certain. We must, therefore, keep it in view while construing the Constitution. . . .

The sovereignty of a State extends to everything which exists by its own authority or is introduced by its permission, but does it extend to those means which are employed by Congress to carry into execution powers conferred on that body by the people of the United States? We think it demonstrable that it does not. Those powers are not given by the people of a single State. They are given by the people of the United States, to a Government whose laws, made in pursuance of the Constitution, are declared to be supreme. Consequently, the people of a single State cannot confer a sovereignty which will extend over them. . . .

We find, then, on just theory, a total failure of this original right to tax the means employed by the Government of the Union, for the execution of its powers. The right never existed, and the question whether it has been surrendered cannot arise.

But, waiving this theory for the present, let us resume the inquiry, whether this power can be exercised by the respective States, consistently with a fair construction of the Constitution?

That the power to tax involves the power to destroy; that the power to destroy may defeat and render useless the power to create; that there is a plain repugnance in conferring on one Government a power to control the constitutional measures of another, which other, with respect to those very measures, is declared to be supreme over that which exerts the control, are propositions not to be denied. But all inconsistencies are to be reconciled by the magic of the word CONFIDENCE. Taxation, it is said, does not necessarily and unavoidably destroy. To carry it to the excess of destruction would be an abuse, to presume which would banish that confidence which is essential to all Government.

But is this a case of confidence? Would the people of any one State trust those of another with a power to control the most insignificant operations of their State Government? We know they would not. Why, then, should we suppose that the people of any one State should be willing to trust those of another with a power to control the operations of a Government to which they have confided their most important and most valuable interests? In the Legislature of the Union alone are all represented. The Legislature of the Union alone, therefore, can be trusted by the people with the power of controlling measures which concern all, in the confidence that it will not be abused. This, then, is not a case of confidence, and we must consider it is as it really is.

If we apply the principle for which the State of Maryland contends, to the Constitution generally, we shall find it capable of changing totally the character of that instrument. We shall find it capable of arresting all the measures of the Government, and of prostrating it at the foot of the States. The American people have declared their Constitution and the laws made in pursuance thereof to be supreme, but this principle would transfer the supremacy, in fact, to the States.

If the States may tax one instrument, employed by the Government in the execution of its powers, they may tax any and every other instrument. They may tax the mail; they may tax the mint; they may tax patent rights; they may tax the papers of the custom house; they may tax judicial process; they may tax all the means employed by the Government to an excess which would defeat all the ends of Government. This was not intended by the American people. They did not design to make their Government dependent on the States. . . .

The Court has bestowed on this subject its most deliberate consideration. The result is a conviction that the States have no power, by taxation or otherwise, to retard, impede, burden, or in any manner control the operations of the constitutional laws enacted by Congress to carry into execution the powers vested in the General Government. This is, we think, the unavoidable consequence of that supremacy which the Constitution has declared.

We are unanimously of opinion that the law passed by the Legislature of Maryland, imposing a tax on the Bank of the United States is unconstitutional and void. . . .

Thomas Jefferson  **NO**

Opinion on the Constitutionality of the Bill for Establishing a National Bank

The bill for establishing a National Bank undertakes, among other things

1. to form the subscribers into a Corporation.
2. to enable them, in their corporate capacities to receive grants of land; and so far is against the laws of *Mortmain.* *
3. to make *alien* subscribers capable of holding lands, and so far is against the laws of *Alienage.*
4. to transmit these lands, on the death of a proprietor, to a certain line of successors: and so far changes the course of *Descents.*
5. to put the lands out of the reach of forfeiture or escheat and so far is against the laws of *Forfeiture and Escheat.*
6. to transmit personal chattels to successors in a certain line: and so far is against the laws of *Distribution.*
7. to give them the sole and exclusive right of banking under the national authority: and so far is against the laws of *Monopoly.*
8. to communicate to them a power to make laws paramount to the laws of the states: for so they must be construed, to protect the institution from the control of the state legislatures; and so, probably they will be construed.

I consider the foundation of the Constitution as laid on this ground that 'all powers not delegated to the U.S. by the Constitution, not prohibited by it to the states, are reserved to the states or to the people'. To take a single step beyond the boundaries thus specially drawn around the powers of Congress, is to take possession of a boundless field of power, no longer susceptible of any definition.

The incorporation of a bank, and other powers assumed by this bill have not, in my opinion, been delegated to the U.S. by the Constitution.

---

*Though the constitution controls the laws of Mortmain so far as to permit Congress itself to hold lands for certain purposes, yet not so far as to permit them to communicate a similar right to other corporate bodies.

From *The Papers of Thomas Jefferson* by Julian P. Boyd et al., eds., 1950, pp. 275–280. Copyright © 1950 by Princeton University Press. Reprinted by permission.

I. They are not among the powers specially enumerated, for these are

1. A power to *lay taxes* for the purpose of paying the debts of the U.S. But no debt is paid by this bill, nor any tax laid. Were it a bill to raise money, its origination in the Senate would condemn it by the constitution.
2. 'to borrow money.' But this bill neither borrows money, nor ensures the borrowing it. The proprietors of the bank will be just as free as any other money holders, to lend or not to lend their money to the public. The operation proposed in the bill, first to lend them two millions, and then borrow them back again, cannot change the nature of the latter act, which will still be a payment, and not a loan, call it by what name you please.
3. 'to regulate commerce with foreign nations, and among the states, and with the Indian tribes.' To erect a bank, and to regulate commerce, are very different acts. He who erects a bank creates a subject of commerce in its bills: so does he who makes a bushel of wheat, or digs a dollar out of the mines. Yet neither of these persons regulates commerce thereby. To erect a thing which may be bought and sold, is not to prescribe regulations for buying and selling. Besides; if this was an exercise of the power of regulating commerce, it would be void, as extending as much to the internal commerce of every state, as to its external. For the power given to Congress by the Constitution, does not extend to the internal regulation of the commerce of a state (that is to say of the commerce between citizen and citizen) which remains exclusively with its own legislature; but to its external commerce only, that is to say, its commerce with another state, or with foreign nations or with the Indian tribes. Accordingly the bill does not propose the measure as a 'regulation of trade,[1] but as 'productive of considerable advantage to trade.'
    Still less are these powers covered by any other of the special enumerations.

II. Nor are they within either of the general phrases, which are the two following.

1. 'To lay taxes to provide for the general welfare of the U.S.' that is to say 'to lay taxes *for the purpose* of providing for the general welfare'. For the laying of taxes is the *power* and the general welfare the *purpose* for which the power is to be exercised. They are not to lay taxes ad libitum *for any purpose they please;* but only to *pay the debts or provide for the welfare of the Union.* In like manner they are not *to do anything they please* to provide for the general welfare, but only *to lay taxes* for that purpose. To consider the latter phrase, not as describing the purpose of the first, but as giving a distinct and independent power to do any act they please, which might be for the good of the Union, would render all the preceding and subsequent enumerations of power completely useless. It would reduce the whole instrument to a single phrase, that of instituting a Congress with power to do whatever would be for the good of the U.S. and as they would be the sole judges of the good or evil, it would be also a power to do

whatever evil they pleased. It is an established rule of construction, where a phrase will bear either of two meanings, to give it that which will allow some meaning to the other parts of the instrument, and not that which would render all the others useless. Certainly no such universal power was meant to be given them. It was intended to lace them up straitly within the enumerated powers, and those without which, as means, these powers could not be carried into effect. It is known that the very power now proposed *as a means,* was rejected *as an end,* by the Convention which formed the constitution. A proposition was made to them to authorize Congress to open canals, and an amendatory one to empower them to incorporate. But the whole was rejected, and one of the reasons of rejection urged in debate was that then they would have a power to erect a bank, which would render the great cities, where there were prejudices and jealousies on that subject adverse to the reception of the constitution.

2. The second general phrase is 'to make all laws *necessary* and proper for carrying into execution the enumerated powers.' But they can all be carried into execution without a bank. A bank therefore is not *necessary,* and consequently not authorised by this phrase.

It has been much urged that a bank will give great facility, or convenience in the collection of taxes. Suppose this were true: yet the constitution allows only the means which are 'necessary' not those which are merely 'convenient' for effecting the enumerated powers. If such a latitude of construction be allowed to this phrase as to give any non-enumerated power, it will go to every one, for these is no one which ingenuity may not torture into a *convenience, in some way or other, to some one* of so long a list of enumerated powers. It would swallow up all the delegated powers, and reduce the whole to one phrase as before observed. Therefore it was that the constitution restrained them to the *necessary* means, that is to say, to those means without which the grant of the power would be nugatory.

But let us examine this *convenience,* and see what it is. The report on this subject states the only *general* convenience to be the preventing the transportation and re-transportation of money between the states and the treasury. (For I pass over the increase of circulating medium ascribed to it as a merit, and which, according to my ideas of paper money is clearly a demerit.) Every state will have to pay a sum of tax-money into the treasury: and the treasury will have to pay, in every state, a part of the interest on the public debt, and salaries to the officers of government resident in that state. In most of the states there will still be a surplus of tax-money to come up to the seat of government for the officers residing there. The payments of interest and salary in each state may be made by treasury-orders on the state collector. This will take up the greater part of the money he has collected in his state, and consequently prevent the great mass of it from being drawn out of the state. If there be a balance of commerce in favour of that state against the one in which the government resides, the surplus of taxes will be remitted by the bills of exchange drawn for that commercial balance. And so it must be if there was a bank. But if there be no balance of commerce, either direct or circuitous, all the banks in the world could not bring up the surplus of taxes but in the form of money. Treasury orders then and bills of exchange may prevent the displacement of the main mass of the money collected, without the aid of any bank: and where these fail, it cannot be prevented even with that aid.

Perhaps indeed bank bills may be a more *convenient* vehicle than treasury orders. But a little *difference* in the degree of *convenience,* cannot constitute the necessity which the constitution makes the ground for assuming any non-enumerated power.

Besides; the existing banks will without a doubt, enter into arrangements for lending their agency: and the more favourable, as there will be a competition among them for it: whereas the bill delivers us up bound to the national bank, who are free to refuse all arrangement, but on their own terms, and the public not free, on such refusal, to employ any other bank. That of Philadelphia, I believe, now does this business, by their post-notes, which by an arrangement with the treasury, are paid by any state collector to whom they are presented. This expedient alone suffices to prevent the existence of that *necessity* which may justify the assumption of a non-enumerated power as a means for carrying into effect an enumerated one. The thing may be done, and has been done, and well done without this assumption; therefore it does not stand on that degree of *necessity* which can honestly justify it.

It may be said that a bank, whose bills would have a currency all over the states, would be more convenient than one whose currency is limited to a single state. So it would be still more convenient that there should be a bank whose bills should have a currency all over the world. But it does not follow from this superior conveniency that there exists anywhere a power to establish such a bank; or that the world may not go on very well without it.

Can it be thought that the Constitution intended that for a shade or two of *convenience,* more or less, Congress should be authorised to break down the most ancient and fundamental laws of the several states, such as those against Mortmain, the laws of alienage, the rules of descent, the acts of distribution, the laws of escheat and forfeiture, the laws of monopoly? Nothing but a necessity invincible by any other means, can justify such a prostration of laws which constitute the pillars of our whole system of jurisprudence. Will Congress be too strait-laced to carry the constitution into honest effect, unless they may pass over the foundation-laws of the state-governments for the slightest convenience to theirs?

The Negative of the President is the shield provided by the constitution to protect against the invasions of the legislature: 1. the rights of the Executive, 2. of the Judiciary, 3. of the states and state legislatures. The present is the case of a right remaining exclusively with the states and is consequently one of those intended by the constitution to be placed under his protection.

It must be added however, that unless the President's mind on a view of every thing which is urged for and against this bill, is tolerably clear that it is unauthorised by the constitution, if the pro and the con hang so even as to balance his judgment, a just respect for the wisdom of the legislature would naturally decide the balance in favour of their opinion. It is chiefly for cases where they are clearly misled by error, ambition, or interest, that the constitution has placed a check in the negative of the President.

Tʜ: Jᴇꜰꜰᴇʀꜱᴏɴ
Feb. 15. 1791.

Notes

PrC (DLC); MS worn on right-hand edges and some parts of words are supplied from Tr (DLC: Washington Papers), which varies slightly in punctuation and capitalization. Entry in SJPL reads: "[Feb.] 15. Op[inio]n Th: J. on the Bank law.—Madison's speech on same subject." This would suggest that TJ enclosed Madison's argument against the constitutionality of the bank (see Madison, *Writings,* ed. Hunt, ᴠɪ, 19–44).

Hamilton's creation of the Bank of the United States—one modelled on the Bank of England, privately directed but inseparably connected with government, capitalized largely on the pyramided public paper made possible by his funding and assumption measures, and believed by opponents to have been designed to support the special interests that controlled its policies—widened and deepened the partisan and sectional cleavage that had long since made its appearance within the government. Joseph Charles, *The Origins of the American Party System* (New York, 1961), p. 26, pointed out that historians had often concerned themselves with the impact of the bank bill on public opinion while neglecting to do so for the funding and assumption measures, which he regarded as the "first milestones in the growth of parties." There is still general agreement that "it was Madison's and Jefferson's opposition to the original charter [of the bank] that marked the birth" of the Republican party and that "Jefferson's attack on the constitutionality of the Bank and his enunciation of a narrow interpretation of the 'necessary and proper' clause of the Constitution became articles of faith in the Republican dogma" (Edward C. Carter, II, "The birth of a political economist: Mathew Carey and the recharter fight of 1810–1811," *Pennsylvania History,* XXXIII [July, 1966], 280; for variant opinions on the politics of the bank issue, see Mitchell, *Hamilton,* II, 86–108; Malone, *Jefferson,* II, 337–50; Brant, *Madison,* II, 327–33; Sehachner, *Jefferson,* I, 416–22; Miller, *Hamilton,* p. 255–77; see also, Stuart Bruchey, "Alexander Hamilton and the State Banks, 1789 to 1795," WMQ, 3rd. ser., xxvii [July, 1970], 347–78, the best analysis of Hamilton's attempt to reconcile—under the broad rubric of the public interest—his conflicting views about rival banking systems chartered under federal and state authority; while just to Hamilton, Bruchey concludes that, in the favoritism shown the Bank of New York, he "acted in ways that deserve to be questioned"; the definitive texts of Hamilton's proposal of the bank and his defense of its constitutionality are presented by Syrett, *Hamilton,* VII, 237–42; VIII, 62–134). Leonard D. White, *The Federalists,* p. 223, concluded that the "first substantial break over public policy occurred . . . when Jefferson declared Hamilton's plan . . . beyond the power of Congress to enact."

But it must be emphasized, first of all, that the contest over the bank did not bring TJ and Hamilton into public view as protagonists of opposing views of public policy. Their opinions were solicited by the President in private and were not known to the contemporary public. "Washington's long delay in signing the bill did, of course, cause much anxiety on the part of Hamilton and others; Madison's impassioned argument in the House of Representatives was a matter of public record; and the constitutional issue was discussed in the press (*Federal Gazette,* 21 Feb. 1791; *Va. Gazette* [Richmond], 16 Mch. 1791). Second, both Madison and TJ, as ardent and consistent nationalists, had frequently upheld the doctrine of implied or inherent powers advanced by Hamilton to defend the bank bill—Madison most conspicuously in *The Federalist* No. 44 and TJ most radically in arguing for a treaty that he considered beyond the powers of the Confederation (TJ to John Adams, 28 July 1785, enclosure; see also TJ's opinion on the constitutionality of the Residence Act, Vol. 17: 197). This very fact, which implied that TJ and Madison were in effect arguing against themselves, obliged TJ also to question the necessity of a national bank since state-chartered institutions were in existence. Third, the constitutional issue was raised belatedly. While both TJ and Madison were undoubtedly disturbed about the tendency of Hamilton's measures and resorted to a strict constructionist position to challenge that tendency, this was primarily a weapon of defense—a wholly inadequate one. Finally, though Washington's doubts may not have been entirely resolved by Hamilton's argument, there are grounds for supposing that southern— especially Virginian—opposition to a national bank chartered for twenty years rested on the suspicion that this was another means of keeping the government in Philadelphia (see Editorial Note to group of documents on the location of the Federal District, under 24 Jan. 1791).

Théophile Cazenove, representative of several Amsterdam firms, was not the only contemporary to observe a connection between the bank and the capital issues: "As those who desire that the seat of government be on the Potomac are united against the Bank, so the opposite party are united in its favor" (Cazenove to his principals, 5 Feb. 1791; Cazenove Letterbook). Fisher Ames declared that the "great point of difficulty was, the effect of the bank law to make the future removal of the government" from Philadelphia less likely. William L. Smith claimed that Virginians had indeed proposed "first by innuendo and finally in direct terms" that if the charter were limited to ten years the bill would be supported, but if not, the constitutional issue would be raised. "Had Pennsylvania acceded to the proposition, which the writer knows was made to this effect," Smith declared, "much discussion and ill humor might have been spared, a prodigious deal of debate respecting the constitutionality of the law would have been avoided, and the painful agitation and disturbed state of mind for many days of a great character [Washington] would not have been excited" (Fisher Ames to George Roberts Minot, 17 Feb. 1791, Ames, *Works,* ed. Seth Ames, I, 95–6; [William L. Smith], *The politicks and views of a certain party displayed* [1792], p. 17; both quotations from Ames and Smith are drawn from an article by Kenneth R. Bowling, "The Bank Bill, the Capital City, and President Washington" (*Capitol Studies,* I [1972]). These observations scarcely did justice to the convictions of those who advanced the constitutional argument and Madison categorically denied Smith's allegation about a proposition to limit the charter to ten years {Madison's "Outline of an Answer to a Pamphlet," 1792; DLC: Madison Papers, cited by Bowling). But there can be no doubt that political maneuvers in which both Washington and TJ were involved did connect the bank bill and the bill to amend the Residence Act (see note to group of documents on the location of the Federal District, under 24 Jan. 1791).

While the partisan and sectional cleavages were exacerbated by the bank issue, the first public break on a fundamental question of policy came with TJ's remarkably blunt report on the whale and cod fisheries. This was a deliberate and conscious effort on his part to force the issue into the open after the lines had been drawn in private. It brought him and Hamilton on the stage as contestants, being none the less a confrontation because TJ was the challenger and Hamilton, confronted with a dilemma, was his silent and covert opponent. Its nature, if not its purpose, was obvious to the public. It therefore created something of a public sensation in a manner that the bank issue did not, for it reaffirmed policies on which there had once been general agreement but on which there was now partisan and sectional divergence. Hamilton had won a crowning victory with his bank bill, but a costly one. He and his followers, at the moment of their triumph, were deeply concerned over the threat implicit in TJ's report and its legislative counterpart, Madison's navigation bill (see Editorial Note to TJ's report on the fisheries, 1 Feb. 1791). Fiscalism, victorious on the domestic scene, was now faced with a serious challenge on a basic question of foreign policy, one not confined to the interests of a special group but concerned with the welfare of the whole economy. Hamilton was well aware that this was less a moment for celebrating triumph than for being politically circumspect. For the challenge that had been made by TJ was issued with the approval of the President, Hamilton's very essential aegis.

POSTSCRIPT

Is Congress Given a Broad Grant of Implied Powers by the Constitution?

Chief Justice John Marshall and founding father Thomas Jefferson have very different viewpoints on this important issue. Marshall's argument in *McCulloch v. Maryland* (1819) was that Article I's "necessary and proper clause" should be interpreted to authorize a broad grant of authority to Congress. The state of Maryland had urged the Supreme Court to adopt a construction of the necessary and proper clause that would give Congress only implied power to pass laws that were "indispensable" for the execution of its enumerated authority. In Maryland's view, establishing a national bank did not satisfy this high standard.

Thus, this critical decision in U.S. constitutional history focused on the meaning of a single word, "necessary." Marshall questioned: "Does [the word necessary] always import an absolute physical necessity so strong that one thing to which another may be termed necessary cannot exist without that other? If reference be had to its use in the common affairs of the world or in approved authors, we find that it frequently imports no more than that one thing is convenient, or useful, or essential to another." Knowing that John Marshall was an ardent federalist, it is not surprising that his interpretation of the necessary and proper clause was one that would expand the power of the national government. The preceding passage also demonstrates another important legal principle: Be careful of the words you use. *McCulloch v. Maryland* illustrates clearly that the outcome of one of the most important cases in U.S. history effectively hinged on the Supreme Court's interpretation of a single seemingly innocuous word.

Thomas Jefferson, in contrast, argued that the enumerated powers of Congress can all be carried into execution without a bank. "A bank is therefore not *necessary* [emphasis in the original], and consequently not authorized by this phrase." The most significant issue in this case, however, was the broader debate on federalism/states' rights. This issue has had a profound impact on U.S. history and has influenced many different areas of American life.

For example, the next issue presented in this volume is the power of the Congress under the Interstate Commerce Clause. As you will learn, the balance of power to regulate even areas traditionally within the discretion of the states has shifted markedly toward the federal government.

Another important issue we will consider later is the extent to which the Constitution's Bill of Rights should be binding on state criminal proceedings. Currently, virtually all of these constitutional protections have been made binding in state courts through the Fourteenth Amendment's Due Process Clause. These include, among others, the exclusionary rule of evidence in search and seizure cases, the privilege against self-incrimination, the right to be free from double jeopardy, the right to counsel, the right to a jury trial, the right to a public trial, and the protection against cruel and unusual punishment.

In addition, the Supreme Court has sanctioned the power of the Congress to condition grant programs on states' willingness to promote federally mandated social policies. For example, in *South Dakota v. Dole*, 403 U.S. 203 (1987), the Congress passed a law that withheld federal highway funds from states that allowed persons under 21 years of age to purchase or possess alcohol in public. The State attempted to justify its 18-year-old drinking age by citing its Tenth Amendment police power authority. The Supreme Court upheld the Congress's authority to spend money in this manner and to place conditions on grants to provide an inducement for the states to adopt federally sponsored social policies.

Even more recently, the Supreme Court has decided *Gonzales v. Raich*, 545 U.S. 1 (2005). A majority of California voters had passed the "Compassionate Use Act" a ballot measure that had legalized the cultivation and use of marijuana for persons with serious illnesses. Angel Raich had used homegrown marijuana under the new law. Medical doctors testified that Raich would have felt severe pain without the marijuana and could possibly die. A second defendant, Monson, had been growing marijuana for medical purposes. Police and federal agents raided Monson's home and destroyed six marijuana plants, which were prohibited by the federal Controlled Substances Act (CSA). Raich and Monson brought an action seeking injunctive and declaratory relief prohibiting the enforcement of the federal law to the extent that it prevented them from possessing, obtaining, or manufacturing cannabis for their personal medical use.

In a seven-to-two decision, the U.S. Supreme Court upheld congressional authority under the Interstate Commerce Clause to ban the cultivation and use of marijuana. Since this case was decided in 2005, however, U.S. Attorney General Eric Holder has issued new guidelines for the prosecution of marijuana cases by the Department of Justice. The new rules state that it will not be a Justice Department priority to prosecute individuals with serious illnesses who use marijuana for medical purposes.

The cases cited above, and many others we will consider in later readings in this volume, make it abundantly clear that during the last 200 years, the debate about the proper distribution of power between the states and the federal government is largely over. Quite clearly, the Marshall/Jefferson debate presented in *McCulloch v. Maryland* has been resolved conclusively in favor of the federal government.

For additional readings on these issues, see: Richard E. Ellis, *Aggressive Nationalism: McCulloch v. Maryland and the Foundation of Federal Authority in the Young Republic* (Oxford University Press, 2007); Kathleen M. Sullivan and Gerald Gunther, *Constitutional Law* (Foundation Press, 15th ed., 2004); Laurence H. Tribe, *American Constitutional Law* (Foundation Press, 2nd ed., 1988); Alpheus

Thomas Mason and Donald Grier Stephenson, Jr., *American Constitutional Law* (Pearson Prentice Hall, 15th ed., 2009); Bernard Schwartz, *A History of the Supreme Court* (Oxford University Press, 1993); Kermit L. Hall, Paul Finkelman, and James Ely, Jr., *American Legal History: Cases and Materials* (Oxford University Press, 3rd ed., 2005); Kermit L. Hall, *The Oxford Companion to the Supreme Court of the United States* (Oxford University Press, 1992); Walter F. Murphy, James E. Fleming, Sotirios A. Barber, and Stephen Macedo, *American Constitutional Interpretation* (Foundation Press, 3rd ed., 2003); David M. O'Brien, *Constitutional Law and Politics: Struggles for Power and Government Accountability* (W.W.Norton, 6th ed., 2005); Craig R. Ducat, *Constitutional Interpretation* (Wadsworth, 9th ed., 2009); John H. Garvey, T. Alexander Aleinikoff, and Daniel A. Farber, *Modern Constitutional Theory: A Reader* (Thompson West, 5th Ed., 2004). See: Randy Barnett, "The Original Meaning of the Commerce Spending, and Necessary and Proper Clauses: The Choice Between Madison and FDR," *Harvard Journal of Law and Public Policy,* vol. 31, p. 1005 (2008); Kurt T. Lash, "The Original Meaning of an Omission: The Tenth Amendment, Popular Sovereignty, and 'Expressly' Delegated Power," *Notre Dame Law Review,* vol. 83, p.1889 (2008); J. Harvie Wilkinson III, "Madison Lecture Toward One America: A Vision in Law," *New York University Law Review,* vol. 83, p. 323 (2008); Sanford Levinson and Jack M. Balkin, "Constitutional Crises," *University of Pennsylvania Law Review,* vol. 157, p. 707 (2009).

ISSUE 6

Should Congress Have Broad Constitutional Power to Regulate the States Under the Interstate Commerce Clause?

YES: Robert H. Jackson, from *Wickard v. Filburn*, 317 U.S. 111 (1942)

NO: William H. Rehnquist, from *United States v. Lopez*, 541 U.S. 549 (1995)

ISSUE SUMMARY

YES: Justice Robert H. Jackson, writing for the Supreme Court in 1942, in the aftermath of the New Deal, asserted that the "power of Congress over interstate commerce is plenary and complete in itself, may be exercised to its utmost extent, and acknowledges no limitations other than are prescribed in the Constitution." Moreover, "no form of state activity can constitutionally thwart the regulatory power granted by the commerce clause to Congress."

NO: Chief Justice William H. Rehnquist, writing for the Supreme Court in 2000, asserted that congressional power to pass laws under the Constitution's Interstate Commerce Clause is limited to cases that demonstrate a direct link to "instrumentalities, channels, or goods involved in interstate commerce." Thus, the passage of laws designed to regulate the possession of guns in school zones should be left to the discretion of the states.

The issue of the power of the U.S. Congress under the Interstate Commerce Clause has been a controversial one throughout U.S. history. The debate reflects a theme we have already encountered in this volume: The proper allocation of powers between the federal and state governments in a governmental system is based on the principle of federalism. These issues remain as relevant today as they were in the early 1940s, when the Supreme Court took a very expansive view of this type of congressional power; however, this controversy has raged since even before the formation of our nation.

By way of introduction, there are two types of cases that may arise under the Interstate Commerce Clause. The first, and most relevant type for purposes of this volume, may be termed an *active* commerce clause case, which always involve the question of whether a law passed by Congress infringes on state sovereignty in some manner. The second, and far less common type of case, presents a *dormant* commerce clause issue. These cases always involve the question of whether a particular state law interferes in some way with interstate commerce. Because the issue in this section focuses on the power of the U.S. Congress to pass laws that impact the states, we will consider only active commerce clause issues.

One of the very early cases to consider the reach of congressional power under the Interstate Commerce Clause was *Gibbons v. Ogden*, 22 U.S. 1 (1824). Ogden had acquired, from the New York legislature, a monopoly to operate steamboat ferries between New York and New Jersey. Thomas Gibbons, a former partner of Ogden, began to operate a competing steamboat operation, in violation of Ogden's monopoly. Gibbons' boats were licensed under a federal law, but Ogden obtained an injunction in the New York courts that ordered Gibbons to stop operating his boats in New York waters.

If you were to be told that Chief Justice John Marshall wrote the Supreme Court's opinion in this case, you may, after having read the first three issues in this volume, be able to guess the outcome. Marshall held that New York's injunction against Gibbons was illegal under the U.S. Constitution's "Supremacy Clause" because it conflicted with a valid federal law. The Supremacy Clause in Article VI provides: "This Constitution, and the Laws of the United States which shall be made in Pursuance thereof; and all Treaties made, or which shall be made, under the Authority of the United States, shall be the supreme law of the land."

In addition, Marshall's opinion took a very expansive view of congressional power under Article I's Interstate Commerce Clause. Stated Marshall:

> [The Commerce power] like all others vested in Congress is complete in itself, may be exercised to its utmost extent, and acknowledges no limitations, other than are prescribed in the Constitution. [If] . . . the sovereignty of congress though limited to specified objects, is plenary as to those objects, [it] is vested in congress as absolutely as it would be in a single government, having in its constitution the same restrictions on the exercise of the power as are found in the constitution of the United States.

Finally, Marshall considered an additional recurrent issue in commerce clause cases: Whether congressional power to regulate interstate commerce may be utilized to regulate economic activities that occur primarily within a single state or "intrastate activity." Marshall implicitly rejected the notion that the Tenth Amendment to the Constitution would prohibit such regulation and concluded that congressional power does extend to intrastate activities as long as there is some reasonable connection to the commercial activities of another state. This view was later promoted by Justice Oliver Wendell Holmes in *Swift & Co. v. U.S.,* 196 U.S. 375 (1905) and has been described as a "stream of commerce" theory.

During this same period, the U.S. Congress began to use its authority under the Interstate Commerce Clause to attempt to regulate matters of social morality. *Champion v. Ames,* 188 U.S. 321 (1903) challenged a federal law that prohibited the interstate shipment of lottery tickets. The justification for this law was that lotteries were considered to be an immoral practice that was an appropriate subject for congressional regulation. The Supreme Court upheld the law because Congress was regulating the interstate shipment of lottery tickets, not interfering with an intrastate practice, which would be more properly left to state control.

Fifteen years later, however, the Supreme Court appeared to signal that it would impose limits on the scope of congressional power under the Interstate Commerce Clause. In *Hammer v. Dagenhart,* 247 U.S. 251 (1918), the Court held unconstitutional a federal law that prohibited the interstate transportation of goods made by child laborers. Unlike the lottery tickets in *Champion v. Ames,* the goods produced by the children were morally neutral and the evil of employing child labor was not related directly to interstate commerce. (*Champion v. Ames* was expressly overruled by *United States v. Darby,* 312 U.S. 100 (1941). The latter case upheld a federal law banning the interstate shipment of goods produced by child labor.)

Justice Oliver Wendell Holmes, dissenting in *Champion,* asserted that as long as a law is authorized under the Interstate Commerce Clause, it does not matter if it has an additional impact on "local" activities such as the development of employment laws. Following Chief Justice Marshall's lead in *Gibbons v. Ogden* (1924), Holmes too implicitly rejected the argument that the Tenth Amendment should limit congressional authority, as long as there is a connection to an enumerated power of Congress. Later, in *Darby,* considered briefly above, the Supreme Court expressly rejected the idea that the Tenth Amendment should act as a limit on congressional authority under the Interstate Commerce Clause.

The Interstate Commerce Clause was also used by the U.S. Congress to help to implement civil rights legislation during the 1960s. For example, in *Heart of Atlanta Motel v. U.S.,* 379 U.S. 241 (1964), a motel owner in downtown Atlanta refused to rent rooms to African Americans. The motel was located adjacent to two interstate highways and was patronized by a large number of interstate guests. The Supreme Court held that the Civil Rights Act of 1964 was applicable to the motel because of its connection to interstate commerce.

While a comprehensive review of the full body of Supreme Court Commerce Clause precedents is beyond the scope of the present initiative, a few important later cases that represent the Court's modern Interstate Commerce Clause jurisprudence merit some attention. In *National League of Cities v. Usery,* 426 U.S. 833 (1976), the Supreme Court appeared to breathe new life into the Tenth Amendment as a limitation on congressional power under the Interstate Commerce Clause. The Court held that the federal wage and overtime law could not be applied constitutionally to state and municipal workers. Writing for the Court, Justice William Rehnquist stated that "Congress may not exercise power in a fashion that impairs the States' integrity or their ability to function effectively in the federal system."

To illustrate just how contentious these issues are, a mere nine years later, the Supreme Court in *Garcia v. San Antonio Metropolitan Transit Authority*, 469 U.S. 528 (1985) overruled *National League of Cities v. Usery*. The majority criticized *Usery* because its emphasis on "traditional" governmental functions, which Congress was not empowered to regulate, invited "an unelected federal judiciary to make decisions about which state policies it favors and which ones it dislikes."

The readings in this section present starkly different perspectives on Interstate Commerce Clause issues. In *Wickard v. Filburn*, 317 U.S. 111 (1942), a federal law allowed the Secretary of Agriculture to set limits on wheat production for every farm in the United States, including not only wheat to be sold in commerce, but also crops that would not be transported and would be *eaten on the farm where they were grown*. Filburn, who owned a small farm, challenged the government's right to set restrictions on his production of wheat for his own family's consumption. In a unanimous decision, Justice Robert H. Jackson upheld the law because wheat eaten on private farms meant that less of the product would be placed into interstate commerce. While Jackson recognized that Filburn's impact on the amount of wheat provided for interstate commerce would be trivial, if it were to be considered in conjunction with that of other farmers who also grew wheat for personal consumption, the cumulative effects would be "far from trivial." Therefore, Congress was authorized to regulate wheat grown for home consumption because it was held to be reasonably related to interstate commerce.

Chief Justice William Rehnquist, in contrast, believes that congressional authority to regulate the states under the Interstate Commerce Clause should be more circumscribed. In *United States v. Lopez*, 541 U.S. 549 (1995), Rehnquist wrote that Congress's commerce power should be restricted to cases that demonstrate a direct link to "instrumentalities, channels, or goods involved in interstate commerce." Therefore, even the passage of laws designed to regulate the possession of guns in school zones should be left to the discretion of the states.

In Your Opinion . . .

- Who do you believe presents the better case, Justice Jackson or Chief Justice Rehnquist?
- If you were a current member of the Supreme Court, how would you vote?
- Are there dangers associated with the expansive use of congressional authority under the Interstate Commerce Clause?
- Should the states be left to decide for themselves major issues of social policy that may impact every state?

YES

Robert H. Jackson

Wickard v. Filburn

Mr. Justice Jackson delivered the opinion of the Court.

The appellee filed his complaint against the Secretary of Agriculture of the United States, three members of the County Agricultural Conservation Committee for Montgomery County, Ohio, and a member of the State Agricultural Conservation Committee for Ohio. He sought to enjoin enforcement against himself of the marketing penalty imposed by the amendment of May 26, 1941, to the Agricultural Adjustment Act of 1938, upon that part of his 1941 wheat crop which was available for marketing in excess of the marketing quota established for his farm. He also sought a declaratory judgment that the wheat marketing quota provisions of the Act as amended and applicable to him were unconstitutional because not sus- [317 U.S. 111, 114] tainable under the Commerce Clause or consistent with the Due Process Clause of the Fifth Amendment.

The Secretary moved to dismiss the action against him for improper venue but later waived his objection and filed an answer. The other appellants moved to dismiss on the ground that they had no power or authority to enforce the wheat marketing quota provisions of the Act, and after their motion was denied they answered, reserving exceptions to the ruling on their motion to dismiss. The case was submitted for decision on the pleadings and upon a stipulation of facts.

The appellee for many years past has owned and operated a small farm in Montgomery County, Ohio, maintaining a herd of dairy cattle, selling milk, raising poultry, and selling poultry and eggs. It has been his practice to raise a small acreage of winter wheat, sown in the Fall and harvested in the following July; to sell a portion of the crop; to feed part to poultry and livestock on the farm, some of which is sold; to use some in making flour for home consumption; and to keep the rest for the following seeding. The intended disposition of the crop here involved has not been expressly stated.

In July of 1940, pursuant to the Agricultural Adjustment Act of 1938, as then amended, there were established for the appellee's 1941 crop a wheat acreage allotment of 11.1 acres and a normal yield of 20.1 bushels of wheat an acre. He was given notice of such allotment in July of 1940 before the Fall planting of his 1941 crop of wheat, and again in July of 1941, before it was harvested. He sowed, however, 23 acres, and harvested from his 11.9 acres of excess acreage 239 bushels, which under the terms of the Act as amended on May 26, 1941, constituted farm [317 U.S. 111, 115] marketing excess, subject to a penalty of 49 cents a bushel, or $117.11 in all. The appellee has not paid the penalty and

Supreme Court of the United States, 1942.

he has not postponed or avoided it by storing the excess under regulations of the Secretary of Agriculture, or by delivering it up to the Secretary. The Committee, therefore, refused him a marketing card, which was, under the terms of Regulations promulgated by the Secretary, necessary to protect a buyer from liability to the penalty and upon its protecting lien.

The general scheme of the Agricultural Adjustment Act of 1938 as related to wheat is to control the volume moving in interstate and foreign commerce in order to avoid surpluses and shortages and the consequent abnormally low or high wheat prices and obstructions to commerce. Within prescribed limits and by prescribed standards the Secretary of Agriculture is directed to ascertain and proclaim each year a national acreage allotment for the next crop of wheat, which is then apportioned to the states and their counties, and is eventually broken up into allotments for individual farms. Loans and payments to wheat farmers are authorized in stated circumstances. . . .

It is urged that under the Commerce Clause of the Constitution, Article I, 8, clause 3, Congress does not possess the power it has in this instance sought to exercise. The question would merit little consideration since our decision in *United States v. Darby*, 312 U.S. 100, 61 S.Ct. 451, 132 A.L.R. 1430, sustaining the federal power to regulate production of goods for commerce except for the fact that this Act extends federal regulation to production not intended in any part for commerce but wholly for consumption on the farm. The Act includes a definition of 'market' and its derivatives so that as related to wheat in addition to its conventional meaning it also means to dispose of by feeding (in any [317 U.S. 111, 119] form) to poultry or livestock which, or the products of which, are sold, bartered, or exchanged, or to be so disposed of.' Hence, marketing quotas not only embrace all that may be sold without penalty but also what may be consumed on the premises. Wheat produced on excess acreage is designated as 'available for marketing' as so defined and the penalty is imposed thereon. Penalties do not depend upon whether any part of the wheat either within or without the quota is sold or intended to be sold. The sum of this is that the Federal Government fixes a quota including all that the farmer may harvest for sale or for his own farm needs, and declares that wheat produced on excess acreage may neither be disposed of nor used except upon payment of the penalty or except it is stored as required by the Act or delivered to the Secretary of Agriculture.

Appellee says that this is a regulation of production and consumption of wheat. Such activities are, he urges, beyond the reach of Congressional power under the Commerce Clause, since they are local in character, and their effects upon interstate commerce are at most 'indirect.' In answer the Government argues that the statute regulates neither production nor consumption, but only marketing; and, in the alternative, that if the Act does go beyond the regulation of marketing it is sustainable as a 'necessary and proper' implementation of the power of Congress over interstate commerce.

The Government's concern lest the Act be held to be a regulation of production or consumption rather than of marketing is attributable to a few dicta and decisions of this Court which might be understood to lay it down that activities such as 'production,' 'manufacturing,' and [317 U.S. 111, 120] 'mining' are strictly 'local' and, except in special circumstances which are not present here, cannot be regulated under the commerce power because their effects upon interstate commerce are, as matter of law, only 'indirect.' Even today, when this power has been held to have great latitude, there is no decision of this Court that such activities may be regulated where no part of the product is intended for interstate commerce or intermingled with the subjects thereof. We believe that a review of the course of decision under the Commerce Clause will make plain, however, that questions of the power of Congress are not to be decided by reference to any formula which would give controlling force to nomenclature such as 'production' and 'indirect' and foreclose consideration of the actual effects of the activity in question upon interstate commerce.

At the beginning Chief Justice Marshall described the Federal commerce power with a breadth never yet exceeded. *Gibbons v. Ogden,* 9 Wheat. 1, 194, 195. He made emphatic the embracing and penetrating nature of this power by warning that effective restraints on its exercise must proceed from political rather than from judicial processes. 9 Wheat. at page 197. [317 U.S. 111, 121] For nearly a century, however, decisions of this Court under the Commerce Clause dealt rarely with questions of what Congress might do in the exercise of its granted power under the Clause and almost entirely with the permissibility of state activity which it was claimed discriminated against or burdened interstate commerce. During this period there was perhaps little occasion for the affirmative exercise of the commerce power, and the influence of the Clause on American life and law was a negative one, resulting almost wholly from its operation as a restraint upon the powers of the states. In discussion and decision, the point of reference instead of being what was 'necessary and proper' to the exercise by Congress of its granted power was often some concept of sovereignty thought to be implicit in the status of statehood. Certain activities such as 'production,' 'manufacturing,' and 'mining' were occasionally said to be within the province of state governments and beyond the power of Congress under the Commerce Clause.

It was not until 1887 with the enactment of the Interstate Commerce Act that the interstate commerce power began to exert positive influence in American law and life. This first important federal resort to the commerce power was followed in 1890 by the Sherman Anti-Trust Act and, thereafter, mainly after 1903, by many others. These statutes ushered in new phases of adjudication, which required the Court to approach the interpretation of the Commerce Clause in the light of an actual exercise by Congress of its power thereunder.

When it first dealt with this new legislation, the Court adhered to its earlier pronouncements, and allowed but [317 U.S. 111, 122] little scope to the power of Congress. *United States v. E. C. Knight Co.*, 156 U.S. 1, 15 S.Ct. 249. These earlier pronouncements also played an important part in several of the five cases in which this Court later held that Acts of Congress under the Commerce Clause were in excess of its power.

Even while important opinions in this line of restrictive authority were being written, however, other cases called forth broader interpretations of the Commerce Clause destined to supersede the earlier ones, and to bring about a return to the principles first enunciated by Chief Justice Marshall in *Gibbons v. Ogden,* supra.

Not long after the decision of *United States v. E. C. Knight Co.*, supra, Mr. Justice Holmes, in sustaining the exercise of national power over intrastate activity, stated for the Court that 'commerce among the states is not a technical legal conception, but a practical one, drawn from the course of business.' *Swift & Co. v. United States,* 196 U.S. 375, 398, 25 S.Ct. 276, 280. It was soon demonstrated that the effects of many kinds of intrastate activity upon interstate commerce were such as to make them a proper subject of federal regulation. In some cases·sustaining the exercise of federal power over intrastate matters the term 'direct' [317 U.S. 111, 123] was used for the purpose of stating, rather than of reaching, a result; in others it was treated as synonymous with 'substantial' or 'material'; and in others it was not used at all. Of late its use has been abandoned in cases dealing with questions of federal power under the Commerce Clause.

In the Shreveport Rate Cases (*Houston, E. & W.T.R. Co. v. United States*), 234 U.S. 342, 34 S.Ct. 833, the Court held that railroad rates of an admittedly intrastate character and fixed by authority of the state might, nevertheless, be revised by the Federal Government because of the economic effects which they had upon interstate commerce. The opinion of Mr. Justice Hughes found federal intervention constitutionally authorized because of 'matters having such a close and substantial relation to interstate traffic that the control is essential or appropriate to the security of that traffic, to the efficiency of the interstate service, and to the maintenance of the conditions under which interstate commerce may be conducted upon fair terms and without molestation or hindrance.' 234 U.S. at page 351, 34 S.Ct. at page 836.

The Court's recognition of the relevance of the economic effects in the application of the Commerce Clause ex- [317 U.S. 111, 124] emplified by this statement has made the mechanical application of legal formulas no longer feasible. Once an economic measure of the reach of the power granted to Congress in the Commerce Clause is accepted, questions of federal power cannot be decided simply by finding the activity in question to be 'production' nor can consideration of its economic effects be foreclosed by calling them 'indirect.' The present Chief Justice has said in summary of the present state of the law: 'The commerce power is not confined in its exercise to the regulation of commerce among the states. It extends to those activities intrastate which so affect interstate commerce, or the exertion of the power of Congress over it, as to make regulation of them appropriate means to the attainment of a legitimate end, the effective execution of the granted power to regulate interstate commerce. . . . The power of Congress over interstate commerce is plenary and complete in itself, may be exercised to its utmost extent, and acknowledges no limitations other than are prescribed in the Constitution. . . . It follows that no form of state activity can constitutionally thwart the regulatory power granted by the commerce clause to Congress. Hence the reach of that power extends to those intrastate activities which in a substantial way interfere with or obstruct the exercise of the granted power.' *United States v. Wrightwood Dairy Co.*, 315 U.S. 110, 119 , 62 S.Ct. 523, 526.

Whether the subject of the regulation in question was 'production,' 'consumption,' or 'marketing' is, therefore, not material for purposes of deciding the question of federal power before us. That an activity is of local character may help in a doubtful case to determine whether Congress intended to reach it. The same consideration might help in determining whether in the absence of Congressional action it would be permissible for the state [317 U.S. 111, 125] to exert its power on the subject matter, even though in so doing it to some degree affected interstate commerce. But even if appellee's activity be local and though it may not be regarded as commerce, it may still, whatever its nature, be reached by Congress if it exerts a substantial economic effect on interstate commerce and this irrespective of whether such effect is what might at some earlier time have been defined as 'direct' or 'indirect.'

The parties have stipulated a summary of the economics of the wheat industry. Commerce among the states in wheat is large and important. Although wheat is raised in every state but one, production in most states is not equal to consumption. Sixteen states on average have had a surplus of wheat above their own requirements for feed, seed, and food. Thirty-two states and the District of Columbia, where production has been below consumption, have looked to these surplus-producing states for their supply as well as for wheat for export and carryover.

The wheat industry has been a problem industry for some years. Largely as a result of increased foreign production and import restrictions, annual exports of wheat and flour from the United States during the ten-year period ending in 1940 averaged less than 10 per cent of total production, while during the 1920s they averaged more than 25 per cent. The decline in the export trade has left a large surplus in production which in connection with an abnormally large supply of wheat and other grains in recent years caused congestion in a number of markets; tied up railroad cars; and caused elevators in some instances to turn away grains, and railroads to institute embargoes to prevent further congestion.

Many countries, both importing and exporting, have sought to modify the impact of the world market conditions on their own economy. Importing countries have taken measures to stimulate production and self-sufficiency. The four large exporting countries of Argen- [317 U.S. 111, 126] tina, Australia, Canada, and the United States have all undertaken various programs for the relief of growers. Such measures have been designed in part at least to protect the domestic price received by producers. Such plans have generally evolved towards control by the central government.

In the absence of regulation the price of wheat in the United States would be much affected by world conditions. During 1941, producers who cooperated with the Agricultural Adjustment program received an average price on the farm of about $1.16 a bushel as compared with the world market price of 40 cents a bushel.

Differences in farming conditions, however, make these benefits mean different things to different wheat growers. There are several large areas of specialization in wheat, and the concentration on this crop reaches 27 percent of the crop land, and the average harvest runs as high as [317 U.S. 111, 127] 155 acres. Except for some use of wheat as stock feed and for seed, the practice is to sell the crop for cash. Wheat from such areas constitutes the bulk of the interstate commerce therein. . . .

The effect of consumption of homegrown wheat on interstate commerce is due to the fact that it constitutes the most variable factor in the disappearance of the wheat crop. Consumption on the farm where grown appears to vary in an amount greater than 20 per cent of average production. The total amount of wheat consumed as food varies but relatively little, and use as seed is relatively constant.

The maintenance by government regulation of a price for wheat undoubtedly can be accomplished as effectively by sustaining or increasing the demand as by limiting the supply. The effect of the statute before us is to restrict the amount which may be produced for market and the extent as well to which one may forestall resort to the market by producing to meet his own needs. That appellee's own contribution to the demand for wheat may be trivial by itself is not enough to remove him from the [317 U.S. 111, 128] scope of federal regulation where, as here, his contribution, taken together with that of many others similarly situated, is far from trivial. *National Labor Relations Board v. Fainblatt,* 306 U.S. 601, 606, et seq., 307 U.S. 609, 59 S.Ct. 668; *United States v. Darby,* supra, 312 U.S. at page 123, 61 S.Ct. 461, 132 A.L.R. 1430.

It is well established by decisions of this Court that the power to regulate commerce includes the power to regulate the prices at which commodities in that commerce are dealt in and practices affecting such prices. One of the primary purposes of the Act in question was to increase the market price of wheat and to that end to limit the volume thereof that could affect the market. It can hardly be denied that a factor of such volume and variability as home-consumed wheat would have a substantial influence on price and market conditions. This may arise because being in marketable condition such wheat overhangs the market and if induced by rising prices tends to flow into the market and check price increases. But if we assume that it is never marketed, it supplies a need of the man who grew it which would otherwise be reflected by purchases in the open market. Home-grown wheat in this sense competes with wheat in commerce. The stimulation of commerce is a use of the regulatory function quite as definitely as prohibitions or restrictions thereon. This record leaves us in no doubt that Congress [317 U.S. 111, 129] may properly have considered that wheat consumed on the farm where grown if wholly outside the scheme of regulation would have a substantial effect in defeating and obstructing its purpose to stimulate trade therein at increased prices.

It is said, however, that this Act, forcing some farmers into the market to buy what they could provide for themselves, is an unfair promotion of the markets and prices of specializing wheat growers. It is of the essence of regulation that it lays a restraining hand on the self-interest of the regulated and that advantages from the regulation commonly fall to others. The conflicts of economic interest between the regulated and those who advantage by it are wisely left under our system to resolution by the Congress under its more flexible and responsible legislative process. Such conflicts rarely lend themselves to judicial determination. And with the wisdom, workability, or fairness, of the plan of regulation we have nothing to do. . . .

William H. Rehnquist

United States v. Lopez

Chief Justice Rehnquist delivered the opinion of the Court.

In the Gun Free School Zones Act of 1990, Congress made it a federal offense "for any individual knowingly to possess a firearm at a place that the individual knows, or has reasonable cause to believe, is a school zone." 18 U.S.C. § 922(q)(1)(A) (1988 ed., Supp. V). The Act neither regulates a commercial activity nor contains a requirement that the possession be connected in any way to interstate commerce. We hold that the Act exceeds the authority of Congress "[t]o regulate Commerce . . . among the several States. . . ." U.S. Const., Art. I, §8, cl. 3.

On March 10, 1992, respondent, who was then a 12th grade student, arrived at Edison High School in San Antonio, Texas, carrying a concealed .38 caliber handgun and five bullets. Acting upon an anonymous tip, school authorities confronted respondent, who admitted that he was carrying the weapon. He was arrested and charged under Texas law with firearm possession on school premises. See Tex. Penal Code Ann. §46.03(a)(1) (Supp. 1994). The next day, the state charges were dismissed after federal agents charged respondent by complaint with violating the Gun Free School Zones Act of 1990. 18 U.S.C. § 922(q)(1)(A) (1988 ed., Supp. V).

A federal grand jury indicted respondent on one count of knowing possession of a firearm at a school zone, in violation of §922(q). Respondent moved to dismiss his federal indictment on the ground that §922(q) "is unconstitutional as it is beyond the power of Congress to legislate control over our public schools." The District Court denied the motion, concluding that §922(q) "is a constitutional exercise of Congress' well defined power to regulate activities in and affecting commerce, and the 'business' of elementary, middle and high schools . . . affects interstate commerce." App. to Pet. for Cert. 55a. Respondent waived his right to a jury trial. The District Court conducted a bench trial, found him guilty of violating §922(q), and sentenced him to six months' imprisonment and two years' supervised release.

On appeal, respondent challenged his conviction based on his claim that §922(q) exceeded Congress' power to legislate under the Commerce Clause. The Court of Appeals for the Fifth Circuit agreed and reversed respondent's conviction. It held that, in light of what it characterized as insufficient congressional findings and legislative history, "section 922(q), in the full reach of its terms, is invalid as beyond the power of Congress under the Commerce Clause." 2 F. 3d

Supreme Court of the United States, April 26, 1995.

1342, 1367–1368 (1993). Because of the importance of the issue, we granted certiorari, 511 U.S. (1994), and we now affirm.

We start with first principles. The Constitution creates a Federal Government of enumerated powers. See U.S. Const., Art. I, §8. As James Madison wrote, "[t]he powers delegated by the proposed Constitution to the federal government are few and defined. Those which are to remain in the State governments are numerous and indefinite." The Federalist No. 45, pp. 292–293 (C. Rossiter ed. 1961). This constitutionally mandated division of authority "was adopted by the Framers to ensure protection of our fundamental liberties." *Gregory v. Ashcroft*, 501 U.S. 452, 458 (1991) (internal quotation marks omitted). "Just as the separation and independence of the coordinate branches of the Federal Government serves to prevent the accumulation of excessive power in any one branch, a healthy balance of power between the States and the Federal Government will reduce the risk of tyranny and abuse from either front." *Ibid.*

The Constitution delegates to Congress the power "[t]o regulate Commerce with foreign Nations, and among the several States, and with the Indian Tribes." U.S. Const., Art. I, §8, cl. 3. The Court, through Chief Justice Marshall, first defined the nature of Congress' commerce power in *Gibbons v. Ogden*, 9 Wheat. 1, 189–190 (1824):

> "Commerce, undoubtedly, is traffic, but it is something more: it is intercourse. It describes the commercial intercourse between nations, and parts of nations, in all its branches, and is regulated by prescribing rules for carrying on that intercourse."

The commerce power "is the power to regulate; that is, to prescribe the rule by which commerce is to be governed. This power, like all others vested in Congress, is complete in itself, may be exercised to its utmost extent, and acknowledges no limitations, other than are prescribed in the constitution." *Id.*, at 196. The *Gibbons* Court, however, acknowledged that limitations on the commerce power are inherent in the very language of the Commerce Clause.

> "It is not intended to say that these words comprehend that commerce, which is completely internal, which is carried on between man and man in a State, or between different parts of the same State, and which does not extend to or affect other States. Such a power would be inconvenient, and is certainly unnecessary.
>
> "Comprehensive as the word 'among' is, it may very properly be restricted to that commerce which concerns more States than one. . . . The enumeration presupposes something not enumerated; and that something, if we regard the language or the subject of the sentence, must be the exclusively internal commerce of a State." *Id.*, at 194–195.

For nearly a century thereafter, the Court's Commerce Clause decisions dealt but rarely with the extent of Congress' power, and almost entirely with the Commerce Clause as a limit on state legislation that discriminated against interstate commerce. See, *e.g.*, *Veazie v. Moor*, 14 How. 568, 573–575 (1853) (upholding a state created steamboat monopoly because it involved regulation of wholly internal commerce); *Kidd v. Pearson*, 128 U.S. 1. 17, 20–22 (1888) (upholding a state prohibition on the manufacture of intoxicating liquor because the commerce power "does not comprehend the purely domestic commerce of a State which is carried on between man and man within a State or between different parts of the same State"); see also L. Tribe, American Constitutional Law 306 (2d ed. 1988). Under this line of precedent, the Court held that certain categories of activity such as "production," "manufacturing," and "mining" were within the province of state governments, and thus were beyond the power of Congress under the Commerce Clause. See *Wickard v. Filburn*, 317 U.S. 111. 121 (1942) (describing development of Commerce Clause jurisprudence).

In 1887, Congress enacted the Interstate Commerce Act, 24 Stat. 379, and in 1890, Congress enacted the Sherman Antitrust Act, 26 Stat. 209, as amended, 15 U.S.C. § 1 *et seq.* These laws ushered in a new era of federal regulation under the commerce power. When cases involving these laws first reached this Court, we imported from our negative Commerce Clause cases the approach that Congress could not regulate activities such as "production," "manufacturing," and "mining." See, *e.g.*, *United States v. E. C. Knight Co.*, 156 U.S. 1, 12 (1895) ("Commerce succeeds to manufacture, and is not part of it"); *Carter v. Carter Coal Co.*, 298 U.S. 238, 304 (1936) ("Mining brings the subject matter of commerce into existence. Commerce disposes of it"). Simultaneously, however, the Court held that, where the interstate and intrastate aspects of commerce were so mingled together that full regulation of interstate commerce required incidental regulation of intrastate commerce, the Commerce Clause authorized such regulation. See, *e.g.*, *Houston, E. & W. T. R. Co. v. United States*, 234 U.S. 342 (1914) (*Shreveport Rate Cases*).

In *A. L. A. Schecter Poultry Corp. v. United States*, 295 U.S. 495, 550 (1935), the Court struck down regulations that fixed the hours and wages of individuals employed by an intrastate business because the activity being regulated related to interstate commerce only indirectly. In doing so, the Court characterized the distinction between direct and indirect effects of intrastate transactions upon interstate commerce as "a fundamental one, essential to the maintenance of our constitutional system." *Id.*, at 548. Activities that affected interstate commerce directly were within Congress' power; activities that affected interstate commerce indirectly were beyond Congress' reach. *Id.*, at 546. The justification for this formal distinction was rooted in the fear that otherwise "there would be virtually no limit to the federal power and for all practical purposes we should have a completely centralized government." *Id.*, at 548.

Two years later, in the watershed case of *NLRB v. Jones & Laughlin Steel Corp.*, 301 U.S. 1 (1937), the Court upheld the National Labor Relations Act against a Commerce Clause challenge, and in the process, departed from the distinction between "direct" and "indirect" effects on interstate commerce. *Id.*, at 36–38 ("The question [of the scope of Congress' power] is necessarily one of degree"). The Court held that intrastate activities that "have such a close and substantial relation to interstate commerce that their control is essential or appropriate to protect that commerce from burdens and obstructions" are within Congress' power to regulate. *Id.*, at 37.

In *United States v. Darby*, 312 U.S. 100 (1941), the Court upheld the Fair Labor Standards Act, stating:

> "The power of Congress over interstate commerce is not confined to the regulation of commerce among the states. It extends to those activities intrastate which so affect interstate commerce or the exercise of the power of Congress over it as to make regulation of them appropriate means to the attainment of a legitimate end, the exercise of the granted power of Congress to regulate interstate commerce." *Id.*, at 118.

See also *United States v. Wrightwood Dairy Co.*, 315 U.S. 110, 119 (1942) (the commerce power "extends to those intrastate activities which in a substantial way interfere with or obstruct the exercise of the granted power").

In *Wickard v. Filburn*, the Court upheld the application of amendments to the Agricultural Adjustment Act of 1938 to the production and consumption of home grown wheat. 317 U.S., at 128–129. The *Wickard* Court explicitly rejected earlier distinctions between direct and indirect effects on interstate commerce, stating:

> "[E]ven if appellee's activity be local and though it may not be regarded as commerce, it may still, whatever its nature, be reached by Congress if it exerts a substantial economic effect on interstate commerce, and this irrespective of whether such effect is what might at some earlier time have been defined as 'direct' or 'indirect.'" *Id.*, at 125.

The *Wickard* Court emphasized that although Filburn's own contribution to the demand for wheat may have been trivial by itself, that was not "enough to remove him from the scope of federal regulation where, as here, his contribution, taken together with that of many others similarly situated, is far from trivial." *Id.*, at 127–128.

Jones & Laughlin Steel, *Darby*, and *Wickard* ushered in an era of Commerce Clause jurisprudence that greatly expanded the previously defined authority of Congress under that Clause. In part, this was a recognition of the great changes that had occurred in the way business was carried on in this country. Enterprises that had once been local or at most regional in nature had become national in scope. But the doctrinal change also reflected a view that earlier Commerce Clause cases artificially had constrained the authority of Congress to regulate interstate commerce.

But even these modern era precedents which have expanded congressional power under the Commerce Clause confirm that this power is subject to outer limits. In *Jones & Laughlin Steel*, the Court warned that the scope of the interstate commerce power "must be considered in the light of our dual system of government and may not be extended so as to embrace effects upon interstate commerce so indirect and remote that to embrace them, in view of our complex society, would effectually obliterate the distinction between what is national and what is local and create a completely centralized government." 301 U.S., at 37; see also *Darby, supra*, at 119–120 (Congress may regulate intrastate activity that has a "substantial effect" on interstate commerce); *Wickard, supra,* at 125 (Congress may regulate activity that "exerts a substantial economic effect on interstate commerce"). Since that time, the Court has heeded that warning and undertaken to decide whether a rational basis existed for concluding that a regulated activity sufficiently affected interstate commerce. See, *e.g., Hodel v. Virginia Surface Mining & Reclamation Assn., Inc.,* 452 U.S. 264, 276–280 (1981); *Perez v. United States,* 402 U.S. 146, 155–156 (1971); *Katzenbach v. McClung,* 379 U.S. 294, 299–301 (1964); *Heart of Atlanta Motel, Inc. v. United States,* 379 U.S. 241, 252–253 (1964).

Similarly, in *Maryland v. Wirtz,* 392 U.S. 183 (1968), the Court reaffirmed that "the power to regulate commerce, though broad indeed, has limits" that "[t]he Court has ample power" to enforce. *Id.,* at 196, overruled on other grounds, *National League of Cities v. Usery,* 426 U.S. 833 (1976), overruled by *Garcia v. San Antonio Metropolitan Transit Authority,* 469 U.S. 528 (1985). In response to the dissent's warnings that the Court was powerless to enforce the limitations on Congress' commerce powers because "[a]ll activities affecting commerce, even in the minutest degree, *[Wickard],* may be regulated and controlled by Congress," 392 U.S., at 204 (Douglas, J., dissenting), the *Wirtz* Court replied that the dissent had misread precedent as "[n]either here nor in *Wickard* has the Court declared that Congress may use a relatively trivial impact on commerce as an excuse for broad general regulation of state or private activities," *id.,* at 197, n. 27. Rather, "[t]he Court has said only that where *a general regulatory statute bears a substantial relation to commerce,* the *de minimis* character of individual instances arising under that statute is of no consequence." *Ibid.* (first emphasis added).

Consistent with this structure, we have identified three broad categories of activity that Congress may regulate under its commerce power. *Perez v. United States, supra,* at 150; see also *Hodel v. Virginia Surface Mining & Reclamation Assn., supra,* at 276–277. First, Congress may regulate the use of the channels of interstate commerce. See, *e.g., Darby,* 312 U.S., at 114; *Heart of Atlanta Motel, supra,* at 256 ("'[T]he authority of Congress to keep the channels of interstate commerce free from immoral and injurious uses has been frequently sustained, and is no longer open to question.'" (quoting *Caminetti v. United States,* 242 U.S. 470, 491 (1917)). Second, Congress is empowered to regulate and protect the instrumentalities of interstate commerce, or persons or things in interstate commerce, even though the threat may come only from intrastate activities. See, *e.g., Shreveport Rate Cases,* 234 U.S. 342 (1914); *Southern R. Co. v. United States,* 222 U.S. 20 (1911) (upholding amendments to Safety Appliance Act as applied to vehicles used in intrastate commerce); *Perez, supra,* at 150 ("[F]or example, the destruction of an aircraft (18 U.S.C. § 32), or . . . thefts from interstate shipments (18 U.S.C. § 659)"). Finally, Congress' commerce authority includes the power to regulate those activities having a substantial relation to interstate commerce, *Jones & Laughlin Steel,* 301 U.S., at 37, *i.e.,* those activities that substantially affect interstate commerce. *Wirtz, supra,* at 196, n. 27.

Within this final category, admittedly, our case law has not been clear whether an activity must "affect" or "substantially affect" interstate commerce in order to be within Congress' power to regulate it under the Commerce

Clause. Compare *Preseault v. ICC,* 494 U.S. 1, 17 (1990), with *Wirtz, supra,* at 196, n. 27 (the Court has never declared that "Congress may use a relatively trivial impact on commerce as an excuse for broad general regulation of state or private activities"). We conclude, consistent with the great weight of our case law, that the proper test requires an analysis of whether the regulated activity "substantially affects" interstate commerce.

We now turn to consider the power of Congress, in the light of this frame-work, to enact §922(q). The first two categories of authority may be quickly disposed of: §922(q) is not a regulation of the use of the channels of interstate commerce, nor is it an attempt to prohibit the interstate transportation of a commodity through the channels of commerce; nor can §922(q) be justified as a regulation by which Congress has sought to protect an instrumentality of interstate commerce or a thing in interstate commerce. Thus, if §922(q) is to be sustained, it must be under the third category as a regulation of an activity that substantially affects interstate commerce.

First, we have upheld a wide variety of congressional Acts regulating intrastate economic activity where we have concluded that the activity sub-stantially affected interstate commerce. Examples include the regulation of intrastate coal mining; *Hodel, supra,* intrastate extortionate credit transactions, *Perez, supra,* restaurants utilizing substantial interstate supplies, *McClung, supra,* inns and hotels catering to interstate guests, *Heart of Atlanta Motel, supra,* and production and consumption of home grown wheat, *Wickard v. Filburn,* 317 U.S. 111 (1942). These examples are by no means exhaustive, but the pattern is clear. Where economic activity substantially affects interstate commerce, legislation regulating that activity will be sustained.

Even *Wickard,* which is perhaps the most far reaching example of Com-merce Clause authority over intrastate activity, involved economic activity in a way that the possession of a gun in a school zone does not. Roscoe Filburn operated a small farm in Ohio, on which, in the year involved, he raised 23 acres of wheat. It was his practice to sow winter wheat in the fall, and after harvesting it in July to sell a portion of the crop, to feed part of it to poultry and livestock on the farm, to use some in making flour for home consump-tion, and to keep the remainder for seeding future crops. The Secretary of Agriculture assessed a penalty against him under the Agricultural Adjustment Act of 1938 because he harvested about 12 acres more wheat than his allot-ment under the Act permitted. The Act was designed to regulate the volume of wheat moving in interstate and foreign commerce in order to avoid surpluses and shortages, and concomitant fluctuation in wheat prices, which had previ-ously obtained. The Court said, in an opinion sustaining the application of the Act to Filburn's activity:

> "One of the primary purposes of the Act in question was to increase the market price of wheat and to that end to limit the volume thereof that could affect the market. It can hardly be denied that a factor of such volume and variability as home consumed wheat would have a substantial influence on price and market conditions. This may arise because being in marketable condition such wheat overhangs the

market and, if induced by rising prices, tends to flow into the market and check price increases. But if we assume that it is never marketed, it supplies a need of the man who grew it which would otherwise be reflected by purchases in the open market. Home grown wheat in this sense competes with wheat in commerce." 317 U.S., at 128.

Section 922(q) is a criminal statute that by its terms has nothing to do with "commerce" or any sort of economic enterprise, however broadly one might define those terms. Section 922(q) is not an essential part of a larger regulation of economic activity, in which the regulatory scheme could be undercut unless the intrastate activity were regulated. It cannot, therefore, be sustained under our cases upholding regulations of activities that arise out of or are connected with a commercial transaction, which viewed in the aggregate, substantially affects interstate commerce.

Second, §922(q) contains no jurisdictional element which would ensure, through case by case inquiry, that the firearm possession in question affects interstate commerce. For example, in *United States v. Bass*, 404 U.S. 336 (1971), the Court interpreted former 18 U.S.C. § 1202(a), which made it a crime for a felon to "receiv[e], posses[s], or transpor[t] in commerce or affecting commerce . . . any firearm." 404 U.S., at 337. The Court interpreted the possession component of §1202(a) to require an additional nexus to interstate commerce both because the statute was ambiguous and because "unless Congress conveys its purpose clearly, it will not be deemed to have significantly changed the federal state balance." *Id.*, at 349. The *Bass* Court set aside the conviction because although the Government had demonstrated that Bass had possessed a firearm, it had failed "to show the requisite nexus with interstate commerce." *Id.*, at 347. The Court thus interpreted the statute to reserve the constitutional question whether Congress could regulate, without more, the "mere possession" of firearms. See *id.*, at 339, n. 4; see also *United States v. Five Gambling Devices*, 346 U.S. 441, 448 (1953) (plurality opinion) ("The principle is old and deeply imbedded in our jurisprudence that this Court will construe a statute in a manner that requires decision of serious constitutional questions only if the statutory language leaves no reasonable alternative"). Unlike the statute in *Bass*, §922(q) has no express jurisdictional element which might limit its reach to a discrete set of firearm possessions that additionally have an explicit connection with or effect on interstate commerce.

Although as part of our independent evaluation of constitutionality under the Commerce Clause we of course consider legislative findings, and indeed even congressional committee findings, regarding effect on interstate commerce, see, *e.g., Preseault v. ICC*, 494 U.S. 1, 17 (1990), the Government concedes that "[n]either the statute nor its legislative history contain[s] express congressional findings regarding the effects upon interstate commerce of gun possession in a school zone." Brief for United States 5–6. We agree with the Government that Congress normally is not required to make formal findings as to the substantial burdens that an activity has on interstate commerce. See *McClung*, 379 U.S., at 304; see also *Perez*, 402 U.S., at 156 ("Congress need [not] make particularized findings in order to legislate"). But to the extent that congressional findings would enable us to evaluate the legislative judgment that the activity in question substantially affected interstate commerce, even though no such substantial effect was visible to the naked eye, they are lacking here.

The Government argues that Congress has accumulated institutional expertise regarding the regulation of firearms through previous enactments. Cf. *Fullilove v. Klutznick,* 448 U.S. 448, 503 (1980) (Powell, J., concurring). We agree, however, with the Fifth Circuit that importation of previous findings to justify §922(q) is especially inappropriate here because the "prior federal enactments or Congressional findings [do not] speak to the subject matter of section 922(q) or its relationship to interstate commerce. Indeed, section 922(q) plows thoroughly new ground and represents a sharp break with the long standing pattern of federal firearms legislation." 2 F. 3d, at 1366.

The Government's essential contention, *in fine,* is that we may determine here that §922(q) is valid because possession of a firearm in a local school zone does indeed substantially affect interstate commerce. Brief for United States 17. The Government argues that possession of a firearm in a school zone may result in violent crime and that violent crime can be expected to affect the functioning of the national economy in two ways. First, the costs of violent crime are substantial, and, through the mechanism of insurance, those costs are spread throughout the population. See *United States v. Evans,* 928 F. 2d 858, 862 (CA9 1991). Second, violent crime reduces the willingness of individuals to travel to areas within the country that are perceived to be unsafe. Cf. *Heart of Atlanta Motel,* 379 U.S., at 253. The Government also argues that the presence of guns in schools poses a substantial threat to the educational process by threatening the learning environment. A handicapped educational process, in turn, will result in a less productive citizenry. That, in turn, would have an adverse effect on the Nation's economic well-being. As a result, the Government argues that Congress could rationally have concluded that §922(q) substantially affects interstate commerce.

We pause to consider the implications of the Government's arguments. The Government admits, under its "costs of crime" reasoning, that Congress could regulate not only all violent crime, but all activities that might lead to violent crime, regardless of how tenuously they relate to interstate commerce. See Tr. of Oral Arg. 8–9. Similarly, under the Government's "national productivity" reasoning, Congress could regulate any activity that it found was related to the economic productivity of individual citizens: family law (including marriage, divorce, and child custody), for example. Under the theories that the Government presents in support of §922(q), it is difficult to perceive any limitation on federal power, even in areas such as criminal law enforcement or education where States historically have been sovereign. Thus, if we were to accept the Government's arguments, we are hard pressed to posit any activity by an individual that Congress is without power to regulate.

Although Justice Breyer argues that acceptance of the Government's rationales would not authorize a general federal police power, he is unable to identify any activity that the States may regulate but Congress may not. Justice Breyer posits that there might be some limitations on Congress' commerce power such as family law or certain aspects of education. *Post,* at 10–11. These suggested limitations, when viewed in light of the dissent's expansive analysis, are devoid of substance.

Justice Breyer focuses, for the most part, on the threat that firearm possession in and near schools poses to the educational process and the potential economic consequences flowing from that threat. *Post,* at 5–9. Specifically, the dissent reasons that (1) gun-related violence is a serious problem; (2) that problem, in turn, has an adverse effect on classroom learning; and (3) that adverse effect on classroom learning, in turn, represents a substantial threat to trade and commerce. *Post,* at 9. This analysis would be equally applicable, if not more so, to subjects such as family law and direct regulation of education.

For instance, if Congress can, pursuant to its Commerce Clause power, regulate activities that adversely affect the learning environment, then, *a fortiori,* it also can regulate the educational process directly. Congress could determine that a school's curriculum has a-significant" effect on the extent of classroom learning. As a result, Congress could mandate a federal curriculum for local elementary and secondary schools because what is taught in local schools has a significant "effect on classroom learning," cf. *post,* at 9, and that, in turn, has a substantial effect on interstate commerce.

Justice Breyer rejects our reading of precedent and argues that "Congress . . . could rationally conclude that schools fall on the commercial side of the line." *Post,* at 16. Again, Justice Breyer's rationale lacks any real limits because, depending on the level of generality, any activity can be looked upon as commercial. Under the dissent's rationale, Congress could just as easily look at child rearing as "fall[ing] on the commercial side of the line" because it provides a "valuable service—namely, to equip [children] with the skills they need to survive in life and, more specifically, in the workplace." *Ibid.* We do not doubt that Congress has authority under the Commerce Clause to regulate numerous commercial activities that substantially affect interstate commerce and also affect the educational process. That authority, though broad, does not include the authority to regulate each and every aspect of local schools.

Admittedly, a determination whether an intrastate activity is commercial or noncommercial may in some cases result in legal uncertainty. But, so long as Congress' authority is limited to those powers enumerated in the Constitution, and so long as those enumerated powers are interpreted as having judicially enforceable outer limits, congressional legislation under the Commerce Clause always will engender "legal uncertainty." *Post,* at 17. As Chief Justice Marshall stated in *McCulloch v. Maryland,* 4 Wheat. 316 (1819):

> "The [federal] government is acknowledged by all to be one of enumerated powers. The principle, that it can exercise only the powers granted to it . . . is now universally admitted. But the question respecting the extent of the powers actually granted, is perpetually arising, and will probably continue to arise, as long as our system shall exist." *Id.,* at 405.

See also *Gibbons v. Ogden,* 9 Wheat., at 195 ("The enumeration presupposes something not enumerated"). The Constitution mandates this uncertainty by withholding from Congress a plenary police power that would authorize enactment of every type of legislation. See U.S. Const., Art. I, §8. Congress has operated within this framework of legal uncertainty ever since this Court determined that it was the judiciary's duty "to say what the law is." *Marbury v. Madison,* 1 Cranch. 137, 177 (1803) (Marshall, C. J.). Any possible benefit from eliminating this "legal uncertainty" would be at the expense of the Constitution's system of enumerated powers.

In *Jones* & *Laughlin Steel,* 301 U.S., at 37, we held that the question of congressional power under the Commerce Clause "is necessarily one of degree." To the same effect is the concurring opinion of Justice Cardozo in *Schecter Poultry:*

> "There is a view of causation that would obliterate the distinction of what is national and what is local in the activities of commerce. Motion at the outer rim is communicated perceptibly, though minutely, to recording instruments at the center. A society such as ours 'is an elastic medium which transmits all tremors throughout its territory; the only question is of their size.'" 295 U.S., at 554 (quoting *United States v. A.L.A. Schecter Poultry Corp,* 76 F. 2d 617, 624 (CA2 1935) (L. Hand, J., concurring)).

These are not precise formulations, and in the nature of things they cannot be. But we think they point the way to a correct decision of this case. The possession of a gun in a local school zone is in no sense an economic activity that might, through repetition elsewhere, substantially affect any sort of interstate commerce. Respondent was a local student at a local school; there is no indication that he had recently moved in interstate commerce, and there is no requirement that his possession of the firearm have any concrete tie to interstate commerce.

To uphold the Government's contentions here, we would have to pile inference upon inference in a manner that would bid fair to convert congressional authority under the Commerce Clause to a general police power of the sort retained by the States. Admittedly, some of our prior cases have taken long steps down that road, giving great deference to congressional action. See *supra,* at 8. The broad language in these opinions has suggested the possibility of additional expansion, but we decline here to proceed any further. To do so would require us to conclude that the Constitution's enumeration of powers does not presuppose something not enumerated, cf. *Gibbons v. Ogden, supra,* at 195, and that there never will be a distinction between what is truly national and what is truly local, cf. *Jones & Laughlin Steel, supra,* at 30. This we are unwilling to do.

POSTSCRIPT

Should Congress Have Broad Constitutional Power to Regulate the States Under the Interstate Commerce Clause?

Justices Robert H. Jackson and William H. Rehnquist present very different viewpoints on this important issue. Significantly, the debate centers on some of the same philosophical issues that had occupied the founding fathers at the very beginning of our nation: Should the states retain a high degree of sovereignty, per the Jeffersonian model, or is a strong national government a better alternative for our nation, per Hamilton, Marshall, and others?

In recent years, this has remained a highly contentious issue among members of the U.S. Supreme Court. As noted previously, *National League of Cities v. Usery* (1976) held that if states are engaged in the performance of "traditional government functions," it is "local activity" that is not subject to congressional regulation under the Interstate Commerce Clause. This case was decided by a five-to-four vote in the Supreme Court.

A mere nine years later, in *Garcia v. San Antonio Metropolitan Transit Authority* (1985), in another five-to-four decision, the Court overruled *Usery*. A majority of the Court concluded that the "traditional governmental functions" test adopted in *Usery* was too subjective and "inevitably invites an unelected federal judiciary to make decisions about which state policies it favors and which ones it dislikes." Moreover, the Court held that state interests are protected adequately by "the structure of the federal government itself," which "was designed in large part to protect the states from overreaching by Congress." These protections include the fact that the states are given a role in both the selection of the executive and legislative branches of the federal government and have direct influence over the House of Representatives and the Presidency "by their control of electoral qualifications and their role in Presidential elections." Moreover, the states "were given more direct influence in the Senate, where each state received equal representation and each Senator was to be elected by the legislature of his state." One of my former law professors summarized these passages by stating: "The States get their protection from their elected representatives. If the people in a state don't like what their representatives are voting for, they get to vote them out of office."

Do you find this argument convincing? In fact, do our elected representatives listen to "the people," or are they more concerned with satisfying lobbyists, enhancing their personal power, and raising money for future elections? These are controversial issues indeed.

Another noteworthy aspect of *Garcia* is the dissenting opinion of Chief Justice Rehnquist, who felt strongly that *National League of Cities v. Usery* should be upheld. He stated: "I do not think it incumbent on those of us in dissent to spell out the fine points of a principle that will, I am confident, in time again command the support of a majority of this Court." What Rehnquist was saying is that the Supreme Court's debate over Congress's commerce clause authority was far from over. He was right.

In several important cases decided since *Garcia v. San Antonio Metropolitan Transit Authority*, the Supreme Court has restricted to some extent the scope of congressional power under the Interstate Commerce Clause. *United States v. Lopez* is one such case, but there have been others as well. For example, in *United States v. Morrison,* Congress had passed a law providing a civil remedy for the victims of gender-motivated violence. Stated Chief Justice Rehnquist: "Gender-motivated crimes of violence are not in any sense of the phrase, economic activity." He continued: "Indeed, if Congress may regulate gender-motivated violence, it would be able to regulate murder or any other type of violence. . . ." Further, although Rehnquist recognized that the victim [who was beaten and raped] in this case should be entitled to a legal remedy, "under our federal system that remedy must be provided by the [State law], and not by the United States."

So, where are we currently with respect to the issue of congressional power under the Interstate Commerce Clause? In this area of constitutional law, there appears to be a serious lack of respect for established precedents by the members of the Supreme Court. We appear to be at the mercy of whoever occupies positions as Supreme Court justices at any given time. It is doubtful that this was ever the intent of the founding fathers when they wrote the Constitution.

For additional readings on these issues, see: Kathleen M. Sullivan and Gerald Gunther, *Constitutional Law* (Foundation Press, 15th ed., 2004); Laurence H. Tribe, *American Constitutional Law* (Foundation Press, 2nd ed., 1988); Alpheus Thomas Mason and Donald Grier Stephenson, Jr., *American Constitutional Law* (Pearson Prentice Hall, 15th ed., 2009); Bernard Schwartz, *A History of the Supreme Court* (Oxford University Press, 1993); Kermit L. Hall, Paul Finkelman, and James Ely, Jr., *American Legal History: Cases and Materials* (Oxford University Press, 3rd ed., 2005); Kermit L. Hall, *The Oxford Companion to the Supreme Court of the United States* (Oxford University Press, 1992); Walter F. Murphy, James E. Fleming, Sotirios A. Barber, and Stephen Macedo, *American Constitutional Interpretation* (Foundation Press, 3rd ed., 2003); David M. O'Brien, *Constitutional Law and Politics: Struggles for Power and Government Accountability* (W.W.Norton, 6th ed., 2005); Craig R. Ducat, *Constitutional Interpretation* (Wadsworth, 9th ed., 2009); John H. Garvey, T. Alexander Aleinikoff, and Daniel A. Farber, *Modern Constitutional Theory: A Reader* (Thompson West, 5th ed., 2004). See also: Henry P. Monaghan, "The Sovereign Immunity Exception," *Harvard Law Review,* vol. 110, p. 102 (1996); John C. Jeffries, "The Right-Remedy Gap in Constitutional Law," *Yale Law Journal,* vol. 109, p. 87 (1999); Michael W. McConnell, "Federalism: Evaluating the Founders' Design," *The University of Chicago Law Review,* vol. 54, p. 1484 (1987); Donald H. Regan, "How to Think About the Federal Commerce Power and Incidentally Rewrite *United States v. Lopez*," *Michigan Law Review,* vol. 94, p. 554 (1995).

ISSUE 7

Should the Bill of Rights be Fully Binding on State Proceedings?

YES: Hugo L. Black, from *Adamson v. California*, 322 U.S. 46 (1947)

NO: Benjamin N. Cardozo, from *Palko v. Connecticut*, 302 U.S. 319 (1937)

ISSUE SUMMARY

YES: Justice Hugo L. Black, in a dissenting opinion in *Adamson v. California* (1947), asserted that the Supreme Court's "selective incorporation" approach to the constitutional protections in the Bill of Rights "degrades" those safeguards. Moreover, the Fifth, Sixth, and Eighth Amendments were specifically designed to confine the exercise of power by judges, particularly in criminal cases.

NO: Justice Benjamin N. Cardozo, writing for the Supreme Court in *Palko v. Connecticut* (1937), asserted that only those Bill of Rights protections that are "implicit in a concept of ordered liberty" are binding on state proceedings through the Due Process Clause of the Fourteenth Amendment.

T he issue of whether the U.S. Constitution's Bill of Rights, the first ten amendments, should be binding on state authorities has been a subject of great controversy since the beginning of the Republic. As interpreted originally, and adopted in 1791 by the founding fathers, the Bill of Rights was intended to protect individuals from encroachment on their constitutional rights by the federal government only. Early in our nation's constitutional history, the Supreme Court recognized this principle in *Barron v. Mayor and City of Baltimore*, 32 U.S. 243 (1833). Barron had sued the city administration for depositing large amounts of sand and harming his wharf in Baltimore harbor by making the water too shallow for most boats. He claimed that the City's actions violated the Fifth Amendment provision that a private property may not be taken for public use "without just compensation." The trial court had awarded Barron $45,000, but the state's appellate court reversed. Writing for the U.S. Supreme Court, Chief Justice John Marshall took a restrictive view of the applicability of the Bill of Rights to state proceedings. Stated Marshall: "[The Bill of Rights] contain no expression indicating an intention to apply them to the state governments. [These protections are] intended solely as a limitation on the exercise of power by the government of the United States, and are not applicable [to the states]." This position became widely known as the "Barron Doctrine."

Three new constitutional amendments were adopted, however, in the aftermath of the Civil War. The Thirteenth Amendment prohibited slavery in the United States and any place subject to its jurisdiction. The Fifteenth Amendment provided that the right of citizens of the United States to vote shall not be denied or abridged by any state "on account of race, color, or previous condition of servitude." For purposes of this discussion, however, the Fourteenth Amendment was the most crucial. It provided, among other things, that "No State shall make or enforce any law which shall abridge the privileges or immunities of citizens of the United States; nor shall any State deprive any person of life, liberty, or property, without due process of law; nor deny to any person within its jurisdiction the equal protection of the laws." Thus, the three essential clauses of Section 1 of the Fourteenth Amendment are (1) the Privileges and Immunities Clause, (2) the Due Process Clause, and (3) the Equal Protection Clause.

To this point in our nation's history, the U.S. Supreme Court has not interpreted the Privileges and Immunities Clause as a broad source of individual's rights. In the *Slaughterhouse Cases*, 83 U.S. 36 (1873), the state of Louisiana had passed a law that gave a certain company a monopoly on butchering animals in New Orleans. Butchers who were prevented from practicing their profession sued, asserting that the Louisiana law denied them the privileges and immunities of law. Writing for the U.S. Supreme Court, Justice Samuel F. Miller held, however, that the first sentence of the Fourteenth Amendment makes a distinction between rights of national and state citizenship. Fundamental civil rights, including the right to practice one's profession, fell within the purview of the states. Therefore, if the butchers' rights were not protected under Louisiana law, there was no protection under the Privileges and Immunities Clause because it prevents state encroachment on rights of "national" citizenship only. According to the Court, these included the use of seaports and "protection on the high seas." This view of the Privileges and Immunities Clause commanded only five votes, however.

Dissenting Justice Joseph P. Bradley asserted that it was the intention of the people of this country in adopting the Fourteenth Amendment to "provide National security by the States of the fundamental rights of the citizen." He then considered the argument that such an interpretation of the Fourteenth Amendment would interfere with the internal affairs of the states. Stated Bradley: "The National will and National interest are of far greater [significance]."

The majority view of the Privileges and Immunities Clause continues to prevail, however. Throughout our history, it has been viewed by the Supreme Court as only a very limited source of individual protections, including among other things the right to engage in interstate travel and the right to vote in national elections. More consistent with Justice Bradley's dissenting opinion, the Fourteenth Amendment's Due Process Clause has proved to be a much more fertile source of protections for those claiming that a state has infringed their rights under the U.S. Constitution.

The extent to which provisions in the Bill of Rights should apply to state proceedings is termed the *incorporation controversy.* Four different approaches to this issue have been embraced by various judges and legal scholars throughout our history.

The *Barron* doctrine asserts and the majority opinion in the *Slaughterhouse Cases* imply that the Bill of Rights should not apply to state proceedings. This may be termed a *states' rights* position on the incorporation controversy.

Selective incorporation asserts that only those rights in the Bill of Rights that are ranked as "fundamental" should be protected against state infringement by the Fourteenth Amendment's Due Process Clause. The term fundamental, in this context, means that the particular right asserted is basic to an American sense of justice and fair play. The task for the Supreme Court, using this model, is to determine whether an asserted right provided in the Bill of Rights merits protection by the Fourteenth Amendment's Due Process Clause on a case-by-case basis. This approach represents an effort by the Supreme Court to balance state interests in the administration of justice with national interests in protecting individual's rights. It is the approach to the incorporation controversy that has been adopted in practice by the U.S. Supreme Court throughout the twentieth century.

Total incorporation, in contrast, asserts that all protections in the Bill of Rights should apply to state proceedings through the Due Process Clause of the Fourteenth Amendment. Proponents of this view argue that selective incorporation's efforts to classify protections in the Bill of Rights as "fundamental" invite judges to inject their personal values and biases into the decision-making process. This approach is viewed as being too close to a "natural law" doctrine, which emphasizes that there are immutable laws in the universe that emerge from a "higher source." The preferred approach is to rule that the entire Bill of Rights is binding on state proceedings through the Due Process Clause of the Fourteenth Amendment. Such an approach would also eliminate the need for the cumbersome process of case by case analysis required by the selective incorporation doctrine.

A fourth approach to the incorporation controversy may be termed *total incorporation plus.* This asserts that the U.S. Constitution should be regarded as a living and flexible document that the founders intended to endure forever. Therefore, not only should the specific protections in the Bill of Rights be incorporated into state proceedings through the Due Process Clause, but also additional rights that should be guaranteed to all Americans, such as the right to a clean water, air, and food. This view of the incorporation controversy has had only a few proponents throughout U.S. Supreme Court history, including such noteworthy figures as Associate Justice William O. Douglas.

Although the Supreme Court has ostensibly followed the selective incorporation doctrine, presently almost all of the provisions in the Bill of Rights have been incorporated into state proceedings. The process began in 1925 with the First Amendment's protection of free expression in *Gitlow v. New York,* 268 U.S. 652 (1925), and has since been extended to include almost all other protections in the Bill of Rights. Most recently, in 2008, the Supreme Court held in *District of Columbia v. Heller,* 554 U.S. ___ (2008), that "the Second Amendment protects an individual's right to possess a firearm unconnected with service in a militia, and to use that arm for traditionally lawful purposes, such as self-defense within the home." That case did not, however, specifically provide that the right to bear arms is incorporated into state proceedings through the Due Process Clause of the Fourteenth Amendment. At the time of this writing, oral arguments have been presented in the U.S. Supreme Court in a case that presents this very issue, *McDonald v. City of Chicago.* This decision is now pending.

The readings included in this area represent two alternative views of the incorporation controversy. Associate Justice Hugo L. Black is perhaps the best-known advocate of the total incorporation approach, which asserts that the entire Bill of Rights should be binding on state proceedings. His dissenting opinion in *Adamson v. California,* 322 U.S. 46 (1947) states: "But to pass upon the constitutionality of statutes by looking to the particular standards enumerated in the Bill of Rights . . . is one thing; to invalidate statutes because of application of 'natural law,' deemed to be above and undefined by the Constitution is another." Black then quoted the Court's decision in *Federal Power Commission v. Pipeline Co.,* 315 U.S. 575 (1942) for the proposition that:

> In the one instance [total incorporation], courts proceeding within clearly marked constitutional boundaries seek to execute policies written into the Constitution; in the other [selective incorporation], they roam at will in the limitless area of their own beliefs as to reasonableness and actually select policies, a responsibility which the Constitution entrusts to the legislative representatives of the people.

In his widely quoted opinion, *Palko v. Connecticut,* 302 U.S. 319 (1937), Associate Justice Benjamin N. Cardozo held that protections contained in the Bill of Rights that are "found to be implicit in the concept of ordered liberty . . . become valid against the states." Thus, Cardozo believed it was possible for judges to develop a hierarchy of constitutional protections. For example, while the right to be free from a state prosecution except as a result of a grand jury indictment may have value and importance, it "is not of the very essence of a scheme of ordered liberty. To abolish them is not to violate a principle of justice so rooted in the traditions and conscience of our people as to be ranked as fundamental."

In Your Opinion . . .

- Which position is the better one?
- Based upon your study of the Constitution thus far, do you feel that total or selective incorporation is the more practical approach to constitutional analysis?

YES

Hugo L. Black

Adamson v. California

Mr. Justice Black dissenting.

The appellant was tried for murder in a California state court. He did not take the stand as a witness in his own behalf. The prosecuting attorney, under purported authority of a California statute, Cal.Penal Code, § 1323 (Hillyer-Lake, 1945), argued to the jury that an inference of guilt could be drawn because of appellant's failure to deny evidence offered against him. The appellant's contention in the state court and here has been that the statute denies him a right guaranteed by the Federal Constitution. The argument is that (1) permitting comment upon his failure to testify has the effect of compelling him to testify, so as to violate that provision of the Bill of Rights contained in the Fifth Amendment that "No person . . . shall be compelled in any criminal case to be a witness against himself," and (2) although this provision of the Fifth Amendment originally applied only as a restraint upon federal courts, *Barron v. Baltimore,* 7 Peters 243, the Fourteenth Amendment was intended to, and did, make the prohibition against compelled testimony applicable to trials in state courts.

The Court refuses to meet and decide the appellant's first contention. But while the Court's opinion, as I read it, strongly implies that the Fifth Amendment does not, of itself, bar comment upon failure to testify in federal courts, the Court nevertheless assumes that it does in order to reach the second constitutional question involved in appellant's case. I must consider the case on the same assumption that the Court does. For the discussion of the second contention turns out to be a decision which reaches far beyond the relatively narrow issues on which this case might have turned.

This decision reasserts a constitutional theory spelled out in *Twining v. New Jersey,* 211 U.S. 78, that this Court is endowed by the Constitution with boundless power under "natural law" periodically to expand and contract constitutional standards to conform to the Court's conception of what, at a particular time, constitutes "civilized decency" and "fundamental liberty and justice." Invoking this *Twining* rule, the Court concludes that, although comment upon testimony in a federal court would violate the Fifth Amendment, identical comment in a state court does not violate today's fashion in civilized decency and fundamentals, and is therefore not prohibited by the Federal Constitution, as amended.

The *Twining* case was the first, as it is the only, decision of this Court which has squarely held that states were free, notwithstanding the Fifth and

Supreme Court of the United States, 1947.

Fourteenth Amendments, to extort evidence from one accused of crime. I agree that, if *Twining* be reaffirmed, the result reached might appropriately follow. But I would not reaffirm the *Twining* decision. I think that decision and the "natural law" theory of the Constitution upon which it relies degrade the constitutional safeguards of the Bill of Rights, and simultaneously appropriate for this Court a broad power which we are not authorized by the Constitution to exercise. Furthermore, the *Twining* decision rested on previous cases and broad hypotheses which have been undercut by intervening decisions of this Court. *See* Corwin, The Supreme Court's Construction of the Self-Incrimination Clause, 29 Mich.L.Rev. 1, 191, 202. My reasons for believing that the *Twining* decision should not be revitalized can best be understood by reference to the constitutional, judicial, and general history that preceded and followed the case. That reference must be abbreviated far more than is justified but for the necessary limitations of opinion-writing.

The first ten amendments were proposed and adopted largely because of fear that Government might unduly interfere with prized individual liberties. The people wanted and demanded a Bill of Rights written into their Constitution. The amendments embodying the Bill of Rights were intended to curb all branches of the Federal Government in the fields touched by the amendments—Legislative, Executive, and Judicial. The Fifth, Sixth, and Eighth Amendments were pointedly aimed at confining exercise of power by courts and judges within precise boundaries, particularly in the procedure used for the trial of criminal cases. Past history provided strong reasons for the apprehensions which brought these procedural amendments into being and attest the wisdom of their adoption. For the fears of arbitrary court action sprang largely from the past use of courts in the imposition of criminal punishments to suppress speech, press, and religion. Hence, the constitutional limitations of courts' powers were, in the view of the Founders, essential supplements to the First Amendment, which was itself designed to protect the widest scope for all people to believe and to express the most divergent political, religious, and other views.

But these limitations were not expressly imposed upon state court action. In 1833, *Barron v. Baltimore, supra,* was decided by this Court. It specifically held inapplicable to the states that provision of the Fifth Amendment which declares: "nor shall private property be taken for public use, without just compensation." In deciding the particular point raised, the Court there said that it could not hold that the first eight amendments applied to the states. This was the controlling constitutional rule when the Fourteenth Amendment was proposed in 1866.

My study of the historical events that culminated in the Fourteenth Amendment, and the expressions of those who sponsored and favored, as well as those who opposed, its submission and passage persuades me that one of the chief objects that the provisions of the Amendment's first section, separately and as a whole, were intended to accomplish was to make the Bill of Rights, applicable to the states. With full knowledge of the import of the *Barron* decision, the framers and backers of the Fourteenth Amendment proclaimed its purpose to be to overturn the constitutional rule that case had announced.

This historical purpose has never received full consideration or exposition in any opinion of this Court interpreting the Amendment. . . .

Investigation of the cases relied upon in *Twining v. New Jersey* to support the conclusion there reached that neither the Fifth Amendment's prohibition of compelled testimony, nor any of the Bill of Rights, applies to the States reveals an unexplained departure from this salutary practice. Neither the briefs nor opinions in any of these cases, except *Maxwell v. Dow*, 176 U.S. 581, make reference to the legislative and contemporary history for the purpose of demonstrating that those who conceived, shaped, and brought about the adoption of the Fourteenth Amendment intended it to nullify this Court's decision in *Barron v. Baltimore, supra,* and thereby to make the Bill of Rights applicable to the States. In *Maxwell v. Dow, supra,* the issue turned on whether the Bill of Rights guarantee of a jury trial was, by the Fourteenth Amendment, extended to trials in state courts. In that case, counsel for appellant did cite from the speech of Senator Howard, Appendix, *infra,* p. 104, which so emphatically stated the understanding of the framers of the Amendment—the Committee on Reconstruction for which he spoke—that the Bill of Rights was to be made applicable to the states by the Amendment's first section. . . .

Id. at 113. Thus, the Court declined, and again today declines, to appraise the relevant historical evidence of the intended scope of the first section of the Amendment. Instead, it relied upon previous cases, none of which had analyzed the evidence showing that one purpose of those who framed, advocated, and adopted the Amendment had been to make the Bill of Rights applicable to the States. None of the cases relied upon by the Court today made such an analysis.

For this reason, I am attaching to this dissent an appendix which contains a resume, by no means complete, of the Amendment's history. In my judgment, that history conclusively demonstrates that the language of the first section of the Fourteenth Amendment, taken as a whole, was thought by those responsible for its submission to the people, and by those who opposed its submission, sufficiently explicit to guarantee that, thereafter, no state could deprive its citizens of the privileges and protections of the Bill of Rights. Whether this Court ever will, or whether it now should, in the light of past decisions, give full effect to what the Amendment was intended to accomplish is not necessarily essential to a decision here. However that may be, our prior decisions, including *Twining,* do not prevent our carrying out that purpose, at least to the extent of making applicable to the states, not a mere part, as the Court has, but the full protection of the Fifth Amendment's provision against compelling evidence from an accused to convict him of crime. And I further contend that the "natural law" formula which the Court uses to reach its conclusion in this case should be abandoned as an incongruous excrescence on our Constitution. I believe that formula to be itself a violation of our Constitution, in that it subtly conveys to courts, at the expense of legislatures, ultimate power over public policies in fields where no specific provision of the Constitution limits legislative power. And my belief seems to be in accord with the views expressed by this Court, at least for the first two decades after the Fourteenth Amendment was adopted. . . .

The foregoing constitutional doctrine, judicially created and adopted by expanding the previously accepted meaning of "due process," marked a complete departure from the *Slaughter-House* philosophy of judicial tolerance of state regulation of business activities. Conversely, the new formula contracted the effectiveness of the Fourteenth Amendment as a protection from state infringement of individual liberties enumerated in the Bill of Rights. Thus, the Court's second-thought interpretation of the Amendment was an about-face from the *Slaughter-House* interpretation and represented a failure to carry out the avowed purpose of the Amendment's sponsors. This reversal is dramatized by the fact that the *Hurtado* case, which had rejected the due process clause as an instrument for preserving Bill of Rights liberties and privileges, was cited as authority for expanding the scope of that clause so as to permit this Court to invalidate all state regulatory legislation it believed to be contrary to "fundamental" principles.

The *Twining* decision, rejecting the compelled testimony clause of the Fifth Amendment, and indeed rejecting all the Bill of Rights, is the end product of one phase of this philosophy. At the same time, that decision consolidated the power of the Court assumed in past cases by laying broader foundations for the Court to invalidate state and even federal regulatory legislation. For the *Twining* decision, giving separate consideration to "due process" and "privileges or immunities," went all the way to say that the "privileges or immunities" clause of the Fourteenth Amendment "did not forbid the States to abridge the personal rights enumerated in the first eight Amendments. . . ." *Twining v. New Jersey, supra,* 99. And in order to be certain, so far as possible, to leave this Court wholly free to reject all the Bill of Rights as specific restraints upon state action, the decision declared that, even if this Court should decide that the due process clause forbids the states to infringe personal liberties guaranteed by the Bill of Rights, it would do so, not

> because those rights are enumerated in the first eight Amendments, but because they are of such a nature that they are included in the conception of due process of law.

Cf. Polko v. Connecticut, 302 U.S. 319, 329

Later decisions of this Court have completely undermined that phase of the *Twining* doctrine which broadly precluded reliance on the Bill of Rights to determine what is and what is not a "fundamental" right. Later cases have also made the *Hurtado* case an inadequate support for this phase of the *Twining* formula. For, despite *Hurtado* and *Twining,* this Court has now held that the Fourteenth Amendment protects from state invasion the following "fundamental" rights safeguarded by the Bill of Rights: right to counsel in criminal cases, *Powell v. Alabama,* 287 U.S. 45, 67, limiting the *Hurtado* case; *see also Betts v. Brady,* 316 U.S. 455, and *De Meerleer v. Michigan,* 329 U.S. 663; freedom of assembly, *De Jonge v. Oregon,* 299 U.S. 353, 364; at the very least, certain types of cruel and unusual punishment and former jeopardy, *State of Louisiana ex rel. Francis v. Resweber,* 329 U.S. 459; the right of an accused in a criminal case to be informed of the charge against him, *see Snyder v. Massachusetts,* 291 U.S. 97, 105;

the right to receive just compensation on account of taking private property for public use, *Chicago, B. & Q. R. Co. v. Chicago,* 166 U.S. 226. And the Court has now through the Fourteenth Amendment literally and emphatically applied the First Amendment to the States in its very terms. *Everson v. Board of Education,* 330 U.S. 1; *Board of Education v. Barnette,* 319 U.S. 624, 639; *Bridges v. California,* 314 U.S. 252, 268. In *Palko v. Connecticut, supra,* a case which involved former jeopardy only, this Court reexamined the path it had traveled in interpreting the Fourteenth Amendment since the *Twining* opinion was written. In *Twining,* the Court had declared that none of the rights enumerated in the first eight amendments were protected against state invasion because they were incorporated in the Bill of Rights. But the Court in *Palko, supra,* at 323, answered a contention that all eight applied with the more guarded statement, similar to that the Court had used in *Maxwell v. Dow, supra,* at 597, that "there is no such general rule." Implicit in this statement, and in the cases decided in the interim between *Twining* and *Palko* and since, is the understanding that some of the eight amendments do apply by their very terms. Thus, the Court said in the *Palko* case that the Fourteenth Amendment may make it unlawful for a state to abridge by its statutes the

> freedom of speech which the First Amendment safeguards against encroachment by the Congress . . . or the like freedom of the press . . . or the free exercise of religion . . . or the right of peaceable assembly . . . or the right of one accused of crime to the benefit of counsel. . . . In these and other situations, immunities that are valid as against the federal government by force of the specific pledges of particular amendments have been found to be implicit in the concept of ordered liberty, and thus, through the Fourteenth Amendment, become valid as against the states.

Id. at 324-325. The Court went on to describe the Amendments made applicable to the States as

> the privileges and immunities that have been taken over from the earlier articles of the federal bill of rights and brought within the Fourteenth Amendment by a process of absorption. . . .

I cannot consider the Bill of Rights to be an outworn 18th century "strait jacket," as the *Twining* opinion did. Its provisions may be thought outdated abstractions by some. And it is true that they were designed to meet ancient evils. But they are the same kind of human evils that have emerged from century to century wherever excessive power is sought by the few at the expense of the many. In my judgment, the people of no nation can lose their liberty so long as a Bill of Rights like ours survives and its basic purposes are conscientiously interpreted, enforced and respected so as to afford continuous protection against old, as well as new, devices and practices which might thwart those purposes. I fear to see the consequences of the Court's practice of substituting its own concepts of decency and fundamental justice for the language of the Bill of Rights as its point of departure in interpreting and enforcing that Bill of

Rights. If the choice must be between the selective process of the *Palko* decision, applying some of the Bill of Rights to the States, or the *Twining* rule, applying none of them, I would choose the *Palko* selective process. But, rather than accept either of these choices, I would follow what I believe was the original purpose of the Fourteenth Amendment—to extend to all the people of the nation the complete protection of the Bill of Rights. To hold that this Court can determine what, if any, provisions of the Bill of Rights will be enforced, and, if so, to what degree, is to frustrate the great design of a written Constitution.

Conceding the possibility that this Court is now wise enough to improve on the Bill of Rights by substituting natural law concepts for the Bill of Rights, I think the possibility is entirely too speculative to agree to take that course. I would therefore hold in this case that the full protection of the Fifth Amendment's proscription against compelled testimony must be afforded by California. This I would do because of reliance upon the original purpose of the Fourteenth Amendment.

It is an illusory apprehension that literal application of some or all of the provisions of the Bill of Rights to the States would unwisely increase the sum total of the powers of this Court to invalidate state legislation. The Federal Government has not been harmfully burdened by the requirement that enforcement of federal laws affecting civil liberty conform literally to the Bill of Rights. Who would advocate its repeal? It must be conceded, of course, that the natural law-due process formula, which the Court today reaffirms, has been interpreted to limit substantially this Court's power to prevent state violations of the individual civil liberties guaranteed by the Bill of Rights. But this formula also has been used in the past, and can be used in the future, to license this Court, in considering regulatory legislation, to roam at large in the broad expanses of policy and morals and to trespass, all too freely, on the legislative domain of the States as well as the Federal Government.

Since *Marbury v. Madison,* 1 Cranch 137, was decided, the practice has been firmly established, for better or worse, that courts can strike down legislative enactments which violate the Constitution. This process, of course, involves interpretation, and since words can have many meanings, interpretation obviously may result in contraction or extension of the original purpose of a constitutional provision, thereby affecting policy. But to pass upon the constitutionality of statutes by looking to the particular standards enumerated in the Bill of Rights and other parts of the Constitution is one thing; to invalidate statutes because of application of "natural law," deemed to be above and undefined by the Constitution, is another.

> In the one instance, courts proceeding within clearly marked constitutional boundaries seek to execute policies written into the Constitution; in the other, they roam at will in the limitless area of their own beliefs as to reasonableness and actually select policies, a responsibility which the Constitution entrusts to the legislative representatives of the people.

Federal Power Commission v. Pipeline Co., 315 U.S. 575, 599, 601, n. 4. . . .

Benjamin N. Cardozo

 **NO**

Palko v. Connecticut

Mr. Justice Cardozo delivered the opinion of the Court.

A statute of Connecticut permitting appeals in criminal cases to be taken by the state is challenged by appellant as an infringement of the Fourteenth Amendment of the Constitution of the United States. Whether the challenge should be upheld is now to be determined.

Appellant was indicted in Fairfield County, Connecticut, for the crime of murder in the first degree. A jury found him guilty of murder in the second degree, and he was sentenced to confinement in the state prison for life. Thereafter, the State of Connecticut, with the permission of the judge presiding at the trial, gave notice of appeal to the Supreme Court of Errors. This it did pursuant to an act adopted in 1886 which is printed in the margin. Public Acts, 1886, p. 560; now § 6494 of the General Statutes. Upon such appeal, the Supreme Court of Errors reversed the judgment and ordered a new trial. *State v. Palko*, 121 Conn. 669, 186 Atl. 657. It found that there had been error of law to the prejudice of the state (1) in excluding testimony as to a confession by defendant, (2) in excluding testimony upon cross-examination of defendant to impeach his credibility, and (3) in the instructions to the jury as to the difference between first and second degree murder.

Pursuant to the mandate of the Supreme Court of Errors, defendant was brought to trial again. Before a jury was impaneled and also at later stages of the case, he made the objection that the effect of the new trial was to place him twice in jeopardy for the same offense, and, in so doing, to violate the Fourteenth Amendment of the Constitution of the United States. Upon the overruling of the objection, the trial proceeded. The jury returned a verdict of murder in the first degree, and the court sentenced the defendant to the punishment of death. The Supreme Court of Errors affirmed the judgment of conviction, 122 Conn. 529, 191 Atl. 320, adhering to a decision announced in 1894, *State v. Lee, 65 Conn. 265, 30 Atl. 1110, which upheld the challenged statute.* Cf. *State v. Muolo*, 118 Conn. 373, 172 Atl. 875. The case is here upon appeal. 28 U.S.C. § 344.

1. The execution of the sentence will not deprive appellant of his life without the process of law assured to him by the Fourteenth Amendment of the Federal Constitution.

The argument for appellant is that whatever is forbidden by the Fifth Amendment is forbidden by the Fourteenth also. The Fifth Amendment,

Supreme Court of the United States, 1937.

which is not directed to the states, but solely to the federal government, creates immunity from double jeopardy. No person shall be "subject for the same offense to be twice put in jeopardy of life or limb." The Fourteenth Amendment ordains, "nor shall any State deprive any person of life, liberty, or property, without due process of law." To retry a defendant, though under one indictment and only one, subjects him, it is said, to double jeopardy in violation of the Fifth Amendment if the prosecution is one on behalf of the United States. From this the consequence is said to follow that there is a denial of life or liberty without due process of law, if the prosecution is one on behalf of the People of a State. Thirty-five years ago, a like argument was made to this court in *Dreyer v. Illinois,* 187 U.S. 71, 85, and was passed without consideration of its merits as unnecessary to a decision. The question is now here.

We do not find it profitable to mark the precise limits of the prohibition of double jeopardy in federal prosecutions. The subject was much considered in *Kepner v. United States,* 195 U.S. 100, decided in 1904 by a closely divided court. The view was there expressed for a majority of the court that the prohibition was not confined to jeopardy in a new and independent case. It forbade jeopardy in the same case if the new trial was at the instance of the government, and not upon defendant's motion. *Cf. Trono v. United States,* 199 U.S. 521. All this may be assumed for the purpose of the case at hand, though the dissenting opinions (195 U.S. 100, 134, 137) show how much was to be said in favor of a different ruling. Right-minded men, as we learn from those opinions, could reasonably, even if mistakenly, believe that a second trial was lawful in prosecutions subject to the Fifth Amendment if it was all in the same case. Even more plainly, right-minded men could reasonably believe that, in espousing that conclusion, they were not favoring a practice repugnant to the conscience of mankind. Is double jeopardy in such circumstances, if double jeopardy it must be called, a denial of due process forbidden to the states? The tyranny of labels, *Snyder v. Massachusetts,* 291 U.S. 97, 114, must not lead us to leap to a conclusion that a word which in one set of facts may stand for oppression or enormity is of like effect in every other.

We have said that, in appellant's view, the Fourteenth Amendment is to be taken as embodying the prohibitions of the Fifth. His thesis is even broader. Whatever would be a violation of the original bill of rights (Amendments I to VIII) if done by the federal government is now equally unlawful by force of the Fourteenth Amendment if done by a state. There is no such general rule.

The Fifth Amendment provides, among other things, that no person shall be held to answer for a capital or otherwise infamous crime unless on presentment or indictment of a grand jury. This court has held that, in prosecutions by a state, presentment or indictment by a grand jury may give way to informations at the instance of a public officer. *Hurtado v. California,* 110 U.S. 516; *Gaines v. Washington,* 277 U.S. 81, 86. The Fifth Amendment provides also that no person shall be compelled in any criminal case to be a witness against himself. This court has said that, in prosecutions by a state, the exemption will fail if the state elects to end it. *Twining v. New Jersey,* 211 U.S. 78, 106, 111, 112. *Cf. Snyder v. Massachusetts, supra,* p. 105; *Brown v. Mississippi,* 297 U.S. 278, 285. The Sixth Amendment calls for a jury trial in criminal cases, and the Seventh for a jury trial in civil cases at common law where the value in controversy shall exceed twenty dollars. This court has ruled that consistently with those amendments trial by jury may be modified by a state or abolished altogether. *Walker v. Sauvinet,* 92 U.S. 90; *Maxwell v. Dow,* 176 U.S. 581; *New York Central R. Co. v. White,* 243 U.S. 188, 208; *Wagner Electric Mfg. Co. v. Lyndon,* 262 U.S. 226, 232. As to the Fourth Amendment, one should refer to *Weeks v. United States,* 232 U.S. 383, 398, and, as to other provisions of the Sixth, to *West v. Louisiana,* 194 U.S. 258.

On the other hand, the due process clause of the Fourteenth Amendment may make it unlawful for a state to abridge by its statutes the freedom of speech which the First Amendment safeguards against encroachment by the Congress, *De Jonge v. Oregon,* 299 U.S. 353, 364; *Herndon v. Lowry,* 301 U.S. 242, 259; or the like freedom of the press, *Grosjean v. American Press Co.,* 297 U.S. 233; *Near v. Minnesota ex rel. Olson,* 283 U.S. 697, 707; or the free exercise of religion, *Hamilton v. Regents,* 293 U.S. 245, 262; *cf. Grosjean v. American Press Co., supra; Pierce v. Society of Sisters,* 268 U.S. 510; or the right of peaceable assembly, without which speech would be unduly trammeled, *De Jonge v. Oregon, supra; Herndon v. Lowry, supra;* or the right of one accused of crime to the benefit of counsel, *Powell v. Alabama,* 287 U.S. 45. In these and other situations, immunities that are valid as against the federal government by force of the specific pledges of particular amendments have been found to be implicit in the concept of ordered liberty, and thus, through the Fourteenth Amendment, become valid as against the states.

The line of division may seem to be wavering and broken if there is a hasty catalogue of the cases on the one side and the other. Reflection and analysis will induce a different view. There emerges the perception of a rationalizing principle which gives to discrete instances a proper order and coherence. The right to trial by jury and the immunity from prosecution except as the result of an indictment may have value and importance. Even so, they are not of the very essence of a scheme of ordered liberty. To abolish them is not to violate a "principle of justice so rooted in the traditions and conscience of our people as to be ranked as fundamental." *Snyder v. Massachusetts, supra,* p. 105; *Brown v. Mississippi, supra,* p. 285; *Hebert v. Louisiana,* 272 U.S. 312, 316. Few would be so narrow or provincial as to maintain that a fair and enlightened system of justice would be impossible without them. What is true of jury trials and indictments is true also, as the cases show, of the immunity from compulsory self-incrimination. *Twining v. New Jersey, supra.* This too might be lost, and justice still be done. Indeed, today, as in the past, there are students of our penal system who look upon the immunity as a mischief, rather than a benefit, and who would limit its scope, or destroy it altogether. No doubt there would remain the need to give protection against torture, physical or mental. *Brown v. Mississippi, supra.* Justice, however, would not perish if the accused were subject to a duty to respond to orderly inquiry. The exclusion of these immunities and privileges from the privileges and immunities protected against the action of the states has not been arbitrary or casual. It has been dictated by a study and appreciation of the meaning, the essential implications, of liberty itself.

We reach a different plane of social and moral values when we pass to the privileges and immunities that have been taken over from the earlier articles of the federal bill of rights and brought within the Fourteenth Amendment by a process of absorption. These, in their origin, were effective against the federal government alone. If the Fourteenth Amendment has absorbed them, the process of absorption has had its source in the belief that neither liberty nor Justice would exist if they were sacrificed. *Twining v. New Jersey, supra,* p. 99. This is true, for illustration, of freedom of thought, and speech. Of that freedom one may say that it is the matrix, the indispensable condition, of nearly every other form of freedom. With rare aberrations, a pervasive recognition of that truth can be traced in our history, political and legal. So it has come about that the domain of liberty, withdrawn by the Fourteenth Amendment from encroachment by the states, has been enlarged by latter-day judgments to include liberty of the mind as well as liberty of action. The extension became, indeed, a logical imperative when once it was recognized, as long ago it was, that liberty is something more than exemption from physical restraint, and that, even in the field of substantive rights and duties, the legislative judgment, if oppressive and arbitrary, may be overridden by the courts. *Cf. Near v. Minnesota ex rel. Olson, supra; De Jonge v. Oregon, supra.* Fundamental too in the concept of due process, and so in that of liberty, is the thought that condemnation shall be rendered only after trial. *Scott v. McNeal,* 154 U.S. 34; *Blackmer v. United States,* 284 U.S. 421. The hearing, moreover, must be a real one, not a sham or a pretense. *Moore v. Dempsey,* 261 U.S. 86; *Mooney v. Holohan,* 294 U.S. 103. For that reason, ignorant defendants in a capital case were held to have been condemned unlawfully when in truth, though not in form, they were refused the aid of counsel. *Powell v. Alabama, supra,* pp. 67, 68. The decision did not turn upon the fact that the benefit of counsel would have been guaranteed to the defendants by the provisions of the Sixth Amendment if they had been prosecuted in a federal court. The decision turned upon the fact that, in the particular situation laid before us in the evidence, the benefit of counsel was essential to the substance of a hearing.

Our survey of the cases serves, we think, to justify the statement that the dividing line between them, if not unfaltering throughout its course, has been true for the most part to a unifying principle. On which side of the line the case made out by the appellant has appropriate location must be the next inquiry, and the final one. Is that kind of double jeopardy to which the statute has subjected him a hardship so acute and shocking that our polity will not endure it? Does it violate those "fundamental principles of liberty and justice which lie at the base of all our civil and political institutions"? *Hebert v. Louisiana, supra.* The answer surely must be "no." What the answer would have to be if the state were permitted after a trial free from error to try the accused over again or to bring another case against him, we have no occasion to consider. We deal with the statute before us, and no other. The state is not attempting to wear the accused out by a multitude of cases with accumulated trials. It asks no more than this, that the case against him shall go on until there shall be a trial free from the corrosion of substantial legal error. *State v. Felch,* 92 Vt. 477, 105 Atl. 23; *State v. Lee, supra.* This is not cruelty at all, nor even vexation in any immoderate degree. If the trial had been infected with error adverse to the accused, there might have been review at his instance, and as often as necessary to purge the vicious taint. A reciprocal privilege, subject at all times to the discretion of the presiding judge, *State v. Carabetta,* 106 Conn. 114, 127 Atl. 394, has now been granted to the state. There is here no seismic innovation. The edifice of justice stands, its symmetry, to many, greater than before.

2. The conviction of appellant is not in derogation of any privileges or immunities that belong to him as a citizen of the United States.

There is argument in his behalf that the privileges and immunities clause of the Fourteenth Amendment as well as the due process clause has been flouted by the judgment.

Maxwell v. Dow, supra, p. 584, gives all the answer that is necessary.

The judgment is

Affirmed.

POSTSCRIPT

Should the Bill of Rights be Fully Binding on State Proceedings?

One of the more enduring themes throughout U.S. history has been the effort to strike a proper balance between federal and state power in our nation. In the previous discussions, we considered the dimensions of this struggle in the context of the exercise of the authority of courts to develop precedents that all states must follow. We too discussed the authority of Congress under the Interstate Commerce Clause to control the states. The issue of whether the Bill of Rights should be binding on the states, however, shifts the focus of the balance between state and federal power away from macrolevel questions of federal governmental authority to individual's rights under the Constitution. In the latter cases, the Supreme Court has been challenged to decide on a case by case basis precisely which individual's rights must be granted to individuals by the states.

The result of this effort is that the U.S. Supreme Court has adopted Justice Cardozo's "ordered liberties" position on the incorporation controversy. From this perspective, the guarantees in the Constitution's Bill of Rights that are ranked as "fundamental" or essential to a "scheme of ordered liberty" are held binding on state proceedings through the Fourteenth Amendment's Due Process Clause. The result has been the gradual assimilation of most of the provisions of the Bill of Rights into state proceedings. Table 1 presents a summary of the major Supreme Court precedents that have incorporated various fundamental rights into state proceedings through the Due Process Clause.

As Table 1 indicates, the selective incorporation process has resulted in a rights-generous application of the Bill of Rights in state proceedings. In fact, as of now, only a few constitutional protections have not been incorporated. These include the Third Amendment's protection against quartering soldiers, the Fifth Amendment's right to a grand jury indictment, the Seventh Amendment's right to a jury trial in civil cases, and the Eighth Amendment's protection against excessive bail and fines.

Moreover, the exclusion of these rights from the protection of the Fourteenth Amendment lends a measure of intuitive appeal to Justice Cardozo's "ordered liberties" approach to deciding if a protection should be applied to state proceedings. In terms of a hierarchy of constitutional rights, the protections to individuals resulting from grand jury indictments, the prohibition against quartering soldiers in private homes, jury trials in civil cases, and the right to be free from excessive bail and fines seem rather insignificant when compared to many of the rights mentioned in Table 1.

Table 1

Noteworthy Constitutional Rights Applied to State Proceedings through the Due Process Clause of the Fourteenth Amendment

Case	Right Incorporated	Amendment
Gitlow v. New York, 268 U.S. 652 (1925)	Freedom of speech	1st
Cantwell v. Connecticut, 310 U.S. 296 (1940)	Free exercise of religion	1st
Everson v. Board of Education, 330 U.S. 1 (1947)	No govt. establishment of religion	1st
Near v. Minnesota, 283 U.S. 697 (1931)	Freedom of the press	1st
DeJonge v. Oregon, 299 U.S. 353 (1937)	Freedom of assembly	1st
McDonald v. City of Chicago, 561 U.S. ___ (2010)	Right to bear arms	2nd
Wolf v. Colorado, 338 U.S. 25 (1949)	Search and seizure	4th
Mapp v. Ohio, 367 U.S. 643 (1961)	Exclusionary rule of evidence	4th
Benton v. Maryland, 395 U.S. 784 (1969)	Double jeopardy	5th
Malloy v. Hogan, 378 U.S. 1 (1964)	Self-incrimination	5th
Klopfer v. N Carolina, 386 U.S. 213 (1967)	Speedy trial	6th
In re Oliver, 333 U.S. 257 (1948)	Public trial, notice of charges	6th
Duncan v. Louisiana, 391 U.S. 145 (1968)	Impartial jury	6th
Pointer v. Texas, 380 U.S. 400 (1965)	Confront adverse witnesses	6th
Washington v. Texas, 388 U.S. 14 (1967)	Compulsory process	6th
Gideon v. Wainright, 372 U.S. 335 (1963)	Counsel	6th
Robinson v. California, 370 U.S. 660 (1962)	Cruel and unusual punishment	8th

After reading the excerpts from the cases in this section, do you believe that Justice Cardozo was correct in extolling the case by case process of selective incorporation? Or, conversely, would the U.S. Supreme Court have saved itself from this rather laborious undertaking, and shielded itself from criticism that it had injected personal values into the constitutional interpretation process, if it had adopted Justice Black's total incorporation approach?

If you are still undecided, the following readings may help you in reaching a conclusion on this important issue. See: Rolando V. del Carmen, *Criminal Procedure: Law and Practice* (Wadsworth, 7th ed., 2006); Kathleen M. Sullivan and Gerald Gunther, *Constitutional Law* (Foundation Press, 15th ed., 2004); Laurence H. Tribe, *American Constitutional Law* (Foundation Press, 2nd ed., 1988); Alpheus Thomas Mason and Donald Grier Stephenson, Jr., *American Constitutional Law* (Pearson Prentice Hall, 15th ed., 2009); Bernard Schwartz, *A History of the Supreme Court* (Oxford University Press, 1993); Kermit L. Hall, Paul Finkelman, and James Ely, Jr., *American Legal History: Cases and Materials* (Oxford University Press, 3rd ed., 2005); Kermit L. Hall, *The Oxford Companion to the Supreme Court of the United States* (Oxford University Press, 1992); Walter F. Murphy, James E. Flemming, Sotirios A. Barber, and Stephen Macedo, *American Constitutional Interpretation* (Foundation Press, 3rd ed., 2003); David M. O'Brien, *Constitutional Law and Politics: Struggles for Power and Government Accountability* (W.W. Norton, 6th ed., 2005); Craig R. Ducat, *Constitutional Interpretation* (Wadsworth, 9th ed., 2009); John H. Garvey, T. Alexander Aleinikoff, and Daniel A. Farber, *Modern Constitutional Theory: A Reader* (Thompson West, 5th ed., (2004). See also: Magliocca, "Why Did the Incorporation of the Bill of Rights Fail in the Late Nineteenth Century?"

Minnesota Law Review, vol. 94, p. 102 (2009); Nelson Lund, "Symposium: District of Columbia v. Heller: Anticipating Second Amendment Incorporation: The Role of the Inferior Courts," *Syracuse Law Review,* vol. 59, p. 185 (2008); Justin F. Marceau, "Criminal Law: Un-incorporating the Bill of Rights: The Tension Between the Fourteenth Amendment and the Federalism Concerns that Underlie Modern Criminal Procedure Reforms," *Journal of Criminal Law and Criminology,* vol. 98, p. 1231 (2008); Morris B. Hoffman, "The Court Says No to 'Incorporation Rebound': Virginia v. Moore," *Baylor Law Review,* vol. 61, p. 818 (2009).

ISSUE 8

Should the States be Permitted to Abolish the Exclusionary Rule of Evidence in Criminal Cases?

YES: Akhil Reed Amar, from "Against Exclusion (Except to Protect Truth or Prevent Privacy Violations)," *Harvard Journal of Law and Public Policy* (Winter 1997)

NO: Yale Kamisar, from "In Defense of the Search and Seizure Exclusionary Rule," *Harvard Journal of Law and Public Policy* (Winter 2003)

ISSUE SUMMARY

YES: Yale law professor Akhil Reed Amar argues that if reliable evidence is excluded from trials, wrongful acquittals and erroneous convictions will result. Moreover, he believes that the exclusionary rule of evidence hurts innocent defendants while helping the guilty ones.

NO: University of Michigan law professor Yale Kamisar contends that the exclusionary rule is the sole effective remedy to secure compliance with the Constitution by the police and that admitting evidence obtained illegally requires courts to condone lawless activities of law enforcement officers.

T he exclusionary rule of evidence is a prophylactic device that has been developed by U.S. courts to ensure that police officers comply with the requirements of the Constitution. It provides that evidence obtained unlawfully may not be used in a criminal proceeding as evidence of guilt. Exclusionary rule issues may arise from violations of a suspect's Fourth Amendment rights by virtue of an illegal search and seizure, Fifth Amendment rights due to a violation of the suspect's privilege against self-incrimination, or Sixth Amendment protections because of a violation of an individual's right to counsel.

Questions about whether we should use an exclusionary rule of evidence have been debated in the U.S. justice system for many years. In *People v. Defore,*

150 N.E. 585 (1926), a case decided by the New York Court of Appeals, Benjamin Cardozo, who later became one of the greatest U.S. Supreme Court justices in U.S. history, posed the exclusionary dilemma as follows: Is the criminal to go free because the constable has blundered? Years later, in *Mapp v. Ohio*, 367 U.S. 643 (1961), Justice Tom C. Clark provided an answer to Justice Cardozo's earlier question, stating: "The criminal goes free, if he must, but it is the law that sets him free. Nothing can destroy a government more quickly than its failure to observe its own laws, or worse, its disregard of the charter of its own existence."

For a number of years prior to *Mapp v. Ohio*, the Supreme Court had appeared reluctant to impose the exclusionary rule on state criminal proceedings. For example, in *Wolf v. Colorado*, 338 U.S. 25 (1949), the Court applied the Fourth Amendment right to be free from unreasonable searches and seizures to the states through the Fourteenth Amendment's due process clause; however, it declined to extend the exclusionary rule to the states at that time because it believed that a vigilant press and public opinion could deter the police from conducting illegal searches and seizures. Three years later, in *Rochin v. California*, 342 U.S. 165 (1952), the Court extended the exclusionary rule protection to state proceedings when the conduct of law enforcement officers "shocks the conscience." Finally, in *Mapp v. Ohio*, a majority of the Court concluded that it was necessary to make the exclusionary rule mandatory in state criminal trials as part of the due process guarantee of the Fourteenth Amendment.

In general, proponents of the exclusionary rule believe that it needed to ensure the integrity of our justice system. Exclusionary rule opponents assert that it deprives society of the opportunity to convict guilty people who have violated its laws. But, what is the true impact of the exclusionary rule of evidence on society? Are legions of factually guilty defendants being released on legal technicalities and allowed to prey on society?

Based on the available evidence, should the United States abolish the exclusionary rule? The authors of the articles in this section provide very different answers to this question. Yale law professor Akhil Reed Amar argues that if reliable evidence is excluded from trials, wrongful acquittals and erroneous convictions will result. Moreover, he believes that the exclusionary rule hurts innocent defendants while helping the guilty ones.

In Your Opinion . . .

- Based on your personal experiences or on what you have read in the newspapers and seen on television, do you believe that without the exclusionary rule, police officers would commit illegal acts in order to enforce the law?
- Think about whether there are any reasonable alternatives to the exclusionary rule. Is there a middle ground between the positions adopted by Professors Amar and Kamisar?

YES

Akhil Reed Amar

Against Exclusion (Except to Protect Truth or Prevent Privacy Violations)

The title of this Panel is a question: "What Belongs in a Criminal Trial?" Now if my mother, who is not a lawyer, asked me what belongs in a criminal trial, I would look her in the eye and say, "Mom, the truth." And if my brother, who is a lawyer, asked me what belongs in a criminal trial, I would say, "Vik, reliable evidence subject to true privacy privileges"—a more elaborate answer, but the same basic idea.

There should be two principles guiding the exclusion of evidence in a criminal trial.[1] First, if the introduction of X where X is testimony or physical evidence, words or things would itself tend to risk a distinctively inaccurate verdict in some very substantial way, then X should be excluded.[2] This is especially true when X creates an unacceptably high risk that an innocent defendant will be erroneously convicted, for our system is, quite properly, particularly concerned with erroneous convictions.[3] When prejudice truly outweighs probative value, there is an argument for exclusion: the evidence is just so unreliable or misleading that the decisionmaker simply cannot assess it fairly. This principle may not apply to a great many situations, but it has normative appeal.

The second principle is that true privacy privileges may constrain the search for truth. Now, in the Anglo-American tradition, we—rightly—believe that trials are public events,[4] and yet we also—rightly—believe that some matters are best kept altogether private. When these beliefs bump up against each other, one can make a good argument that certain things simply should not come into the public trial at all, and thus should remain private. These exclusions prevent private facts from ever becoming public. They do not remedy an out-of-court privacy violation, they prevent an in-court privacy violation. These exclusions exist in order to protect some valuable social relationships such as the spousal relationship, or the priest–penitent, lawyer–client, and doctor–patient relationships. These relationships implicate true privacy privileges.

Now, one might ask, what is a true privacy privilege? One test is that a true privacy privilege is one that applies to all witnesses, not merely defendants, and in all actions, not just criminal cases.[5] On this account, the Fifth Amendment[6] privilege against self-incrimination is not a true privacy privilege, because it

From *Harvard Journal of Law & Public Policy*, vol. 20, no. 2, Winter 1997, pp. 457–466. Copyright © 1997 by Harvard Journal of Law and Public Policy. Reprinted by permission.

can be overcome by immunity. Furthermore, it applies only in criminal, but not civil, cases. So, for instance, Oliver North has no Fifth Amendment privacy privilege. If we want his "private" story badly enough, we can force him to give it. All we have to do is grant him a certain kind of criminal immunity. The key question is, then, what kind of immunity do we have to give him? The question of immunity does not even arise in priest–penitent or doctor–patient or spousal or attorney–client relationships, because these implicate true privacy privileges: one has an absolute right to keep these conversations private, and so the privacy violation is the compelled statement itself. The test of universal applicability also explains why the Fourth Amendment exclusionary rule is not a true privacy privilege: if introduction of illegally found evidence were itself a privacy violation, exclusion would be required in all civil as well as criminal cases, and yet this has never been the law. A true privacy privilege is one where courtroom exclusion prevents the privacy violation—exposure in court—from ever occurring, rather than "remedying" an antecedent breach of privacy that has already occurred, out of court.[7]

Let me now try to elaborate on my general vision of what does belong in a criminal trial by going through the Fourth[8], Fifth, and Sixth[9] Amendments. Remember, the subtitle of our Panel is "The Role of Exclusionary Rules"—a plural word—and exclusionary rules derive not just from the Fourth but also from the Fifth and Sixth Amendments. These Amendments have been misunderstood in their purpose and effect.

Let us start with the Fourth. The Fourth Amendment generally does not require, does not call for, does not even invite, the exclusion of evidence as a remedy for an unconstitutional search or seizure. Nowhere does the text say such a thing. Indeed, the text never distinguishes between civil and criminal cases, yet exclusionary rule doctrine always has. When we do exclude, we exclude in criminal cases but never, as a general matter, in civil cases. So, the text obviously does not support the current exclusionary rule.

What about history? The history emphatically rejects any idea of exclusion.[10] The English common law cases underlying the Fourth Amendment never recognized exclusion. England still does not recognize exclusion. Canada, until the 1980s, resisted the temptation. None of the Founders ever linked the Fourth Amendment to exclusion. In the first century after independence, no federal court ever recognized exclusion. No state court—and remember, virtually every State's constitution had a counterpart to the Fourth Amendment—ever excluded evidence in this first century.

When the most thoughtful judges of the era were presented with the case for exclusion—and it came up rarely, because it was so outlandish—they dismissed it out of hand. Joseph Story, who was no slouch as a scholar, confronted the argument for exclusion, and said that he had never heard of a case in the Anglo-American world excluding evidence on the ground that it was illegally obtained.[11] The Massachusetts Supreme Judicial Court reached the same conclusion a generation later, in a case presided over by its great Chief Justice Lemuel Shaw.[12]

So much for text. So much for history. How about structure? The structure of our Constitution generally, and of our criminal procedure provisions in particular, corresponds to my principles. The structure of the Constitution basically advocates truthseeking procedures constrained by privacy privileges, and so Fourth Amendment exclusion derives no support from a proper understanding of the Fourth, Fifth, and Sixth Amendments.

One obvious question is, then, where did this exclusion doctrine come from? It did not develop, as is taught in law schools, as a deterrence-based remedy for an antecedent Fourth Amendment violation. Rather, in about twenty United States Supreme Court cases—landmark cases beginning with Boyd in 1886[13] and continuing to the 1960s—judicial proponents of exclusion put forth an argument combining the Fourth Amendment and the Fifth Amendment privilege against self-incrimination.[14] This combination swayed the Court. It drives Justice Hugo Black's fifth vote in Mapp[15] and appears no less than six times, if one reads carefully, in Justice Clark's majority opinion in Mapp.[16] It goes as follows.

Consider a diary. (Most of these early cases involved personal papers.) When the government illegally grabs your most personal papers and your diaries, and then seeks to introduce all this stuff in a criminal proceeding, the introduction of that diary is itself a new Fifth Amendment-like constitutional violation (the argument goes). In effect, you are being made an involuntary witness against yourself when your personal papers testify against you. That was the theory, anyway.

So, exclusion was not designed to remedy an antecedent violation, but to prevent a new one from occurring in the courtroom itself, a violation rooted in Fifth Amendment self-incrimination concerns. This explains: (1) where the exclusionary rule came from; (2) why it has always applied in criminal cases but never in civil cases[17] (because the Fifth Amendment applies only in criminal cases); (3) why illegally obtained evidence could always be used against any defendant other than the searchee[18] (because your papers, as an extension of your person, your voice, your testimony, could not be made to testify against you—but, just as you could be forced to testify against someone else, so could your papers); and finally, (4) why the courts have always treated illegal seizures of persons differently from illegal searches and seizures of objects (because the Fifth Amendment self-incrimination idea did not apply to the body of the defendant and we never exclude the body of the defendant from the trial).[19]

Now, this doctrine of Fourth–Fifth fusion, which is the only principled—if incorrect—constitutional basis for exclusion, has been plainly repudiated by the recent Supreme Court. The Court repudiated it in both the Fisher and Leon cases,[20] leaving us only with three more modern arguments for exclusion. First, some claim that the exclusionary rule preserves judicial integrity. This argument is hard to take seriously, because the rule does not apply to civil cases. Furthermore, other countries with judicial systems characterized by integrity do not exclude evidence. In fact, integrity is also threatened when we exclude true evidence, and thereby deprive the trial and the world of relevant facts.

Second, there is the non-profit principle—the idea that government should not profit from its own wrong. This is incorrect as a constitutional rule, both factually and normatively. Factually, it simply is not true that the government is always actually and clearly better off because, and only because, it violated the Fourth Amendment. In many cases, even though the Constitution was violated, the violation was not the but-for cause of the government's later possession of the evidence. Often, it could have gotten the evidence utterly lawfully. Suppose, for example, that law enforcement officers had probable cause but did not obtain a warrant before conducting a search for a bloody knife. If they found the knife, under current exclusionary rules, judges would still suppress it as the fruit of an illegal search. This result is disturbing because the police (by hypothesis) easily could have gotten a warrant. Frank Easterbrook has written thoughtfully on just this problem in a Seventh Circuit opinion.[21] So, the standard of inevitable discovery discussed by Carol Steiker[22] actually is not overbroad, but rather is radically underinclusive. After all, there are many situations with a seventy percent likelihood that the government would have found the evidence. But unless that likelihood is ninety-nine percent, judges tend to say that the government can never use that evidence. The criminal, therefore, is the one affirmatively better off, because once the government initially acquires something illegal, it rarely can be used against the defendant. In short, there is a huge causation gap.

But there is also a normative problem, because the government always has been able, in some sense, to profit from its wrongs. It does not have to give stolen goods back to a thief. It does not have to give drugs back to a drug dealer or contraband back to a smuggler. This is basically because the thief is not entitled, morally or legally speaking, to the stolen goods, nor to the drug dealer to the drugs, nor the smuggler to the contraband. Similarly, they are not entitled to the evidence of their crimes. The law is entitled to every person's evidence; so, normatively, the government should be able to use the evidence just as it is able to keep the stolen goods.

Finally, there is the third modern argument for the exclusionary rule—deterrence. Here I disagree with Bill Stuntz.[23] Every scheme of deterrence will prevent some inappropriate searches and seizures. But not every deterrence scheme is sensible. The Founders knew about deterrence and talked about it a great deal. They never talked about exclusion, though. Instead, they talked about punitive damages and civil tort suits. Those schemes of deterrence have huge advantages over the exclusionary rule. They focus on the scope of the violation, which occurs when the search and seizure takes place, rather than when it happens to come up with otherwise admissible evidence.[24] If the police bop me on the nose, their action is not really related to whether or not they find evidence. Bopping me on the nose is, however, an independent constitutional wrong.

Tort law and deterrence remedies can focus on that independent wrong. We could enforce punitive damages. If there is too little or too much deterrence, we could raise the punitive damages or lower them as needed. Such remedies would also change the distribution of the benefits of deterrence. Right now, the benefits of deterrence go to the guilty more than the innocent. If the police know you are innocent and just want to hassle you because of your race, your sex, your politics, and the search—predictably—finds no evidence, the exclusionary rule is no deterrent whatsoever. It is no help for you at all. In Stanley Surrey's phrase, the distribution of benefits under the exclusionary rule is "upside down," helping the guilty, not the innocent.[25] This is why many countries around the world do not have our exclusionary scheme. The Founders did not intend to enact our scheme, and, with all due respect, they understood deterrence better than Bill Stuntz does. I should say that Bill Stuntz has written very thoughtfully about all of this. I just disagree with his judgment about what is the most functionally desirable system. But even if I am wrong about that, there remain these small matters of text, history, and structure to contend with.

Now let us turn to the Fifth Amendment. This Amendment is a rule requiring exclusion, but only of words, of testimony, of witnessing. The Amendment applies in criminal, and only criminal, cases. It can be overcome by immunity. And it does not apply to objects. (Schmerber[26] tells us that we can force people to give up a sample of their own blood, even if it might hang them.)

What is the reason for the Fifth Amendment rule of exclusion, then? The reason is reliability. One basic concern is that when words are coerced from suspects—especially in a preGideon[27] world—the suspects might not have the advice of a lawyer. If suspects were forced to take the stand, clever prosecutors could make them look guilty even if they are not. The cruelty is in forcing the innocent to take the stand, twisting their own words against them, making them look guilty, and thus making them effectively hang themselves. If that is the account, it is easy to understand why the privilege applies to criminal, rather than civil, cases. After all, we are far more concerned about erroneous convictions in criminal contexts. Moreover, it is clear why immunity overcomes the privilege, because immunity insures that your words will never be introduced against you in a criminal trial. Finally, it explains why the Self-Incrimination Clause does not apply to objects, because physical evidence such as blood is far more reliable than words.

Using this analysis, we can actually compel Oliver North to testify before Congress—that is not a criminal case—and so long as his words are never introduced in a criminal case in which he is a defendant, no Fifth Amendment violation will ever have occurred. Simply put, he will never have been made a witness against himself in a criminal trial. Similarly, outside the trial of a criminal defendant, we can actually force the defendant to disclose where the body is buried or where the bloody knife is hidden, and the defendant must tell us, under penalty of perjury. The lawyer is there to provide advice, just as in civil discovery, and the actual words will never be introduced at trial. So long as only the fruit of this discovery is introduced—the body and the bloody knife, with defendant's fingerprints all over them—there will never be any Fifth Amendment violation.

The Fourth Amendment is about things—houses, papers, effects, stuff—but it is not about exclusion. The Fifth Amendment is about exclusion in criminal cases—but only about excluding words, because they can be unreliable.

I am not going to be able to go into Sixth Amendment doctrine in detail here, but there are rules of exclusion there too, based both on the attorney–client privilege and the speedy trial ideal. As I have explained elsewhere,[28] Sixth Amendment exclusion doctrine is defensible only to the extent it prevents unreliable adjudication or preserves legitimate privacy.

The current rules, which exclude much too much reliable physical evidence on Fourth Amendment, Fifth Amendment, and Sixth Amendment speedy trial grounds—are upside down in two ways. And here I do agree with Bill Stuntz's biggest point:[29] these rules do have the unfortunate effect of letting guilty people go free, but more significantly, they also often make innocent people affirmatively worse off.

The exclusionary rule often leads judges to constrict what counts as a Fourth Amendment violation, and that hurts innocent people. Similarly, because we have such overbroad principles of exclusion under the Fifth Amendment Self-Incrimination Clause, innocent defendants actually suffer because they cannot compel the production of witnesses in their favor. Even if I as an innocent defendant actually know who did it, I cannot currently put that person on the stand if that person takes the Fifth. Under a proper reading of the Fifth Amendment, that would change.[30]

When truth is excluded from trials, there will be two types of systemic errors: wrongful, erroneous convictions and erroneous acquittals. The rules hurt innocent defendants while helping the guilty ones. And I have a hard time explaining to my mother or my brother why that makes sense.

Notes

1. My remarks summarize themes developed in much greater detail in AKHIL REED AMAR, THE CONSTITUTION AND CRIMINAL PROCEDURE: FIRST PRINCIPLES (1997). Instead of cluttering my summary presentation here with excessive footnotes, I have tried to steer the interested reader to the relevant passages of this book, which contains much more elaboration and documentation.

2. In many situations, properly instructed juries might be able to assess and properly discount partially unreliable evidence. See AMAR, supra note 1, at 131. Cf. id. at 203-04 n. 21 (suggesting that properly crafted instructions may not always work).

3. See, e.g., id. at 90-92, 154-55, 191 n.124, 214 n.1g1.

4. See id. at 117-19 (describing the concept of the public trial).

5. See id. at 65-66, 69-70 (critiquing a privacy rationale for the Self-Incrimination Clause).

6. U.S. CONST. amend. V (". . . [N]or shall [any person] be compelled in any criminal case to be a witness against himself. . . .").

7. See AMAR, supra note 1, at 137-38 (further discussing privacy privileges).

8. U.S. CONST. amend. IV ("The right of the people to be secure in their persons, houses, papers, and effects, against unreasonable searches and seizures, shall not be violated. . . .").

9. U.S. CONST. amend. VI ("In all criminal prosecutions, the accused shall enjoy the right to a speedy and public trial . . . and to have the Assistance of Counsel for his defense.").

10. See generally id. at 20-25, 191 n.132 (discussing historical attitudes toward the exclusionary rule, both in the U.S. and abroad).

11. *United States v. La Jeune Eugenie*, 26 F. Cas. 832, 84344 (C.C.D. Mass. 1822) (No. 15,551) (stating that "the right of using evidence does not depend, nor, as far as I have any recollection, has ever been supposed to

depend, upon the lawfulness or unlawfulness of the mode, by which it is obtained").

12. *Commonwealth v. Dana,* 43 Mass. (2 Met.) 329, 337-38 (1841) ("When papers are offered in evidence, the court can take no notice how they were obtained, whether lawfully or unlawfully; nor would they form a collateral issue to determine that question.") The opinion was actually written by Justice Wilde, see id. at 333, but Chief Justice Shaw then overruled the defendant's motion to arrest the judgment. See id. at 343.

13. See *Boyd v. United States,* 116 U.S. 616, 630, 633-36 (1886) (holding that compulsory production of private papers for use against their owner is prohibited both by the Fourth Amendment privilege against unreasonable search and seizure and by the Fifth Amendment privilege against self-incrimination). The case is discussed in AMAR, supra note 1, at 22-25.

14. These cases are listed in AMAR, supra note 1, at 250 n.28.

15. See *Mapp v. Ohio,* 367 U.S. 643, 661-66 (1961) (Black, J., concurring) (incorporating the exclusionary rules against the States).

16. See id. at 646-47, 646 n.5, 655-57 (opinion of the Court). For a list of the six passages, see AMAR, supra note 1, at 251 n.33.

17. See generally *United States v. Janis,* 428 U.S. 433, 447 (1976) ("In the complex and turbulent history of the [exclusionary] rule, the Court has never applied it to exclude evidence from a civil proceeding, federal or state.").

18. See *Agnello v. United States,* 269 U.S. 20, 35 (1925) (refusing to grant a new trial to co-defendants of a person against whom an unlawful search had been made, even though their convictions depended in part on the unlawfully-found evidence, because the constitutional rights of the co-defendants had not been violated); *Alderman v. United States,* 394 U.S. 165, 171-76 (1969) (restricting exclusionary rule standing to those whose rights were violated by the search itself).

19. See, e.g., *Holt v. United States,* 218 U.S. 245, 252-53 (1910) (holding that requiring a defendant to put on a shirt, in order to prove that it fit him, was not prohibited by the Fifth Amendment, because "the prohibition of compelling a man in a criminal court to be witness against himself is a prohibition of the use of physical or moral compulsion to extort communications from him, not an exclusion of his body as evidence when it may be material"); *Schmerber v. California,* 384 U.S. 757, 760-72 (1966) (holding that the Constitution does not prohibit the use of involuntarily-given blood samples from a criminal defendant). These cases are discussed in AMAR, supra note 1, at 23, 62-63. If the government kidnapped you utterly illegally, a court would never "exclude" your body and hold that the government had to dismiss the charges, let you go, close its eyes, count to 20, and then try to catch you again. See id. at 108, 236-37 n.84 (citing and discussing cases).

20. See *Fisher v. United States,* 425 U.S. 391, 40708 (1976) (repudiating Boyd); *United States v. Leon,* 468 U.S. 897, 905-06 (1984) (same).

21. See *United States v. Brown,* 64 F.3d 1083, 1084-86 (7th Cir. 1995) (permitting use of evidence discovered, though not seized, in a warrantless search of a defendant's home, because the police had believed the apartment did not belong to the defendant and had conducted the search for safety reasons).

22. See Carol S. Steiker, Counter-Revolution in Constitutional Criminal Procedure? 20 HARV. J.L. & PUB. POL'Y 435 (1997).

23. See William J. Stuntz, The Virtues and Vices of the Exclusionary Rule, 20 HARV. J.L. & PUB. POL'Y 443 (1997).

24. For more analysis on this point, see AMAR at supra note 1, at 15658.

25. See generally STANLEY S. SURREY, PATHWAYS TO TAX REFORM: THE CONCEPT OF TAX EXPENDITURES (1973).

26. See *Schmerber v. California,* 384 U.S. 757 (1966).

27. See *Gideon v. Wainwright,* 372 U.S. 335 (1963) (instituting the right to state-paid counsel for indigent defendants in all criminal felony trials, federal and state).

28. See AMAR, supra note 1, at 96-116, 136-38.

29. See Stuntz, supra note 23, at 454.

30. See AMAR, supra note 1, at 49-51, 71-73, 134-36 (explaining how narrower Fifth Amendment immunity would lead to broader rights of defendants to compel other witnesses to testify against themselves).

In Defense of the Search and Seizure Exclusionary Rule

Introduction[1]

About a quarter-century ago, after my co-authors and I had published the fourth edition of our criminal procedure casebook,[2] I attended a conference with A. Kenneth Pye, then the Dean of the Duke Law School. During a break in the conference proceedings, Dean Pye, a strong admirer of the Warren Court,[3] took me aside to give me some advice about casebook writing. This is a fairly accurate recollection of what Dean Pye said:

> On thumbing through the new edition of your casebook, I couldn't help noticing that you have eliminated a number of the pre-Warren Court cases you had in the earlier editions. I realize you were responding to the need to add a good deal of new material to the book without letting an already big book get any larger. But taking out the old cases has serious costs. In the years ahead, as more and more interesting new cases are handed down, you will feel much pressure to take out still more older cases. But this is a process you must resist.
>
> Otherwise, by the time you and your co-authors publish your eighth or tenth edition, the confessions chapter will begin with Miranda[4] and the search and seizure chapter with Mapp.[5] This would be calamitous. For many law students (and a few young criminal procedure professors) won't appreciate Mapp and Miranda—won't really understand why the Court felt the need to take the big steps it did—unless casebooks like yours contain material that enables readers of the books to get some idea of how unsatisfactory the prevailing rules and doctrines were before the Warren Court arrived on the scene.

I think Dean Pye's advice about casebook writing was sound,[6] and what he had to say also applies to discussions and debates about such issues as the search and seizure exclusionary rule. We cannot (at least we should not) begin with *Mapp v. Ohio*. We need a prelude.

The Pre-*Mapp* Era

Perhaps we should begin with *People v. Cahan*,[7] the pre-*Mapp* case in which California adopted the exclusionary rule on its own initiative.[8] At first, Justice Roger Traynor, who wrote the majority opinion, had not been a proponent of

From *Harvard Journal of Law & Public Policy*, vol. 26, no. 1, Winter 2003, p. 119. Copyright © 2003 by Harvard Journal of Law and Public Policy. Reprinted by permission.

the exclusionary rule. Indeed, thirteen years earlier, he had written the opinion of the California Supreme Court reaffirming the admissibility of illegally seized evidence.[9] By 1955, he and a majority of his colleagues felt compelled to overrule state precedents and adopt the exclusionary rule. Why? The Cahan majority explained:

> [O]ther remedies have completely failed to secure compliance with the constitutional provisions on the part of police officers with the attendant result that the courts under the old rule [of admissibility] have been constantly required to participate in, and in effect condone, the lawless activities of law enforcement officers.[10]

Justice Traynor and his colleagues seemed astounded by how casually and routinely illegally seized evidence was being offered and admitted in the California courts. After noting that Los Angeles police had candidly admitted that they had illegally installed listening devices in the defendants' homes and had described, with equal candor, how they had forcibly entered buildings without bothering to obtain warrants by breaking windows and kicking in doors,[11] Justice Traynor observed:

> [W]ithout fear of criminal punishment or other discipline, law enforcement officers . . . frankly admit their deliberate, flagrant [unconstitutional] acts. . . . It is clearly apparent from their testimony that [Los Angeles police officers] casually regard [their illegal acts] as nothing, more than the performance of their ordinary duties for which the City employs and pays them.[12]

Perhaps we should go back in time still further, three-quarters of a century, to *People v. Defore*,[13] the occasion for Judge (later Justice) Cardozo's famous opinion explaining why New York would not adopt the federal exclusionary rule. Cardozo maintained, as have most critics of the exclusionary rule ever since, that excluding the illegally seized evidence was not the only effective way to enforce the Fourth Amendment (or its state constitutional counterpart): "The [offending] officer might have been resisted, or sued for damages, or even prosecuted for oppression. He was subject to removal or other discipline at the hands of his superiors."[14]

Two decades later, in *Wolf v. Colorado*,[15] when the Supreme Court declined to impose the federal exclusionary rule on the states as a matter of Fourteenth Amendment Due Process, the Wolf majority, per Justice Frankfurter, made a similar argument. Indeed, the Court relied partly on what it called Cardozo's "[w]eighty testimony" about the availability of various alternatives to the exclusionary rule.[16]

The states that had rejected the federal exclusionary rule, Justice Frankfurter assured us, had "not left the right to privacy without other means of protection."[17] "It could not, therefore, be regard[ed] as a departure from basic standards to remand [victims of unlawful searches and seizures] to the remedies of private action and such protection as the internal discipline of the police, under the eyes of an alert public opinion, may afford."[18]

A majority of the Court took a very different view of the various alternatives (perhaps one should say, theoretical alternatives) to the exclusionary rule a dozen years later when it handed down *Mapp v. Ohio*,[19] overruling *Wolf*. This time the Court dismissed alternatives to the exclusionary rule, noting that "[t]he experience of California that such other remedies have been worthless and futile is buttressed by the experience of other States."[20] But the Court had nothing specific to say about the experience in any state other than California nor did it rely on empirical studies. Instead, the Court relied on comments by Justice Traynor in Cahan.

Asserting that the various alternatives to the exclusionary rule are worthless (or quoting statements by the California Supreme Court to the same effect) does not necessarily make them so—just as asserting (or assuming) that alternative remedies are meaningful (as both Cardozo and Frankfurter did) does not make that so. Fortunately, impressive evidence of the ineffectiveness of the so-called alternatives to the exclusionary rule does exist. But it is not to be found in the *Mapp* opinion itself. It is to be found rather in the reaction of law enforcement officials to the *Mapp* decision. To borrow a phrase, this reaction is the "weighty testimony"[21] that (despite the claims of Cardozo, Frankfurter, and others) reliance on tort remedies, criminal prosecutions, and the internal discipline of the police indeed left "the right to privacy without other means of protection."[22]

The Law Enforcement Community's Reaction to *Mapp*

Although Michael Murphy, the police commissioner of New York City at the time, did not say so in so many words, he left no doubt that because New York courts (relying on the *Defore* case) had permitted the prosecution to use illegally seized evidence up to the time of *Mapp*, neither the commissioner nor the thousands of officers who worked for him had been taking the law of search and seizure at all seriously. As the commissioner recalled some time later:

> I can think of no decision in recent times in the field of law enforcement which had such a dramatic and traumatic effect as [*Mapp*]. As the then commissioner of the largest police force in this country I was immediately caught up in the entire problem of reevaluating our procedures, which had followed the *Defore* rule, and . . . creating new policies and new instructions for the implementation of *Mapp*. . . . [Decisions such as *Mapp*] create tidal waves and earthquakes which require rebuilding of our institutions sometimes from their very foundations upward. Retraining sessions had to be held from the very top administrators down to each of the thousands of foot patrolmen and detectives engaged in the daily basic enforcement function.[23]

Why was *Mapp's* effect so "dramatic and traumatic"? Why did it create "tidal waves and earthquakes"? Why did it require "retraining" from top to bottom? Had there been any search and seizure training before *Mapp*?

What did the commissioner mean when he told us that prior to *Mapp* his police department's procedures "had followed the *Defore* case"? *Defore* did not set forth any procedures or permit the police to establish any procedures other than those that complied with the Fourth Amendment. It did allow New York prosecutors to use illegally seized evidence, but it did not (as the commissioner seemed to think) allow New York police to commit illegal searches and seizures. Is there any better evidence of the inadequacies of the existing alternatives to the exclusionary rule than the police reaction to the imposition of the rule?[24]

It appears that, prior to *Mapp*, New York prosecutors were also unfamiliar with and uninterested in the law of search and seizure. Professor Richard Uviller, a New York prosecuting attorney at the time *Mapp* was handed down, recalled that he "cranked out a crude summary" of federal search and seizure law just in time for the next state convention of district attorneys and that summary turned out to be "an instant runaway best seller. It was as though we had made a belated discovery that the fourth amendment applied in the State of New York . . .".[25] That, I think, says it all.

The response of New York law enforcement officials to the imposition of the search and seizure rule is hardly unique. Six years earlier, when the California Supreme Court adopted the exclusionary rule on its own initiative in *People v. Cahan*,[26] the reaction of the Los Angeles Chief of Police, William Parker, had been quite similar to the one his New York City counterpart displayed when *Mapp* was decided.[27]

In Pennsylvania—another state whose courts had admitted illegally seized evidence prior to *Mapp*—a young Philadelphia assistant district attorney (and a future U.S. Senator), Arlen Specter, left little doubt that in this state, too, the so-called alternative remedies to the exclusionary rule had had virtually no effect. Commissioner Murphy had likened *Mapp* to a "tidal wave" and an "earthquake"; Mr. Specter compared it to a revolution:

> Police practices and prosecution procedures were revolutionized in many states by the holding in . . . *Mapp v. Ohio* that evidence obtained from an illegal search and seizure cannot be used in a criminal proceeding. . . . [There are indications] that the imposition of the exclusionary rule upon the states is the most significant event in criminal law since the adoption of the fourteenth amendment. . . . *Mapp* has rewritten the criminal law treatise for states which had admitted evidence regardless of how it was obtained.[28]

Mr. Specter, like Commissioner Murphy, seemed to equate the relevance of the law of search and seizure with the presence or absence of the exclusionary rule, a remedy for the violation of a body of law the police were supposed to be obeying all along: [T]he *Mapp* decision has significantly impaired the ability of the police to secure evidence to convict the guilty. . . . The law abiding citizen who must walk on some Philadelphia streets at two o'clock in the morning would doubtless prefer to be subjected to a search, without any cause, and have the police do the same to the man standing idly at a corner; but that cannot be done under *Mapp*.[29]

Has the Exclusionary Rule Inhibited the Development of Alternative Remedies?

One can hear the critics of the exclusionary rule now. *Mapp v. Ohio*, some say, removed both the incentive and the opportunity to develop effective alternative means of enforcing the Fourth Amendment. Indeed, Chief Justice Warren Burger once said that "the continued existence of [the exclusionary rule] inhibits the development of rational alternatives."[30] However, it is hard to take this argument seriously.

First of all, as opponents of the exclusionary rule never tire of telling us, large portions of police activity relating to the seizing of criminal property do not produce (and may not even have been designed to produce) incriminating evidence, and thus do not result in criminal prosecutions.[31] Whatever the reason for the failure to impose direct sanctions on the offending officers in these instances, it cannot be the existence of the exclusionary rule. The issue need not, and should not, be framed in terms of whether we should enforce the Fourth Amendment by an exclusionary rule or tort remedies against the offending officers or departmental sanctions. Nothing prevents the use of "internal sanctions" against the police "simultaneously with the use of the exclusionary rule."[32] After all, "[n]o proponent of the exclusionary rule has suggested that it should act in isolation."[33]

Moreover, blaming the failure to develop any effective "direct sanctions" against offending police officers on the exclusionary rule itself, to borrow a phrase from Carol Steiker, "ignores history."[34] For many decades a large number of states had no exclusionary rule, yet none of them produced any meaningful alternatives to the rule. Almost half a century passed between the time the federal courts adopted the exclusionary rule[35] and the time the Court finally imposed the rule on the states. But in all that time, not one of the twenty-four states that still admitted illegally seized evidence on the eve of *Mapp* had developed an effective alternative to the rule.[36] Thus, five decades of post-Weeks "freedom" from the inhibiting effect of the federal exclusionary rule failed to produce any meaningful alternative to the exclusionary rule in any jurisdiction.

One can hear the critics of the exclusionary rule again. Some of them are telling us that times have changed. Have they?

Are Today's Politicians More Likely to Impose Effective "Direct Sanctions" against the Police Than the Politicians of Yesteryear?

Is there any reason to believe that today's or tomorrow's politicians are, or will be, any less fearful of appearing "soft on crime" or any more interested in protecting people under investigation by the police than the politicians of any other era? Is there any reason to think that the lawmakers of our day are any more willing than their predecessors to invigorate tort remedies (or any other "direct sanction") against police officers who act overzealously in the pursuit of "criminals"?

"If anything," observes Carol Steiker, "the escalating public hysteria over violent crime from the 1960s through the present makes it is [sic] even more 'politically suicidal' today to support restrictions on police behavior than it was before 1961."[37] Consider, too, the disheartening comments of Donald Dripps:

> American legislatures consistently have failed to address defects in the criminal process, even when they rise to crisis-level proportions. For example, when the Miranda Court invited Congress and the states to experiment with alternatives to traditional backroom police interrogation, Congress responded by adopting Title II [of the Omnibus Crime Control and Safe Streets Act of 1968], which stubbornly insisted on the traditional practice. To this day only two American jurisdictions, Alaska and Minnesota, require taping interrogations. In both instances the state courts, rather than the state legislature, were the source of reform.
>
> Legislatures across the United States have found billions of dollars for prisons, but the support for indigent defense is shamefully inadequate.[38] No legislature has adopted reforms of police identification procedures, even though we have known since the 1930s that mistaken identification is the leading cause of false convictions.[39] Legislatures . . . have not adopted statutory requirements for judicial warrants, or the preservation of exculpatory evidence, or plugged holes in the exclusionary rule, let alone delivered the effective tort remedy exclusionary rule critics have advocated for decades.
>
> The record is not an accident, but the product of rational political incentives. Almost everyone has an interest in controlling crime. Only young men, disproportionately black, are at significant risk of erroneous prosecution for garden-variety felonies. Abuses of police search and seizure or interrogation powers rarely fall upon middle-aged, middle-class citizens. . . . [S]o long as the vast bulk of police and prosecutorial power targets the relatively powerless (and when will that ever be otherwise?), criminal procedure rules that limit public power will come from the courts or they will come from nowhere.[40]

A new book by Welsh White relates an incident that illustrates the formidable political power possessed by the law enforcement community.[41] As the result of a lawsuit brought by an alleged victim of abusive police interrogation practices, a police investigator looked into charges against a Chicago police commander and those working for him. He concluded that for a period of more than ten years the commander and his men had been torturing suspects into confessing. In 1993, the commander was dismissed from the police force.[42] But allegations of police misconduct continued to fill the air. For example, ten Illinois prisoners on death row maintained that the Chicago commander and his men had extracted confessions from them by torture.[43]

In the wake of the controversy surrounding these alleged police torture cases, the Illinois legislature at one point seemed prepared to enact a law requiring the police to video or audiotape their interrogation practices. But the law enforcement community expressed its strong opposition to the bill, claiming that it would create new obstacles and expand the rights of the accused "at the expense of crime victims, public safety and law enforcement."[44] The bill died in committee.[45]

As Justice Traynor noted long ago in Cahan, "even when it becomes generally known that the police conduct illegal searches and seizures, public opinion is not aroused as it is in the case of other violations of constitutional rights" because illegal arrests and unlawful searches "lack the obvious brutality of coerced confessions and the third degree and do not so clearly strike at the very basis of our civil liberties as do unfair trials. . . ."[46] Moreover, unlike the Chicago torture cases, illegal searches and seizures do not raise doubts as to a defendant's innocence. If the police and their allies can crush legislative reform efforts in the confessions area as decisively as they did in the wake of the Chicago police scandal—despite serious questions about the guilt of a number of people on death row—how much difficulty will they have defeating legislative proposals to impose direct sanctions on them for committing Fourth Amendment violations?

One half of Judge Guido Calabresi's proposed alternative to the exclusionary rule is to impose a system of "direct punishment" on the offending police officer.[47] Perhaps Judge Calabresi has in mind the imposition of substantial fines, suspensions without pay, or dismissal from the force, depending on the seriousness of the officer's Fourth Amendment violation. One fails to see, however, why this part of his proposal will fare any better in the political arena than many other "direct sanction" proposals that have failed over the years.

Police Perjury and Judicial "Winking"

As other critics of the exclusionary rule have done,[48] Judge Calabresi notes that the police frequently lie in court to evade the exclusionary rule.[49] Still worse, there is good reason to believe that in a significant number of cases, judges "knowingly accept police perjury as truthful."[50] There are at least two responses to this criticism of the exclusionary rule.

First, Myron Orfield's interviews with approximately forty Chicago criminal division judges, prosecutors, and public defenders left no doubt that police perjury and judicial toleration of it were widespread, but he concluded:

> Although recognizing the [exclusionary] rule's imperfections, respondents believe it is the only mechanism that injects any restraint in the system, or any respect for rights. Though often evaded, the respondents believe that by creating a possibility of suppression, the rule makes the Fourth Amendment a factor in police and judicial thinking. . . .[51]

Critics might also argue that pervasive perjury is a cost of the exclusionary rule, and as such, outweighs any incremental benefit gained by the rule's uneven deterrent effect. Respondents . . . nevertheless believe that the exclusionary rule has dramatically improved police behavior and should be retained. . . . Today, while police often perjure themselves, they also, because of the exclusionary rule, often obey the Fourth Amendment. By any measure, this is an improvement [over pre-*Mapp* days].[52]

Second, as Laurie Levenson recently observed, there is no evidence and no reason to believe "that a police officer will be any less motivated to lie in an administrative hearing, where [his] reputation and job position are at risk, than in a criminal proceeding where the court threatens to exclude evidence."[53] "[I]t is important to realize," admonishes Orfield, in the course of concluding his study of Chicago narcotics officers, "that any remedial scheme that imposes a personal sanction on an officer is likely to encourage perjury."[54]

The Costs of the Exclusionary Rule

[Many critics of the exclusionary role have assumed][55] that the criminal defendant who benefits from the application of the search and seizure exclusionary rule will often be a murderer or rapist.[56] However, an empirical study by Thomas Davies, called "[t]he most careful and balanced assessment conducted to date of all available empirical data,"[57] reveals that the exclusion of evidence in murder, rape, and other violent cases is exceedingly rare.[58] "The most striking feature of the data," reports Davies, "is the concentration of illegal searches in drug arrests (and possibly weapons possession arrests) and the extremely small effects in arrests for other offenses, including violent crimes."[59]

It may be that search and seizure problems arise much less frequently in murder, forcible rape, and other violent crime cases than they do in drug and weapons possession cases. Myron Orfield furnishes two other explanations, one encouraging, the other not.

The first explanation is that the more serious the crime, the greater the officer's desire to see the perpetrator convicted and, because the police care more about convictions in these cases, the more potent the exclusionary rule's deterrent effects.[60] Moreover, "big cases" are more likely to involve officers in specialized units "who are more likely to take the time and care necessary to comply with the Fourth Amendment."[61]

The second explanation is that in "heater" cases (i.e., big cases that have "the potential to arouse public ire" if the defendant "goes free" because the police violated the Fourth Amendment),[62] many judges will feel tremendous pressure to admit the illegally seized evidence and will often find a way to do so.[63] It is almost as if many judges, at least those who have to run for re-election, have informally adopted one law professor's proposal to make an exception to the exclusionary rule in prosecutions for treason, espionage, murder, armed robbery, and kidnapping.[64] I find this an unfortunate and dispiriting development,[65] but it is only one of a number of ways in which the courts have accommodated the needs of law enforcement in the exclusionary rule era.

The Warren Court has been disbanded for more than thirty years. Since then, with only a few exceptions,[66] the Burger and Rehnquist Courts have waged a kind of "guerilla warfare" against the law of search and seizure.[67] As a result, Judge Cardozo's oft-quoted criticism of the exclusionary rule—"[t]he criminal is to go free because the constable has blundered"[68]—is out of date. The Court has taken a grudging view of what amounts to a "search" or "seizure" within the meaning of the Fourth Amendment and has taken a relaxed view of what constitutes consent to an otherwise illegal search or seizure; it has so softened the "probable cause" requirement, so increased the occasions on which the police may act on the basis of "reasonable suspicion" or in the absence of any reasonable suspicion, and so narrowed the thrust of the exclusionary rule that nowadays the criminal only "goes free" if and when the constable has blundered badly.[69]

Judge Calabresi argues that the downsizing of the Fourth Amendment and the protections to privacy it provides, because of the pressure the exclusionary rule puts on courts to avoid freeing a guilty defendant, should make liberals hate the exclusionary rule.[70] I think not.

A meaningful tort remedy or administrative sanction or any other effective alternative to the exclusionary rule would also exert strong pressure on courts to make the rules governing search and seizure more "police-friendly." As Monrad Paulsen noted on the eve of the Mapp case: "Whenever the rules are enforced by meaningful sanctions, our attention is drawn to their content. The comfort of Freedom's words spoken in the abstract is always disturbed by their application to a contested instance. Any rule of police regulation enforced in fact will generate pressures to weaken the rule."[71]

There is no denying that one of the effects of the exclusionary rule has been to diminish the protection provided by the Fourth Amendment. But this is probably the price we would have had to pay for any means of enforcing the Amendment that had a bite—one that actually worked.

The only time the Amendment would not impose the societal costs that critics of the exclusionary rule complain about—and the only time it would not put pressure on the courts to water down the rules governing search and seizure—would be if it were "an unenforced honor code that the police may follow in their discretion."[72]

Judge Calabresi's Proposal

As Tracey Maclin has reminded us,[73] ever since the 1930s,[74] commentators have deplored the inadequacies of existing tort remedies against offending police officers and proposed various ways to invigorate these remedies (although nothing seems to have come of it). Therefore, I find quite noteworthy Judge Calabresi's view that, in the ordinary unlawful arrest or illegal search case, tort remedies will not work.[75] I agree with him that, although jurors often identify with the plaintiff in a tort action, they are unlikely to do so when the plaintiff is a criminal or a suspected criminal.[76] However, I find the alternative to the exclusionary rule that Judge Calabresi proposes disappointing.

Judge Calabresi's proposal has two parts: First, after the person has been convicted, a hearing would take place to determine whether the police had obtained evidence illegally and, if so, whether the officer(s) had done so inadvertently, negligently, willfully, or wantonly. Based on the flagrancy of the police misconduct, the defendant would then be given a reduction of two, three, or four points on the sentencing guidelines.[77] Second, the officer or officers who were found to have violated the Fourth Amendment would then be subjected to a separate system of direct punishment which would vary, depending upon the flagrancy of the misconduct.[78] I assume that one or more of the officer's superiors would determine what the punishment should be.

A reduction of the prison sentence, based on the degree to which the police violated the defendant's rights, is an unusual aspect of Judge Calabresi's proposal. He assures us that this feature would provide the defendant with a significant incentive to bring up the fact that the evidence introduced by the state was obtained illegally. Perhaps so,[79] but the more relevant question is how, if at all, this part of the judge's proposal would influence the police. Would it constitute a disincentive—a means of eliminating, or at least reducing, significant police incentives to illegal searches where the police contemplate prosecution and conviction?[80] I think not. This feature of Judge Calabresi's proposal would likely have no impact on the police at all.

Chief Justice Burger once argued that the exclusionary rule does not affect police officers' behavior.[81] However, Myron Orfield's Chicago study strongly indicates otherwise.[82] Every judge, prosecutor, and public defender he interviewed expressed the belief that "officers care about convictions and experience adverse personal reactions when they lose evidence."[83]

Under Judge Calabresi's proposal, however, the victim of the police misconduct could be, and would be, convicted on the basis of evidence the police obtained in violation of the Fourth Amendment, even when the violation was gross or willful. I am convinced that the police do care whether the evidence they obtained leads to a conviction or whether such evidence is thrown out by the court. But a conviction is one thing; the length of the sentence is something else. I find it hard to believe that the police care one whit whether the person convicted on the basis of their unlawful acquisition of evidence is sentenced to four years or five, ten months or twelve. From the perspective of the police, the important thing—perhaps the only thing—is that their actions resulted in the conviction of a criminal and a substantial stretch of prison time for him. In other words, their illegal actions "paid off."

Therefore, the efficacy of Judge Calabresi's proposed alternative to the exclusionary rule must turn on the other half of his proposal—what he calls a separate system of direct punishment of the individual officer after a post-trial determination that the officer committed a search and seizure violation.[84]

We can be fairly certain that if the police believed Judge Calabresi's system of direct punishment for Fourth Amendment violations would really work, they would resist its adoption for the same reasons they would be unhappy about other systems of "direct sanctions" against them (such as tort remedies) that really worked. They would argue forcefully, and with some plausibility, that if six-month suspensions without pay and/or substantial fines were imposed on them for search and seizure violations (presumably the kind of "direct punishments" Judge Calabresi contemplates), they "would be afraid to conduct the searches they should make."[85]

Orfield's study of Chicago narcotics officers discloses that they clearly preferred the exclusionary rule to a system of "direct sanctions" against them.[86] This finding may be somewhat misleading. Few police are enamored of the exclusionary rule. If they had their druthers, most would prefer the pre-*Mapp* days, when, in many states, no viable means of enforcing the protection against unreasonable search and seizure existed.[87] However, the police would rather live with an "indirect" sanction, like the exclusionary rule, than a direct one. Moreover, the exclusionary rule is not something the police can fight and defeat in the political arena—it is a remedy that judges control and can apply "without being dependent upon the actions of other branches of government."[88]

The police can, however, have a large effect on the alternatives to the exclusionary rule, because other actors such as legislators, prosecutors, and police brass control these.[89] For one thing, the police can invoke their formidable political clout [90] to prevent a plan like Judge Calabresi's from ever being adopted. Moreover, even if such a plan were adopted, the police could prevent it from being applied in appropriate cases.

Judge Calabresi's proposed system would probably not overcome the resulting police resistance. But the greater danger is that a plan like the judge's might be adopted, displacing the exclusionary rule, yet rarely be enforced. It might turn out to exist only on paper.

One cannot help thinking of *INS v. Lopez-Mendoza*,[91] a case that declined to apply the exclusionary rule to civil deportation proceedings. One reason the Court gave for the conclusion it reached was that the Immigration and Naturalization Services ("INS") "has its own comprehensive scheme for deterring Fourth Amendment violations by its officers"[92]—a system of rules and regulations restricting INS agents' conduct in dealing with aliens, a program for giving new officers "instruction and examination in Fourth Amendment law," and "a procedure for investigating and punishing immigration officers who commit Fourth Amendment violations."[93] These programs and procedures, the Court assured us, "reduce the likely deterrent value of the exclusionary rule."[94]

The trouble was, as dissenting Justice White was quick to point out, that the *Lopez-Mendoza* majority failed to cite "a single instance" in which the INS procedures had been invoked.[95] Moreover, other portions of the majority opinion were likely to shake one's confidence in the vaunted procedures the INS was supposed to have in place for deterring, investigating, and punishing Fourth Amendment violations. Even an "occasional invocation of the exclusionary rule might significantly change and complicate the character of [deportation] proceedings," the Court told us, because "[n]either the hearing officers nor the attorneys participating in those hearings are likely to be well versed in the intricacies of Fourth Amendment law."[96] The Court also indicated that application of the exclusionary rule to deportation proceedings "might well result in the suppression of large amounts of information that had been obtained entirely lawfully," because "INS arrests occur in crowded and confused circumstances."[97] Moreover, the Court told us that requiring INS agents to keep "a precise account of exactly what happened in each particular arrest" would be impractical, considering the "massed numbers of ascertainably illegal aliens. . . ."[98]

To avoid a replay of the paper procedures for deterring Fourth Amendment violations in place at the INS, I suggest that we proceed slowly and cautiously with [proposals to change the exclusionary rule]. As noted earlier, many unlawful arrests and searches do not turn up any incriminating evidence or result in any criminal prosecutions.[99] In the unlikely event that Judge Calabresi's scheme of directly punishing the offending officer is put in place, a better plan is to keep the exclusionary rule in the first three to five years for instances of police misconduct that result in criminal prosecutions and to use the new administrative sanctions against those officers whose misconduct failed to produce any incriminating evidence. In the unlikely event that an appraisal of the situation three or five years later demonstrates that the judge's system of direct punishment really works—that police officers are regularly punished for "the frequent infringements [of the Fourth Amendment] motivated by commendable zeal" as well as for "the grossest of violations"[100]—there will be time enough to abolish the exclusionary rule.

Notes

1. There is a vast literature on this subject. For a good sampling, see WAYNE R. LAFAVE, SEARCH AND SEIZURE: A TREATISE ON THE FOURTH AMENDMENT 1-373 (3d ed. 1996); Francis A. Allen, Federalism and the Fourth Amendment: A Requiem for Wolf, 1961 SUP. CT. REV. 1; Akhil Reed Amar, Fourth Amendment First Principles, 107 HARV. L. REV. 757 (1994); Anthony G. Amsterdam, Perspectives on the Fourth Amendment, 58 MINN. L. REV. 349 (1974); Edward L. Barrett, Jr., Exclusion of Evidence Obtained by Illegal Searches—A Comment on People vs. Cahan, 43 CAL. L. REV. 565 (1955); Yale Kamisar, Does (Did) (Should) the Exclusionary Rule Rest on a "Principled Basis" Rather than an "Empirical Proposition"? 16 CREIGHTON L. REV. 565 (1983); Tracey Maclin, When the Cure for the Fourth Amendment is Worse than the Disease, 68 S. CAL. L. REV. 1 (1994); Dallin H. Oaks, Studying the Exclusionary Rule in Search and Seizure, 37 U. CHI. L. REV. 665 (1970); Monrad G. Paulsen, The Exclusionary Rule and Misconduct by the Police, 52 J. CRIM. L.C. & P.S. 255 (1961); Christopher Slobogin, Why Liberals Should Chuck the Exclusionary Rule, 1999 U. ILL. L. REV. 363; Carol S. Steiker, Second Thoughts About First Principles, 107 HARV. L. REV. 820 (1994); Potter Stewart, The Road to Mapp v. Ohio and Beyond: The Origins, Development and Future of the Exclusionary Rule in Search-and-Seizure Cases, 83 COLUM. L. REV. 1365 (1983); John Barker Waite, Judges and the Crime Burden, 54 MICH. L. REV. 169 (1955); Silas Wasserstrom & William J. Mertens, The Exclusionary Rule on the Scaffold: But Was It a Fair Trial? 22 AM. GRIM. L. REV. 85 (1984); John H. Wigmore, Using Evidence Obtained by Illegal Search and Seizure, 8 A.B.A. J. 479 (1922). It is very hard to select the best long article ever written on the exclusionary rule, but it is relatively easy to pick the best short one—William J. Stuntz, The Virtues and Vices of the Exclusionary Rule, 20 HARV. J.L. & PUB. POL'Y 443 (1997).

2. YALE KAMISAR ET AL., MODERN CRIMINAL PROCEDURE (4th ed. 1974).

3. See, e.g., A. Kenneth Pye, The Warren Court and Criminal Procedure, 67 MICH. L. REV. 249 (1968). At the time he gave me advice about writing criminal procedure casebooks, Pye was one of the nation's leading criminal procedure commentators, but in later years Pye's administrative obligations as law school dean, university chancellor and university president diverted his efforts from legal scholarship. See generally Francis A. Allen, The Scholarship of Kenneth Pye, 49 SMU L. REV. 439 (1996).

4. Miranda v. Arizona, 384 U.S. 436 (1966).

5. Mapp v. Ohio, 367 U.S. 643 (1961).

6. Our casebook is now in its tenth edition. See YALE KAMISAR ET AL., MODERN CRIMINAL PROCEDURE (10th ed. 2002). The chapter on search and seizure still does not begin with Mapp; the chapter on confessions still does not begin with Miranda.

7. 282 P.2d 905 (Cal. 1955).

8. Prior to Mapp, state courts were free to admit or to exclude illegally seized evidence. In 1949, thirty-one states declined to exclude such evidence. A decade later, on the eve of Mapp, twenty-four states still rejected the exclusionary rule. See Yale Kamisar, The Exclusionary Rule in Historical Perspective: The Struggle to Make the Fourth Amendment More than "an Empty Blessing", 62 JUDICATURE 337, 346 (1979).

9. See People v. Gonzales, 124 P.2d 44 (Cal. 1942). What is even more ironic is that in 1942 Earl Warren was the California Attorney General who successfully urged Justice Traynor and his colleagues to reaffirm the rule permitting the use of illegally seized evidence. See id.

10. Cahan, 282 P.2d at 911-12.

11. See id. at 906 (citation omitted).

12. Id. at 907. See also Roger Traynor, Mapp v. Ohio at Large in the Fifty States, 1962 DUKE L. J. 319 (1962): My misgivings about [the admissibility of illegally seized evidence] grew as I observed that time after time it was being offered and admitted as routine procedure. It became impossible to ignore the corollary that illegal searches and seizures were also a routine procedure subject to no effective deterrent; else how could illegally obtained evidence come into court with such regularity? Id. At 321-22.

13. 150 N.E. 585 (NY App. Ct. 1926).

14. Id. at 586-87.

15. 338 U.S. 25 (1949).

16. Id. at 31. The Court quoted from Judge Cardozo's Defore opinion at considerable length. See id. at 31-32 n.2.

17. Id. at 30.

18. Id. at 31.

19. 367 U.S. 643 (1961).

20. Id. at 652.

21. Wolf, 338 U.S. at 31.

22. Id. at 30.

23. Michael Murphy, Judicial Review of Police Methods in Law Enforcement: The Problem of Compliance by Police Departments, 44 TEX. L. REV. 939, 941 (1966) (citation omitted) (emphasis added).

24. If any police official's post-Mapp comments are more revealing than Commissioner Murphy's, it may be those of New York City Deputy Police Commissioner Leonard Reisman. Reisman told a large group of police officers why they had to learn the law of seizure at such a late date in their careers: "[In the past] nobody bothered to take out search warrants. . . . [T]he Supreme Court had ruled that evidence obtained without a warrant—illegally if you

will—was admissible in state courts. So the feeling was, why bother?" Sidney E. Zion, Detectives Get a Course in Law, N.Y. TIMES, Apr. 28, 1965, at A50.

25. H. Richard Uviller, The Acquisition of Evidence for Criminal Prosecution: Some Constitutional Premises and Practices in Transition, 35 VAND. L. REV. 501, 502 (1982).

26. 282 P.2d 905 (Cal. 1955); see supra note 7 and accompanying text.

27. Chief Parker told the public that the commission of a serious crime would no longer "justify affirmative police action until such time as the police have armed themselves with sufficient information to constitute 'probable cause.'" WILLIAM H. PARKER, POLICE 117 (Wilson ed., 1957), quoted in Yale Kamisar, Wolf and Lustig Ten Years Later: Illegal State Evidence in State and Federal Courts, 43 MINN. L. REV. 1083, 1153-54 (1959). He also pledged that he and his officers would work "within the framework of limitations" imposed by the law of search and seizure "[a]s long as the Exclusionary Rule is the law of California." Id. at 131. For substantial extracts from Chief Parker's responses to the Cahan decision and for comments on his reaction, see Kamisar, supra, at 1153-54.

28. Arlen Specter, Mapp v. Ohio: Pandora's Problems for the Prosecutor, 111 U. PA. L. REV. 4(1962).

29. Id. at 42.

30. Stone v. Powell, 428 U.S. 465, 500 (1976) (Burger, C.J., concurring).

31. See, e.g., Akhil Reed Amar, Against Exclusion (Except to Protect Truth or Prevent Privacy Violations), 20 HARV. J.L. & PUB. POL'Y 457, 463-64 (1997) (describing alternate benefits of illegal evidence seizure).

32. Cf. A. Kenneth Pye, Charles Fahy and the Criminal Law, 54 GEO. L.J. 1055, 1072 (1966) (explaining that exclusionary rule is invoked because of failure of "internal sanctions" above).

33. Id.

34. Steiker, supra note 1, at 849; see also Kamisar, supra note 8, at 346, 350 (describing lack of initiative on part of states to develop alternatives between adoption of federal exclusionary rule and decisions of Mapp, 367 U.S. 643 (1961) and Wolf, 338 U.S. 25 (1949)).

35. See Weeks v. United States, 232 U.S. 383 (1914).

36. See Elkins v. United States, 364 U.S. 206, 224-25 (1960).

37. Steiker, supra note 1, at 850 (citation omitted); see also Amsterdam, supra note 1, at 379 ("[T]here will remain more than enough crime and fear of it in American society to keep our legislatures from the politically suicidal undertaking of police control.").

38. See, e.g., Note, Gideon's Promise Unfulfilled: The Need for Litigated Reform of Indigent Defense, 113 HARV. L. REV. 2062, 2067 (2000) (alluding to congressional and local jurisdictional decreases in resources devoted to indigent defense).

39. See also Francis A. Allen, The Judicial Quest for Penal Justice: The Warren Court and the Criminal Cases, 1975 U. ILL. L.F. 518, 542 (1975) (deploring the fact that Congress simply attempted to repeal the 1967 Supreme Court cases extending right to counsel to police lineups without offering anything in their place).

40. Donald A. Dripps, Constitutional Theory for Criminal Procedure: Dickerson, Miranda, and the Continuing Quest for Broad-But-Shallow, 43 WM. & MARY L. REV. 1, 45-46 (2001) (citations omitted).

41. See WELSH S. WHITE, MIRANDA'S WANING PROTECTIONS 128-36 (2001).

42. See id. at 130.

43. See id. at 130-31.

44. Id. at 136.

45. See id.

46. 282 P.2d 905, 913 (Cal. 1955).

47. Guido Calabresi, The Exclusionary Rule, 26 HARV. J.L. & PUB. POL'Y 111, 116 (2002).

48. See, e.g., L. Timothy Perrin, et al., If It's Broken, Fix It: Moving Beyond the Exclusionary Rule, 83 IOWA L. REV. 669, 677 (1998).

49. See Calabresi, supra note 47, at 113.

50. Myron W. Orfield, Jr., Deterrence, Perjury, and the Heater Factor: An Exclusionary Rule in the Chicago Criminal Courts, 63 U. COLO. L. REV. 75, 83 (1992). The study was based on interviews with thirteen judges, eleven prosecutors, and fourteen public defenders in the Chicago criminal court system. See id. at 81.

51. Id. at 123.

52. Id. at 132.

53. Laurie L. Levenson, Administrative Replacements: How Much Can They Do?, 26 PEPP. L. REV. 879, 881 (1999).

54. Myron W. Orfield, Jr., Comment, The Exclusionary Rule and Deterrence: An Empirical Study of Chicago Narcotics Officers, 54 U. CHI. L. REV. 1016, 1055 (1987). This study, based on interviews with twenty-six narcotics officers in the Chicago Police Department, was conducted while Orfield was still a law student. Seven years later when Orfield published his second empirical study, he reported that "many" of the judges, prosecutors and public defenders interviewed expressed the view "that to the extent a tort remedy would actually impose damages on police officers, it would cause the police to perjure themselves even more frequently [than they do now to thwart the impact of the exclusionary rule]." Orfield, supra note 50, at 126.
　　It strikes me that what Orfield has to say about tort actions applies to administrative sanctions as well. An officer is likely to be just as fearful about being dismissed or suspended (without pay) from the police force, or forced to pay a substantial fine, as he is about having to pay tort damages.

55. See California v. Minjares, 443 U.S. 916, 927 (1979) (Rehnquist, J., dissenting from denial of stay); Stone v. Powell, 428 U.S 465, 501 (1976) (Burger, C.J., concurring); Bivens v. Six Unknown Named Agents, 403 U.S. 388, 413 (1971) (Burger, C.J., dissenting); Amar, supra note 1, at 793-98; Stephen J. Markman, Six Observations on the Exclusionary Rule, 20 HARV. J.L. & PUB. POL'Y 425, 432-33 (1997).

56. See Calabresi, supra note 47, at 115.

57. LAFAVE, supra note 1, at 58.

58. See Thomas Y. Davies, A Hard Look at What We Know (and Still Need to Learn) About the "Costs" of the Exclusionary Rule: The NIJ Study and Other Studies of "Lost" Arrests, 1983 AM. B. FOUND. RES. J. 611, 640, 645. According to a five-year study of California data, illegal search and seizure problems were given as the reason for the rejection of only thirteen of more than 14,000 forcible rape arrests (0.09%) and only eight of approximately 12,000 homicide arrests (0.06%). See id. Another study, a three-state (Illinois, Michigan and Pennsylvania) study by Peter Nardulli involving some 7,500 cases, disclosed that none of the successful motions to exclude illegally seized evidence "involved exceptionally serious cases such as murder, rape, armed robbery, or even unarmed robbery." Peter F. Nardulli, The Societal Cost of the Exclusionary Rule: An Empirical Assessment, 1983 AM. B. FOUND. RES. J. 585, 596 n.47.

59. Davies, supra note 58, at 680. The California data reveals that less than 0.3% (fewer than three in 1,000) of arrests for all non-drug offenses are rejected by prosecutors because of illegal searches. Id. at 619. Davies estimates that "the cumulative loss of drug arrests at all stages of felony processing in California is around 7.1%." Id. at 681. In United States v. Leon, the Court, per Justice White, estimated that "the cumulative loss due to nonprosecution or nonconviction of individuals arrested on felony drug charges is probably in the range of 2.8% to 7.1%." 468 U.S. 897, 907 n.6 (1984). One may argue, as the Court did in Leon, that the small percentages of cases lost because of the exclusionary rule "mask a large absolute number." Id. at 907 n.6. As Davies has pointed out, however, "raw numbers are not as useful for policy evaluation as percentages. In a system as large as the American criminal justice system . . . almost any nationwide measurement or estimate will look large if expressed in raw numbers." Davies, supra note 58, at 670.

60. See Orfield, supra note 50, at 82, 85, 115.

61. Id. at 115.

62. Id. at 116.

63. See id. at 115-23.

64. See John Kaplan, The Limits of the Exclusionary Rule, 26 STAN. L. REV. 1027, 1046-49 (1974).

65. For extensive criticism of Professor Kaplan's proposal to limit the impact of the exclusionary rule see Yale Kamisar, "Comparative Reprehensibility" and the Fourth Amendment Exclusionary Rule, 86 MICH. L. REV. 1 (1987). But see Stuntz, supra note 1, at 447 ("[T]he visibility of the criminal who walks away [because of the exclusionary rule] . . . makes courts see the consequences of [their rulings and may be] . . . a way of limiting counter-majoritarian excess.").

66. See, e.g., Kyllo v. United States, 533 U.S. 27, 34 (2001) (holding that the use of a thermal imager or, more generally, any "sense-enhancing" technology to obtain "any information regarding the interior of the home that could not otherwise have been obtained without physical 'intrusion into a constitutionally protected area' constitutes a search—at least where (as here) the technology in question is not in general use") (citation omitted).

67. Albert W. Alschuler, Failed Pragmatism: Reflections on the Burger Court, 100 HARV. L. REV. 1436, 1442 (1987).

68. People v. Defore, 150 N.E. 585, 587 (N.Y. 1926).

69. A dozen cases should suffice. See, e.g., Pa. Bd. of Prob. & Parole v. Scott, 524 U.S. 357 (1998) (concluding that exclusionary rule does not apply to parole revocation hearings even when officer who conducted illegal search was aware of person's parole status); Whren v. United States, 517 U.S. 806 (1996) (ruling that police may stop a motorist where there are adequate grounds to believe that some traffic violation has occurred, even though the stop is pretextual); Illinois v. Rodriguez, 497 U.S. 177 (1990) (ruling that police may search dwelling house on "apparent authority" of a third party who lacks actual authority to consent); Mich. Dep't of State Police v. Sitz, 496 U.S. 444 (1990) (holding that in order to combat drunk driving, police may stop all motorists at sobriety checkpoints absent any individualized suspicion); Alabama v. White, 496 U.S. 325 (1990) (illustrating how little is needed to constitute "reasonable suspicion" to stop suspect's car and to question her); California v. Greenwood, 486 U.S. 35 (1988) (finding that police examination, for evidence of crime, of contents of opaque sealed plastic trash bags left for collection not a "search"); California v. Ciraolo, 476 U.S. 207 (1986) (holding that police aerial surveillance of a fenced-in backyard not a "search"); Illinois v. LaFayette, 462 U.S. 640 (1983) (finding that police may search through shoulder bag at stationhouse inventory of arrestee's effects, even though all the inventory objectives could be achieved "in a less intrusive manner"); Illinois v. Gates, 462 U.S. 213 (1983) (replacing existing probable cause structure with "totality-of-circumstances" test and stressing that probable cause is a "fluid concept" and that it requires only a "substantial chance of criminal activity"); Florida v. Royer, 460 U.S. 491 (1983) (stating in passing that certain police–citizen "encounters" or "contacts," such as asking a person at an airport to show her driver's license and airline ticket, were not a "seizure"); New York v. Belton, 453 U.S. 454 (1981) (finding that even though police lack any reason to believe that a car contains evidence of crime, if they have adequate grounds to make a custodial arrest of driver, they may search the entire interior of the car, including closed containers found in that area, even after the driver has been removed from the car and handcuffed); Schneckloth v. Bustamonte, 412 U.S. 218 (1973) (holding that suspect may effectively consent to an otherwise unlawful search even though he was never informed, and no evidence existed that he was ever aware, of his right to refuse officer's request).

70. See Calabresi, supra note 47, at 112. See also Slobogin, supra note 1 (arguing that the exclusionary rule is systemically harmful to Fourth Amendment values).

71. Paulsen, supra note 1, at 256.

72. U.S. v. Leon, 468 U.S. 897, 978 (1984) (Stevens, J., dissenting).

73. See Maclin, supra note 1, at 60 n.289.

74. See Jerome Hall, The Law of Arrest in Relation to Contemporary Social Problems, 3 U. CHI. L. REV. 345 (1936); William T. Plumb, Jr., Illegal Enforcement of the Law, 24 CORNELL L.Q. 337 (1939).

75. See Calabresi, supra note 47, at 114.

76. See id.

77. See id. at 116.

78. See id. at 116-17.

79. Judge Calabresi assures us that since, under his proposal, the legality of the police conduct would not be examined until the trial was over and the defendant convicted, the prosecutor would lack any incentive to charge more. See id. at 116. But every conscientious prosecutor would know at the outset, long before a post-trial hearing took place, whether or not the police acted illegally in the case, or, at the very least, whether or not there was a serious possibility that, at a post-trial hearing, one or more officers might be found to have acted illegally.

80. See generally Amsterdam, supra note 1, at 431-32; Phillip Johnson, New Approaches to Enforcing the Fourth Amendment 4 (Working Papers, Sept. 1978) (on file in the University of Michigan Law Library), quoted in YALE KAMISAR ET AL., MODERN CRIMINAL PROCEDURE 229-30 (5th ed. 1980) and cited in United States v. Leon, 468 U.S. 897, 916 n.14 (1984).

81. See Bivens v. Six Unknown Named Agents, 403 U.S. 388, 416-17 (Burger, C.J., dissenting).

82. See Orfield, supra note 50 and accompanying text.

83. Id. at 82. Those interviewed also believed that "police change their behavior in response to the suppression of evidence" and that the operation of the exclusionary rule "effectively educated officers in the law of search and seizure and that the law is not too complicated for police officers to do their jobs effectively." Id.

    For an earlier study by the same author of Chicago narcotics officers see the discussion in note 54, revealing that officers experience "personal disappointment at the loss of a potential conviction" and that "[t]he significant amount of time spent on these investigations, together with their danger and uncertainty, create a strong emotional commitment to conviction." Orfield, supra note 54, at 1042.

84. See Calabresi, supra note 47, at 116.

85. For an example of this line of thought, see Orfield, supra note 54, at 1053. See also Stuntz, supra note 1: [O]verdeterrence is a danger because the police have no strong incentive to undertake the marginal (legal) search or arrest. The result is that the usual legal tool—damages, fines, criminal punishment—are likely to cause more harm than good if they are widely used. If an officer faces serious loss whenever he makes a bad arrest, he will make fewer bad arrests, but also many fewer good ones. Id. at 445.

86. See Orfield, supra note 54, at 1051-54.

87. See supra notes 10-29. But see Milton A. Loewenthal, Evaluating the Exclusionary Rule in Search and Seizure, 49 UMKC L. REV. 24 (1980). This is, so far as I know, the most comprehensive study of police attitudes toward the exclusionary rule. Loewenthal, who taught police officer students at John Jay College of the City University of New York at the time, conducted many interviews with police commanders on all levels, as well as with the police officer students. He was also a participant–observer on forty tours of duty concerning various phases of police work. Professor Loewenthal found "strong evidence that, regardless of the effectiveness of direct sanctions, police officers could neither understand nor respect a

Court which purported to impose constitutional standards on the police without excluding evidence obtained in violation of those standards." Id. at 29. He also found that the police "have great difficulty believing that standards can have any real meaning if the government can profit from violating them," id. at 39, and that regardless of what substitute remedies may be provided, the police "are bound to view the elimination of the exclusionary rule as an indication that the fourth amendment is not a serious matter, if indeed it applies to them at all." Id. at 30. See also Orfield, supra note 50, at 128 ("None of the narcotics officers previously interviewed believed that the exclusionary rule should be abolished. Several officers said they appreciated the rule because it gave them a reason, within their peer group, to act properly. Some thought a 'good faith exception' would be appropriate."); Orfield, supra note 54, at 1051-52 (same).

88. Morgan Cloud, Judicial Review and the Exclusionary Rule, 26 PEPP. L. REV. 835, 838 (1999).

89. See id.

90. See supra notes 37-46 and accompanying text.

91. 468 U.S. 1032 (1984).

92. Id. at 1044.

93. Id. at 1044-45.

94. Id. at 1045.

95. Id. at 1054 (White, J., dissenting). Nor did the INS claim that any of the eleven officers terminated and any of the nine officers suspended in recent years for misconduct toward aliens had been disciplined for Fourth Amendment violations, and it appears that all the officers terminated "were terminated for rape or assault." Id. at 1055 n.2.

   One of the exclusionary rule's virtues is that "[c]laims are inexpensive to raise, and the facts on which they rest usually do not involve much independent digging by defense counsel." Stuntz, supra note 1, at 453. Moreover, the fact that the exclusionary rule is tied to criminal prosecutions "ensures that lots of claims are raised, which in turn allows courts to serve as reasonably good watchdogs for certain kinds of police misbehavior." Id. at 455.

96. Lopez-Mendoza, 468 U.S. at 1048.

97. Id. at 1049.

98. Id. at 1049-50. This led dissenting Justice White to say: Rather than constituting a rejection of the application of the exclusionary rule in civil deportation proceedings, however, [the majority's] argument amounts to a rejection of the application of the Fourth Amendment to the activities of INS agents. If the pandemonium attending immigration arrests is so great that violations of the Fourth Amendment cannot be ascertained for the purpose of applying the exclusionary rule, there is no reason to think that such violations can be ascertained for purposes of civil suits or internal disciplinary proceedings, both of which are proceedings that the majority suggests provide adequate deterrence against Fourth Amendment violations. Id. at 1059 (White, J., dissenting).

99. See supra note 31.

100. I have borrowed language from the lectures on search and seizure delivered
     by Justice Potter Stewart shortly after he stepped down from the Supreme
     Court. Stewart, supra note 1: "Taken together, the currently available alter-
     natives to the exclusionary rule . . . punish and perhaps deter the grossest
     of violations. . . . But they do little, if anything, to reduce the likelihood of
     the vast majority of fourth amendment violations—the frequent infringe-
     ments motivated by commendable zeal, not condemnable malice." Id. at
     1388-89. See also Cloud, supra note 88: "Remedies aimed directly at offi-
     cers who break the law . . . are rational methods for pursuing the goal of
     deterring misconduct. Undoubtedly, they are more likely to get the atten-
     tion of individual officers than is the suppression of evidence in criminal
     prosecutions. The problem, of course, is that no one seriously expects that
     those remedies will be rigorously enforced in any but the most egregious
     cases. This is true, in part, because enforcing those remedies is a task for
     other government actors, including police departments and prosecutors.
     It is not a task for judges. . . ." Id. at 853.

POSTSCRIPT

Should the States be Permitted to Abolish the Exclusionary Rule of Evidence in Criminal Cases?

The potential abolition of the exclusionary rule of evidence has been a controversial issue in the U.S. justice system. On one hand, the exclusionary rule prevents a judge or jury from considering highly credible evidence of a defendant's guilt. Proponents of the exclusionary rule in its present form believe, however, that it is needed to guarantee the legitimacy of the justice system itself. From this perspective, it is never acceptable for the police to break the law in order to enforce it.

The introduction to this issue asked you to think about a possible middle ground between the positions advocated by Professors Akhil Reed Amar and Yale Kamisar. Over the years, scholars and justice system practitioners have proposed a variety of alternatives to the exclusionary rule in its present form.

One such alternative has been described as "the Former British Model." Under this system, illegally obtained evidence could be used at trial. However, the police officers who obtained the illegal evidence were subject to internal departmental discipline. More recently, British law has been changed to give judges the discretion to refuse to admit illegally obtained evidence.

A second alternative to the exclusionary rule is civil tort lawsuits against the police. In theory, a person who is victimized by an illegal search and seizure could sue the police officer for monetary damages. Most experienced attorneys would reject this alternative, however, because in practice it is very difficult to successfully sue police officers.

A third alternative that has been suggested is the use of civilian review panels composed of citizens who examine alleged instances of police misconduct. Such panels have proved unpopular with police agencies, however, because many officers believe that panel members have unrealistic expectations for the police.

Do you believe that any of the alternatives considered above would constitute a reasonable alternative to the exclusionary rule of evidence? Can you think of another alternative? Do you agree with Professor Amar or Professor Kamisar's position on these issues?

Since the Supreme Court decided *Mapp v. Ohio* in 1961, a number of more recent cases have restricted the scope of the rule's protections for criminal defendants. In the final analysis, the Court may have settled on the best approach of all—maintain the rule in its present form, but restrict its application in cases when the police are acting in good faith.

Fortunately, there are a large number of excellent resources that can shed additional light on these issues. See: Rolando V. del Carmen, *Criminal Procedure,* 6th ed. (Wadsworth, 2004); Yale Kamisar, Wayne R. LaFave, Jerold H. Israel, and Nancy J. King, *Modern Criminal Procedure,* 11th ed. (West, 2005); Thomas J. Hickey, *Criminal Procedure* (McGraw-Hill, 2001); and George F. Cole and Christopher E. Smith, *Introduction to Criminal Justice,* 10th ed. (Wadsworth, 2004).

See, as well, the following articles: Raymond A. Atkins and Paul H. Rubin, "Effects of Criminal Procedure on Crime Rates: Mapping out the Consequences of the Exclusionary Rule," *Journal of Law and Economics,* vol. 46 no. 1 (2003); American Bar Association Special Committee on Criminal Justice in a Free Society, "Criminal Justice in Crisis," vol. 21, no. 844 (1988); Donald Dripps, "The Case for the Contingent Exclusionary Rule," *The American Criminal Law Review,* vol. 38, no. 1 (2001); Jeffrey Standen, "The Exclusionary Rule and Damages: An Economic Comparison of Private Remedies for Unconstitutional Police Conduct," *Brigham Young University Law Review,* vol. 2000, no. 4 (2000); L. Timothy Perrin, H. Mitchell Caldwell, and Carol A. Chase, "If It's Broken, Fix It: Moving Beyond the Exclusionary Rule," *Search & Seizure Law Report,* vol. 26, no. 7 (1999); Evan Osborne, "Is the Exclusionary Rule Worthwhile?" *Contemporary Economic Policy,* vol. 17, no. 3 (1999); Stephen J. Markman, "Six Observations on the Exclusionary Rule," *Harvard Journal of Law and Public Policy,* vol. 20, no. 2 (1997); Heather A. Jackson, "Arizona v. Evans: Expanding Exclusionary Rule Exceptions and Contracting Fourth Amendment Protection," *Journal of Criminal Law & Criminology,* vol. 86, no. 4 (1996); James J. Fyfe, "Stops, Frisks, Searches, and the Constitution," *Criminology & Public Policy,* vol. 3, no. 3 (2004); Zack Bray, "Appellate Review and the Exclusionary Rule," *The Yale Law Journal,* vol. 113, no. 5 (2004); and Marvin Zalman and Elsa Shartsis, "A Roadblock too Far? Justice O'Connor's Left Turn on the Fourth," *Journal of Contemporary Criminal Justice,* vol. 19, no. 2 (2003).

Internet References . . .

Academy of Criminal Justice Sciences

This Web site is an excellent resource for a wide variety of information about the U.S. justice system. It provides links to a number of resources that consider various aspects of justice system processes, including the police, the courts, punishment, and corrections.

http://www.acjs.org/

American Civil Liberties Unions (ACLU)

The ACLU is an organization dedicated to protecting Americans' constitutional freedoms.

http://www.aclu.org/

American Correctional Association (ACA)

The ACA is the oldest and largest international correctional association in the world. ACA serves all disciplines within the corrections profession and is dedicated to excellence in every aspect of the field.

http://www.aca.org/

National Criminal Justice Reference Service (NCJRS)

This very comprehensive database provides a wealth of information about justice system processes. Topics include corrections, courts, crime prevention, crime rates, drugs, the criminal justice system, juvenile justice, law enforcement, and the victims of crime. It also provides links to NCJRS-sponsored research on virtually every aspect of the criminal justice system.

http://www.ncjrs.org/

Privacy and Civil Liberties

*S*ome *of the more fascinating issues in U.S. constitutional law have developed in the area of individual privacy and civil liberties. A central issue revolves around the fact that the Constitution's text does not expressly mention a right to privacy, which leads logically to the question of whether other provisions in the Bill of Rights may imply privacy rights. Moreover, this section focuses on the Supreme Court's interpretation of provisions in the Bill of Rights that form the foundation for constitutional protections in the United States.*

- Does the Bill of Rights to the U.S. Constitution Guarantee a Right to Privacy?

- Does a Constitutional Right to Privacy Protect a Woman's Right to Obtain a Lawful Abortion?

- Does a Constitutional Right to Privacy Protect the Rights of Homosexual Couples to Engage in Intimate Personal Relationships?

- Does the Constitution Protect the Right to Possess a Firearm Unconnected With Service in a Militia?

- Does Confining Sex Offenders Indefinitely in Mental Hospitals After They Have Served Their Prison Sentences Violate the Constitution?

- Is the Death Penalty an Unconstitutional Punishment for Juvenile Offenders?

ISSUE 9

Does the Bill of Rights to the U.S. Constitution Guarantee a Right to Privacy?

YES: William O. Douglas, from *Griswold v. Connecticut*, 381 U.S. 479 (1965)

NO: Hugo L. Black, from *Griswold v. Connecticut*, 381 U.S. 479 (1965)

ISSUE SUMMARY

YES: Justice William O. Douglas asserted that the Constitution has rights that emanate from certain amendments that form a "penumbra," which provides a right to privacy protected from governmental interference.

NO: Justice Hugo L. Black, in contrast, asserted that a constitutional right to privacy is not found in any explicit provision in the Bill of Rights. Therefore, he would vote to uphold the Connecticut law prohibiting contraceptives.

Americans enjoy their privacy. Most people realize, however, that personal privacy may under some circumstances be limited by the government for good cause. For example, if there were evidence that a fire was burning your home, police officers would be justified in coming onto your property to try to warn you of the potential danger. Likewise, even in the privacy of your own home, federal and state laws prohibit the possession of pornographic images depicting children. In these instances, society has made a judgment that intrusion on your privacy is less important than other significant social interests.

There are a few different ways to look at privacy in the legal sense that focus on *due process* of law. The due process clauses are found in the Fifth and Fourteenth Amendments to the U.S. Constitution. The Fifth Amendment Due Process Clause provides that no person shall "be deprived of life, liberty, or property, without due process of law." As you may already know, the Fifth Amendment's guarantee applies this standard to the federal government. The Fourteenth Amendment provides that *no state* shall "deprive any person of life, liberty, or property, without due process of law." Taking the term "due process" literally, it would appear to imply that the authorities must grant process or procedures to persons in danger of having their life, liberty, or property taken from them by the government. This could become an issue in a criminal case, which could result in the death penalty, imprisonment, or a fine. Likewise, if the government were to initiate a civil proceeding against someone to confiscate their property for nonpayment of taxes, or to terminate their welfare benefits, the due process clauses would apply as well.

The vast majority of the due process issues the U.S. Supreme Court has considered throughout our nation's history have involved cases like those discussed above. Such cases, which involve *procedural due process*, ask whether governmental authorities have followed the proper procedures when they have tried to take away someone's life, liberty, or property.

For example, *Mapp v. Ohio*, 367 U.S. 643 (1961), which has been discussed extensively in the last issue, presented the question of whether the exclusionary rule of evidence should be applied to state proceedings through the Fourteenth Amendment's Due Process Clause. Likewise, in another widely known case, *Miranda v. Arizona*, 384 U.S. 436 (1966), the Supreme Court held that defendants undergoing custodial interrogation by the police during state criminal proceedings must be advised of their right to remain silent and their right to counsel. These cases present clearly procedural due process issues that were resolved by the Supreme Court in a rights-expansive way.

Procedural due process is not the only way to look at the issue, however. On several different occasions throughout our history, the Supreme Court has held that the Fourteenth Amendment's Due Process Clause also limits the substance of state regulation. The *substantive due process* doctrine asserts that state governments may not pass legislation that interferes improperly with an individual's liberty or privacy. In other words, someone using the substantive due process doctrine to challenge a state law would assert that the legislature had gone too far and intruded into an area of life that the state has no right to regulate.

A person challenging the law would assert that the state's law has violated a "fundamental" constitutional right. If the Supreme Court finds that the purported constitutional right is a fundamental one, it will use an analytical device termed *strict scrutiny* to review the law. This requires the state to demonstrate a "compelling interest" that supports the statute. The state too must show that there is almost no better way to accomplish its objective than the one the statute has adopted.

In contrast, if the Supreme Court decides that an asserted constitutional right is not a fundamental one, it will use a much more deferential standard of review to analyze the state law. This is termed *rationality review*. To survive rationality review a state needs only to demonstrate that it has a legitimate interest supported by the challenged law and that it is a rational way of accomplishing its objective.

When the Court uses strict scrutiny analysis to review a state law, it is almost always declared unconstitutional. Such cases are far less common than those presenting procedural due process issues. When they do arise they normally present highly important and contentious constitutional issues.

One of the most famous early cases to use the substantive due process doctrine to strike down a state law was *Lochner v. New York*, 198 U.S. 45 (1905). The state of New York had passed a labor law that regulated working conditions and limited the number of hours that bakers could work. This was because the New York legislature had determined that baking was a relatively hazardous occupation that often had an adverse impact on bakers' health.

The U.S. Supreme Court held that New York's law violated the rights of bakers and their employers to "liberty of contract," which was a fundamental constitutional right. It therefore violated the Due Process Clause. The Court concluded that "it is not possible in fact to discover the connection between the number of hours a baker may work in the bakery and the healthful quality of the bread" that was produced. In one of the most famous dissenting opinions in U.S. Supreme Court history, Justice Oliver Wendell Holmes asserted that the Court had exceeded its authority by imposing its views of proper social policy on the state legislature. In other words, the Court's majority had substituted their personal views for the judgment of the legislature on the issue of labor conditions in the baking industry.

Justice Holmes' opinion illustrates one of the most important criticisms of the substantive due process doctrine: Opponents of Supreme Court decisions that use this doctrine to strike down state legislation argue that substantive due process merely substitutes the personal views of a majority of the Court for the decision of a state's legislature. They would further argue that such an improper use of the power of judicial review is a clear violation of the separation of powers.

Moreover, opponents of substantive due process believe that it creates an inherently unstable body of constitutional law because conceptions of the types of conduct that are "private," and outside state regulatory power, change over time. For example, in *Lochner*, the Supreme Court used the substantive due process doctrine to strike down a state's labor law. Thus, in 1905, "freedom of contract" was considered a "private" matter and a fundamental right that a state's legislature had no power to control. In 2010, state and federal laws that regulate almost every aspect of the employment process, workplace conditions, and the economy are commonplace and are considered important matters of social concern. Moreover, state laws that regulate such economic matters are almost certain to be upheld by modern courts.

More recently, the Supreme Court has used the substantive due process doctrine to strike down state legislation that intrudes into areas of fundamental individual rights. In contrast to the *Lochner*-era philosophy that economic rights were private and therefore not subject to legislative control, more modern Supreme Court cases emphasize self-direction as matters within a private realm withdrawn from state legislative direction.

In *Griswold v. Connecticut*, 381 U.S. 479 (1965), the Supreme Court was asked to review the constitutionality of a Connecticut statute that provided: "Any person who uses any drug, medicinal article or instrument for the purpose of preventing conception shall be fined not less than fifty dollars or imprisoned not less than sixty days nor more than one year or be both fined and imprisoned." It continued: "Any person who assists, abets, counsels, hires or commands another to commit any offense may be prosecuted and punished as if he were the principal offender." Appellant Griswold was the Executive Director of the Planned Parenthood League of Connecticut. Appellant Buxton was a licensed physician and a professor at the Yale Medical School who served as Medical Director for the League. They gave information, instruction, and medical advice to married persons as to how to prevent conception. Griswold and Buxton were found guilty as accessories and fined $100 each. On appeal to the Supreme Court, they claimed the statute at issue violated the Fourteenth Amendment's Due Process Clause.

Justice William O. Douglas held that "the First Amendment has a penumbra where privacy is protected from governmental intrusion." He therefore held that the state law invaded an area of "protected freedoms," and was unconstitutional. Justice Douglas concluded:

> We deal with a right of privacy older than the Bill of Rights—older than our political parties, older than our school system. Marriage is a coming together for better or for worse, hopefully enduring, and intimate to the degree of being sacred. It is an association that promotes a way of life, not causes; a harmony in living, not political faiths; a bilateral loyalty, not commercial or social projects. Yet it is an association for as noble a purpose as any involved in our prior decisions.

Justice Hugo L. Black, dissenting, had a very different perspective on the issues presented in this case, however. Stated Justice Black:

> I get nowhere in this case by talk about a constitutional right of 'privacy' as an emanation from one or more constitutional provisions. I like my privacy as well as the next one, but I am nevertheless compelled to admit that government has a right to invade it unless prohibited by some specific constitutional provision.

Thus, Justice Black would have voted to affirm the law and defer to the judgment of the Connecticut legislature.

In Your Opinion . . .

- Do you feel that Justice Douglas or Justice Black states the better position on using the substantive due process doctrine to strike down the Connecticut statute that prohibited medical professionals from giving advice to married persons as to the means for preventing conception?
- What about the broader issue of the substantive due process doctrine?
- Is it thinly veiled means for judges to substitute their views of proper social policy for those of state legislatures, or a proper exercise of the power of judicial review?
- Do you feel that the Supreme Court should have used strict scrutiny, or rationality review, to analyze the Connecticut law?

YES

William O. Douglas

Griswold v. Connecticut

MR. JUSTICE DOUGLAS delivered the opinion of the Court.

Appellant Griswold is Executive Director of the Planned Parenthood League of Connecticut. Appellant Buxton is a licensed physician and a professor at the Yale Medical School who served as Medical Director for the League at its Center in New Haven—a center open and operating from November 1 to November 10, 1961, when appellants were arrested.

They gave information, instruction, and medical advice to *married persons* as to the means of preventing conception. They examined the wife and prescribed the best contraceptive device or material for her use. Fees were usually charged, although some couples were serviced free.

The statutes whose constitutionality is involved in this appeal are §§ 53-32 and 54-196 of the General Statutes of Connecticut (1958 rev.). The former provides:

> Any person who uses any drug, medicinal article or instrument for the purpose of preventing conception shall be fined not less than fifty dollars or imprisoned not less than sixty days nor more than one year or be both fined and imprisoned.

Section 54-196 provides:

> Any person who assists, abets, counsels, causes, hires or commands another to commit any offense may be prosecuted and punished as if he were the principal offender.

The appellants were found guilty as accessories and fined $100 each, against the claim that the accessory statute, as so applied, violated the Fourteenth Amendment. The Appellate Division of the Circuit Court affirmed. The Supreme Court of Errors affirmed that judgment. 151 Conn. 544, 200 A.2d 479. We noted probable jurisdiction. 379 U.S. 926.

We think that appellants have standing to raise the constitutional rights of the married people with whom they had a professional relationship. *Tileston v. Ullman,* 318 U.S. 44, is different, for there the plaintiff seeking to represent others asked for a declaratory judgment. In that situation, we thought that the requirements of standing should be strict, lest the standards of "case or controversy" in Article III of the Constitution become blurred. Here, those doubts are removed by reason of a criminal conviction for serving married

Supreme Court of the United States, 1965.

couples in violation of an aiding-and-abetting statute. Certainly the accessory should have standing to assert that the offense which he is charged with assisting is not, or cannot constitutionally be, a crime.

This case is more akin to *Truax v. Raich,* 239 U.S. 33, where an employee was permitted to assert the rights of his employer; to *Pierce v. Society of Sisters,* 268 U.S. 510, where the owners of private schools were entitled to assert the rights of potential pupils and their parents; and to *Barrows v. Jackson,* 346 U.S. 249, where a white defendant, party to a racially restrictive covenant, who was being sued for damages by the covenantors because she had conveyed her property to Negroes, was allowed to raise the issue that enforcement of the covenant violated the rights of prospective Negro purchasers to equal protection, although no Negro was a party to the suit. *And see Meyer v. Nebraska,* 262 U.S. 390; *Adler v. Board of Education,* 342 U.S. 485; *NAACP v. Alabama,* 357 U.S. 449; *NAACP v. Button,* 371 U.S. 415. The rights of husband and wife, pressed here, are likely to be diluted or adversely affected unless those rights are considered in a suit involving those who have this kind of confidential relation to them.

Coming to the merits, we are met with a wide range of questions that implicate the Due Process Clause of the Fourteenth Amendment. Overtones of some arguments suggest that *Lochner v. New York,* 198 U.S. 45, should be our guide. But we decline that invitation, as we did in *West Coast Hotel Co. v. Parrish,* 300 U.S. 379; *Olsen v. Nebraska,* 313 U.S. 236; *Lincoln Union v. Northwestern Co.,* 335 U.S. 525; *Williamson v. Lee Optical Co.,* 348 U.S. 483; *Giboney v. Empire Storage Co.,* 336 U.S. 490. We do not sit as a super-legislature to determine the wisdom, need, and propriety of laws that touch economic problems, business affairs, or social conditions. This law, however, operates directly on an intimate relation of husband and wife and their physician's role in one aspect of that relation.

The association of people is not mentioned in the Constitution nor in the Bill of Rights. The right to educate a child in a school of the parents' choice—whether public or private or parochial—is also not mentioned. Nor is the right to study any particular subject or any foreign language. Yet the First Amendment has been construed to include certain of those rights.

By *Pierce v. Society of Sisters, supra,* the right to educate one's children as one chooses is made applicable to the States by the force of the First and Fourteenth Amendments. By *Meyer v. Nebraska, supra,* the same dignity is given the right to study the German language in a private school. In other words, the State may not, consistently with the spirit of the First Amendment, contract the spectrum of available knowledge. The right of freedom of speech and press includes not only the right to utter or to print, but the right to distribute, the right to receive, the right to read (*Martin v. Struthers,* 319 U.S. 141, 143) and freedom of inquiry, freedom of thought, and freedom to teach (*see Wiemann v. Updegraff,* 344 U.S. 183, 195)—indeed, the freedom of the entire university community. *Sweezy v. New Hampshire,* 354 U.S. 234, 249–250, 261–263; *Barenblatt v. United States,* 360 U.S. 109, 112; *Baggett v. Bullitt,* 377 U.S. 360, 369. Without those peripheral rights, the specific rights would be less secure. And so we reaffirm the principle of the *Pierce* and the *Meyer* cases.

In *NAACP v. Alabama,* 357 U.S. 449, 462 we protected the "freedom to associate and privacy in one's associations," noting that freedom of association was a peripheral First Amendment right. Disclosure of membership lists of a constitutionally valid association, we held, was invalid

> as entailing the likelihood of a substantial restraint upon the exercise by petitioner's members of their right to freedom of association.

Ibid. In other words, the First Amendment has a penumbra where privacy is protected from governmental intrusion. In like context, we have protected forms of "association" that are not political in the customary sense, but pertain to the social, legal, and economic benefit of the members. *NAACP v. Button,* 371 U.S. 415, 430–431. In *Schware v. Board of Bar Examiners,* 353 U.S. 232, we held it not permissible to bar a lawyer from practice because he had once been a member of the Communist Party. The man's "association with that Party" was not shown to be "anything more than a political faith in a political party" (*id.* at 244), and was not action of a kind proving bad moral character. *Id.* at 245–246.

Those cases involved more than the "right of assembly"—a right that extends to all, irrespective of their race or ideology. *De Jonge v. Oregon,* 299 U.S. 353. The right of "association," like the right of belief (*Board of Education v. Barnette,* 319 U.S. 624), is more than the right to attend a meeting; it includes the right to express one's attitudes or philosophies by membership in a group or by affiliation with it or by other lawful means. Association in that context is a form of expression of opinion, and, while it is not expressly included in the First Amendment, its existence is necessary in making the express guarantees fully meaningful.

The foregoing cases suggest that specific guarantees in the Bill of Rights have penumbras, formed by emanations from those guarantees that help give them life and substance. *See Poe v. Ullman,* 367 U.S. 497, 516–522 (dissenting opinion). Various guarantees create zones of privacy. The right of association contained in the penumbra of the First Amendment is one, as we have seen. The Third Amendment, in its prohibition against the quartering of soldiers "in any house" in time of peace without the consent of the owner, is another facet of that privacy. The Fourth Amendment explicitly affirms the "right of the people to be secure in their persons, houses, papers, and effects, against unreasonable searches and seizures." The Fifth Amendment, in its Self-Incrimination Clause, enables the citizen to create a zone of privacy which government may not force him to surrender to his detriment. The Ninth Amendment provides: "The enumeration in the Constitution, of certain rights, shall not be construed to deny or disparage others retained by the people."

The Fourth and Fifth Amendments were described in *Boyd v. United States,* 116 U.S. 616, 630, as protection against all governmental invasions "of the sanctity of a man's home and the privacies of life."[1] We recently referred in *Mapp v. Ohio,* 367 U.S. 643, 656, to the Fourth Amendment as creating a "right to privacy, no less important than any other right carefully an particularly reserved to the people." *See* Beaney, The Constitutional Right to Privacy, 1962 *Sup. Ct. Rev.* 212; Griswold, The Right to be Let Alone, 55 *Nw. U.L. Rev.* 216 (1960).

We have had many controversies over these penumbral rights of "privacy and repose." *See, e.g., Breard v. Alexandria,* 341 U.S. 622, 626, 644; *Public Utilities*

Commvn v. Pollak, 343 U.S. 451; *Monroe v. Pape,* 365 U.S. 167; *Lanza v. New York,* 370 U.S. 139; *Frank v. Maryland,* 359 U.S. 360; *Skinner v. Oklahoma,* 316 U.S. 535, 541. These cases bear witness that the right of privacy which presses for recognition here is a legitimate one.

The present case, then, concerns a relationship lying within the zone of privacy created by several fundamental constitutional guarantees. And it concerns a law which, in forbidding the use of contraceptives, rather than regulating their manufacture or sale, seeks to achieve its goals by means having a maximum destructive impact upon that relationship. Such a law cannot stand in light of the familiar principle, so often applied by this Court, that a

> governmental purpose to control or prevent activities constitutionally subject to state regulation may not be achieved by means which sweep unnecessarily broadly and thereby invade the area of protected freedoms.

NAACP v. Alabama, 377 U.S. 288, 307. Would we allow the police to search the sacred precincts of marital bedrooms for telltale signs of the use of contraceptives? The very idea is repulsive to the notions of privacy surrounding the marriage relationship.

We deal with a right of privacy older than the Bill of Rights—older than our political parties, older than our school system. Marriage is a coming together for better or for worse, hopefully enduring, and intimate to the degree of being sacred. It is an association that promotes a way of life, not causes; a harmony in living, not political faiths; a bilateral loyalty, not commercial or social projects. Yet it is an association for as noble a purpose as any involved in our prior decisions.

Reversed.

Notes

1. The Court said in full about this right of privacy:

> The principles laid down in this opinion [by Lord Camden in *Entick v. Carrington,* 19 How.St.Tr. 1029] affect the very essence of constitutional liberty and security. They reach farther than the concrete form of the case then before the court, with its adventitious circumstances; they apply to all invasions on the part of the government and its employes of the sanctity of a man's home and the privacies of life. It is not the breaking of his doors, and the rummaging of his drawers, that constitutes the essence of the offence; but it is the invasion of his indefeasible right of personal security, personal liberty and private property, where that right has never been forfeited by his conviction of some public offence—it is the invasion of this sacred right which underlies and constitutes the essence of Lord Camden's judgment. Breaking into a house and opening boxes and drawers are circumstances of aggravation; but any forcible and compulsory extortion of a man's own testimony or of his private papers to be used as evidence to convict him of crime or to forfeit his goods is within the condemnation of that judgment. In this regard, the Fourth and Fifth Amendments run almost into each other.

116 U.S. at 630.

 **NO**

Griswold v. Connecticut

$\mathbf{M}$R. JUSTICE BLACK, with whom MR. JUSTICE STEWART joins, dissenting.

I agree with my Brother STEWART's dissenting opinion. And, like him, I do not to any extent whatever base my view that this Connecticut law is constitutional on a belief that the law is wise, or that its policy is a good one. In order that there may be no room at all to doubt why I vote as I do, I feel constrained to add that the law is every bit as offensive to me as it is to my Brethren of the majority and my Brothers HARLAN, WHITE and GOLDBERG, who, reciting reasons why it is offensive to them, hold it unconstitutional. There is no single one of the graphic and eloquent strictures and criticisms fired at the policy of this Connecticut law either by the Court's opinion or by those of my concurring Brethren to which I cannot subscribe—except their conclusion that the evil qualities they see in the law make it unconstitutional.

Had the doctor defendant here, or even the nondoctor defendant, been convicted for doing nothing more than expressing opinions to persons coming to the clinic that certain contraceptive devices, medicines or practices would do them good and would be desirable, or for telling people how devices could be used, I can think of no reasons at this time why their expressions of views would not be protected by the First and Fourteenth Amendments, which guarantee freedom of speech. *Cf. Brotherhood of Railroad Trainmen v. Virginia ex rel. Virginia State Bar*, 377 U.S. 1; *NAACP v. Button*, 371 U.S. 415. But speech is one thing; conduct and physical activities are quite another. *See, e.g., Cox v. Louisiana*, 379 U.S. 536, 554–555; *Cox v. Louisiana*, 379 U.S. 559, 563–564; *id.* 575–584 (concurring opinion); *Giboney v. Empire Storage & Ice Co.*, 336 U.S. 490; *cf. Reynolds v. United States*, 98 U.S. 145, 163–164. The two defendants here were active participants in an organization which gave physical examinations to women, advised them what kind of contraceptive devices or medicines would most likely be satisfactory for them, and then supplied the devices themselves, all for a graduated scale of fees, based on the family income. Thus, these defendants admittedly engaged with others in a planned course of conduct to help people violate the Connecticut law. Merely because some speech was used in carrying on that conduct—just as, in ordinary life, some speech accompanies most kinds of conduct—we are not, in my view, justified in holding that the First Amendment forbids the State to punish their conduct. Strongly as I desire to protect all First Amendment freedoms, I am unable to stretch the Amendment so as to afford protection to the conduct of

Supreme Court of the United States, 1965.

these defendants in violating the Connecticut law. What would be the constitutional fate of the law if hereafter applied to punish nothing but speech is, as I have said, quite another matter. The Court talks about a constitutional "right of privacy" as though there is some constitutional provision or provisions forbidding any law ever to be passed which might abridge the "privacy" of individuals. But there is not. There are, of course, guarantees in certain specific constitutional provisions which are designed in part to protect privacy at certain times and places with respect to certain activities. Such, for example, is the Fourth Amendment's guarantee against "unreasonable searches and seizures." But I think it belittles that Amendment to talk about it as though it protects nothing but "privacy." To treat it that way is to give it a niggardly interpretation, not the kind of liberal reading I think any Bill of Rights provision should be given. The average man would very likely not have his feelings soothed any more by having his property seized openly than by having it seized privately and by stealth. He simply wants his property left alone. And a person can be just as much, if not more, irritated, annoyed and injured by an unceremonious public arrest by a policeman as he is by a seizure in the privacy of his office or home.

One of the most effective ways of diluting or expanding a constitutionally guaranteed right is to substitute for the crucial word or words of a constitutional guarantee another word or words, more or less flexible and more or less restricted in meaning. This fact is well illustrated by the use of the term "right of privacy" as a comprehensive substitute for the Fourth Amendment's guarantee against "unreasonable searches and seizures." "Privacy" is a broad, abstract and ambiguous concept which can easily be shrunken in meaning but which can also, on the other hand, easily be interpreted as a constitutional ban against many things other than searches and seizures. I have expressed the view many times that First Amendment freedoms, for example, have suffered from a failure of the courts to stick to the simple language of the First Amendment in construing it, instead of invoking multitudes of words substituted for those the Framers used. *See, e.g., New York Times Co. v. Sullivan,* 376 U.S. 254, 293 (concurring opinion); cases collected in *City of El Paso v. Simmons,* 379 U.S. 497, 517, n. 1 (dissenting opinion); Black, The Bill of Rights, 35 N.Y.U.L.Rev. 865. For these reasons, I get nowhere in this case by talk about a constitutional "right of privacy" as an emanation from one or more constitutional provisions. I like my privacy as well as the next one, but I am nevertheless compelled to admit that government has a right to invade it unless prohibited by some specific constitutional provision. For these reasons, I cannot agree with the Court's judgment and the reasons it gives for holding this Connecticut law unconstitutional.

This brings me to the arguments made by my Brothers HARLAN, WHITE and GOLDBERG for invalidating the Connecticut law. Brothers HARLAN and WHITE would invalidate it by reliance on the Due Process Clause of the Fourteenth Amendment, but Brother GOLDBERG, while agreeing with Brother HARLAN, relies also on the Ninth Amendment. I have no doubt that the Connecticut law could be applied in such a way as to abridge freedom of speech and press, and therefore violate the First and Fourteenth Amendments.

My disagreement with the Court's opinion holding that there is such a violation here is a narrow one, relating to the application of the First Amendment to the facts and circumstances of this particular case. But my disagreement with Brothers HARLAN, WHITE and GOLDBERG is more basic. I think that, if properly construed, neither the Due Process Clause nor the Ninth Amendment, nor both together, could under any circumstances be a proper basis for invalidating the Connecticut law. I discuss the due process and Ninth Amendment arguments together because, on analysis, they turn out to be the same thing—merely using different words to claim for this Court and the federal judiciary power to invalidate any legislative act which the judges find irrational, unreasonable or offensive.

The due process argument which my Brothers HARLAN and WHITE adopt here is based, as their opinions indicate, on the premise that this Court is vested with power to invalidate all state laws that it considers to be arbitrary, capricious, unreasonable, or oppressive, or on this Court's belief that a particular state law under scrutiny has no "rational or justifying" purpose, or is offensive to a "sense of fairness and justice." If these formulas based on "natural justice," or others which mean the same thing, are to prevail, they require judges to determine what is or is not constitutional on the basis of their own appraisal of what laws are unwise or unnecessary. The power to make such decisions is, of course, that of a legislative body. Surely it has to be admitted that no provision of the Constitution specifically gives such blanket power to courts to exercise such a supervisory veto over the wisdom and value of legislative policies and to hold unconstitutional those laws which they believe unwise or dangerous. I readily admit that no legislative body, state or national, should pass laws that can justly be given any of the invidious labels invoked as constitutional excuses to strike down state laws. But perhaps it is not too much to say that no legislative body ever does pass laws without believing that they will accomplish a sane, rational, wise and justifiable purpose. While I completely subscribe to the holding of *Marbury v. Madison,* 1 Cranch 137, and subsequent cases, that our Court has constitutional power to strike down statutes, state or federal, that violate commands of the Federal Constitution, I do not believe that we are granted power by the Due Process Clause or any other constitutional provision or provisions to measure constitutionality by our belief that legislation is arbitrary, capricious or unreasonable, or accomplishes no justifiable purpose, or is offensive to our own notions of "civilized standards of conduct." Such an appraisal of the wisdom of legislation is an attribute of the power to make laws, not of the power to interpret them. The use by federal courts of such a formula or doctrine or whatnot to veto federal or state laws simply takes away from Congress and States the power to make laws based on their own judgment of fairness and wisdom, and transfers that power to this Court for ultimate determination—a power which was specifically denied to federal courts by the convention that framed the Constitution.

My Brother GOLDBERG has adopted the recent discovery that the Ninth Amendment as well as the Due Process Clause can be used by this Court as authority to strike down all state legislation which this Court thinks violates "fundamental principles of liberty and justice," or is contrary to the "traditions and [collective] conscience of our people." He also states, without proof satisfactory to me, that, in making decisions on this basis, judges will not consider "their personal and private notions." One may ask how they can avoid considering them. Our Court certainly has no machinery with which to take a Gallup Poll. And the scientific miracles of this age have not yet produced a gadget which the Court can use to determine what traditions are rooted in the "[collective] conscience of our people." Moreover, one would certainly have to look far beyond the language of the Ninth Amendment to find that the Framers vested in this Court any such awesome veto powers over lawmaking, either by the States or by the Congress. Nor does anything in the history of the Amendment offer any support for such a shocking doctrine. The whole history of the adoption of the Constitution and Bill of Rights points the other way, and the very material quoted by my Brother GOLDBERG shows that the Ninth Amendment was intended to protect against the idea that, "by enumerating particular exceptions to the grant of power" to the Federal Government, "those rights which were not singled out were intended to be assigned into the hands of the General Government [the United States], and were consequently insecure." That Amendment was passed not to broaden the powers of this Court or any other department of "the General Government," but, as every student of history knows, to assure the people that the Constitution in all its provisions was intended to limit the Federal Government to the powers granted expressly or by necessary implication. If any broad, unlimited power to hold laws unconstitutional because they offend what this Court conceives to be the "[collective] conscience of our people" is vested in this Court by the Ninth Amendment, the Fourteenth Amendment, or any other provision of the Constitution, it was not given by the Framers, but rather has been bestowed on the Court by the Court. This fact is perhaps responsible for the peculiar phenomenon that, for a period of a century and a half, no serious suggestion was ever made that the Ninth Amendment, enacted to protect state powers against federal invasion, could be used as a weapon of federal power to prevent state legislatures from passing laws they consider appropriate to govern local affairs. Use of any such broad, unbounded judicial authority would make of this Court's members a day-to-day constitutional convention.

I repeat, so as not to be misunderstood, that this Court does have power, which it should exercise, to hold laws unconstitutional where they are forbidden by the Federal Constitution. My point is that there is no provision of the Constitution which either expressly or impliedly vests power in this Court to sit as a supervisory agency over acts of duly constituted legislative bodies and set aside their laws because of the Court's belief that the legislative policies adopted are unreasonable, unwise, arbitrary, capricious or irrational. The adoption of such a loose, flexible, uncontrolled standard for holding laws unconstitutional, if ever it is finally achieved, will amount to a great unconstitutional shift of power to the courts which I believe and am constrained to say will be bad for the courts, and worse for the country. Subjecting federal and state laws to such an unrestrained and unrestrainable judicial control as to the wisdom of legislative enactments would, I fear, jeopardize the separation of governmental powers that the Framers set up, and, at the same time, threaten to take away much of the power of States to govern themselves which the Constitution plainly intended them to have.

I realize that many good and able men have eloquently spoken and written, sometimes in rhapsodical strains, about the duty of this Court to keep the Constitution in tune with the times. The idea is that the Constitution must be changed from time to time, and that this Court is charged with a duty to make those changes. For myself, I must, with all deference, reject that philosophy. The Constitution makers knew the need for change, and provided for it. Amendments suggested by the people's elected representatives can be submitted to the people or their selected agents for ratification. That method of change was good for our Fathers, and, being somewhat old-fashioned, I must add it is good enough for me. And so I cannot rely on the Due Process Clause or the Ninth Amendment or any mysterious and uncertain natural law concept as a reason for striking down this state law. The Due Process Clause, with an "arbitrary and capricious" or "shocking to the conscience" formula, was liberally used by this Court to strike down economic legislation in the early decades of this century, threatening, many people thought, the tranquility and stability of the Nation. *See, e.g., Lochner v. New York,* 198 U.S. 45. That formula, based on subjective considerations of "natural justice," is no less dangerous when used to enforce this Court's views about personal rights than those about economic rights. I had thought that we had laid that formula, as a means for striking down state legislation, to rest once and for all in cases like *West Coast Hotel Co. v. Parrish,* 300 U.S. 379; *Olsen v. Nebraska ex rel. Western Reference & Bond Assn.,* 313 U.S. 236, and many other opinions. *See also Lochner v. New York,* 198 U.S. 45, 74 (Holmes, J., dissenting). . . .

POSTSCRIPT

Does the Bill of Rights to the U.S. Constitution Guarantee a Right to Privacy?

This is a challenging question. Justice William O. Douglas contends that the Constitution has rights that emanate from certain amendments in the Bill of Rights that form a "penumbra," which provides a right to privacy protected from governmental interference. Conversely, Justice Hugo L. Black maintains that a constitutional right to privacy is not found in any explicit provision in the Bill of Rights. Therefore, the Supreme Court should have deferred to the judgment of the Connecticut legislature, even though Justice Black believed that the law was highly objectionable as a personal matter.

After reading the case excerpts in this section, who do you believe presents the more compelling case, Justice Douglas or Justice Black? Is Justice Douglas' position that "specific guarantees in the Bill of Rights have penumbras, formed by emanations from those guarantees that help give them life and substance," and also "create zones of privacy," a compelling one? Or, are you persuaded by Justice Black's assertion that:

> The due process argument which my Brothers . . . adopt here is based . . . on the premise that this Court is vested with power to invalidate all state laws that it considers to be arbitrary, capricious, unreasonable, or oppressive, or on this Court's belief that a particular state law under scrutiny has no 'rational or justifying' purpose, or is offensive to a 'sense of fairness and justice.' If these formulas based on 'natural justice,' or others which mean the same thing, are to prevail, they required judges to determine what is or is not constitutional on the basis of their own appraisal of what laws are unwise or unnecessary. The power to make such decisions is, of course, that of a legislative body.

Another important issue concerns the logical limits to the extension of the *Griswold* principle. Seven years following *Griswold*, in *Eisenstadt v. Baird*, 405 U.S. 438 (1972), the Supreme Court considered whether the right to privacy should be extended to unmarried persons. Massachusetts law provided that contraceptives could only be distributed by physicians or pharmacists, and only to married persons. The defendant, William Baird, was convicted for providing contraceptive foam to an unmarried person during a lecture at Boston University. A Massachusetts appellate court partially overturned his conviction and held that the lectures were protected by the First Amendment. The United States Court of Appeals later held that the law infringed on fundamental human rights of unmarried persons under the Fourteenth Amendment's

Due Process Clause. The U.S. Supreme Court held that the Massachusetts law violated the Equal Protection Clause, because it was not designed to protect public health and had no rational basis. It did not reach the due process issue. Stated Justice William J. Brennan: "If the right of privacy means anything, it is the right of the individual, married or single, to be free from unwarranted governmental intrusion into matters so fundamentally affecting a person as the decision whether to bear or beget a child."

Five years later, the Supreme Court considered the constitutionality of a New York law that prohibited all persons other than licensed pharmacists from distributing contraceptives to persons over 16 years of age and also forbid the sale or distribution of contraceptives to anyone under the age of 16, without a prescription. In *Carey v. Population Services International*, 431 U.S. 678 (1977), the Court held that because the provision restricting contraceptive distribution to pharmacists attempted to restrict the exercise of a fundamental right, the state of New York was required to demonstrate a compelling interest that would support its law. This it failed to do, and the provision prohibiting anyone but pharmacists from distributing contraceptives was unconstitutional. A plurality of the Court held too that the provision that barred the sale or distribution of contraceptives to those under age 16 was irrational and increased the risks of pregnancy and sexually transmitted diseases.

Eisenstadt v. Baird and *Carey v. Population Services International*, then, present the next logical steps in the evolution of the privacy doctrine: the extension of the right to privacy to sexual relationships between unmarried persons, including minors. Noted legal scholar Laurence Tribe has described these important principles as the right to reproductive autonomy. Issue 10 in this volume will consider another highly controversial issue implicating reproductive autonomy: whether *Griswold*'s recognition of a constitutional right to privacy should be extended to a woman's right to obtain a lawful abortion.

Earlier in this volume we considered Justice Benjamin Cardozo's highly astute observation that, once developed, a legal principle has a "tendency to expand itself to the limit of its logic." What, then, is the practical limit to the logic of the principle that courts using a substantive due process doctrine may strike down laws passed by legislatures because they violate individual rights to privacy? Even though the outcomes of these cases may be attractive, for example, striking down laws prohibiting the sale and use of contraceptives, following Justice Black's line of thought it seems prudent to inquire about whether this is a proper role for the judicial branch. Or, are decisions such as these best left to legislative bodies?

These are difficult questions. A considerable number of legal scholars have weighed in on these questions since *Griswold* was decided. The following readings may help to shed some light on these questions. See: Kathleen M. Sullivan and Gerald Gunther, *Constitutional Law* (Foundation Press, 15th ed., 2004); Laurence H. Tribe, *American Constitutional Law* (Foundation Press, 2nd ed., 1988); Alpheus Thomas Mason and Donald Grier Stephenson, Jr., *American Constitutional Law* (Pearson Prentice Hall, 15th ed., 2009); Bernard Schwartz, *A History of the Supreme Court* (Oxford University Press, 1993); Kermit L. Hall, Paul Finkelman, and James Ely, Jr., *American Legal History: Cases and*

Materials (Oxford University Press, 3rd ed., 2005); Kermit L. Hall, *The Oxford Companion to the Supreme Court of the United States* (Oxford University Press, 1992); Walter F. Murphy, James E. Fleming, Sotirios A. Barber, and Stephen Macedo, *American Constitutional Interpretation* (Foundation Press, 3rd ed., 2003); David M. O'Brien, *Constitutional Law and Politics: Struggles for Power and Government Accountability* (W.W. Norton, 6th ed., 2005); Craig R. Ducat, *Constitutional Interpretation* (Wadsworth, 9th ed., 2009); John H. Garvey, T. Alexander Aleinikoff, and Daniel A. Farber, *Modern Constitutional Theory: A Reader* (Thompson West, 5th ed., 2004). See also: Jamal Greene, "Symposium: Liberty—The So-Called Right to Privacy?" *UC Davis Law Review*, vol. 43, p. 715 (2010); Caitlin E. Borgmann, "Abortion, the Undue Burden Standard, and the Evisceration of Womens' Privacy," *William & Mary Journal of Women and the Law*, vol. 16, p. 291 (2010); Radhika Rao, "Conflicting Interests in Reproductive Autonomy and Their Impact on New Technologies: The Personal Right: Privacy, Property, or Child?: Equal Liberty: Assisted Reproductive Technology and Reproductive Equality," *The George Washington Law Review*, vol. 76, p. 1457 (2008); John C. Toro, "The Charade of Tradition-Based Substantive Due Process," *The NYU Journal of Law & Liberty*, vol. 4, p. 172 (2009).

ISSUE 10

Does a Constitutional Right to Privacy Protect a Woman's Right to Obtain a Lawful Abortion?

YES: Harry A. Blackmun, from *Roe v. Wade,* 410 U.S. 113 (1973)

NO: William H. Rehnquist, from *Roe v. Wade,* 410 U.S. 113 (1973)

ISSUE SUMMARY

YES: Justice Harry A. Blackmun, writing for the U.S. Supreme Court in *Roe v. Wade* (1973), asserted that the constitutional right to privacy, established in *Griswold v. Connecticut* (1965), is sufficiently broad to protect a woman's right to terminate her pregnancy.

NO: Justice William H. Rehnquist, dissenting in *Roe v. Wade* (1973), asserted that although privacy may be a form of liberty protected by the Fourteenth Amendment, such an interest is protected only against state actions without due process of law. Moreover, the right to an abortion is not "so rooted in the traditions and conscience of our people as to be ranked as fundamental."

A woman's right to obtain a lawful abortion is a highly contentious issue in American society. In fact, many writers have suggested that *Roe v. Wade,* 410 U.S. 113 (1973), may have been the most controversial case the Supreme Court has considered during the latter portion of the twentieth century. As opposed to most issues, where reasonable persons with opposing viewpoints often appear able to forge a compromise over time, there still appears to be little middle ground in the abortion debate.

Even in 2010, it is not uncommon to witness protestors picketing abortion clinics carrying placards depicting various stages of the abortion process and describing it as a legally sanctioned form of murder. It is also not uncommon to see pro-choice advocates in face-to-face emotionally charged confrontations with abortion foes.

One example of just how contentious the abortion issue has become occurred in 2009, when Dr. George Tiller, one of the few physicians to perform late-term abortions in the United States, was shot to death in

Wichita, Kansas, while attending Sunday church services. Scott Roeder was charged with first-degree murder for killing Dr. Tiller. Roeder's defense team attempted to use a *necessity defense* to the murder charge at trial. This justification for criminal conduct asserts that the harm to be prevented by the act of the defendant was greater than the harm that he had caused. Therefore, his actions were justified and no criminal liability should be imposed. Judge Warren Wilbert, however, declined to permit Roeder to use the necessity defense. Judge Wilbert asserted that if he were to permit Roeder to use this defense it would "not only lead to chaos but would be tantamount to sanctioning anarchy."

Roeder was convicted of first-degree murder for shooting Dr. Tiller in the head, ostensibly, "to save the lives of unborn babies." The evidence at trial revealed that Roeder had stalked Dr. Tiller for months. Judge Wilbert sentenced the 52-year-old Roeder to a sentence of life in prison for first-degree murder and declared that he would not be eligible for parole for 50 years.

Prior to his sentencing, Roeder told the court that he did not regret killing Dr. Tiller. Stated Roeder: "I stopped him so he could not dismember another innocent baby. Wichita is a far safer place for unborn babies without George Tiller." (*B.B.C. News*, 4/2/2010.) An attorney for the Tiller family, Lee Thompson, described the murder as a form of "domestic terrorism," and stated: "[Dr. Tiller] respected and trusted the right of women to make their own decisions. He gave his life to the rights of women." (*Id.*)

The reactions to Scott Roeder's conviction for first-degree murder varied considerably throughout U.S. society. While many people applauded the life sentence he received, others believed that Roeder was a hero whose crime was justified by his desire to protect the unborn. In any event, this case demonstrates clearly just how polarizing the abortion debate has become.

Another very interesting issue concerns the reasons why women seek abortions at 16 or more weeks of the gestation process. According to one study conducted by the Guttmacher Institute, 71% of women reported that they did not know they were pregnant. Forty-eight percent found it hard to make arrangements to have an abortion and 33% indicated that they were afraid to tell their partner or parents.

Public support for a woman's right to obtain an abortion has remained remarkably stable over time. A CNN/USA Today/Gallup poll conducted in January 2003 inquired about whether people felt that abortion should be legal during the first, second, and third trimesters of the gestation process. The poll had been conducted previously in 2000, and in 1996. In 2003, 66% of those surveyed believed that first trimester abortions should be legal. The 2000 poll produced the same result. The 1996 poll had indicated that 64% of those surveyed believed that abortion should be legal. [Editor's note: The difference between the 1996 poll and the later surveys was not likely to be statistically significant.] (Saad, *The Gallup Poll Monthly*, April 2000). The overall stability of public support for a woman's right to obtain an abortion may be an indication of just how entrenched attitudes on this topic really are. People have strong opinions about abortion and once these attitudes are established, it seems unlikely that they will change over time.

It is also interesting to note that according to the U.S. Centers for Disease Control, in 1974, the year after the Supreme Court decided *Roe v. Wade*, there were approximately 763,000 lawful abortions. That number increased over the next several years and eventually peaked at a high of approximately 1,429,000 in 1990. In 2005, however, the number of lawful abortions had declined to approximately 820,000. This may illustrate that state efforts to curtail the number of abortions by passing laws to make them more difficult to obtain are working.

After looking at the data presented here, do you believe that it should be a woman's constitutional right to be able to obtain a lawful abortion, or should the courts defer to state legislative judgments about what restrictions may be placed on this medical practice? Justices Blackmun and Rehnquist provide very different answers to these questions in *Roe v. Wade*.

Justice Harry A. Blackmun, writing for the Supreme Court, asserted that state abortion laws that criminalize abortion except in cases where a mother's life is endangered without regard to the stage of her pregnancy violate a woman's constitutional right to privacy. Notwithstanding the woman's privacy rights, however, the states have a legitimate interest in protecting both a woman's health and a potentially viable human being. Each of these interests reaches a compelling point at different stages of the gestation process.

In discussing a woman's right to obtain a lawful abortion, Justice Blackmun stated:

> The right of privacy, whether it be founded in the Fourteenth Amendment's concept of personal liberty and restrictions upon state action . . . is broad enough to encompass a woman's decision whether or not to terminate her pregnancy. The detriment that the state would impose upon the pregnant woman by denying this choice altogether is apparent. Specific and direct harm medically diagnosable even in early pregnancy may be involved. Maternity, or additional offspring, may force upon the woman a distressful life and future. Psychological harm may be imminent. . . . All these factors the woman and her responsible physician necessarily will consider in consultation.

Moreover, Justice Blackmun concluded that "the word 'person' in the Fourteenth Amendment does not include the unborn." In addition, although a woman's right to obtain an abortion is a fundamental one protected by the Fourteenth Amendment, it is not "unqualified." This right must be balanced against a state's "important and legitimate interest in protecting the health of the pregnant woman . . . [and] in protecting the potentiality of human life." Blackmun continued: "With respect to the State's important and legitimate interest in potential life, the 'compelling' point is at viability." He therefore concluded that the Texas abortion statute swept "too broadly," because it made no distinction between abortions performed early in the pregnancy and those performed later and it limited to a single factor, saving a mother's life, a legal justification for the procedure.

Justice William H. Rehnquist, dissenting, asserted that the Texas statute criminalizing abortion should be analyzed by asking if there was a rational relationship between the law and a valid state objective. Stated Rehnquist:

> [T]he Court's sweeping invalidation of any restrictions on abortion during the first trimester is impossible to justify under that standard, and the conscious weighing of competing factors that the Court's opinion apparently substitutes for the established test is far more appropriate to a legislative judgment than to a judicial one.

In Your Opinion . . .

- Who presents the more compelling argument, Justice Blackmun or Justice Rehnquist?
- One of the areas of disagreement between these jurists involved the issue of whether the Court should even consider *Roe v. Wade* due to the mootness doctrine. Try to understand the basis for this argument and decide if you believe that the Court should have ruled that *Roe v. Wade* was moot.
- Try to decide if you believe that *Roe v. Wade* represented a clear "victory" for "pro-choice" or "pro-life" advocates.
- Was it an effective balancing of a woman's constitutional right to privacy with legitimate state interests in maternal health and the lives of the unborn?

YES

Harry A. Blackmun

Roe v. Wade

Mr. Justice Blackmun delivered the opinion of the Court. . . .

We forthwith acknowledge our awareness of the sensitive and emotional nature of the abortion controversy, of the vigorous opposing views, even among physicians, and of the deep and seemingly absolute convictions that the subject inspires. One's philosophy, one's experiences, one's exposure to the raw edges of human existence, one's religious training, one's attitudes toward life and family and their values, and the moral standards one establishes and seeks to observe, are all likely to influence and to color one's thinking and conclusions about abortion.

In addition, population growth, pollution, poverty, and racial overtones tend to complicate and not to simplify the problem.

Our task, of course, is to resolve the issue by constitutional measurement, free of emotion and of predilection. We seek earnestly to do this, and, because we do, we have inquired into, and in this opinion place some emphasis upon, medical and medical-legal history and what that history reveals about man's attitudes toward the abortion procedure over the centuries. We bear in mind, too, Mr. Justice Holmes' admonition in his now-vindicated dissent in *Lochner v. New York,* 198 U.S. 45, 76 (1905):

> [The Constitution] is made for people of fundamentally differing views, and the accident of our finding certain opinions natural and familiar or novel and even shocking ought not to conclude our judgment upon the question whether statutes embodying them conflict with the Constitution of the United States.

I

The Texas statutes that concern us here are Arts. 1191-1194 and 1196 of the State's Penal Code. These make it a crime to "procure an abortion," as therein defined, or to attempt one, except with respect to "an abortion procured or attempted by medical advice for the purpose of saving the life of the mother." Similar statutes are in existence in a majority of the States. . . .

Supreme Court of the United States, 1973.

II

Jane Roe, a single woman who was residing in Dallas County, Texas, instituted this federal action in March 1970 against the District Attorney of the county. She sought a declaratory judgment that the Texas criminal abortion statutes were unconstitutional on their face, and an injunction restraining the defendant from enforcing the statutes.

Roe alleged that she was unmarried and pregnant; that she wished to terminate her pregnancy by an abortion "performed by a competent, licensed physician, under safe, clinical conditions"; that she was unable to get a "legal" abortion in Texas because her life did not appear to be threatened by the continuation of her pregnancy; and that she could not afford to travel to another jurisdiction in order to secure a legal abortion under safe conditions. She claimed that the Texas statutes were unconstitutionally vague and that they abridged her right of personal privacy, protected by the First, Fourth, Fifth, Ninth, and Fourteenth Amendments. By an amendment to her complaint, Roe purported to sue "on behalf of herself and all other women" similarly situated.

James Hubert Hallford, a licensed physician, sought and was granted leave to intervene in Roe's action. In his complaint, he alleged that he had been arrested previously for violations of the Texas abortion statutes, and that two such prosecutions were pending against him. He described conditions of patients who came to him seeking abortions, and he claimed that for many cases he, as a physician, was unable to determine whether they fell within or outside the exception recognized by Article 1196. He alleged that, as a consequence, the statutes were vague and uncertain, in violation of the Fourteenth Amendment, and that they violated his own and his patients' rights to privacy in the doctor–patient relationship and his own right to practice medicine, rights he claimed were guaranteed by the First, Fourth, Fifth, Ninth, and Fourteenth Amendments.

John and Mary Doe, a married couple, filed a companion complaint to that of Roe. They also named the District Attorney as defendant, claimed like constitutional deprivations, and sought declaratory and injunctive relief. The Does alleged that they were a childless couple; that Mrs. Doe was suffering from a "neural-chemical" disorder; that her physician had "advised her to avoid pregnancy until such time as her condition has materially improved" (although a pregnancy at the present time would not present "a serious risk" to her life); that, pursuant to medical advice, she had discontinued use of birth control pills; and that, if she should become pregnant, she would want to terminate the pregnancy by an abortion performed by a competent, licensed physician under safe, clinical conditions. By an amendment to their complaint, the Does purported to sue "on behalf of themselves and all couples similarly situated."

The two actions were consolidated and heard together by a duly convened three-judge district court. The suits thus presented the situations of the pregnant single woman, the childless couple, with the wife not pregnant, and the licensed practicing physician, all joining in the attack on the Texas criminal abortion statutes. Upon the filing of affidavits, motions were made for dismissal and for summary judgment. The court held that Roe and members of her class, and Dr. Hallford, had standing to sue and presented justiciable controversies, but that the Does had failed to allege facts sufficient to state a present controversy, and did not have standing. It concluded that, with respect to the requests for a declaratory judgment, abstention was not warranted. On the merits, the District Court held that the

> fundamental right of single women and married persons to choose whether to have children is protected by the Ninth Amendment, through the Fourteenth Amendment,

and that the Texas criminal abortion statutes were void on their face because they were both unconstitutionally vague and constituted an over-broad infringement of the plaintiffs' Ninth Amendment rights. The court then held that abstention was warranted with respect to the requests for an injunction. It therefore dismissed the Does' complaint, declared the abortion statutes void, and dismissed the application for injunctive relief. 314 F.Supp. 1217, 1225 (ND Tex. 1970).

The plaintiffs Roe and Doe and the intervenor Hallford, pursuant to 28 U.S.C. § 1253 have appealed to this Court from that part of the District Court's judgment denying the injunction. The defendant District Attorney has purported to cross-appeal, pursuant to the same statute, from the court's grant of declaratory relief to Roe and Hallford. Both sides also have taken protective appeals to the United States Court of Appeals for the Fifth Circuit. That court ordered the appeals held in abeyance pending decision here. We postponed decision on jurisdiction to the hearing on the merits. 402 U.S. 941 (1971)

IV

We are next confronted with issues of justiciability, standing, and abstention. Have Roe and the Does established that "personal stake in the outcome of the controversy," *Baker v. Carr*, 369 U.S. 186, 204 (1962), that ensures that

> the dispute sought to be adjudicated will be presented in an adversary context and in a form historically viewed as capable of judicial resolution,

Flast v. Cohen, 392 U.S. 83, 101 (1968), and *Sierra Club v. Morton*, 405 U.S. 727, 732 (1972)? And what effect did the pendency of criminal abortion charges against Dr. Hallford in state court have upon the propriety of the federal court's granting relief to him as a plaintiff-intervenor?

A. *Jane Roe.* Despite the use of the pseudonym, no suggestion is made that Roe is a fictitious person. For purposes of her case, we accept as true, and as established, her existence; her pregnant state, as of the inception of her suit in March 1970 and as late as May 21 of that year when she filed an alias affidavit with the District Court; and her inability to obtain a legal abortion in Texas.

Viewing Roe's case as of the time of its filing and thereafter until as late a May, there can be little dispute that it then presented a case or controversy and that, wholly apart from the class aspects, she, as a pregnant single woman thwarted by the Texas criminal abortion laws, had standing to challenge those statutes. *Abele v. Markle,* 452 F.2d 1121, 1125 (CA2 1971); *Crossen v. Breckenridge,* 446 F.2d 833, 838-839 (CA6 1971); *Poe v. Menghini,* 339 F.Supp. 986, 990-991 (Kan. 1972). *See Truax v. Raich,* 239 U.S. 33 (1915). Indeed, we do not read the appellee's brief as really asserting anything to the contrary. The "logical nexus between the status asserted and the claim sought to be adjudicated," *Flast v. Cohen,* 392 U.S. at 102, and the necessary degree of contentiousness, *Golden v. Zwickler,* 394 U.S. 103 (1969), are both present.

The appellee notes, however, that the record does not disclose that Roe was pregnant at the time of the District Court hearing on May 22, 1970, or on the following June 17 when the court's opinion and judgment were filed. And he suggests that Roe's case must now be moot because she and all other members of her class are no longer subject to any 1970 pregnancy.

The usual rule in federal cases is that an actual controversy must exist at stages of appellate or certiorari review, and not simply at the date the action is initiated. *United States v. Munsingwear, Inc.,* 340 U.S. 36 (1950); *Golden v. Zwickler, supra; SEC v. Medical Committee for Human Rights,* 404 U.S. 403 (1972).

But when, as here, pregnancy is a significant fact in the litigation, the normal 266-day human gestation period is so short that the pregnancy will come to term before the usual appellate process is complete. If that termination makes a case moot, pregnancy litigation seldom will survive much beyond the trial stage, and appellate review will be effectively denied. Our law should not be that rigid. Pregnancy often comes more than once to the same woman, and in the general population, if man is to survive, it will always be with us. Pregnancy provides a classic justification for a conclusion of nonmootness. It truly could be "capable of repetition, yet evading review." *Southern Pacific Terminal Co. v. ICC,* 219 U.S. 498, 515 (1911). *See Moore v. Ogilvie,* 394 U.S. 814, 816 (1969); *Carroll v. Princess Anne,* 393 U.S. 175, 178-179 (1968); *United States v. W. T. Grant Co.,* 345 U.S. 629, 632-633 (1953).

We, therefore, agree with the District Court that Jane Roe had standing to undertake this litigation, that she presented a justiciable controversy, and that the termination of her 1970 pregnancy has not rendered her case moot. . . .

C. *The Does.* In view of our ruling as to Roe's standing in her case, the issue of the Does' standing in their case has little significance. The claims they assert are essentially the same as those of Roe, and they attack the same statutes. . . .

V

The principal thrust of appellant's attack on the Texas statutes is that they improperly invade a right, said to be possessed by the pregnant woman, to choose to terminate her pregnancy. Appellant would discover this right in the concept of personal "liberty" embodied in the Fourteenth Amendment's Due Process Clause; or in personal, marital, familial, and sexual privacy said to be protected by the Bill of Rights or its penumbras, *see Griswold v. Connecticut,* 381 U.S. 479 (1965); *Eisenstadt v. Baird,* 405 U.S. 438 (1972); *id.* at 460 (WHITE, J., concurring in result); or among those rights reserved to the people by the Ninth Amendment, *Griswold v. Connecticut,* 381 U.S. at 486 (Goldberg, J., concurring). Before addressing this claim, we feel it desirable briefly to survey, in several aspects, the history of abortion, for such insight as that history may afford us, and then to examine the state purposes and interests behind the criminal abortion laws.

VI

It perhaps is not generally appreciated that the restrictive criminal abortion laws in effect in a majority of States today are of relatively recent vintage. Those laws, generally proscribing abortion or its attempt at any time during pregnancy except when necessary to preserve the pregnant woman's life, are not of ancient or even of common law origin. Instead, they derive from statutory changes effected, for the most part, in the latter half of the 19th century.

1. *Ancient attitudes.*   These are not capable of precise determination. We are told that, at the time of the Persian Empire, abortifacients were known, and that criminal abortions were severely punished. We are also told, however, that abortion was practiced in Greek times as well as in the Roman Era, and that "it was resorted to without scruple." The Ephesian, Soranus, often described as the greatest of the ancient gynecologists, appears to have been generally opposed to Rome's prevailing free-abortion practices. He found it necessary to think first of the life of the mother, and he resorted to abortion when, upon this standard, he felt the procedure advisable. Greek and Roman law afforded little protection to the unborn. If abortion was prosecuted in some places, it seems to have been based on a concept of a violation of the father's right to his offspring. Ancient religion did not bar abortion.

2. *The Hippocratic Oath.*   What then of the famous Oath that has stood so long as the ethical guide of the medical profession and that bears the name of the great Greek (460(?)–377(?) B. C.), who has been described as the Father of Medicine, the "wisest and the greatest practitioner of his art," and the "most important and most complete medical personality of antiquity," who dominated the medical schools of his time, and who typified the sum of the medical knowledge of the past? The Oath varies somewhat according to the particular translation, but in any translation the content is clear:

> I will give no deadly medicine to anyone if asked, nor suggest any such counsel; and in like manner, I will not give to a woman a pessary to produce abortion,

or

> I will neither give a deadly drug to anybody if asked for it, nor will I make a suggestion to this effect. Similarly, I will not give to a woman an abortive remedy.

Although the Oath is not mentioned in any of the principal briefs in this case or in *Doe v. Bolton, post,* p. 179, it represents the apex of the development of strict ethical concepts in medicine, and its influence endures to this day. Why did not the authority of Hippocrates dissuade abortion practice in his time and that of Rome? The late Dr. Edelstein provides us with a theory: The Oath was not uncontested even in Hippocrates' day; only the Pythagorean school of philosophers frowned upon the related act of suicide. Most Greek thinkers, on the other hand, commended abortion, at least prior to viability. *See* Plato, Republic, V, 461; Aristotle, Politics, VII, 1335b 25. For the Pythagoreans, however, it was a matter of dogma. For them, the embryo was animate from the moment of conception, and abortion meant destruction of a living being. The abortion clause of the Oath, therefore, "echoes Pythagorean doctrines," and "[i]n no other stratum of Greek opinion were such views held or proposed in the same spirit of uncompromising austerity." . . .

This, it seems to us, is a satisfactory and acceptable explanation of the Hippocratic Oath's apparent rigidity. It enables us to understand, in historical context, a long-accepted and revered statement of medical ethics.

3. *The common law.* It is undisputed that, at common law, abortion performed before "quickening"—the first recognizable movement of the fetus *in utero,* appearing usually from the 16th to the 18th week of pregnancy—was not an indictable offense. The absence of a common law crime for pre-quickening abortion appears to have developed from a confluence of earlier philosophical, theological, and civil and canon law concepts of when life begins. These disciplines variously approached the question in terms of the point at which the embryo or fetus became "formed" or recognizably human, or in terms of when a "person" came into being, that is, infused with a "soul" or "animated." A loose consensus evolved in early English law that these events occurred at some point between conception and live birth. This was "mediate animation." Although Christian theology and the canon law came to fix the point of animation at 40 days for a male and 80 days for a female, a view that persisted until the 19th century, there was otherwise little agreement about the precise time of formation or animation. There was agreement, however, that, prior to this point, the fetus was to be regarded as part of the mother, and its destruction, therefore, was not homicide. Due to continued uncertainty about the precise time when animation occurred, to the lack of any empirical basis for the 40–80-day view, and perhaps to Aquinas' definition of movement as one of the two first principles of life, Bracton focused upon quickening as the critical point. The significance of quickening was echoed by later common law scholars, and found its way into the received common law in this country.

Whether abortion of a quick fetus was a felony at common law, or even a lesser crime, is still disputed. Bracton, writing early in the 13th century, thought it homicide. But the later and predominant view, following the great common law scholars, has been that it was, at most, a lesser offense. In a frequently cited passage, Coke took the position that abortion of a woman "quick with childe" is "a great misprision, and no murder." Blackstone followed, saying that, while abortion after quickening had once been considered manslaughter (though not murder), "modern law" took a less severe view. A recent review of the common law precedents argues, however, that those precedents contradict Coke, and that even post-quickening abortion was never established as a common law crime. This is of some importance, because, while most American courts ruled, in holding or dictum, that abortion of an unquickened fetus was not criminal under their received common law, others followed Coke in stating that abortion of a quick fetus was a "misprision," a term they translated to mean "misdemeanor." That their reliance on Coke on this aspect of the law was uncritical and, apparently in all the reported cases, dictum (due probably to the paucity of common law prosecutions for post-quickening abortion), makes it now appear doubtful that abortion was ever firmly established as a common law crime even with respect to the destruction of a quick fetus. . . .

5. The American law.   In this country, the law in effect in all but a few States until mid-19th century was the preexisting English common law. Connecticut, the first State to enact abortion legislation, adopted in 1821 that part of Lord Ellenborough's Act that related to a woman "quick with child." The death penalty was not imposed. Abortion before quickening was made a crime in that State only in 1860. In 1828, New York enacted legislation that, in two respects, was to serve as a model for early anti-abortion statutes. First, while barring destruction of an unquickened fetus as well as a quick fetus, it made the former only a misdemeanor, but the latter second-degree manslaughter. Second, it incorporated a concept of therapeutic abortion by providing that an abortion was excused if it

> shall have been necessary to preserve the life of such mother, or shall have been advised by two physicians to be necessary for such purpose.

By 1840, when Texas had received the common law, only eight American States had statutes dealing with abortion. It was not until after the War Between the States that legislation began generally to replace the common law. Most of these initial statutes dealt severely with abortion after quickening, but were lenient with it before quickening. Most punished attempts equally with completed abortions. While many statutes included the exception for an abortion thought by one or more physicians to be necessary to save the mother's life, that provision soon disappeared, and the typical law required that the procedure actually be necessary for that purpose. Gradually, in the middle and late 19th century, the quickening distinction disappeared from the statutory law of most States and the degree of the offense and the penalties were increased. By the end of the 1950s, a large majority of the jurisdictions banned abortion, however and whenever performed, unless done to save or preserve the life of the mother. The exceptions, Alabama and the District of Columbia, permitted abortion to preserve the mother's health. Three States permitted abortions that were not "unlawfully" performed or that were not "without lawful justification," leaving interpretation of those standards to the courts. In the past several years, however, a trend toward liberalization of abortion statutes has resulted in adoption, by about one-third of the States, of less stringent laws, most of them patterned after the ALI Model Penal Code, § 230.3, set forth as Appendix B to the opinion in *Doe v. Bolton, post,* p. 205.

It is thus apparent that, at common law, at the time of the adoption of our Constitution, and throughout the major portion of the 19th century, abortion was viewed with less disfavor than under most American statutes currently in effect. Phrasing it another way, a woman enjoyed a substantially broader right to terminate a pregnancy than she does in most States today. At least with respect to the early stage of pregnancy, and very possibly without such a limitation, the opportunity to make this choice was present in this country well into the 19th century. Even later, the law continued for some time to treat less punitively an abortion procured in early pregnancy.

6. *The position of the American Medical Association.* The anti-abortion mood prevalent in this country in the late 19th century was shared by the medical profession. Indeed, the attitude of the profession may have played a significant role in the enactment of stringent criminal abortion legislation during that period.

An AMA Committee on Criminal Abortion was appointed in May, 1857. It presented its report, 12 Trans, of the Am.Med.Assn. 778 (1859), to the Twelfth Annual Meeting. That report observed that the Committee had been appointed to investigate criminal abortion "with a view to its general suppression." It deplored abortion and its frequency and it listed three causes of "this general demoralization":

> The first of these causes is a widespread popular ignorance of the true character of the crime—a belief, even among mothers themselves, that the foetus is not alive till after the period of quickening.
>
> The second of the agents alluded to is the fact that the profession themselves are frequently supposed careless of foetal life. . . .
>
> The third reason of the frightful extent of this crime is found in the grave defects of our laws, both common and statute, as regards the independent and actual existence of the child before birth, as a living being. These errors, which are sufficient in most instances to prevent conviction, are based, and only based, upon mistaken and exploded medical dogmas. With strange inconsistency, the law fully acknowledges the foetus *in utero* and its inherent rights, for civil purposes; while personally and as criminally affected, it fails to recognize it, and to its life as yet denies all protection.

Id. at 776. The Committee then offered, and the Association adopted, resolutions protesting "against such unwarrantable destruction of human life," calling upon state legislatures to revise their abortion laws, and requesting the cooperation of state medical societies "in pressing the subject." *Id.* at 28, 78.

In 1871, a long and vivid report was submitted by the Committee on Criminal Abortion. It ended with the observation,

> We had to deal with human life. In a matter of less importance, we could entertain no compromise. An honest judge on the bench would call things by their proper names. We could do no less.

22 Trans. of the Am.Med.Assn. 268 (1871). It proffered resolutions, adopted by the Association, *id.* at 38–39, recommending, among other things, that it

> be unlawful and unprofessional for any physician to induce abortion or premature labor without the concurrent opinion of at least one respectable consulting physician, and then always with a view to the safety of the child—if that be possible,

and calling

> the attention of the clergy of all denominations to the perverted views of morality entertained by a large class of females—aye, and men also, on this important question.

Except for periodic condemnation of the criminal abortionist, no further formal AMA action took place until 1967. In that year, the Committee on Human Reproduction urged the adoption of a stated policy of opposition to induced abortion except when there is "documented medical evidence" of a threat to the health or life of the mother, or that the child "may be born with incapacitating physical deformity or mental deficiency," or that a pregnancy "resulting from legally established statutory or forcible rape or incest may constitute a threat to the mental or physical health of the patient," two other physicians "chosen because of their recognized professional competence have examined the patient and have concurred in writing," and the procedure "is performed in a hospital accredited by the Joint Commission on Accreditation of Hospitals." The providing of medical information by physicians to state legislatures in their consideration of legislation regarding therapeutic abortion was "to be considered consistent with the principles of ethics of the American Medical Association." This recommendation was adopted by the House of Delegates. Proceedings of the AMA House of Delegates 40–51 (June 1967).

In 1970, after the introduction of a variety of proposed resolutions and of a report from its Board of Trustees, a reference committee noted "polarization of the medical profession on this controversial issue"; division among those who had testified; a difference of opinion among AMA councils and committees; "the remarkable shift in testimony" in six months, felt to be influenced "by the rapid changes in state laws and by the judicial decisions which tend to make abortion more freely available"; and a feeling "that this trend will continue." On June 25, 1970, the House of Delegates adopted preambles and most of the resolutions proposed by the reference committee. The preambles emphasized "the best interests of the patient," "sound clinical judgment," and "informed patient consent," in contrast to "mere acquiescence to the patient's demand." The resolutions asserted that abortion is a medical procedure that should be performed by a licensed physician in an accredited hospital only after consultation with two other physicians and in conformity with state law, and that no party to the procedure should be required to violate personally held moral principles. Proceedings of the AMA House of Delegates 220 (June 1970). The AMA Judicial Council rendered a complementary opinion. . . .

VII

Three reasons have been advanced to explain historically the enactment of criminal abortion laws in the 19th century and to justify their continued existence.

It has been argued occasionally that these laws were the product of a Victorian social concern to discourage illicit sexual conduct. Texas, however, does not advance this justification in the present case, and it appears that no court or commentator has taken the argument seriously. The appellants and *amici* contend, moreover, that this is not a proper state purpose, at all and suggest that, if it were, the Texas statutes are overbroad in protecting it, since the law fails to distinguish between married and unwed mothers.

A second reason is concerned with abortion as a medical procedure. When most criminal abortion laws were first enacted, the procedure was a hazardous one for the woman. This was particularly true prior to the development of antisepsis. Antiseptic techniques, of course, were based on discoveries by Lister, Pasteur, and others first announced in 1867, but were not generally accepted and employed until about the turn of the century. Abortion mortality was high. Even after 1900, and perhaps until as late as the development of antibiotics in the 1940s, standard modern techniques such as dilation and curettage were not nearly so safe as they are today. Thus, it has been argued that a State's real concern in enacting a criminal abortion law was to protect the pregnant woman, that is, to restrain her from submitting to a procedure that placed her life in serious jeopardy.

Modern medical techniques have altered this situation. Appellants and various *amici* refer to medical data indicating that abortion in early pregnancy, that is, prior to the end of the first trimester, although not without its risk, is now relatively safe. Mortality rates for women undergoing early abortions, where the procedure is legal, appear to be as low as or lower than the rates for normal childbirth. Consequently, any interest of the State in protecting the woman from an inherently hazardous procedure, except when it would be equally dangerous for her to forgo it, has largely disappeared. Of course, important state interests in the areas of health and medical standards do remain. The State has a legitimate interest in seeing to it that abortion, like any other medical procedure, is performed under circumstances that ensure maximum safety for the patient. This interest obviously extends at least to the performing physician and his staff, to the facilities involved, to the availability of after-care, and to adequate provision for any complication or emergency that might arise. The prevalence of high mortality rates at illegal "abortion mills" strengthens, rather than weakens, the State's interest in regulating the conditions under which abortions are performed. Moreover, the risk to the woman increases as her pregnancy continues. Thus, the State retains a definite interest in protecting the woman's own health and safety when an abortion is proposed at a late stage of pregnancy.

The third reason is the State's interest—some phrase it in terms of duty—in protecting prenatal life. Some of the argument for this justification rests on the theory that a new human life is present from the moment of conception.

The State's interest and general obligation to protect life then extends, it is argued, to prenatal life. Only when the life of the pregnant mother herself is at stake, balanced against the life she carries within her, should the interest of the embryo or fetus not prevail. Logically, of course, a legitimate state interest in this area need not stand or fall on acceptance of the belief that life begins at conception or at some other point prior to live birth. In assessing the State's interest, recognition may be given to the less rigid claim that as long as at least potential life is involved, the State may assert interests beyond the protection of the pregnant woman alone.

Parties challenging state abortion laws have sharply disputed in some courts the contention that a purpose of these laws, when enacted, was to protect prenatal life. Pointing to the absence of legislative history to support the contention, they claim that most state laws were designed solely to protect the woman. Because medical advances have lessened this concern, at least with respect to abortion in early pregnancy, they argue that with respect to such abortions the laws can no longer be justified by any state interest. There is some scholarly support for this view of original purpose. The few state courts called upon to interpret their laws in the late 19th and early 20th centuries did focus on the State's interest in protecting the woman's health, rather than in preserving the embryo and fetus. Proponents of this view point out that in many States, including Texas, by statute or judicial interpretation, the pregnant woman herself could not be prosecuted for self-abortion or for cooperating in an abortion performed upon her by another. They claim that adoption of the "quickening" distinction through received common law and state statutes tacitly recognizes the greater health hazards inherent in late abortion and impliedly repudiates the theory that life begins at conception.

It is with these interests, and the eight to be attached to them, that this case is concerned.

VIII

The Constitution does not explicitly mention any right of privacy. In a line of decisions, however, going back perhaps as far as *Union Pacific R. Co. v. Botsford,* 141 U.S. 250, 251 (1891), the Court has recognized that a right of personal privacy, or a guarantee of certain areas or zones of privacy, does exist under the Constitution. In varying contexts, the Court or individual Justices have, indeed, found at least the roots of that right in the First Amendment, *Stanley v. Georgia,* 394 U.S. 557, 564 (1969); in the Fourth and Fifth Amendments, *Terry v. Ohio,* 392 U.S. 1, 8–9 (1968), *Katz v. United States,* 389 U.S. 347, 350 (1967), *Boyd v. United States,* 116 U.S. 616 (1886), *see Olmstead v. United States,* 277 U.S. 438, 478 (1928) (Brandeis, J., dissenting); in the penumbras of the Bill of Rights, *Griswold v. Connecticut,* 381 U.S. at 484–485; in the Ninth Amendment, *id.* at 486 (Goldberg, J., concurring); or in the concept of liberty guaranteed by the first section of the Fourteenth Amendment, *see Meyer v. Nebraska,* 262 U.S. 390, 399 (1923). These decisions make it clear that only personal rights that can be deemed "fundamental" or "implicit in the concept of ordered liberty," *Palko v. Connecticut,* 302 U.S. 319, 325 (1937), are included in this guarantee of personal privacy. They also make it clear that the right has some extension to activities relating to marriage, *Loving v. Virginia*, 388 U.S. 1, 12 (1967); procreation, *Skinner v. Oklahoma*, 316 U.S. 535, 541–542 (1942); contraception, *Eisenstadt v. Baird*, 405 U.S. at 453–454; *id.* at 460, 463–465 (WHITE, J., concurring in result); family relationships, *Prince v. Massachusetts*, 321 U.S. 158, 166 (1944); and childrearing and education, *Pierce v. Society of Sisters*, 268 U.S. 510, 535 (1925), *Meyer v. Nebraska, supra*.

This right of privacy, whether it be founded in the Fourteenth Amendment's concept of personal liberty and restrictions upon state action, as we feel it is, or, as the District Court determined, in the Ninth Amendment's reservation of rights to the people, is broad enough to encompass a woman's decision whether or not to terminate her pregnancy. The detriment that the State would impose upon the pregnant woman by denying this choice altogether is apparent. Specific and direct harm medically diagnosable even in early pregnancy may be involved. Maternity, or additional offspring, may force upon the woman a distressful life and future. Psychological harm may be imminent. Mental and physical health may be taxed by child care. There is also the distress, for all concerned, associated with the unwanted child, and there is the problem of bringing a child into a family already unable, psychologically and otherwise, to care for it. In other cases, as in this one, the additional difficulties and continuing stigma of unwed motherhood may be involved. All these are factors the woman and her responsible physician necessarily will consider in consultation.

On the basis of elements such as these, appellant and some *amici* argue that the woman's right is absolute and that she is entitled to terminate her pregnancy at whatever time, in whatever way, and for whatever reason she alone chooses. With this we do not agree. Appellant's arguments that Texas either has no valid interest at all in regulating the abortion decision, or no interest strong enough to support any limitation upon the woman's sole determination, are unpersuasive. The Court's decisions recognizing a right of privacy also acknowledge that some state regulation in areas protected by that right is appropriate. As noted above, a State may properly assert important interests in safeguarding health, in maintaining medical standards, and in protecting potential life. At some point in pregnancy, these respective interests become sufficiently compelling to sustain regulation of the factors that govern the abortion decision. The privacy right involved, therefore, cannot be said to be absolute. In fact, it is not clear to us that the claim asserted by some *amici* that one has an unlimited right to do with one's body as one pleases bears a close relationship to the right of privacy previously articulated in the Court's decisions. The Court has refused to recognize an unlimited right of this kind in the past. *Jacobson v. Massachusetts*, 197 U.S. 11 (1905) (vaccination); *Buck v. Bell*, 274 U.S. 200 (1927) (sterilization).

We, therefore, conclude that the right of personal privacy includes the abortion decision, but that this right is not unqualified, and must be considered against important state interests in regulation. . . .

Where certain "fundamental rights" are involved, the Court has held that regulation limiting these rights may be justified only by a "compelling state interest," *Kramer v. Union Free School District,* 395 U.S. 621, 627 (1969); *Shapiro v. Thompson,* 394 U.S. 618, 634 (1969), *Sherbert v. Verner,* 374 U.S. 398, 406 (1963), and that legislative enactments must be narrowly drawn to express only the legitimate state interests at stake. *Griswold v. Connecticut,* 381 U.S. at 485; *Aptheker v. Secretary of State,* 378 U.S. 500, 508 (1964); *Cantwell v. Connecticut,* 310 U.S. 296, 307–308 (1940); *see Eisenstadt v. Baird,* 405 U.S. at 460, 463–464 (WHITE, J., concurring in result).

In the recent abortion cases cited above, courts have recognized these principles. Those striking down state laws have generally scrutinized the State's interests in protecting health and potential life, and have concluded that neither interest justified broad limitations on the reasons for which a physician and his pregnant patient might decide that she should have an abortion in the early stages of pregnancy. Courts sustaining state laws have held that the State's determinations to protect health or prenatal life are dominant and constitutionally justifiable.

IX

The District Court held that the appellee failed to meet his burden of demonstrating that the Texas statute's infringement upon Roe's rights was necessary to support a compelling state interest, and that, although the appellee presented "several compelling justifications for state presence in the area of abortions," the statutes outstripped these justifications and swept "far beyond any areas of compelling state interest." 314 F.Supp. at 1222–1223. Appellant and appellee both contest that holding. Appellant, as has been indicated, claims an absolute right that bars any state imposition of criminal penalties in the area. Appellee argues that the State's determination to recognize and protect prenatal life from and after conception constitutes a compelling state interest. As noted above, we do not agree fully with either formulation.

A. The appellee and certain *amici* argue that the fetus is a "person" within the language and meaning of the Fourteenth Amendment. In support of this, they outline at length and in detail the well-known facts of fetal development. If this suggestion of personhood is established, the appellant's case, of course, collapses, for the fetus' right to life would then be guaranteed specifically by the Amendment. The appellant conceded as much on reargument. On the other hand, the appellee conceded on reargument that no case could be cited that holds that a fetus is a person within the meaning of the Fourteenth Amendment.

The Constitution does not define "person" in so many words. Section 1 of the Fourteenth Amendment contains three references to "person." The first, in defining "citizens," speaks of "persons born or naturalized in the United States." The word also appears both in the Due Process Clause and in the Equal Protection Clause. "Person" is used in other places in the Constitution: in the listing of qualifications for Representatives and Senators, Art. I, § 2, cl. 2, and § 3, cl. 3; in the Apportionment Clause, Art. I, § 2, cl. 3; in the Migration and Importation provision, Art. I, § 9, cl. 1; in the Emolument Clause, Art. I, § 9, cl. 8; in the Electors provisions, Art. II, § 1, cl. 2, and the superseded cl. 3; in the provision outlining qualifications for the office of President, Art. II, § 1, cl. 5; in the Extradition provisions, Art. IV, § 2, cl. 2, and the superseded Fugitive Slave Clause 3; and in the Fifth, Twelfth, and Twenty-second Amendments, as well as in §§ 2 and 3 of the Fourteenth Amendment. But in nearly all these instances, the use of the word is such that it has application only postnatally. None indicates, with any assurance, that it has any possible prenatal application.

All this, together with our observation, *supra,* that, throughout the major portion of the 19th century, prevailing legal abortion practices were far freer than they are today, persuades us that the word "person," as used in the Fourteenth Amendment, does not include the unborn. This is in accord with the results reached in those few cases where the issue has been squarely presented. *McGarvey v. Magee-Womens Hospital,* 340 F.Supp. 751 (WD Pa.1972); *Byrn v. New York City Health & Hospitals Corp.,* 31 N.Y.2d 194, 286 N.E.2d 887 (1972), *appeal docketed,* No. 72-434; *Abele v. Markle,* 351 F.Supp. 224 (Conn. 1972), *appeal docketed,* No. 72-730. *Cf. Cheaney v. State,* ___ Ind. at ___, 285 N.E.2d at 270; *Montana v. Rogers,* 278 F.2d 68, 72 (CA7 1960), *aff'd sub nom. Montana v. Kennedy,* 366 U.S. 308 (1961); *Keeler v. Superior Court,* 2 Cal.3d 619, 470 P.2d 617 (1970); *State v. Dickinson,* 28 Ohio St.2d 65, 275 N.E.2d 599 (1971). Indeed, our decision in *United States v. Vuitch,* 402 U.S. 62 (1971), inferentially is to the same effect, for we there would not have indulged in statutory interpretation favorable to abortion in specified circumstances if the necessary consequence was the termination of life entitled to Fourteenth Amendment protection.

This conclusion, however, does not of itself fully answer the contentions raised by Texas, and we pass on to other considerations.

B. The pregnant woman cannot be isolated in her privacy. She carries an embryo and, later, a fetus, if one accepts the medical definitions of the developing young in the human uterus. *See Dorland's Illustrated Medical Dictionary* 478–479, 547 (24th ed., 1965). The situation therefore is inherently different from marital intimacy, or bedroom possession of obscene material, or marriage, or procreation, or education, with which Eisenstadt and Griswold, Stanley, Loving, Skinner, and Pierce and Meyer were respectively concerned. As we have intimated above, it is reasonable and appropriate for a State to decide that, at some point in time another interest, that of health of the mother or that of potential human life, becomes significantly involved. The woman's privacy is no longer sole and any right of privacy she possesses must be measured accordingly.

Texas urges that, apart from the Fourteenth Amendment, life begins at conception and is present throughout pregnancy, and that, therefore, the State has a compelling interest in protecting that life from and after conception. We need not resolve the difficult question of when life begins. When those trained in the respective disciplines of medicine, philosophy, and theology are unable to arrive at any consensus, the judiciary, at this point in the development of man's knowledge, is not in a position to speculate as to the answer.

It should be sufficient to note briefly the wide divergence of thinking on this most sensitive and difficult quesion. There has always been strong support for the view that life does not begin until live birth. . . .

In areas other than criminal abortion, the law has been reluctant to endorse any theory that life, as we recognize it, begins before live birth, or to accord legal rights to the unborn except in narrowly defined situations and except when the rights are contingent upon live birth. For example, the traditional rule of tort law denied recovery for prenatal injuries even though the child was born alive. That rule has been changed in almost every jurisdiction. In most States, recovery is said to be permitted only if the fetus was viable, or at least quick, when the injuries were sustained, though few courts have squarely so held. In a recent development, generally opposed by the commentators, some States permit the parents of a stillborn child to maintain an action for wrongful death because of prenatal injuries. Such an action, however, would appear to be one to vindicate the parents' interest and is thus consistent with the view that the fetus, at most, represents only the potentiality of life. Similarly, unborn children have been recognized as acquiring rights or interests by way of inheritance or other devolution of property, and have been represented by guardians *ad litem*. Perfection of the interests involved, again, has generally been contingent upon live birth. In short, the unborn have never been recognized in the law as persons in the whole sense.

X

In view of all this, we do not agree that, by adopting one theory of life, Texas may override the rights of the pregnant woman that are at stake. We repeat, however, that the State does have an important and legitimate interest in preserving and protecting the health of the pregnant woman, whether she be a resident of the State or a nonresident who seeks medical consultation and treatment there, and that it has still *another* important and legitimate interest in protecting the potentiality of human life. These interests are separate and distinct. Each grows in substantiality as the woman approaches term and, at a point during pregnancy, each becomes "compelling."

With respect to the State's important and legitimate interest in the health of the mother, the "compelling" point, in the light of present medical knowledge, is at approximately the end of the first trimester. This is so because of the now-established medical fact, referred to above at 149, that, until the end of the first trimester mortality in abortion may be less than mortality in normal childbirth. It follows that, from and after this point, a State may regulate the abortion procedure to the extent that the regulation reasonably relates to the preservation and protection of maternal health. Examples of permissible state regulation in this area are requirements as to the qualifications of the person who is to perform the abortion; as to the licensure of that person; as to the facility in which the procedure is to be performed, that is, whether it must be a hospital or may be a clinic or some other place of less-than-hospital status; as to the licensing of the facility; and the like.

This means, on the other hand, that, for the period of pregnancy prior to this "compelling" point, the attending physician, in consultation with his patient, is free to determine, without regulation by the State, that, in his medical judgment, the patient's pregnancy should be terminated. If that decision is reached, the judgment may be effectuated by an abortion free of interference by the State.

With respect to the State's important and legitimate interest in potential life, the "compelling" point is at viability. This is so because the fetus then presumably has the capability of meaningful life outside the mother's womb. State regulation protective of fetal life after viability thus has both logical and biological justifications. If the State is interested in protecting fetal life after viability, it may go so far as to proscribe abortion during that period, except when it is necessary to preserve the life or health of the mother.

Measured against these standards, Art. 1196 of the Texas Penal Code, in restricting legal abortions to those "procured or attempted by medical advice for the purpose of saving the life of the mother," sweeps too broadly. The statute makes no distinction between abortions performed early in pregnancy and those performed later, and it limits to a single reason, "saving" the mother's life, the legal justification for the procedure. The statute, therefore, cannot survive the constitutional attack made upon it here.

This conclusion makes it unnecessary for us to consider the additional challenge to the Texas statute asserted on grounds of vagueness. *See United States v. Vuitch,* 402 U.S. at 67-72.

XI

To summarize and to repeat:

1. A state criminal abortion statute of the current Texas type, that excepts from criminality only a lifesaving procedure on behalf of the mother, without regard to pregnancy stage and without recognition of the other interests involved, is violative of the Due Process Clause of the Fourteenth Amendment.
   (a) For the stage prior to approximately the end of the first trimester, the abortion decision and its effectuation must be left to the medical judgment of the pregnant woman's attending physician.
   (b) For the stage subsequent to approximately the end of the first trimester, the State, in promoting its interest in the health of the mother, may, if it chooses, regulate the abortion procedure in ways that are reasonably related to maternal health.
   (c) For the stage subsequent to viability, the State in promoting its interest in the potentiality of human life may, if it chooses, regulate, and even proscribe, abortion except where it is necessary, in appropriate medical judgment, for the preservation of the life or health of the mother.
2. The State may define the term "physician," as it has been employed in the preceding paragraphs of this Part XI of this opinion, to mean only a physician currently licensed by the State, and may proscribe any abortion by a person who is not a physician as so defined.

In *Doe v. Bolton, post,* p. 179, procedural requirements contained in one of the modern abortion statutes are considered. That opinion and this one, of course, are to be read together.

This holding, we feel, is consistent with the relative weights of the respective interests involved, with the lessons and examples of medical and legal history, with the lenity of the common law, and with the demands of the profound problems of the present day. The decision leaves the State free to place increasing restrictions on abortion as the period of pregnancy lengthens, so long as those restrictions are tailored to the recognized state interests. The decision vindicates the right of the physician to administer medical treatment according to his professional judgment up to the points where important state interests provide compelling justifications for intervention. Up to those points, the abortion decision in all its aspects is inherently, and primarily, a medical decision, and basic responsibility for it must rest with the physician. If an individual practitioner abuses the privilege of exercising proper medical judgment, the usual remedies, judicial and intra-professional, are available.

XII

Our conclusion that Art. 1196 is unconstitutional means, of course, that the Texas abortion statutes, as a unit, must fall. The exception of Art. 1196 cannot be struck down separately, for then the State would be left with a statute proscribing all abortion procedures no matter how medically urgent the case. . . .

William H. Rehnquist

Roe v. Wade

Mr. Justice Rehnquist, dissenting.

The Court's opinion brings to the decision of this troubling question both extensive historical fact and a wealth of legal scholarship. While the opinion thus commands my respect, I find myself nonetheless in fundamental disagreement with those parts of it that invalidate the Texas statute in question, and therefore dissent.

I

The Court's opinion decides that a State may impose virtually no restriction on the performance of abortions during the first trimester of pregnancy. Our previous decisions indicate that a necessary predicate for such an opinion is a plaintiff who was in her first trimester of pregnancy at some time during the pendency of her lawsuit. While a party may vindicate his own constitutional rights, he may not seek vindication for the rights of others. *Moose Lodge v. Irvis,* 407 U.S. 163 (1972); *Sierra Club v. Morton,* 405 U.S. 727 (1972). The Court's statement of facts in this case makes clear, however, that the record in no way indicates the presence of such a plaintiff. We know only that plaintiff Roe at the time of filing her complaint was a pregnant woman; for aught that appears in this record, she may have been in her last trimester of pregnancy as of the date the complaint was filed.

Nothing in the Court's opinion indicates that Texas might not constitutionally apply its proscription of abortion as written to a woman in that stage of pregnancy. Nonetheless, the Court uses her complaint against the Texas statute as a fulcrum for deciding that States may impose virtually no restrictions on medical abortions performed during the first trimester of pregnancy. In deciding such a hypothetical lawsuit, the Court departs from the longstanding admonition that it should never "formulate a rule of constitutional law broader than is required by the precise facts to which it is to be applied." *Liverpool, New York & Philadelphia S.S. Co. v. Commissioners of Emigration,* 113 U.S. 33, 39 (1885). *See also Ashwander v. TVA,* 297 U.S. 288, 345 (1936) (Brandeis, J., concurring).

Supreme Court of the United States, 1973.

II

Even if there were a plaintiff in this case capable of litigating the issue which the Court decides, I would reach a conclusion opposite to that reached by the Court. I have difficulty in concluding, as the Court does, that the right of "privacy" is involved in this case. Texas, by the statute here challenged, bars the performance of a medical abortion by a licensed physician on a plaintiff such as Roe. A transaction resulting in an operation such as this is not "private" in the ordinary usage of that word. Nor is the "privacy" that the Court finds here even a distant relative of the freedom from searches and seizures protected by the Fourth Amendment to the Constitution, which the Court has referred to as embodying a right to privacy. *Katz v. United States,* 389 U.S. 347 (1967).

If the Court means by the term "privacy" no more than that the claim of a person to be free from unwanted state regulation of consensual transactions may be a form of "liberty" protected by the Fourteenth Amendment, there is no doubt that similar claims have been upheld in our earlier decisions on the basis of that liberty. I agree with the statement of MR. JUSTICE STEWART in his concurring opinion that the "liberty," against deprivation of which without due process the Fourteenth Amendment protects, embraces more than the rights found in the Bill of Rights. But that liberty is not guaranteed absolutely against deprivation, only against deprivation without due process of law. The test traditionally applied in the area of social and economic legislation is whether or not a law such as that challenged has a rational relation to a valid state objective. *Williamson v. Lee Optical Co.,* 348 U.S. 483, 491 (1955). The Due Process Clause of the Fourteenth Amendment undoubtedly does place a limit, albeit a broad one, on legislative power to enact laws such as this. If the Texas statute were to prohibit an abortion even where the mother's life is in jeopardy, I have little doubt that such a statute would lack a rational relation to a valid state objective under the test stated in *Williamson, supra.* But the Court's sweeping invalidation of any restrictions on abortion during the first trimester is impossible to justify under that standard, and the conscious weighing of competing factors that the Court's opinion apparently substitutes for the established test is far more appropriate to a legislative judgment than to a judicial one.

The Court eschews the history of the Fourteenth Amendment in its reliance on the "compelling state interest" test. *See Weber v. Aetna Casualty & Surety Co.,* 406 U.S. 164, 179 (1972) (dissenting opinion). But the Court adds a new wrinkle to this test by transposing it from the legal considerations associated with the Equal Protection Clause of the Fourteenth Amendment to this case arising under the Due Process Clause of the Fourteenth Amendment. Unless I misapprehend the consequences of this transplanting of the "compelling state interest test," the Court's opinion will accomplish the seemingly impossible feat of leaving this area of the law more confused than it found it.

While the Court's opinion quotes from the dissent of Mr. Justice Holmes in *Lochner v. New York,* 198 U.S. 45, 74 (1905), the result it reaches is more closely attuned to the majority opinion of Mr. Justice Peckham in that case. As in *Lochner* and similar cases applying substantive due process standards to economic and social welfare legislation, the adoption of the compelling state interest standard will inevitably require this Court to examine the legislative policies and pass on the wisdom of these policies in the very process of deciding whether a particular state interest put forward may or may not be "compelling." The decision here to break pregnancy into three distinct terms and to outline the permissible restrictions the State may impose in each one, for example, partakes more of judicial legislation than it does of a determination of the intent of the drafters of the Fourteenth Amendment.

The fact that a majority of the States reflecting, after all, the majority sentiment in those States, have had restrictions on abortions for at least a century is a strong indication, it seems to me, that the asserted right to an abortion is not "so rooted in the traditions and conscience of our people as to be ranked as fundamental," *Snyder v. Massachusetts,* 291 U.S. 97, 105 (1934). Even today, when society's views on abortion are changing, the very existence of the debate is evidence that the "right" to an abortion is not so universally accepted as the appellant would have us believe.

To reach its result, the Court necessarily has had to find within the scope of the Fourteenth Amendment a right that was apparently completely unknown to the drafters of the Amendment. As early as 1821, the first state law dealing directly with abortion was enacted by the Connecticut Legislature. Conn.Stat., Tit. 22, §§ 14, 16. By the time of the adoption of the Fourteenth Amendment in 1868, there were at least 36 laws enacted by state or territorial legislatures limiting abortion. While many States have amended or updated their laws, 21 of the laws on the books in 1868 remain in effect today. Indeed, the Texas statute struck down today was, as the majority notes, first enacted in 1857, and "has remained substantially unchanged to the present time." *Ante* at 119.

There apparently was no question concerning the validity of this provision or of any of the other state statutes when the Fourteenth Amendment was adopted. The only conclusion possible from this history is that the drafters did not intend to have the Fourteenth Amendment withdraw from the States the power to legislate with respect to this matter.

III

Even if one were to agree that the case that the Court decides were here, and that the enunciation of the substantive constitutional law in the Court's opinion were proper, the actual disposition of the case by the Court is still difficult to justify. The Texas statute is struck down *in toto,* even though the Court apparently concedes that, at later periods of pregnancy Texas might impose these self-same statutory limitations on abortion. My understanding of past practice is that a statute found to be invalid as applied to a particular plaintiff, but not unconstitutional as a whole, is not simply "struck down" but is, instead, declared unconstitutional as applied to the fact situation before the Court. *Yick Wo v. Hopkins,* 118 U.S. 356 (1886); *Street v. New York,* 394 U.S. 576 (1969).

For all of the foregoing reasons, I respectfully dissent.

POSTSCRIPT

Does a Constitutional Right to Privacy Protect a Woman's Right to Obtain a Lawful Abortion?

This may be one of the more controversial questions presented in this volume. Justice Harry A. Blackmun contends that the constitutional right to privacy, established in *Griswold v. Connecticut* (1965), is sufficiently broad to protect a woman's decision to terminate an unwanted pregnancy. Justice William H. Rehnquist, in contrast, maintains that although privacy may be a form of liberty protected by the Fourteenth Amendment, such an interest is safeguarded only against state actions without due process of law. Moreover, he believes that the right to an abortion is no "so rooted in the traditions and conscience of our people as to be ranked fundamental." Whichever side of the abortion debate one embraces, however, it is difficult to deny that *Roe v. Wade* has exerted a significant impact on U.S. law and society.

At this point in our discussion, it may be instructive to focus briefly on the essential holding and trimester framework established in *Roe v. Wade*. State abortion laws that criminalize abortion except to save a mother's life without regard to the stage of her pregnancy violate the Due Process Clause of the Fourteenth Amendment, which protects a woman's right to privacy and to terminate an unwanted pregnancy. A state, too, has legitimate interests in protecting both maternal health and potential human life. Each of these interests reaches a "compelling" point as the gestation process advances. For the stage before approximately the end of the first trimester, the abortion decision must be left to the judgment of the pregnant woman and her physician. For the stage approximately following the end of the first trimester, a state, in order to promote its interest in maternal health, may regulate the abortion procedure in a manner that is reasonably related to that interest. For the stage after the fetus becomes viable (typically the third trimester), a state, in order to promote its interest in potential human life, may regulate, and even ban abortion, except when necessary to preserve the life or health of the mother.

When *Roe v. Wade* was issued in 1973, it invalidated the abortion laws of many different states. At the time, a significant number of states had laws that permitted abortion only when necessary to protect maternal life. Others had less restrictive laws that would permit abortion under somewhat broader circumstances, such as when the fetus was seriously deformed or when a pregnancy had resulted from rape or incest. *Roe* mandated changes in such restrictive laws and set the stage for continuing battles over the abortion issue.

Over the next several years, it became clear that a number of states, particularly in traditionally conservative areas of the United States, were committed to limiting the exercise of a woman's right to obtain a lawful abortion by passing laws designed to restrict this practice by chipping away at *Roe v. Wader*'s trimester framework. The abortion debate was far from over. Although a comprehensive review of the Supreme Court's decisions since *Roe v. Wade* is beyond the scope of the present initiative, it is important to consider a few important precedents that have helped to shape the contemporary law of abortion in the United States.

In *Akron v. Akron Center for Reproductive Health, Inc.*, 462 U.S. 416 (1983), the state of Ohio had passed a law requiring that all abortions after the first trimester be performed in a hospital. This law effectively prevented second-trimester abortions from being performed in outpatient facilities, which were much more convenient for many women. The U.S. Supreme Court held that the state's law was unconstitutional. Although a state may require that all second-trimester abortions be performed in a licensed clinic, it could not mandate that they be performed in a fully equipped hospital.

In another important case, *Webster v. Reproductive Health Services*, 492 U.S. 490 (1989), a Missouri statute prohibited the use of public facilities and public employees for the performance of any abortion that was not necessary to save a mother's life. It also stated that if a doctor believed that a fetus was 20 or more weeks old, he or she was required to conduct viability testing before performing an abortion. Moreover, the preamble to the statute declared that "life begins at conception."

The Supreme Court upheld the provision that prohibited the use of public facilities and public employees for performing abortions. It held that a state is not constitutionally required to assist women seeking to have an abortion. It further held that the law's viability testing provision was permissible. Moreover, a three-justice plurality asserted that *Roe v. Wade*'s trimester framework for analyzing abortion statutes should be abandoned. A legal principle that does not have the support of a majority of the justices, as in the case of a plurality decision, does not constitute a binding precedent for future cases; however, a plurality position remains highly useful to attorneys and others who are interested in developing future arguments in similar cases. Thus, although a majority of the Court in *Webster* did not vote to overturn *Roe v. Wade,* its trimester framework was left hanging by a thread.

Also noteworthy is that Justice Sandra D. O'Connor, writing separately, asserted a new standard for analyzing a state's restrictions on abortions. Justice O'Connor stated that abortion regulations were lawful unless they placed an "undue burden" on a woman's privacy right. This standard has become highly important in subsequent abortion cases.

Shortly after the *Webster* decision, Justices William J. Brennan and Thurgood Marshall, two strong advocates for *Roe v. Wade,* retired from the Court. They were replaced by Clarence Thomas and David Souter, men whose judicial philosophies were very different from those of Brennan and Marshall.

Planned Parenthood of Southeastern Pennsylvania v. Casey, 505 U.S. 833 (1992) demonstrated the impact that the new members of the Supreme Court would have on abortion cases. A Pennsylvania statute had imposed several different conditions on a woman's ability to obtain an abortion, including providing her with information about the abortion process, so-called "informed consent"; a 24-hour waiting period after providing her with the preceding information; spousal consent; parental consent for minors, which also contained a "judicial bypass" procedure to permit minors to seek a judge's permission to obtain an abortion as an alternative to parental consent; and recordkeeping requirements for medical staff.

The Supreme Court upheld all of the statute's requirements, except the provision requiring spousal consent. The strong desire of abortion opponents for the Supreme Court to conclusively overturn *Roe v. Wade* had failed to occur yet again, however, as *Casey* reaffirmed *Roe*'s essential holding. (*Gonzales v. Carhart*, 505 U.S. 124 (2007)).

In 2003, the U.S. Congress passed a federal abortion law, the Partial-Birth Abortion Ban Act, 18 U.S.C. Section 1531. The statute prohibits "partial-birth abortions," which are defined as:

> An abortion in which the person performing the abortion, deliberately and intentionally vaginally delivers a living fetus until, in the case of a head-first presentation, the entire fetal head is outside the body of the mother, or, in the case of breech presentation, any part of the fetal trunk past the navel is outside the body of the mother, for the purpose of performing an overt act that the person knows will kill the partially delivered living fetus; and performs the overt act, other than completion of delivery, that kills the partially delivered human fetus.

Partial-birth abortions are normally utilized during the second trimester of pregnancy and a fetus may be viable at this stage. The statutory penalty for any physician who performs a partial-birth abortion is a fine and imprisonment for not more than 2 years.

Gonzales v. Carhart, 550 U.S. 124 (2007), presented the issue of the constitutionality of the Partial-Birth Abortion Ban Act. The Supreme Court held first that the statute was not void for vagueness. The *void for vagueness doctrine* asserts that a statute is unconstitutionally vague if it fails to provide persons "of ordinary intelligence a reasonable opportunity to know what is prohibited," thus lending itself to "arbitrary or discriminatory enforcement." Second, the Court held that the statute did not impose an undue burden on a woman's right to obtain an abortion. Its restrictions on second-trimester abortions were not too broad.

So, where are we now with regard to the status of abortion laws in the United States following *Casey* and *Carhart?* Professors Mason and Stephenson have cogently summarized it as follows:

> First, abortion no longer has status as a fundamental right but enjoys a kind of intermediate constitutional protection. Second, and as a consequence of the first, total or near-total bans on previability abortions are almost certainly unconstitutional. Third, the Court will accept restrictions on abortions that would have been quickly rejected just two decades ago. However, just how numerous and how burdensome such restrictions may be, beyond the terms of the 2003 statute, still remains

to be seen. Finally, more than at any time since 1973, a woman's freedom to terminate a pregnancy now depends largely on what state legislatures, Congress, and the president allow. The court may now tolerate more regulations, but it does not require them (Mason & Stephenson, 2009: 586).

Abortion presents a host of difficult questions for scholars and students alike. Fortunately, there are a considerable number of additional resources to pursue further study in this area, including: Kathleen M. Sullivan and Gerald Gunther, *Constitutional Law* (Foundation Press, 15th ed., 2004); Laurence H. Tribe, *American Constitutional Law* (Foundation Press, 2nd ed., 1988); Alpheus Thomas Mason and Donald Grier Stephenson, Jr., *American Constitutional Law* (Pearson Prentice Hall, 15th ed., 2009; 14th ed., 2005); Bernard Schwartz, *A History of the Supreme Court* (Oxford University Press, 1993); Kermit L. Hall, Paul Finkelman, and James Ely, Jr., *American Legal History: Cases and Materials* (Oxford University Press, 3rd ed., 2005); Kermit L. Hall, *The Oxford Companion to the Supreme Court of the United States* (Oxford University Press, 1992); Walter F. Murphy, James E. Flemming, Sotirios A. Barber, and Stephen Macedo, *American Constitutional Interpretation* (Foundation Press, 3rd ed., 2003); David M. O'Brien, *Constitutional Law and Politics: Struggles for Power and Government Accountability* (W.W. Norton, 6th ed., 2005); Craig R. Ducat, *Constitutional Interpretation* (Wadsworth, 9th ed., 2009); John H. Garvey, T. Alexander Aleinikoff, and Daniel A. Farber, *Modern Constitutional Theory: A Reader* (Thompson West, 5th ed., 2004). See also: Janessa L. Bernstein, "The Underground Railroad to Reproductive Freedom: Restrictive Abortion Laws and the Resulting Backlash," *Brooklyn Law Review,* vol. 73, p. 1463 (2008); Neal Devins, "How Planned Parenthood *v.* Casey (Pretty Much) Settled the Abortion Wars," *Yale Law Journal,* vol. 118, p. 1318 (2009); Caitlin Borgmann, "Abortion, the Undue Burden Standard, and the Evisceration of Women's Privacy," *William and Mary Journal of Women and the Law,* vol. 16, p. 291 (2010); and Teresa Stanton Collett, "Judicial Modesty and Abortion," *South Carolina Law Review,* vol. 59, p. 701 (2008).

ISSUE 11

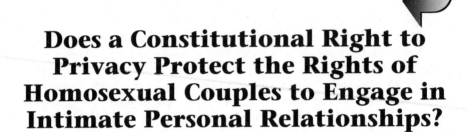

Does a Constitutional Right to Privacy Protect the Rights of Homosexual Couples to Engage in Intimate Personal Relationships?

YES: Anthony M. Kennedy, from Majority Opinion, *Lawrence v. Texas,* 539 U.S. 558 (2003)

NO: Antonin E. Scalia, from Dissenting Opinion, *Lawrence v. Texas,* 539 U.S. 558 (2003)

ISSUE SUMMARY

YES: Justice Anthony M. Kennedy, writing for the U.S. Supreme Court in *Lawrence v. Texas* (2003), held that a Texas law making it a crime for two persons of the same sex to engage in intimate sexual conduct violates the Fourteenth Amendment's Due Process Clause.

NO: Justice Antonin E. Scalia, dissenting in *Lawrence v. Texas* (2003), asserted that the Texas law does not infringe a "fundamental right." Moreover, it bears a rational relationship to what the Constitution considers a legitimate state interest and does not deny the equal protection of the laws.

Society, through the legal system, regulates many aspects of our lives. There is an old saying that if you look long and hard enough, you can find a law somewhere that will prohibit almost anything. It seems reasonable to ask if state and federal legislatures have developed "too much law." Are there areas of human life that legislatures should not attempt to regulate? If so, is there an intelligible principle that courts should use to determine precisely what those areas are?

In the mid-nineteenth century, the celebrated British philosopher and author John Stuart Mill wrote a now-famous essay *On Liberty,* which may have developed such a principle. In the portion of his essay titled "Of the Limits to the Authority of Society over the Individual," Mill asked:

> Where does the authority of society begin? How much of human life should be assigned to individuality, and how much to society? [E]very one who receives the protection of society owes a return for the benefit,

238

and the fact of living in society renders it indispensable that each should be bound to observe a certain line of conduct towards the rest. This conduct consists first, in not injuring the interests of one another . . . But when a person's conduct affects the interests of no persons besides himself . . . there should be perfect freedom, legal and social, to do the action and stand the consequences.

Based on the passage above, how do you think John Stuart Mill would respond to the question posed in this issue? It seems very likely that he would agree that homosexuals should have a constitutional right to privacy that protects their rights to engage in intimate sexual activities: When two individuals freely consent to engage in sexual activity that harms no persons besides themselves, there should be "perfect freedom" to do what they wish. One could also argue, however, that homosexual activity, even between consenting individuals, harms society by eroding its moral standards. Moreover, the issue of whether society should use its legal system to enforce popular conceptions of morality is an important one.

In the United States, homosexual activity has been proscribed throughout much of our history. Most prosecutions of homosexuals for having intimate relations have used state sodomy laws. *Sodomy* is defined in *Black's Law Dictionary* (1979) as "oral or anal copulation between persons who are not husband and wife or consenting adult members of the opposite sex, or between a person and an animal, or coitus with an animal." Following the recommendations of the American Law Institute's Model Penal Code, many states repealed their sodomy laws in the 1970s. A number of commentators at that time also raised the difficult issue of whether it was fair to prosecute homosexuals for engaging in sodomy while heterosexuals were very rarely prosecuted for the same behavior.

The state of Georgia, however, did not repeal its sodomy law. In 1982, Michael Hardwick was arrested for violating the Georgia sodomy law, after a police officer observed him engaged in oral sex with another man. A houseguest had admitted the officer into Hardwick's apartment. The Georgia statute provided that it was a crime to perform or submit to a "sexual act involving the sex organs of one person and the mouth or anus of another"; it did not, however, distinguish between heterosexual and homosexual sodomy. The officer arrested Hardwick and the other man for sodomy. The local prosecutor declined to prosecute the case, however, or present it to a grand jury. Hardwick then sued Georgia's Attorney General, Michael Bowers, in the U.S. District Court and requested a declaratory judgment that Georgia's sodomy law was unconstitutional. When the case was dismissed by that court, Hardwick appealed to the U.S. Court of Appeals, which held that the law was an unconstitutional violation of his right to privacy.

Bowers v. Hardwick, 478 U.S. 186 (1986) presented the U.S. Supreme Court with the issue of whether the constitutional right to privacy, established in *Griswold v. Connecticut,* should be extended to the private consensual sexual conduct of homosexuals. In a five-to-four vote, the Supreme Court upheld Georgia's sodomy statute. Writing for the majority, Justice Byron R. White phrased the issue in this case as follows: "Does the Federal Constitution confer a fundamental right upon homosexuals to engage in sodomy"? Justice White asserted that the right to engage in homosexual sodomy is not one that is "deeply rooted in our Nation's history and tradition" or "implicit in a concept of ordered liberty." In fact, White stated that prohibitions against homosexual sodomy have ancient roots and "to claim that a right to engage in such conduct is 'deeply rooted in this Nation's history and tradition' . . . is, at best, facetious."

You may recall from our discussion of *Griswold v. Connecticut* that the Supreme Court uses different analytical techniques to analyze state laws that implicate constitutional rights. If the purported right at issue is determined to be a fundamental one, the Supreme Court will use strict scrutiny to analyze it. When the Court uses strict scrutiny, it usually holds that the law is unconstitutional. When it decides that a purported right is not a fundamental one, however, the Court will analyze it using rationality review. A state needs only to demonstrate a rational basis for its law. . . .

In *Bowers v. Hardwick,* once the Court had decided that the right to engage in homosexual sodomy was not fundamental, the Georgia statute had only to survive rationality review. Hardwick had argued that the Georgia sodomy law lacked any rational basis, other than the belief of a majority of the electorate that homosexual sodomy is immoral. Justice White responded, however, that laws are "constantly based on notions of morality, and if all laws representing essentially moral choices are to be invalidated under the Due Process Clause, the courts will be very busy indeed." Thus, the statute was upheld because it had a rational basis.

Justice Harry A. Blackmun, dissenting, took issue with the way that the majority had formulated the legal issue in this case. Justice Blackmun asserted that the case was not so much about a right to engage in homosexual sodomy as much as it was about the right to be left alone by the government.

Bowers v. Hardwick, then, upheld the rights of states to develop laws to regulate homosexual sodomy. Do you believe that the Court's majority was correct to cast the issue in this case as the right to engage in homosexual sodomy, or was Justice Blackmun's statement of the issue a more compelling one? In any event, *Bowers v. Hardwick* has generated substantial controversy. Some commentators had even described it as "our generation's *Korematsu,*" the case in which the U.S. Supreme Court had upheld the internment of persons of Japanese ancestry in relocation camps during World War II.

The Supreme Court was asked to revisit the issue presented in *Bowers v. Hardwick* approximately 24 years later. In *Lawrence v. Texas,* 539 U.S. 538 (2003), a Harris County deputy sheriff entered Lawrence's apartment in response to a report of a weapons disturbance. The right of the police to enter was not questioned at trial. The officer observed Lawrence and another man, Tyron Garner, engaging in a sexual act. The men were arrested, charged, and convicted before a justice of the peace for engaging in "deviate sexual intercourse, namely anal sex, with a member of the same sex (man)." The Texas law provided: "A person commits an offense if he engages in deviate sexual intercourse with another individual of the same sex." At trial, the defendants were convicted of violating this law and were each fined $200. The Texas Court of Appeals affirmed the convictions.

Writing for the U.S. Supreme Court, Justice Anthony M. Kennedy held that the Texas law was unconstitutional because it violated the Due Process Clause of the Fourteenth Amendment. The Court also overturned *Bowers v. Hardwick* because its "rationale [did] not withstand careful analysis." Moreover, the Court observed that since *Bowers* had been decided, "criticism . . . [was] substantial and continuing, disapproving of its reasoning in all respects. . . ." Justice Kennedy concluded:

> [This] case involve[s] two adults who, with full and mutual consent from each other, engaged in sexual practices common to a homosexual lifestyle. The petitioners are entitled to respect for their private lives. The State cannot demean their existence or control their destiny by making their private sexual conduct a crime. Their right to liberty under the Due Process Clause gives them the full right to engage in their conduct without intervention of the government. . . . The Texas statute furthers no legitimate state interest which can justify its intrusion into the personal and private life of the individual.

Justice Antonin E. Scalia, in a dissenting opinion, asserted that the Court's opinion in *Bowers v. Hardwick* should have been upheld. Stated Scalia:

> Today's opinion is the product of a Court, which is the product of a law-profession culture, that has largely signed on to the so-called homosexual agenda, by which I mean the agenda promoted by some homosexual activists directed at eliminating the moral opprobrium that has traditionally attached to homosexual conduct. . . . It is clear from this that the Court has taken sides in the culture war, departing from its role of assuring, as neutral observer, that the democratic rules of engagement are observed.

In Your Opinion . . .

- Who presents the better position, Justice Kennedy or Justice Scalia?
- Do you believe that *Bowers v. Hardwick* should have been overturned, or should it have remained a binding precedent?
- Should the right to engage in intimate sexual relations be protected by the Due Process Clause of the Fourteenth Amendment?

YES

Anthony M. Kennedy

Majority Opinion, *Lawrence v. Texas*

J ustice Kennedy delivered the opinion of the Court.

Liberty protects the person from unwarranted government intrusions into a dwelling or other private places. In our tradition the State is not omnipresent in the home. And there are other spheres of our lives and existence, outside the home, where the State should not be a dominant presence. Freedom extends beyond spatial bounds. Liberty presumes an autonomy of self that includes freedom of thought, belief, expression, and certain intimate conduct. The instant case involves liberty of the person both in its spatial and more transcendent dimensions.

I

The question before the Court is the validity of a Texas statute making it a crime for two persons of the same sex to engage in certain intimate sexual conduct.

In Houston, Texas, officers of the Harris County Police Department were dispatched to a private residence in response to a reported weapons disturbance. They entered an apartment where one of the petitioners, John Geddes Lawrence, resided. The right of the police to enter does not seem to have been questioned. The officers observed Lawrence and another man, Tyron Garner, engaging in a sexual act. The two petitioners were arrested, held in custody over night, and charged and convicted before a Justice of the Peace.

The complaints described their crime as "deviate sexual intercourse, namely anal sex, with a member of the same sex (man)." App. to Pet. for Cert. 127a, 139a. The applicable state law is Tex. Penal Code Ann. §21.06(a) (2003). It provides: "A person commits an offense if he engages in deviate sexual intercourse with another individual of the same sex." The statute defines "[d]eviate sexual intercourse" as follows:

"(A) any contact between any part of the genitals of one person and the mouth or anus of another person; or

(B) the penetration of the genitals or the anus of another person with an object." §21.01(1).

The petitioners exercised their right to a trial *de novo* in Harris County Criminal Court. They challenged the statute as a violation of the Equal Protection

Supreme Court of the United States, 539 U.S. 588, 2003.

Clause of the Fourteenth Amendment and of a like provision of the Texas Constitution. Tex. Const., Art. 1, §3a. Those contentions were rejected. The petitioners, having entered a plea of *nolo contendere,* were each fined $200 and assessed court costs of $141.25. App. to Pet. for Cert. 107a–110a.

The Court of Appeals for the Texas Fourteenth District considered the petitioners' federal constitutional arguments under both the Equal Protection and Due Process Clauses of the Fourteenth Amendment. After hearing the case en banc the court, in a divided opinion, rejected the constitutional arguments and affirmed the convictions. 41 S. W. 3d 349 (Tex. App. 2001). The majority opinion indicates that the Court of Appeals considered our decision in *Bowers v. Hardwick,* 478 U.S. 186 (1986), to be controlling on the federal due process aspect of the case. *Bowers* then being authoritative, this was proper.

We granted certiorari, 537 U.S. 1044 (2002), to consider three questions:

1. Whether Petitioners' criminal convictions under the Texas "Homosexual Conduct" law—which criminalizes sexual intimacy by same-sex couples, but not identical behavior by different-sex couples—violate the Fourteenth Amendment guarantee of equal protection of laws?
2. Whether Petitioners' criminal convictions for adult consensual sexual intimacy in the home violate their vital interests in liberty and privacy protected by the Due Process Clause of the Fourteenth Amendment?
3. Whether Bowers *v. Hardwick,* 478 U.S. 186 (1986), should be overruled? Pet. for Cert. i.

The petitioners were adults at the time of the alleged offense. Their conduct was in private and consensual.

II

We conclude the case should be resolved by determining whether the petitioners were free as adults to engage in the private conduct in the exercise of their liberty under the Due Process Clause of the Fourteenth Amendment to the Constitution. For this inquiry we deem it necessary to reconsider the Court's holding in *Bowers.*

There are broad statements of the substantive reach of liberty under the Due Process Clause in earlier cases, including *Pierce v. Society of Sisters,* 268 U.S. 510 (1925), and *Meyer v. Nebraska,* 262 U.S. 390 (1923); but the most pertinent beginning point is our decision in *Griswold v. Connecticut,* 381 U.S. 479 (1965).

In *Griswold* the Court invalidated a state law prohibiting the use of drugs or devices of contraception and counseling or aiding and abetting the use of contraceptives. The Court described the protected interest as a right to privacy and placed emphasis on the marriage relation and the protected space of the marital bedroom. *Id.,* at 485.

After *Griswold* it was established that the right to make certain decisions regarding sexual conduct extends beyond the marital relationship. In *Eisenstadt v. Baird,* 405 U.S. 438 (1972), the Court invalidated a law prohibiting the distribution of contraceptives to unmarried persons. The case was decided under the

Equal Protection Clause, *id.*, at 454; but with respect to unmarried persons, the Court went on to state the fundamental proposition that the law impaired the exercise of their personal rights, *ibid.* It quoted from the statement of the Court of Appeals finding the law to be in conflict with fundamental human rights, and it followed with this statement of its own:

> "It is true that in *Griswold* the right of privacy in question inhered in the marital relationship. . . . If the right of privacy means anything, it is the right of the *individual,* married or single, to be free from unwarranted governmental intrusion into matters so fundamentally affecting a person as the decision whether to bear or beget a child." *Id.*, at 453.

The opinions in *Griswold* and *Eisenstadt* were part of the background for the decision in *Roe v. Wade*, 410 U.S. 113 (1973). As is well known, the case involved a challenge to the Texas law prohibiting abortions, but the laws of other States were affected as well. Although the Court held the woman's rights were not absolute, her right to elect an abortion did have real and substantial protection as an exercise of her liberty under the Due Process Clause. The Court cited cases that protect spatial freedom and cases that go well beyond it. *Roe* recognized the right of a woman to make certain fundamental decisions affecting her destiny and confirmed once more that the protection of liberty under the Due Process Clause has a substantive dimension of fundamental significance in defining the rights of the person.

In *Carey v. Population Services Int'l*, 431 U.S. 678 (1977), the Court confronted a New York law forbidding sale or distribution of contraceptive devices to persons under 16 years of age. Although there was no single opinion for the Court, the law was invalidated. Both *Eisenstadt* and *Carey*, as well as the holding and rationale in *Roe*, confirmed that the reasoning of *Griswold* could not be confined to the protection of rights of married adults. This was the state of the law with respect to some of the most relevant cases when the Court considered *Bowers v. Hardwick.*

The facts in *Bowers* had some similarities to the instant case. A police officer, whose right to enter seems not to have been in question, observed Hardwick, in his own bedroom, engaging in intimate sexual conduct with another adult male. The conduct was in violation of a Georgia statute making it a criminal offense to engage in sodomy. One difference between the two cases is that the Georgia statute prohibited the conduct whether or not the participants were of the same sex, while the Texas statute, as we have seen, applies only to participants of the same sex. Hardwick was not prosecuted, but he brought an action in federal court to declare the state statute invalid. He alleged he was a practicing homosexual and that the criminal prohibition violated rights guaranteed to him by the Constitution. The Court, in an opinion by Justice White, sustained the Georgia law. Chief Justice Burger and Justice Powell joined the opinion of the Court and filed separate, concurring opinions. Four Justices dissented. 478 U.S., at 199 (opinion of Blackmun, J., joined by Brennan, Marshall, and Stevens, JJ.); *id.*, at 214 (opinion of Stevens, J., joined by Brennan and Marshall, JJ.).

The Court began its substantive discussion in *Bowers* as follows: "The issue presented is whether the Federal Constitution confers a fundamental right upon homosexuals to engage in sodomy and hence invalidates the laws of the many States that still make such conduct illegal and have done so for a very long time." *Id.*, at 190. That statement, we now conclude, discloses the Court's own failure to appreciate the extent of the liberty at stake. To say that the issue in *Bowers* was simply the right to engage in certain sexual conduct demeans the claim the individual put forward, just as it would demean a married couple were it to be said marriage is simply about the right to have sexual intercourse. The laws involved in *Bowers* and here are, to be sure, statutes that purport to do no more than prohibit a particular sexual act. Their penalties and purposes, though, have more far-reaching consequences, touching upon the most private human conduct, sexual behavior, and in the most private of places, the home. The statutes do seek to control a personal relationship that, whether or not entitled to formal recognition in the law, is within the liberty of persons to choose without being punished as criminals.

This, as a general rule, should counsel against attempts by the State, or a court, to define the meaning of the relationship or to set its boundaries absent injury to a person or abuse of an institution the law protects. It suffices for us to acknowledge that adults may choose to enter upon this relationship in the confines of their homes and their own private lives and still retain their dignity as free persons. When sexuality finds overt expression in intimate conduct with another person, the conduct can be but one element in a personal bond that is more enduring. The liberty protected by the Constitution allows homosexual persons the right to make this choice.

Having misapprehended the claim of liberty there presented to it, and thus stating the claim to be whether there is a fundamental right to engage in consensual sodomy, the *Bowers* Court said: "Proscriptions against that conduct have ancient roots." *Id.*, at 192. In academic writings, and in many of the scholarly *amicus* briefs filed to assist the Court in this case, there are fundamental criticisms of the historical premises relied upon by the majority and concurring opinions in *Bowers*. Brief for Cato Institute as *Amicus Curiae* 16–17; Brief for American Civil Liberties Union et al. as *Amici Curiae* 15–21; Brief for Professors of History et al. as *Amici Curiae* 3–10. We need not enter this debate in the attempt to reach a definitive historical judgment, but the following considerations counsel against adopting the definitive conclusions upon which *Bowers* placed such reliance.

At the outset it should be noted that there is no longstanding history in this country of laws directed at homosexual conduct as a distinct matter. Beginning in colonial times there were prohibitions of sodomy derived from the English criminal laws passed in the first instance by the Reformation Parliament of 1533. The English prohibition was understood to include relations between men and women as well as relations between men and men. See, *e.g.*, *King v. Wiseman*, 92 Eng. Rep. 774, 775 (K. B. 1718) (interpreting "mankind" in Act of 1533 as including women and girls). Nineteenth-century commentators similarly read American sodomy, buggery, and crime-against-nature statutes as criminalizing certain relations between men and women and between men and men. See, *e.g.*, 2 J. Bishop, Criminal Law §1028 (1858); 2 J. Chitty, Criminal Law 47–50 (5th Am. ed. 1847); R. Desty, A Compendium of American Criminal

Law 143 (1882); J. May, The Law of Crimes §203 (2nd ed. 1893). The absence of legal prohibitions focusing on homosexual conduct may be explained in part by noting that according to some scholars the concept of the homosexual as a distinct category of person did not emerge until the late 19th century. See, e.g., J. Katz, The Invention of Heterosexuality 10 (1995); J. D'Emilio & E. Freedman, Intimate Matters: A History of Sexuality in America 121 (2nd ed. 1997) ("The modern terms *homosexuality* and *heterosexuality* do not apply to an era that had not yet articulated these distinctions"). Thus, early American sodomy laws were not directed at homosexuals as such but instead sought to prohibit nonprocreative sexual activity more generally. This does not suggest approval of homosexual conduct. It does tend to show that this particular form of conduct was not thought of as a separate category from like conduct between heterosexual persons.

Laws prohibiting sodomy do not seem to have been enforced against consenting adults acting in private. A substantial number of sodomy prosecutions and convictions for which there are surviving records were for predatory acts against those who could not or did not consent, as in the case of a minor or the victim of an assault. As to these, one purpose for the prohibitions was to ensure there would be no lack of coverage if a predator committed a sexual assault that did not constitute rape as defined by the criminal law. Thus, the model sodomy indictments presented in a 19th-century treatise, see 2 Chitty, *supra*, at 49, addressed the predatory acts of an adult man against a minor girl or minor boy. Instead of targeting relations between consenting adults in private, 19th-century sodomy prosecutions typically involved relations between men and minor girls or boys, relations between adults involving force, relations between adults implicating disparity in status, or relations between men and animals.

To the extent that there were any prosecutions for the acts in question, 19th-century evidence rules imposed a burden that would make a conviction more difficult to obtain even taking into account the problems always inherent in prosecuting consensual acts committed in private. Under then-prevailing standards, a man could not be convicted of sodomy based upon testimony of a consenting partner, because the partner was considered an accomplice. A partner's testimony, however, was admissible if he or she had not consented to the act or was a minor, and therefore incapable of consent. See, *e.g.*, F. Wharton, Criminal Law 443 (2nd ed. 1852); 1 F. Wharton, Criminal Law 512 (8th ed. 1880). The rule may explain in part the infrequency of these prosecutions. In all events that infrequency makes it difficult to say that society approved of a rigorous and systematic punishment of the consensual acts committed in private and by adults. The longstanding criminal prohibition of homosexual sodomy upon which the *Bowers* decision placed such reliance is as consistent with a general condemnation of nonprocreative sex as it is with an established tradition of prosecuting acts because of their homosexual character.

The policy of punishing consenting adults for private acts was not much discussed in the early legal literature. We can infer that one reason for this was the very private nature of the conduct. Despite the absence of prosecutions, there may have been periods in which there was public criticism of

YES / Anthony M. Kennedy   **247**

homosexuals as such and an insistence that the criminal laws be enforced to discourage their practices. But far from possessing "ancient roots," *Bowers*, 478 U.S., at 192, American laws targeting same-sex couples did not develop until the last third of the 20th century. The reported decisions concerning the prosecution of consensual, homosexual sodomy between adults for the years 1880–1995 are not always clear in the details, but a significant number involved conduct in a public place. See Brief for American Civil Liberties Union et al. as *Amici Curiae* 14–15, and n. 18.

It was not until the 1970s that any State singled out same-sex relations for criminal prosecution, and only nine States have done so. See 1977 Ark. Gen. Acts no. 828; 1983 Kan. Sess. Laws p. 652; 1974 Ky. Acts p. 847; 1977 Mo. Laws p. 687; 1973 Mont. Laws p. 1339; 1977 Nev. Stats, p. 1632; 1989 Tenn. Pub. Acts ch. 591; 1973 Tex. Gen. Laws ch. 399; see also *Post v. State*, 715 P.2nd 1105 (Okla. Crim. App. 1986) (sodomy law invalidated as applied to different-sex couples). Post-Bowers even some of these States did not adhere to the policy of suppressing homosexual conduct. Over the course of the last decades, States with same-sex prohibitions have moved toward abolishing them. See, *e.g.*, *Jegley v. Picado*, 349 Ark. 600, 80 S. W. 3d 332 (2002); *Gryczan v. State*, 283 Mont. 433, 942 P.2nd 112 (1997); *Campbell v. Sundquist*, 926 S. W. 2nd 250 (Tenn. App. 1996); *Commonwealth v. Wasson*, 842 S. W. 2nd 487 (Ky. 1992); see also 1993 Nev. Stats. p. 518 (repealing Nev. Rev. Stat. §201.193).

In summary, the historical grounds relied upon in *Bowers* are more complex than the majority opinion and the concurring opinion by Chief Justice Burger indicate. Their historical premises are not without doubt and, at the very least, are overstated.

It must be acknowledged, of course, that the Court in *Bowers* was making the broader point that for centuries there have been powerful voices to condemn homosexual conduct as immoral. The condemnation has been shaped by religious beliefs, conceptions of right and acceptable behavior, and respect for the traditional family. For many persons these are not trivial concerns but profound and deep convictions accepted as ethical and moral principles to which they aspire and which thus determine the course of their lives. These considerations do not answer the question before us, however. The issue is whether the majority may use the power of the State to enforce these views on the whole society through operation of the criminal law. "Our obligation is to define the liberty of all, not to mandate our own moral code." *Planned Parenthood of Southeastern Pa. v. Casey*, 505 U.S. 833, 850 (1992).

Chief Justice Burger joined the opinion for the Court in *Bowers* and further explained his views as follows: "Decisions of individuals relating to homosexual conduct have been subject to state intervention throughout the history of Western civilization. Condemnation of those practices is firmly rooted in Judeao-Christian moral and ethical standards." 478 U.S., at 196. As with Justice White's assumptions about history, scholarship casts some doubt on the sweeping nature of the statement by Chief Justice Burger as it pertains to private homosexual conduct between consenting adults. See, *e.g.*, Eskridge, Hardwick and Historiography, 1999 U. Ill. L. Rev. 631, 656. In all events we think that our laws and traditions in the past half century are of most relevance here. These references show an emerging awareness that liberty gives substantial protection to adult persons in deciding how to conduct their private lives in matters pertaining to sex. "[H]istory and tradition are the starting point but not in all cases the ending point of the substantive due process inquiry." *County of Sacramento v. Lewis,* 523 U.S. 833, 857 (1998) (Kennedy, J., concurring).

This emerging recognition should have been apparent when *Bowers* was decided. In 1955, the American Law Institute promulgated the Model Penal Code and made clear that it did not recommend or provide for "criminal penalties for consensual sexual relations conducted in private." ALI, Model Penal Code §213.2, Comment 2, p. 372 (1980). It justified its decision on three grounds: (1) The prohibitions undermined respect for the law by penalizing conduct many people engaged in; (2) the statutes regulated private conduct not harmful to others; and (3) the laws were arbitrarily enforced and thus invited the danger of blackmail. ALI, Model Penal Code, Commentary 277–280 (Tent. Draft No. 4, 1955). In 1961, Illinois changed its laws to conform to the Model Penal Code. Other States soon followed. Brief for Cato Institute as *Amicus Curiae* 15–16.

In *Bowers* the Court referred to the fact that before 1961 all 50 States had outlawed sodomy, and that at the time of the Court's decision 24 States and the District of Columbia had sodomy laws. 478 U.S., at 192–193. Justice Powell pointed out that these prohibitions often were being ignored, however. Georgia, for instance, had not sought to enforce its law for decades. *Id.,* at 197–198, n. 2 ("The history of nonenforcement suggests the moribund character today of laws criminalizing this type of private, consensual conduct").

The sweeping references by Chief Justice Burger to the history of Western civilization and to Judeo-Christian moral and ethical standards did not take account of other authorities pointing in an opposite direction. A committee advising the British Parliament recommended in 1957 repeal of laws punishing homosexual conduct. The Wolfenden Report: Report of the Committee on Homosexual Offenses and Prostitution (1963). Parliament enacted the substance of those recommendations 10 years later. Sexual Offences Act 1967, §.

Of even more importance, almost five years before *Bowers* was decided, the European Court of Human Rights considered a case with parallels to *Bowers* and to today's case. An adult male resident in Northern Ireland alleged he was a practicing homosexual who desired to engage in consensual homosexual conduct. The laws of Northern Ireland forbade him that right. He alleged that he had been questioned, his home had been searched, and he feared criminal prosecution. The court held that the laws proscribing the conduct were invalid under the European Convention on Human Rights. *Dudgeon v. United Kingdom,* 45 *Eur. Ct. H. R.* (1981) ¶52. Authoritative in all countries that are members of the Council of Europe (21 nations then, 45 nations now), the decision is at odds with the premise in *Bowers* that the claim put forward was insubstantial in our Western civilization.

In our own constitutional system the deficiencies in *Bowers* became even more apparent in the years following its announcement. The 25 States with laws prohibiting the relevant conduct referenced in the *Bowers* decision are reduced now to 13, of which 4 enforce their laws only against homosexual conduct. In those States where sodomy is still proscribed, whether for same-sex or heterosexual conduct, there is a pattern of nonenforcement with respect to consenting adults acting in private. The State of Texas admitted in 1994 that as of that date it had not prosecuted anyone under those circumstances. *State v. Morales,* 869 S. W. 2nd 941, 943.

Two principal cases decided after *Bowers* cast its holding into even more doubt. In *Planned Parenthood of Southeastern Pa. v. Casey,* 505 U.S. 833 (1992), the Court reaffirmed the substantive force of the liberty protected by the Due Process Clause. The *Casey* decision again confirmed that our laws and tradition afford constitutional protection to personal decisions relating to marriage, pro-creation, contraception, family relationships, child rearing, and education. *Id.,* at 851. In explaining the respect the Constitution demands for the autonomy of the person in making these choices, we stated as follows:

> "These matters, involving the most intimate and personal choices a person may make in a lifetime, choices central to personal dignity and autonomy, are central to the liberty protected by the Fourteenth Amendment. At the heart of liberty is the right to define one's own concept of existence, of meaning, of the universe, and of the mys-tery of human life. Beliefs about these matters could not define the attributes of personhood were they formed under compulsion of the State." *Ibid.*

Persons in a homosexual relationship may seek autonomy for these pur-poses, just as heterosexual persons do. The decision in *Bowers* would deny them this right.

The second post-*Bowers* case of principal relevance is *Romer v. Evans,* 517 U.S. 620 (1996). There the Court struck down class-based legislation directed at homosexuals as a violation of the Equal Protection Clause. *Romer* invali-dated an amendment to Colorado's constitution which named as a solitary class persons who were homosexuals, lesbians, or bisexual either by "orienta-tion, conduct, practices or relationships," *id.,* at 624 (internal quotation marks omitted), and deprived them of protection under state antidiscrimination laws. We concluded that the provision was "born of animosity toward the class of persons affected" and further that it had no rational relation to a legitimate governmental purpose. *Id.,* at 634.

As an alternative argument in this case, counsel for the petitioners and some *amici* contend that *Romer* provides the basis for declaring the Texas stat-ute invalid under the Equal Protection Clause. That is a tenable argument, but we conclude the instant case requires us to address whether *Bowers* itself has continuing validity. Were we to hold the statute invalid under the Equal Protection Clause some might question whether a prohibition would be valid if drawn differently, say, to prohibit the conduct both between same-sex and different-sex participants.

Equality of treatment and the due process right to demand respect for conduct protected by the substantive guarantee of liberty are linked in important respects, and a decision on the latter point advances both interests. If protected conduct is made criminal and the law which does so remains unexamined for its substantive validity, its stigma might remain even if it were not enforceable as drawn for equal protection reasons. When homosexual conduct is made criminal by the law of the State, that declaration in and of itself is an invitation to subject homosexual persons to discrimination both in the public and in the private spheres. The central holding of *Bowers* has been brought in question by this case, and it should be addressed. Its continuance as precedent demeans the lives of homosexual persons.

The stigma this criminal statute imposes, moreover, is not trivial. The offense, to be sure, is but a class C misdemeanor, a minor offense in the Texas legal system. Still, it remains a criminal offense with all that imports for the dignity of the persons charged. The petitioners will bear on their record the history of their criminal convictions. Just this Term we rejected various challenges to state laws requiring the registration of sex offenders. *Smith v. Doe,* 538 U.S. _ (2003); *Connecticut Dept. of Public Safety v. Doe,* 538 U.S. 1 (2003). We are advised that if Texas convicted an adult for private, consensual homosexual conduct under the statute here in question the convicted person would come within the registration laws of a least four States were he or she to be subject to their jurisdiction. Pet. for Cert. 13, and n. 12 (citing Idaho Code §§18–8301 to 18–8326 (Cum. Supp. 2002); La. Code Crim. Proc. Ann., §§15:540–15:549 (West 2003); Miss. Code Ann. §§45–33–21 to 45–33–57 (Lexis 2003); S. C. Code Ann. §§23–3–400 to 23–3–490 (West 2002)). This underscores the consequential nature of the punishment and the state-sponsored condemnation attendant to the criminal prohibition. Furthermore, the Texas criminal conviction carries with it the other collateral consequences always following a conviction, such as notations on job application forms, to mention but one example.

The foundations of *Bowers* have sustained serious erosion from our recent decisions in *Casey* and *Romer.* When our precedent has been thus weakened, criticism from other sources is of greater significance. In the United States criticism of *Bowers* has been substantial and continuing, disapproving of its reasoning in all respects, not just as to its historical assumptions. See, *e.g.,* C. Fried, Order and Law: Arguing the Reagan Revolution—A Firsthand Account 81–84 (1991); R. Posner, Sex and Reason 341–350 (1992). The courts of five different States have declined to follow it in interpreting provisions in their own state constitutions parallel to the Due Process Clause of the Fourteenth Amendment, see *Jegley v. Picado,* 349 Ark. 600, 80 S. W. 3d 332 (2002); *Powell v. State,* 270 Ga. 327, 510 S. E. 2nd 18, 24 (1998); *Gryczan v. State,* 283 Mont. 433, 942 P.2nd 112 (1997); *Campbell v. Sundquist,* 926 S. W. 2nd 250 (Tenn. App. 1996); *Commonwealth v. Wasson,* 842 S. W. 2nd 487 (Ky. 1992).

To the extent *Bowers* relied on values we share with a wider civilization, it should be noted that the reasoning and holding in *Bowers* have been rejected elsewhere. The European Court of Human Rights has followed not *Bowers* but its own decision in *Dudgeon v. United Kingdom.* See *P. G. & J. H. v. United Kingdom,* App. No. 00044787/98, ¶56 (*Eur. Ct. H. R.,* Sept. 25, 2001); *Modinos v. Cyprus,* 259 *Eur. Ct. H. R.* (1993); *Norris v. Ireland,* 142 *Eur. Ct. H. R.* (1988). Other nations, too, have taken action consistent with an affirmation of the protected right of homosexual adults to engage in intimate, consensual conduct. See Brief for Mary Robinson et al. as *Amici Curiae* 11–12. The right the petitioners seek in this case has been accepted as an integral part of human freedom in many other countries. There has been no showing that in this country the governmental interest in circumscribing personal choice is somehow more legitimate or urgent.

The doctrine of *stare decisis* is essential to the respect accorded to the judgments of the Court and to the stability of the law. It is not, however, an inexorable command. *Payne v. Tennessee,* 501 U.S. 808, 828 (1991) ("*Stare decisis* is not an inexorable command; rather, it 'is a principle of policy and not a mechanical formula of adherence to the latest decision'") (quoting *Helvering v. Hallock,* 309 U.S. 106, 119 (1940))). In *Casey* we noted that when a Court is asked to overrule a precedent recognizing a constitutional liberty interest, individual or societal reliance on the existence of that liberty cautions with particular strength against reversing course. 505 U.S., at 855–856; see also *id.,* at 844 ("Liberty finds no refuge in a jurisprudence of doubt"). The holding in *Bowers,* however, has not induced detrimental reliance comparable to some instances where recognized individual rights are involved. Indeed, there has been no individual or societal reliance on *Bowers* of the sort that could counsel against overturning its holding once there are compelling reasons to do so. *Bowers* itself causes uncertainty, for the precedents before and after its issuance contradict its central holding.

The rationale of *Bowers* does not withstand careful analysis. In his dissenting opinion in *Bowers* Justice Stevens came to these conclusions:

> "Our prior cases make two propositions abundantly clear. First, the fact that the governing majority in a State has traditionally viewed a particular practice as immoral is not a sufficient reason for upholding a law prohibiting the practice; neither history nor tradition could save a law prohibiting miscegenation from constitutional attack. Second, individual decisions by married persons, concerning the intimacies of their physical relationship, even when not intended to produce offspring, are a form of "liberty" protected by the Due Process Clause of the Fourteenth Amendment. Moreover, this protection extends to intimate choices by unmarried as well as married persons." 478 U.S., at 216 (footnotes and citations omitted).

Justice Stevens' analysis, in our view, should have been controlling in *Bowers* and should control here.

Bowers was not correct when it was decided, and it is not correct today. It ought not to remain binding precedent. *Bowers v. Hardwick* should be and now is overruled.

The present case does not involve minors. It does not involve persons who might be injured or coerced or who are situated in relationships where consent might not easily be refused. It does not involve public conduct or prostitution. It does not involve whether the government must give formal recognition to any relationship that homosexual persons seek to enter. The case does involve two adults who, with full and mutual consent from each other, engaged in sexual practices common to a homosexual lifestyle. The petitioners are entitled to respect for their private lives. The State cannot demean their existence or control their destiny by making their private sexual conduct a crime. Their right to liberty under the Due Process Clause gives them the full right to engage in their conduct without intervention of the government. "It is a promise of the Constitution that there is a realm of personal liberty which the government may not enter." *Casey, supra,* at 847. The Texas statute furthers no legitimate state interest which can justify its intrusion into the personal and private life of the individual.

Had those who drew and ratified the Due Process Clauses of the Fifth Amendment or the Fourteenth Amendment known the components of liberty in its manifold possibilities, they might have been more specific. They did not presume to have this insight. They knew times can blind us to certain truths and later generations can see that laws once thought necessary and proper in fact serve only to oppress. As the Constitution endures, persons in every generation can invoke its principles in their own search for greater freedom.

The judgment of the Court of Appeals for the Texas Fourteenth District is reversed, and the case is remanded for further proceedings not inconsistent with this opinion.

It is so ordered.

Antonin E. Scalia  **NO**

Dissenting Opinion, *Lawrence v. Texas*

J ustice Scalia, with whom the Chief Justice and Justice Thomas join, dissenting.

"Liberty finds no refuge in a jurisprudence of doubt." *Planned Parenthood of Southeastern Pa. v. Casey,* 505 U.S. 833, 844 (1992). That was the Court's sententious response, barely more than a decade ago, to those seeking to overrule *Roe v. Wade,* 410 U.S. 113 (1973). The Court's response today, to those who have engaged in a 17-year crusade to overrule *Bowers v. Hardwick,* 478 U.S. 186 (1986), is very different. The need for stability and certainty presents no barrier.

Most of the rest of today's opinion has no relevance to its actual holding—that the Texas statute "furthers no legitimate state interest which can justify" its application to petitioners under rational-basis review. *Ante,* at 18 (overruling *Bowers* to the extent it sustained Georgia's anti-sodomy statute under the rational-basis test). Though there is discussion of "fundamental proposition[s]," *ante,* at 4, and "fundamental decisions," *ibid.* nowhere does the Court's opinion declare that homosexual sodomy is a "fundamental right" under the Due Process Clause; nor does it subject the Texas law to the standard of review that would be appropriate (strict scrutiny) if homosexual sodomy *were* a "fundamental right." Thus, while overruling the *outcome* of *Bowers,* the Court leaves strangely untouched its central legal conclusion: "[R]espondent would have us announce . . . a fundamental right to engage in homosexual sodomy. This we are quite unwilling to do." 478 U.S., at 191. Instead the Court simply describes petitioners' conduct as "an exercise of their liberty"—which it undoubtedly is—and proceeds to apply an unheard-of form of rational-basis review that will have far-reaching implications beyond this case. *Ante,* at 3.

I

I begin with the Court's surprising readiness to reconsider a decision rendered a mere 17 years ago in *Bowers v. Hardwick.* I do not myself believe in rigid adherence to *stare decisis* in constitutional cases; but I do believe that we should be consistent rather than manipulative in invoking the doctrine. Today's opinions in support of reversal do not bother to distinguish—or indeed, even bother to mention—the paean to *stare decisis* coauthored by three Members of today's majority in *Planned Parenthood v. Casey.* There, when *stare decisis* meant

Supreme Court of the United States, 2003.

preservation of judicially invented abortion rights, the widespread criticism of *Roe* was strong reason to *reaffirm* it:

> "Where, in the performance of its judicial duties, the Court decides a case in such a way as to resolve the sort of intensely divisive controversy reflected in *Roe*[,] . . . its decision has a dimension that the resolution of the normal case does not carry. . . . [T]o overrule under fire in the absence of the most compelling reason . . . would subvert the Court's legitimacy beyond any serious question." 505 U.S., at 866–867.

Today, however, the widespread opposition to *Bowers,* a decision resolving an issue as "intensely divisive" as the issue in *Roe,* is offered as a reason in favor of *overruling* it. See *ante,* at 15–16. Gone, too, is any "enquiry" (of the sort conducted in *Casey*) into whether the decision sought to be overruled has "proven 'unworkable,'" *Casey, supra,* at 855.

Today's approach to *stare decisis* invites us to overrule an erroneously decided precedent (including an "intensely divisive" decision) *if:* (1) its foundations have been "eroded" by subsequent decisions, *ante,* at 15; (2) it has been subject to "substantial and continuing" criticism, *ibid.*; and (3) it has not induced "individual or societal reliance" that counsels against overturning, *ante,* at 16. The problem is that *Roe* itself—which today's majority surely has no disposition to overrule—satisfies these conditions to at least the same degree as *Bowers.*

(1) A preliminary digressive observation with regard to the first factor: The Court's claim that *Planned Parenthood v. Casey, supra,* "casts some doubt" upon the holding in *Bowers* (or any other case, for that matter) does not withstand analysis. *Ante,* at 10. As far as its holding is concerned, *Casey* provided a *less* expansive right to abortion than did *Roe, which was already on the books when Bowers was decided.* And if the Court is referring not to the holding of *Casey,* but to the dictum of its famed sweet-mystery-of-life passage, *ante,* at 13 ("At the heart of liberty is the right to define one's own concept of existence, of meaning, of the universe, and of the mystery of human life"): That "casts some doubt" upon either the totality of our jurisprudence or else (presumably the right answer) nothing at all. I have never heard of a law that attempted to restrict one's "right to define" certain concepts; and if the passage calls into question the government's power to regulate *actions based on* one's self-defined "concept of existence, etc.," it is the passage that ate the rule of law.

I do not quarrel with the Court's claim that *Romer v. Evans,* 517 U.S. 620 (1996), "eroded" the "foundations" of *Bowers'* rational-basis holding. See *Romer, supra,* at 640–643 (Scalia, J., dissenting). But *Roe* and *Casey* have been equally "eroded" by *Washington v. Glucksberg,* 521 U.S. 702, 721 (1997), which held that *only* fundamental rights which are "deeply rooted in this Nation's history and tradition" qualify for anything other than rational basis scrutiny under the doctrine of "substantive due process." *Roe* and *Casey,* of course, subjected the restriction of abortion to heightened scrutiny without even attempting to establish that the freedom to abort *was* rooted in this Nation's tradition.

(2) *Bowers,* the Court says, has been subject to "substantial and continuing [criticism], disapproving of its reasoning in all respects, not just as

to its historical assumptions." *Ante,* at 15. Exactly what those nonhistorical criticisms are, and whether the Court even agrees with them, are left unsaid, although the Court does cite two books. See *ibid.* (citing C. Fried, Order and Law: Arguing the Reagan Revolution—A Firsthand Account 81–84 (1991); R. Posner, Sex and Reason 341–350 (1992)). Of course, *Roe* too (and by extension *Casey*) had been (and still is) subject to unrelenting criticism, including criticism from the two commentators cited by the Court today. See Fried, *supra,* at 75 ("*Roe* was a prime example of twisted judging"); Posner, *supra,* at 337 ("[The Court's] opinion in *Roe* . . . fails to measure up to professional expectations regarding judicial opinions"); Posner, Judicial Opinion Writing, 62 U. Chi. L. Rev. 1421, 1434 (1995) (describing the opinion in *Roe* as an "embarrassing performanc[e]").

(3) That leaves, to distinguish the rock-solid, unamendable disposition of *Roe* from the readily overrulable *Bowers,* only the third factor. "[T]here has been," the Court says, "no individual or societal reliance on *Bowers* of the sort that could counsel against overturning its holding. . . ." *Ante,* at 16. It seems to me that the "societal reliance" on the principles confirmed in *Bowers* and discarded today has been overwhelming. Countless judicial decisions and legislative enactments have relied on the ancient proposition that a governing majority's belief that certain sexual behavior is "immoral and unacceptable" constitutes a rational basis for regulation. See, *e.g., Williams v. Pryor,* 240 F.3d 944, 949 (CA11 2001) (citing *Bowers* in upholding Alabama's prohibition on the sale of sex toys on the ground that "[t]he crafting and safeguarding of public morality . . . indisputably is a legitimate government interest under rational basis scrutiny"); *Milner v. Apfel,* 148 F.3d 812, 814 (CA7 1998) (citing *Bowers* for the proposition that "[l]egislatures are permitted to legislate with regard to morality . . . rather than confined to preventing demonstrable harms"); *Holmes v. California Army National Guard* 124 F.3d 1126, 1136 (CA9 1997) (relying on *Bowers* in upholding the federal statute and regulations banning from military service those who engage in homosexual conduct); *Owens v. State,* 352 Md. 663, 683, 724 A. 2nd 43, 53 (1999) (relying on *Bowers* in holding that "a person has no constitutional right to engage in sexual intercourse, at least outside of marriage"); *Sherman v. Henry,* 928 S. W. 2nd 464, 469–473 (Tex. 1996) (relying on *Bowers* in rejecting a claimed constitutional right to commit adultery). We ourselves relied extensively on *Bowers* when we concluded, in *Barnes v. Glen Theatre, Inc.,* 501 U.S. 560, 569 (1991), that Indiana's public indecency statute furthered "a substantial government interest in protecting order and morality," *ibid.,* (plurality opinion); see also *id.,* at 575 (Scalia, J., concurring in judgment). State laws against bigamy, same-sex marriage, adult incest, prostitution, masturbation, adultery, fornication, bestiality, and obscenity are likewise sustainable only in light of *Bowers'* validation of laws based on moral choices. Every single one of these laws is called into question by today's decision; the Court makes no effort to cabin the scope of its decision to exclude them from its holding. See *ante,* at 11 (noting "an emerging awareness that liberty gives substantial protection to adult persons in deciding how to conduct their private lives *in matters pertaining to sex*" (emphasis added)). The impossibility of distinguishing homosexuality from other traditional "morals" offenses is

precisely why *Bowers* rejected the rational-basis challenge. "The law," it said, "is constantly based on notions of morality, and if all laws representing essentially moral choices are to be invalidated under the Due Process Clause, the courts will be very busy indeed." 478 U.S., at 196.

What a massive disruption of the current social order, therefore, the overruling of *Bowers* entails. Not so the overruling of *Roe*, which would simply have restored the regime that existed for centuries before 1973, in which the permissibility of and restrictions upon abortion were determined legislatively State-by-State. *Casey*, however, chose to base its *stare decisis* determination on a different "sort" of reliance. "[P]eople," it said, "have organized intimate relationships and made choices that define their views of themselves and their places in society, in reliance on the availability of abortion in the event that contraception should fail." 505 U.S., at 856. This falsely assumes that the consequence of overruling *Roe* would have been to make abortion unlawful. It would not; it would merely have *permitted* the States to do so. Many States would unquestionably have declined to prohibit abortion, and others would not have prohibited it within six months (after which the most significant reliance interests would have expired). Even for persons in States other than these, the choice would not have been between abortion and childbirth, but between abortion nearby and abortion in a neighboring State.

To tell the truth, it does not surprise me, and should surprise no one, that the Court has chosen today to revise the standards of *stare decisis* set forth in *Casey*. It has thereby exposed *Casey's* extraordinary deference to precedent for the result-oriented expedient that it is.

II

Having decided that it need not adhere to *stare decisis*, the Court still must establish that *Bowers* was wrongly decided and that the Texas statute, as applied to petitioners, is unconstitutional.

Texas Penal Code Ann. §21.06(a) (2003) undoubtedly imposes constraints on liberty. So do laws prohibiting prostitution, recreational use of heroin, and, for that matter, working more than 60 hours per week in a bakery. But there is no right to "liberty" under the Due Process Clause, though today's opinion repeatedly makes that claim. *Ante,* at 6 ("The liberty protected by the Constitution allows homosexual persons the right to make this choice"); *ante,* at 13 ("These matters . . . are central to the liberty protected by the Fourteenth Amendment"); *ante,* at 17 ("Their right to liberty under the Due Process Clause gives them the full right to engage in their conduct without intervention of the government"). The Fourteenth Amendment *expressly allows* States to deprive their citizens of "liberty," so long as "due process of law" is provided:

> "No state shall . . . deprive any person of life, liberty, or property, *without due process of law*." Amdt. 14 (emphasis added).

Our opinions applying the doctrine known as "substantive due process" hold that the Due Process Clause prohibits States from infringing *fundamental* liberty interests, unless the infringement is narrowly tailored to serve a compelling state interest. *Washington v. Glucksberg,* 521 U.S., at 721. We have held repeatedly, in cases the Court today does not overrule, that *only* fundamental rights qualify for this so-called "heightened scrutiny" protection—that is, rights which are "deeply rooted in this Nation's history and tradition," *ibid.* See *Reno v. Flores,* 507 U.S. 292, 303 (1993) (fundamental liberty interests must be "so rooted in the traditions and conscience of our people as to be ranked as fundamental" (internal quotation marks and citations omitted)); *United States v. Salerno,* 481 U.S. 739, 751 (1987) (same). See also *Michael H. v. Gerald D.,* 491 U.S. 110, 122 (1989) ("[W]e have insisted not merely that the interest denominated as a 'liberty' be 'fundamental'. . . but also that it be an interest traditionally protected by our society"); *Moore v. East Cleveland,* 431 U.S. 494, 503 (1977) (plurality opinion); *Meyer v. Nebraska,* 262 U.S. 390, 399 (1923) (Fourteenth Amendment protects "those privileges *long recognized at common law* as essential to the orderly pursuit of happiness by free men" (emphasis added)). All other liberty interests may be abridged or abrogated pursuant to a validly enacted state law if that law is rationally related to a legitimate state interest.

 Bowers held, first, that criminal prohibitions of homosexual sodomy are not subject to heightened scrutiny because they do not implicate a "fundamental right" under the Due Process Clause, 478 U.S., at 191–194. Noting that "[p]roscriptions against that conduct have ancient roots," *id.,* at 192, that "[s]odomy was a criminal offense at common law and was forbidden by the laws of the original 13 States when they ratified the Bill of Rights," *ibid.,* and that many States had retained their bans on sodomy, *id.,* at 193, *Bowers* concluded that a right to engage in homosexual sodomy was not "deeply rooted in this Nation's history and tradition," *id.,* at 192.

 The Court today does not overrule this holding. Not once does it describe homosexual sodomy as a "fundamental right" or a "fundamental liberty interest," nor does it subject the Texas statute to strict scrutiny. Instead, having failed to establish that the right to homosexual sodomy is "deeply rooted in this Nation's history and tradition," the Court concludes that the application of Texas's statute to petitioners' conduct fails the rational-basis test, and overrules *Bowers'* holding to the contrary, see *id.,* at 196. "The Texas statute furthers no legitimate state interest which can justify its intrusion into the personal and private life of the individual." *Ante,* at 18.

 I shall address that rational-basis holding presently. First, however, I address some aspersions that the Court casts upon *Bowers'* conclusion that homosexual sodomy is not a "fundamental right"—even though, as I have said, the Court does not have the boldness to reverse that conclusion.

III

The Court's description of "the state of the law" at the time of *Bowers* only confirms that *Bowers* was right. *Ante,* at 5. The Court points to *Griswold v. Connecticut,* 381 U.S. 479, 481–482 (1965). But that case *expressly disclaimed* any reliance on the doctrine of "substantive due process," and grounded the so-called "right to privacy" in penumbras of constitutional provisions *other than* the Due Process Clause. *Eisenstadt v. Baird,* 405 U.S. 438 (1972), likewise had nothing to do with "substantive due process"; it invalidated a Massachusetts law prohibiting the distribution of contraceptives to unmarried persons solely on the basis of the Equal Protection Clause. Of course *Eisenstadt* contains well known dictum relating to the "right to privacy," but this referred to the right recognized in *Griswold*—a right penumbral to the *specific* guarantees in the Bill of Rights, and not a "substantive due process" right.

Roe v. Wade recognized that the right to abort an unborn child was a "fundamental right" protected by the Due Process Clause. 410 U.S., at 155. The *Roe* Court, however, made no attempt to establish that this right was "deeply rooted in this Nation's history and tradition"; instead, it based its conclusion that "the Fourteenth Amendment's concept of personal liberty . . . is broad enough to encompass a woman's decision whether or not to terminate her pregnancy" on its own normative judgment that anti-abortion laws were undesirable. See *id.,* at 153. We have since rejected *Roe's* holding that regulations of abortion must be narrowly tailored to serve a compelling state interest, see *Planned Parenthood v. Casey,* 505 U.S., at 876 (joint opinion of O'Connor, Kennedy, and Souter, JJ.); *id.,* at 951–953 (Rehnquist, C. J., concurring in judgment in part and dissenting in part)—and thus, by logical implication, *Roe's* holding that the right to abort an unborn child is a "fundamental right." See 505 U.S., at 843–912 (joint opinion of O'Connor, Kennedy, and Souter, JJ.) (not once describing abortion as a "fundamental right" or a "fundamental liberty interest").

After discussing the history of antisodomy laws, *ante,* at 7–10, the Court proclaims that, "it should be noted that there is no longstanding history in this country of laws directed at homosexual conduct as a distinct matter," *ante,* at 7. This observation in no way casts into doubt the "definitive [historical] conclusion," *id.,* on which *Bowers* relied: that our Nation has a longstanding history of laws prohibiting *sodomy in general*—regardless of whether it was performed by same-sex or opposite-sex couples:

> "It is obvious to us that neither of these formulations would extend a fundamental right to homosexuals to engage in acts of consensual sodomy. Proscriptions against that conduct have ancient roots. *Sodomy* was a criminal offense at common law and was forbidden by the laws of the original 13 States when they ratified the Bill of Rights. In 1868, when the Fourteenth Amendment was ratified, all but 5 of the 37 States in the Union had *criminal sodomy laws*. In fact, until 1961, all 50 States outlawed *sodomy,* and today, 24 States and the District of Columbia continue to provide criminal penalties for *sodomy* performed in private and between consenting adults. Against this background, to claim that a right to engage in such conduct is 'deeply rooted in this Nation's history and tradition' or 'implicit in the concept of ordered liberty' is, at best, facetious." 478 U.S., at 192–194 (citations and footnotes omitted; emphasis added).

It is (as *Bowers* recognized) entirely irrelevant whether the laws in our long national tradition criminalizing homosexual sodomy were "directed at homosexual conduct as a distinct matter." *Ante,* at 7. Whether homosexual sodomy was prohibited by a law targeted at same-sex sexual relations or by a more general law prohibiting both homosexual and heterosexual sodomy, the only relevant point is that it *was* criminalized—which suffices to establish that homosexual sodomy is not a right "deeply rooted in our Nation's history and tradition." The Court today agrees that homosexual sodomy was criminalized and thus does not dispute the facts on which *Bowers actually* relied.

Next the Court makes the claim, again unsupported by any citations, that "[l]aws prohibiting sodomy do not seem to have been enforced against consenting adults acting in private." *Ante,* at 8. The key qualifier here is "acting in private"—since the Court admits that sodomy laws *were* enforced against consenting adults (although the Court contends that prosecutions were "infrequent," *ante,* at 9). I do not know what "acting in private" means; surely consensual sodomy, like heterosexual intercourse, is rarely performed on stage. If all the Court means by "acting in private" is "on private premises, with the doors closed and windows covered," it is entirely unsurprising that evidence of enforcement would be hard to come by. (Imagine the circumstances that would enable a search warrant to be obtained for a residence on the ground that there was probable cause to believe that consensual sodomy was then and there occurring.) Surely that lack of evidence would not sustain the proposition that consensual sodomy on private premises with the doors closed and windows covered was regarded as a "fundamental right," even though all other consensual sodomy was criminalized. There are 203 prosecutions for consensual, adult homosexual sodomy reported in the West Reporting system and official state reporters from the years 1880 to 1995. See W. Eskridge, Gaylaw: Challenging the Apartheid of the Closet 375 (1999) (hereinafter Gaylaw). There are also records of 20 sodomy prosecutions and 4 executions during the colonial period. J. Katz, Gay/Lesbian Almanac 29, 58, 663 (1983). *Bowers'* conclusion that homosexual sodomy is not a fundamental right "deeply rooted in this Nation's history and tradition" is utterly unassailable.

Realizing that fact, the Court instead says: "[W]e think that our laws and traditions in the past half century are of most relevance here. These references show *an emerging awareness* that liberty gives substantial protection to adult persons in deciding how to conduct their private lives *in matters pertaining to sex." Ante,* at 11 (emphasis added). Apart from the fact that such an "emerging awareness" does not establish a "fundamental right," the statement is factually false. States continue to prosecute all sorts of crimes by adults "in matters pertaining to sex": prostitution, adult incest, adultery, obscenity, and child pornography. Sodomy laws, too, have been enforced "in the past half century," in which there have been 134 reported cases involving prosecutions for consensual, adult, homosexual sodomy. Gaylaw 375. In relying, for evidence of an "emerging recognition," upon the American Law Institute's 1955 recommendation not to criminalize "consensual sexual relations conducted in private," *ante,* at 11, the Court ignores the fact that this recommendation was "a point of resistance in most of the states that considered adopting the Model Penal Code." Gaylaw 159.

In any event, an "emerging awareness" is by definition not "deeply rooted in this Nation's history and tradition[s]," as we have said "fundamental right" status requires. Constitutional entitlements do not spring into existence because some States choose to lessen or eliminate criminal sanctions on certain behavior. Much less do they spring into existence, as the Court seems to believe, because *foreign nations* decriminalize conduct. The *Bowers* majority opinion *never* relied on "values we share with a wider civilization," *ante,* at 16, but rather rejected the claimed right to sodomy on the ground that such a right was not "deeply rooted in *this Nation's* history and tradition," 478 U.S., at 193–194 (emphasis added). *Bowers'* rational-basis holding is likewise devoid of any reliance on the views of a "wider civilization," see *id.,* at 196. The Court's discussion of these foreign views (ignoring, of course, the many countries that have retained criminal prohibitions on sodomy) is therefore meaningless dicta. Dangerous dicta, however, since "this Court . . . should not impose foreign moods, fads, or fashions on Americans." *Foster v. Florida,* 537 U.S. 990, n. (2002) (Thomas, J., concurring in denial of certiorari).

IV

I turn now to the ground on which the Court squarely rests its holding: the contention that there is no rational basis for the law here under attack. This proposition is so out of accord with our jurisprudence—indeed, with the jurisprudence of *any* society we know—that it requires little discussion.

The Texas statute undeniably seeks to further the belief of its citizens that certain forms of sexual behavior are "immoral and unacceptable," *Bowers, supra,* at 196—the same interest furthered by criminal laws against fornication, bigamy, adultery, adult incest, bestiality, and obscenity. *Bowers* held that this *was* a legitimate state interest. The Court today reaches the opposite conclusion. The Texas statute, it says, "furthers *no legitimate state interest* which can justify its intrusion into the personal and private life of the individual," *ante,* at 18 (emphasis added). The Court embraces instead Justice Stevens' declaration in his *Bowers* dissent, that "the fact that the governing majority in a State has traditionally viewed a particular practice as immoral is not a sufficient reason for upholding a law prohibiting the practice," *ante,* at 17. This effectively decrees the end of all morals legislation. If, as the Court asserts, the promotion of majoritarian sexual morality is not even a *legitimate* state interest, none of the above-mentioned laws can survive rational-basis review.

V

Finally, I turn to petitioners' equal-protection challenge, which no Member of the Court save Justice O'Connor, *ante,* at 1 (opinion concurring in judgment), embraces: On its face §21.06(a) applies equally to all persons. Men and women, heterosexuals and homosexuals, are all subject to its prohibition of deviate sexual intercourse with someone of the same sex. To be sure, §21.06 does distinguish between the sexes insofar as concerns the partner with whom the sexual acts are performed: men can violate the law only with other men, and women only with other women. But this cannot itself be a denial of equal protection, since it is precisely the same distinction regarding partner that is drawn in state laws prohibiting marriage with someone of the same sex while permitting marriage with someone of the opposite sex.

The objection is made, however, that the antimiscegenation laws invalidated in *Loving v. Virginia,* 388 U.S. 1, 8 (1967), similarly were applicable to whites and blacks alike, and only distinguished between the races insofar as the *partner* was concerned. In *Loving,* however, we correctly applied heightened scrutiny, rather than the usual rational-basis review, because the Virginia statute was "designed to maintain White Supremacy." *Id.,* at 6, 11. A racially discriminatory purpose is always sufficient to subject a law to strict scrutiny, even a facially neutral law that makes no mention of race. See *Washington v. Davis,* 426 U.S. 229, 241–242 (1976). No purpose to discriminate against men or women as a class can be gleaned from the Texas law, so rational-basis review applies. That review is readily satisfied here by the same rational basis that satisfied it in *Bowers*—society's belief that certain forms of sexual behavior are "immoral and unacceptable," 478 U.S., at 196. This is the same justification that supports many other laws regulating sexual behavior that make a distinction based upon the identity of the partner—for example, laws against adultery, fornication, and adult incest, and laws refusing to recognize homosexual marriage.

Justice O'Connor argues that the discrimination in this law which must be justified is not its discrimination with regard to the sex of the partner but its discrimination with regard to the sexual proclivity of the principal actor.

"While it is true that the law applies only to conduct, the conduct targeted by this law is conduct that is closely correlated with being homosexual. Under such circumstances, Texas' sodomy law is targeted at more than conduct. It is instead directed toward gay persons as a class." *Ante,* at 5.

Of course the same could be said of any law. A law against public nudity targets "the conduct that is closely correlated with being a nudist," and hence "is targeted at more than conduct"; it is "directed toward nudists as a class." But be that as it may. Even if the Texas law *does* deny equal protection to "homosexuals as a class," that denial *still* does not need to be justified by anything more than a rational basis, which our cases show is satisfied by the enforcement of traditional notions of sexual morality.

Justice O'Connor simply decrees application of "a more searching form of rational basis review" to the Texas statute. *Ante,* at 2. The cases she cites do not recognize such a standard, and reach their conclusions only after finding, as required by conventional rational-basis analysis, that no conceivable legitimate state interest supports the classification at issue. See *Romer v. Evans,* 517 U.S., at 635; *Cleburne v. Cleburne Living Center, Inc.,* 473 U.S. 432, 448–450 (1985); *Department of Agriculture v. Moreno,* 413 U.S. 528, 534–538 (1973). Nor does Justice O'Connor explain precisely what her "more searching form" of rational-basis review consists of. It must at least mean, however, that laws exhibiting "a . . . desire to harm a politically unpopular group," *ante,* at 2, are invalid *even though* there may be a conceivable rational basis to support them.

This reasoning leaves on pretty shaky grounds state laws limiting marriage to opposite-sex couples. Justice O'Connor seeks to preserve them by the conclusory statement that "preserving the traditional institution of marriage" is a legitimate state interest. *Ante,* at 7. But "preserving the traditional institution of marriage" is just a kinder way of describing the State's *moral disapproval* of same-sex couples. Texas's interest in §21.06 could be recast in similarly euphemistic terms: "preserving the traditional sexual mores of our society." In the jurisprudence Justice O'Connor has seemingly created, judges can validate laws by characterizing them as "preserving the traditions of society" (good); or invalidate them by characterizing them as "expressing moral disapproval" (bad).

* * *

Today's opinion is the product of a Court, which is the product of a law-profession culture, that has largely signed on to the so-called homosexual agenda, by which I mean the agenda promoted by some homosexual activists directed at eliminating the moral opprobrium that has traditionally attached to homosexual conduct. I noted in an earlier opinion the fact that the American Association of Law Schools (to which any reputable law school *must* seek to belong) excludes from membership any school that refuses to ban from its job-interview facilities a law firm (no matter how small) that does not wish to hire as a prospective partner a person who openly engages in homosexual conduct. See *Romer, supra,* at 653.

One of the most revealing statements in today's opinion is the Court's grim warning that the criminalization of homosexual conduct is "an invitation to subject homosexual persons to discrimination both in the public and in the private spheres." *Ante,* at 14. It is clear from this that the Court has taken sides in the culture war, departing from its role of assuring, as neutral observer, that the democratic rules of engagement are observed. Many Americans do not want persons who openly engage in homosexual conduct as partners in their business, as scoutmasters for their children, as teachers in their children's schools, or as boarders in their home. They view this as protecting themselves and their families from a lifestyle that they believe to be immoral and destructive. The Court views it as "discrimination" which it is the function of our judgments to deter. So imbued is the Court with the law profession's anti-anti-homosexual culture, that it is seemingly unaware that the attitudes of that culture are not obviously "mainstream"; that in most States what the Court calls "discrimination" against those who engage in homosexual acts is perfectly legal; that proposals to ban such "discrimination" under Title VII have repeatedly been rejected by Congress, see Employment Non-Discrimination Act of 1994, S. 2238, 103d Cong., 2nd Sess. (1994); Civil Rights Amendments, H. R. 5452, 94th Cong., 1st Sess. (1975); that in some cases such "discrimination" is *mandated* by federal statute, see 10 U.S.C. § 654(b)(1) (mandating discharge from the armed forces of any service member who engages in or intends to engage in homosexual acts); and that in some cases such "discrimination" is a constitutional right, see *Boy Scouts of America v. Dale,* 530 U.S. 640 (2000).

Let me be clear that I have nothing against homosexuals, or any other group, promoting their agenda through normal democratic means. Social perceptions of sexual and other morality change over time, and every group has the right to persuade its fellow citizens that its view of such matters is the best.

That homosexuals have achieved some success in that enterprise is attested to by the fact that Texas is one of the few remaining States that criminalize private, consensual homosexual acts. But persuading one's fellow citizens is one thing, and imposing one's views in absence of democratic majority will is something else. I would no more *require* a State to criminalize homosexual acts—or, for that matter, display *any* moral disapprobation of them—than I would *forbid* it to do so. What Texas has chosen to do is well within the range of traditional democratic action, and its hand should not be stayed through the invention of a brand-new "constitutional right" by a Court that is impatient of democratic change. It is indeed true that "later generations can see that laws once thought necessary and proper in fact serve only to oppress," *ante,* at 18; and when that happens, later generations can repeal those laws. But it is the premise of our system that those judgments are to be made by the people, and not imposed by a governing caste that knows best.

One of the benefits of leaving regulation of this matter to the people rather than to the courts is that the people, unlike judges, need not carry things to their logical conclusion. The people may feel that their disapprobation of homosexual conduct is strong enough to disallow homosexual marriage, but not strong enough to criminalize private homosexual acts—and may legislate accordingly. The Court today pretends that it possesses a similar freedom of action, so that that we need not fear judicial imposition of homosexual marriage, as has recently occurred in Canada (in a decision that the Canadian Government has chosen not to appeal). See *Halpern v. Toronto,* 2003 WL 34950 (Ontario Ct. App.); Cohen, Dozens in Canada Follow Gay Couple's Lead, Washington Post, June 12, 2003, p. A25. At the end of its opinion—after having laid waste the foundations of our rational-basis jurisprudence—the Court says that the present case "does not involve whether the government must give formal recognition to any relationship that homosexual persons seek to enter." *Ante,* at 17. Do not believe it. More illuminating than this bald, unreasoned disclaimer is the progression of thought displayed by an earlier passage in the Court's opinion, which notes the constitutional protections afforded to "personal decisions relating to *marriage,* procreation, contraception, family relationships, child rearing, and education," and then declares that "[p]ersons in a homosexual relationship may seek autonomy for these purposes, just as heterosexual persons do." *Ante,* at 13 (emphasis added). Today's opinion dismantles the structure of constitutional law that has permitted a distinction to be made between heterosexual and homosexual unions, insofar as formal recognition in marriage is concerned. If moral disapprobation of homosexual conduct is "no legitimate state interest" for purposes of proscribing that conduct, *ante,* at 18; and if, as the Court coos (casting aside all pretense of neutrality), "[w]hen sexuality finds overt expression in intimate conduct with another person, the conduct can be but one element in a personal bond that is more enduring," *ante,* at 6; what justification could there possibly be for denying the benefits of marriage to homosexual couples exercising "[t]he liberty protected by the Constitution," *ibid.?* Surely not the encouragement of procreation, since the sterile and the elderly are allowed to marry. This case "does not involve" the issue of homosexual marriage only if one entertains the belief that principle and logic have nothing to do with the decisions of this Court. Many will hope that, as the Court comfortingly assures us, this is so.

The matters appropriate for this Court's resolution are only three: Texas's prohibition of sodomy neither infringes a "fundamental right" (which the Court does not dispute), nor is unsupported by a rational relation to what the Constitution considers a legitimate state interest, nor denies the equal protection of the laws. I dissent.

POSTSCRIPT

Does a Constitutional Right to Privacy Protect the Rights of Homosexual Couples to Engage in Intimate Personal Relationships?

This is yet another challenging question. Justice Anthony M. Kennedy, writing for the Court in *Lawrence v. Texas* (2003), held that a Texas law making it a crime for two persons of the same sex to engage in intimate sexual conduct violates the Fourteenth Amendment's Due Process Clause. Moreover, the Court appeared to imply that the Texas law could not even survive rationality review because it furthered "no legitimate state interest that could justify its intrusion into the personal and private life of the individual." Justice Antonin E. Scalia, dissenting in *Lawrence v. Texas* (2003), asserted that the Texas law does not infringe a "fundamental right." Scalia also believed that the law bears a rational relationship to what the Constitution considers a legitimate state interest and does not deny the equal protection of the laws.

Justice Scalia's dissenting opinion therefore considered an issue that the majority opinion did not decide in *Lawrence v. Texas* (2003): whether statutes such as the one in this case violate the Fourteenth Amendment's Equal Protection Clause. The Supreme Court's analysis of cases under the Equal Protection Clause proceeds in a manner that is similar, but not identical, to substantive due process analysis. An equal protection challenge to a state's law would assert that it assigned benefits or liabilities to a particular identifiable group of persons in a discriminatory manner, without a reasonable basis for doing so. In *Lawrence v. Texas*, the petitioners had argued that the Texas law discriminated against homosexuals because it prohibited only persons of the same sex from engaging in intimate sexual conduct. The same standard did not apply to heterosexuals who engaged in the same intimate sexual conduct. A similar equal protection issue had been considered in an earlier case, *Romer v. Evans*, 517 U.S. 620 (1996), which struck down a Colorado constitutional amendment that had singled out homosexuals and deprived them of protection under state antidiscrimination laws. There the Supreme Court held that the amendment was "born of animosity" toward homosexuals and that it had no rational relation to a legitimate governmental objective.

Justice Kennedy's opinion for the Court in *Lawrence* considered the equal protection argument only briefly. Rather than deciding this issue, Kennedy stated that it was better to determine if *Bowers v. Hardwick* (1989) had "continuing vitality." Stated Justice Kennedy: "Were we to hold the statute invalid under the Equal Protection Clause some might question whether a prohibition would be valid if drawn differently, say, to prohibit the conduct both between same-sex and different-sex participants." Overruling *Bowers v. Hardwick*, Kennedy asserted that "[i]ts continuance as precedent demeans the lives of homosexual persons."

Justice Scalia responded that the Texas law did not demonstrate a "purpose to discriminate against men or women as a class . . . so rational-basis review applies." "That review is readily satisfied here by . . . [a] belief that certain forms of sexual behavior are 'immoral and unacceptable.'"

Justice Scalia's dissenting opinion raised another interesting issue as well: Whether *Lawrence v. Texas* (2003) will lead the Supreme Court to sanction homosexual marriage based on a similar rationale at some future date. Stated Scalia:

> Today's opinion dismantles the structure of constitutional law that has permitted a distinction to be made between heterosexual unions, insofar as formal recognition in marriage is concerned. If moral disapprobation of homosexual conduct is 'no legitimate state interest' for purposes of proscribing that conduct . . . and if, as the Court coos (casting aside all pretense of neutrality), '[w]hen sexuality finds overt expression in intimate conduct with another person, the conduct can be but one element in a personal bond that is more enduring'; what justification could there possibly be for denying the benefits of marriage to homosexual couples exercising '[t]he liberty protected by the Constitution'?

Justice Scalia's assertion brings to mind Justice Benjamin J. Cardozo's famous statement about the tendency of a legal principle once developed to expand itself "to the limits of its logic." Do you believe that the next step in the substantive due process chain in cases involving human sexuality will be to recognize a constitutional right for homosexuals to marry? Should the U.S. Constitution guarantee a right to form such unions? Remember that marriage as an institution carries with it a host of rights and duties that do not apply to persons involved in less formal unions. These include, among other things, the right to inherit and own property together, receive life insurance benefits, participate in a spouse's health insurance plan, and make determinations about a partner's health care in the event that he or she becomes incapacitated. Do you feel that homosexuals should have the same rights as heterosexuals with regard to such critical issues?

Proponents of a federal constitutional right to same-sex marriage will face a statutory obstacle as well. In 1996, the U.S. Congress passed the Defense of Marriage Act (DOMA), 1 U.S.C. Section 7; 28 U.S.C. 1738 C. It defines marriage as a "union of one man and one woman as husband and wife." It further authorizes states to deny the rights of married persons to a homosexual couple that has been granted those rights in a different state. This is a statutorily created exception to the Constitution's "full faith and credit clause," which requires states to recognize the laws and contracts of other states.

A mere 6 months after the *Lawrence* decision, the Massachusetts Supreme Judicial Court, in *Goodridge v. Department of Public Health*, 798 N.E.2nd 941 (Mass. 2003), upheld the right of homosexual couples to engage in "civil" marriages. The Court defined civil marriage as "the voluntary union of two persons as spouses, to the exclusion of all others."

Even more recently, the Supreme Court of the state of New York for New York County held that the New York State Constitution gave homosexual couples the right to obtain marriage licenses and become married in *Hernandez v. Robles*, 2005 N.Y. Slip Opinion 25057 (*Sup. Ct. N.Y. Feb.* 4, 2005). The Court stated: "[Marriage] is a unique expression of a private bond and profound love between a couple, and a life dream shared by many in our culture. It is also society's most significant public proclamation of commitment to another person for life."

Do you agree with the viewpoints expressed by these courts? To this point in time, the U.S. Supreme Court has not ruled on the right of homosexual couples to marry. It will be very interesting to see if the Court will sanction such a constitutional right. Attorney and law professor Jack B. Harrison contends: "Simply no argument other than animus toward gay and lesbian persons explains excluding gay and lesbian persons from the institution of marriage." Do you agree with Professor Harrison's position?

The issues discussed in this section present a host of challenging questions. Additional resources to pursue further study in this area include: Kathleen M. Sullivan and Gerald Gunther, *Constitutional Law* (Foundation Press, 15th ed., 2004); Laurence H. Tribe, *American Constitutional Law* (Foundation Press, 2nd ed., 1988); Alpheus Thomas Mason and Donald Grier Stephenson, Jr., *American Constitutional Law* (Pearson Prentice Hall, 15th ed., 2009; 14th ed., 2005); Bernard Schwartz, *A History of the Supreme Court* (Oxford University Press, 1993); Kermit L. Hall, Paul Finkelman, and James Ely, Jr., *American Legal History: Cases and Materials* (Oxford University Press, 3rd ed., 2005); Kermit L. Hall, *The Oxford Companion to the Supreme Court of the United States* (Oxford University Press, 1992); Walter F. Murphy, James E. Fleming, Sotirios A. Barber, and Stephen Macedo, *American Constitutional Interpretation* (Foundation Press, 3rd ed., 2003); David M. O'Brien, *Constitutional Law and Politics: Struggles for Power and Government Accountability* (W.W. Norton, 6th ed., 2005); Craig R. Ducat, *Constitutional Interpretation* (Wadsworth, 9th ed., 2009); John H. Garvey, T. Alexander Aleinikoff, and Daniel A. Farber, *Modern Constitutional Theory: A Reader* (Thompson West, 5th ed., (2004). See also: Jack B. Harrison, "The Future of Same-Sex Marriage after *Lawrence v. Texas* and the Election of 2004," *University of Dayton Law Review*, vol. 30, no. 3 (2005); Daniel Allender, "Applying Lawrence: Teenagers and the Crime Against Nature," *Duke Law Journal*, vol. 58, p. 1825 (2009); Matthew W. Green, "Lawrence: An Unlikely Catalyst for Massive Disruption in the Sphere of Government Employee Privacy and Intimate Association Claims," *Berkeley Journal of Employment and Labor Law*, vol. 29, p. 311 (2008); Erwin Chemerinsky, "*Washington v. Glucksburg* Was Tragically Wrong," *Michigan Law Review*, vol. 106, p. 1501 (2008); Yale Kamisar, "Can *Glucksburg* Survive *Lawrence?* Another Look at the End of Life and Personal Autonomy," *Michigan Law Review*, vol. 106, p. 1453 (2008); Kristin Fasullo, "Beyond *Lawrence v. Texas*: Crafting a Fundamental Right to Sexual Privacy," *Fordham Law Review*, vol. 77, p. 2997 (2009).

ISSUE 12

Does the Constitution Protect the Right to Possess a Firearm Unconnected With Service in a Militia?

YES: Antonin E. Scalia, from Majority Opinion, *District of Columbia v. Heller*, 554 U.S.__ (2008).

NO: John Paul Stevens, from Dissenting Opinion, *District of Columbia v. Heller*, 554 U.S.__ (2008).

ISSUE SUMMARY

YES: Justice Antonin E. Scalia, writing for the U.S. Supreme Court in *District of Columbia v. Heller* (2008), held that a District of Columbia law making it a crime to carry an unregistered handgun and prohibiting the registration of handguns, but that authorizes the police chief to issue one-year licenses and requires residents to keep lawfully owned handgun unloaded and dissembled or bound by a trigger lock or similar device, violates the Second Amendment.

NO: Justice John Paul Stevens, dissenting in *District of Columbia v. Heller* (2008), argued that neither the text of the Second Amendment nor the arguments advanced by its proponents evidenced the slightest interest in limiting any legislature's authority to regulate private civilian uses of firearms. Moreover, there is no indication that the framers intended to enshrine the common-law right of self-defense in the Constitution.

The right to bear arms may well be one of the more controversial issues in this volume. Proponents of such a right, including powerful lobbying interests such as the National Rifle Association (NRA), believe that the right to bear arms is a fundamental one. Firearms ownership should be an individual right guaranteed by the Second Amendment to the U.S. Constitution. Opponents of an individual right to bear arms contend that the Second Amendment refers to the right of a citizen militia to possess guns and that states and the federal government may justifiably regulate the ownership of firearms. This controversy is further exacerbated by the text of the Second Amendment, which on its face is not entirely clear:

> A well regulated Militia, being necessary to the security of a free State, the right of the people to keep and bear Arms, shall not be infringed.

Does the wording of this amendment imply that only persons who are part of a "well regulated militia" have a right to keep and bear arms? Or, does it imply that the "people" have a "right to keep and bear Arms," independent of their association with a militia? These are questions that have challenged U.S. courts throughout U.S. history.

In *United States v. Emerson*, 270 F. 3d 203 (5th Cir. 2001), the U.S. Court of Appeals identified three different basic interpretations of the Second Amendment. First, the "Second Amendment does not apply to individuals, rather it merely recognizes the right of a state to arm its militia."

Advocates of the second model of the Second Amendment assert that it recognizes some limited individual rights. "However, this supposedly 'individual' right to bear arms can only be exercised by members of a functioning, organized state militia who bear the arms while and as a part of actively participating in the organized militia's activities." It applies only if the federal or state governments fail to provide the firearms necessary for such militia service. The Court asserted too that the only such organized and actively functioning militia is the National Guard. Moreover, "under this model, the Second Amendment poses no obstacle to the wholesale disarmament of the American people." This perspective on the Second Amendment is often termed "the collective rights model."

The third model emphasizes that the Second Amendment provides a right for individuals to keep and bear arms. This view has received considerable academic endorsement, "especially in the last two decades." The U.S. Court of Appeals agreed with this perspective and held that the Second Amendment to the U.S. Constitution guarantees individuals the right to keep and bear arms.

The U.S. Court of Appeals for the Ninth Circuit has a different view of the Second Amendment, however. *Silveira v. Lockyear*, 312 F.3d 1052 (9th Cir. 2002), presented a challenge to California's gun control laws that placed restrictions on the possession, use, and transfer of semiautomatic weapons, often called "assault weapons." The plaintiff asserted, among other things, that the Second Amendment conferred an individual right to own and possess firearms. The U.S. Court of Appeals held, however, that "[t]he Amendment protects the people's right to maintain an effective state militia, and does not establish an individual right to own or possess firearms for personal or other use."

Both of the decisions cited above considered an important, but somewhat cryptic, Supreme Court precedent interpreting the Second Amendment. In *United States v. Miller*, 307 U.S. 174 (1939), the defendant was charged with possessing and transporting in interstate commerce a sawed-off shotgun with a barrel less than 18 inches long, without having registered it and without having in his possession a stamp-affixed written order for it, as required by the National Firearms Act. At his trial in the U.S. District Court, Western District of Arkansas, the defendant alleged that the statute was an unconstitutional violation of the Tenth Amendment because it usurped states' "police power." The defendant further argued that the statute violated the Second Amendment to the U.S. Constitution. The U.S. District Court agreed and held that the National Firearms Act violated the Second Amendment.

On appeal, Justice James C. McReynolds, writing for the U.S. Supreme Court, quickly dismissed the defendant's Tenth Amendment claim. The defendant's Second Amendment claim was somewhat more compelling; however, Justice McReynolds held:

> In the absence of any evidence tending to show that possession or use of a 'shotgun having a barrel of less than eighteen inches in length' at this time has some reasonable relationship to the preservation or efficiency of a well-regulated militia, we cannot say that the Second Amendment guarantees the right to keep and bear such an instrument.

Justice McReynolds also presented a detailed historical analysis of what the framers of the Second Amendment considered a "militia" to be. He stated that the militia in colonial America was composed of "all males physically capable of acting in concert for the common defense." Further, when these individuals were called for service, they "were expected to appear bearing arms supplied by themselves and of the kind in common use at that time." Therefore, the Court held that because the Second Amendment did not protect an individual's right to own firearms, the National Firearms Act was a lawful exercise of congressional authority.

In 2008, the U.S. Supreme Court considered the case excerpted in this section, *District of Columbia v. Heller,* 554 U.S.___ (2008). In *Heller,* the Court was asked to reconsider *U.S. v. Miller*'s holding that the Second Amendment did not protect an individual's right to own firearms. The facts that gave rise to *Heller* are as follows: The *District of Columbia* had passed a law making it a crime to carry an unregistered handgun and prohibiting the registration of handguns, but that authorized the police chief to issue one-year licenses, and required residents to keep lawfully owned handguns unloaded and dissembled or bound by a trigger lock or similar device. *Heller,* a District of Columbia special policeman, applied to register a handgun he wished to keep at home, but the city denied his application. He then filed suit in U.S. District Court to prevent the city from enforcing the ban on handgun registration, the licensing requirement insofar as it prohibits carrying an unlicensed firearm in the home, and the trigger-lock requirement insofar as it prohibits the use of functional firearms in the home. The District Court dismissed the suit, but the U.S. Court of Appeals (D.C. Cir.) reversed, holding that the Second Amendment protects an individual's right to possess firearms and that the city's total ban on handguns, as well as its requirement that firearms in the home be kept nonfunctional even when needed for self-defense, violated that right.

The U.S. Supreme Court granted certiorari and held that the Second Amendment protects an individual right to possess a firearm unconnected with service in a militia, and to use that weapon for traditionally lawful purposes, such as self-defense. Accordingly, Justice Scalia, writing for a five-to-four majority, concluded:

> We are aware of the problem of handgun violence in this country, and we take seriously the concerns raised by the many amici who believe that prohibition of handgun ownership is the solution. The Constitution leaves the District of Columbia a variety of tools for combating that problem, including some measures regulating handguns. But the enshrinement of constitutional rights necessarily takes certain policy choices off the table. These include the absolute prohibition of handguns held and used for self-defense in the home. . . . it is not the role of this Court to pronounce the Second Amendment extinct.

In a compelling dissenting opinion, Justice John Paul Stevens took issue with the majority's conclusion. Stated Justice Stevens:

> The court properly disclaims any interest in evaluating the wisdom of the specific policy choice challenged in this case, but it fails to pay heed to a far more important policy choice—the choice made by the Framers themselves. The Court would have us believe that over 200 years ago, the Framers made a choice to limit the tools available to elected officials wishing to regulate civilian uses of weapons, and to authorize this Court to use the common-law process of case-by-case judicial lawmaking to define the contours of acceptable gun control policy. Absent compelling evidence that is nowhere to be found in the Court's opinion, I could not possibly conclude that the Framers made such a choice.

In Your Opinion . . .

- Who presents the more compelling view of the rights guaranteed by the Second Amendment, Justice Scalia or Justice Stevens?
- If you agree with Justice Scalia, what, if any, limitations would you allow society to place on firearms ownership?
- Should one consider whether society should be able to limit other aspects of firearms ownership, such as the possession of Teflon-coated bullets, which can penetrate the bulletproof vests worn by many police officers?

YES

Antonin E. Scalia

Majority Opinion, *District of Columbia v. Heller*

Justice Scalia delivered the opinion of the Court.

We consider whether a District of Columbia prohibition on the possession of usable handguns in the home violates the Second Amendment to the Constitution.

I

The District of Columbia generally prohibits the possession of handguns. It is a crime to carry an unregistered firearm, and the registration of handguns is prohibited. See D. C. Code §§7-2501.01(12), 7-2502.01(a), 7-2502.02(a)(4) (2001). Wholly apart from that prohibition, no person may carry a handgun without a license, but the chief of police may issue licenses for 1-year periods. See §§22-4504(a), 22-4506. District of Columbia law also requires residents to keep their lawfully owned firearms, such as registered long guns, "unloaded and dissembled or bound by a trigger lock or similar device" unless they are located in a place of business or are being used for lawful recreational activities. See §7-2507.02.

Respondent Dick Heller is a D.C. special police officer authorized to carry a handgun while on duty at the Federal Judicial Center. He applied for a registration certificate for a handgun that he wished to keep at home, but the District refused. He thereafter filed a lawsuit in the Federal District Court for the District of Columbia seeking, on Second Amendment grounds, to enjoin the city from enforcing the bar on the registration of handguns, the licensing requirement insofar as it prohibits the carrying of a firearm in the home without a license, and the trigger-lock requirement insofar as it prohibits the use of "functional firearms within the home." App. 59a. The District Court dismissed respondent's complaint, see *Parker v. District of Columbia*, 311 F. Supp. 2d 103, 109 (2004). The Court of Appeals for the District of Columbia Circuit, construing his complaint as seeking the right to render a firearm operable and carry it about his home in that condition only when necessary for self-defense, reversed, see *Parker v. District of Columbia*, 478 F. 3d 370, 401 (2007). It held that the Second Amendment protects an individual right to possess firearms and that the city's total ban on handguns, as well as its requirement that firearms in the home be kept nonfunctional even when necessary for self-defense,

Supreme Court of the United States, 2008.

violated that right. See *id.*, at 395, 399–401. The Court of Appeals directed the District Court to enter summary judgment for respondent.

We granted certiorari. 552 U. S. ___ (2007).

II

We turn first to the meaning of the Second Amendment.

A

The Second Amendment provides: "A well regulated Militia, being necessary to the security of a free State, the right of the people to keep and bear Arms, shall not be infringed." In interpreting this text, we are guided by the principle that "[t]he Constitution was written to be understood by the voters; its words and phrases were used in their normal and ordinary as distinguished from technical meaning." *United States v. Sprague,* 282 U. S. 716, 731 (1931); see also *Gibbons v. Ogden,* 9 Wheat. 1, 188 (1824). Normal meaning may of course include an idiomatic meaning, but it excludes secret or technical meanings that would not have been known to ordinary citizens in the founding generation.

The two sides in this case have set out very different interpretations of the Amendment. Petitioners and today's dissenting Justices believe that it protects only the right to possess and carry a firearm in connection with militia service. See Brief for Petitioners 11-12; *post,* at 1 (Stevens, J., dissenting). Respondent argues that it protects an individual right to possess a firearm unconnected with service in a militia, and to use that arm for traditionally lawful purposes, such as self-defense within the home. See Brief for Respondent 2-4.

The Second Amendment is naturally divided into two parts: its prefatory clause and its operative clause. The former does not limit the latter grammatically, but rather announces a purpose. The Amendment could be rephrased, "Because a well regulated Militia is necessary to the security of a free State, the right of the people to keep and bear Arms shall not be infringed." See J. Tiffany, A Treatise on Government and Constitutional Law §585, p. 394 (1867); Brief for Professors of Linguistics and English as *Amici Curiae* 3 (hereinafter Linguists' Brief). Although this structure of the Second Amendment is unique in our Constitution, other legal documents of the founding era, particularly individual-rights provisions of state constitutions, commonly included a prefatory statement of purpose. See generally Volokh, The Commonplace Second Amendment, 73 N. Y. U. L. Rev. 793, 814–821 (1998).

Logic demands that there be a link between the stated purpose and the command. The Second Amendment would be nonsensical if it read, "A well regulated Militia, being necessary to the security of a free State, the right of the people to petition for redress of grievances shall not be infringed." That requirement of logical connection may cause a prefatory clause to resolve an ambiguity in the operative clause ("The separation of church and state being an important objective, the teachings of canons shall have no place in our jurisprudence." The preface makes clear that the operative clause refers not to canons of interpretation but to clergymen.) But apart from that clarifying function, a prefatory clause does not limit or expand the scope of the operative clause. See F. Dwarris, A General Treatise on Statutes, 268–269 (P. Potter ed. 1871) (hereinafter Dwarris); T. Sedgwick, The Interpretation and Construction of Statutory and Constitutional Law, 42-45 (2d ed. 1874). "It is nothing unusual in acts . . . for the enacting part to go beyond the preamble; the remedy often extends beyond the particular act or mischief which first suggested the necessity of the law." J. Bishop, Commentaries on Written Laws and Their Interpretation §51, p. 49 (1882) (quoting *Rex v. Marks,* 3 East, 157, 165 (K. B. 1802)). Therefore, while we will begin our textual analysis with the operative clause, we will return to the prefatory clause to ensure that our reading of the operative clause is consistent with the announced purpose.

1. Operative Clause.
a. "Right of the People." The first salient feature of the operative clause is that it codifies a "right of the people." The unamended Constitution and the Bill of Rights use the phrase "right of the people" two other times, in the First Amendment's Assembly-and-Petition Clause and in the Fourth Amendment's Search-and-Seizure Clause. The Ninth Amendment uses very similar terminology ("The enumeration in the Constitution, of certain rights, shall not be construed to deny or disparage others retained by the people"). All three of these instances unambiguously refer to individual rights, not "collective" rights, or rights that may be exercised only through participation in some corporate body.

Three provisions of the Constitution refer to "the people" in a context other than "rights"—the famous preamble ("We the people"), §2 of Article I (providing that "the people" will choose members of the House), and the Tenth Amendment (providing that those powers not given the Federal Government remain with "the States" or "the people"). Those provisions arguably refer to "the people" acting collectively—but they deal with the exercise or reservation of powers, not rights. Nowhere else in the Constitution does a "right" attributed to "the people" refer to anything other than an individual right.

What is more, in all six other provisions of the Constitution that mention "the people," the term unambiguously refers to all members of the political community, not an unspecified subset. As we said in *United States v. Verdugo-Urquidez,* 494 U. S. 259, 265 (1990):

> "'[T]he people' seems to have been a term of art employed in select parts of the Constitution. . . . [Its uses] sugges[t] that 'the people' protected by the Fourth Amendment, and by the First and Second Amendments, and to whom rights and powers are reserved in the Ninth and Tenth Amendments, refers to a class of persons who are part of a national community or who have otherwise developed sufficient connection with this country to be considered part of that community."

This contrasts markedly with the phrase "the militia" in the prefatory clause. As we will describe below, the "militia" in colonial America consisted of a subset of "the people"—those who were male, able bodied, and within a certain age range. Reading the Second Amendment as protecting only the right to "keep and bear Arms" in an organized militia therefore fits poorly with the operative clause's description of the holder of that right as "the people."

We start therefore with a strong presumption that the Second Amendment right is exercised individually and belongs to all Americans.

b. "Keep and bear Arms." We move now from the holder of the right— "the people"—to the substance of the right: "to keep and bear Arms."

Before addressing the verbs "keep" and "bear," we interpret their object: "Arms." The 18th-century meaning is no different from the meaning today. The 1773 edition of Samuel Johnson's dictionary defined "arms" as "weapons of offence, or armour of defence." 1 *Dictionary of the English Language* 107 (4th ed.) (hereinafter Johnson). Timothy Cunningham's important 1771 legal dictionary defined "arms" as "any thing that a man wears for his defence, or takes into his hands, or useth in wrath to cast at or strike another." 1 *A New and Complete Law Dictionary* (1771); see also N. Webster, American Dictionary of the English Language (1828) (reprinted 1989) (hereinafter Webster) (similar).

The term was applied, then as now, to weapons that were not specifically designed for military use and were not employed in a military capacity. For instance, Cunningham's legal dictionary gave as an example of usage: "Servants and labourers shall use bows and arrows on *Sundays,* &c. and not bear other arms." See also, e.g., An Act for the trial of Negroes, 1797 Del. Laws ch. XLIII, §6, p. 104, in *First Laws of the state of Delaware* 102, 104 (J. Cushing ed. 1981 (pt. 1)); see generally *State v. Duke,* 42Tex. 455, 458 (1874) (citing decisions of state courts construing "arms"). Although one founding-era thesaurus limited "arms" (as opposed to "weapons") to "instruments of offence *generally* made use of in war," even that source stated that all firearms constituted "arms." 1 J. Trusler, The Distinction Between Words Esteemed Synonymous in the English Language 37 (1794) (emphasis added).

Some have made the argument, bordering on the frivolous, that only those arms in existence in the 18th century are protected by the Second Amendment. We do not interpret constitutional rights that way. Just as the First Amendment protects modern forms of communications, e.g., *Reno v. American Civil Liberties Union,* 521 U. S. 844, 849 (1997), and the Fourth Amendment applies to modern forms of search, e.g., *Kyllo v. United States,* 533 U. S. 27, 35–36 (2001), the Second Amendment extends, prima facie, to all instruments that constitute bearable arms, even those that were not in existence at the time of the founding.

We turn to the phrases "keep arms" and "bear arms." Johnson defined "keep" as, most relevantly, "[t]o retain; not to lose," and "[t]o have in custody." Johnson 1095. Webster defined it as "[t]o hold; to retain in one's power or possession." No party has apprised us of an idiomatic meaning of "keep Arms." Thus, the most natural reading of "keep Arms" in the Second Amendment is to "have weapons."

The phrase "keep arms" was not prevalent in the written documents of the founding period that we have found, but there are a few examples, all of which favor viewing the right to "keep Arms" as an individual right unconnected with militia service. William Blackstone, for example, wrote that Catholics convicted of not attending service in the Church of England suffered certain penalties, one of which was that they were not permitted to "keep arms in their houses." 4 Commentaries on the Laws of England 55 (1769) (hereinafter Blackstone); see also 1 W. & M., c. 15, §4, in 3 Eng. Stat. at Large 422 (1689) ("[N]o Papist . . . shall or may have or keep in his House . . . any Arms . . . "); 1 Hawkins, Treatise on the Pleas of the Crown 26 (1771) (similar). Petitioners point to militia laws of the founding period that required militia members to "keep" arms in connection with militia service, and they conclude from this that the phrase "keep Arms" has a militia-related connotation. See Brief for Petitioners 16-17 (citing laws of Delaware, New Jersey, and Virginia). This is rather like saying that, since there are many statutes that authorize aggrieved employees to "file complaints" with federal agencies, the phrase "file complaints" has an employment-related connotation. "Keep arms" was simply a common way of referring to possessing arms, for militiamen and everyone else.

At the time of the founding, as now, to "bear" meant to "carry." See Johnson 161; Webster; T. Sheridan, A Complete Dictionary of the English Language (1796); 2 Oxford English Dictionary 20 (2d ed. 1989) (hereinafter Oxford). When used with "arms," however, the term has a meaning that refers to carrying for a particular purpose—confrontation. In *Muscarello v. United States,* 524 U. S. 125 (1998), in the course of analyzing the meaning of "carries a firearm" in a federal criminal statute, Justice Ginsburg wrote that "[s]urely a most familiar meaning is, as the Constitution's Second Amendment . . . indicate[s]: 'wear, bear, or carry . . . upon the person or in the clothing or in a pocket, for the purpose . . . of being armed and ready for offensive or defensive action in a case of conflict with another person.'" *Id.,* at 143 (dissenting opinion) (quoting *Black's Law Dictionary* 214 (6th ed. 1998)). We think that Justice Ginsburg accurately captured the natural meaning of "bear arms." Although the phrase implies that the carrying of the weapon is for the purpose of "offensive or defensive action," it in no way connotes participation in a structured military organization. . . .

c. Meaning of the Operative Clause. Putting all of these textual elements together, we find that they guarantee the individual right to possess and carry weapons in case of confrontation. This meaning is strongly confirmed by the historical background of the Second Amendment. We look to this because it has always been widely understood that the Second Amendment, like the First and Fourth Amendments, codified a *pre-existing* right. The very text of the Second Amendment implicitly recognizes the pre-existence of the right and declares only that it "shall not be infringed." As we said in *United States v. Cruikshank,* 92 U. S. 542, 553 (1876), "[t]his is not a right granted by the Constitution. Neither is it in any manner dependent upon that instrument for its existence. The Second amendment declares that it shall not be infringed. . . ."

There seems to us no doubt, on the basis of both text and history, that the Second Amendment conferred an individual right to keep and bear arms. Of course the right was not unlimited, just as the First Amendment's right of free speech was not, see, e.g., *United States v. Williams,* 553 U.S.___ (2008). Thus, we do not read the Second Amendment to protect the right of citizens to carry arms for *any sort* of confrontation, just as we do not read the First

Amendment to protect the right of citizens to speak for *any purpose*. Before turning to limitations upon the individual right, however, we must determine whether the prefatory clause of the Second Amendment comports with our interpretation of the operative clause.

2. Prefatory Clause.

The prefatory clause reads: "A well regulated Militia, being necessary to the security of a free State. . . ."

a. "Well-Regulated Militia." In *United States v. Miller,* 307 U. S. 174, 179 (1939), we explained that "the Militia comprised all males physically capable of acting in concert for the common defense." That definition comports with founding-era sources. See, e.g., Webster ("The militia of a country are the able bodied men organized into companies, regiments and brigades . . . and required by law to attend military exercises on certain days only, but at other times left to pursue their usual occupations"); *The Federalist* No. 46, pp. 329, 334 (B. Wright ed. 1961) (J. Madison) ("near half a million of citizens with arms in their hands"); Letter to Destutt de Tracy (Jan. 26, 1811), in *The Portable Thomas Jefferson* 520, 524 (M. Peterson ed. 1975) ("[T]he militia of the State, that is to say, of every man in it able to bear arms").

Petitioners take a seemingly narrower view of the militia, stating that "[m]ilitias are the state-and congressionally-regulated military forces described in the Militia Clauses (art. I, §8, cls. 15-16)." Brief for Petitioners 12. Although we agree with petitioners' interpretive assumption that "militia" means the same thing in Article I and the Second Amendment, we believe that petitioners identify the wrong thing, namely, the organized militia. Unlike armies and navies, which Congress is given the power to create ("to raise . . . Armies"; "to provide . . . a Navy," Art. I, §8, cls. 12-13), the militia is assumed by Article I already to be *in existence*. Congress is given the power to "provide for calling forth the militia," §8, cl. 15; and the power not to create, but to "organiz[e]" it—and not to organize "a" militia, which is what one would expect if the militia were to be a federal creation, but to organize "the" militia, connoting a body already in existence, *ibid.,* cl. 16. This is fully consistent with the ordinary definition of the militia as all able-bodied men. From that pool, Congress has plenary power to organize the units that will make up an effective fighting force. That is what Congress did in the first militia Act, which specified that "each and every free able-bodied white male citizen of the respective states, resident therein, who is or shall be of the age of eighteen years, and under the age of forty-five years (except as is herein after excepted) shall severally and respectively be enrolled in the militia." Act of May 8, 1792, 1 Stat. 271. To be sure, Congress need not conscript every able-bodied man into the militia, because nothing in Article I suggests that in exercising its power to organize, discipline, and arm the militia, Congress must focus upon the entire body. Although the militia consists of all able-bodied men, the federally organized militia may consist of a subset of them.

Finally, the adjective "well-regulated" implies nothing more than the imposition of proper discipline and training. See Johnson 1619 ("Regulate": "To adjust by rule or method"); Rawle 121–122; cf. Va. Declaration of Rights

§13 (1776), in 7 Thorpe 3812, 3814 (referring to "a well-regulated militia, composed of the body of the people, trained to arms").

b. "Security of a Free State." The phrase "security of a free state" meant "security of a free polity," not security of each of the several States as the dissent below argued, see 478 F. 3d, at 405, and n. 10. Joseph Story wrote in his treatise on the Constitution that "the word 'state' is used in various senses [and in] its most enlarged sense, it means the people composing a particular nation or community." 1 Story §208; see also 3 *id.*, §1890 (in reference to the Second Amendment's prefatory clause: "The militia is the natural defence of a free country"). It is true that the term "State" elsewhere in the Constitution refers to individual States, but the phrase "security of a free state" and close variations seem to have been terms of art in 18th-century political discourse, meaning a "free country" or free polity. See Volokh, "Necessary to the Security of a Free State," 83 *Notre Dame L. Rev.* 1, 5 (2007); see, e.g., 4 Blackstone 151 (1769); Brutus Essay III (Nov. 15, 1787), in *The Essential Antifederalist* 251, 253 (W. Allen & G. Lloyd eds., 2d ed. 2002). Moreover, the other instances of "state" in the Constitution are typically accompanied by modifiers making clear that the reference is to the several States—"each state," "several states," "any state," "that state," "particular states," "one state," "no state." And the presence of the term "foreign state" in Article I and Article III shows that the word "state" did not have a single meaning in the Constitution.

There are many reasons why the militia was thought to be "necessary to the security of a free state." See 3 Story §1890. First, of course, it is useful in repelling invasions and suppressing insurrections. Second, it renders large standing armies unnecessary—an argument that Alexander Hamilton made in favor of federal control over the militia. The Federalist No. 29, pp. 226, 227 (B. Wright ed. 1961) (A. Hamilton). Third, when the able-bodied men of a nation are trained in arms and organized, they are better able to resist tyranny.

3. Relationship between Prefatory Clause and Operative Clause

We reach the question, then: Does the preface fit with an operative clause that creates an individual right to keep and bear arms? It fits perfectly, once one knows the history that the founding generation knew and that we have described above. That history showed that the way tyrants had eliminated a militia consisting of all the able-bodied men was not by banning the militia but simply by taking away the people's arms, enabling a select militia or standing army to suppress political opponents. This is what had occurred in England that prompted codification of the right to have arms in the English Bill of Rights. . . .

It is therefore entirely sensible that the Second Amendment's prefatory clause announces the purpose for which the right was codified: to prevent elimination of the militia. The prefatory clause does not suggest that preserving the militia was the only reason Americans valued the ancient right; most undoubtedly thought it even more important for self-defense and hunting. But the threat that the new Federal Government would destroy the citizens' militia by taking away their arms was the reason that right—unlike some other English rights—was codified in a written Constitution. Justice Breyer's assertion that individual self-defense is merely a "subsidiary interest" of the right to keep and bear arms, see *post,* at 36, is profoundly mistaken. He bases that assertion solely upon the prologue—but that can only show that self-defense had little to do with the right's *codification;* it was the *central component* of the right itself.

Besides ignoring the historical reality that the Second Amendment was not intended to lay down a "novel principl[e]" but rather codified a right "inherited from our English ancestors," *Robertson v. Baldwin,* 165 U. S. 275, 281 (1897), petitioners' interpretation does not even achieve the narrower purpose that prompted codification of the right. If, as they believe, the Second Amendment right is no more than the right to keep and use weapons as a member of an organized militia, see *Brief for Petitioners* 8—if, that is, the *organized* militia is the sole institutional beneficiary of the Second Amendment's guarantee—it does not assure the existence of a "citizens' militia" as a safeguard against tyranny. For Congress retains plenary authority to organize the militia, which must include the authority to say who will belong to the organized force. That is why the first Militia Act's requirement that only whites enroll caused States to amend their militia laws to exclude free blacks. See Siegel, The Federal Government's Power to Enact Color-Conscious Laws, 92 *Nw. U. L. Rev.* 477, 521 (1998). Thus, if petitioners are correct, the Second Amendment protects citizens' right to use a gun in an organization from which Congress has plenary authority to exclude them. It guarantees a select militia of the sort the Stuart kings found useful, but not the people's militia that was the concern of the founding generation.

B

Our interpretation is confirmed by analogous arms-bearing rights in state constitutions that preceded and immediately followed adoption of the Second Amendment. Four States adopted analogues to the Federal Second Amendment in the period between independence and the ratification of the Bill of Rights. Two of them—Pennsylvania and Vermont—clearly adopted individual rights unconnected to militia service. Pennsylvania's Declaration of Rights of 1776 said: "That the people have a right to bear arms *for the defence of themselves,* and the state. . . ." §XIII, in 5 Thorpe 3082, 3083 (emphasis added). In 1777, Vermont adopted the identical provision, except for inconsequential differences in punctuation and capitalization. See Vt. Const., ch. 1, §15, in 6 *id.,* at 3741. . . .

We therefore believe that the most likely reading of all four of these pre-Second Amendment state constitutional provisions is that they secured an individual right to bear arms for defensive purposes. Other States did not include rights to bear arms in their pre-1789 constitutions—although in Virginia a Second Amendment analogue was proposed (unsuccessfully) by Thomas Jefferson. (It read: "No freeman shall ever be debarred the use of arms [within his own lands or tenements]." 1 The Papers of Thomas Jefferson 344 (J. Boyd ed. 1950)). . . .

The historical narrative that petitioners must endorse would thus treat the Federal Second Amendment as an odd outlier, protecting a right unknown in state constitutions or at English common law, based on little more than an overreading of the prefatory clause.

C

Justice Stevens relies on the drafting history of the Second Amendment—the various proposals in the state conventions and the debates in Congress. It is dubious to rely on such history to interpret a text that was widely understood to codify a pre-existing right, rather than to fashion a new one. But even assuming that this legislative history is relevant, Justice Stevens flatly misreads the historical record. . . .

D

1. Post-ratification Commentary
[I]mportant founding-era legal scholars interpreted the Second Amendment in published writings. All three understood it to protect an individual right unconnected with militia service. . . .

We have found only one early 19th-century commentator who clearly conditioned the right to keep and bear arms upon service in the militia—and he recognized that the prevailing view was to the contrary. "The provision of the constitution, declaring the right of the people to keep and bear arms, Etc. was probably intended to apply to the right of the people to bear arms for such [militia-related] purposes only, and not to prevent congress or the legislatures of the different states from enacting laws to prevent the citizens from always going armed. A different construction however has been given to it." B. Oliver, The Rights of an American Citizen 177 (1832). . . .

4. Post-Civil War Commentators
Every late 19th-century legal scholar that we have read interpreted the Second Amendment to secure an individual right unconnected with militia service. The most famous was the judge and professor Thomas Cooley, who wrote a massively popular 1868 Treatise on Constitutional Limitations. Concerning the Second Amendment it said:

> "Among the other defences to personal liberty should be mentioned the right of the people to keep and bear arms. . . . The alternative to a standing army is 'a well-regulated militia,' but this cannot exist unless the people are trained to bearing arms. How far it is in the power of the legislature to regulate this right, we shall not undertake to say, as happily there has been very little occasion to discuss that subject by the courts." *Id.*, at 350. . . .
> "[The purpose of the Second Amendment is] to secure a well-armed militia. . . . But a militia would be useless unless the citizens were enabled to exercise themselves in the use of warlike weapons. To preserve this privilege, and to secure to the people the ability to oppose themselves in military force against the usurpations of government, as well as against enemies from without, that government is forbidden by any law or proceeding to invade or destroy the right to keep and bear arms . . . . The clause is analogous to the one securing the freedom of speech and of

the press. Freedom, not license, is secured; the fair use, not the libellous abuse, is protected." J. Pomeroy, An Introduction to the Constitutional Law of the United States 152–153 (1868) (hereinafter Pomeroy). . . .

"The right to bear arms has always been the distinctive privilege of freemen. Aside from any necessity of self-protection to the person, it represents among all nations power coupled with the exercise of a certain jurisdiction. . . . [I]t was not necessary that the right to bear arms should be granted in the Constitution, for it had always existed." J. Ordronaux, Constitutional Legislation in the United States 241–242 (1891).

E

We now ask whether any of our precedents forecloses the conclusions we have reached about the meaning of the Second Amendment. . . .

Justice Stevens places overwhelming reliance upon this Court's decision in *United States v. Miller*, 307 U. S. 174 (1939). "[H]undreds of judges," we are told, "have relied on the view of the amendment we endorsed there," *post*, at 2, and "[e]ven if the textual and historical arguments on both side of the issue were evenly balanced, respect for the well-settled views of all of our predecessors on this Court, and for the rule of law itself . . . would prevent most jurists from endorsing such a dramatic upheaval in the law," *post*, at 4. And what is, according to Justice Stevens, the holding of *Miller* that demands such obeisance? That the Second Amendment "protects the right to keep and bear arms for certain military purposes, but that it does not curtail the legislature's power to regulate the nonmilitary use and ownership of weapons." *Post*, at 2.

Nothing so clearly demonstrates the weakness of Justice Stevens' case. *Miller* did not hold that and cannot possibly be read to have held that. The judgment in the case upheld against a Second Amendment challenge two men's federal convictions for transporting an unregistered short-barreled shotgun in interstate commerce, in violation of the National Firearms Act, 48 Stat. 1236. It is entirely clear that the Court's basis for saying that the Second Amendment did not apply was *not* that the defendants were "bear[ing] arms" not "for . . . military purposes" but for "nonmilitary use," *post*, at 2. Rather, it was that the *type of weapon at issue* was not eligible for Second Amendment protection: "In the absence of any evidence tending to show that the possession or use of a [short-barreled shotgun] at this time has some reasonable relationship to the preservation or efficiency of a well regulated militia, we cannot say that the Second Amendment guarantees the right to keep and bear *such an instrument*." 307 U. S., at 178 (emphasis added). "Certainly," the Court continued, "it is not within judicial notice that this weapon is any part of the ordinary military equipment or that its use could contribute to the common defense." *Ibid.* Beyond that, the opinion provided no explanation of the content of the right.

This holding is not only consistent with, but positively suggests, that the Second Amendment confers an individual right to keep and bear arms (though only arms that "have some reasonable relationship to the preservation or efficiency of a well regulated militia"). Had the Court believed that the Second Amendment protects only those serving in the militia, it would have been odd to examine the character of the weapon rather than simply note that the two crooks were not militiamen. Justice Stevens can say again and again that *Miller* did "not turn on the difference between muskets and sawed-off shotguns, it turned, rather, on the basic difference between the military and nonmilitary use and possession of guns," *post,* at 42–43, but the words of the opinion prove otherwise. The most Justice Stevens can plausibly claim for *Miller* is that it declined to decide the nature of the Second Amendment right, despite the Solicitor General's argument (made in the alternative) that the right was collective, see Brief for United States, O. T. 1938, No. 696, pp. 4–5. *Miller* stands only for the proposition that the Second Amendment right, whatever its nature, extends only to certain types of weapons. . . .

We may as well consider at this point (for we will have to consider eventually) *what* types of weapons *Miller* permits. Read in isolation, *Miller's* phrase "part of ordinary military equipment" could mean that only those weapons useful in warfare are protected. That would be a startling reading of the opinion, since it would mean that the National Firearms Act's restrictions on machineguns (not challenged in *Miller)* might be unconstitutional, machineguns being useful in warfare in 1939. We think that *Miller's* "ordinary military equipment" language must be read in tandem with what comes after: "[O]rdinarily when called for [militia] service [able-bodied] men were expected to appear bearing arms supplied by themselves and of the kind in common use at the time." 307 U. S., at 179. The traditional militia was formed from a pool of men bringing arms "in common use at the time" for lawful purposes like self-defense. "In the colonial and revolutionary war era, [small-arms] weapons used by militiamen and weapons used in defense of person and home were one and the same." *State v. Kessler,* 289 Ore. 359, 368, 614 P. 2d 94, 98 (1980) (citing G. Neumann, Swords and Blades of the American Revolution 6–15, 252–254 (1973)). Indeed, that is precisely the way in which the Second Amendment's operative clause furthers the purpose announced in its preface. We therefore read *Miller* to say only that the Second Amendment does not protect those weapons not typically possessed by law-abiding citizens for lawful purposes, such as short-barreled shotguns. That accords with the historical understanding of the scope of the right, see Part III, infra.

We conclude that nothing in our precedents forecloses our adoption of the original understanding of the Second Amendment. It should be unsurprising that such a significant matter has been for so long judicially unresolved. For most of our history, the Bill of Rights was not thought applicable to the States, and the Federal Government did not significantly regulate the possession of firearms by law-abiding citizens. Other provisions of the Bill of Rights have similarly remained unilluminated for lengthy periods. This Court first held a law to violate the First Amendment's guarantee of freedom of speech in 1931, almost 150 years after the Amendment was ratified, see *Near v. Minnesota ex rel. Olson,* 283 U.S. 697 (1931), and it was not until after World War II that we held a law invalid under the Establishment Clause, see *Illinois ex rel. McCollum v. Board of Ed. of School Dist. No. 71, Champaign Cty.,* 333 U. S. 203 (1948). Even a question as basic as the scope of proscribable libel was not addressed by this Court until 1964, nearly two centuries after the founding. See *New York Times Co. v. Sullivan,* 376 U. S. 254 (1964). It is demonstrably not true that, as Justice Stevens claims, *post,* at 41-42, "for most of our history, the invalidity of Second-Amendment-based objections to firearms regulations has been well settled and uncontroversial." For most of our history the question did not present itself.

III

Like most rights, the right secured by the Second Amendment is not unlimited. From Blackstone through the 19th-century cases, commentators and courts routinely explained that the right was not a right to keep and carry any weapon whatsoever in any manner whatsoever and for whatever purpose. See, e.g., *Sheldon,* in 5 Blume 346; Rawle 123; Pomeroy 152–153; Abbott 333. For example, the majority of the 19th-century courts to consider the question held that prohibitions on carrying concealed weapons were lawful under the Second Amendment or state analogues. See, e.g., *State v. Chandler,* 5 La. Ann., at 489–490; *Nunn v. State,* 1 Ga., at 251; see generally 2 Kent *340, n. 2; The American Students' Blackstone 84, n. 11 (G. Chase ed. 1884). Although we do not undertake an exhaustive historical analysis today of the full scope of the Second Amendment, nothing in our opinion should be taken to cast doubt on longstanding prohibitions on the possession of firearms by felons and the mentally ill, or laws forbidding the carrying of firearms in sensitive places such as schools and government buildings, or laws imposing conditions and qualifications on the commercial sale of arms.

We also recognize another important limitation on the right to keep and carry arms. *Miller* said, as we have explained, that the sorts of weapons protected were those "in common use at the time." 307 U.S., at 179. We think that limitation is fairly supported by the historical tradition of prohibiting the carrying of "dangerous and unusual weapons." . . .

IV

We turn finally to the law at issue here. As we have said, the law totally bans handgun possession in the home. It also requires that any lawful firearm in the home be disassembled or bound by a trigger lock at all times, rendering it inoperable.

As the quotations earlier in this opinion demonstrate, the inherent right of self-defense has been central to the Second Amendment right. The handgun ban amounts to a prohibition of an entire class of "arms" that is overwhelmingly chosen by American society for that lawful purpose. The prohibition extends, moreover, to the home, where the need for defense of self, family, and property is most acute. Under any of the standards of scrutiny that we have applied to enumerated constitutional rights, banning from the home "the most preferred firearm in the nation to 'keep' and use for protection of one's home and family," 478 F. 3d, at 400, would fail constitutional muster.

Few laws in the history of our Nation have come close to the severe restriction of the District's handgun ban. And some of those few have been struck down. In *Nunn v. State,* the Georgia Supreme Court struck down a prohibition on carrying pistols openly (even though it upheld a prohibition on carrying concealed weapons). See 1 Ga., at 251. In *Andrews v. State,* the Tennessee Supreme Court likewise held that a statute that forbade openly carrying a pistol "publicly or privately, without regard to time or place, or circumstances," 50 Tenn., at 187, violated the state constitutional provision (which the court equated with the Second Amendment). That was so even though the statute did not restrict the carrying of long guns. *Ibid.* See also *State v. Reid,* 1 Ala. 612, 616-617 (1840) ("A statute which, under the pretence of regulating, amounts to a destruction of the right, or which requires arms to be so borne as to render them wholly useless for the purpose of defence, would be clearly unconstitutional").

It is no answer to say, as petitioners do, that it is permissible to ban the possession of handguns so long as the possession of other firearms (i.e., long guns) is allowed. It is enough to note, as we have observed, that the American people have considered the handgun to be the quintessential self-defense weapon. There are many reasons that a citizen may prefer a handgun for home defense: It is easier to store in a location that is readily accessible in an emergency; it cannot easily be redirected or wrestled away by an attacker; it is easier to use for those without the upper-body strength to lift and aim a long gun; it can be pointed at a burglar with one hand while the other hand dials the police. Whatever the reason, handguns are the most popular weapon chosen by Americans for self-defense in the home, and a complete prohibition of their use is invalid.

We must also address the District's requirement (as applied to respondent's handgun) that firearms in the home be rendered and kept inoperable at all times. This makes it impossible for citizens to use them for the core lawful purpose of self-defense and is hence unconstitutional. The District argues that we should interpret this element of the statute to contain an exception for self-defense. See *Brief for Petitioners* 56–57. But we think that is precluded by the unequivocal text, and by the presence of certain other enumerated exceptions: "Except for law enforcement personnel . . ., each registrant shall keep any firearm in his possession unloaded and disassembled or bound by a trigger lock or similar device unless such firearm is kept at his place of business, or while being used for lawful recreational purposes within the District of Columbia." D. C. Code §7-2507.02. The nonexistence of a self-defense exception is also suggested by the D. C. Court of Appeals' statement that the statute forbids residents to use firearms to stop intruders, see *McIntosh v. Washington,* 395 A. 2d 744, 755–756 (1978). . . .

In sum, we hold that the District's ban on handgun possession in the home violates the Second Amendment, as does its prohibition against rendering any lawful firearm in the home operable for the purpose of immediate self-defense. Assuming that Heller is not disqualified from the exercise of Second Amendment rights, the District must permit him to register his handgun and must issue him a license to carry it in the home.

*   *   *

We are aware of the problem of handgun violence in this country, and we take seriously the concerns raised by the many *amici* who believe that prohibition of handgun ownership is a solution. The Constitution leaves the District of Columbia a variety of tools for combating that problem, including some measures regulating handguns, see *supra*, at 54–55, and n. 26. But the enshrinement of constitutional rights necessarily takes certain policy choices off the table. These include the absolute prohibition of handguns held and used for self-defense in the home. Undoubtedly some think that the Second Amendment is outmoded in a society where our standing army is the pride of our Nation, where well-trained police forces provide personal security, and where gun violence is a serious problem. That is perhaps debatable, but what is not debatable is that it is not the role of this Court to pronounce the Second Amendment extinct.

We affirm the judgment of the Court of Appeals.

It is so ordered.

John Paul Stevens  **NO**

Dissenting Opinion, *District of Columbia v. Heller*

Supreme Court of the United States
District of Columbia, *et al.*, Petitioners *v.* Dick Anthony Heller

Justice Stevens, **with whom** Justice Souter, Justice Ginsburg, **and** Justice Breyer **join, dissenting.**

The question presented by this case is not whether the Second Amendment protects a "collective right" or an "individual right." Surely it protects a right that can be enforced by individuals. But a conclusion that the Second Amendment protects an individual right does not tell us anything about the scope of that right.

Guns are used to hunt, for self-defense, to commit crimes, for sporting activities, and to perform military duties. The Second Amendment plainly does not protect the right to use a gun to rob a bank; it is equally clear that it *does* encompass the right to use weapons for certain military purposes. Whether it also protects the right to possess and use guns for nonmilitary purposes like hunting and personal self-defense is the question presented by this case. The text of the Amendment, its history, and our decision in *United States v. Miller*, 307 U. S. 174 (1939), provide a clear answer to that question.

The Second Amendment was adopted to protect the right of the people of each of the several States to maintain a well-regulated militia. It was a response to concerns raised during the ratification of the Constitution that the power of Congress to disarm the state militias and create a national standing army posed an intolerable threat to the sovereignty of the several States. Neither the text of the Amendment nor the arguments advanced by its proponents evidenced the slightest interest in limiting any legislature's authority to regulate private civilian uses of firearms. Specifically, there is no indication that the Framers of the Amendment intended to enshrine the common-law right of self-defense in the Constitution.

In 1934, Congress enacted the National Firearms Act, the first major federal firearms law. Upholding a conviction under that Act, this Court held that, "[i]n the absence of any evidence tending to show that possession or use of a 'shotgun having a barrel of less than eighteen inches in length' at this time has some reasonable relationship to the preservation or efficiency of a well regulated militia, we cannot say that the Second Amendment guarantees the right to keep and bear such

Supreme Court of the United States, 2008.

an instrument." *Miller,* 307 U.S., at 178. The view of the Amendment we took in *Miller*—that it protects the right to keep and bear arms for certain military purposes, but that it does not curtail the Legislature's power to regulate the nonmilitary use and ownership of weapons—is both the most natural reading of the Amendment's text and the interpretation most faithful to the history of its adoption.

Since our decision in *Miller,* hundreds of judges have relied on the view of the Amendment we endorsed there; we ourselves affirmed it in 1980. See *Lewis v. United States,* 445 U.S. 55 , n. 8 (1980). No new evidence has surfaced since 1980 supporting the view that the Amendment was intended to curtail the power of Congress to regulate civilian use or misuse of weapons. Indeed, a review of the drafting history of the Amendment demonstrates that its Framers *rejected* proposals that would have broadened its coverage to include such uses.

The opinion the Court announces today fails to identify any new evidence supporting the view that the Amendment was intended to limit the power of Congress to regulate civilian uses of weapons. Unable to point to any such evidence, the Court stakes its holding on a strained and unpersuasive reading of the Amendment's text; significantly different provisions in the 1689 English Bill of Rights, and in various 19th-century State Constitutions; postenactment commentary that was available to the Court when it decided *Miller;* and, ultimately, a feeble attempt to distinguish *Miller* that places more emphasis on the Court's decisional process than on the reasoning in the opinion itself.

Even if the textual and historical arguments on both sides of the issue were evenly balanced, respect for the well-settled views of all of our predecessors on this Court, and for the rule of law itself, see *Mitchell v. W. T. Grant Co.,* 416 U. S. 600, 636 (1974) (Stewart, J., dissenting), would prevent most jurists from endorsing such a dramatic upheaval in the law. As Justice Cardozo observed years ago, the "labor of judges would be increased almost to the breaking point if every past decision could be reopened in every case, and one could not lay one's own course of bricks on the secure foundation of the courses laid by others who had gone before him." The Nature of the Judicial Process 149 (1921).

In this dissent I shall first explain why our decision in *Miller* was faithful to the text of the Second Amendment and the purposes revealed in its drafting history. I shall then comment on the postratification history of the Amendment, which makes abundantly clear that the Amendment should not be interpreted as limiting the authority of Congress to regulate the use or possession of firearms for purely civilian purposes.

I

The text of the Second Amendment is brief. It provides: "A well regulated Militia, being necessary to the security of a free State, the right of the people to keep and bear Arms, shall not be infringed."

Three portions of that text merit special focus: the introductory language defining the Amendment's purpose, the class of persons encompassed within its reach, and the unitary nature of the right that it protects.

"A well regulated Militia, being necessary to the security of a free State"

The preamble to the Second Amendment makes three important points. It identifies the preservation of the militia as the Amendment's purpose; it explains that the militia is necessary to the security of a free State; and it recognizes that the militia must be "well regulated." In all three respects it is comparable to provisions in several State Declarations of Rights that were adopted roughly contemporaneously with the Declaration of Independence. Those state provisions highlight the importance members of the founding generation attached to the maintenance of state militias; they also underscore the profound fear shared by many in that era of the dangers posed by standing armies. While the need for state militias has not been a matter of significant public interest for almost two centuries, that fact should not obscure the contemporary concerns that animated the Framers. . . .

"The right of the people."

. . . The Court overlooks the significance of the way the Framers used the phrase "the people" in these constitutional provisions. In the First Amendment, no words define the class of individuals entitled to speak, to publish, or to worship; in that Amendment it is only the right peaceably to assemble, and to petition the Government for a redress of grievances, that is described as a right of "the people." These rights contemplate collective action. While the right peaceably to assemble protects the individual rights of those persons participating in the assembly, its concern is with action engaged in by members of a group, rather than any single individual. Likewise, although the act of petitioning the Government is a right that can be exercised by individuals, it is primarily collective in nature. For if they are to be effective, petitions must involve groups of individuals acting in concert.

Similarly, the words "the people" in the Second Amendment refer back to the object announced in the Amendment's preamble. They remind us that it is the collective action of individuals having a duty to serve in the militia that the text directly protects and, perhaps more importantly, that the ultimate purpose of the Amendment was to protect the States' share of the divided sovereignty created by the Constitution. . . .

"To keep and bear Arms"

Although the Court's discussion of these words treats them as two "phrases"—as if they read "to keep" and "to bear"—they describe a unitary right: to possess arms if needed for military purposes and to use them in conjunction with military activities.

As a threshold matter, it is worth pausing to note an oddity in the Court's interpretation of "to keep and bear arms." Unlike the Court of Appeals, the Court does not read that phrase to create a right to possess arms for "lawful, private purposes." *Parker v. District of Columbia*, 478 F. 3d 370, 382 (CADC 2007). Instead, the Court limits the Amendment's protection to the right "to possess and carry weapons in case of confrontation." *Ante*, at 19. No party or *amicus* urged this interpretation; the Court appears to have fashioned it out of whole cloth. But although this novel limitation lacks support in the text of the Amendment, the Amendment's text *does* justify a different limitation: the "right to keep and bear arms" protects only a right to possess and use firearms in connection with service in a state-organized militia.

The term "bear arms" is a familiar idiom; when used unadorned by any additional words, its meaning is "to serve as a soldier, do military service, fight." 1 *Oxford English Dictionary* 634 (2d ed. 1989). It is derived from the Latin *arma ferre*, which, translated literally, means "to bear *[ferre]* war equipment *[arma]*." Brief for Professors of Linguistics and English as *Amici Curiae* 19. One 18th-century dictionary defined "arms" as "weapons of offence, or armour of defence," 1 S. Johnson, *A Dictionary of the English Language* (1755), and another contemporaneous source explained that "[b]y *arms*, we understand those instruments of offence generally made use of in war; such as firearms, swords, & c. By *weapons*, we more particularly mean instruments of other kinds (exclusive of fire-arms), made use of as offensive, on special occasions." 1 J. Trusler, The Distinction Between Words Esteemed Synonymous in the English Language 37 (1794). Had the Framers wished to expand the meaning of the phrase "bear arms" to encompass civilian possession and use, they could have done so by the addition of phrases such as "for the defense of themselves," as was done in the Pennsylvania and Vermont Declarations of Rights. The *unmodified* use of "bear arms," by contrast, refers most naturally to a military purpose, as evidenced by its use in literally dozens of contemporary texts. The absence of any reference to civilian uses of weapons tailors the text of the Amendment to the purpose identified in its preamble. But when discussing these words, the Court simply ignores the preamble. . . .

This reading is confirmed by the fact that the clause protects only one right, rather than two. It does not describe a right "to keep arms" and a separate right "to bear arms." Rather, the single right that it does describe is both a duty and a right to have arms available and ready for military service, and to use them for military purposes when necessary. Different language surely would have been used to protect nonmilitary use and possession of weapons from regulation if such an intent had played any role in the drafting of the Amendment.

*　*　*

When each word in the text is given full effect, the Amendment is most naturally read to secure to the people a right to use and possess arms in conjunction with service in a well-regulated militia. So far as appears, no more than that was contemplated by its drafters or is encompassed within its terms. Even if the meaning of the text were genuinely susceptible to more than one interpretation, the burden would remain on those advocating a departure from the purpose identified in the preamble and from settled law to come forward with persuasive new arguments or evidence. The textual analysis offered by respondent and embraced by the Court falls far short of sustaining that heavy burden. And the Court's emphatic reliance on the claim "that the Second Amendment . . . codified a *pre-existing* right," *ante,* at 19, is of course beside the point because the right to keep and bear arms for service in a state militia was also a pre-existing right.

Indeed, not a word in the constitutional text even arguably supports the Court's overwrought and novel description of the Second Amendment as "elevat[ing] above all other interests" "the right of law-abiding, responsible citizens to use arms in defense of hearth and home." *Ante,* at 63.

II

The proper allocation of military power in the new Nation was an issue of central concern for the Framers. The compromises they ultimately reached, reflected in Article I's Militia Clauses and the Second Amendment, represent quintessential examples of the Framers' "splitting the atom of sovereignty." . . .

Madison, charged with the task of assembling the proposals for amendments sent by the ratifying States, was the principal draftsman of the Second Amendment. He had before him, or at the very least would have been aware of, all of these proposed formulations. In addition, Madison had been a member, some years earlier, of the committee tasked with drafting the Virginia Declaration of Rights. That committee considered a proposal by Thomas Jefferson that would have included within the Virginia Declaration the following language: "No freeman shall ever be debarred the use of arms [within his own lands or tenements]." 1 Papers of Thomas Jefferson 363 (J. Boyd ed. 1950). . . .

With all of these sources upon which to draw, it is strikingly significant that Madison's first draft omitted any mention of nonmilitary use or possession of weapons. Rather, his original draft repeated the essence of the two proposed amendments sent by Virginia, combining the substance of the two provisions succinctly into one, which read: "The right of the people to keep and bear arms shall not be infringed; a well armed, and well regulated militia being the best security of a free country; but no person religiously scrupulous of bearing arms, shall be compelled to render military service in person." Cogan 169.

Madison's decision to model the Second Amendment on the distinctly military Virginia proposal is therefore revealing, since it is clear that he considered and rejected formulations that would have unambiguously protected civilian uses of firearms. When Madison prepared his first draft, and when that draft was debated and modified, it is reasonable to assume that all participants in the drafting process were fully aware of the other formulations that would have protected civilian use and possession of weapons and that their choice to craft the Amendment as they did represented a rejection of those alternative formulations.

Madison's initial inclusion of an exemption for conscientious objectors sheds revelatory light on the purpose of the Amendment. It confirms an intent to describe a duty as well as a right, and it unequivocally identifies the military character of both. The objections voiced to the conscientious-objector clause only confirm the central meaning of the text. Although records of the debate in the Senate, which is where the conscientious-objector clause was removed, do not survive, the arguments raised in the House illuminate the perceived problems with the clause: Specifically, there was concern that Congress "can declare who are those religiously scrupulous, and prevent them from bearing arms." The ultimate removal of the clause, therefore, only serves to confirm the purpose of the Amendment—to protect against congressional disarmament, by whatever means, of the States' militias. . . .

The history of the adoption of the Amendment thus describes an overriding concern about the potential threat to state sovereignty that a federal standing army would pose, and a desire to protect the States' militias as the means by which to guard against that danger. But state militias could not effectively check the prospect of a federal standing army so long as Congress retained the power to disarm them, and so a guarantee against such disarmament was needed. As we explained in *Miller:* "With obvious purpose to assure the continuation and render possible the effectiveness of such forces the declaration and guarantee of the Second Amendment were made. It must be interpreted and applied with that end in view." 307 U.S., at 178. The evidence plainly refutes the claim that the Amendment was motivated by the Framers' fears that Congress might act to regulate any civilian uses of weapons. And even if the historical record were genuinely ambiguous, the burden would remain on the parties advocating a change in the law to introduce facts or arguments "newly ascertained," *Vasquez,* 474 U.S., at 266; the Court is unable to identify any such facts or arguments.

III

Although it gives short shrift to the drafting history of the Second Amendment, the Court dwells at length on four other sources: the 17th-century English Bill of Rights; Blackstone's Commentaries on the Laws of England; postenactment commentary on the Second Amendment; and post-Civil War legislative history. All of these sources shed only indirect light on the question before us, and in any event offer little support for the Court's conclusion. . . .

Thus, for most of our history, the invalidity of Second-Amendment-based objections to firearms regulations has been well settled and uncontroversial. Indeed, the Second Amendment was not even mentioned in either full House of Congress during the legislative proceedings that led to the passage of the 1934 Act. Yet enforcement of that law produced the judicial decision that confirmed the status of the Amendment as limited in reach to military usage. After reviewing many of the same sources that are discussed at greater length by the Court today, the *Miller* Court unanimously concluded that the Second Amendment did not apply to the possession of a firearm that did not have "some reasonable relationship to the preservation or efficiency of a well regulated militia." 307 U.S., at 178.

The key to that decision did not, as the Court belatedly suggests, *ante,* at 49–51, turn on the difference between muskets and sawed-off shotguns; it turned, rather, on the basic difference between the military and nonmilitary use and possession of guns. Indeed, if the Second Amendment were not limited in its coverage to military uses of weapons, why should the Court in *Miller* have suggested that some weapons but not others were eligible for

Second Amendment protection? If use for self-defense were the relevant stand-ard, why did the Court not inquire into the suitability of a particular weapon for self-defense purposes? . . .

The Court is simply wrong when it intones that *Miller* contained *"not a word"* about the Amendment's history. *Ante,* at 52. The Court plainly looked to history to construe the term "Militia," and, on the best reading of *Miller,* the entire guarantee of the Second Amendment. After noting the original Consti-tution's grant of power to Congres and to the States over the militia, the Court explained:

> "With obvious purpose to assure the continuation and render possi-ble the effectiveness of such forces the declaration and guarantee of the Second Amendment were made. It must be interpreted and applied with that end in view."
>
> "The Militia which the States were expected to maintain and train is set in contrast with Troops which they were forbidden to keep without the consent of Congress. The sentiment of the time strongly disfavored standing armies; the common view was that adequate defense of country and laws could be secured through the Militia—civilians primarily, soldiers on occasion."
>
> "The signification attributed to the term Militia appears from the debates in the Convention, the history and legislation of Colonies and States, and the writings of approved commentators." *Miller,* 307 U.S., at 178–179.

The majority cannot seriously believe that the *Miller* Court did not consider any relevant evidence; the majority simply does not approve of the conclusion the *Miller* Court reached on that evidence. Standing alone, that is insufficient reason to disregard a unanimous opinion of this Court, upon which substantial reliance has been placed by legislators and citizens for nearly 70 years.

V

The Court concludes its opinion by declaring that it is not the proper role of this Court to change the meaning of rights "enshrine[d]" in the Constitution. *Ante,* at 64. But the right the Court announces was not "enshrined" in the Second Amendment by the Framers; it is the product of today's law-changing decision. The majority's exegesis has utterly failed to establish that as a matter of text or history, "the right of law-abiding, responsible citizens to use arms in defense of hearth and home" is "elevate[d] above all other interests" by the Second Amendment. *Ante,* at 64.

Until today, it has been understood that legislatures may regulate the civilian use and misuse of firearms so long as they do not interfere with the preservation of a well-regulated militia. The Court's announcement of a new constitutional right to own and use firearms for private purposes upsets that settled understanding, but leaves for future cases the formidable task of defin-ing the scope of permissible regulations. Today judicial craftsmen have con-fidently asserted that a policy choice that denies a "law-abiding, responsible citize[n]" the right to keep and use weapons in the home for self-defense is "off the table." *Ante,* at 64. Given the presumption that most citizens are law abiding, and the reality that the need to defend oneself may suddenly arise in a host of locations outside the home, I fear that the District's policy choice may well be just the first of an unknown number of dominoes to be knocked off the table.

I do not know whether today's decision will increase the labor of federal judges to the "breaking point" envisioned by Justice Cardozo, but it will surely give rise to a far more active judicial role in making vitally important national policy decisions than was envisioned at any time in the 18th, 19th, or 20th centuries.

The Court properly disclaims any interest in evaluating the wisdom of the specific policy choice challenged in this case, but it fails to pay heed to a far more important policy choice—the choice made by the Framers themselves. The Court would have us believe that over 200 years ago, the Framers made a choice to limit the tools available to elected officials wishing to regulate civilian uses of weapons, and to authorize this Court to use the common-law process of case-by-case judicial lawmaking to define the contours of acceptable gun control policy. Absent compelling evidence that is nowhere to be found in the Court's opinion, I could not possibly conclude that the Framers made such a choice.

For these reasons, I respectfully dissent.

POSTSCRIPT

Does the Constitution Protect the Right to Possess a Firearm Unconnected With Service in a Militia?

This issue presents one of the more controversial debates considered in this volume. Many Americans love guns. In fact, recent studies have indicated that there are more than 200,000,000 guns owned privately in the United States. That is almost one gun for every 1.5 Americans. What explains this fascination with guns?

Some persons believe that America has a "gun culture." The image of the United States as a frontier nation with a history of gun usage for self-defense, the acquisition of food, and as a part of the cultural heritage of the wild west is a compelling one. America's love affair with guns has come at a substantial cost, however.

Professor Franklin E. Zimring asserts that while guns are used in only about 4 percent of all crimes, and only about 20 percent of all violent crimes, they are involved in almost 70 percent of all criminal homicides. States Zimring: "If the problem is lethal violence, the market share for firearms is 70 percent. Guns alone account for twice as many criminal deaths as all other means of killing combined (Zimring, 2004: 34)." In response to the question: Can gun control work? Professor Zimring states:

> The answer to this general question is a highly qualified 'yes, but.' If and to the extent that regulation reduces the use of loaded guns in crimes it will save American lives. But reducing the share of violence with guns is not an easy task to achieve in urban environments with large inventories of available handguns. Most gun control efforts do not make measurable impacts on gun use, particularly low budget symbolic legislation. If Congress when creating what it called a 'gun-free school zone' by legislation did reduce firearms violence, the result would be on par with that of the miracle of loaves and fishes. But New York City's effort to tightly enforce one of the nation's most restrictive handgun laws did apparently have a substantial payoff in reduced shootings that saved many lives.

Professor Lance K. Stell responds, however:

> Strict gun control, by effect if not intent, institutionalizes the natural predatory advantages of larger, stronger, violence-prone persons or gangs

of such persons, and yet its proponents incur no liability to offset resulting risks. . . . Prohibiting competent, adult, non-felons to possess 'equalizers' also has distributional wealth effects not only between criminals and the law-abiding, but also among the law-abiding. Strict gun control disproportionately increases the risks of violent victimization for less well-off law-abiding citizens who cannot take advantage of the privileged connections to officials that wealthier citizens take for granted.

As you can see, the gun control debate is not an easy one. Is it better to restrict the number of guns in the population, or to arm everyone in the interests of having a "fair fight?" These are difficult questions that seem unable to produce little compromise among even very rational proponents of different viewpoints.

Moreover, the gun control debate appears to be raging within the U.S. Supreme Court as well. The Court's five-to-four decision in *District of Columbia v. Heller* appears to reflect the cultural divide in the nation as a whole.

It seems important to recognize, however, that *Heller* does not appear to have opened the floodgates to unrestricted private firearms ownership, however. Justice Scalia stated: "[W]e do not read the Second Amendment to protect the right of citizens to carry arms for any sort of confrontation just as we do not read the First Amendment to protect the right of citizens to speak for any purpose." He continued:

[T]he right [to bear arms is] not a right to keep and carry any weapon whatsoever in any manner whatsoever and for whatever purpose . . . [N]othing in our opinion should be taken to cast doubt on longstanding prohibitions on the possession of firearms by felons and the mentally ill, or laws forbidding the carrying of firearms in sensitive places such as schools and government building, or laws imposing conditions and qualification on the commercial sale of firearms.

Therefore, it appears that *Heller* will not mean that Americans will witness persons sauntering down Main Street with high-powered assault rifles, such as AK-47s, sawed-off shotguns, or fully automatic weapons, anytime soon. Stated Justice Scalia in *Heller:* "[W]e therefore read *Miller* to say only that the Second Amendment does not protect those weapons not typically possessed by law-abiding citizens for lawful purposes, such as short-barreled shotguns." Moreover, it seems to indicate as well that governments will continue to be able to impose meaningful "time, place, and manner," restrictions on firearms possession. For example, laws prohibiting firearms possession in places such as bars and taverns, where alcohol is sold, are likely to continue to be upheld by U.S. courts. However, now that the Supreme Court has recognized an individual right to possess firearms under the Second Amendment, where do we go from here?

At the time of this writing, a case is pending in the U.S. Supreme Court that may have further implications for the development of a constitutional right to bear arms. In March 2010, the Supreme Court heard oral arguments in *McDonald v. City of Chicago,* Docket No. 08-1521 (2010), a case that presents a challenge to the city of Chicago's gun control law. Specifically, the plaintiff has challenged the following aspects of the City's law: (1) its prohibition on the registration of handguns; (2) its requirement for gun registration before they can be purchased by Chicago residents; (3) the City's requirement for the re-registration of guns on an annual basis, along with the payment of an annual fee; and (4) the city's declaration that if the registration lapses on any gun, it may never be registered again.

An important distinction between *District of Columbia v. Heller* and *McDonald v. City of Chicago* is that the former case involved a federal jurisdiction, the District of Columbia, whereas the latter one originated in the state of Illinois. The distinction is crucial because the *Heller* court's recognition of an individual right to bear arms under the Second Amendment has not yet been applied to the state and local governments, which, at least for now, are free to maintain restrictive firearms laws.

Moreover, in *McDonald,* the plaintiff has argued that the Second Amendment's Right to Bear Arms should be applied to the states, or incorporated, through the Due Process Clause of the Fourteenth Amendment. Essentially, the plaintiff is arguing that the right to bear arms is "implicit in the concept of ordered liberty," and is thus a "fundamental" right that the states may not deny. In any event it will be interesting to see what the U.S. Supreme Court will decide in *McDonald v. City of Chicago.*

The issues discussed in this section present a great many challenging questions. Additional resources to pursue further study in this area include: Kathleen M. Sullivan and Gerald Gunther, *Constitutional Law* (Foundation Press, 15th ed., 2004); Laurence H. Tribe, *American Constitutional Law* (Foundation Press, 2nd ed., 1988); Alpheus Thomas Mason and Donald Grier Stephenson, Jr., *American Constitutional Law* (Pearson Prentice Hall, 15th ed., 2009; 14th ed., 2005); Bernard Schwartz, *A History of the Supreme Court* (Oxford University Press, 1993); Kermit L. Hall, Paul Finkelman, and James Ely, Jr., *American Legal History: Cases and Materials* (Oxford University Press, 3rd ed., 2005); Kermit L. Hall, *The Oxford Companion to the Supreme Court of the United States* (Oxford University Press, 1992); Walter F. Murphy, James E. Fleming, Sotirios A. Barber, and Stephen Macedo, *American Constitutional Interpretation* (Foundation Press, 3rd ed., 2003); David M. O'Brien, *Constitutional Law and Politics: Struggles for Power and Government Accountability* (W.W. Norton, 3rd ed., 6th ed., 2005); Craig R. Ducat, *Constitutional Interpretation* (Wadsworth, 9th ed., 2009); John H. Garvey, T. Alexander Aleinikoff, and Daniel A. Farber, *Modern Constitutional Theory: A Reader* (Thompson West, 5th ed., 2004). See also: Clayton E. Cramer and Joseph Edward Olson, "What did 'Bear Arms' Mean in the Second Amendment?" *Georgetown Journal of Law & Public Policy,* vol. 6, p. 511 (2008); Clayton E. Cramer, Nicholas J. Johnson, and George A. Mocsary, "This Right is Not Allowed by Governments That Are Afraid of the People: The Public Meaning of the Second Amendment," *George Mason Law Review,* vol. 17, p.823 (2010); Dennis A. Henigan, "The Second Amendment and the Right to Bear Arms After D.C. *v.* Heller: The Heller Paradox," *UCLA Law Review,* vol. 56, p. 1171

(2009); Franklin E. Zimring, "Firearms, Violence, and the Potential Impact of Firearms Control," *Journal of Law Medicine & Ethics,* vol. 32, p. 1 (2004); Lance K. Stell, "The Production of Criminal Violence in America: Is Strict Gun Control the Solution?" *Journal of Law Medicine & Ethics,* vol. 32, p. 1 (2004); Mark Tushnet, *"Heller* and the New Originalism," *Ohio State Law Journal,* vol. 69, p. 609 (2008).

ISSUE 13

Does Confining Sex Offenders Indefinitely in Mental Hospitals After They Have Served Their Prison Sentences Violate the Constitution?

YES: Stephen Breyer, from Dissenting Opinion, *Kansas v. Hendricks,* 521 U.S. 346 (1997)

NO: Clarence Thomas, from Majority Opinion, *Kansas v. Hendricks,* 521 U.S. 346 (1997)

ISSUE SUMMARY

YES: Associate Justice Stephen Breyer asserts that if a state's law attempts to inflict additional punishment on an offender after he has served a prison sentence, it will violate the U.S. Constitution.

NO: Justice Clarence Thomas, in contrast, contends that post-imprisonment civil confinement laws do not violate the Constitution.

Imagine for a moment that you are a criminal who has been sentenced to a term of incarceration in a state prison and that you have almost completed your sentence. One month before you are to be released, you learn that the state alleges that you pose a continuing threat to society and will initiate a civil commitment proceeding designed to confine you indefinitely in a state mental hospital. How would you react? Would you attempt to challenge the state's authority to keep you confined beyond your original prison term? Which legal theories would you use?

One possible legal theory is that the potential commitment is a violation of the Fifth Amendment's double jeopardy clause. The Supreme Court has held that the double jeopardy protection extends not only to two trials for the same offense but also to two punishments for the same crime. Would it seem like a "slam dunk" argument that a mandatory confinement in a mental institution after someone has served their full prison sentence for the same crime violates the double jeopardy clause? Don't bet on it.

Kansas v. Hendricks, 521 U.S. 346 (1997) presented similar facts. Shortly before he was to be released from a Kansas prison to a halfway house from his sentence for taking indecent liberties with two adolescents, Hendricks was found by a jury to be a sexually violent predator. During the trial, he agreed with the state physician's diagnosis that he suffered from pedophilia. The trial judge ordered Hendricks, under the Kansas Sexually Violent Predator Act, committed to a mental institution for an indefinite period, although the continuing necessity of his confinement was subject to an annual review by the court. On appeal, the Kansas Supreme Court held that the commitment violated Hendricks' Fourteenth Amendment due process rights.

The Court held too that a confinement in a state mental institution after the completion of an offender's original prison sentence does not violate the Fifth Amendment's double jeopardy clause because that provision prohibits only a second *punishment* for the same offense. Stated Thomas: "The State may take measures to restrict the freedom of the dangerously mentally ill. This is a legitimate nonpunitive governmental objective and has been historically so regarded."

Are you persuaded by the Court's reasoning? Justice Thomas contends that Hendricks' indefinite incarceration, after he had completed his state prison sentence for the *same offenses,* did not violate the double jeopardy clause. As a number of commentators have pointed out, the line between punishment and indefinite commitment to a mental institution may be a difficult one to identify.

Justice Stephen Breyer's dissenting opinion disagrees with the majority's holding that Hendricks' later confinement in a state mental institution did not constitute punishment. Stated Justice Breyer: "The statutory provisions before us do amount to punishment primarily because, as I have said, the legislature did not tailor the statute to fit the nonpunitive civil aim of treatment, which it concedes exists in Hendricks' case."

It is sometimes said that "hard cases make bad law." This may be a case where we like the results of the decision, even though the legal reasoning supporting the decision is less than completely persuasive.

In Your Opinion . . .

- Is it fundamentally fair to apply to a convict a statute passed after they had committed their offense?
- Does society have a right to protect itself from dangerous sexual predators by keeping them confined?
- As a member of the U.S. Supreme Court, how would you decide this case?

YES

Stephen Breyer

Dissenting Opinion,
Kansas v. Hendricks

I agree with the majority that the Kansas Act's "definition of 'mental abnormality'" satisfies the "substantive" requirements of the Due Process Clause. Kansas, however, concedes that Hendricks' condition is treatable; yet the Act did not provide Hendricks (or others like him) with any treatment until after his release date from prison and only inadequate treatment thereafter. These, and certain other special features of the Act convince me that it was not simply an effort to commit Hendricks civilly, but rather an effort to inflict further punishment upon him. The *Ex Post Facto* Clause therefore prohibits the Act's application to Hendricks, who committed his crimes prior to its enactment.

I

I begin with the area of agreement. This Court has held that the civil commitment of a "mentally ill" and "dangerous" person does not automatically violate the Due Process Clause provided that the commitment takes place pursuant to proper procedures and evidentiary standards. The Kansas Supreme Court, however, held that the Due Process Clause forbids application of the Act to Hendricks for "substantive" reasons, *i.e.*, irrespective of the procedures or evidentiary standards used. The court reasoned that Kansas had not satisfied the "mentally ill" requirement of the Due Process Clause because Hendricks was not "mentally ill." Moreover, Kansas had not satisfied what the court believed was an additional "substantive due process" requirement, namely the provision of treatment. I shall consider each of these matters briefly.

A

In my view, the Due Process Clause permits Kansas to classify Hendricks as a mentally ill and dangerous person for civil commitment purposes. I agree with the majority that the Constitution gives States a degree of leeway in making this kind of determination. But, because I do not subscribe to all of its reasoning, I shall set forth three sets of circumstances that, taken together, convince me that Kansas has acted within the limits that the Due Process Clause substantively sets.

First, the psychiatric profession itself classifies the kind of problem from which Hendricks suffers as a serious mental disorder. But the very presence and

Supreme Court of the United States, 521 U.S. 346, 1997.

vigor of this debate is important. The Constitution permits a State to follow one reasonable professional view, while rejecting another. The psychiatric debate, therefore, helps to inform the law by setting the bounds of what is reasonable, but it cannot here decide just how States must write their laws within those bounds.

Second, Hendricks' abnormality does not consist simply of a long course of antisocial behavior, but rather it includes a specific, serious, and highly unusual inability to control his actions. (For example, Hendricks testified that, when he gets "stressed out," he cannot "control the urge" to molest children.) The law traditionally has considered this kind of abnormality akin to insanity for purposes of confinement. Indeed, the notion of an "irresistible impulse" often has helped to shape criminal law's insanity defense and to inform the related recommendations of legal experts as they seek to translate the insights of mental health professionals into workable legal rules.

Third, Hendricks' mental abnormality also makes him dangerous. Hendricks "has been convicted of . . . a sexually violent offense," and a jury found that he "suffers from a mental abnormality . . . which makes" him "likely to engage" in similar "acts of sexual violence" in the future. The evidence at trial favored the State. Dr. Befort, for example, explained why Hendricks was likely to commit further acts of sexual violence if released. And Hendricks' own testimony about what happens when he gets "stressed out" confirmed Dr. Befort's diagnosis.

Because (1) many mental health professionals consider pedophilia a serious mental disorder; and (2) Hendricks suffers from a classic case of irresistible impulse, namely he is so afflicted with pedophilia that he cannot "control the urge" to molest children; and (3) his pedophilia presents a serious danger to those children; I believe that Kansas can classify Hendricks as "mentally ill" and "dangerous" as this Court used those terms in *Foucha*.

The Kansas Supreme Court's contrary conclusion rested primarily upon that court's view that Hendricks would not qualify for civil commitment under Kansas' own state civil commitment statute. The issue before us, however, is one of constitutional interpretation. The Constitution does not require Kansas to write all of its civil commitment rules in a single statute or forbid it to write two separate statutes each covering somewhat different classes of committable individuals. Moreover, Hendricks apparently falls outside the scope of the Kansas general civil commitment statute because that statute permits confinement only of those who "lack capacity to make an informed decision concerning treatment." The statute does not tell us why it imposes this requirement. Capacity to make an informed decision about treatment is not always or obviously incompatible with severe mental illness. Neither Hendricks nor his *amici* point to a uniform body of professional opinion that says as much, and we have not found any. Consequently, the boundaries of the federal Constitution and those of Kansas' general civil commitment statute are not congruent.

B

The Kansas Supreme Court also held that the Due Process Clause requires a State to provide treatment to those whom it civilly confines (as "mentally ill" and "dangerous"). It found that Kansas did not provide Hendricks with significant treatment. And it concluded that Hendricks' confinement violated the Due Process Clause for this reason as well.

This case does not require us to consider whether the Due Process Clause *always* requires treatment—whether, for example, it would forbid civil confinement of an *untreatable* mentally ill, dangerous person. To the contrary, Kansas argues that pedophilia is an "abnormality" or "illness" that can be treated. Two groups of mental health professionals agree. Indeed, no one argues the contrary. Hence the legal question before us is whether the Clause forbids Hendricks' confinement unless Kansas provides him with treatment *that it concedes is available.*

Nor does anyone argue that Kansas somehow could have violated the Due Process Clause's *treatment* concerns had it provided Hendricks with the treatment that is potentially available (and I do not see how any such argument could succeed). Rather, the basic substantive due process treatment question is whether that Clause requires Kansas to provide treatment that it concedes is potentially available to a person whom it concedes is treatable. This same question is at the heart of my discussion of whether Hendricks' confinement violates the Constitution's *Ex Post Facto* Clause. For that reason, I shall not consider the substantive due process treatment question separately, but instead shall simply turn to the *Ex Post Facto* Clause discussion.

II

Kansas' 1994 Act violates the Federal Constitution's prohibition of "any . . . *ex post facto* Law" if it "inflicts" upon Hendricks "a greater punishment" than did the law "annexed to" his "crimes" when he "committed" those crimes in 1984. The majority agrees that the Clause "'forbids the application of *any new punitive measure* to a crime already consummated.'" But it finds the Act is not "punitive." With respect to that basic question, I disagree with the majority.

Certain resemblances between the Act's "civil commitment" and traditional criminal punishments are obvious. Like criminal imprisonment, the Act's civil commitment amounts to "secure" confinement, and "incarceration against one's will." In addition, a basic objective of the Act is incapacitation, which, as Blackstone said in describing an objective of criminal law, is to "deprive the party injuring of the power to do future mischief."

Moreover, the Act, like criminal punishment, imposes its confinement (or sanction) only upon an individual who has previously committed a criminal offense. And the Act imposes that confinement through the use of persons (county prosecutors), procedural guarantees (trial by jury, assistance of counsel, psychiatric evaluations), and standards ("beyond a reasonable doubt") traditionally associated with the criminal law.

These obvious resemblances by themselves, however, are not legally sufficient to transform what the Act calls "civil commitment" into a criminal punishment. Civil commitment of dangerous, mentally ill individuals by its very nature involves confinement and incapacitation. Yet "civil commitment," from a constitutional perspective, nonetheless remains civil. Nor does the fact that criminal behavior triggers the Act make the critical difference.

The Act's insistence upon a prior crime, by screening out those whose past behavior does not concretely demonstrate the existence of a mental problem or potential future danger, may serve an important noncriminal evidentiary purpose. Neither is the presence of criminal law-type procedures determinative. Those procedures can serve an important purpose that in this context one might consider noncriminal, namely helping to prevent judgmental mistakes that would wrongly deprive a person of important liberty.

If these obvious similarities cannot by themselves prove that Kansas' "civil commitment" statute is criminal, neither can the word "civil" written into the statute, by itself prove the contrary. This Court has said that only the "clearest proof" could establish that a law the legislature called "civil," was, in reality a "punitive" measure. But the Court has also reiterated that a "civil label is not always dispositive"; it has said that in close cases the label is "'not of paramount importance'"; and it has looked behind a "civil" label fairly often.

In this circumstance, with important features of the Act pointing in opposite directions, I would place particular importance upon those features that would likely distinguish between a basically punitive and a basically nonpunitive purpose. And I note that the Court, in an earlier civil commitment case, looked primarily to the law's concern for treatment as an important distinguishing feature. I do not believe that *Allen* means that a particular law's lack of concern for treatment, by itself, is enough to make an incapacitative law punitive. But, for reasons I will point out, when a State believes that treatment does exist, and then couples that admission with a legislatively required delay of such treatment until a person is at the end of his jail term (so that further incapacitation is therefore necessary), such a legislative scheme begins to look punitive.

In *Allen*, the Court considered whether, for Fifth Amendment purposes, proceedings under an Illinois statute were civil or "criminal." The Illinois statute, rather like the Kansas statute here, authorized the confinement of persons who were sexually dangerous, who had committed at least one prior sexual assault, and who suffered from a "mental disorder." The *Allen* Court, looking behind the statute's "civil commitment" label, found the statute civil—in important part because the State had "provided for the treatment of those it commits." (also referring to facts that the State had "disavowed any interest in punishment" and that it had "established a system under which committed persons may be released after the briefest time in confinement").

In reaching this conclusion, the Court noted that the State Supreme Court had found the proceedings "essentially civil" because the statute's aim was to provide "treatment, not punishment." It observed that the State had "a statutory obligation to provide 'care and treatment . . . designed to effect recovery'" in a "facility set aside to provide psychiatric care." And it referred to the State's purpose as one of "*treating* rather than punishing sexually dangerous persons."

The *Allen* Court's focus upon treatment, as a kind of touchstone helping to distinguish civil from punitive purposes, is not surprising, for one would expect a nonpunitive statutory scheme to confine, not simply in order to protect, but also in order to cure. That is to say, one would expect a nonpunitively motivated legislature that confines *because of* a dangerous mental abnormality to seek to help the individual himself overcome that abnormality (at least insofar as professional treatment for the abnormality exists and is potentially helpful, as Kansas, supported by some groups of mental health professionals, argues is the case here). Conversely, a statutory scheme that provides confinement that does not reasonably fit a practically available, medically oriented treatment objective, more likely reflects a primarily punitive legislative purpose.

Several important treatment-related factors—factors of a kind that led the five-member *Allen* majority to conclude that the Illinois' legislature's purpose was primarily civil, not punitive—in this case suggest precisely the opposite. First, the State Supreme Court here, unlike the state court in *Allen,* has held that treatment is not a significant objective of the Act. The Kansas court wrote that the Act's purpose is "segregation of sexually violent offenders," with "treatment" a matter that was "incidental at best." By way of contrast, in *Allen* the Illinois court had written that "treatment, not punishment" was "the aim of the statute."

We have generally given considerable weight to the findings of state and lower federal courts regarding the intent or purpose underlying state officials' actions, although the level of deference given to such findings varies with the circumstances, and is not always as conclusive as a state court's construction of one of its statutes. For example, *Allen's* dissenters, as well as its majority, considered the state court's characterization of the state law's purpose an important factor in determining the constitutionality of that statute.

The record provides support for the Kansas court's conclusion. The court found that, as of the time of Hendricks' commitment, the State had not funded treatment, it had not entered into treatment contracts, and it had little, if any, qualified treatment staff. Indeed, were we to follow the majority's invitation to look beyond the record in this case, an invitation with which we disagree, it would reveal that Hendricks, according to the commitment program's own director, was receiving "essentially no treatment."

It is therefore not surprising that some of the Act's official supporters had seen in it an opportunity permanently to confine dangerous sex offenders. Others thought that effective treatment did not exist—a view, by the way, that the State of Kansas, supported by groups of informed mental health professionals, here strongly denies.

The Kansas court acknowledged the existence of "provisions of the Act for treatment" (although it called them "somewhat disingenuous"). Nor did the court deny that Kansas could later increase the amount of treatment it provided. But the Kansas Supreme Court could, and did, use the Act's language, history, and initial implementation to help it characterize the Act's primary purposes.

Second, the Kansas statute insofar as it applies to previously convicted offenders, such as Hendricks, commits, confines, and treats those offenders *after* they have served virtually their entire criminal sentence. That timerelated circumstance seems deliberate. The Act explicitly defers diagnosis, evaluation, and commitment proceedings until a few weeks prior to the "anticipated release" of a previously convicted offender from prison. But why, one might ask, does the Act not commit and require treatment of sex offenders sooner, say soon after they begin to serve their sentences?

An Act that simply seeks confinement, of course, would not need to begin civil commitment proceedings sooner. Such an Act would have to begin proceedings only when an offender's prison term ends, threatening his release from the confinement that imprisonment assures. But it is difficult to see why rational legislators who seek treatment would write the Act in this way—providing treatment years after the criminal act that indicated its necessity. And it is particularly difficult to see why legislators who specifically wrote into the statute a finding that "prognosis for rehabilitating . . . in a prison setting is poor" would leave an offender in that setting for months or years before beginning treatment. This is to say, the timing provisions of the statute confirm the Kansas Supreme Court's view that treatment was not a particularly important legislative objective.

I recognize one possible counter-argument. A State, wanting both to punish Hendricks (say, for deterrence purposes) and also to treat him, might argue that it should be permitted to postpone treatment until after punishment in order to make certain that the punishment in fact occurs. But any such reasoning is out of place here. Much of the treatment that Kansas offered here (called "ward milieu" and "group therapy") can be given at the same time as, and in the same place where, Hendricks serves his punishment. The evidence adduced at the state habeas proceeding, were we to assume it properly before the Court, see *infra*, at 20–21, supports this conclusion as well. Hence, assuming arguendo that it would be otherwise permissible, Kansas need not postpone treatment in order to make certain that sex offenders serve their full terms of imprisonment, *i.e.*, to make certain that they receive the entire punishment that Kansas criminal law provides. To the contrary, the statement in the Act itself, that the Act aims to respond to special "long term" "treatment needs," suggests that treatment should begin during imprisonment. It also suggests that, were those long-term treatment needs (rather than further punishment) Kansas' primary aim, the State would require that treatment begin soon after conviction, not 10 or more years later.

Third, the statute, at least as of the time Kansas applied it to Hendricks, did not require the committing authority to consider the possibility of using less restrictive alternatives, such as postrelease supervision, halfway houses, or other methods that *amici* supporting Kansas here have mentioned. The laws of many other States require such consideration. This Court has said that a failure to consider, or to use, "alternative and less harsh methods" to achieve a nonpunitive objective can help to show that legislature's "purpose . . . was to punish." And one can draw a similar conclusion here. Legislation that seeks to help the individual offender as well as to protect the public would avoid significantly greater restriction of an individual's liberty than public safety requires. Legislation that seeks almost exclusively to incapacitate the individual through confinement, however, would not necessarily concern itself with potentially less restrictive forms of incapacitation. I would reemphasize that this is not a case in which the State claims there is no treatment potentially available. Rather, Kansas, and supporting *amici*, argue that pedophilia is treatable.

Fourth, the laws of other States confirm, through comparison, that Kansas' "civil commitment" objectives do not require the statutory features that indicate a punitive purpose. I have found 17 States with laws that seek to protect the public from mentally abnormal, sexually dangerous individuals through civil commitment or other mandatory treatment programs. Ten of those statutes, unlike the Kansas statute, begin treatment of an offender soon after he has been apprehended and charged with a serious sex offense. Only seven, like Kansas, delay "civil" commitment (and treatment) until the offender has served his criminal sentence (and this figure includes the Acts of Minnesota and New Jersey, both of which generally do not delay treatment). Of these seven, however, six (unlike Kansas) require consideration of less restrictive alternatives. Only one State other than Kansas, namely Iowa, both delays civil commitment (and consequent treatment) and does not explicitly consider less restrictive alternatives. But the law of that State applies prospectively only, thereby avoiding *ex post facto* problems. Thus the practical experience of other States, as revealed by their statutes, confirms what the Kansas Supreme Court's finding, the timing of the civil commitment proceeding, and the failure to consider less restrictive alternatives, themselves suggest, namely, that for *Ex Post Facto* Clause purposes, the purpose of the Kansas Act (as applied to previously convicted offenders) has a punitive, rather than a purely civil, purpose.

Kansas points to several cases as support for a contrary conclusion. It points to *Allen*—which is, as we have seen, a case in which the Court concluded that Illinois' "civil commitment" proceedings were not criminal. I have explained in detail, however, how the statute here differs from that in *Allen,* and why *Allen's* reasoning leads to a different conclusion in this litigation.

Kansas also points to *Addington v. Texas,* where the Court held that the Constitution does not require application of criminal law's "beyond a reasonable doubt" standard in a civil commitment proceeding. Nothing I say here would change the reach or holding of *Addington* in any way. That is, a State is free to commit those who are dangerous and mentally ill in order to treat them. Nor does my decision preclude a State from deciding that a certain subset of people are mentally ill, dangerous, and untreatable, and that confinement of this subset is therefore necessary (again, assuming that all the procedural safeguards of *Addington* are in place). But when a State decides offenders can be treated and confines an offender to provide that treatment, but then refuses to provide it, the refusal to treat while a person is fully incapacitated begins to look punitive.

The majority suggests that this is the very case I say it is not, namely a case of a mentally ill person who is *untreatable.* And it quotes a long excerpt from the Kansas Supreme Court's opinion in support. That court, however, did not find that Hendricks was untreat*able;* it found that he was untreat*ed*—quite a different matter. Had the Kansas Supreme Court thought that Hendricks, or others like him, are untreatable, it could not have written the words that follow that excerpt, adopting by reference the words of another court opinion:

> "The statute forecloses the possibility that offenders will be evaluated and treated until after they have been punished. . . . Setting aside the question of whether a prison term exacerbates or minimizes the mental

condition of a sex offender, it plainly delays the treatment that must constitutionally accompany commitment pursuant to the Statute. The failure of the Statute to provide for examination or treatment prior to the completion of the punishment phase strongly suggests that treatment is of secondary, rather than primary, concern."

This quotation, and the rest of the opinion, make clear that the court is finding it objectionable that the Statute, among other things, has not provided adequate treatment to one who, all parties here concede, *can* be treated. . . .

. . . We have found no evidence in the record to support the conclusion that Kansas was in fact providing the treatment that all parties agree that it could provide. Thus, even had the Kansas Supreme Court considered the majority's new evidence—which it did not—it is not likely to have changed its characterization of the Act's treatment provisions as "somewhat disingenuous."

Regardless, the Kansas Supreme Court did so to characterize the Act's treatment provisions and did find that treatment was "at best" an "incidental" objective. Thus, the circumstances here are different from *Allen,* where the Illinois Supreme Court explicitly found that the statute's aim was to provide treatment, not punishment. There is no evidence in the record that contradicts the finding of the Kansas court. Thus, *Allen's* approach—its reliance on the State court—if followed here would mean the Act as applied to *Leroy Hendricks* (as opposed to others who may have received treatment or who were sentenced after the effective date of the Act), is punitive.

Finally, Kansas points to *United States v. Salerno,* a case in which this Court held preventive detention of a dangerous accused person pending trial constitutionally permissible. *Salerno,* however, involved the brief detention of that person, after a finding of "probable cause" that he had committed a crime that would justify further imprisonment, and only pending a speedy judicial determination of guilt or innocence. This Court, in *Foucha,* emphasized the fact that the confinement at issue in *Salerno* was "strictly limited in duration." 504 U.S. at 82. It described that "pretrial detention of arrestees" as "one of those carefully limited exceptions permitted by the Due Process Clause." And it held that *Salerno* did not authorize the indefinite detention, on grounds of dangerousness, of "insanity acquittees who are not mentally ill but who do not prove they would not be dangerous to others." Whatever *Salerno's* "due process" implications may be, it does not focus upon, nor control, the question at issue here, the question of "punishment" for purposes of the *Ex Post Facto* Clause.

One other case warrants mention. In *Kennedy v. Mendoza-Martinez,* this Court listed seven factors that helped it determine whether a particular statute was primarily punitive for purposes of applying the Fifth and Sixth Amendments. Those factors include whether a sanction involves an affirmative restraint, how history has regarded it, whether it applies to behavior already a crime, the need for a finding of scienter, its relationship to a traditional aim of punishment, the presence of a nonpunitive alternative purpose, and whether it is excessive in relation to that purpose. This Court has said that these seven factors are "neither exhaustive nor dispositive," but nonetheless "helpful."

308

ISSUE 13 / Does Confining Sex Offenders Indefinitely in Mental . . . ?

Ward, 448 U.S. at 249. Paraphrasing them here, I believe the Act before us involves an affirmative restraint historically regarded as punishment; imposed upon behavior already a crime after a finding of scienter; which restraint, namely confinement, serves a traditional aim of punishment, does not primarily serve an alternative purpose (such as treatment) and is excessive in relation to any alternative purpose assigned.

This is to say that each of the factors the Court mentioned in *Martinez-Mendoza* on balance argues here in favor of a constitutional characterization as "punishment." It is not to say that I have found "a single 'formula' for identifying those legislative changes that have a sufficient effect on substantive crimes or punishments to fall within the constitutional prohibition." We have not previously done so, and I do not do so here. Rather, I have pointed to those features of the Act itself, in the context of this litigation, that lead me to conclude, in light of our precedent, that the added confinement the Act imposes upon Hendricks is basically punitive. This analysis, rooted in the facts surrounding Kansas' failure to treat Hendricks, cannot answer the question whether the Kansas Act, as it now stands, and in light of its current implementation, is punitive towards people other than he. And I do not attempt to do so here.

III

To find that the confinement the Act imposes upon Hendricks is "punishment" is to find a violation of the *Ex Post Facto* Clause. Kansas does not deny that the 1994 Act changed the legal consequences that attached to Hendricks earlier crimes, and in a way that significantly "disadvantaged the offender."

To find a violation of that Clause here, however, is not to hold that the Clause prevents Kansas, or other States, from enacting dangerous sexual offender statutes. A statute that operates prospectively, for example, does not offend the *Ex Post Facto* Clause. Neither does it offend the *Ex Post Facto* Clause for a State to sentence offenders to the fully authorized sentence, to seek consecutive, rather than concurrent, sentences, or to invoke recidivism statutes to lengthen imprisonment. Moreover, a statute that operates retroactively, like Kansas' statute, nonetheless does not offend the Clause *if the confinement that it imposes is not punishment*—if, that is to say, the legislature does not simply add a later criminal punishment to an earlier one.

The statutory provisions before us do amount to punishment primarily because, as I have said, the legislature did not tailor the statute to fit the nonpunitive civil aim of treatment, which it concedes exists in Hendricks' case. The Clause in these circumstances does not stand as an obstacle to achieving important protections for the public's safety; rather it provides an assurance that, where so significant a restriction of an individual's basic freedoms is at issue, a State cannot cut corners. Rather, the legislature must hew to the Constitution's liberty-protecting line.

Majority Opinion, *Kansas v. Hendricks*

J ustice Thomas delivered the opinion of the Court.

In 1994, Kansas enacted the Sexually Violent Predator Act, which establishes procedures for the civil commitment of persons who, due to a "mental abnormality" or a "personality disorder," are likely to engage in "predatory acts of sexual violence." The State invoked the Act for the first time to commit Leroy Hendricks, an inmate who had a long history of sexually molesting children, and who was scheduled for release from prison shortly after the Act became law. Hendricks challenged his commitment on, *inter alia*, "substantive" due process, double jeopardy, and *ex post facto* grounds. The Kansas Supreme Court invalidated the Act, holding that its precommitment condition of a "mental abnormality" did not satisfy what the court perceived to be the "substantive" due process requirement that involuntary civil commitment must be predicated on a finding of "mental illness." The State of Kansas petitioned for certiorari.

I

A

The Kansas Legislature enacted the Sexually Violent Predator Act (Act) in 1994 to grapple with the problem of managing repeat sexual offenders. Although Kansas already had a statute addressing the involuntary commitment of those defined as "mentally ill," the legislature determined that existing civil commitment procedures were inadequate to confront the risks presented by "sexually violent predators." In the Act's preamble, the legislature explained:

> "[A] small but extremely dangerous group of sexually violent predators exist who do not have a mental disease or defect that renders them appropriate for involuntary treatment pursuant to the [general involuntary civil commitment statute]. . . . In contrast to persons appropriate for civil commitment under the [general involuntary civil commitment statute], sexually violent predators generally have anti-social personality features which are unamenable to existing mental illness treatment modalities and those features render them likely to engage in sexually violent behavior. The legislature further finds that sexually violent predators' likelihood of engaging in repeat acts of predatory sexual violence is high. The existing involuntary commitment procedure . . . is

Supreme Court of the United States, 521 U.S. 346, 1997.

inadequate to address the risk these sexually violent predators pose to society. The legislature further finds that the prognosis for rehabilitating sexually violent predators in a prison setting is poor, the treatment needs of this population are very long term and the treatment modalities for this population are very different than the traditional treatment modalities for people appropriate for commitment under the [general involuntary civil commitment statute]."

As a result, the Legislature found it necessary to establish "a civil commitment procedure for the long-term care and treatment of the sexually violent predator." The Act defined a "sexually violent predator" as:

"any person who has been convicted of or charged with a sexually violent offense and who suffers from a mental abnormality or personality disorder which makes the person likely to engage in the predatory acts of sexual violence."

A "mental abnormality" was defined, in turn, as a "congenital or acquired condition affecting the emotional or volitional capacity which predisposes the person to commit sexually violent offenses in a degree constituting such person a menace to the health and safety of others."

As originally structured, the Act's civil commitment procedures pertained to: (1) a presently confined person who, like Hendricks, "has been convicted of a sexually violent offense" and is scheduled for release; (2) a person who has been "charged with a sexually violent offense" but has been found incompetent to stand trial; (3) a person who has been found "not guilty by reason of insanity of a sexually violent offense"; and (4) a person found "not guilty" of a sexually violent offense because of a mental disease or defect.

The initial version of the Act, as applied to a currently confined person such as Hendricks, was designed to initiate a specific series of procedures. The custodial agency was required to notify the local prosecutor 60 days before the anticipated release of a person who might have met the Act's criteria. The prosecutor was then obligated, within 45 days, to decide whether to file a petition in state court seeking the person's involuntary commitment. If such a petition were filed, the court was to determine whether "probable cause" existed to support a finding that the person was a "sexually violent predator" and thus eligible for civil commitment. Upon such a determination, transfer of the individual to a secure facility for professional evaluation would occur. After that evaluation, a trial would be held to determine beyond a reasonable doubt whether the individual was a sexually violent predator. If that determination were made, the person would then be transferred to the custody of the Secretary of Social and Rehabilitation Services (Secretary) for "control, care and treatment until such time as the person's mental abnormality or personality disorder has so changed that the person is safe to be at large."

In addition to placing the burden of proof upon the State, the Act afforded the individual a number of other procedural safeguards. In the case of an indigent person, the State was required to provide, at public expense, the assistance of counsel and an examination by mental health care professionals. The individual also received the right to present and cross-examine witnesses, and the opportunity to review documentary evidence presented by the State.

Once an individual was confined, the Act required that "the involuntary detention or commitment . . . shall conform to constitutional requirements for care and treatment." Confined persons were afforded three different avenues of review: First, the committing court was obligated to conduct an annual review to determine whether continued detention was warranted. Second, the Secretary was permitted, at any time, to decide that the confined individual's condition had so changed that release was appropriate, and could then authorize the person to petition for release. Finally, even without the Secretary's permission, the confined person could at any time file a release petition. If the court found that the State could no longer satisfy its burden under the initial commitment standard, the individual would be freed from confinement.

B

In 1984, Hendricks was convicted of taking "indecent liberties" with two 13-year-old boys. After serving nearly 10 years of his sentence, he was slated for release to a halfway house. Shortly before his scheduled release, however, the State filed a petition in state court seeking Hendricks' civil confinement as a sexually violent predator. On August 19, 1994, Hendricks appeared before the court with counsel and moved to dismiss the petition on the grounds that the Act violated various federal constitutional provisions. Although the court reserved ruling on the Act's constitutionality, it concluded that there was probable cause to support a finding that Hendricks was a sexually violent predator, and therefore ordered that he be evaluated at the Larned State Security Hospital.

Hendricks subsequently requested a jury trial to determine whether he qualified as a sexually violent predator. During that trial, Hendricks' own testimony revealed a chilling history of repeated child sexual molestation and abuse, beginning in 1955 when he exposed his genitals to two young girls. At that time, he pleaded guilty to indecent exposure. Then, in 1957, he was convicted of lewdness involving a young girl and received a brief jail sentence. In 1960, he molested two young boys while he worked for a carnival. After serving two years in prison for that offense, he was paroled, only to be rearrested for molesting a 7-year-old girl. Attempts were made to treat him for his sexual deviance, and in 1965 he was considered "safe to be at large," and was discharged from a state psychiatric hospital.

Shortly thereafter, however, Hendricks sexually assaulted another young boy and girl—he performed oral sex on the 8-year-old girl and fondled the 11-year-old boy. He was again imprisoned in 1967, but refused to participate in a sex offender treatment program, and thus remained incarcerated until his parole in 1972. Diagnosed as a pedophile, Hendricks entered into, but then abandoned, a treatment program. He testified that despite having received professional help for his pedophilia, he continued to harbor sexual desires for children. Indeed, soon after his 1972 parole, Hendricks began to abuse his own stepdaughter and stepson. He forced the children to engage in sexual activity with him over a period of approximately four years. Then, as noted above, Hendricks was convicted of "taking indecent liberties" with two adolescent boys after he attempted to fondle them. As a result of that conviction, he was once again imprisoned, and was serving that sentence when he reached his conditional release date in September 1994.

Hendricks admitted that he had repeatedly abused children whenever he was not confined. He explained that when he "gets stressed out," he "can't control the urge" to molest children. Although Hendricks recognized that his behavior harms children, and he hoped he would not sexually molest children again, he stated that the only sure way he could keep from sexually abusing children in the future was "to die." Hendricks readily agreed with the state physician's diagnosis that he suffers from pedophilia and that he is not cured of the condition; indeed, he told the physician that "treatment is bull—." The jury unanimously found beyond a reasonable doubt that Hendricks was a sexually violent predator. The trial court subsequently determined, as a matter of state law, that pedophilia qualifies as a "mental abnormality" as defined by the Act, and thus ordered Hendricks committed to the Secretary's custody.

Hendricks appealed, claiming, among other things, that application of the Act to him violated the Federal Constitution's Due Process, Double Jeopardy, and *Ex Post Facto* Clauses. The Kansas Supreme Court accepted Hendricks' due process claim. The court declared that in order to commit a person involuntarily in a civil proceeding, a State is required by "substantive" due process to prove by clear and convincing evidence that the person is both (1) mentally ill, and (2) a danger to himself or to others. The court then determined that the Act's definition of "mental abnormality" did not satisfy what it perceived to be this Court's "mental illness" requirement in the civil commitment context. As a result, the court held that "the Act violates Hendricks' substantive due process rights."

The majority did not address Hendricks' *ex post facto* or double jeopardy claims. The dissent, however, considered each of Hendricks' constitutional arguments and rejected them.

II

A

Kansas argues that the Act's definition of "mental abnormality" satisfies "substantive" due process requirements. We agree. Although freedom from physical restraint "has always been at the core of the liberty protected by the Due Process Clause from arbitrary governmental action," that liberty interest is not absolute. The Court has recognized that an individual's constitutionally protected interest in avoiding physical restraint may be overridden even in the civil context:

> "The liberty secured by the Constitution of the United States to every person within its jurisdiction does not import an absolute right in each person to be, at all times and in all circumstances, wholly free from restraint. There are manifold restraints to which every person is

necessarily subject for the common good. On any other basis organized society could not exist with safety to its members."

Accordingly, States have in certain narrow circumstances provided for the forcible civil detainment of people who are unable to control their behavior and who thereby pose a danger to the public health and safety. We have consistently upheld such involuntary commitment statutes provided the confinement takes place pursuant to proper procedures and evidentiary standards. It thus cannot be said that the involuntary civil confinement of a limited subclass of dangerous persons is contrary to our understanding of ordered liberty.

The challenged Act unambiguously requires a finding of dangerousness either to one's self or to others as a prerequisite to involuntary confinement. Commitment proceedings can be initiated only when a person "has been convicted of or charged with a sexually violent offense," and "suffers from a mental abnormality or personality disorder which makes the person likely to engage in the predatory acts of sexual violence." The statute thus requires proof of more than a mere predisposition to violence; rather, it requires evidence of past sexually violent behavior and a present mental condition that creates a likelihood of such conduct in the future if the person is not incapacitated. As we have recognized, "previous instances of violent behavior are an important indicator of future violent tendencies." A finding of dangerousness, standing alone, is ordinarily not a sufficient ground upon which to justify indefinite involuntary commitment. We have sustained civil commitment statutes when they have coupled proof of dangerousness with the proof of some additional factor, such as a "mental illness" or "mental abnormality." These added statutory requirements serve to limit involuntary civil confinement to those who suffer from a volitional impairment rendering them dangerous beyond their control. The Kansas Act is plainly of a kind with these other civil commitment statutes: It requires a finding of future dangerousness, and then links that finding to the existence of a "mental abnormality" or "personality disorder" that makes it difficult, if not impossible, for the person to control his dangerous behavior. The precommitment requirement of a "mental abnormality" or "personality disorder" is consistent with the requirements of these other statutes that we have upheld in that it narrows the class of persons eligible for confinement to those who are unable to control their dangerousness.

Hendricks nonetheless argues that our earlier cases dictate a finding of "mental illness" as a prerequisite for civil commitment. He then asserts that a "mental abnormality" is *not* equivalent to a "mental illness" because it is a term coined by the Kansas Legislature, rather than by the psychiatric community. Contrary to Hendricks' assertion, the term "mental illness" is devoid of any talismanic significance. Not only do "psychiatrists disagree widely and frequently on what constitutes mental illness," but the Court itself has used a variety of expressions to describe the mental condition of those properly subject to civil confinement.

To the extent that the civil commitment statutes we have considered set forth criteria relating to an individual's inability to control his dangerousness, the Kansas Act sets forth comparable criteria and Hendricks' condition doubtless satisfies those criteria. The mental health professionals who evaluated Hendricks diagnosed him as suffering from pedophilia, a condition the psychiatric profession itself classifies as a serious mental disorder. Hendricks even conceded that, when he becomes "stressed out," he cannot "control the urge" to molest children. This admitted lack of volitional control, coupled with a prediction of future dangerousness, adequately distinguishes Hendricks from other dangerous persons who are perhaps more properly dealt with exclusively through criminal proceedings. Hendricks' diagnosis as a pedophile, which qualifies as a "mental abnormality" under the Act, thus plainly suffices for due process purposes.

B

We granted Hendricks' cross-petition to determine whether the Act violates the Constitution's double jeopardy prohibition or its ban on *ex post facto* lawmaking. The thrust of Hendricks' argument is that the Act establishes criminal proceedings; hence confinement under it necessarily constitutes punishment. He contends that where, as here, newly enacted "punishment" is predicated upon past conduct for which he has already been convicted and forced to serve a prison sentence, the Constitution's Double Jeopardy and *Ex Post Facto* Clauses are violated. We are unpersuaded by Hendricks' argument that Kansas has established criminal proceedings.

The categorization of a particular proceeding as civil or criminal "is first of all a question of statutory construction." We must initially ascertain whether the legislature meant the statute to establish "civil" proceedings. If so, we ordinarily defer to the legislature's stated intent. Here, Kansas' objective to create a civil proceeding is evidenced by its placement of the Sexually Violent Predator Act within the Kansas probate code, instead of the criminal code, as well as its description of the Act as creating a *"civil commitment procedure."* Nothing on the face of the statute suggests that the legislature sought to create anything other than a civil commitment scheme designed to protect the public from harm.

Although we recognize that a "civil label is not always dispositive," we will reject the legislature's manifest intent only where a party challenging the statute provides "the clearest proof" that "the statutory scheme [is] so punitive either in purpose or effect as to negate [the State's] intention" to deem it "civil." In those limited circumstances, we will consider the statute to have established criminal proceedings for constitutional purposes. Hendricks, however, has failed to satisfy this heavy burden.

As a threshold matter, commitment under the Act does not implicate either of the two primary objectives of criminal punishment: retribution or deterrence. The Act's purpose is not retributive because it does not affix culpability for prior criminal conduct. Instead, such conduct is used solely for evidentiary purposes, either to demonstrate that a "mental abnormality" exists or to support a finding of future dangerousness. We have previously concluded that an Illinois statute was nonpunitive even though it was triggered by the commission of a sexual assault, explaining that evidence of the prior criminal conduct was "received not to punish past misdeeds, but primarily to show the accused's mental condition and to predict future behavior." In addition, the Kansas Act does not make a criminal conviction a prerequisite for commitment—persons absolved of criminal responsibility may nonetheless be subject to confinement under the Act. An absence of the necessary criminal responsibility suggests that the State is not seeking retribution for a past misdeed. Thus, the fact that the Act may be "tied to criminal activity" is "insufficient to render the statute punitive."

Moreover, unlike a criminal statute, no finding of scienter is required to commit an individual who is found to be a sexually violent predator; instead, the commitment determination is made based on a "mental abnormality" or "personality disorder" rather than on one's criminal intent. The existence of a scienter requirement is customarily an important element in distinguishing criminal from civil statutes. The absence of such a requirement here is evidence that confinement under the statute is not intended to be retributive.

Nor can it be said that the legislature intended the Act to function as a deterrent. Those persons committed under the Act are, by definition, suffering from a "mental abnormality" or a "personality disorder" that prevents them from exercising adequate control over their behavior. Such persons are therefore unlikely to be deterred by the threat of confinement. And the conditions surrounding that confinement do not suggest a punitive purpose on the State's part. The State has represented that an individual confined under the Act is not subject to the more restrictive conditions placed on state prisoners, but instead experiences essentially the same conditions as any involuntarily committed patient in the state mental institution. Because none of the parties argues that people institutionalized under the Kansas general civil commitment statute are subject to punitive conditions, even though they may be involuntarily confined, it is difficult to conclude that persons confined under this Act are being "punished."

Although the civil commitment scheme at issue here does involve an affirmative restraint, "the mere fact that a person is detained does not inexorably lead to the conclusion that the government has imposed punishment." The State may take measures to restrict the freedom of the dangerously mentally ill. This is a legitimate nonpunitive governmental objective and has been historically so regarded. The Court has, in fact, cited the confinement of "mentally unstable individuals who present a danger to the public" as one classic example of nonpunitive detention. If detention for the purpose of protecting the community from harm *necessarily* constituted punishment, then all involuntary civil commitments would have to be considered punishment. But we have never so held.

Hendricks focuses on his confinement's potentially indefinite duration as evidence of the State's punitive intent. That focus, however, is misplaced. Far from any punitive objective, the confinement's duration is instead linked to the stated purposes of the commitment, namely, to hold the person until his mental abnormality no longer causes him to be a threat to others. If, at any time, the confined person is adjudged "safe to be at large," he is statutorily entitled to immediate release.

Furthermore, commitment under the Act is only *potentially* indefinite. The maximum amount of time an individual can be incapacitated pursuant to a single judicial proceeding is one year. If Kansas seeks to continue the detention beyond that year, a court must once again determine beyond a reasonable doubt that the detainee satisfies the same standards as required for the initial confinement. This requirement again demonstrates that Kansas does not intend an individual committed pursuant to the Act to remain confined any longer than he suffers from a mental abnormality rendering him unable to control his dangerousness.

Hendricks next contends that the State's use of procedural safeguards traditionally found in criminal trials makes the proceedings here criminal rather than civil. In *Allen,* we confronted a similar argument. There, the petitioner "placed great reliance on the fact that proceedings under the Act are accompanied by procedural safeguards usually found in criminal trials" to argue that the proceedings were civil in name only. We rejected that argument, however, explaining that the State's decision "to provide some of the safeguards applicable in criminal trials cannot itself turn these proceedings into criminal prosecutions." The numerous procedural and evidentiary protections afforded here demonstrate that the Kansas Legislature has taken great care to confine only a narrow class of particularly dangerous individuals, and then only after meeting the strictest procedural standards. That Kansas chose to afford such procedural protections does not transform a civil commitment proceeding into a criminal prosecution.

Finally, Hendricks argues that the Act is necessarily punitive because it fails to offer any legitimate "treatment." Without such treatment, Hendricks asserts, confinement under the Act amounts to little more than disguised punishment. Hendricks' argument assumes that treatment for his condition is available, but that the State has failed (or refused) to provide it. The Kansas Supreme Court, however, apparently rejected this assumption, explaining:

> "It is clear that the overriding concern of the legislature is to continue the segregation of sexually violent offenders from the public. Treatment with the goal of reintegrating them into society is incidental, at best. The record reflects that treatment for sexually violent predators is all but nonexistent. The legislature concedes that sexually violent predators are not amenable to treatment under [the existing Kansas involuntary commitment statute]. If there is nothing to treat under [that statute], then there is no mental illness. In that light, the provisions of the Act for treatment appear somewhat disingenuous."

It is possible to read this passage as a determination that Hendricks' condition was *untreatable* under the existing Kansas civil commitment statute, and thus the Act's sole purpose was incapacitation. Absent a treatable mental illness, the Kansas court concluded, Hendricks could not be detained against his will.

Accepting the Kansas court's apparent determination that treatment is not possible for this category of individuals does not obligate us to adopt its legal conclusions. We have already observed that, under the appropriate circumstances and when accompanied by proper procedures, incapacitation may be a legitimate end of the civil law. Accordingly, the Kansas court's determination that the Act's "overriding concern" was the continued "segregation of sexually violent offenders" is consistent with our conclusion that the Act establishes civil proceedings, especially when that concern is coupled with the State's ancillary goal of providing treatment to those offenders, if such is possible. While we have upheld state civil commitment statutes that aim both to incapacitate and to treat, see *Allen, supra,* we have never held that the Constitution prevents a State from civilly detaining those for whom no treatment is available, but who nevertheless pose a danger to others. A State could hardly be seen as furthering a "punitive" purpose by involuntarily confining persons afflicted with an untreatable, highly contagious disease. Similarly, it would be of little value to require treatment as a precondition for civil confinement of the dangerously insane when no acceptable treatment existed. To conclude otherwise would obligate a State to release certain confined individuals who were both mentally ill and dangerous simply because they could not be successfully treated for their afflictions. . . .

Although the treatment program initially offered Hendricks may have seemed somewhat meager, it must be remembered that he was the first person committed under the Act. That the State did not have all of its treatment procedures in place is thus not surprising. What is significant, however, is that Hendricks was placed under the supervision of the Kansas Department of Health and Social and Rehabilitative Services, housed in a unit segregated from the general prison population and operated not by employees of the Department of Corrections, but by other trained individuals. And, before this Court, Kansas declared "absolutely" that persons committed under the Act are now receiving in the neighborhood of "31.5 hours of treatment per week."

Where the State has "disavowed any punitive intent"; limited confinement to a small segment of particularly dangerous individuals; provided strict procedural safeguards; directed that confined persons be segregated from the general prison population and afforded the same status as others who have been civilly committed; recommended treatment if such is possible; and permitted immediate release upon a showing that the individual is no longer dangerous or mentally impaired, we cannot say that it acted with punitive intent. We therefore hold that the Act does not establish criminal proceedings and that involuntary confinement pursuant to the Act is not punitive. Our conclusion that the Act is nonpunitive thus removes an essential prerequisite for both Hendricks' double jeopardy and *ex post facto* claims.

1

The Double Jeopardy Clause provides: "Nor shall any person be subject for the same offence to be twice put in jeopardy of life or limb." Although generally understood to preclude a second prosecution for the same offense, the Court has also interpreted this prohibition to prevent the State from "punishing twice, or attempting a second time to punish criminally, for the same offense." Hendricks argues that, as applied to him, the Act violates double jeopardy principles because his confinement under the Act, imposed after a conviction and a term of incarceration, amounted to both a second prosecution and a second punishment for the same offense. We disagree.

Because we have determined that the Kansas Act is civil in nature, initiation of its commitment proceedings does not constitute a second prosecution. Moreover, as commitment under the Act is not tantamount to "punishment," Hendricks' involuntary detention does not violate the Double Jeopardy Clause, even though that confinement may follow a prison term. Indeed, in *Baxstrom v. Herold,* we expressly recognized that civil commitment could follow the expiration of a prison term without offending double jeopardy principles. We reasoned that "there is no conceivable basis for distinguishing the commitment of a person who is nearing the end of a penal term from all other civil commitments." If an individual otherwise meets the requirements for involuntary civil commitment, the State is under no obligation to release that individual simply because the detention would follow a period of incarceration. . . .

2

Hendricks' *ex post facto* claim is similarly flawed. The *Ex Post Facto* Clause, which "forbids the application of any new punitive measure to a crime already consummated," has been interpreted to pertain exclusively to penal statutes. As we have previously determined, the Act does not impose punishment; thus, its application does not raise *ex post facto* concerns. Moreover, the Act clearly does not have retroactive effect. Rather, the Act permits involuntary confinement based upon a determination that the person *currently* both suffers from a "mental abnormality" or "personality disorder" and is likely to pose a future danger to the public. To the extent that past behavior is taken into account, it is used, as noted above, solely for evidentiary purposes. Because the Act does not criminalize conduct legal before its enactment, nor deprive Hendricks of any defense that was available to him at the time of his crimes, the Act does not violate the *Ex Post Facto* Clause.

III

We hold that the Kansas Sexually Violent Predator Act comports with due process requirements and neither runs afoul of double jeopardy principles nor constitutes an exercise in impermissible *ex post facto* lawmaking. Accordingly, the judgment of the Kansas Supreme Court is reversed.

POSTSCRIPT

Does Confining Sex Offenders Indefinitely in Mental Hospitals After They Have Served Their Prison Sentences Violate the Constitution?

The readings in this section are excerpts from the U.S. Supreme Court's decision in *Kansas v. Hendricks*. If you were a member of the Court, would you have joined the majority opinion, or would you have joined Justice Breyer's dissent? Do you agree with Justice Stephen Breyer's assertion that the Kansas Sexually Violent Predator Act is an unconstitutional *ex post facto* law as applied in this case?

Moreover, are you convinced by Justice Thomas' contention that committing someone to confinement in a state mental institution after they have completed their prison sentence does not constitute *punishment*? Rather, according to the Court, confining someone in this manner is therapeutic *treatment*. Therefore, the Fifth Amendment's double jeopardy clause does not bar the additional confinement. Is the distinction that the Court has drawn between punishment and treatment a matter of form triumphing over substance? Is this a case where you agree with the result—dangerous pedophiles should not be allowed to prey on our children, but disagree with how the court reached their conclusion?

What if a state were to pass a law providing that after receiving a complete psychiatric exam, a certified pedophile about to be released from prison could have the choice of undergoing physical castration in lieu of an indefinite commitment to a mental institution? What constitutional issues would you raise as the attorney for the sex offender faced with this difficult choice?

Another interesting issue concerns the sex offender's Sixth Amendment right to counsel. Suppose that as an attorney you were appointed by a court to represent someone like Leroy Hendricks in a proceeding to determine whether he would be indefinitely confined to a mental hospital following the completion of his sentence. Would you accept the case? The Rules of Professional Responsibility that govern the conduct of attorneys provide that if you accept the case, you must defend the offender's interest to the best of your ability. The Rules provide as well that if you cannot do so, you must refuse to take the case. What would you do?

The issue considered in this section is a challenging one. Fortunately, there are additional resources that add substantially to the discussion of these matters. See American Psychiatric Association, *Dangerous Sex Offenders: A Task Force Report of the American Psychiatric Association* (American Psychiatric Press, 1999);

Lisa L. Sample and Timothy M. Bray, "Are Sex Offenders Dangerous?" *Criminology & Public Policy*, vol. 3, no. 1 (2003); Holly A. Miller, Amy E. Amenta, and Mary Alice Conroy, "Sexually Violent Predator Evaluations: Empirical Evidence, Strategies for Professionals, and Research Directions," *Law & Human Behavior*, vol. 29, no. 1 (2005); Leam A. Craig, Kevin D. Browne, Ian Stringer, and Anthony Beech, "Limitations in Actuarial Rist Assessment of Sexual Offenders: A Methodological Note," *The British Journal of Forensic Practice*, vol. 6, no. 1 (2004); Wanda D. Beyer Kendall and Monit Cheung, "Sexually Violent Predators and Civil Commitment Laws," *Journal of Child Sexual Abuse*, vol. 13, no. 2 (2004).

Additional resources include Ron Langevin, Suzanne Cumoe, Paul Federoff, and Renee Bennett, et al., "Lifetime Sex Offender Recidivism: A 25-Year Follow-Up Study," *Canadian Journal of Criminology and Criminal Justice*, vol. 46, no. 5 (2004); Kyron Huigens, "Dignity and Desert in Punishment Theory," *Harvard Journal of Law and Public Policy*, vol. 27, no. 1 (2003); Patricia E. Erickson, "The Legal Standard of Volitional Impairment: An Analysis of Substantive Due Process and the United States Supreme Court's Decision in *Kansas v. Hendricks*," *Journal of Criminal Justice*, vol. 30, no. 1 (2002); and Eric S. Janus, "Sex Predator Commitment Laws: Constitutional but Unwise," *Psychiatric Annals*, vol. 30, no. 6 (2000).

ISSUE 14

Is the Death Penalty an Unconstitutional Punishment for Juvenile Offenders?

YES: Anthony M. Kennedy, from Majority Opinion, *Roper v. Simmons,* U.S. Supreme Court (2005)

NO: Antonin E. Scalia, from Dissenting Opinion, *Roper v. Simmons,* U.S. Supreme Court (2005)

ISSUE SUMMARY

YES: Associate Justice Anthony M. Kennedy, writing for the Court, asserts that the death penalty is an unacceptable punishment for juveniles who commit murder because it constitutes cruel and unusual punishment in violation of the Eighth and Fourteenth Amendments.

NO: Associate Justice Antonin E. Scalia, dissenting in the same case, argues that there is no clear social consensus that would favor abolishing the death penalty in these cases and that in doing so the Court's majority is usurping the powers of state legislatures.

Perhaps the single-most controversial issue concerning U.S. justice system policy is the use of the death penalty. A significant percentage of Americans appear to support capital punishment. A 2005 ABC News/Washington Post Poll showed that approximately 65 percent of adults surveyed nationwide favor the death penalty, while 29 percent oppose it, and 6 percent remain unsure. But, as pollsters know, how they ask the death penalty question has a great deal to do with the responses they receive. A 2005 CBS News Poll asked: "What do you think should be the penalty for persons convicted of murder: the death penalty, life in prison with no chance of parole, or a long prison sentence with a chance of parole?" Thirty-nine percent of the respondents selected the death penalty, 39 percent chose life in prison with no chance of parole, 6 percent indicated a long prison sentence with a chance of parole, and 3 percent were unsure.

What these polls show is that while death penalty proponents are quick to point to polls showing that a majority of Americans support capital punishment, the reality is that many people are somewhat ambivalent about it. When penal alternatives to capital punishment are offered, support for the death penalty is much more equivocal.

But, how do Americans feel about executing juvenile offenders? A significant majority clearly do not support it. A 2001 University of Chicago study found that while 62 percent of those surveyed supported the death penalty, only 34 percent supported it for juvenile offenders. A 2002 Gallup Poll showed similar results: While 72 percent of Americans supported the death penalty, only 26 percent supported it for juvenile offenders.

What are the arguments on both sides of the juvenile death penalty debate? One argument favoring the juvenile death penalty is that if the offender is old enough to commit a heinous crime, he or she is old enough to pay the consequences. Another related argument is based on the doctrine of "just deserts"—the offender should receive the death penalty because the act that he or she committed deserves to be punished by death. Likewise, by virtue of committing a violent murder, the juvenile offender has demonstrated that he or she is "unfit" to live and that society is justified in applying the punishment of death.

On the other side, juvenile death penalty opponents note that children have less cognitive capacity than adults. That is why our legal system assumes that children who commit crimes are less responsible for their offenses than mature adults. Accordingly, scientific research appears to indicate that the portions of the human brain that control thinking and impulsiveness are not developed until a person reaches his or her early twenties. Moreover, a strong case can be made that executing offenders for crimes committed as juveniles is simply barbaric and, according to Justice Anthony M. Kennedy's majority opinion in *Roper v. Simmons*, places the United States in the same category with the Democratic Republic of Congo, Iran, Nigeria, Pakistan, Saudi Arabia, and Yemen as the only countries that execute juvenile offenders.

So, should the death penalty be an unacceptable punishment for juvenile offenders? The Supreme Court justices who authored the majority and dissenting opinions in *Roper v. Simmons* have very different views of this controversy. Justice Kennedy, writing for the Court, asserted that persons should not be eligible for the death penalty if they committed their crimes as juveniles. Justice Antonin E. Scalia, however, believed that decisions about whether to execute juveniles should be left to state legislatures.

In Your Opinion . . .

- Based on what you know about the death penalty, should society be permitted to execute persons who committed murder as juveniles?
- Is the death penalty a barbaric practice that is inconsistent with American values and ideals?
- Is there a less drastic alternative method of punishing juvenile murderers?

YES

Anthony M. Kennedy

Majority Opinion, *Roper v. Simmons*

Justice Kennedy delivered the opinion of the Court.

This case requires us to address, for the second time in a decade and a half, whether it is permissible under the Eighth and Fourteenth Amendments to the Constitution of the United States to execute a juvenile offender who was older than 15 but younger than 18 when he committed a capital crime. In *Stanford v. Kentucky*, 492 U.S. 361, 106 L. Ed. 2d 306, 109 S. Ct. 2969 (1989), a divided Court rejected the proposition that the Constitution bars capital punishment for juvenile offenders in this age group. We reconsider the question. . . .

I

The Eighth Amendment provides: "Excessive bail shall not be required, nor excessive fines imposed, nor cruel and unusual punishments inflicted." The provision is applicable to the States through the Fourteenth Amendment. As the Court explained in *Atkins*, the Eighth Amendment guarantees individuals the right not to be subjected to excessive sanctions. The right flows from the basic "'precept of justice that punishment for crime should be graduated and proportioned to [the] offense.'" By protecting even those convicted of heinous crimes, the Eighth Amendment reaffirms the duty of the government to respect the dignity of all persons.

The prohibition against "cruel and unusual punishments," like other expansive language in the Constitution, must be interpreted according to its text, by considering history, tradition, and precedent, and with due regard for its purpose and function in the constitutional design. To implement this framework we have established the propriety and affirmed the necessity of referring to "the evolving standards of decency that mark the progress of a maturing society" to determine which punishments are so disproportionate as to be cruel and unusual.

In *Thompson v. Oklahoma*, a plurality of the Court determined that our standards of decency do not permit the execution of any offender under the age of 16 at the time of the crime. The plurality opinion explained that no death penalty State that had given express consideration to a minimum age for the death penalty had set the age lower than 16. The plurality also observed that "[t]he conclusion that it would offend civilized standards of decency to execute a person who was less than 16 years old at the time of his or her

Supreme Court of the United States, March 1, 2005.

offense is consistent with the views that have been expressed by respected professional organizations, by other nations that share our Anglo-American heritage, and by the leading members of the Western European community." The opinion further noted that juries imposed the death penalty on offenders under 16 with exceeding rarity; the last execution of an offender for a crime committed under the age of 16 had been carried out in 1948, 40 years prior.

Bringing its independent judgment to bear on the permissibility of the death penalty for a 15-year-old offender, the *Thompson* plurality stressed that "[t]he reasons why juveniles are not trusted with the privileges and responsibilities of an adult also explain why their irresponsible conduct is not as morally reprehensible as that of an adult." According to the plurality, the lesser culpability of offenders under 16 made the death penalty inappropriate as a form of retribution, while the low likelihood that offenders under 16 engaged in "the kind of cost-benefit analysis that attaches any weight to the possibility of execution" made the death penalty ineffective as a means of deterrence. With Justice O'Connor concurring in the judgment on narrower grounds, the Court set aside the death sentence that had been imposed on the 15-year-old offender.

The next year, in *Stanford v. Kentucky*, the Court, over a dissenting opinion joined by four justices, referred to contemporary standards of decency in this country and concluded the Eighth and Fourteenth Amendments did not proscribe the execution of juvenile offenders over 15 but under 18. The Court noted that 22 of the 37 death penalty States permitted the death penalty for 16-year-old offenders, and, among these 37 States, 25 permitted it for 17-year-old offenders. These numbers, in the Court's view, indicated there was no national consensus "sufficient to label a particular punishment cruel and unusual." A plurality of the Court also "emphatically reject[ed]" the suggestion that the Court should bring its own judgment to bear on the acceptability of the juvenile death penalty.

The same day the Court decided *Stanford*, it held that the Eighth Amendment did not mandate a categorical exemption from the death penalty for the mentally retarded. In reaching this conclusion it stressed that only two States had enacted laws banning the imposition of the death penalty on a mentally retarded person convicted of a capital offense. According to the Court, "the two state statutes prohibiting execution of the mentally retarded, even when added to the 14 States that have rejected capital punishment completely, [did] not provide sufficient evidence at present of a national consensus."

Three Terms ago the subject was reconsidered in *Atkins*. We held that standards of decency have evolved since *Penry* and now demonstrate that the execution of the mentally retarded is cruel and unusual punishment. The Court noted objective indicia of society's standards, as expressed in legislative enactments and state practice with respect to executions of the mentally retarded. When *Atkins* was decided only a minority of States permitted the practice, and even in those States it was rare. On the basis of these indicia the Court determined that executing mentally retarded offenders "has become truly unusual, and it is fair to say that a national consensus has developed against it." . . .

Just as the *Atkins* Court reconsidered the issue decided in *Penry*, we now reconsider the issue decided in *Stanford*. The beginning point is a review of objective indicia of consensus, as expressed in particular by the enactments of legislatures that have addressed the question. This data gives us essential instruction. We then must determine, in the exercise of our own independent judgment, whether the death penalty is a disproportionate punishment for juveniles.

II

A

The evidence of national consensus against the death penalty for juveniles is similar, and in some respects parallel, to the evidence *Atkins* held sufficient to demonstrate a national consensus against the death penalty for the mentally retarded. When *Atkins* was decided, 30 States prohibited the death penalty for the mentally retarded. This number comprised 12 that had abandoned the death penalty altogether, and 18 that maintained it but excluded the mentally retarded from its reach. By a similar calculation in this case, 30 States prohibit the juvenile death penalty, comprising 12 that have rejected the death penalty altogether and 18 that maintain it but, by express provision or judicial interpretation, exclude juveniles from its reach. *Atkins* emphasized that even in the 20 States without formal prohibition, the practice of executing the mentally retarded was infrequent. Since *Penry*, only five States had executed offenders known to have an IQ under 70. In the present case, too, even in the 20 States without a formal prohibition on executing juveniles, the practice is infrequent. Since *Stanford*, six States have executed prisoners for crimes committed as juveniles. In the past 10 years, only three have done so: Oklahoma, Texas, and Virginia. In December 2003, the Governor of Kentucky decided to spare the life of Kevin Stanford and commuted his sentence to one of life imprisonment without parole, with the declaration that "'[w]e ought not be executing people who, legally, were children.'" By this act the Governor ensured Kentucky would not add itself to the list of States that have executed juveniles within the last 10 years even by the execution of the very defendant whose death sentence the Court had upheld in *Stanford v. Kentucky*.

There is, to be sure, at least one difference between the evidence of consensus in *Atkins* and in this case. Impressive in *Atkins* was the rate of abolition of the death penalty for the mentally retarded. Sixteen States that permitted the execution of the mentally retarded at the time of *Penry* had prohibited the practice by the time we heard *Atkins*. By contrast, the rate of change in reducing the incidence of the juvenile death penalty, or in taking specific steps to abolish it, has been slower. Five States that allowed the juvenile death penalty at the time of *Stanford* have abandoned it in the intervening 15 years—four through legislative enactments and one through judicial decision.

Though less dramatic than the change from *Penry* to *Atkins* ("telling," to borrow the word *Atkins* used to describe this difference), we still consider the change from *Stanford* to this case to be significant. As noted in *Atkins*, with respect to the States that had abandoned the death penalty for the mentally retarded since *Penry*, "[i]t is not so much the number of these States that is significant, but the consistency of the direction of change." In particular we found it significant that, in the wake of *Penry*, no State that had already prohibited the execution of the mentally retarded had passed legislation to reinstate the penalty. The number of States that have abandoned capital punishment for juvenile offenders since *Stanford* is smaller than the number of States that abandoned capital punishment for the mentally retarded after *Penry*; yet we think the same consistency of direction of change has been demonstrated. Since *Stanford*, no State that previously prohibited capital punishment for juveniles has reinstated it. This fact, coupled with the trend toward abolition of the juvenile death penalty, carries special force in light of the general popularity of anticrime legislation, and in light of the particular trend in recent years toward cracking down on juvenile crime in other respects. Any difference between this case and *Atkins* with respect to the pace of abolition is thus counterbalanced by the consistent direction of the change. . . .

As in *Atkins*, the objective indicia of consensus in this case—the rejection of the juvenile death penalty in the majority of States; the infrequency of its use even where it remains on the books; and the consistency in the trend toward abolition of the practice—provide sufficient evidence that today our society views juveniles, in the words *Atkins* used respecting the mentally retarded, as "categorically less culpable than the average criminal."

B

A majority of States have rejected the imposition of the death penalty on juvenile offenders under 18, and we now hold this is required by the Eighth Amendment.

Because the death penalty is the most severe punishment, the Eighth Amendment applies to it with special force. Capital punishment must be limited to those offenders who commit "a narrow category of the most serious crimes" and whose extreme culpability makes them "the most deserving of execution." This principle is implemented throughout the capital sentencing process. States must give narrow and precise definition to the aggravating factors that can result in a capital sentence. In any capital case a defendant has wide latitude to raise as a mitigating factor "any aspect of [his or her] character or record and any of the circumstances of the offense that the defendant proffers as a basis for a sentence less than death." There are a number of crimes that beyond question are severe in absolute terms, yet the death penalty may not be imposed for their commission. The death penalty may not be imposed on certain classes of offenders, such as juveniles under 16, the insane, and the mentally retarded, no matter how heinous the crime. These rules vindicate the underlying principle that the death penalty is reserved for a narrow category of crimes and offenders.

Three general differences between juveniles under 18 and adults demonstrate that juvenile offenders cannot with reliability be classified among the worst offenders. First, as any parent knows and as the scientific and sociological studies respondent and his *amici* cite tend to confirm, "[a] lack of maturity and an underdeveloped sense of responsibility are found in youth more often than in adults and are more understandable among the young. These qualities often result in impetuous and ill-considered actions and decisions." It has been noted that "adolescents are overrepresented statistically in virtually every category of reckless behavior." In recognition of the comparative immaturity and irresponsibility of juveniles, almost every State prohibits those under 18 years of age from voting, serving on juries, or marrying without parental consent.

The second area of difference is that juveniles are more vulnerable or susceptible to negative influences and outside pressures, including peer pressure. ("[Y]outh is more than a chronological fact. It is a time and condition of life when a person may be most susceptible to influence and to psychological damage"). This is explained in part by the prevailing circumstance that juveniles have less control, or less experience with control, over their own environment.

The third broad difference is that the character of a juvenile is not as well formed as that of an adult. The personality traits of juveniles are more transitory, less fixed.

These differences render suspect any conclusion that a juvenile falls among the worst offenders. The susceptibility of juveniles to immature and irresponsible behavior means "their irresponsible conduct is not as morally reprehensible as that of an adult." Their own vulnerability and comparative lack of control over their immediate surroundings mean juveniles have a greater claim than adults to be forgiven for failing to escape negative influences in their whole environment. The reality that juveniles still struggle to define their identity means it is less supportable to conclude that even a heinous crime committed by a juvenile is evidence of irretrievably depraved character. From a moral standpoint it would be misguided to equate the failings of a minor with those of an adult, for a greater possibility exists that a minor's character deficiencies will be reformed. Indeed, "[t]he relevance of youth as a mitigating factor derives from the fact that the signature qualities of youth are transient; as individuals mature, the impetuousness and recklessness that may dominate in younger years can subside."

Once the diminished culpability of juveniles is recognized, it is evident that the penological justifications for the death penalty apply to them with lesser force than to adults. We have held there are two distinct social purposes served by the death penalty: "'retribution and deterrence of capital crimes by prospective offenders.'" As for retribution, we remarked in *Atkins* that "[i]f the culpability of the average murderer is insufficient to justify the most extreme sanction available to the State, the lesser culpability of the mentally retarded offender surely does not merit that form of retribution." The same conclusions follow from the lesser culpability of the juvenile offender. Whether viewed as an attempt to express the community's moral outrage or as an attempt to right the balance for the wrong to the victim, the case for retribution is not as strong with a minor as with an adult. Retribution is not proportional if the law's most severe penalty is imposed on one whose culpability or blameworthiness is diminished, to a substantial degree, by reason of youth and immaturity.

As for deterrence, it is unclear whether the death penalty has a significant or even measurable deterrent effect on juveniles, as counsel for the petitioner acknowledged at oral argument. In general we leave to legislatures the assessment of the efficacy of various criminal penalty schemes. Here, however, the absence of evidence of deterrent effect is of special concern because the same characteristics that render juveniles less culpable than adults suggest as well that juveniles will be less susceptible to deterrence. In particular, as the plurality observed in *Thompson*, "[t]he likelihood that the teenage offender has made the kind of cost-benefit analysis that attaches any weight to the possibility of execution is so remote as to be virtually nonexistent." To the extent the juvenile death penalty might have residual deterrent effect, it is worth noting that the punishment of life imprisonment without the possibility of parole is itself a severe sanction, in particular for a young person.

In concluding that neither retribution nor deterrence provides adequate justification for imposing the death penalty on juvenile offenders, we cannot deny or overlook the brutal crimes too many juvenile offenders have committed. Certainly it can be argued, although we by no means concede the point, that a rare case might arise in which a juvenile offender has sufficient psychological maturity, and at the same time demonstrates sufficient depravity, to merit a sentence of death. Indeed, this possibility is the linchpin of one contention pressed by petitioner and his *amici*. They assert that even assuming the truth of the observations we have made about juveniles' diminished culpability in general, jurors nonetheless should be allowed to consider mitigating arguments related to youth on a case-by-case basis, and in some cases to impose the death penalty if justified. A central feature of death penalty sentencing is a particular assessment of the circumstances of the crime and the characteristics of the offender. The system is designed to consider both aggravating and mitigating circumstances, including youth, in every case. Given this Court's own insistence on individualized consideration, petitioner maintains that it is both arbitrary and unnecessary to adopt a categorical rule barring imposition of the death penalty on any offender under 18 years of age.

We disagree. The differences between juvenile and adult offenders are too marked and well understood to risk allowing a youthful person to receive the death penalty despite insufficient culpability. An unacceptable likelihood exists that the brutality or cold-blooded nature of any particular crime would overpower mitigating arguments based on youth as a matter of course, even where the juvenile offender's objective immaturity, vulnerability, and lack of true depravity should require a sentence less severe than death. In some cases a defendant's youth may even be counted against him. In this very case, as we noted above, the prosecutor argued Simmons' youth was aggravating rather than mitigating. While this sort of overreaching could be corrected by a particular rule to ensure that the mitigating force of youth is not overlooked, that would not address our larger concerns.

It is difficult even for expert psychologists to differentiate between the juvenile offender whose crime reflects unfortunate yet transient immaturity, and the rare juvenile offender whose crime reflects irreparable corruption. As we understand it, this difficulty underlies the rule forbidding psychiatrists from diagnosing any patient under 18 as having antisocial personality disorder, a disorder also referred to as psychopathy or sociopathy, and which is characterized by callousness, cynicism, and contempt for the feelings, rights, and suffering of others. If trained psychiatrists with the advantage of clinical testing and observation refrain, despite diagnostic expertise, from assessing any juvenile under 18 as having antisocial personality disorder, we conclude that States should refrain from asking jurors to issue a far graver condemnation—that a juvenile offender merits the death penalty. When a juvenile offender commits a heinous crime, the State can exact forfeiture of some of the most basic liberties, but the State cannot extinguish his life and his potential to attain a mature understanding of his own humanity.

Drawing the line at 18 years of age is subject, of course, to the objections always raised against categorical rules. The qualities that distinguish juveniles from adults do not disappear when an individual turns 18. By the same token, some under 18 have already attained a level of maturity some adults will never reach. For the reasons we have discussed, however, a line must be drawn. The plurality opinion in *Thompson* drew the line at 16. In the intervening years the *Thompson* plurality's conclusion that offenders under 16 may not be executed has not been challenged. The logic of *Thompson* extends to those who are under 18. The age of 18 is the point where society draws the line for many purposes between childhood and adulthood. It is, we conclude, the age at which the line for death eligibility ought to rest. . . .

III

Our determination that the death penalty is disproportionate punishment for offenders under 18 finds confirmation in the stark reality that the United States is the only country in the world that continues to give official sanction to the juvenile death penalty. This reality does not become controlling, for the task of interpreting the Eighth Amendment remains our responsibility. Yet at least from the time of the Court's decision in *Trop*, the Court has referred to the laws of other countries and to international authorities as instructive for its interpretation of the Eighth Amendment's prohibition of "cruel and unusual punishments." . . .

As respondent and a number of *amici* emphasize, Article 37 of the United Nations Convention on the Rights of the Child, which every country in the world has ratified save for the United States and Somalia, contains an express prohibition on capital punishment for crimes committed by juveniles under 18. No ratifying country has entered a reservation to the provision prohibiting the execution of juvenile offenders. Parallel prohibitions are contained in other significant international covenants.

Respondent and his *amici* have submitted, and petitioner does not contest, that only seven countries other than the United States have executed juvenile offenders since 1990: Iran, Pakistan, Saudi Arabia, Yemen, Nigeria, the Democratic Republic of Congo, and China. Since then each of these countries has either abolished capital punishment for juveniles or made public disavowal of the practice. Brief for Respondent 49–50. In sum, it is fair to say that the United States now stands alone in a world that has turned its face against the juvenile death penalty.

Though the international covenants prohibiting the juvenile death penalty are of more recent date, it is instructive to note that the United Kingdom abolished the juvenile death penalty before these covenants came into being. The United Kingdom's experience bears particular relevance here in light of the historic ties between our countries and in light of the Eighth Amendment's own origins. The Amendment was modeled on a parallel provision in the English Declaration of Rights of 1689, which provided: "[E]xcessive Bail ought not to be required nor excessive Fines imposed; nor cruel and unusual Punishments inflicted." As of now, the United Kingdom has abolished the death penalty in its entirety; but, decades before it took this step, it recognized the disproportionate nature of the juvenile death penalty; and it abolished that penalty as a separate matter.

It is proper that we acknowledge the overwhelming weight of international opinion against the juvenile death penalty, resting in large part on the understanding that the instability and emotional imbalance of young people may often be a factor in the crime. The opinion of the world community, while not controlling our outcome, does provide respected and significant confirmation for our own conclusions.

Over time, from one generation to the next, the Constitution has come to earn the high respect and even, as Madison dared to hope, the veneration of the American people. The document sets forth, and rests upon, innovative principles original to the American experience, such as federalism; a proven balance in political mechanisms through separation of powers; specific guarantees for the accused in criminal cases; and broad provisions to secure individual freedom and preserve human dignity. These doctrines and guarantees are central to the American experience and remain essential to our present-day self-definition and national identity. Not the least of the reasons we honor the Constitution, then, is because we know it to be our own. It does not lessen our fidelity to the Constitution or our pride in its origins to acknowledge that the express affirmation of certain fundamental rights by other nations and peoples simply underscores the centrality of those same rights within our own heritage of freedom. . . .

Antonin E. Scalia  **NO**

Dissenting Opinion, *Roper v. Simmons*

J ustice Scalia, with whom the Chief Justice and Justice Thomas join, dissenting.

In urging approval of a Constitution that gave life-tenured judges the power to nullify laws enacted by the people's representatives, Alexander Hamilton assured the citizens of New York that there was little risk in this, since "[t]he judiciary . . . ha[s] neither FORCE nor WILL but merely judgment." But Hamilton had in mind a traditional judiciary, "bound down by strict rules and precedents which serve to define and point out their duty in every particular case that comes before them." Bound down, indeed. What a mockery today's opinion makes of Hamilton's expectation, announcing the Court's conclusion that the meaning of our Constitution has changed over the past 15 years—not, mind you, that this Court's decision 15 years ago was *wrong*, but that the Constitution *has changed*. The Court reaches this implausible result by purporting to advert, not to the original meaning of the Eighth Amendment, but to "the evolving standards of decency," of our national society. It then finds, on the flimsiest of grounds, that a national consensus which could not be perceived in our people's laws barely 15 years ago now solidly exists. Worse still, the Court says in so many words that what our people's laws say about the issue does not, in the last analysis, matter: "[I]n the end our own judgment will be brought to bear on the question of the acceptability of the death penalty under the Eighth Amendment." The Court thus proclaims itself sole arbiter of our Nation's moral standards—and in the course of discharging that awesome responsibility purports to take guidance from the views of foreign courts and legislatures. Because I do not believe that the meaning of our Eighth Amendment, any more than the meaning of other provisions of our Constitution, should be determined by the subjective views of five Members of this Court and like-minded foreigners, I dissent.

I

In determining that capital punishment of offenders who committed murder before age 18 is "cruel and unusual" under the Eighth Amendment, the Court first considers, in accordance with our modern (though in my view mistaken) jurisprudence, whether there is a "national consensus," that laws allowing such executions contravene our modern "standards of decency." We have held that this determination should be based on "objective indicia that reflect the

Supreme Court of the United States, March 1, 2005.

public attitude toward a given sanction"—namely, "statutes passed by society's elected representatives." As in *Atkins v. Virginia,* the Court dutifully recites this test and claims halfheartedly that a national consensus has emerged since our decision in *Stanford,* because 18 States—or 47% of States that permit capital punishment—now have legislation prohibiting the execution of offenders under 18, and because all of four States have adopted such legislation since *Stanford.*

Words have no meaning if the views of less than 50% of death penalty States can constitute a national consensus. Our previous cases have required overwhelming opposition to a challenged practice, generally over a long period of time. In *Coker v. Georgia,* a plurality concluded the Eighth Amendment prohibited capital punishment for rape of an adult woman where only one jurisdiction authorized such punishment. The plurality also observed that "[a]t no time in the last 50 years ha[d] a majority of States authorized death as a punishment for rape." In *Ford v. Wainwright,* we held execution of the insane unconstitutional, tracing the roots of this prohibition to the common law and noting that "no State in the union permits the execution of the insane." In *Enmund v. Florida,* we invalidated capital punishment imposed for participation in a robbery in which an accomplice committed murder, because 78% of all death penalty States prohibited this punishment. Even there we expressed some hesitation, because the legislative judgment was "neither 'wholly unanimous among state legislatures,' . . . nor as compelling as the legislative judgments considered in *Coker.*" By contrast, agreement among 42% of death penalty States in *Stanford,* which the Court appears to believe was correctly decided at the time, was insufficient to show a national consensus.

In an attempt to keep afloat its implausible assertion of national consensus, the Court throws overboard a proposition well established in our Eighth Amendment jurisprudence. "It should be observed," the Court says, "that the *Stanford* Court should have considered those States that had abandoned the death penalty altogether as part of the consensus against the juvenile death penalty . . .; a State's decision to bar the death penalty altogether of necessity demonstrates a judgment that the death penalty is inappropriate for all offenders, including juveniles." The insinuation that the Court's new method of counting contradicts only "the *Stanford* Court" is misleading. *None* of our cases dealing with an alleged constitutional limitation upon the death penalty has counted, as States supporting a consensus in favor of that limitation, States that have eliminated the death penalty entirely. And with good reason. Consulting States that bar the death penalty concerning the necessity of making an exception to the penalty for offenders under 18 is rather like including old-order Amishmen in a consumer-preference poll on the electric car. Of *course* they don't like it, but that sheds no light whatever on the point at issue. That 12 States favor *no* executions says something about consensus against the death penalty, but nothing—absolutely nothing—about consensus that offenders under 18 deserve special immunity from such a penalty. In repealing the death penalty, those 12 States considered *none* of the factors that the Court puts forth as determinative of the issue before us today—lower culpability of the young, inherent recklessness, lack of capacity for considered judgment, etc. What might be relevant, perhaps, is how many of those States permit 16- and 17-year-old offenders to be treated as adults with respect to noncapital offenses. (They all do; indeed, some even *require* that juveniles as young as 14 be tried as adults if they are charged with murder.) The attempt by the Court to turn its remarkable minority consensus into a faux majority by counting Amishmen is an act of nomological desperation.

Recognizing that its national-consensus argument was weak compared with our earlier cases, the *Atkins* Court found additional support in the fact that 16 States had prohibited execution of mentally retarded individuals since *Penry v. Lynaugh.* Indeed, the *Atkins* Court distinguished *Stanford* on that very ground, explaining that "[a]lthough we decided *Stanford* on the same day as *Penry,* apparently *only two* state legislatures have raised the threshold age for imposition of the death penalty." Now, the Court says a legislative change in four States is "significant" enough to trigger a constitutional prohibition. It is amazing to think that this subtle shift in numbers can take the issue entirely off the table for legislative debate.

I also doubt whether many of the legislators who voted to change the laws in those four States would have done so if they had known their decision would (by the pronouncement of this Court) be rendered irreversible. After all, legislative support for capital punishment, in any form, has surged and ebbed throughout our Nation's history. As Justice O'Connor has explained:

> "The history of the death penalty instructs that there is danger in inferring a settled societal consensus from statistics like those relied on in this case. In 1846, Michigan became the first State to abolish the death penalty. . . . In succeeding decades, other American States continued the trend towards abolition. . . . Later, and particularly after World War II, there ensued a steady and dramatic decline in executions. . . . In the 1950s and 1960s, more States abolished or radically restricted capital punishment, and executions ceased completely for several years beginning in 1968. . . .
>
> "In 1972, when this Court heard arguments on the constitutionality of the death penalty, such statistics might have suggested that the practice had become a relic, implicitly rejected by a new societal consensus. . . . We now know that any inference of a societal consensus rejecting the death penalty would have been mistaken. But had this Court then declared the existence of such a consensus, and outlawed capital punishment, legislatures would very likely not have been able to revive it. The mistaken premise of the decision would have been frozen into constitutional law, making it difficult to refute and even more difficult to reject."

Relying on such narrow margins is especially inappropriate in light of the fact that a number of legislatures and voters have expressly affirmed their support for capital punishment of 16- and 17-year-old offenders since *Stanford.* Though the Court is correct that no State has lowered its death penalty age, both the Missouri and Virginia Legislatures—which, at the time of *Stanford,* had no minimum age requirement—expressly established 16 as the minimum. The people of Arizona and Florida have done the same by ballot initiative. Thus, even States that have not executed an under-18 offender in recent years unquestionably favor the possibility of capital punishment in some circumstances.

The Court's reliance on the infrequency of executions, for under-18 murderers, credits an argument that this Court considered and explicitly rejected in *Stanford*. That infrequency is explained, we accurately said, both by "the undisputed fact that a far smaller percentage of capital crimes are committed by persons under 18 than over 18," and by the fact that juries are required at sentencing to consider the offender's youth as a mitigating factor. Thus, "it is not only possible, but overwhelmingly probable, that the very considerations which induce [respondent] and [his] supporters to believe that death should *never* be imposed on offenders under 18 cause prosecutors and juries to believe that it should *rarely* be imposed."

It is, furthermore, unclear that executions of the relevant age group have decreased since we decided *Stanford*. Between 1990 and 2003, 123 of 3,599 death sentences, or 3.4%, were given to individuals who committed crimes before reaching age 18. By contrast, only 2.1% of those sentenced to death between 1982 and 1988 committed the crimes when they were under 18. As for actual executions of under-18 offenders, they constituted 2.4% of the total executions since 1973. In *Stanford*, we noted that only 2% of the executions between 1642 and 1986 were of under-18 offenders and found that lower number did not demonstrate a national consensus against the penalty. Thus, the numbers of under-18 offenders subjected to the death penalty, though low compared with adults, have either held steady or slightly increased since *Stanford*. These statistics in no way support the action the Court takes today.

II

Of course, the real force driving today's decision is not the actions of four state legislatures, but the Court's "own judgment" that murderers younger than 18 can never be as morally culpable as older counterparts. The Court claims that this usurpation of the role of moral arbiter is simply a "retur[n] to the rul[e] established in decisions predating *Stanford*." That supposed rule—which is reflected solely in dicta and never once in a *holding* that purports to supplant the consensus of the American people with the justices' views—was repudiated in *Stanford* for the very good reason that it has no foundation in law or logic. If the Eighth Amendment set forth an ordinary rule of law, it would indeed be the role of this Court to say what the law is. But the Court having pronounced that the Eighth Amendment is an ever-changing reflection of "the evolving standards of decency" of our society, it makes no sense for the justices then to *prescribe* those standards rather than discern them from the practices of our people. On the evolving-standards hypothesis, the only legitimate function of this Court is to identify a moral consensus of the American people. By what conceivable warrant can nine lawyers presume to be the authoritative conscience of the Nation?

The reason for insistence on legislative primacy is obvious and fundamental: "'[I]n a democratic society legislatures, not courts, are constituted to respond to the will and consequently the moral values of the people.'" For a similar reason we have, in our determination of society's moral standards, consulted the practices of sentencing juries: Juries "'maintain a link between contemporary community values and the penal system'" that this Court cannot claim for itself.

Today's opinion provides a perfect example of why judges are ill equipped to make the type of legislative judgments the Court insists on making here. To support its opinion that States should be prohibited from imposing the death penalty on anyone who committed murder before age 18, the Court looks to scientific and sociological studies, picking and choosing those that support its position. It never explains why those particular studies are methodologically sound; none was ever entered into evidence or tested in an adversarial proceeding. As the Chief Justice has explained:

> "[M]ethodological and other errors can affect the reliability and validity of estimates about the opinions and attitudes of a population derived from various sampling techniques. Everything from variations in the survey methodology, such as the choice of the target population, the sampling design used, the questions asked, and the statistical analyses used to interpret the data can skew the results."

In other words, all the Court has done today, to borrow from another context, is to look over the heads of the crowd and pick out its friends.

We need not look far to find studies contradicting the Court's conclusions. As petitioner points out, the American Psychological Association (APA), which claims in this case that scientific evidence shows persons under 18 lack the ability to take moral responsibility for their decisions, has previously taken precisely the opposite position before this very Court. In its brief in *Hodgson v. Minnesota,* the APA found a "rich body of research" showing that juveniles are mature enough to decide whether to obtain an abortion without parental involvement. The APA brief, citing psychology treatises and studies too numerous to list here, asserted: "[B]y middle adolescence (age 14–15) young people develop abilities similar to adults in reasoning about moral dilemmas, understanding social rules and laws, [and] reasoning about interpersonal relationships and interpersonal problems." Given the nuances of scientific methodology and conflicting views, courts—which can only consider the limited evidence on the record before them—are ill equipped to determine which view of science is the right one. Legislatures "are better qualified to weigh and 'evaluate the results of statistical studies in terms of their own local conditions and with a flexibility of approach that is not available to the courts.'"

Even putting aside questions of methodology, the studies cited by the Court offer scant support for a categorical prohibition of the death penalty for murderers under 18. At most, these studies conclude that, *on average,* or *in most cases,* persons under 18 are unable to take moral responsibility for their actions. Not one of the cited studies opines that all individuals under 18 are unable to appreciate the nature of their crimes.

Moreover, the cited studies describe only adolescents who engage in risky or antisocial behavior, as many young people do. Murder, however, is more than just risky or antisocial behavior. It is entirely consistent to believe that young people often act impetuously and lack judgment, but, at the same time, to believe that those who commit premeditated murder are—at least sometimes—just as culpable as adults. Christopher Simmons, who was only seven months shy of his 18th birthday when he murdered Shirley Crook, described to his friends *beforehand*—"[i]n chilling, callous terms," as the Court puts it—the murder he planned to commit. He then broke into the home of an innocent woman, bound her with duct tape and electrical wire, and threw her off a bridge alive and conscious. In their *amici* brief, the States of Alabama, Delaware, Oklahoma, Texas, Utah, and Virginia offer additional examples of murders committed by individuals under 18 that involve truly monstrous acts. In Alabama, two 17-year-olds, one 16-year-old, and one 19-year-old picked up a female hitchhiker, threw bottles at her, and kicked and stomped her for approximately 30 minutes until she died. They then sexually assaulted her lifeless body and, when they were finished, threw her body off a cliff. They later returned to the crime scene to mutilate her corpse. Other examples in the brief are equally shocking. Though these cases are assuredly the exception rather than the rule, the studies the Court cites in no way justify a constitutional imperative that prevents legislatures and juries from treating exceptional cases in an exceptional way—by determining that some murders are not just the acts of happy-go-lucky teenagers, but heinous crimes deserving of death.

That "almost every State prohibits those under 18 years of age from voting, serving on juries, or marrying without parental consent," is patently irrelevant—and is yet another resurrection of an argument that this Court gave a decent burial in *Stanford*. (What kind of Equal Justice under Law is it that—without so much as a "Sorry about that"—gives as the basis for sparing one person from execution arguments *explicitly rejected* in refusing to spare another?) As we explained in *Stanford*, it is "absurd to think that one must be mature enough to drive carefully, to drink responsibly, or to vote intelligently, in order to be mature enough to understand that murdering another human being is profoundly wrong, and to conform one's conduct to that most minimal of all civilized standards." Serving on a jury or entering into marriage also involve decisions far more sophisticated than the simple decision not to take another's life.

Moreover, the age statutes the Court lists "set the appropriate ages for the operation of a system that makes its determinations in gross, and that does not conduct individualized maturity tests." The criminal justice system, by contrast, provides for individualized consideration of each defendant. In capital cases, this Court requires the sentencer to make an individualized determination, which includes weighing aggravating factors and mitigating factors, such as youth. In other contexts where individualized consideration is provided, we have recognized that at least some minors will be mature enough to make difficult decisions that involve moral considerations. For instance, we have struck down abortion statutes that do not allow minors deemed mature by courts to bypass parental notification provisions. It is hard to see why this context should be any different. Whether to obtain an abortion is surely a much more complex decision for a young person than whether to kill an innocent person in cold blood.

The Court concludes, however, that juries cannot be trusted with the delicate task of weighing a defendant's youth along with the other mitigating and aggravating factors of his crime. This startling conclusion undermines the very foundations of our capital sentencing system, which entrusts juries with "mak[ing] the difficult and uniquely human judgments that defy codification and that 'buil[d] discretion, equity, and flexibility into a legal system.'" The Court says that juries will be unable to appreciate the significance of a defendant's youth when faced with details of a brutal crime. This assertion is based on no evidence; to the contrary, the Court itself acknowledges that the execution of under-18 offenders is "infrequent" even in the States "without a formal prohibition on executing juveniles," suggesting that juries take seriously their responsibility to weigh youth as a mitigating factor.

Nor does the Court suggest a stopping point for its reasoning. If juries cannot make appropriate determinations in cases involving murderers under 18, in what other kinds of cases will the Court find jurors deficient? We have already held that no jury may consider whether a mentally deficient defendant can receive the death penalty, irrespective of his crime. Why not take other mitigating factors, such as considerations of childhood abuse or poverty, away from juries as well? Surely jurors "overpower[ed]" by "the brutality or cold-blooded nature" of a crime, could not adequately weigh these mitigating factors either.

The Court's contention that the goals of retribution and deterrence are not served by executing murderers under 18 is also transparently false. The argument that "[r]etribution is not proportional if the law's most severe penalty is imposed on one whose culpability or blameworthiness is diminished," is simply an extension of the earlier, false generalization that youth *always* defeats culpability. The Court claims that "juveniles will be less susceptible to deterrence," because "'[t]he likelihood that the teenage offender has made the kind of cost-benefit analysis that attaches any weight to the possibility of execution is so remote as to be virtually nonexistent.'" The Court unsurprisingly finds no support for this astounding proposition, save its own case law. The facts of this very case show the proposition to be false. Before committing the crime, Simmons encouraged his friends to join him by assuring them that they could "get away with it" because they were minors. This fact may have influenced the jury's decision to impose capital punishment despite Simmons' age. Because the Court refuses to entertain the possibility that its own unsubstantiated generalization about juveniles could be wrong, it ignores this evidence entirely.

III

Though the views of our own citizens are essentially irrelevant to the Court's decision today, the views of other countries and the so-called international community take center stage.

The Court begins by noting that "Article 37 of the United Nations Convention on the Rights of the Child, which every country in the world has ratified *save for the United States* and Somalia, contains an express prohibition on capital punishment for crimes committed by juveniles under 18." ...

Unless the Court has added to its arsenal the power to join and ratify treaties on behalf of the United States, I cannot see how this evidence favors, rather than refutes, its position. That the Senate and the President—those actors our Constitution empowers to enter into treaties, see Art. II, § 2—have declined to join and ratify treaties prohibiting execution of under-18 offenders can only suggest that *our country* has either not reached a national consensus on the question, or has reached a consensus contrary to what the Court announces. That the reservation to the ICCPR was made in 1992 does not suggest otherwise, since the reservation still remains in place today. It is also worth noting that, in addition to barring the execution of under-18 offenders, the United Nations Convention on the Rights of the Child prohibits punishing them with life in prison without the possibility of release. If we are truly going to get in line with the international community, then the Court's reassurance that the death penalty is really not needed, since "the punishment of life imprisonment without the possibility of parole is itself a severe sanction," gives little comfort.

It is interesting that whereas the Court is not content to accept what the States of our Federal Union *say*, but insists on inquiring into what they *do* (specifically, whether they in fact *apply* the juvenile death penalty that their laws allow), the Court is quite willing to believe that every foreign nation—of whatever tyrannical political makeup and with however subservient or incompetent a court system—in fact *adheres* to a rule of no death penalty for offenders under 18. Nor does the Court inquire into how many of the countries that have the death penalty, but have forsworn (on paper at least) imposing that penalty on offenders under 18, have what no State of this country can constitutionally have: a *mandatory* death penalty for certain crimes, with no possibility of mitigation by the sentencing authority, for youth or any other reason. I suspect it is most of them. To forbid the death penalty for juveniles under such a system may be a good idea, but it says nothing about our system, in which the sentencing authority, typically a jury, always can, and almost always does, withhold the death penalty from an under-18 offender except, after considering all the circumstances, in the rare cases where it is warranted. The foreign authorities, in other words, do not even speak to the issue before us here.

More fundamentally, however, the basic premise of the Court's argument—that American law should conform to the laws of the rest of the world—ought to be rejected out of hand. In fact the Court itself does not believe it. In many significant respects the laws of most other countries differ from our law—including not only such explicit provisions of our Constitution as the right to jury trial and grand jury indictment, but even many interpretations of the Constitution prescribed by this Court itself. ...

The Court has been oblivious to the views of other countries when deciding how to interpret our Constitution's requirement that "Congress shall make no law respecting an establishment of religion. . . ." Most other countries—including those committed to religious neutrality—do not insist on the degree of separation between church and state that this Court requires. . . .

And let us not forget the Court's abortion jurisprudence, which makes us one of only six countries that allow abortion on demand until the point of viability. . . .

The Court's special reliance on the laws of the United Kingdom is perhaps the most indefensible part of its opinion. It is of course true that we share a common history with the United Kingdom, and that we often consult English sources when asked to discern the meaning of a constitutional text written against the backdrop of 18th-century English law and legal thought. If we applied that approach today, our task would be an easy one. . . . It is beyond comprehension why we should look, for that purpose, to a country that has developed, in the centuries since the Revolutionary War—and with increasing speed since the United Kingdom's recent submission to the jurisprudence of European courts dominated by continental jurists—a legal, political, and social culture quite different from our own. If we took the Court's directive seriously, we would also consider relaxing our double jeopardy prohibition, since the British Law Commission recently published a report that would significantly extend the rights of the prosecution to appeal cases where an acquittal was the result of a judge's ruling that was legally incorrect. . . .

The Court should either profess its willingness to reconsider all these matters in light of the views of foreigners, or else it should cease putting forth foreigners' views as part of the *reasoned basis* of its decisions. To invoke alien law when it agrees with one's own thinking, and ignore it otherwise, is not reasoned decisionmaking, but sophistry.

The Court responds that "[i]t does not lessen our fidelity to the Constitution or our pride in its origins to acknowledge that the express affirmation of certain fundamental rights by other nations and peoples simply underscores the centrality of those same rights within our own heritage of freedom." To begin with, I do not believe that approval by "other nations and peoples" should buttress our commitment to American principles any more than (what should logically follow) disapproval by "other nations and peoples" should weaken that commitment. More importantly, however, the Court's statement flatly misdescribes what is going on here. Foreign sources are cited today, *not* to underscore our "fidelity" to the Constitution, our "pride in its origins," and "our own [American] heritage." To the contrary, they are cited *to set aside* the centuries-old American practice—a practice still engaged in by a large majority of the relevant States—of letting a jury of 12 citizens decide whether, in the particular case, youth should be the basis for withholding the death penalty. What these foreign sources "affirm," rather than repudiate, is the justices' own notion of how the world ought to be, and their diktat that it shall be so henceforth in America. The Court's parting attempt to downplay the significance of its extensive discussion of foreign law is unconvincing. "Acknowledgment" of foreign approval has no place in the legal opinion of this Court *unless it is part of the basis for the Court's judgment*—which is surely what it parades as today.

IV

To add insult to injury, the Court affirms the Missouri Supreme Court without even admonishing that court for its flagrant disregard of our precedent in *Stanford*. Until today, we have always held that "it is this Court's prerogative alone to overrule one of its precedents." That has been true even where "'changes in judicial doctrine' ha[ve] significantly undermined" our prior holding, and even where our prior holding "appears to rest on reasons rejected in some other line of decisions." Today, however, the Court silently approves a state-court decision that blatantly rejected controlling precedent.

One must admit that the Missouri Supreme Court's action, and this Court's indulgent reaction, are, in a way, understandable. In a system based upon constitutional and statutory text democratically adopted, the concept of "law" ordinarily signifies that particular words have a fixed meaning. Such law does not change, and this Court's pronouncement of it therefore remains authoritative until (confessing our prior error) we overrule. The Court has purported to make of the Eighth Amendment, however, a mirror of the passing and changing sentiment of American society regarding penology. The lower courts can look into that mirror as well as we can; and what we saw 15 years ago bears no necessary relationship to what they see today. Since they are not looking at the same text, but at a different scene, why should our earlier decision control their judgment?

However sound philosophically, this is no way to run a legal system. We must disregard the new reality that, to the extent our Eighth Amendment decisions constitute something more than a show of hands on the current justices' current personal views about penology, they purport to be nothing more than a snapshot of American public opinion at a particular point in time (with the timeframes now shortened to a mere 15 years). We must treat these decisions just as though they represented *real* law, *real* prescriptions democratically adopted by the American people, as conclusively (rather than sequentially) construed by this Court. Allowing lower courts to reinterpret the Eighth Amendment whenever they decide enough time has passed for a new snapshot leaves this Court's decisions without any force—especially since the "evolution" of our Eighth Amendment is no longer determined by objective criteria. To allow lower courts to behave as we do, "updating" the Eighth Amendment as needed, destroys stability and makes our case law an unreliable basis for the designing of laws by citizens and their representatives, and for action by public officials. The result will be to crown arbitrariness with chaos.

POSTSCRIPT

Is the Death Penalty an Unconstitutional Punishment for Juvenile Offenders?

The opinion poll results we examined in the introduction to this issue provided some very interesting information. First, support for the death penalty when the alternative of sentencing someone to a life term in prison without the possibility of parole was provided was equivocal—as many Americans supported the imprisonment option as favored the death penalty. Second, only a small number of Americans support using the death penalty for criminals who committed their crimes as juveniles. This would seem to support Justice Anthony M. Kennedy's position that the "evolving standards of decency that mark the progress of a maturing society" would counsel against imposition of the death penalty for juveniles.

Moreover, the United States was the only Western nation that still permitted individuals to be executed for the crimes they committed as juveniles. Although this factor did not appear to be the sole motivation for the Court's decision in *Roper v. Simmons,* that fact did seem to influence some of the justices. Justice Kennedy noted this fact:

> Article 37 of the United Nations Convention on the Rights of the Child, which every country in the world has ratified save for the United States and Somalia, contains an express prohibition on capital punishment for crimes committed by juveniles under 18. . . . [O]nly seven countries other than the United States have executed juvenile offenders since 1990: Iran, Pakistan, Saudi Arabia, Yemen, Nigeria, the Democratic Republic of Congo, and China. Since then each of these countries has either abolished capital punishment for juveniles or made public disavowal of the practice.

Do you think that the justice system policies of other nations should influence penal practices in the United States? If the United States is out of step with the world community, should we not search consciences to determine if we have made a serious mistake?

Another significant issue surrounding the use of capital punishment that has become prominent in recent years is the fact that our justice system has made mistakes in the past. A 2002 study conducted by Columbia Law School Professor James Liebman concluded that "aggressive death sentencing is a magnet for serious error." Liebman's study, which tried to answer the question of why so many mistakes happen in death penalty cases, found that 68 percent of all death verdicts reviewed from 1973 to 1995 were reversed by courts.

Of these reversals, 82 percent resulted in less severe sentences, and 9 percent of these individuals were found not guilty. Moreover, Liebman observes that since the death penalty was reinstituted in the United States in 1973, 99 death row inmates have been found innocent and released.

These data indicate that our justice system makes mistakes. If a convicted offender is sentenced to prison and it later becomes clear that he or she did not commit the crime, society can release the individual and provide appropriate compensation. If we have executed the accused, however, there is no way to rectify the mistake. The finality of the death penalty thus makes it unlike any other type of sentence in our justice system. This fact may make this punishment even more questionable in cases involving juvenile offenders.

There are many additional resources that shed light on the issues considered in this section. See: Mary Ann Mason, "The U.S. and the International Children's Rights Crusade: Leader or Laggard," *Journal of Social History*, vol. 38, no. 4 (2005); Robert H. Bork, "Travesty Time, Again," *National Review*, vol. 57, no. 5 (2005); Kenneth Anderson, "Foreign Law and the U.S. Constitution," *Policy Review*, vol. 131 (2005); Jeffrey Fagan and Valerie West, "The Decline of the Juvenile Death Penalty: Scientific Evidence of Evolving Norms," *Journal of Criminal Law & Criminology*, vol. 95, no. 2 (2005); James Liebman, Andrew Gelman, Alexander Kiss, and Valerie West, "A Broken System: The Persistent Pattern of Reversals of Death Penalty Cases," *Journal of Empirical Legal Studies*, vol. 1, no. 209 (2004); James D. Unnever and Francis Cullen, "Executing the Innocent and Support for Capital Punishment: Implications for Public Policy," *Criminology & Public Policy*, vol. 4, no. 1 (2005); Lucy C. Ferguson, "The Implications of Developmental Cognitive Research on 'Evolving Standards of Decency' and the Imposition of the Death Penalty on Juveniles," *American University Law Review*, vol. 54, no. 2 (2004); Donna M. Bishop, "Injustice and Irrationality in Contemporary Youth Policy," *Criminology & Public Policy*, vol. 3, no. 4 (2004); Scott Vollum, Dennis R. Longmire, and Jacqueline Buffinton-Vollum, "Confidence in the Death Penalty and Support for Its Use: Exploring the Value-Expressive Dimension of Death Penalty Attitudes," *Justice Quarterly*, vol. 21, no. 3 (2004); and Michael E. Antonio, Benjamin D. Fleury-Steiner, Valerie P. Hans, and William J. Bowers, "Capital Jurors as the Litmus Test of Community Conscience for the Juvenile Death Penalty," *Judicature*, vol. 87, no. 6 (2004).

Internet References . . .

United States Courts

This Web site provides information from and about the Judicial Branch of the U.S. government.

http://www.uscourts.gov/Home.aspx

The Oyez Project

Multimedia archive devoted to the Supreme Court and its work.

http://www.oyez.org/

Equal Protection of Law

*T*he Equal Protection Clause of the Fourteenth Amendment provides that no state shall "deny to any person within its jurisdiction the
equal protection of the laws." U.S. Supreme Court interpretations of this
important source of rights have been controversial and highly compelling
throughout our history. Many would argue that some of the brightest
moments in Supreme Court history have resulted from its equal protection
jurisprudence and efforts to ensure equality for all persons throughout our
nation.

- Does the U.S. Constitution Require that Public Institutions and Facilities be Racially Integrated?

- Are "Affirmative Action" Admissions Policies at Public Universities Permitted by the Constitution?

- Does the Fourteenth Amendment Require the States to Use a "One Person, One Vote" Standard for Apportioning Legislative Districts?

ISSUE 15

Does the U.S. Constitution Require that Public Institutions and Facilities be Racially Integrated?

YES: Earl Warren, from Majority Opinion, *Brown v. Board of Education of Topeka, Kansas,* 347 U.S. 483 (1954)

NO: Henry B. Brown, from Majority Opinion, *Plessy v. Ferguson,* 163 U.S. 537 (1896)

ISSUE SUMMARY

YES: Chief Justice Earl Warren, writing for the U.S. Supreme Court in *Brown v. Board of Education of Topeka,* held that state laws that segregate white and black children solely on the basis of race deny to African American children their Fourteenth Amendment right to the equal protection of law. Warren also expressly rejected the "separate but equal" doctrine developed in *Plessy v. Ferguson* (1896).

NO: In contrast, Justice Henry B. Brown, writing for the Court in *Plessy v. Ferguson,* held that Louisiana's law providing for "separate but equal" accommodations for persons of different races on passenger trains does not violate the Thirteenth or Fourteenth Amendment to the U.S. Constitution.

$\mathbf{F}$ew issues in U.S. history have been as divisive socially as those involving race. In 1868, in the aftermath of the Civil War, the United States adopted the Thirteenth, Fourteenth, and Fifteenth Amendments to the U.S. Constitution. These "post–Civil War Amendments" were designed specifically to address issues involving the assimilation of former slaves as full persons and active participants in American society. You may recall that the Supreme Court had held in the infamous *Dred Scott* case (*Scott v. Sandford,* 60 U.S. 393 (1856)) that "descendents of Africans, [who] were sold as slaves" were not U.S. citizens entitled to use the federal courts to sue for their freedom.

The Thirteenth Amendment, ratified in 1865, provided: "Neither slavery nor involuntary servitude, except as a punishment for crime," shall exist in the

United States, or any place subject to its jurisdiction. The Fourteenth Amendment, ratified in 1868, placed specific restrictions on state laws. Section 1 provides: "No State shall make or enforce any law which shall abridge the privileges or immunities of citizens of the United States; nor shall any State deprive any person of life, liberty, or property without due process of law; nor deny to any person within its jurisdiction the equal protection of the laws." The Fifteenth Amendment, ratified in 1870, provided that a person's right to vote could not be denied or abridged "on account of race, color, or previous condition of servitude."

Following the conclusion of the Civil War, many of the former slave-holding states did not give up the institution of slavery easily, however. In the aftermath of the War, many of them had passed laws designed to keep the former slaves from exercising their rights as citizens. *Jim Crow laws* were developed throughout the South to disenfranchise many African Americans and uneducated white people through a variety of devices including, among other things, poll taxes and literacy tests that were required to cast their votes in all elections. In addition, many of the same states had passed racial segregation laws to separate whites from blacks.

In 1890, the state of Louisiana had passed a law that required separate accommodations for whites and blacks on public railroad trains. Two years later, Homer Plessy, who was one-eighth African American and appeared to be "white," decided to test the law and purchased a first-class ticket on a railroad train traveling to New Orleans. After he had boarded the train and sat in the "whites only" car, he informed the conductor of his heritage. When Plessy refused to leave the car, he was arrested and confined in a New Orleans jail to await trial for violating the Louisiana segregation law.

On appeal to the U.S. Supreme Court, Justice Henry B. Brown held that the "separate but equal" principle did not violate the U.S. Constitution. Plessy had argued that the Louisiana law had violated both the Thirteenth and Fourteenth Amendments. Addressing Plessy's Thirteenth Amendment argument, Justice Brown, quoting an earlier Supreme Court case, stated:

> It would be running the slavery argument into the ground to make every act of discrimination which a person may see fit to make as to the guests he will entertain, or as to the people he will take into his coach or cab or car, or admit to his concert or theatre, or deal with in other matters of intercourse or business.

Justice Brown concluded further that the Louisiana law did not violate the Fourteenth Amendment as well. Stated Brown:

> The object of the amendment was undoubtedly to enforce the absolute equality of the two races before the law, but, in the nature of things, it could not have been intended to abolish distinctions based upon color, or to enforce social, as distinguished from political, equality or a commingling of the two races upon terms unsatisfactory to either. Laws permitting, and even requiring, their separation in places where they are liable to be brought into contact do not necessarily imply the inferiority of either race to the other, and have been generally, if not

universally, recognized as within the competency of the state legislatures in the exercise of their police power.

    Plessy v. Ferguson then held that the Fourteenth Amendment's Equal Protection Clause protected African Americans only from legal inequality, but not from the pernicious effects of social inequality. Moreover, its "separate but equal" doctrine would continue to guide state laws for approximately the next 50 years.

    Another aspect of *Plessy v. Ferguson* that should be noted is Justice John Marshall Harlan's prescient dissenting opinion. Stated Justice Harlan:

> Everyone knows that the statute in question had its origin in the purpose not to exclude white persons from railroad cars occupied by blacks as to exclude colored people from coaches occupied by or assigned to white persons. The thing to accomplish was, under the guise of giving equal accommodation for whites and blacks, to compel the latter to keep to themselves while traveling in railroad passenger coaches. . . . The fundamental objection, therefore, to the statute is that it interferes with the personal freedom of citizens. . . . If a white man and a black man choose to occupy the same public conveyance on a public highway, it is their right to do so, and no government, proceeding alone on the grounds of race, can prevent it without infringing the personal liberty of each.

    Justice Harlan's opinion was way ahead of its time. When you read the excerpts from *Brown v. Board of Education of Topeka* (1954), which was written approximately 58 years after *Plessy*, you will notice a strong similarity between Justice Harlan's reasoning and that of Chief Justice Earl Warren, the author of *Brown*. Before considering *Brown* in more detail, however, it seems appropriate to present a brief overview of the Supreme Court's analytical framework for analyzing cases that present Fourteenth Amendment Equal Protection Clause issues.

    The Equal Protection Clause, as interpreted throughout U.S. history, requires legislatures to treat different groups of people in the same manner, unless there is a compelling reason for treating them differently. Thus, in approaching cases arising under the Equal Protection Clause that challenge the constitutionality of state or federal laws, the Supreme Court will first consider the type of trait the legislature is trying to use to distinguish between the different groups, or that try to "classify" them. Based on numerous cases that have been decided over the years, the Supreme Court has developed an effective analytical formula, or different *tiers of scrutiny*, to be applied in equal protection cases.

    Strict scrutiny will be conducted to analyze laws that use race or national origin to classify people into different groups. It will require a state to demonstrate a very compelling interest to justify its law and virtually no better way to accomplish its objective. This is an extremely difficult standard to satisfy and most laws to which strict scrutiny is applied are held unconstitutional. For example, suppose a state were to pass a law that limited attendance at a state university to white students. Assume further that it tried to justify such a law by asserting that the state university system was experiencing financial difficulty. Such a law will almost certainly be struck down by a reviewing court. First, although preserving limited financial resources may be a legitimate goal for a state's legislature, there are better ways to accomplish such a goal that do not discriminate against persons due to race, such as by limiting the salaries of overpaid university administrators.

The second tier of analysis that the Supreme Court will use in equal protection cases is termed *intermediate level scrutiny*. This is used most often for cases involving gender. It requires that the law must be substantially related to an important governmental objective. Unlike cases involving strict scrutiny, in which a law is almost certain to be held unconstitutional, the Supreme Court in these cases will scrutinize the motive behind the law as well as whether it is an effective and reasonable way to accomplish the state's objective. For example, in *Craig v. Boren*, 429 U.S. 190 (1976), the Supreme Court considered an Oklahoma law that prohibited the sale of low-alcohol beer to males under 21 and females under age 18. It held that the law was unconstitutional because it denied equal protection to males. Although the Supreme Court recognized that Oklahoma's objective of promoting traffic safety was an important one, the means it chose to accomplish its goal were "too tenuous."

The third tier of equal protection analysis is *rationality review*. To survive this analysis, a state must only demonstrate a legitimate interest to support its law and that the means it has chosen to accomplish its objective is a rational one. For example, all states have laws that provide that physicians may prescribe drugs to ill persons. If a lay person attempts to challenge this law based on the fact that it discriminates against nonphysicians, a reviewing court will uphold it: States have a legitimate interest in controlling prescription drugs and this law would be a reasonable means to accomplish the objective. Laws that regulate economic relations receive this very deferential standard of review and are almost always upheld by reviewing courts.

In contrast to the standard of review described in the preceding paragraph, the Supreme Court in *Brown v. Board of Education of Topeka* (1954) used strict scrutiny to strike down a Kansas law that mandated "separate but equal" public educational facilities for white and black students. Writing for a unanimous Supreme Court, Chief Justice Earl Warren overturned the separate but equal doctrine of *Plessy v. Ferguson*. Stated Justice Warren:

> [I]n the field of public education, the doctrine of 'separate but equal' has no place. . . . Therefore, we hold that the plaintiffs and others similarly situated . . . [have been] deprived of the equal protection of the laws guaranteed by the Fourteenth Amendment.

Brown v. Board of Education of Topeka (1954) is widely considered to be a shining moment in U.S. Supreme Court history. In a now-famous passage, Chief Justice Warren also stated: "Segregation with the sanction of law . . . has a tendency to [retard] the educational and mental development of Negro children and to deprive them of . . . the benefits they would receive in an integrated school. . . . Separate educational facilities are inherently unequal."

In Your Opinion . . .

- When you read Chief Justice Warren's majority opinion, try to discern the reasons why he concludes that separate facilities are unequal.
- Do you agree with Chief Justice Warren's reasoning?
- Could there possibly be any rational way to support *Plessy v. Ferguson's* "separate but equal" principle in modern America?

YES

Earl Warren

Majority Opinion, *Brown v. Board of Education of Topeka*

• • • **M**R. CHIEF JUSTICE WARREN delivered the opinion of the Court.

These cases come to us from the States of Kansas, South Carolina, Virginia, and Delaware. They are premised on different facts and different local conditions, but a common legal question justifies their consideration together in this consolidated opinion.[1]

In each of the cases, minors of the Negro race, through their legal representatives, seek the aid of the courts in obtaining admission to the public schools of their community on a nonsegregated basis. In each instance, they had been denied admission to schools attended by white children under laws requiring or permitting segregation according to race. This segregation was alleged to deprive the plaintiffs of the equal protection of the laws under the Fourteenth Amendment. In each of the cases other than the Delaware case, a three-judge federal district court denied relief to the plaintiffs on the so-called "separate but equal" doctrine announced by this Court in *Plessy v. Ferguson*, 163 U.S. 537. Under that doctrine, equality of treatment is accorded when the races are provided substantially equal facilities, even though these facilities be separate. In the Delaware case, the Supreme Court of Delaware adhered to that doctrine, but ordered that the plaintiffs be admitted to the white schools because of their superiority to the Negro schools.

The plaintiffs contend that segregated public schools are not "equal" and cannot be made "equal," and that hence they are deprived of the equal protection of the laws. Because of the obvious importance of the question presented, the Court took jurisdiction.[2] Argument was heard in the 1952 Term, and reargument was heard this Term on certain questions propounded by the Court.[3]

Reargument was largely devoted to the circumstances surrounding the adoption of the Fourteenth Amendment in 1868. It covered exhaustively consideration of the Amendment in Congress, ratification by the states, then-existing practices in racial segregation, and the views of proponents and opponents of the Amendment. This discussion and our own investigation convince us that, although these sources cast some light, it is not enough to resolve the problem with which we are faced. At best, they are inconclusive. The most avid proponents of the post-War Amendments undoubtedly intended them to remove all legal distinctions among "all persons born or naturalized in the

Supreme Court of the United States, 1954.

United States." Their opponents, just as certainly, were antagonistic to both the letter and the spirit of the Amendments and wished them to have the most limited effect. What others in Congress and the state legislatures had in mind cannot be determined with any degree of certainty.

An additional reason for the inconclusive nature of the Amendment's history with respect to segregated schools is the status of public education at that time.[4] In the South, the movement toward free common schools, supported by general taxation, had not yet taken hold. Education of white children was largely in the hands of private groups. Education of Negroes was almost nonexistent, and practically all of the race were illiterate. In fact, any education of Negroes was forbidden by law in some states. Today, in contrast, many Negroes have achieved outstanding success in the arts and sciences, as well as in the business and professional world. It is true that public school education at the time of the Amendment had advanced further in the North, but the effect of the Amendment on Northern States was generally ignored in the congressional debates. Even in the North, the conditions of public education did not approximate those existing today. The curriculum was usually rudimentary; ungraded schools were common in rural areas; the school term was but three months a year in many states, and compulsory school attendance was virtually unknown. As a consequence, it is not surprising that there should be so little in the history of the Fourteenth Amendment relating to its intended effect on public education.

In the first cases in this Court construing the Fourteenth Amendment, decided shortly after its adoption, the Court interpreted it as proscribing all state-imposed discriminations against the Negro race.[5] The doctrine of "separate but equal" did not make its appearance in this Court until 1896 in the case of *Plessy v. Ferguson, supra,* involving not education but transportation.[6] American courts have since labored with the doctrine for over half a century. In this Court, there have been six cases involving the "separate but equal" doctrine in the field of public education.[7] In *Cumming v. Richmond County Board of Education,* 175 U.S. 528, and *Gong Lum v. Rice,* 275 U.S. 78, the validity of the doctrine itself was not challenged.[8] In more recent cases, all on the graduate school level, inequality was found in that specific benefits enjoyed by white students were denied to Negro students of the same educational qualifications. *Missouri ex rel. Gaines v. Canada,* 305 U.S. 337; *Sipuel v. Board of Regents of University of Oklahoma,* 332 U.S. 631; *Sweatt v. Painter,* 339 U.S. 629; *McLaurin v. Oklahoma State Regents,* 339 U.S. 637. In none of these cases was it necessary to reexamine the doctrine to grant relief to the Negro plaintiff. And in *Sweatt v. Painter, supra,* the Court expressly reserved decision on the question whether *Plessy v. Ferguson* should be held inapplicable to public education.

In the instant cases, that question is directly presented. Here, unlike *Sweatt v. Painter,* there are findings below that the Negro and white schools involved have been equalized, or are being equalized, with respect to buildings, curricula, qualifications and salaries of teachers, and other "tangible" factors.[9] Our decision, therefore, cannot turn on merely a comparison of these tangible factors in the Negro and white schools involved in each of the cases. We must look instead to the effect of segregation itself on public education.

In approaching this problem, we cannot turn the clock back to 1868, when the Amendment was adopted, or even to 1896, when *Plessy v. Ferguson* was written. We must consider public education in the light of its full development and its present place in American life throughout the Nation. Only in this way it can be determined if segregation in public schools deprives these plaintiffs of the equal protection of the laws.

Today, education is perhaps the most important function of state and local governments. Compulsory school attendance laws and the great expenditures for education both demonstrate our recognition of the importance of education to our democratic society. It is required in the performance of our most basic public responsibilities, even service in the armed forces. It is the very foundation of good citizenship. Today it is a principal instrument in awakening the child to cultural values, in preparing him for later professional training, and in helping him to adjust normally to his environment. In these days, it is doubtful that any child may reasonably be expected to succeed in life if he is denied the opportunity of an education. Such an opportunity, where the state has undertaken to provide it, is a right which must be made available to all on equal terms.

We come then to the question presented: Does segregation of children in public schools solely on the basis of race, even though the physical facilities and other "tangible" factors may be equal, deprive the children of the minority group of equal educational opportunities? We believe that it does.

In *Sweatt v. Painter, supra,* in finding that a segregated law school for Negroes could not provide them equal educational opportunities, this Court relied in large part on "those qualities which are incapable of objective measurement but which make for greatness in a law school." In *McLaurin v. Oklahoma State Regents, supra,* the Court, in requiring that a Negro admitted to a white graduate school be treated like all other students, again resorted to intangible considerations: ". . . his ability to study, to engage in discussions and exchange views with other students, and, in general, to learn his profession." Such considerations apply with added force to children in grade and high schools. To separate them from others of similar age and qualifications solely because of their race generates a feeling of inferiority as to their status in the community that may affect their hearts and minds in a way unlikely ever to be undone. The effect of this separation on their educational opportunities was well stated by a finding in the Kansas case by a court which nevertheless felt compelled to rule against the Negro plaintiffs: Segregation of white and colored children in public schools has a detrimental effect upon the colored children. The impact is greater when it has the sanction of the law, for the policy of separating the races is usually interpreted as denoting the inferiority of the negro group. A sense of inferiority affects the motivation of a child to learn. Segregation with the sanction of law, therefore, has a tendency to [retard] the educational and mental development of negro children and to deprive them of some of the benefits they would receive in a racial[ly] integrated school system.[10] Whatever may have been the extent of psychological knowledge at the time of *Plessy v. Ferguson,* this finding is amply supported by modern authority.[11] Any language in *Plessy v. Ferguson* contrary to this finding is rejected.

We conclude that, in the field of public education, the doctrine of "separate but equal" has no place. Separate educational facilities are inherently unequal. Therefore, we hold that the plaintiffs and others similarly situated for whom the actions have been brought are, by reason of the segregation complained of, deprived of the equal protection of the laws guaranteed by the Fourteenth Amendment. This disposition makes unnecessary any discussion whether such segregation also violates the Due Process Clause of the Fourteenth Amendment.[12]

Because these are class actions, because of the wide applicability of this decision, and because of the great variety of local conditions, the formulation of decrees in these cases presents problems of considerable complexity. On reargument, the consideration of appropriate relief was necessarily subordinated to the primary question—the constitutionality of segregation in public education. We have now announced that such segregation is a denial of the equal protection of the laws. In order that we may have the full assistance of the parties in formulating decrees, the cases will be restored to the docket, and the parties are requested to present further argument on Questions 4 and 5 previously propounded by the Court for the reargument this Term.[13] The Attorney General of the United States is again invited to participate. The Attorneys General of the states requiring or permitting segregation in public education will also be permitted to appear as *amici curiae* upon request to do so by September 15, 1954, and submission of briefs by October 1, 1954.[14]

It is so ordered.

*Together with No. 2, *Briggs et al. v. Elliott et al.*, on appeal from the United States District Court for the Eastern District of South Carolina, argued December 9–10, 1952, reargued December 7–8, 1953; No. 4, *Davis et al. v. County School Board of Prince Edward County, Virginia, et al.*, on appeal from the United States District Court for the Eastern District of Virginia, argued December 10, 1952, reargued December 7–8, 1953, and No. 10, *Gebhart et al. v. Belton et al.*, on certiorari to the Supreme Court of Delaware, argued December 11, 1952, reargued December 9, 1953.

Notes

1. In the Kansas case, *Brown v. Board of Education*, the plaintiffs are Negro children of elementary school age residing in Topeka. They brought this action in the United States District Court for the District of Kansas to enjoin enforcement of a Kansas statute which permits, but does not require, cities of more than 15,000 population to maintain separate school facilities for Negro and white students. *Kan. Gen.Stat.* § 72-1724 (1949). Pursuant to that authority, the Topeka Board of Education elected to establish segregated elementary schools. Other public schools in the community, however, are operated on a nonsegregated basis. The three-judge District Court, convened under 28 U.S.C. §§ 2281 and 2284, found that segregation in public education has a detrimental effect upon Negro children, but denied relief on the ground that the Negro and white schools were substantially equal with respect to buildings,

transportation, curricula, and educational qualifications of teachers. 98 *F. Supp.* 797. The case is here on direct appeal under 28 U.S.C. § 1253.

In the South Carolina case, *Briggs v. Elliott,* the plaintiffs are Negro children of both elementary and high school age residing in Clarendon County. They brought this action in the United States District Court for the Eastern District of South Carolina to enjoin enforcement of provisions in the state constitution and statutory code which require the segregation of Negroes and whites in public schools. S.C.Const., Art. XI, § 7; S.C.Code § 5377 (1942). The three-judge District Court, convened under 28 U.S.C. §§ 2281 and 2284, denied the requested relief. The court found that the Negro schools were inferior to the white schools, and ordered the defendants to begin immediately to equalize the facilities. But the court sustained the validity of the contested provisions and denied the plaintiffs admission to the white schools during the equalization program. 98 F.Supp. 529. This Court vacated the District Court's judgment and remanded the case for the purpose of obtaining the court's views on a report filed by the defendants concerning the progress made in the equalization program. 342 U.S. 350. On remand, the District Court found that substantial equality had been achieved except for buildings and that the defendants were proceeding to rectify this inequality as well. 103 F.Supp. 920. The case is again here on direct appeal under 28 U.S.C. § 1253.

In the Virginia case, *Davis v. County School Board,* the plaintiffs are Negro children of high school age residing in Prince Edward County. They brought this action in the United States District Court for the Eastern District of Virginia to enjoin enforcement of provisions in the state constitution and statutory code which require the segregation of Negroes and whites in public schools. Va.Const., § 140; Va.Code § 22-221 (1950). The three-judge District Court, convened under 28 U.S.C. §§ 2281 and 2284, denied the requested relief. The court found the Negro school inferior in physical plant, curricula, and transportation, and ordered the defendants forthwith to provide substantially equal curricula and transportation and to "proceed with all reasonable diligence and dispatch to remove" the inequality in physical plant. But, as in the South Carolina case, the court sustained the validity of the contested provisions and denied the plaintiffs admission to the white schools during the equalization program. 103 *F.Supp.* 337. The case is here on direct appeal under 28 U.S.C. § 1253.

In the Delaware case, *Gebhart v. Belton,* the plaintiffs are Negro children of both elementary and high school age residing in New Castle County. They brought this action in the Delaware Court of Chancery to enjoin enforcement of provisions in the state constitution and statutory code which require the segregation of Negroes and whites in public schools. *Del.Const.,* Art. X, § 2; *Del.Rev. Code* § 2631 (1935). The Chancellor gave judgment for the plaintiffs and ordered their immediate admission to schools previously attended only by white children, on the ground that the Negro schools were inferior with respect to teacher training, pupil-teacher ratio, extracurricular activities, physical plant, and time and distance involved in travel. 87 A.2d 862. The Chancellor also found that segregation itself results in an inferior education for Negro children (*see* note 10, *infra*), but did not rest his decision on that ground. *Id.* at 865. The Chancellor's decree was affirmed by the Supreme Court of Delaware, which intimated, however, that the defendants might be able to obtain a modification of the decree after equalization of the Negro and white schools had been accomplished. 91 A.2d 137, 152. The defendants, contending only that the Delaware courts had erred in ordering the immediate admission of the Negro plaintiffs to the white schools, applied to this Court for certiorari. The writ was granted, 344 U.S. 891. The plaintiffs, who were successful below, did not submit a cross-petition.

2. 344 U.S. 1, 141, 891.

3. 345 U.S. 972. The Attorney General of the United States participated both Terms as amicus curiae.

4. For a general study of the development of public education prior to the Amendment, see Butts and Cremin, A History of Education in American Culture (1953), Pts. I, II; Cubberley, Public Education in the United States (1934 ed.), cc. II-XII. School practices current at the time of the adoption of the Fourteenth Amendment are described in Butts and Cremin, supra, at 269–275; Cubberley, supra, at 288–339, 408–431; Knight, Public Education in the South (1922), cc. VIII, IX. See also H. Ex.Doc. No. 315, 41st Cong., 2d Sess. (1871). Although the demand for free public schools followed substantially the same pattern in both the North and the South, the development in the South did not begin to gain momentum until about 1850, some twenty years after that in the North. The reasons for the somewhat slower development in the South (e.g., the rural character of the South and the different regional attitudes toward state assistance) are well explained in Cubberley, supra, at 408–423. In the country as a whole, but particularly in the South, the War virtually stopped all progress in public education. Id, at 427–428. The low status of Negro education in all sections of the country, both before and immediately after the War, is described in Beale, A History of Freedom of Teaching in American Schools (1941), 112–132, 175–195. Compulsory school attendance laws were not generally adopted until after the ratification of the Fourteenth Amendment, and it was not until 1918 that such laws were in force in all the states. Cubberley, supra, at 563–565.

5. Slaughter-House Cases, 16 Wall. 36, 67–72 (1873); *Strauder v. West Virginia*, 100 U.S. 303, 307–308 (1880): It ordains that no State shall deprive any person of life, liberty, or property, without due process of law, or deny to any person within its jurisdiction the equal protection of the laws. What is this but declaring that the law in the States shall be the same for the black as for the white; that all persons, whether colored or white, shall stand equal before the laws of the States, and, in regard to the colored race, for whose protection the amendment was primarily designed, that no discrimination shall be made against them by law because of their color? The words of the amendment, it is true, are prohibitory, but they contain a necessary implication of a positive immunity, or right, most valuable to the colored race—the right to exemption from unfriendly legislation against them distinctively as colored—exemption from legal discriminations, implying inferiority in civil society, lessening the security of their enjoyment of the rights which others enjoy, and discriminations which are steps towards reducing them to the condition of a

subject race. See also *Virginia v. Rives,* 100 U.S. 313, 318 (1880); Ex parte Virginia, 100 U.S. 339, 344–345 (1880).

6. The doctrine apparently originated in *Roberts v. City of Boston,* 59 Mass. 198, 206 (1850), upholding school segregation against attack as being violative of a state constitutional guarantee of equality. Segregation in Boston public schools was eliminated in 1855. Mass. Acts 1855, c. 256. But elsewhere in the North, segregation in public education has persisted in some communities until recent years. It is apparent that such segregation has long been a nationwide problem, not merely one of sectional concern.

7. See also *Berea College v. Kentucky,* 211 U.S. 45 (1908).

8. In the *Cumming* case, Negro taxpayers sought an injunction requiring the defendant school board to discontinue the operation of a high school for white children until the board resumed operation of a high school for Negro children. Similarly, in the *Gong Lum* case, the plaintiff, a child of Chinese descent, contended only that state authorities had misapplied the doctrine by classifying him with Negro children and requiring him to attend a Negro school.

9. In the Kansas case, the court below found substantial equality as to all such factors. 98 F.Supp. 797, 798. In the South Carolina case, the court below found that the defendants were proceeding "promptly and in good faith to comply with the court's decree." 103 F. Supp. 920, 921. In the Virginia case, the court below noted that the equalization program was already "afoot and progressing" (103 *F.Supp.* 337, 341); since then, we have been advised, in the Virginia Attorney General's brief on reargument, that the program has now been completed. In the Delaware case, the court below similarly noted that the state's equalization program was well under way. 91 A. 2d 137, 149.

10. A similar finding was made in the Delaware case: I conclude from the testimony that, in our Delaware society, State-imposed segregation in education itself results in the Negro children, as a class, receiving educational opportunities which are substantially inferior to those available to white children otherwise similarly situated. 87 A.2d 862, 865.

11. K.B. Clark, Effect of Prejudice and Discrimination on Personality Development (Mid-century White House Conference on Children and Youth, 1950); Witmer and Kotinsky, Personality in the Making (1952), c. VI; Deutscher and Chein, The Psychological Effects of Enforced Segregation: A Survey of Social Science Opinion, 26 *J. Psychol.* 259 (1948); Chein, What are the Psychological Effects of Segregation Under Conditions of Equal Facilities?, 3 *Int. J. Opinion and Attitude Res.* 229 (1949); Brameld, *Educational Costs, in Discrimination and National Welfare* (MacIver, ed., 1949), 44–48; Frazier, *The Negro in the United States* (1949), 674–681. And see generally Myrdal, *An American Dilemma* (1944).

12. See *Bolling v. Sharpe,* post, p. 497, concerning the Due Process Clause of the Fifth Amendment.

13. Assuming it is decided that segregation in public schools violates the Fourteenth Amendment (a) would a decree necessarily follow providing that, within the limits set by normal geographic school districting, Negro children should forthwith be admitted to schools of their choice, or

(b) may this Court, in the exercise of its equity powers, permit an effective gradual adjustment to be brought about from existing segregated systems to a system not based on color distinctions? 5. On the assumption on which questions 4(a) and (b) are based, and assuming further that this Court will exercise its equity powers to the end described in question 4 (b),(a) should this Court formulate detailed decrees in these cases; (b) if so, what specific issues should the decrees reach; (c) should this Court appoint a special master to hear evidence with a view to recommending specific terms for such decrees; (d) should this Court remand to the courts of first instance with directions to frame decrees in these cases and, if so, what general directions should the decrees of this Court include and what procedures should the courts of first instance follow in arriving at the specific terms of more detailed decrees?

14. See Rule 42, Revised Rules of this Court (effective July 1, 1954).

Henry B. Brown

 **NO**

Majority Opinion, *Plessy v. Ferguson*

MR. JUSTICE BROWN, after stating the case, delivered the opinion of the court.
This case turns upon the constitutionality of an act of the General Assembly of the State of Louisiana, passed in 1890, providing for separate railway carriages for the white and colored races. Acts 1890, No. 111, p. 152.

The first section of the statute enacts

> that all railway companies carrying passengers in their coaches in this State shall provide equal but separate accommodations for the white and colored races by providing two or more passenger coaches for each passenger train, or by dividing the passenger coaches by a partition so as to secure separate accommodations: *Provided,* That this section shall not be construed to apply to street railroads. No person or persons, shall be admitted to occupy seats in coaches other than the ones assigned to them on account of the race they belong to.

By the second section, it was enacted

> that the officers of such passenger trains shall have power and are hereby required to assign each passenger to the coach or compartment used for the race to which such passenger belongs; any passenger insisting on going into a coach or compartment to which by race he does not belong shall be liable to a fine of twenty-five dollars, or in lieu thereof to imprisonment for a period of not more than twenty days in the parish prison, and any officer of any railroad insisting on assigning a passenger to a coach or compartment other than the one set aside for the race to which said passenger belongs shall be liable to a fine of twenty-five dollars, or in lieu thereof to imprisonment for a period of not more than twenty days in the parish prison; and should any passenger refuse to occupy the coach or compartment to which he or she is assigned by the officer of such railway, said officer shall have power to refuse to carry such passenger on his train, and for such refusal neither he nor the railway company which he represents shall be liable for damages in any of the courts of this State.

The third section provides penalties for the refusal or neglect of the officers, directors, conductors, and employees of railway companies to comply with the act, with a proviso that "nothing in this act shall be construed as

Supreme Court of the United States, 1896.

applying to nurses attending children of the other race." The fourth section is immaterial.

The information filed in the criminal District Court charged in substance that Plessy, being a passenger between two stations within the State of Louisiana, was assigned by officers of the company to the coach used for the race to which he belonged, but he insisted upon going into a coach used by the race to which he did not belong. Neither in the information nor plea was his particular race or color averred. The petition for the writ of prohibition averred that petitioner was seven-eighths Caucasian and one-eighth African blood; that the mixture of colored blood was not discernible in him, and that he was entitled to every right, privilege and immunity secured to citizens of the United States of the white race; and that, upon such theory, he took possession of a vacant seat in a coach where passengers of the white race were accommodated, and was ordered by the conductor to vacate said coach and take a seat in another assigned to persons of the colored race, and, having refused to comply with such demand, he was forcibly ejected with the aid of a police officer, and imprisoned in the parish jail to answer a charge of having violated the above act.

The constitutionality of this act is attacked upon the ground that it conflicts both with the Thirteenth Amendment of the Constitution, abolishing slavery, and the Fourteenth Amendment, which prohibits certain restrictive legislation on the part of the States.

1. That it does not conflict with the Thirteenth Amendment, which abolished slavery and involuntary servitude, except as a punishment for crime, is too clear for argument. Slavery implies involuntary servitude—a state of bondage; the ownership of mankind as a chattel, or at least the control of the labor and services of one man for the benefit of another, and the absence of a legal right to the disposal of his own person, property and services. This amendment was said in the *Slaughterhouse Cases,* 16 Wall. 36, to have been intended primarily to abolish slavery as it had been previously known in this country, and that it equally forbade Mexican peonage or the Chinese coolie trade when they amounted to slavery or involuntary servitude, and that the use of the word "servitude" was intended to prohibit the use of all forms of involuntary slavery, of whatever class or name. It was intimated, however, in that case that this amendment was regarded by the statesmen of that day as insufficient to protect the colored race from certain laws which had been enacted in the Southern States, imposing upon the colored race onerous disabilities and burdens and curtailing their rights in the pursuit of life, liberty and property to such an extent that their freedom was of little value; and that the Fourteenth Amendment was devised to meet this exigency.

So, too, in the *Civil Rights Cases,* 109 U.S. 3, 24, it was said that the act of a mere individual, the owner of an inn, a public conveyance or place of amusement, refusing accommodations to colored people cannot be justly regarded as imposing any badge of slavery or servitude upon the applicant, but only as involving an ordinary civil injury, properly cognizable by the laws of the State and presumably subject to redress by those laws until the contrary appears.

"It would be running the slavery argument into the ground," said Mr. Justice Bradley,

> to make it apply to every act of discrimination which a person may see fit to make as to the guests he will entertain, or as to the people he will take into his coach or cab or car, or admit to his concert or theatre, or deal with in other matters of intercourse or business.

A statute which implies merely a legal distinction between the white and colored races—a distinction which is founded in the color of the two races and which must always exist so long as white men are distinguished from the other race by color—has no tendency to destroy the legal equality of the two races, or reestablish a state of involuntary servitude. Indeed, we do not understand that the Thirteenth Amendment is strenuously relied upon by the plaintiff in error in this connection.

2. By the Fourteenth Amendment, all persons born or naturalized in the United States and subject to the jurisdiction thereof are made citizens of the United States and of the State wherein they reside, and the States are forbidden from making or enforcing any law which shall abridge the privileges or immunities of citizens of the United States, or shall deprive any person of life, liberty, or property without due process of law, or deny to any person within their jurisdiction the equal protection of the laws.

The proper construction of this amendment was first called to the attention of this court in the *Slaughterhouse Cases,* 16 Wall. 36, which involved, however, not a question of race, but one of exclusive privileges. The case did not call for any expression of opinion as to the exact rights it was intended to secure to the colored race, but it was said generally that its main purpose was to establish the citizenship of the negro, to give definitions of citizenship of the United States and of the States, and to protect from the hostile legislation of the States the privileges and immunities of citizens of the United States, as distinguished from those of citizens of the States.

The object of the amendment was undoubtedly to enforce the absolute equality of the two races before the law, but, in the nature of things, it could not have been intended to abolish distinctions based upon color, or to enforce social, as distinguished from political, equality, or a commingling of the two races upon terms unsatisfactory to either. Laws permitting, and even requiring, their separation in places where they are liable to be brought into contact do not necessarily imply the inferiority of either race to the other, and have been generally, if not universally, recognized as within the competency of the state legislatures in the exercise of their police power. The most common instance of this is connected with the establishment of separate schools for white and colored children, which has been held to be a valid exercise of the legislative power even by courts of States where the political rights of the colored race have been longest and most earnestly enforced.

One of the earliest of these cases is that of *Roberts v. City of Boston,* 5 Cush. 19, in which the Supreme Judicial Court of Massachusetts held that the general school committee of Boston had power to make provision for the instruction of colored children in separate schools established exclusively for them, and to prohibit their attendance upon the other schools. "The great principle," said Chief Justice Shaw, p. 206, "advanced by the learned and eloquent advocate for the plaintiff" (Mr. Charles Sumner),

> is that, by the constitution and laws of Massachusetts, all persons without distinction of age or sex, birth or color, origin or condition, are equal before the law. . . . But when this great principle comes to be applied to the actual and various conditions of persons in society, it will not warrant the assertion that men and women are legally clothed with the same civil and political powers, and that children and adults are legally to have the same functions and be subject to the same treatment, but only that the rights of all, as they are settled and regulated by law, are equally entitled to the paternal consideration and protection of the law for their maintenance and security.

It was held that the powers of the committee extended to the establishment of separate schools for children of different ages, sexes and colors, and that they might also establish special schools for poor and neglected children, who have become too old to attend the primary school and yet have not acquired the rudiments of learning to enable them to enter the ordinary schools. Similar laws have been enacted by Congress under its general power of legislation over the District of Columbia, Rev.Stat.D.C. §§ 281, 282, 283, 310, 319, as well as by the legislatures of many of the States, and have been generally, if not uniformly, sustained by the courts. *State v. McCann,* 21 Ohio St. 198; *Lehew v. Brummell,* 15 S.W.Rep. 765; *Ward v. Flood,* 48 California 36; *Bertonneau v. School Directors,* 3 Woods 177; *People v. Gallagher,* 93 N.Y. 438; *Cory v. Carter,* 48 Indiana 897; *Dawson v. Lee,* 3 Kentucky 49.

Laws forbidding the intermarriage of the two races may be said in a technical sense to interfere with the freedom of contract, and yet have been universally recognized as within the police power of the State. *State v. Gibson,* 36 Indiana 389.

The distinction between laws interfering with the political equality of the negro and those requiring the separation of the two races in schools, theatres and railway carriages has been frequently drawn by this court. Thus, in *Strauder v. West Virginia,* 100 U.S. 303, it was held that a law of West Virginia limiting to white male persons, 21 years of age and citizens of the State, the right to sit upon juries was a discrimination which implied a legal inferiority in civil society, which lessened the security of the right of the colored race, and was a step toward reducing them to a condition of servility. Indeed, the right of a colored man that, in the selection of jurors to pass upon his life, liberty and property, there shall be no exclusion of his race and no discrimination against them because of color has been asserted in a number of cases. *Virginia v. Rives,* 100 U.S. 313; *Neal v. Delaware,* 103 U.S. 370; *Bush v. Kentucky,* 107 U.S. 110; *Gibson v. Mississippi,* 162 U.S. 565. So, where the laws of a particular locality or the charter of a particular railway corporation has provided that no person shall be excluded from the cars on account of color, we have held that this meant that persons of color should travel in the same car as white ones, and that the enactment was not satisfied by the company's providing cars assigned exclusively to people of color, though they were as good as those which they assigned exclusively to white persons. *Railroad Company v. Brown,* 17 Wall. 445.

Upon the other hand, where a statute of Louisiana required those engaged in the transportation of passengers among the States to give to all persons traveling within that State, upon vessels employed in that business, equal rights and privileges in all parts of the vessel, without distinction on account of race or color, and subjected to an action for damages the owner of such a vessel, who excluded colored passengers on account of their color from the cabin set aside by him for the use of whites, it was held to be, so far as it applied to interstate commerce, unconstitutional and void. *Hall v. De Cuir,* 95 U.S. 48. The court in this case, however, expressly disclaimed that it had anything whatever to do with the statute as a regulation of internal commerce, or affecting anything else than commerce among the States.

In the *Civil Rights Case,* 109 U.S. 3, it was held that an act of Congress entitling all persons within the jurisdiction of the United States to the full and equal enjoyment of the accommodations, advantages, facilities and privileges of inns, public conveyances, on land or water, theatres and other places of public amusement, and made applicable to citizens of every race and color, regardless of any previous condition of servitude, was unconstitutional and void upon the ground that the Fourteenth Amendment was prohibitory upon the States only, and the legislation authorized to be adopted by Congress for enforcing it was not direct legislation on matters respecting which the States were prohibited from making or enforcing certain laws, or doing certain acts, but was corrective legislation such as might be necessary or proper for counteracting and redressing the effect of such laws or acts. In delivering the opinion of the court, Mr. Justice Bradley observed that the Fourteenth Amendment

> does not invest Congress with power to legislate upon subjects that are within the domain of state legislation, but to provide modes of relief against state legislation or state action of the kind referred to. It does not authorize Congress to create a code of municipal law for the regulation of private rights, but to provide modes of redress against the operation of state laws and the action of state officers, executive or judicial, when these are subversive of the fundamental rights specified in the amendment. Positive rights and privileges are undoubtedly secured by the Fourteenth Amendment, but they are secured by way of prohibition against state laws and state proceedings affecting those rights and privileges, and by power given to Congress to legislate for the purpose of carrying such prohibition into effect, and such legislation must necessarily be predicated upon such supposed state laws or state proceedings, and be directed to the correction of their operation and effect.

Much nearer, and, indeed, almost directly in point is the case of the *Louisville, New Orleans & Texas Railway Co. v. Mississippi,* 133 U.S. 587, wherein the railway company was indicted for a violation of a statute of Mississippi enacting that all railroads carrying passengers should provide equal but separate accommodations for the white and colored races by providing two or more passenger cars for each passenger train, or by dividing the passenger cars by a partition so as to secure separate accommodations. The case was presented in a different aspect from the one under consideration, inasmuch as it was an indictment against the railway company for failing to provide the separate accommodations, but the question considered was the constitutionality of the law. In that case, the Supreme Court of Mississippi, 66 Mississippi 662, had held that the statute applied solely to commerce within the State, and that, being the construction of the state statute by its highest court, was accepted as conclusive. "If it be a matter," said the court, p. 591,

> respecting commerce wholly within a State, and not interfering with commerce between the States, then obviously there is no violation of the commerce clause of the Federal Constitution. . . . No question arises under this section as to the power of the State to separate in different compartments interstate passengers or affect in any manner the privileges and rights of such passengers. All that we can consider is whether the State has the power to require that railroad trains within her limits shall have separate accommodations for the two races; that affecting only commerce within the State is no invasion of the power given to Congress by the commerce clause.

A like course of reasoning applies to the case under consideration, since the Supreme Court of Louisiana in the case of the *State ex rel. Abbott v. Hicks, Judge, et al.,* 44 La.Ann. 770, held that the statute in question did not apply to interstate passengers, but was confined in its application to passengers traveling exclusively within the borders of the State. The case was decided largely upon the authority of *Railway Co. v. State,* 66 Mississippi 662, and affirmed by this court in 133 U.S. 587. In the present case, no question of interference with interstate commerce can possibly arise, since the East Louisiana Railway appears to have been purely a local line, with both its termini within the State of Louisiana. Similar statutes for the separation of the [two] races upon public conveyances were held to be constitutional in *West Chester &c. Railroad v. Miles,* 55 Penn. St. 209; *Day v. Owen,* 5 Michigan 520; *Chicago &c. Railway v. Williams,* 5 Illinois 185; *Chesapeake &c. Railroad v. Wells,* 85 Tennessee 613; *Memphis &c. Railroad v. Benson,* 85 Tennessee 627; *The Sue,* 22 Fed.Rep. 83; *Logwood v. Memphis &c. Railroad,* 23 Fed.Rep. 318; *McGuinn v. Forbes,* 37 Fed.Rep. 639; *People v. King,* 18 N.E.Rep. 245; *Houck v. South Pac. Railway,* 38 Fed.Rep. 226; *Heard v. Georgia Railroad Co.,* 3 Int.Com.Com'n 111; S.C., 1 *Ibid.* 428.

While we think the enforced separation of the races, as applied to the internal commerce of the State, neither abridges the privileges or immunities of the colored man, deprives him of his property without due process of law, nor denies him the equal protection of the laws within the meaning of the Fourteenth Amendment, we are not prepared to say that the conductor, in assigning passengers to the coaches according to their race, does not act at his peril, or that the provision of the second section of the act that denies to the passenger compensation in damages for a refusal to receive him into the coach in which he properly belongs is a valid exercise of the legislative power. Indeed, we understand it to be conceded by the State's Attorney that such part of the act as exempts from liability the railway company and its officers is unconstitutional. The power to assign to a particular coach obviously implies the power to determine to which race the passenger belongs, as well as the power to determine who, under the laws of the particular State, is to be deemed a white and who a colored person. This question, though indicated in the brief of the plaintiff in error, does not properly arise upon the record in this case, since the only issue made is as to the unconstitutionality of the act so far as it requires the railway to provide separate accommodations and the conductor to assign passengers according to their race.

It is claimed by the plaintiff in error that, in any mixed community, the reputation of belonging to the dominant race, in this instance the white race, is property in the same sense that a right of action or of inheritance is property. Conceding this to be so for the purposes of this case, we are unable to see how this statute deprives him of, or in any way affects his right to, such property. If he be a white man and assigned to a colored coach, he may have his action for damages against the company for being deprived of his so-called property. Upon the other hand, if he be a colored man and be so assigned, he has been deprived of no property, since he is not lawfully entitled to the reputation of being a white man.

In this connection, it is also suggested by the learned counsel for the plaintiff in error that the same argument that will justify the state legislature in requiring railways to provide separate accommodations for the two races will also authorize them to require separate cars to be provided for people whose hair is of a certain color, or who are aliens, or who belong to certain nationalities, or to enact laws requiring colored people to walk upon one side of the street and white people upon the other, or requiring white men's houses to be painted white and colored men's black, or their vehicles or business signs to be of different colors, upon the theory that one side of the street is as good as the other, or that a house or vehicle of one color is as good as one of another color. The reply to all this is that every exercise of the police power must be reasonable, and extend only to such laws as are enacted in good faith for the promotion for the public good, and not for the annoyance or oppression of a particular class. Thus, in *Yick Wo v. Hopkins,* 118 U.S. 356, it was held by this court that a municipal ordinance of the city of San Francisco to regulate the carrying on of public laundries within the limits of the municipality violated the provisions of the Constitution of the United States if it conferred upon the municipal authorities arbitrary power, at their own will and without regard to discretion, in the legal sense of the term, to give or withhold consent as to persons or places without regard to the competency of the persons applying or the propriety of the places selected for the carrying on of the business. It was held to be a covert attempt on the part of the municipality to make an arbitrary and unjust discrimination against the Chinese race. While this was the case of a municipal ordinance, a like principle has been held to apply to acts of a state legislature passed in the exercise of the police power. *Railroad Company v. Husen,* 95 U.S. 465; *Louisville & Nashville Railroad v. Kentucky,* 161 U.S. 677, and cases cited on p. 700; *Duggett v. Hudson,* 43 Ohio St. 548; *Capen v. Foster,* 12 Pick. 48;

State ex rel. Wood v. Baker, 38 Wisconsin 71; *Monroe v. Collins,* 17 Ohio St. 66; *Hulseman v. Rems,* 41 Penn. St. 396; *Orman v. Riley,* 1 California 48.

So far, then, as a conflict with the Fourteenth Amendment is concerned, the case reduces itself to the question whether the statute of Louisiana is a reasonable regulation, and, with respect to this, there must necessarily be a large discretion on the part of the legislature. In determining the question of reasonableness, it is at liberty to act with reference to the established usages, customs, and traditions of the people, and with a view to the promotion of their comfort and the preservation of the public peace and good order. Gauged by this standard, we cannot say that a law which authorizes or even requires the separation of the two races in public conveyances is unreasonable, or more obnoxious to the Fourteenth Amendment than the acts of Congress requiring separate schools for colored children in the District of Columbia, the constitutionality of which does not seem to have been questioned, or the corresponding acts of state legislatures.

We consider the underlying fallacy of the plaintiff's argument to consist in the assumption that the enforced separation of the two races stamps the colored race with a badge of inferiority. If this be so, it is not by reason of anything found in the act, but solely because the colored race chooses to put that construction upon it. The argument necessarily assumes that if, as has been more than once the case and is not unlikely to be so again, the colored race should become the dominant power in the state legislature, and should enact a law in precisely similar terms, it would thereby relegate the white race to an inferior position. We imagine that the white race, at least, would not acquiesce in this assumption. The argument also assumes that social prejudices may be overcome by legislation, and that equal rights cannot be secured to the negro except by an enforced commingling of the two races. We cannot accept this proposition. If the two races are to meet upon terms of social equality, it must be the result of natural affinities, a mutual appreciation of each other's merits, and a voluntary consent of individuals. As was said by the Court of Appeals of New York in *People v. Gallagher,* 93 N.Y. 438, 448,

> this end can neither be accomplished nor promoted by laws which conflict with the general sentiment of the community upon whom they are designed to operate. When the government, therefore, has secured to each of its citizens equal rights before the law and equal opportunities for improvement and progress, it has accomplished the end for which it was organized, and performed all of the functions respecting social advantages with which it is endowed.

Legislation is powerless to eradicate racial instincts or to abolish distinctions based upon physical differences, and the attempt to do so can only result in accentuating the difficulties of the present situation. If the civil and political rights of both races be equal, one cannot be inferior to the other civilly or politically. If one race be inferior to the other socially, the Constitution of the United States cannot put them upon the same plane.

It is true that the question of the proportion of colored blood necessary to constitute a colored person, as distinguished from a white person, is one upon which there is a difference of opinion in the different States, some holding that any visible admixture of black blood stamps the person as belonging to the colored race *(State v. Chaver,* 5 Jones [N.C.] 1, p. 11); others that it depends upon the preponderance of blood *(Gray v. State,* 4 Ohio 354; *Monroe v. Collins,* 17 Ohio St. 665); and still others that the predominance of white blood must only be in the proportion of three-fourths *(People v. Dean,* 4 Michigan 406; *Jones v. Commonwealth,* 80 Virginia 538). But these are questions to be determined under the laws of each State, and are not properly put in issue in this case. Under the allegations of his petition, it may undoubtedly become a question of importance whether, under the laws of Louisiana, the petitioner belongs to the white or colored race.

The judgment of the court below is, therefore,

Affirmed.

POSTSCRIPT

Does the U.S. Constitution Require that Public Institutions and Facilities be Racially Integrated?

This is an easy question in 2010. Unfortunately, however, the question was not such an easy one during earlier portions of our history. We discussed earlier the notion that some states were not pleased to relinquish the institution of slavery, and during Reconstruction era they had developed laws designed to disenfranchise the former slaves who were now full legal citizens. In a similar fashion, a number of states were hesitant to comply with the mandate of *Brown v. Board of Education of Topeka* (1954) and did their absolute best to resist its implementation. Chief Justice Earl Warren was not about to let the reluctant states frustrate *Brown's* desegregation mandate, however.

Approximately one year following the issuance of *Brown v. Board of Education of Topeka (Brown I)*, *Brown v. Board of Education of Topeka* (1955) *(Brown II)* came before the Supreme Court again. The Court in *Brown I* had requested further argument on the question of relief for the aggrieved parties. That is what led to *Brown II*, commonly called the "implementation decision." In the latter case, Chief Justice Warren held:

> [These] cases are remanded to the District Courts to take such proceedings and enter such orders and decrees consistent with this opinion as are necessary and proper to admit to public schools on a racially non-discriminatory basis with all deliberate speed the parties to these cases.

Thus, the U.S. District Courts were given the responsibility to supervise the implementation of public school desegregation efforts by using principles of "equity," or common sense and fairness. Moreover, the Court decided to allow the states and school boards some flexibility to implement its desegregation mandate, but required that it should be carried out "with all deliberate speed."

Issue 2 in this volume presented the question of whether U.S. Supreme Court decisions become binding precedents for future cases. Excerpts from the Court's decision in *Cooper v. Aaron*, 358 U.S. 1 (1958), also authored by Chief Justice Earl Warren, were presented and discussed. The facts giving rise to *Cooper v. Aaron* had developed in a direct response to the Supreme Court's desegregation principle established in *Brown I*. In *Cooper*, Arkansas Governor Faubus had called out the National Guard to prevent desegregation efforts in the Little Rock School system. The state and the school board had requested a two-and-a-half-year delay in implementing its desegregation plan. The Supreme Court refused to permit the Arkansas Legislature and the Governor to stonewall its desegregation efforts, however. The state had argued as well that it was not bound by the *Brown* decision because its holding governed only the immediate parties to that particular case. In other words, *Brown* had not established a precedent that nonparties were required to follow. Stated Chief Justice Warren:

> [T]he constitutional rights of children not to be discriminated against in school admission on grounds of race or color declared by this Court in the Brown case can neither be nullified openly and directly by state legislators or state executive or judicial officers, nor nullified indirectly by them through evasive schemes for segregation whether attempted "ingeniously or ingenuously."

Chief Justice Warren continued:

> The principles announced in [*Brown I*] and the obedience of the States to them, according to the command of the Constitution, are indispensable for the protection of the freedoms guaranteed by our fundamental charter for all of us. Our constitutional ideal of equal justice under law is thus made a living truth.

Cooper v. Aaron then established a limit for the Supreme Court's patience with those who had attempted to circumvent the *Brown* desegregation principle. Moreover, it settled another important constitutional issue as well: U.S. Supreme Court decisions constitute binding precedents for future cases involving persons who were not parties to the original case. Had the Supreme Court ruled otherwise, it would have wreaked havoc throughout the U.S. judicial system. Moreover, it seems plausible that if the Court had permitted the state of Arkansas to ignore *Brown*, in some regions of this country schools and other public institutions would have remained segregated well into the latter portion of the twentieth century.

Another fascinating aspect of *Brown v. Board of Education of Topeka (Brown I)* was its express rejection of *Plessy v. Ferguson's* assertion that the Constitution makes a distinction between legal and social equality. In *Plessy*, Justice Brown had stated:

> A statute which implies merely a legal distinction between the white and colored races—a distinction which is founded in the color of the two races and which must always exist so long as white men are distinguished from the other race by color—has no tendency to destroy the legal equality of the two races, or reestablish a state of involuntary servitude.

In *Brown*, Chief Justice Warren rejected this distinction by focusing on the impact of social equality on young students. Stated Warren:

> To separate [students] from others of similar age and qualifications solely because of their race generates a feeling of inferiority as to their

status in the community that may affect their hearts and minds in a way unlikely ever to be undone.

It is clear, then, that in the 58-year-period between *Plessy v. Ferguson* (1896) and *Brown v. Board of Education* (1954), the United States had evolved in its views of race relations. That progress continued in the aftermath of *Brown*, including the Civil Rights Act of 1964, the Voting Rights Act of 1965, and the development of additional important precedents by the Supreme Court.

For example, in *Loving v. Virginia*, a state law prohibited marriage between members of different races. The U.S. Supreme Court used strict scrutiny to analyze the law and held that it was unconstitutional. The statute's history had made it clear that its sole purpose was to preserve "racial integrity." It therefore violated the Equal Protection Clause of the Fourteenth Amendment.

This issue has considered the early history of the desegregation movement. Issue 16 will consider another related and challenging issue: May states make special efforts to dismantle the past vestiges of racial discrimination by developing "affirmative action" programs? This is yet another fascinating legal issue that is almost certain to generate a substantial controversy among students and teachers alike.

The issues considered in this section present a host of challenging questions. Additional resources to pursue further study in this area include: Kathleen M. Sullivan and Gerald Gunther, *Constitutional Law* (Foundation Press, 15th ed., 2004); Laurence H. Tribe, *American Constitutional Law* (Foundation Press, 2nd ed., 1988); Alpheus Thomas Mason and Donald Grier Stephenson, Jr., *American Constitutional Law* (Pearson Prentice Hall, 15th ed., 2009; 14th ed., 2005); Bernard Schwartz, *A History of the Supreme Court* (Oxford University Press, 1993); Kermit L. Hall, Paul Finkelman, and James Ely, Jr., *American Legal History: Cases and Materials* (Oxford University Press, 3rd ed., 2005); Kermit L. Hall, *The Oxford Companion to the Supreme Court of the United States* (Oxford University Press, 1992); Walter F. Murphy, James E. Fleming, Sotirios A. Barber, and Stephen Macedo, *American Constitutional Interpretation* (Foundation Press, 3rd ed., 2003); David M. O'Brien, *Constitutional Law and Politics: Struggles for Power and Government Accountability* (W.W. Norton, 6th ed., 2005); Craig R. Ducat, *Constitutional Interpretation* (Wadsworth, 9th ed., 2009); John H. Garvey, T. Alexander Aleinikoff, and Daniel A. Farber, *Modern Constitutional Theory: A Reader* (Thompson West, 5th ed., 2004). See also: Mark A. Graber, "The Price of Fame: Brown as Celebrity," *The Ohio State Law Journal*, vol. 69, p. 939 (2008); Vincent James Strickler, "Green-lighting Brown: A Cumulative-Process Conception of Judicial Impact," *The Georgia Law Review*, vol. 43, p. 785 (2009); Wendy Parker, "Limiting the Equal Protection Clause Roberts Style," *University of Miami Law Review*, vol. 63, p. 507 (2009); Randall T. Shepard, "The Changing Nature of Judicial Leadership," *Indiana Law Review*, vol. 42, p. 767 (2009); Meaghan Hines, "Fulfilling the Promise of Brown? What Parents Involved Means for Louisville and the Future of Race in Public Education," *The Notre Dame Law Review*, vol. 83, p. 2173 (2008); Angelo Ancheta, "A Constitutional Analysis of Parents Involved in *Community Schools v. Seattle School District No.1* and Voluntary School Integration Policies," *Rutgers Race & The Law Review*, vol. 10, p. 2173 (2008).

ISSUE 16

Are "Affirmative Action" Admissions Policies at Public Universities Permitted by the Constitution?

YES: **Sandra D. O'Connor,** from Majority Opinion, *Grutter v. Bollinger,* 539 U.S. 306 (2003)

NO: **William H. Rehnquist,** from Dissenting Opinion, *Grutter v. Bollinger,* 539 U.S. 306 (2003)

ISSUE SUMMARY

YES: Associate Justice Sandra D. O'Connor, writing for the U.S. Supreme Court in *Grutter v. Bollinger* (2003), held that a state law school's narrowly tailored use of race in admissions decision to further a compelling state interest in obtaining the educational benefits that flow from a diverse student body is not prohibited by the Equal Protection Clause of the Fourteenth Amendment or federal statutes.

NO: Chief Justice William H. Rehnquist, dissenting in *Grutter v. Bollinger* (2003), asserted that when it comes to the use of race, the connection between a state's interest and the means used to attain them must be precise. In this case, it is not; therefore, the use of race as an admissions criterion violates the Equal Protection Clause.

The preceding issue in this volume considered whether the Equal Protection Clause of the Fourteenth Amendment requires that public institutions and facilities be racially integrated. This issue presents a related question: the constitutionality of the use of state-sponsored affirmative action programs to attain the benefits of a diverse student body in a state law school. Just as the Supreme Court's decision in *Brown v. Board of Education of Topeka* was very controversial in 1954, its more recent treatment of "affirmative action" programs remains highly contentious today.

Affirmative action may be defined as "a special effort to recruit, hire, train, and promote members of traditionally disadvantaged groups in an attempt to remedy past and present sources of discrimination." It may be difficult to rectify past discrimination against groups of people, however, without providing them with some form of prospective advantage in current competitive social situations. When such programs are adopted, however, it is sometimes difficult to candidly rebut accusations that they constitute a reverse form of discrimination, which may also be prohibited by the Fourteenth Amendment.

The U.S. Supreme Court has attempted to navigate this difficult area of the law by striking a balance between society's efforts to rectify its past mistakes without causing an additional injustice for persons who may never have committed any form of racial discrimination whatsoever. That this effort by the Court has been somewhat successful is evidenced by the fact that an early and important precedent in this area, Justice Louis F. Powell's opinion in *Regents of the University of California v. Bakke,* 438 U.S. 265 (1978), continues to guide the analysis of these cases, many years later.

The facts that gave rise to *Bakke* focused on the admissions program at the UC Davis School of Medicine. It had reserved 16 seats in each entering class of 100 students for members of minority groups, including African Americans, Hispanics, and Asian Americans. If an applicant was a member of one of the specified groups, his or her application would then be scrutinized to determine if it reflected a past economic or educational disadvantage. Allan Bakke, a white applicant, sued the university claiming that this affirmative action program violated the Equal Protection Clause of the Fourteenth Amendment. He asserted that disadvantaged students with grade point averages and admissions test results that were lower than his had been accepted due to the program.

Although there was no formal majority opinion in *Bakke* because six of the nine justices wrote separate opinions, Justice Powell was able to forge a majority coalition for certain key propositions. First, Justice Powell held that while a university may consider race in making an admissions decision, it may not use a racial "quota" system. The university's approach in *Bakke* violated the Equal Protection Clause, because it used an inflexible reservation approach. Second, Justice Powell asserted that all racial and ethnic classifications will be subjected to strict scrutiny. You may recall from our discussion of equal protection analysis in the previous section that when the Supreme Court utilizes strict scrutiny, the challenged law or policy is often overturned. Third, and significantly for analyzing future affirmative action cases arising in educational institutions, Justice Powell held that the university's asserted goal, the "educational benefits that flow from an ethnically diverse student body," was a legitimate and important state interest; however, it was not one that was justified by the use of an inflexible racial quota system. Rather, asserted Justice Powell, an admissions system such as the one used at Harvard University provided a better model. Under this plan, race could be considered as a "plus" factor in making an admissions decision. Moreover, the Harvard Plan was viewed as superior to the one at UC Davis School of Medicine, because it had properly treated each applicant as an "individual" in the admissions process.

Bakke also had a happy ending. As a result of his lawsuit, Allan Bakke was ordered admitted to the UC Davis School of Medicine, graduated in 1982, and is currently a licensed physician.

Since *Bakke* was decided, the Supreme Court has considered many additional cases focusing on affirmative action programs sponsored by the states as well as the federal governments. In general, it has adhered to *Bakke's framework* for analyzing these cases. Although a comprehensive review of the Court's affirmative action precedents is beyond the scope of this initiative, several important cases will be considered briefly.

In *Richmond v. J.A. Croson,* 488 U.S. 469 (1989), the Supreme Court invalidated a preferential set-aside program for minority contractors under which a general contractor was required to subcontract a minimum of 30 percent of the dollar amount of all contracts with the City to Minority Business Enterprises (MBE). Justice Sandra D. O'Connor, writing for a plurality, used strict scrutiny to assess the plan and held that it was unconstitutional. The City had made no showing of the number of minority businesses *qualified to* undertake the projects, demonstrate a compelling need to remedy past discrimination, or show that the plan was sufficiently narrowly tailored to accomplish its objectives.

Likewise, *Adarand Constructors v. Pena,* 515 U.S. 200 (1995), held that federal affirmative action programs will also be subjected to strict scrutiny. This case is significant because it demonstrates that the Supreme Court will apply the same standard of review to programs developed by the federal government as it does to those sponsored by the states.

Moreover, in a more recent case, the Supreme Court, using strict scrutiny, has invalidated state programs designed to remedy racial imbalances in public school enrollments. *Parents Involved v. Seattle School District No. 1,* 127 S.Ct. 2735 (2007), held that unless there was evidence of intentional segregation, a state may not use race to assign students to public schools.

U.S. courts have also revisited the issue of affirmative action policies at state universities since *Bakke.* One such case was *Hopwood v. Texas,* 78 F.3d 932 (5th Cir. 1996). This case was decided by the U.S. Court of Appeals for the Fifth Circuit, and the U.S. Supreme Court declined to review it.

Cheryl Hopwood filed a federal lawsuit after she was rejected for admission to the University of Texas's School of Law. Hopwood asserted that while she had been denied admission, a number of minority applicants with lower test scores and grade point averages were admitted. The trial judge ruled in favor of the university and asserted that it could continue to use its race-conscious affirmative action program. The U.S. Court of Appeals struck down the use of this program, however, and held that the university could not use race as a factor in deciding which applicants to admit. Because the U.S. Supreme Court declined to review the judgment, it became the law in the Fifth Circuit, which includes the States of Texas, Louisiana, and Mississippi.

More recently, the Supreme Court considered two cases that focused on affirmative action policies used by different and highly competitive colleges at the University of Michigan. *Gratz v. Bollinger,* 539 U.S. 244 (2003), challenged Michigan's admissions policy in its College of Literature, Science, and the Arts (LSA). The class action lawsuit alleged that the plaintiffs had been denied the Equal Protection of Law under the Fourteenth Amendment. At trial, the plaintiffs established that the University of Michigan had used a 150-point scale to measure applicants. One hundred points were needed to guarantee admission and the university awarded automatically a 20-point boost to student applicants from underrepresented groups, including African Americans, Native Americans, and Hispanics.

The U.S. Supreme Court held that the point system used by the College of Literature, Science, and the Arts violated the Equal Protection Clause. Chief Justice William H. Rehnquist stated that this affirmative action policy, which automatically gave 20 points to every minority candidate for admission, was not narrowly tailored to achieve educational diversity. The Court noted that any student with a perfect SAT score received only a 12-point bonus. Quoting from *Adarand Constructors,* Chief Justice Rehnquist stated: "[A]ny person, of whatever race, has the right to demand that any governmental actor subject to the Constitution justify any racial classification subjecting that person to unequal treatment under the strictest of judicial scrutiny." The policy violated the Equal Protection Clause because it did not provide "individualized consideration" to each applicant. It was therefore not sufficiently narrowly tailored to achieve the university's compelling interest in promoting educational diversity.

In Your Opinion . . .

- As you read *Grutter v. Bollinger,* try to determine why the Supreme Court upheld the admissions program at the law school, but held that the policy violated the Equal Protection Clause.
- Do you agree with the Court's reasoning?
- Do you believe that affirmative action policies in public universities should be permitted?

YES

Sandra D. O'Connor

Majority Opinion, *Grutter v. Bollinger*

Justice O'Connor delivered the opinion of the Court.

This case requires us to decide whether the use of race as a factor in student admissions by the University of Michigan Law School (Law School) is unlawful.

I

A

The Law School ranks among the Nation's top law schools. It receives more than 3,500 applications each year for a class of around 350 students. Seeking to "admit a group of students who individually and collectively are among the most capable," the Law School looks for individuals with "substantial promise for success in law school" and "a strong likelihood of succeeding in the practice of law and contributing in diverse ways to the well-being of others." App. 110. More broadly, the Law School seeks "a mix of students with varying backgrounds and experiences who will respect and learn from each other." *Ibid.* In 1992, the dean of the Law School charged a faculty committee with crafting a written admissions policy to implement these goals. In particular, the Law School sought to ensure that its efforts to achieve student body diversity complied with this Court's most recent ruling on the use of race in university admissions. See *Regents of Univ. of Cal. v. Bakke,* 438 U.S. 265 (1978). Upon the unanimous adoption of the committee's report by the Law School faculty, it became the Law School's official admissions policy.

The hallmark of that policy is its focus on academic ability coupled with a flexible assessment of applicants' talents, experiences, and potential "to contribute to the learning of those around them." App. 111. The policy requires admissions officials to evaluate each applicant based on all the information available in the file, including a personal statement, letters of recommendation, and an essay describing the ways in which the applicant will contribute to the life and diversity of the Law School. *Id.,* at 83–84, 114–121. In reviewing an applicant's file, admissions officials must consider the applicant's undergraduate grade point average (GPA) and Law School Admissions Test (LSAT) score because they are important (if imperfect) predictors of academic success in law school. *Id.,* at 112. The policy stresses that "no applicant should be

Supreme Court of the United States, June 23, 2003.

admitted unless we expect that applicant to do well enough to graduate with no serious academic problems." *Id.*, at 111.

The policy makes clear, however, that even the highest possible score does not guarantee admission to the Law School. *Id.*, at 113. Nor does a low score automatically disqualify an applicant. *Ibid.* Rather, the policy requires admissions officials to look beyond grades and test scores to other criteria that are important to the Law School's educational objectives. *Id.*, at 114. So-called "'soft' variables" such as "the enthusiasm of recommenders, the quality of the undergraduate institution, the quality of the applicant's essay, and the areas and difficulty of undergraduate course selection" are all brought to bear in assessing an "applicant's likely contributions to the intellectual and social life of the institution." *Ibid.*

The policy aspires to "achieve that diversity which has the potential to enrich everyone's education and thus make a law school class stronger than the sum of its parts." *Id.*, at 118. The policy does not restrict the types of diversity contributions eligible for "substantial weight" in the admissions process, but instead recognizes "many possible bases for diversity admissions." *Id.*, at 118, 120. The policy does, however, reaffirm the Law School's longstanding commitment to "one particular type of diversity," that is, "racial and ethnic diversity with special reference to the inclusion of students from groups which have been historically discriminated against, like African-Americans, Hispanics and Native Americans, who without this commitment might not be represented in our student body in meaningful numbers." *Id.*, at 120. By enrolling a "'critical mass' of [underrepresented] minority students," the Law School seeks to "ensur[e] their ability to make unique contributions to the character of the Law School." *Id.*, at 120–121.

The policy does not define diversity "solely in terms of racial and ethnic status." *Id.*, at 121. Nor is the policy "insensitive to the competition among all students for admission to the [L]aw [S]chool." *Ibid.* Rather, the policy seeks to guide admissions officers in "producing classes both diverse and academically outstanding, classes made up of students who promise to continue the tradition of outstanding contribution by Michigan Graduates to the legal profession." *Ibid.*

B

Petitioner Barbara Grutter is a white Michigan resident who applied to the Law School in 1996 with a 3.8 grade point average and 161 LSAT score. The Law School initially placed petitioner on a waiting list, but subsequently rejected her application. In December 1997, petitioner filed suit in the United States District Court for the Eastern District of Michigan against the Law School, the Regents of the University of Michigan, Lee Bollinger (Dean of the Law School from 1987 to 1994, and President of the University of Michigan from 1996 to 2002), Jeffrey Lehman (Dean of the Law School), and Dennis Shields (Director of Admissions at the Law School from 1991 until 1998). Petitioner alleged that respondents discriminated against her on the basis of race in violation of the Fourteenth Amendment; Title VI of the Civil Rights Act of 1964, 78 Stat. 252, 42 U.S.C. § 2000d; and Rev. Stat. §1977, as amended, 42 U.S.C. §1981.

Petitioner further alleged that her application was rejected because the Law School uses race as a "predominant" factor, giving applicants who belong to certain minority groups "a significantly greater chance of admission than students with similar credentials from disfavored racial groups." App. 33–34. Petitioner also alleged that respondents "had no compelling interest to justify their use of race in the admissions process." *Id.*, at 34. Petitioner requested compensatory and punitive damages, an order requiring the Law School to offer her admission, and an injunction prohibiting the Law School from continuing to discriminate on the basis of race. *Id.*, at 36. Petitioner clearly has standing to bring this lawsuit. *Northeastern Fla. Chapter, Associated Gen. Contractors of America v. Jacksonville,* 508 U.S. 656, 666 (1993).

The District Court granted petitioner's motion for class certification and for bifurcation of the trial into liability and damages phases. The class was defined as "'all persons who (A) applied for and were not granted admission to the University of Michigan Law School for the academic years since (and including) 1995 until the time that judgment is entered herein; and (B) were members of those racial or ethnic groups, including Caucasian, that Defendants treated less favorably in considering their applications for admission to the Law School.'" *App. to Pet. for Cert.* 191a–192a.

The District Court heard oral argument on the parties' cross-motions for summary judgment on December 22, 2000. Taking the motions under advisement, the District Court indicated that it would decide as a matter of law whether the Law School's asserted interest in obtaining the educational benefits that flow from a diverse student body was compelling. The District Court also indicated that it would conduct a bench trial on the extent to which race was a factor in the Law School's admissions decisions, and whether the Law School's consideration of race in admissions decisions constituted a race-based double standard.

During the 15-day bench trial, the parties introduced extensive evidence concerning the Law School's use of race in the admissions process. Dennis Shields, Director of Admissions when petitioner applied to the Law School, testified that he did not direct his staff to admit a particular percentage or number of minority students, but rather to consider an applicant's race along with all other factors. *Id.*, at 206a. Shields testified that at the height of the admissions season, he would frequently consult the so-called "daily reports" that kept track of the racial and ethnic composition of the class (along with other information such as residency status and gender). *Id.*, at 207a. This was done, Shields testified, to ensure that a critical mass of underrepresented minority students would be reached so as to realize the educational benefits of a diverse student body. *Ibid.* Shields stressed, however, that he did not seek to admit any particular number or percentage of underrepresented minority students. *Ibid.*

Erica Munzel, who succeeded Shields as Director of Admissions, testified that "'critical mass'" means "'meaningful numbers'" or "'meaningful representation,'" which she understood to mean a number that encourages underrepresented minority students to participate in the classroom and not feel isolated. *Id.*, at 208a–209a. Munzel stated there is no number, percentage, or range of numbers or percentages that constitute critical mass. *Id.*, at 209a. Munzel also asserted that she must consider the race of applicants because a critical mass of underrepresented minority students could not be enrolled if admissions decisions were based primarily on undergraduate GPAs and LSAT scores. *Ibid.*

The current Dean of the Law School, Jeffrey Lehman, also testified. Like the other Law School witnesses, Lehman did not quantify critical mass in terms of numbers or percentages. *Id.,* at 211a. He indicated that critical mass means numbers such that underrepresented minority students do not feel isolated or like spokespersons for their race. *Ibid.* When asked about the extent to which race is considered in admissions, Lehman testified that it varies from one applicant to another. *Ibid.* In some cases, according to Lehman's testimony, an applicant's race may play no role, while in others it may be a "'determinative'" factor. *Ibid.*

The District Court heard extensive testimony from Professor Richard Lempert, who chaired the faculty committee that drafted the 1992 policy. Lempert emphasized that the Law School seeks students with diverse interests and backgrounds to enhance classroom discussion and the educational experience both inside and outside the classroom. *Id.,* at 213a. When asked about the policy's "'commitment to racial and ethnic diversity with special reference to the inclusion of students from groups which have been historically discriminated against,'" Lempert explained that this language did not purport to remedy past discrimination, but rather to include students who may bring to the Law School a perspective different from that of members of groups which have not been the victims of such discrimination. *Ibid.* Lempert acknowledged that other groups, such as Asians and Jews, have experienced discrimination, but explained they were not mentioned in the policy because individuals who are members of those groups were already being admitted to the Law School in significant numbers. *Ibid.*

Kent Syverud was the final witness to testify about the Law School's use of race in admissions decisions. Syverud was a professor at the Law School when the 1992 admissions policy was adopted and is now Dean of Vanderbilt Law School. In addition to his testimony at trial, Syverud submitted several expert reports on the educational benefits of diversity. Syverud's testimony indicated that when a critical mass of underrepresented minority students is present, racial stereotypes lose their force because nonminority students learn there is no "'minority viewpoint'" but rather a variety of viewpoints among minority students. *Id.,* at 215a. . . .

In the end, the District Court concluded that the Law School's use of race as a factor in admissions decisions was unlawful. Applying strict scrutiny, the District Court determined that the Law School's asserted interest in assembling a diverse student body was not compelling because "the attainment of a racially diverse class . . . was not recognized as such by *Bakke* and is not a remedy for past discrimination." *Id.,* at 246a. The District Court went on to hold that even if diversity were compelling, the Law School had not narrowly tailored its use of race to further that interest. The District Court granted petitioner's request for declaratory relief and enjoined the Law School from using race as a factor in its admissions decisions. The Court of Appeals entered a stay of the injunction pending appeal.

Sitting en banc, the Court of Appeals reversed the District Court's judgment and vacated the injunction. The Court of Appeals first held that Justice Powell's opinion in *Bakke* was binding precedent establishing diversity as a compelling state interest. According to the Court of Appeals, Justice Powell's opinion with respect to diversity comprised the controlling rationale for the judgment of this Court under the analysis set forth in *Marks v. United States*, 430 U.S. 188 (1977). The Court of Appeals also held that the Law School's use of race was narrowly tailored because race was merely a "potential 'plus' factor" and because the Law School's program was "virtually identical" to the Harvard admissions program described approvingly by Justice Powell and appended to his *Bakke* opinion. 288 F.3d 732, 746, 749 (CA6 2002).

Four dissenting judges would have held the Law School's use of race unconstitutional. Three of the dissenters, rejecting the majority's *Marks* analysis, examined the Law School's interest in student body diversity on the merits and concluded it was not compelling. The fourth dissenter, writing separately, found it unnecessary to decide whether diversity was a compelling interest because, like the other dissenters, he believed that the Law School's use of race was not narrowly tailored to further that interest.

We granted certiorari, 537 U.S. 1043 (2002), to resolve the disagreement among the Courts of Appeals on a question of national importance: Whether diversity is a compelling interest that can justify the narrowly tailored use of race in selecting applicants for admission to public universities. Compare *Hopwood v. Texas*, 78 F.3d 932 (CA5 1996) *(Hopwood I)* (holding that diversity is not a compelling state interest), with *Smith v. University of Wash. Law School*, 233 F.3d 1188 (CA9 2000) (holding that it is).

II

A

We last addressed the use of race in public higher education over 25 years ago. In the landmark *Bakke* case, we reviewed a racial set-aside program that reserved 16 out of 100 seats in a medical school class for members of certain minority groups. 438 U.S. 265 (1978). The decision produced six separate opinions, none of which commanded a majority of the Court. Four Justices would have upheld the program against all attack on the ground that the government can use race to "remedy disadvantages cast on minorities by past racial prejudice." *Id.,* at 325 (joint opinion of Brennan, White, Marshall, and Blackmun, JJ., concurring in judgment in part and dissenting in part). Four other Justices avoided the constitutional question altogether and struck down the program on statutory grounds. *Id.,* at 408 (opinion of Stevens, J., joined by Burger, C. J., and Stewart and Rehnquist, JJ., concurring in judgment in part and dissenting in part). Justice Powell provided a fifth vote not only for invalidating the set-aside program, but also for reversing the state court's injunction against any use of race whatsoever. The only holding for the Court in *Bakke* was that a "State has a substantial interest that legitimately may be served by a properly devised admissions program involving the competitive consideration of race and ethnic origin." *Id.*, at 320. Thus, we reversed that part of the lower court's judgment that enjoined the university "from any consideration of the race of any applicant." *Ibid.*

Since this Court's splintered decision in *Bakke*, Justice Powell's opinion announcing the judgment of the Court has served as the touchstone for constitutional analysis of race-conscious admissions policies. Public and private universities across the Nation have modeled their own admissions programs on Justice Powell's views on permissible race-conscious policies. See, *e.g.*, Brief for Judith Areen et al. as *Amici Curiae* 12–13 (law school admissions programs employ "methods designed from and based on Justice Powell's opinion in *Bakke*"); Brief for Amherst College et al. as *Amici Curiae 27* ("After *Bakke*, each of the *amici* (and undoubtedly other selective colleges and universities as well) reviewed their admissions procedures in light of Justice Powell's opinion . . . and set sail accordingly"). We therefore discuss Justice Powell's opinion in some detail.

Justice Powell began by stating that "[t]he guarantee of equal protection cannot mean one thing when applied to one individual and something else when applied to a person of another color. If both are not accorded the same protection, then it is not equal." *Bakke*, 438 U.S., at 289–290. In Justice Powell's view, when governmental decisions "touch upon an individual's race or ethnic background, he is entitled to a judicial determination that the burden he is asked to bear on that basis is precisely tailored to serve a compelling governmental interest." *Id.*, at 299. Under this exacting standard, only one of the interests asserted by the university survived Justice Powell's scrutiny.

First, Justice Powell rejected an interest in "'reducing the historic deficit of traditionally disfavored minorities in medical schools and in the medical profession'" as an unlawful interest in racial balancing. *Id.*, at 306–307. Second, Justice Powell rejected an interest in remedying societal discrimination because such measures would risk placing unnecessary burdens on innocent third parties "who bear no responsibility for whatever harm the beneficiaries of the special admissions program are thought to have suffered." *Id.*, at 310. Third, Justice Powell rejected an interest in "increasing the number of physicians who will practice in communities currently underserved," concluding that even if such an interest could be compelling in some circumstances the program under review was not "geared to promote that goal." *Id.*, at 306, 310.

Justice Powell approved the university's use of race to further only one interest: "the attainment of a diverse student body." *Id.*, at 311. With the important proviso that "constitutional limitations protecting individual rights may not be disregarded," Justice Powell grounded his analysis in the academic freedom that "long has been viewed as a special concern of the First Amendment." *Id.*, at 312, 314. Justice Powell emphasized that nothing less than the "'nation's future depends upon leaders trained through wide exposure' to the ideas and mores of students as diverse as this Nation of many peoples." *Id.*, at 313 (quoting *Keyishian v. Board of Regents of Univ. of State of N.Y.*, 385 U.S. 589, 603 (1967)). In seeking the "right to select those students who will contribute the most to the 'robust exchange of ideas,'" a university seeks "to achieve a goal that is of paramount importance in the fulfillment of its mission."

438 U.S., at 313. Both "tradition and experience lend support to the view that the contribution of diversity is substantial." *Ibid.*

Justice Powell was, however, careful to emphasize that in his view race "is only one element in a range of factors a university properly may consider in attaining the goal of a heterogeneous student body." *Id.,* at 314. For Justice Powell, "[i]t is not an interest in simple ethnic diversity, in which a specified percentage of the student body is in effect guaranteed to be members of selected ethnic groups," that can justify the use of race. *Id.,* at 315. Rather, "[t] he diversity that furthers a compelling state interest encompasses a far broader array of qualifications and characteristics of which racial or ethnic origin is but a single though important element." *Ibid.* . . .

More important, for the reasons set out below, today we endorse Justice Powell's view that student body diversity is a compelling state interest that can justify the use of race in university admissions.

B

The Equal Protection Clause provides that no State shall "deny to any person within its jurisdiction the equal protection of the laws." U.S. Const., Amdt. 14, §2. Because the Fourteenth Amendment "protect[s] *persons,* not *groups,*" all "governmental action based on race—a *group* classification long recognized as in most circumstances irrelevant and therefore prohibited—should be subjected to detailed judicial inquiry to ensure that the *personal* right to equal protection of the laws has not been infringed." *Adarand Constructors, Inc. v. Peña,* 515 U.S. 200, 227 (1995) (emphasis in original; internal quotation marks and citation omitted). We are a "free people whose institutions are founded upon the doctrine of equality." *Loving v. Virginia,* 388 U.S. 1, 11 (1967) (internal quotation marks and citation omitted). It follows from that principle that "government may treat people differently because of their race only for the most compelling reasons." *Adarand Constructors, Inc. v. Peña,* 515 U.S., at 227.

We have held that all racial classifications imposed by government "must be analyzed by a reviewing court under strict scrutiny." *Ibid.* This means that such classifications are constitutional only if they are narrowly tailored to further compelling governmental interests. "Absent searching judicial inquiry into the justification for such race-based measures," we have no way to determine what "classifications are 'benign' or 'remedial' and what classifications are in fact motivated by illegitimate notions of racial inferiority or simple racial politics." *Richmond v. J. A. Croson Co.,* 488 U.S. 469, 493 (1989) (plurality opinion). We apply strict scrutiny to all racial classifications to "'smoke out' illegitimate uses of race by assuring that [government] is pursuing a goal important enough to warrant use of a highly suspect tool," *Ibid.*

Strict scrutiny is not "strict in theory, but fatal in fact." *Adarand Constructors, Inc. v. Peña, supra,* at 237 (internal quotation marks and citation omitted). Although all governmental uses of race are subject to strict scrutiny, not all are invalidated by it. As we have explained, "whenever the government treats any person unequally because of his or her race, that person has suffered an injury that falls squarely within the language and spirit of the Constitution's guarantee of equal protection." 515 U.S., at 229–230. But that observation "says nothing about the ultimate validity of any particular law; that determination is the job of the court applying strict scrutiny." *Id.*, at 230. When race-based action is necessary to further a compelling governmental interest, such action does not violate the constitutional guarantee of equal protection so long as the narrow tailoring requirement is also satisfied.

Context matters when reviewing race-based governmental action under the Equal Protection Clause. See *Gomillion v. Lightfoot,* 364 U.S. 339, 343–344 (1960) (admonishing that, "in dealing with claims under broad provisions of the Constitution, which derive content by an interpretive process of inclusion and exclusion, it is imperative that generalizations, based on and qualified by the concrete situations that gave rise to them, must not be applied out of context in disregard of variant controlling facts"). In *Adarand Constructors, Inc. v. Peña,* we made clear that strict scrutiny must take "'relevant differences' into account." 515 U.S., at 228. Indeed, as we explained, that is its "fundamental purpose." *Ibid.* Not every decision influenced by race is equally objectionable and strict scrutiny is designed to provide a framework for carefully examining the importance and the sincerity of the reasons advanced by the governmental decisionmaker for the use of race in that particular context.

III

A

With these principles in mind, we turn to the question whether the Law School's use of race is justified by a compelling state interest. Before this Court, as they have throughout this litigation, respondents assert only one justification for their use of race in the admissions process: obtaining "the educational benefits that flow from a diverse student body." Brief for Respondents Bollinger et al. In other words, the Law School asks us to recognize, in the context of higher education, a compelling state interest in student body diversity.

We first wish to dispel the notion that the Law School's argument has been foreclosed, either expressly or implicitly, by our affirmative-action cases decided since *Bakke.* It is true that some language in those opinions might be read to suggest that remedying past discrimination is the only permissible justification for race-based governmental action. See, *e.g., Richmond v. J. A. Croson Co., supra,* at 493 (plurality opinion) (stating that unless classifications based on race are "strictly reserved for remedial settings, they may in fact promote notions of racial inferiority and lead to a politics of racial hostility"). But we have never held that the only governmental use of race that can survive strict scrutiny is remedying past discrimination. Nor, since *Bakke,* have we directly addressed the use of race in the context of public higher education. Today, we hold that the Law School has a compelling interest in attaining a diverse student body.

The Law School's educational judgment that such diversity is essential to its educational mission is one to which we defer. The Law School's assessment that diversity will, in fact, yield educational benefits is substantiated by respondents and their *amici*. Our scrutiny of the interest asserted by the Law School is no less strict for taking into account complex educational judgments in an area that lies primarily within the expertise of the university. Our holding today is in keeping with our tradition of giving a degree of deference to a university's academic decisions, within constitutionally prescribed limits. See *Regents of Univ. of Mich. v. Ewing*, 474 U.S. 214, 225 (1985); *Board of Curators of Univ. of Mo. v. Horowitz*, 435 U.S. 78, 96, n. 6 (1978); *Bakke*, 438 U.S., at 319, n. 53 (opinion of Powell, J.).

We have long recognized that, given the important purpose of public education and the expansive freedoms of speech and thought associated with the university environment, universities occupy a special niche in our constitutional tradition. See, *e.g.*, *Wieman v. Updegraff*, 344 U.S. 183, 195 (1952) (Frankfurter, J., concurring); *Sweezy v. New Hampshire*, 354 U.S. 234, 250 (1957); *Shelton v. Tucker*, 364 U.S. 479, 487 (1960); *Keyishian v. Board of Regents of Univ. of State of N.Y.*, 385 U.S., at 603. In announcing the principle of student body diversity as a compelling state interest, Justice Powell invoked our cases recognizing a constitutional dimension, grounded in the First Amendment, of educational autonomy: "The freedom of a university to make its own judgments as to education includes the selection of its student body." *Bakke*, supra, at 312. From this premise, Justice Powell reasoned that by claiming "the right to select those students who will contribute the most to the 'robust exchange of ideas,'" a university "seek[s] to achieve a goal that is of paramount importance in the fulfillment of its mission." 438 U.S., at 313 (quoting *Keyishian v. Board of Regents of Univ. of State of N.Y.*, supra, at 603). Our conclusion that the Law School has a compelling interest in a diverse student body is informed by our view that attaining a diverse student body is at the heart of the Law School's proper institutional mission, and that "good faith" on the part of a university is "presumed" absent "a showing to the contrary." 438 U.S., at 318–319.

As part of its goal of "assembling a class that is both exceptionally academically qualified and broadly diverse," the Law School seeks to "enroll a 'critical mass' of minority students." Brief for Respondents Bollinger et al. The Law School's interest is not simply "to assure within its student body some specified percentage of a particular group merely because of its race or ethnic origin." *Bakke*, 438 U.S., at 307 (opinion of Powell, J.). That would amount to outright racial balancing, which is patently unconstitutional. *Ibid.; Freeman v. Pitts*, 503 U.S. 467, 494 (1992) ("Racial balance is not to be achieved for its own sake"); *Richmond v. J. A. Croson Co.*, 488 U.S., at 507. Rather, the Law School's concept of critical mass is defined by reference to the educational benefits that diversity is designed to produce.

These benefits are substantial. As the District Court emphasized, the Law School's admissions policy promotes "cross-racial understanding," helps to break down racial stereotypes, and "enables [students] to better understand persons of different races." *App. to Pet. for Cert.* 246a. These benefits are "important and laudable," because "classroom discussion is livelier, more spirited, and simply more enlightening and interesting" when the students have "the greatest possible variety of backgrounds." *Id.*, at 246a, 244a.

The Law School's claim of a compelling interest is further bolstered by its *amici,* who point to the educational benefits that flow from student body diversity. In addition to the expert studies and reports entered into evidence at trial, numerous studies show that student body diversity promotes learning outcomes, and "better prepares students for an increasingly diverse workforce and society, and better prepares them as professionals." Brief for American Educational Research Association et al. as *Amici Curiae* 3; see, *e.g.,* W. Bowen & D. Bok, The Shape of the River (1998); Diversity Challenged: Evidence on the Impact of Affirmative Action (G. Orfield & M. Kurlaender eds., 2001); Compelling Interest: Examining the Evidence on Racial Dynamics in Colleges and Universities (M. Chang, D. Witt, J. Jones, & K. Hakuta eds., 2003).

These benefits are not theoretical but real, as major American businesses have made clear that the skills needed in today's increasingly global marketplace can only be developed through exposure to widely diverse people, cultures, ideas, and viewpoints. Brief for 3M et al. as *Amici Curiae* 5; Brief for General Motors Corp. as *Amicus Curiae* 3–4. What is more, high-ranking retired officers and civilian leaders of the United States military assert that, "[b]ased on [their] decades of experience," a "highly qualified, racially diverse officer corps . . . is essential to the military's ability to fulfill its principal mission to provide national security." Brief for Julius W. Becton, Jr. et al. as *Amici Curiae* 27. The primary sources for the Nation's officer corps are the service academies and the Reserve Officers Training Corps (ROTC), the latter comprising students already admitted to participating colleges and universities. *Id.,* at 5. At present, "the military cannot achieve an officer corps that is *both* highly qualified *and* racially diverse unless the service academies and the ROTC used limited race-conscious recruiting and admissions policies." *Ibid.* (emphasis in original). To fulfill its mission, the military "must be selective in admissions for training and education for the officer corps, *and* it must train and educate a highly qualified, racially diverse officer corps in a racially diverse setting." *Id.,* at 29 (emphasis in original). We agree that "[i]t requires only a small step from this analysis to conclude that our country's other most selective institutions must remain both diverse and selective." *Ibid.*

We have repeatedly acknowledged the overriding importance of preparing students for work and citizenship, describing education as pivotal to "sustaining our political and cultural heritage" with a fundamental role in maintaining the fabric of society. *Plyler v. Doe,* 457 U.S. 202, 221 (1982). This Court has long recognized that "education . . . is the very foundation of good citizenship." *Brown v. Board of Education,* 347 U.S. 483, 493 (1954). For this reason, the diffusion of knowledge and opportunity through public institutions of higher education must be accessible to all individuals regardless of race or ethnicity. The United States, as *amicus curiae,* affirms that "[e]nsuring that public institutions are open and available to all segments of American society, including people of all races and ethnicities, represents a paramount government objective." Brief for United States as *Amicus Curiae* 13. And, "[n]owhere is the importance of such openness more acute than in the context of higher education." *Ibid.* Effective participation by members of all racial and ethnic groups in the civic life of our Nation is essential if the dream of one Nation, indivisible, is to be realized.

Moreover, universities, and in particular, law schools, represent the training ground for a large number of our Nation's leaders. *Sweatt v. Painter*, 339 U.S. 629, 634 (1950) (describing law school as a "proving ground for legal learning and practice"). Individuals with law degrees occupy roughly half the state governorships, more than half the seats in the United States Senate, and more than a third of the seats in the United States House of Representatives. See Brief for Association of American Law Schools as *Amicus Curiae* 5–6. The pattern is even more striking when it comes to highly selective law schools. A handful of these schools accounts for 25 of the 100 United States Senators, 74 United States Courts of Appeals judges, and nearly 200 of the more than 600 United States District Court judges. *Id.*, at 6.

In order to cultivate a set of leaders with legitimacy in the eyes of the citizenry, it is necessary that the path to leadership be visibly open to talented and qualified individuals of every race and ethnicity. All members of our heterogeneous society must have confidence in the openness and integrity of the educational institutions that provide this training. As we have recognized, law schools "cannot be effective in isolation from the individuals and institutions with which the law interacts." See *Sweatt v. Painter, supra,* at 634. Access to legal education (and thus the legal profession) must be inclusive of talented and qualified individuals of every race and ethnicity, so that all members of our heterogeneous society may participate in the educational institutions that provide the training and education necessary to succeed in America.

The Law School does not premise its need for critical mass on "any belief that minority students always (or even consistently) express some characteristic minority viewpoint on any issue." Brief for Respondent Bollinger et al. To the contrary, diminishing the force of such stereotypes is both a crucial part of the Law School's mission, and one that it cannot accomplish with only token numbers of minority students. Just as growing up in a particular region or having particular professional experiences is likely to affect an individual's views, so too is one's own, unique experience of being a racial minority in a society, like our own, in which race unfortunately still matters. The Law School has determined, based on its experience and expertise, that a "critical mass" of underrepresented minorities is necessary to further its compelling interest in securing the educational benefits of a diverse student body.

B

Even in the limited circumstance when drawing racial distinctions is permissible to further a compelling state interest, government is still "constrained in how it may pursue that end: [T]he means chosen to accomplish the [government's] asserted purpose must be specifically and narrowly framed to accomplish that purpose." *Shaw v. Hunt,* 517 U.S. 899, 908 (1996) (internal quotation marks and citation omitted). The purpose of the narrow tailoring requirement is to ensure that "the means chosen 'fit' . . . th[e] compelling goal so closely that there is little or no possibility that the motive for the classification was illegitimate racial prejudice or stereotype." *Richmond v. J. A. Croson Co.,* 488 U.S., at 493 (plurality opinion). . . .

To be narrowly tailored, a race-conscious admissions program cannot use a quota system—it cannot "insulat[e] each category of applicants with certain desired qualifications from competition with all other applicants." *Bakke, supra,* at 315 (opinion of Powell, J.). Instead, a university may consider race or ethnicity only as a "'plus' in a particular applicant's file," without "insulat[ing] the individual from comparison with all other candidates for the available seats." *Id.,* at 317. In other words, an admissions program must be "flexible enough to consider all pertinent elements of diversity in light of the particular qualifications of each applicant, and to place them on the same footing for consideration, although not necessarily according them the same weight." *Ibid.*

We find that the Law School's admissions program bears the hallmarks of a narrowly tailored plan. As Justice Powell made clear in *Bakke,* truly individualized consideration demands that race be used in a flexible, nonmechanical way. It follows from this mandate that universities cannot establish quotas for members of certain racial groups or put members of those groups on separate admissions tracks. See *id.,* at 315–316. Nor can universities insulate applicants who belong to certain racial or ethnic groups from the competition for admission. *Ibid.* Universities can, however, consider race or ethnicity more flexibly as a "plus" factor in the context of individualized consideration of each and every applicant. *Ibid.*

We are satisfied that the Law School's admissions program, like the Harvard plan described by Justice Powell, does not operate as a quota. Properly understood, a "quota" is a program in which a certain fixed number or proportion of opportunities are "reserved exclusively for certain minority groups." *Richmond v. J. A. Croson Co., supra,* at 496 (plurality opinion). Quotas "'impose a fixed number or percentage which must be attained, or which cannot be exceeded,'" *Sheet Metal Workers v. EEOC,* 478 U.S. 421, 495 (1986) (O'Connor, J., concurring in part and dissenting in part), and "insulate the individual from comparison with all other candidates for the available seats." *Bakke, supra,* at 317 (opinion of Powell, J.). In contrast, "a permissible goal . . . require[s] only a good-faith effort . . . to come within a range demarcated by the goal itself," *Sheet Metal Workers v. EEOC, supra,* at 495, and permits consideration of race as a "plus" factor in any given case while still ensuring that each candidate "compete[s] with all other qualified applicants," *Johnson v. Transportation Agency, Santa Clara Cty.,* 480 U.S. 616, 638 (1987).

Justice Powell's distinction between the medical school's rigid 16-seat quota and Harvard's flexible use of race as a "plus" factor is instructive. Harvard certainly had minimum *goals* for minority enrollment, even if it had no specific number firmly in mind. See *Bakke, supra,* at 323 (opinion of Powell, J.) ("10 or 20 black students could not begin to bring to their classmates and to each other the variety of points of view, backgrounds and experiences of blacks in the United States"). What is more, Justice Powell flatly rejected the argument that Harvard's program was "the functional equivalent of a quota" merely because it had some "'plus'" for race, or gave greater "weight" to race than to some other factors, in order to achieve student body diversity. 438 U.S., at 317–318.

The Law School's goal of attaining a critical mass of underrepresented minority students does not transform its program into a quota. As the Harvard plan described by Justice Powell recognized, there is of course "some relationship between numbers and achieving the benefits to be derived from a diverse student body, and between numbers and providing a reasonable environment for those students admitted." *Id.*, at 323. "[S]ome attention to numbers," without more, does not transform a flexible admissions system into a rigid quota. *Ibid.* Nor, as Justice Kennedy posits, does the Law School's consultation of the "daily reports," which keep track of the racial and ethnic composition of the class (as well as of residency and gender), "suggest there was no further attempt at individual review save for race itself" during the final stages of the admissions process. See *post*, at 6 (dissenting opinion). To the contrary, the Law School's admissions officers testified without contradiction that they never gave race any more or less weight based on the information contained in these reports. Brief for Respondents Bollinger et al. n. 70 (citing App. in Nos. 01–1447 and 01–1516 (CA6), p. 7336). Moreover, as Justice Kennedy concedes, see *post*, at 4, between 1993 and 2000, the number of African-American, Latino, and Native-American students in each class at the Law School varied from 13.5 to 20.1 percent, a range inconsistent with a quota.

The Chief Justice believes that the Law School's policy conceals an attempt to achieve racial balancing, and cites admissions data to contend that the Law School discriminates among different groups within the critical mass. *Post*, at 3–9 (dissenting opinion). But, as the Chief Justice concedes, the number of underrepresented minority students who ultimately enroll in the Law School differs substantially from their representation in the applicant pool and varies considerably for each group from year to year. See *post*, at 8 (dissenting opinion).

That a race-conscious admissions program does not operate as a quota does not, by itself, satisfy the requirement of individualized consideration. When using race as a "plus" factor in university admissions, a university's admissions program must remain flexible enough to ensure that each applicant is evaluated as an individual and not in a way that makes an applicant's race or ethnicity the defining feature of his or her application. The importance of this individualized consideration in the context of a race-conscious admissions program is paramount. See *Bakke, supra*, at 318, n. 52 (opinion of Powell, J.) (identifying the "denial . . . of th[e] right to individualized consideration" as the "principal evil" of the medical school's admissions program).

Here, the Law School engages in a highly individualized, holistic review of each applicant's file, giving serious consideration to all the ways an applicant might contribute to a diverse educational environment. The Law School affords this individualized consideration to applicants of all races. There is no policy, either *de jure* or *de facto*, of automatic acceptance or rejection based on any single "soft" variable. Unlike the program at issue in *Gratz v. Bollinger, ante,* the Law School awards no mechanical, predetermined diversity "bonuses" based on race or ethnicity. See *ante*, at 23 (distinguishing a race-conscious admissions program that automatically awards 20 points based on race from the Harvard plan, which considered race but "did not contemplate that any single characteristic automatically ensured a specific and identifiable contribution to a university's diversity"). Like the Harvard plan, the Law School's admissions policy "is flexible enough to consider all pertinent elements of diversity in light of the particular qualifications of each applicant, and to place them on the same footing for consideration, although not necessarily according them the same weight." *Bakke, supra,* at 317 (opinion of Powell, J.).

We also find that, like the Harvard plan Justice Powell referenced in *Bakke,* the Law School's race-conscious admissions program adequately ensures that all factors that may contribute to student body diversity are meaningfully considered alongside race in admissions decisions. With respect to the use of race itself, all underrepresented minority students admitted by the Law School have been deemed qualified. By virtue of our Nation's struggle with racial inequality, such students are both likely to have experiences of particular importance to the Law School's mission, and less likely to be admitted in meaningful numbers on criteria that ignore those experiences. See App. 120.

The Law School does not, however, limit in any way the broad range of qualities and experiences that may be considered valuable contributions to student body diversity. To the contrary, the 1992 policy makes clear "[t]here are many possible bases for diversity admissions," and provides examples of admittees who have lived or traveled widely abroad, are fluent in several languages, have overcome personal adversity and family hardship, have exceptional records of extensive community service, and have had successful careers in other fields. *Id.,* at 118–119. The Law School seriously considers each "applicant's promise of making a notable contribution to the class by way of a particular strength, attainment, or characteristic—*e.g.,* an unusual intellectual achievement, employment experience, nonacademic performance, or personal background." *Id.,* at 83–84. All applicants have the opportunity to highlight their own potential diversity contributions through the submission of a personal statement, letters of recommendation, and an essay describing the ways in which the applicant will contribute to the life and diversity of the Law School.

What is more, the Law School actually gives substantial weight to diversity factors besides race. The Law School frequently accepts nonminority applicants with grades and test scores lower than underrepresented minority applicants (and other nonminority applicants) who are rejected. See Brief for Respondents Bollinger et al. App. 121–122. This shows that the Law School seriously weighs many other diversity factors besides race that can make a real and dispositive difference for nonminority applicants as well. By this flexible approach, the Law School sufficiently takes into account, in practice as well as in theory, a wide variety of characteristics besides race and ethnicity that contribute to a diverse student body. Justice Kennedy speculates that "race is likely outcome determinative for many members of minority groups" who do not fall within the upper range of LSAT scores and grades. *Post,* at 3 (dissenting opinion). But the same could be said of the Harvard plan discussed approvingly by Justice Powell in *Bakke,* and indeed of any plan that uses race as one of many factors. See 438 U.S., at 316 ("'When the Committee on Admissions reviews the large middle group of applicants who are "admissible" and deemed capable of doing good work in their courses, the race of an applicant may tip the balance in his favor'").

Petitioner and the United States argue that the Law School's plan is not narrowly tailored because race-neutral means exist to obtain the educational benefits of student body diversity that the Law School seeks. We disagree. Narrow tailoring does not require exhaustion of every conceivable race-neutral alternative. Nor does it require a university to choose between maintaining a reputation for excellence or fulfilling a commitment to provide educational opportunities to members of all racial groups. See *Wygant v. Jackson Bd. of Ed.,* 476 U.S. 267, 280, n. 6 (1986) (alternatives must serve the interest "'about as well'"); *Richmond v. J. A. Croson Co.,* 488 U.S., at 509–510 (plurality opinion) (city had a "whole array of race-neutral" alternatives because changing requirements "would have [had] little detrimental effect on the city's interests"). Narrow tailoring does, however, require serious, good faith consideration of workable race-neutral alternatives that will achieve the diversity the university seeks. See *id.,* at 507 (set-aside plan not narrowly tailored where "there does not appear to have been any consideration of the use of race-neutral means"); *Wygant v. Jackson Bd. of Ed., supra,* at 280, n. 6 (narrow tailoring "require[s] consideration" of "lawful alternative and less restrictive means").

We agree with the Court of Appeals that the Law School sufficiently considered workable race-neutral alternatives. The District Court took the Law School to task for failing to consider race-neutral alternatives such as "using a lottery system" or "decreasing the emphasis for all applicants on undergraduate GPA and LSAT scores." *App. to Pet. for Cert.* 251a. But these alternatives would require a dramatic sacrifice of diversity, the academic quality of all admitted students, or both.

The Law School's current admissions program considers race as one factor among many, in an effort to assemble a student body that is diverse in ways broader than race. Because a lottery would make that kind of nuanced judgment impossible, it would effectively sacrifice all other educational values, not to mention every other kind of diversity. So too with the suggestion that the Law School simply lower admissions standards for all students, a drastic remedy that would require the Law School to become a much different institution and sacrifice a vital component of its educational mission. The United States advocates "percentage plans," recently adopted by public undergraduate institutions in Texas, Florida, and California to guarantee admission to all students above a certain class-rank threshold in every high school in the State. Brief for United States as *Amicus Curiae* 14–18. The United States does not, however, explain how such plans could work for graduate and professional schools. Moreover, even assuming such plans are race-neutral, they may preclude the university from conducting the individualized assessments necessary to assemble a student body that is not just racially diverse, but diverse along all the qualities valued by the university. We are satisfied that the Law School adequately considered race-neutral alternatives currently capable of producing a critical mass without forcing the Law School to abandon the academic selectivity that is the cornerstone of its educational mission.

We acknowledge that "there are serious problems of justice connected with the idea of preference itself." *Bakke,* 438 U.S., at 298 (opinion of Powell, J.). Narrow tailoring, therefore, requires that a race-conscious admissions program not unduly harm members of any racial group. Even remedial race-based governmental action generally "remains subject to continuing oversight to assure that it will work the least harm possible to other innocent persons competing for the benefit." *Id.*, at 308. To be narrowly tailored, a race-conscious admissions program must not "unduly burden individuals who are not members of the favored racial and ethnic groups." *Metro Broadcasting, Inc. v. FCC*, 497 U.S. 547, 630 (1990) (O'Connor, J., dissenting).

We are satisfied that the Law School's admissions program does not. Because the Law School considers "all pertinent elements of diversity," it can (and does) select nonminority applicants who have greater potential to enhance student body diversity over underrepresented minority applicants. See *Bakke, supra,* at 317 (opinion of Powell, J.). As Justice Powell recognized in *Bakke,* so long as a race-conscious admissions program uses race as a "plus" factor in the context of individualized consideration, a rejected applicant "will not have been foreclosed from all consideration for that seat simply because he was not the right color or had the wrong surname. . . . His qualifications would have been weighed fairly and competitively, and he would have no basis to complain of unequal treatment under the Fourteenth Amendment." 438 U.S., at 318.

We agree that, in the context of its individualized inquiry into the possible diversity contributions of all applicants, the Law School's race-conscious admissions program does not unduly harm nonminority applicants.

We are mindful, however, that "[a] core purpose of the Fourteenth Amendment was to do away with all governmentally imposed discrimination based on race." *Palmore v. Sidoti,* 466 U.S. 429, 432 (1984). Accordingly, race-conscious admissions policies must be limited in time. This requirement reflects that racial classifications, however compelling their goals, are potentially so dangerous that they may be employed no more broadly than the interest demands. Enshrining a permanent justification for racial preferences would offend this fundamental equal protection principle. We see no reason to exempt race-conscious admissions programs from the requirement that all governmental use of race must have a logical end point. The Law School, too, concedes that all "race-conscious programs must have reasonable durational limits." Brief for Respondents Bollinger et al.

In the context of higher education, the durational requirement can be met by sunset provisions in race-conscious admissions policies and periodic reviews to determine whether racial preferences are still necessary to achieve student body diversity. Universities in California, Florida, and Washington State, where racial preferences in admissions are prohibited by state law, are currently engaged in experimenting with a wide variety of alternative approaches. Universities in other States can and should draw on the most promising aspects of these race-neutral alternatives as they develop. Cf. *United States v. Lopez,* 514 U.S. 549, 581 (1995) (Kennedy, J., concurring) ("[T]he States may perform their role as laboratories for experimentation to devise various solutions where the best solution is far from clear").

The requirement that all race-conscious admissions programs have a termination point "assure[s] all citizens that the deviation from the norm of equal treatment of all racial and ethnic groups is a temporary matter, a measure taken in the service of the goal of equality itself." *Richmond v. J. A. Croson Co.*, 488 U.S., at 510 (plurality opinion); see also Nathanson & Bartnik, The Constitutionality of Preferential Treatment for Minority Applicants to Professional Schools, 58 *Chicago Bar Rec.* 282, 293 (May–June 1977) ("It would be a sad day indeed, were America to become a quota-ridden society, with each identifiable minority assigned proportional representation in every desirable walk of life. But that is not the rationale for programs of preferential treatment; the acid test of their justification will be their efficacy in eliminating the need for any racial or ethnic preferences at all").

We take the Law School at its word that it would "like nothing better than to find a race-neutral admissions formula" and will terminate its race-conscious admissions program as soon as practicable. See Brief for Respondents Bollinger et al. *Bakke, supra,* at 317–318 (opinion of Powell, J.) (presuming good faith of university officials in the absence of a showing to the contrary). It has been 25 years since Justice Powell first approved the use of race to further an interest in student body diversity in the context of public higher education. Since that time, the number of minority applicants with high grades and test scores has indeed increased. See Tr. of Oral Arg. 43. We expect that 25 years from now, the use of racial preferences will no longer be necessary to further the interest approved today.

IV

In summary, the Equal Protection Clause does not prohibit the Law School's narrowly tailored use of race in admissions decisions to further a compelling interest in obtaining the educational benefits that flow from a diverse student body. Consequently, petitioner's statutory claims based on Title VI and 42 U.S.C. § 1981 also fail. See *Bakke, supra,* at 287 (opinion of Powell, J.) ("Title VI . . . proscribe[s] only those racial classifications that would violate the Equal Protection Clause or the Fifth Amendment"); *General Building Contractors Assn., Inc. v. Pennsylvania,* 458 U.S. 375, 389–391 (1982) (the prohibition against discrimination in §1981 is co-extensive with the Equal Protection Clause). The judgment of the Court of Appeals for the Sixth Circuit, accordingly, is affirmed.

It is so ordered.

William H. Rehnquist

NO

Dissenting Opinion, *Grutter v. Bollinger*

Chief Justice Rehnquist, with whom Justice Scalia, Justice Kennedy, and Justice Thomas join, dissenting.

I agree with the Court that, "in the limited circumstance when drawing racial distinctions is permissible," the government must ensure that its means are narrowly tailored to achieve a compelling state interest. *Ante*, at 21; see also *Fullilove v. Klutznick*, 448 U.S. 448, 498 (1980) (Powell, J., concurring) ("[E]ven if the government proffers a compelling interest to support reliance upon a suspect classification, the means selected must be narrowly drawn to fulfill the governmental purpose"). I do not believe, however, that the University of Michigan Law School's (Law School) means are narrowly tailored to the interest it asserts. The Law School claims it must take the steps it does to achieve a "'critical mass'" of underrepresented minority students. Brief for Respondents Bollinger et al. But its actual program bears no relation to this asserted goal. Stripped of its "critical mass" veil, the Law School's program is revealed as a naked effort to achieve racial balancing.

As we have explained many times, ""[a]ny preference based on racial or ethnic criteria must necessarily receive a most searching examination."'" *Adarand Constructors, Inc. v. Peña*, 515 U.S. 200, 223 (1995) (quoting *Wygant v. Jackson Bd. of Ed.*, 476 U.S. 267, 273 (1986) (plurality opinion of Powell, J.)). Our cases establish that, in order to withstand this demanding inquiry, respondents must demonstrate that their methods of using race "'fit'" a compelling state interest "with greater precision than any alternative means." *Id.*, at 280, n. 6; *Regents of Univ. of Cal. v. Bakke*, 438 U.S. 265, 299 (1978) (opinion of Powell, J.) ("When [political judgments] touch upon an individual's race or ethnic background, he is entitled to a judicial determination that the burden he is asked to bear on that basis is precisely tailored to serve a compelling governmental interest").

Before the Court's decision today, we consistently applied the same strict scrutiny analysis regardless of the government's purported reason for using race and regardless of the setting in which race was being used. We rejected calls to use more lenient review in the face of claims that race was being used in "good faith" because "'[m]ore than good motives should be required when government seeks to allocate its resources by way of an explicit racial classification system.'" *Adarand, supra*, at 226; *Fullilove, supra*, at 537 (Stevens, J., dissenting) ("Racial classifications are simply too pernicious to permit any but the

Supreme Court of the United States, 2003.

most exact connection between justification and classification"). We likewise rejected calls to apply more lenient review based on the particular setting in which race is being used. Indeed, even in the specific context of higher education, we emphasized that "constitutional limitations protecting individual rights may not be disregarded." *Bakke, supra,* at 314.

Although the Court recites the language of our strict scrutiny analysis, its application of that review is unprecedented in its deference.

Respondents' asserted justification for the Law School's use of race in the admissions process is "obtaining 'the educational benefits that flow from a diverse student body.'" *Ante,* at 15 (quoting Brief for Respondents Bollinger et al.). They contend that a "critical mass" of underrepresented minorities is necessary to further that interest. *Ante,* at 17. Respondents and school administrators explain generally that "critical mass" means a sufficient number of underrepresented minority students to achieve several objectives: To ensure that these minority students do not feel isolated or like spokespersons for their race; to provide adequate opportunities for the type of interaction upon which the educational benefits of diversity depend; and to challenge all students to think critically and reexamine stereotypes. See App. to Pet. for Cert. 211a; Brief for Respondents Bollinger et al. These objectives indicate that "critical mass" relates to the size of the student body. *Id.,* at 5 (claiming that the Law School has enrolled "critical mass," or "enough minority students to provide meaningful integration of its classrooms and residence halls"). Respondents further claim that the Law School is achieving "critical mass." *Id.,* at 4 (noting that the Law School's goals have been "greatly furthered by the presence of . . . a 'critical mass' of" minority students in the student body).

In practice, the Law School's program bears little or no relation to its asserted goal of achieving "critical mass." Respondents explain that the Law School seeks to accumulate a "critical mass" of *each* underrepresented minority group. See, *e.g., id.,* at 49, n. 79 ("The Law School's . . . current policy . . . provide[s] a special commitment to enrolling a 'critical mass' of 'Hispanics'"). But the record demonstrates that the Law School's admissions practices with respect to these groups differ dramatically and cannot be defended under any consistent use of the term "critical mass."

From 1995 through 2000, the Law School admitted between 1,130 and 1,310 students. Of those, between 13 and 19 were Native American, between 91 and 108 were African-Americans, and between 47 and 56 were Hispanic. If the Law School is admitting between 91 and 108 African-Americans in order to achieve "critical mass," thereby preventing African-American students from feeling "isolated or like spokespersons for their race," one would think that a number of the same order of magnitude would be necessary to accomplish the same purpose for Hispanics and Native Americans. Similarly, even if all of the Native American applicants admitted in a given year matriculate, which the record demonstrates is not at all the case, how can this possibly constitute a "critical mass" of Native Americans in a class of over 350 students? In order for this pattern of admission to be consistent with the Law School's explanation of "critical mass," one would have to believe that the objectives of "critical mass" offered by respondents are achieved with only half the number of Hispanics and one-sixth the number of Native Americans as compared to African-Americans. But respondents offer no race-specific reasons for such disparities. Instead, they simply emphasize the importance of achieving "critical mass," without any explanation of why that concept is applied differently among the three underrepresented minority groups.

These different numbers, moreover, come only as a result of substantially different treatment among the three underrepresented minority groups, as is apparent in an example offered by the Law School and highlighted by the Court: The school asserts that it "frequently accepts nonminority applicants with grades and test scores lower than underrepresented minority applicants (and other nonminority applicants) who are rejected." *Ante,* at 26 (citing Brief for Respondents Bollinger et al.). Specifically, the Law School states that "[s]ixty-nine minority applicants were rejected between 1995 and 2000 with at least a 3.5 [Grade Point Average (GPA)] and a [score of] 159 or higher on the [Law School Admissions Test (LSAT)]" while a number of Caucasian and Asian-American applicants with similar or lower scores were admitted. Brief for Respondents Bollinger et al.

Review of the record reveals only 67 such individuals. Of these 67 individuals, 56 were Hispanic, while only 6 were African-American, and only 5 were Native American. This discrepancy reflects a consistent practice. For example, in 2000, 12 Hispanics who scored between a 159–160 on the LSAT and earned a GPA of 3.00 or higher applied for admission and only 2 were admitted. App. 200–201. Meanwhile, 12 African-Americans in the same range of qualifications applied for admission and all 12 were admitted. *Id.,* at 198. Likewise, that same year, 16 Hispanics who scored between a 151–153 on the LSAT and earned a 3.00 or higher applied for admission and only 1 of those applicants was admitted. *Id.,* at 200–201. Twenty-three similarly qualified African-Americans applied for admission and 14 were admitted. *Id.,* at 198.

These statistics have a significant bearing on petitioner's case. Respondents have *never* offered any race-specific arguments explaining why significantly more individuals from one underrepresented minority group are needed in order to achieve "critical mass" or further student body diversity. They certainly have not explained why Hispanics, who they have said are among "the groups most isolated by racial barriers in our country," should have their admission capped out in this manner. Brief for Respondents Bollinger et al. True, petitioner is neither Hispanic nor Native American. But the Law School's disparate admissions practices with respect to these minority groups demonstrate that its alleged goal of "critical mass" is simply a sham. Petitioner may use these statistics to expose this sham, which is the basis for the Law School's admission of less qualified underrepresented minorities in preference to her. Surely strict scrutiny cannot permit these sort of disparities without at least some explanation.

Only when the "critical mass" label is discarded does a likely explanation for these numbers emerge. The Court states that the Law School's goal of attaining a "critical mass" of underrepresented minority students is not an interest in merely "'assur[ing] within its student body some specified percentage of a particular group merely because of its race or ethnic origin.'" *Ante,* at 17 (quoting *Bakke,* 438 U.S., at 307 (opinion of Powell, J.)). The Court recognizes that such an interest "would amount to outright racial balancing, which is patently unconstitutional." *Ante,* at 17. The Court concludes, however, that the Law School's use of race in admissions, consistent with Justice Powell's opinion in *Bakke,* only pays "'[s]ome attention to numbers.'" *Ante,* at 23 (quoting *Bakke, supra,* at 323).

But the correlation between the percentage of the Law School's pool of applicants who are members of the three minority groups and the percentage of the admitted applicants who are members of these same groups is far too precise to be dismissed as merely the result of the school paying "some attention to [the] numbers." As the tables below show, from 1995 through 2000 the percentage of admitted applicants who were members of these minority groups closely tracked the percentage of individuals in the school's applicant pool who were from the same groups.

Table 1

Year	Number of law school applicants	Number of African-American applicants	% of applicants who were African-American	Number of applicants admitted by the law school	Number of African-American applicants admitted	% of admitted applicants who were African-American
1995	4147	404	9.7%	1130	106	9.4%
1996	3677	342	9.3%	1170	108	9.2%
1997	3429	320	9.3%	1218	101	8.3%
1998	3537	304	8.6%	1310	103	7.9%
1999	3400	247	7.3%	1280	91	7.1%
2000	3432	259	7.5%	1249	91	7.3%

Table 2

Year	Number of law school applicants	Number of Hispanic applicants	% of applicants who were Hispanic	Number of applicants admitted by the law school	Number of Hispanic applicants admitted	% of admitted applicants who were Hispanic
1995	4147	213	5.1%	1130	56	5.0%
1996	3677	186	5.1%	1170	54	4.6%
1997	3429	163	4.8%	1218	47	3.9%
1998	3537	150	4.2%	1310	55	4.2%
1999	3400	152	4.5%	1280	48	3.8%
2000	3432	168	4.9%	1249	53	4.2%

Table 3

Year	Number of law school applicants	Number of Native American applicants	% of applicants who were Native American	Number of applicants admitted by the law school	Number of Native American applicants admitted	% of admitted applicants who were Native American
1995	4147	45	1.1%	1130	14	1.2%
1996	3677	31	0.8%	1170	13	1.1%
1997	3429	37	1.1%	1218	19	1.6%
1998	3537	40	1.1%	1310	18	1.4%
1999	3400	25	0.7%	1280	13	1.0%
2000	3432	35	1.0%	1249	14	1.1%

For example, in 1995, when 9.7% of the applicant pool was African-American, 9.4% of the admitted class was African-American. By 2000, only 7.5% of the applicant pool was African-American, and 7.3% of the admitted class was African-American. This correlation is striking. Respondents themselves emphasize that the number of underrepresented minority students admitted to the Law School would be significantly smaller if the race of each applicant were not considered. See *App. to Pet. for Cert.* 223a; Brief for Respondents Bollinger et al. (quoting App. to Pet. for Cert, of Bollinger et al.). But, as the examples above illustrate, the measure of the decrease would differ dramatically among the groups. The tight correlation between the percentage of applicants and admittees of a given race, therefore, must result from careful race-based planning by the Law School. It suggests a formula for admission based on the aspirational assumption that all applicants are equally qualified academically, and therefore that the proportion of each group admitted should be the same as the proportion of that group in the applicant pool. See Brief for Respondents Bollinger et al. n. 70 (discussing admissions officers' use of "periodic reports" to track "the racial composition of the developing class").

Not only do respondents fail to explain this phenomenon, they attempt to obscure it. See *id.*, at 32, n. 50 ("The Law School's minority enrollment percentages . . . diverged from the percentages in the applicant pool by as much as 17.7% from 1995–2000"). But the divergence between the percentages of underrepresented minorities in the applicant pool and in the *enrolled* classes is not the only relevant comparison. In fact, it may not be the most relevant comparison. The Law School cannot precisely control which of its admitted applicants decide to attend the university. But it can and, as the numbers demonstrate, clearly does employ racial preferences in extending offers of admission. Indeed, the ostensibly flexible nature of the Law School's admissions program that the Court finds appealing, see *ante,* at 24–26, appears to be, in practice, a carefully managed program designed to ensure proportionate representation of applicants from selected minority groups.

I do not believe that the Constitution gives the Law School such free rein in the use of race. The Law School has offered no explanation for its actual admissions practices and, unexplained, we are bound to conclude that the Law School has managed its admissions program, not to achieve a "critical mass," but to extend offers of admission to members of selected minority groups in proportion to their statistical representation in the applicant pool. But this is precisely the type of racial balancing that the Court itself calls "patently unconstitutional." *Ante,* at 17.

Finally, I believe that the Law School's program fails strict scrutiny because it is devoid of any reasonably precise time limit on the Law School's use of race in admissions. We have emphasized that we will consider "the planned duration of the remedy" in determining whether a race-conscious program is constitutional. *Fullilove,* 448 U.S., at 510 (Powell, J. concurring); see also *United States v. Paradise,* 480 U.S. 149, 171 (1987) ("In determining whether race-conscious remedies are appropriate, we look to several factors, including the . . . duration of the relief"). Our previous cases have required some limit on the duration of programs such as this because discrimination on the basis of race is invidious.

The Court suggests a possible 25-year limitation on the Law School's current program. See *ante,* at 30. Respondents, on the other hand, remain more ambiguous, explaining that "the Law School of course recognizes that race-conscious programs must have reasonable durational limits, and the Sixth Circuit properly found such a limit in the Law School's resolve to cease considering race when genuine race-neutral alternatives become available." Brief for Respondents Bollinger et al. These discussions of a time limit are the vaguest of assurances. In truth, they permit the Law School's use of racial preferences on a seemingly permanent basis. Thus, an important component of strict scrutiny—that a program be limited in time—is casually subverted.

The Court, in an unprecedented display of deference under our strict scrutiny analysis, upholds the Law School's program despite its obvious flaws. We have said that when it comes to the use of race, the connection between the ends and the means used to attain them must be precise. But here the flaw is deeper than that; it is not merely a question of "fit" between ends and means. Here the means actually used are forbidden by the Equal Protection Clause of the Constitution.

POSTSCRIPT

Are "Affirmative Action" Admissions Policies at Public Universities Permitted by the Constitution?

Affirmative action programs are a controversial practice. While some persons argue that these programs are needed to rectify problems associated with past racial discrimination and finally bring everyone onto a "level playing field," opponents respond that the practice intentionally skews the competition by ignoring merit-based measures. Moreover, many argue that it is wrong to attempt to address past discrimination with programs that expressly discriminate against whites. It seems plausible that overall social support for affirmative action programs would be enhanced if it could be demonstrated that they are an effective device for helping members of traditionally disadvantaged groups to participate as full and productive members of U.S. society.

Scholars have sought to determine the impact of affirmative action programs on minority group members as well as the costs and benefits of racial preferences in admissions. The available evidence appears to be somewhat inconclusive. In an article published in the *Stanford Law Review,* vol. 57, p. 367 (2004), Richard H. Sander, a UCLA law professor, analyzed affirmative action programs in American law schools. His study, which was based on a large, longitudinal data set on white and black law students and lawyers, sought to determine the overall effects of affirmative action policies. Sander's conclusions included the following:

- The levels of racial preferences at American law schools are very large;
- Black students admitted through preferential admissions programs generally have low grades in law school, because the preferences put them at a large academic disadvantage. Moreover, the median black student starting law school in 1991 received first-year grades comparable to a white student at the 7th or 8th percentile;
- Low grades hinder black students in their efforts to complete law school and pass the bar. Only 45% of black law students in a 1991 cohort completed law school and passed the bar on their first attempt (Sander estimates that without preferential admissions programs that rate would rise to 74%);
- The job market benefits of attending an elite law school have been overestimated; the data strongly suggest that most black lawyers entering the job market would have higher earnings in the absence of preferential admissions, because better grades would trump the prestige of attending an elite school;

- It is not clear that preferential admissions policies actually cause the legal education system to produce a larger number of black lawyers. His analysis indicates that 86% of blacks currently enrolled in law schools would have been admitted to some law school under merit-based admissions policies. The much lower attrition rates that would result from merit-based policies would be likely to produce larger groups of black lawyers than the current system;
- In the case of blacks, the objective costs of affirmative action programs appear to "substantially" outweigh the benefits. Sander describes the basic theory as the "academic mismatch" mechanism; attending an elite school where one's credential are far below one's peers has negative effects on learning, motivation, and goals that harm the beneficiary of the preference.

These are daunting criticisms of the use of affirmative action admissions programs in the law school admissions process; however, Professor Sander's work has received substantial criticism in the literature. A working paper, published at the University of Michigan Law School in direct response to Sander's article, asserted that his methodology was flawed and that his study has not been replicated. Moreover, the authors assert that Sander has stated his conclusions with "great confidence. This confidence is unwarranted, and the truth we believe is often the opposite of what Sander posits."

The debate on the effectiveness of affirmative action programs is certain to continue. For now, the safest conclusion is that the "jury is still out" on the empirical effectiveness of these programs; however, it remains clear that many colleges and universities for the time being remain committed in principle to affirmative action programs as a means of providing the benefits of diverse cultural perspectives to their students. It does appear, however, that the Supreme Court will not continue to permit affirmative action programs to last indefinitely.

Justice O'Connor's majority opinion in *Grutter* seems to predict an eventual end to affirmative action. Stated Justice O'Connor:

We take the Law School at its word that it would 'like nothing better than to find a race-neutral admissions formula' and will terminate its race-conscious admissions program as soon as practicable [citations omitted]. It has been 25 years since Justice Powell first approved the use of race to further an interest in student body diversity in the context of public higher education. Since that time, the number of minority applicants with high grades and test scores had indeed increased. We expect that 25 years from now, the use of racial preferences will no longer be necessary to further the interest approved today.

After reading the excerpts from *Grutter,* do you believe that affirmative action programs should be continued? Or, conversely, are they simply a form of reverse discrimination that the Fourteenth Amendment's Equal Protection Clause was designed to prevent?

These are compelling questions. Fortunately, there are a large number of additional resources to pursue further study in this area, including: Kathleen

M. Sullivan and Gerald Gunther, *Constitutional Law* (Foundation Press, 15th ed., 2004); Laurence H. Tribe, *American Constitutional Law* (Foundation Press, 2nd ed., 1988); Alpheus Thomas Mason and Donald Grier Stephenson, Jr., *American Constitutional Law* (Pearson Prentice Hall, 15th ed., 2009; 14th ed., 2005); Bernard Schwartz, *A History of the Supreme Court* (Oxford University Press, 1993); Kermit L. Hall, Paul Finkelman, and James Ely, Jr., *American Legal History: Cases and Materials* (Oxford University Press, 3rd ed., 2005); Kermit L. Hall, *The Oxford Companion to the Supreme Court of the United States* (Oxford University Press, 1992); Walter F. Murphy, James E. Fleming, Sotirios A. Barber, and Stephen Macedo, *American Constitutional Interpretation* (Foundation Press, 3rd ed., 2003); David M. O'Brien, *Constitutional Law and Politics: Struggles for Power and Government Accountability* (W.W. Norton & Company, 6th ed., 2005); Craig R. Ducat, *Constitutional Interpretation* (Wadsworth, 9th ed., 2009); John H. Garvey, T. Alexander Aleinikoff, and Daniel A. Farber, *Modern Constitutional Theory: A Reader* (Thompson West, 5th ed., 2004). See also: Sander, "A Systematic Analysis of Affirmative Action in American Law Schools," *Stanford Law Review*, vol. 57, p. 367 (2004); Lempert, Kidder, Clydesdale, and Chambers, "The John M. Olin Center for Law & Economics Working Paper Series," *University of Michigan Law School, Paper 60* (2006); West-Faulcon, "The River Runs Dry: When Title VI Trumps State Anti-Affirmative Action Laws," *The University of Pennsylvania Law Review*, vol. 157, p. 1075 (2009); Planer, "The Death of Diversity? Affirmative Action in the Workplace After Parents Involved," *Seton Hall Law Review*, vol. 39, p. 1333 (2009); Baldwin, "The Changing Significance of 'Race' in the Post-Bakke Era," *The Alberta Law Review*, vol. 72, p. 803 (2009); Dominguez, "Legal Education and the Ecology of Cultural Justice: How Affirmative Action Can Become Race-Neutral by 2028," *Oregon Law Review*, vol. 88, p. 177 (2009).

ISSUE 17

Does the Fourteenth Amendment Require the States to Use a "One Person, One Vote" Standard for Apportioning Legislative Districts?

YES: Earl H. Warren, from Majority Opinion, *Reynolds v. Sims*, 377 U.S. 533 (1963)

NO: John M. Harlan, from Dissenting Opinion, *Reynolds v. Sims*, 377 U.S. 533 (1963)

ISSUE SUMMARY

YES: Chief Justice Earl H. Warren, writing for the U.S. Supreme Court in *Reynolds v. Sims* (1963), held that both houses of a state's legislature must be apportioned on an equal population basis. The Equal Protection Clause requires an honest and good-faith effort by the states to do so.

NO: Justice John M. Harlan, in contrast, believes that *Reynolds v. Sims*, which involved congressional districting by the states, has the effect of placing basic aspects of state political systems under "the pervasive overlordship of the federal judiciary."

The issues in this section have considered various issues that arise under the Equal Protection Clause of the Fourteenth Amendment. First, we discussed the issue of segregated public facilities. Next, we considered the legality of state-sponsored affirmative action programs. This issue examines another early and important issue that arose in the context of the Civil Rights era—whether the Equal Protection Clause requires the states to apportion its legislative districts according to a "one person, one vote" standard.

On a very fundamental level, apportionment is about how power is distributed in a community (Cortner, 1972). This issue is somewhat more theoretical than the preceding questions in this section and a hypothetical example may help to clarify things. Suppose that a state's legislature were to develop, or *apportion*, two different legislative districts, each represented by a single congressperson. Legislative district "A" is predominantly composed of African

Americans. Legislative district "B" is composed mostly of whites. An Equal Protection Clause problem arises when there is a population imbalance in these districts. Suppose that legislative district "A" has approximately 300,000 registered voters, whereas legislative district "B" has 100,000 registered voters. Each of these districts has the power to elect only one congressional representative. If this situation were to be held lawful, the vote of each person registered in district "B" would be worth three times more than that of someone in district "A." At the risk of oversimplification, this situation is similar to the problem faced by the African American voters in *Reynolds v. Sims* (1963).

Although the hypothetical example presented above seems at first glance to be somewhat extreme, an examination of the pre-*Reynolds* apportionment disparities shows that reality is sometimes stranger than fiction. Then Congressman Morris "Mo" K. Udall compiled the following list to illustrate the scope of the problem:

- In Connecticut, one house district had 191 people; another had 81,000;
- In New Hampshire, one township with three people had a state assemblyman; another town also had one assemblyman. A resident's vote in the first town was 108,000 percent more powerful;
- In Utah, the smallest district had 164 people, the largest 32,280 (?8 times the population of the other);
- In Vermont, the smallest district had 36 people, the largest 35,000, a ratio of almost 1,000 to 1;
- In California, the 14,000 people of one small county had one state senator. The 6,000,000 people of Los Angeles also had one state senator,
- In Idaho, the smallest senate district had 951 people; the largest had 93,400;
- Nevada's 17 state senators represented as many as 127,000 or as few as 568 people—a ratio of 224 to 1 (http://www.economicexpert.com/a/Reynolds:v:Sims.html).

Under the Voting Rights Act of 1965, revised in 2006, the states must conduct legislative apportionment after each 10-year decennial census. This is to ensure that every person's vote has an equal weight.

The Supreme Court's approach to state legislative apportionment cases before the advent of the Civil Rights era was to hold that these issues were nonjusticiable political questions—they were primarily matters of state concern that the federal courts should not decide. For example, in *Colegrove v. Green*, 328 U.S. 549 (1946), Justice Felix Frankfurter asserted that it is inappropriate for the judiciary to become involved in "the politics of the people." He believed that the resolution of apportionment cases was better left to the state legislatures, or to Congress.

In 1962, however, the Supreme Court's approach to apportionment cases took a dramatic turn. *Baker v. Carr*, 369 U.S. 186 (1962), squarely presented yet again the issue of whether legislative apportionment schemes are political questions the courts should refuse to decide. The case involved the apportionment of the Tennessee Assembly, which had last undergone apportionment almost 60 years earlier, in spite of the fact that the Tennessee Constitution required that it be apportioned according to population. As you might imagine, the composition of the state's population had changed significantly over the 60-year period. The Supreme Court held that the issue of legislative apportionment does not present a political question. Therefore, the courts were empowered to hear these cases. In addition, the Supreme Court outlined several factors that courts should consider in determining if a case presents a nonjusticiable political question:

1. Whether the issue is clearly assigned to another coequal branch;
2. Whether there is a lack of judicial standards for deciding the issue;
3. Whether the issue involves a policy determination better left to another branch of government;
4. Whether deciding the case would demonstrate a lack of respect for a coequal branch of government;
5. Whether there is a need to abide by a political decision that has already been made; and
6. Whether there is the potential for embarrassment resulting from multiple pronouncements on one question by different governmental departments.

Baker v. Carr was clearly a case whose time had finally come. By deciding that legislative apportionment cases may be decided by the courts, *Baker v. Carr* helped to pave the way for the Court's seminal apportionment decision in *Reynolds v. Sims*, which was decided one year later, and developed a clear standard for courts to use in deciding legislative apportionment cases.

You should also note that while legislative apportionment decisions have been held to be justiciable issues, *political gerrymandering*, the development of legislative district lines to benefit a particular political party, has received more deferential treatment by the Supreme Court. In *League of United Latin American Citizens v. Perry*, 548 U.S. 399 (2006), Texas democrats challenged a mid-decade legislative redistricting scheme developed by the Republican-controlled state legislature. The Supreme Court upheld the principle that gerrymandering claims are justiciable issues; however, it did not provide a clear set of standards to be used to decide when political gerrymandering violates the Equal Protection Clause.

Political gerrymandering, which receives this more deferential standard of review, may be contrasted with racial gerrymandering, whereby a state legislature attempts to draw electoral districts based on race. In cases of suspected racial gerrymandering, the states are required to follow the "one person, one vote" principle and the courts will use strict scrutiny to analyze the challenged statute.

Reynolds v. Sims presented the latter type of case—a challenge to the apportionment scheme in the Alabama Legislature. It held that the Equal Protection Clause of the Fourteenth Amendment mandates that seats in both houses of a bicameral state legislature must be apportioned on a population basis. Stated Chief Justice Earl Warren:

> The right to vote freely for the candidate of one's choice is of the essence of a democratic society, and any restrictions on that right strike at the heart of representative government. And the right of suffrage can be

denied by a debasement or dilution of the weight of a citizen's vote just as effectively as by wholly prohibiting the free exercise of the franchise.

Chief Justice Warren took note as well of the Court's earlier pronouncement in *Baker v. Carr* (1962) of the need for "discoverable and manageable" standards to be used by lower courts to determine the constitutionality of a state legislative apportionment scheme. The Equal Protection Clause provided such a standard: Courts must determine "if [on the particular facts of the case at bar an act of discrimination] reflects no policy, but simply arbitrary and capricious action [by a state legislature]."

When you read the excerpts from *Reynolds v. Sims*, try to remember that this case arose during a turbulent time in our nation's history. A number of states that had tried to circumvent federal law and Supreme Court Equal Protection Clause precedents were not going to let go of segregation easily. *Reynolds* represents another round in the fight to guarantee equal rights to all Americans.

In Your Opinion . . .

- Do you see any parallels between the issues presented in *Reynolds* and those in *Brown v. Board of Education of Topeka* (1954)?
- Do you agree that the judiciary's involvement in legislative apportionment cases has "the effect of placing basic aspects of state political systems under the pervasive overlordship of the federal judiciary?"
- Should the courts defer to state legislative determinations in these areas?

Majority Opinion, *Reynolds v. Sims*

MR. CHIEF JUSTICE WARREN delivered the opinion of the Court.

Involved in these cases are an appeal and two cross-appeals from a decision of the Federal District Court for the Middle District of Alabama holding invalid, under the Equal Protection Clause of the Federal Constitution, the existing and two legislatively proposed plans for the apportionment of seats in the two houses of the Alabama Legislature, and ordering into effect a temporary reapportionment plan comprised of parts of the proposed but judicially disapproved measures.

I

On August 26, 1961, the original plaintiffs (appellees in No. 23), residents, taxpayers and voters of Jefferson County, Alabama, filed a complaint in the United States District Court for the Middle District of Alabama, in their own behalf and on behalf of all similarly situated Alabama voters, challenging the apportionment of the Alabama Legislature. Defendants below (appellants in No. 23), sued in their representative capacities, were various state and political party officials charged with the performance of certain duties in connection with state elections. The complaint alleged a deprivation of rights under the Alabama Constitution and under the Equal Protection Clause of the Fourteenth Amendment, and asserted that the District Court had jurisdiction under provisions of the Civil Rights Act, 42 U.S.C. §§ 1983, 1988, as well as under 28 U.S.C. § 1343(3).

The complaint stated that the Alabama Legislature was composed of a Senate of 35 members and a House of Representatives of 106 members. It set out relevant portions of the 1901 Alabama Constitution, which prescribe the number of members of the two bodies of the State Legislature and the method of apportioning the seats among the State's 67 counties. . . .

On July 21, 1962, the District Court held that the inequality of the existing representation in the Alabama Legislature violated the Equal Protection Clause of the Fourteenth Amendment, a finding which the Court noted had been "generally conceded" by the parties to the litigation, since population growth and shifts had converted the 1901 scheme, as perpetuated some 60 years later, into an invidiously discriminatory plan completely lacking in rationality. 208 F.Supp. 431. Under the existing provisions, applying

Supreme Court of the United States, 1963.

1960 census figures, only 25.1% of the State's total population resided in districts represented by a majority of the members of the Senate, and only 25.7% lived in counties which could elect a majority of the members of the House of Representatives. Population variance ratios of up to about 41-to-1 existed in the Senate, and up to about 16-to-1 in the House. Bullock County, with a population of only 13,462, and Henry County, with a population of only 15,286, each were allocated two seats in the Alabama House, whereas Mobile County, with a population of 314,301, was given only three seats, and Jefferson County, with 634,864 people, had only seven representatives. With respect to senatorial apportionment, since the pertinent Alabama constitutional provisions had been consistently construed as prohibiting the giving of more than one Senate seat to any one county, Jefferson County, with over 600,000 people, was given only one senator, as was Lowndes County, with a 1960 population of only 15,417, and Wilcox County, with only 18,739 people. . . .

The District Court then directed its concern to the providing of an effective remedy. It indicated that it was adopting and ordering into effect for the November, 1962, election a provisional and temporary reapportionment plan composed of the provisions relating to the House of Representatives contained in the 67-Senator Amendment and the provisions of the Crawford-Webb Act relating to the Senate, . . .

It enjoined the defendant state officials from holding any future elections under any of the apportionment plans that it had found invalid, and stated that the 1962 election of Alabama legislators could validly be conducted only under the apportionment scheme specified in the Court's order. . . .

No effective political remedy to obtain relief against the alleged malapportionment of the Alabama Legislature appears to have been available. No initiative procedure exists under Alabama law. Amendment of the State Constitution can be achieved only after a proposal is adopted by three-fifths of the members of both houses of the legislature and is approved by a majority of the people, or as a result of a constitutional convention convened after approval by the people of a convention call initiated by a majority of both houses of the Alabama Legislature. Notices of appeal to this Court from the District Court's decision were timely filed by defendants below (appellants in No. 23) and by two groups of intervenor-plaintiffs (cross appellants in Nos. 27 and 41). Appellants in No. 23 contend that the District Court erred in holding the existing and the two proposed plans for the apportionment of seats in the Alabama Legislature unconstitutional, and that a federal court lacks the power to affirmatively reapportion seats in a state legislature. Cross-appellants in No. 27 assert that the court below erred in failing to compel reapportionment of the Alabama Senate on a population basis, as allegedly required by the Alabama Constitution and the Equal Protection Clause of the Federal Constitution. Cross-appellants in No. 41 contend that the District Court should have required and ordered into effect the apportionment of seats in both houses of the Alabama Legislature on a population basis. We noted probable jurisdiction on June 10, 1963. 374 U.S. 802.

II

Undeniably, the Constitution of the United States protects the right of all qualified citizens to vote in state as well as in federal elections. A consistent line of decisions by this Court in cases involving attempts to deny or restrict the right of suffrage has made this indelibly clear. It has been repeatedly recognized that all qualified voters have a constitutionally protected right to vote, *Ex parte Yarbrough,* 110 U.S. 651, and to have their votes counted, *United States v. Mosley,* 238 U.S. 383. In *Mosley,* the Court stated that it is "as equally unquestionable that the right to have one's vote counted is as open to protection . . . as the right to put a ballot in a box." 238 U.S. at 386. The right to vote can neither be denied outright, *Guinn v. United States,* 238 U.S. 347, *Lane v. Wilson,* 307 U.S. 268, nor destroyed by alteration of ballots, see *United States v. Classic,* 313 U.S. 299, 315, nor diluted by ballot box stuffing, *Ex parte Siebold,* 100 U.S. 371, *United States v. Saylor,* 322 U.S. 385. As the Court stated in *Classic,*

> Obviously included within the right to choose, secured by the Constitution, is the right of qualified voters within a state to cast their ballots and have them counted. . . .

313 U.S. at 315. Racially based gerrymandering, *Gomillion v. Lightfoot,* 364 U.S. 339, and the conducting of white primaries, *Nixon v. Herndon,* 273 U.S. 536, *Nixon v. Condon,* 286 U.S. 73, *Smith v. Allwright,* 321 U.S. 649, *Terry v. Adams,* 345 U.S. 461, both of which result in denying to some citizens their right to vote, have been held to be constitutionally impermissible. And history has seen a continuing expansion of the scope of the right of suffrage in this country. The right to vote freely for the candidate of one's choice is of the essence of a democratic society, and any restrictions on that right strike at the heart of representative government. And the right of suffrage can be denied by a debasement or dilution of the weight of a citizen's vote just as effectively as by wholly prohibiting the free exercise of the franchise.

In *Baker v. Carr,* 369 U.S. 186, we held that a claim asserted under the Equal Protection Clause challenging the constitutionality of a State's apportionment of seats in its legislature, on the ground that the right to vote of certain citizens was effectively impaired, since debased and diluted, in effect presented a justiciable controversy subject to adjudication by federal courts. The spate of similar cases filed and decided by lower courts since our decision in *Baker* amply shows that the problem of state legislative malapportionment is one that is perceived to exist in a large number of the States. In *Baker,* a suit involving an attack on the apportionment of seats in the Tennessee Legislature, we remanded to the District Court, which had dismissed the action, for consideration on the merits. We intimated no view as to the proper constitutional standards for evaluating the validity of a state legislative apportionment scheme. Nor did we give any consideration to the question of appropriate remedies. Rather, we simply stated:

> Beyond noting that we have no cause at this stage to doubt the District
> Court will be able to fashion relief if violations of constitutional rights

are found, it is improper now to consider what remedy would be most appropriate if appellants prevail at the trial.

We indicated in *Baker,* however, that the Equal Protection Clause provides discoverable and manageable standards for use by lower courts in determining the constitutionality of a state legislative apportionment scheme, and we stated:

> Nor need the appellants, in order to succeed in this action, ask the Court to enter upon policy determinations for which judicially manageable standards are lacking. Judicial standards under the Equal Protection Clause are well developed and familiar, and it has been open to courts since the enactment of the **Fourteenth Amendment** to determine if, on the particular facts they must, that a discrimination reflects no policy, but simply arbitrary and capricious action.

Subsequent to *Baker,* we remanded several cases to the courts below for reconsideration in light of that decision.

In *Gray v. Sanders,* 372 U.S. 368, we held that the Georgia county unit system, applicable in statewide primary elections, was unconstitutional, since it resulted in a dilution of the weight of the votes of certain Georgia voters merely because of where they resided. After indicating that the Fifteenth and Nineteenth Amendments prohibit a State from overweighting or diluting votes on the basis of race or sex, we stated:

> How, then, can one person be given twice or ten times the voting power of another person in a statewide election merely because he lives in a rural area or because he lives in the smallest rural county? Once the geographical unit for which a representative is to be chosen is designated, all who participate in the election are to have an equal vote—whatever their race, whatever their sex, whatever their occupation, whatever their income and wherever their home may be in that geographical unit. This is required by the Equal Protection Clause of the **Fourteenth Amendment**. The concept of "we the people" under the Constitution visualizes no preferred class of voters, but equality among those who meet the basic qualifications. The idea that every voter is equal to every other voter in his State, when he casts his ballot in favor of one of several competing candidates, underlies many of our decisions.

Continuing, we stated that

> there is no indication in the Constitution that homesite or occupation affords a permissible basis for distinguishing between qualified voters within the State.

And, finally, we concluded:

> The conception of political equality from the Declaration of Independence, to Lincoln's Gettysburg Address, to the Fifteenth, Seventeenth,

and Nineteenth Amendments can mean only one thing—one person, one vote.

We stated in *Gray,* however, that that case,

> unlike *Baker v. Carr,* . . . does not involve a question of the degree to which the Equal Protection Clause of the **Fourteenth Amendment** limits the authority of a State Legislature in designing the geographical districts from which representatives are chosen either for the State Legislature or for the Federal House of Representatives. . . . Nor does it present the question, inherent in the bicameral form of our Federal Government, whether a State may have one house chosen without regard to population. Of course, in these cases, we are faced with the problem not presented in *Gray*—that of determining the basic standards and stating the applicable guidelines for implementing our decision in *Baker v. Carr.*

In *Wesberry v. Sanders,* 376 U.S. 1, decided earlier this Term, we held that attacks on the constitutionality of congressional districting plans enacted by state legislatures do not present nonjusticiable questions, and should not be dismissed generally for "want of equity." We determined that the constitutional test for the validity of congressional districting schemes was one of substantial equality of population among the various districts established by a state legislature for the election of members of the Federal House of Representatives.

In that case, we decided that an apportionment of congressional seats which "contracts the value of some votes and expands that of others" is unconstitutional, since

> the Federal Constitution intends that, when qualified voters elect members of Congress, each vote be given as much weight as any other vote. . . .

We concluded that the constitutional prescription for election of members of the House of Representatives "by the People," construed in its historical context, "means that, as nearly as is practicable, one man's vote in a congressional election is to be worth as much as another's." We further stated:

> It would defeat the principle solemnly embodied in the Great Compromise—equal representation in the House for equal numbers of people—for us to hold that, within the States, legislatures may draw the lines of congressional districts in such a way as to give some voters a greater voice in choosing a Congressman than others.

We found further, in *Wesberry,* that "our Constitution's plain objective" was that "of making equal representation for equal numbers of people the fundamental goal. . . ." We concluded by stating:

> No right is more precious in a free country than that of having a voice in the election of those who make the laws under which, as good citizens,

we must live. Other rights, even the most basic, are illusory if the right to vote is undermined. Our Constitution leaves no room for classification of people in a way that unnecessarily abridges this right. . . .

III

A predominant consideration in determining whether a State's legislative apportionment scheme constitutes an invidious discrimination violative of rights asserted under the Equal Protection Clause is that the rights allegedly impaired are individual and personal in nature. As stated by the Court in *United States v. Bathgate,* 246 U.S. 220, 227, "[t]he right to vote is personal. . . ." While the result of a court decision in a state legislative apportionment controversy may be to require the restructuring of the geographical distribution of seats in a state legislature, the judicial focus must be concentrated upon ascertaining whether there has been any discrimination against certain of the State's citizens which constitutes an impermissible impairment of their constitutionally protected right to vote. Like *Skinner v. Oklahoma,* 316 U.S. 535, such a case "touches a sensitive and important area of human rights," and "involves one of the basic civil rights of man," presenting questions of alleged "invidious discriminations . . . against groups or types of individuals in violation of the constitutional guaranty of just and equal laws." 316 U.S. at 536, 541. Undoubtedly, the right of suffrage is a fundamental matter in a free and democratic society. Especially since the right to exercise the franchise in a free and unimpaired manner is preservative of other basic civil and political rights, any alleged infringement of the right of citizens to vote must be carefully and meticulously scrutinized. Almost a century ago, in *Yick Wo v. Hopkins,* 118 U.S. 356, the Court referred to "the political franchise of voting" as "a fundamental political right, because preservative of all rights." 118 U.S. at 370.

Legislators represent people, not trees or acres. Legislators are elected by voters, not farms or cities or economic interests. As long as ours is a representative form of government, and our legislatures are those instruments of government elected directly by and directly representative of the people, the right to elect legislators in a free and unimpaired fashion is a bedrock of our political system. It could hardly be gainsaid that a constitutional claim had been asserted by an allegation that certain otherwise qualified voters had been entirely prohibited from voting for members of their state legislature. And, if a State should provide that the votes of citizens in one part of the State should be given two times, or five times, or 10 times the weight of votes of citizens in another part of the State, it could hardly be contended that the right to vote of those residing in the disfavored areas had not been effectively diluted. It would appear extraordinary to suggest that a State could be constitutionally permitted to enact a law providing that certain of the State's voters could vote two, five, or 10 times for their legislative representatives, while voters living elsewhere could vote only once. And it is inconceivable that a state law to the effect that, in counting votes for legislators, the votes of citizens in one part of the State would be multiplied by two, five, or 10, while the votes of persons in another area would be counted only at face value, could be constitutionally sustainable. Of course, the effect of state legislative districting schemes which give the same number of representatives to unequal numbers of constituents is identical. Overweighting and overvaluation of the votes of those living here has the certain effect of dilution and undervaluation of the votes of those living there. The resulting discrimination against those individual voters living in disfavored areas is easily demonstrable mathematically. Their right to vote is simply not the same right to vote as that of those living in a favored part of the State. Two, five, or 10 of them must vote before the effect of their voting is equivalent to that of their favored neighbor. Weighting the votes of citizens differently, by any method or means, merely because of where they happen to reside, hardly seems justifiable. One must be ever aware that the Constitution forbids "sophisticated, as well as simple-minded, modes of discrimination." *Lane v. Wilson*, 307 U.S. 268, 275; *Gomillion v. Lightfoot,* 364 U.S. 339, 342. As we stated in *Wesberry v. Sanders, supra:*

> We do not believe that the Framers of the Constitution intended to permit the same vote-diluting discrimination to be accomplished through the device of districts containing widely varied numbers of inhabitants. To say that a vote is worth more in one district than in another would . . . run counter to our fundamental ideas of democratic government. . . .

State legislatures are, historically, the fountainhead of representative government in this country. A number of them have their roots in colonial times, and substantially antedate the creation of our Nation and our Federal Government. In fact, the first formal stirrings of American political independence are to be found, in large part, in the views and actions of several of the colonial legislative bodies. With the birth of our National Government, and the adoption and ratification of the Federal Constitution, state legislatures retained a most important place in our Nation's governmental structure. But representative government is, in essence, self-government through the medium of elected representatives of the people, and each and every citizen has an inalienable right to full and effective participation in the political processes of his State's legislative bodies. Most citizens can achieve this participation only as qualified voters through the election of legislators to represent them. Full and effective participation by all citizens in state government requires, therefore, that each citizen have an equally effective voice in the election of members of his state legislature. Modern and viable state government needs, and the Constitution demands, no less.

Logically, in a society ostensibly grounded on representative government, it would seem reasonable that a majority of the people of a State could elect a majority of that State's legislators. To conclude differently, and to sanction minority control of state legislative bodies, would appear to deny majority rights in a way that far surpasses any possible denial of minority rights that might otherwise be thought to result. Since legislatures are responsible for enacting laws by which all citizens are to be governed, they should be bodies which are collectively responsive to the popular will. And the concept of equal protection has been traditionally viewed as requiring the uniform treatment of persons standing in the same relation to the governmental action questioned or challenged. With respect to the allocation of legislative representation, all voters, as citizens of a State, stand in the same relation regardless of where they live. Any suggested criteria for the differentiation of citizens are insufficient to justify any discrimination, as to the weight of their votes, unless relevant to the permissible purposes of legislative apportionment. Since the achieving of fair and effective representation for all citizens is concededly the basic aim of legislative apportionment, we conclude that the Equal Protection Clause guarantees the opportunity for equal participation by all voters in the election of state legislators. Diluting the weight of votes because of place of residence impairs basic constitutional rights under the Fourteenth Amendment just as much as invidious discriminations based upon factors such as race, *Brown v. Board of Education,* 347 U.S. 483, or economic status, *Griffin v. Illinois,* 351 U.S. 12, *Douglas v. California,* 372 U.S. 353. Our constitutional system amply provides for the protection of minorities by means other than giving them majority control of state legislatures. And the democratic ideals of equality and majority rule, which have served this Nation so well in the past, are hardly of any less significance for the present and the future.

We are told that the matter of apportioning representation in a state legislature is a complex and many-faceted one. We are advised that States can rationally consider factors other than population in apportioning legislative representation. We are admonished not to restrict the power of the States to impose differing views as to political philosophy on their citizens. We are cautioned about the dangers of entering into political thickets and mathematical quagmires. Our answer is this: a denial of constitutionally protected rights demands judicial protection; our oath and our office require no less of us. As stated in *Gomillion v. Lightfoot, supra:*

> When a State exercises power wholly within the domain of state interest, it is insulated from federal judicial review. But such insulation is not carried over when state power is used as an instrument for circumventing a federally protected right. To the extent that a citizen's right to vote is debased, he is that much less a citizen. The fact that an individual lives here or there is not a legitimate reason for overweighting or diluting the efficacy of his vote. The complexions of societies and civilizations change, often with amazing rapidity. A nation once primarily rural in character becomes predominantly urban. Representation schemes once fair and equitable become archaic and outdated. But the basic principle of representative government remains, and must remain, unchanged—the weight of a citizen's vote cannot be made to depend on where he lives. Population is, of necessity, the starting point for consideration and the controlling criterion for judgment in legislative apportionment controversies. A citizen, a qualified voter, is no more nor no less so because he lives in the city or on the farm. This is the clear and strong command of our Constitution's Equal Protection Clause. This is an essential part of the concept of a government of laws, and not men. This is at the heart of Lincoln's vision of "government of the people, by the people, [and] for the people." The Equal Protection Clause demands no less than substantially equal state legislative representation for all citizens, of all places as well as of all races.

IV

We hold that, as a basic constitutional standard, the Equal Protection Clause requires that the seats in both houses of a bicameral state legislature must be apportioned on a population basis. Simply stated, an individual's right to vote for state legislators is unconstitutionally impaired when its weight is in a substantial fashion diluted when compared with votes of citizens living in other parts of the State. Since under neither the existing apportionment provisions nor either of the proposed plans was either of the houses of the Alabama Legislature apportioned on a population basis, the District Court correctly held that all three of these schemes were constitutionally invalid. Furthermore, the existing apportionment, and also, to a lesser extent, the apportionment under the Crawford-Webb Act, presented little more than crazy quilts, completely lacking in rationality, and could be found invalid on that basis alone. Although the District Court presumably found the apportionment of the Alabama House of Representatives under the 67-Senator Amendment to be acceptable, we conclude that the deviations from a strict population basis are too egregious to permit us to find that that body, under this proposed plan, was apportioned sufficiently on a population basis so as to permit the arrangement to be constitutionally sustained. Although about 43% of the State's total population would be required to comprise districts which could elect a majority in that body, only 39 of the 106 House seats were actually to be distributed on a population basis, as each of Alabama's 67 counties was given at least one representative, and population variance ratios of close to 5-to-1 would have existed. While mathematical nicety is not a constitutional requisite, one could hardly conclude that the Alabama House, under the proposed constitutional amendment, had been apportioned sufficiently on a population basis to be sustainable under the requirements of the Equal Protection Clause. And none of the other apportionments of seats in either of the bodies of the Alabama Legislature, under the three plans considered by the District Court, came nearly as close to approaching the required constitutional standard as did that of the House of Representatives under the 67-Senator Amendment.

Legislative apportionment in Alabama is signally illustrative and symptomatic of the seriousness of this problem in a number of the States. At the time this litigation was commenced, there had been no reapportionment of seats in the Alabama Legislature for over 60 years. Legislative inaction, coupled with the unavailability of any political or Judicial remedy, had resulted, with the passage of years, in the perpetuated scheme becoming little more than an irrational anachronism. Consistent failure by the Alabama Legislature to comply with state constitutional requirements as to the frequency of reapportionment and the bases of legislative representation resulted in a minority strangle hold on the State Legislature. Inequality of representation in one house added to the inequality in the other. With the crazy-quilt existing apportionment virtually conceded to be invalid, the Alabama Legislature offered two proposed plans for consideration by the District Court, neither of which was to be effective until 1966 and neither of which provided for the apportionment of even one of the two houses on a population basis. We find that the court below did not err in holding that neither of these proposed reapportionment schemes, considered as a whole, "meets the necessary constitutional requirements." And we conclude that the District Court acted properly in considering these two proposed plans, although neither was to become effective until the 1966 election and the proposed constitutional amendment was scheduled to be submitted to the State's voters in November 1962. Consideration by the court below of the two proposed plans was clearly necessary in determining whether the Alabama Legislature had acted effectively to correct the admittedly existing malapportionment, and in ascertaining what sort of judicial relief, if any, should be afforded. . . .

VI

By holding that, as a federal constitutional requisite, both houses of a state legislature must be apportioned on a population basis, we mean that the Equal Protection Clause requires that a State make an honest and good faith effort to construct districts, in both houses of its legislature, as nearly of equal population as is practicable. We realize that it is a practical impossibility to arrange legislative districts so that each one has an identical number of residents, or citizens, or voters. Mathematical exactness or precision is hardly a workable constitutional requirement. . . .

A State may legitimately desire to maintain the integrity of various political subdivisions, insofar as possible, and provide for compact districts of contiguous territory in designing a legislative apportionment scheme. Valid considerations may underlie such aims. Indiscriminate districting, without any regard for political subdivision or natural or historical boundary lines, may be little more than an open invitation to partisan gerrymandering. Single-member districts may be the rule in one State, while another State might desire to achieve some flexibility by creating multi-member or floterial districts. Whatever the means of accomplishment, the overriding objective must be substantial equality of population among the various districts, so that the vote of any citizen is approximately equal in weight to that of any other citizen in the State.

History indicates, however, that many States have deviated, to a greater or lesser degree, from the equal population principle in the apportionment of seats in at least one house of their legislatures. So long as the divergences from a strict population standard are based on legitimate considerations incident to the effectuation of a rational state policy, some deviations from the equal population principle are constitutionally permissible with respect to the apportionment of seats in either or both of the two houses of a bicameral state legislature. But neither history alone, nor economic or other sorts of group interests, are permissible factors in attempting to justify disparities from population-based representation. Citizens, not history or economic interests, cast votes. Considerations of area alone provide an insufficient justification for deviations from the equal population principle. Again, people, not land or trees or pastures, vote. Modern developments and improvements in transportation and communications make rather hollow, in the mid-1960's, most claims that deviations from population-based representation can validly be based solely on geographical considerations. Arguments for allowing such deviations in order to insure effective representation for sparsely settled areas and to prevent legislative districts from becoming so large that the availability of access of citizens to their representatives is impaired are today, for the most part, unconvincing. . . .

VIII

That the Equal Protection Clause requires that both houses of a state legislature be apportioned on a population basis does not mean that States cannot adopt some reasonable plan for periodic revision of their apportionment schemes. Decennial reapportionment appears to be a rational approach to readjustment of legislative representation in order to take into account population shifts and growth. Reallocation of legislative seats every 10 years coincides with the prescribed practice in 41 of the States, often honored more in the breach than the observance, however. Illustratively, the Alabama Constitution requires decennial reapportionment, yet the last reapportionment of the Alabama Legislature, when this suit was brought, was in 1901. Limitations on the frequency of reapportionment are justified by the need for stability and continuity in the organization of the legislative system, although undoubtedly reapportioning no more frequently than every 10 years leads to some imbalance in the population of districts toward the end of the decennial period, and also to the development of resistance to change on the part of some incumbent legislators. In substance, we do not regard the Equal Protection Clause as requiring daily, monthly, annual or biennial reapportionment, so long as a State has a reasonably conceived plan for periodic readjustment of legislative representation. While we do not intend to indicate that decennial reapportionment is a constitutional requisite, compliance with such an approach would clearly meet the minimal requirements for maintaining a reasonably current scheme of legislative representation. And we do not mean to intimate that more frequent reapportionment would not be constitutionally permissible or practicably desirable. But if reapportionment were accomplished with less frequency, it would assuredly be constitutionally suspect. . . .

X

. . . We find, therefore, that the action taken by the District Court in this case, in ordering into effect a reapportionment of both houses of the Alabama Legislature for purposes of the 1962 primary and general elections, by using the best parts of the two proposed plans which it had found, as a whole, to be invalid, was an appropriate and well considered exercise of judicial power. Admittedly, the lower court's ordered plan was intended only as a temporary and provisional measure, and the District Court correctly indicated that the plan was invalid as a permanent apportionment. In retaining jurisdiction while deferring a hearing on the issuance of a final injunction in order to give the provisionally reapportioned legislature an opportunity to act effectively, the court below proceeded in a proper fashion. Since the District Court evinced its realization that its ordered reapportionment could not be sustained as the basis for conducting the 1966 election of Alabama legislators, and avowedly intends to take some further action should the reapportioned Alabama Legislature fail to enact a constitutionally valid, permanent apportionment scheme in the interim, we affirm the judgment below and remand the cases for further proceedings consistent with the views stated in this opinion.

It is so ordered. . . .

Dissenting Opinion, *Reynolds v. Sims*

MR. JUSTICE HARLAN, dissenting.

In these cases, the Court holds that seats in the legislatures of six States are apportioned in ways that violate the Federal Constitution. Under the Court's ruling, it is bound to follow that the legislatures in all but a few of the other 44 States will meet the same fate. These decisions, with *Wesberry v. Sanders,* 376 U.S. 1, involving congressional districting by the States, and *Gray v. Sanders,* 372 U.S. 368, relating to elections for statewide office, have the effect of placing basic aspects of state political systems under the pervasive overlordship of the federal judiciary. Once again, I must register my protest.

Preliminary Statement

Today's holding is that the Equal Protection Clause of the Fourteenth Amendment requires every State to structure its legislature so that all the members of each house represent substantially the same number of people; other factors may be given play only to the extent that they do not significantly encroach on this basic "population" principle. Whatever may be thought of this holding as a piece of political ideology—and even on that score, the political history and practices of this country from its earliest beginnings leave wide room for debate (*see* the dissenting opinion of Frankfurter, J., in *Baker v. Carr,* 369 U.S. 186, 266, 301–323)—I think it demonstrable that the Fourteenth Amendment does not impose this political tenet on the States or authorize this Court to do so.

The Court's constitutional discussion, found in its opinion in the Alabama cases (Nos. 23, 27, 41, *ante,* p. 533) and more particularly at pages 561–568 thereof, is remarkable (as, indeed, is that found in the separate opinions of my Brothers STEWART and CLARK, *ante,* pp. 588, 587) for its failure to address itself at all to the Fourteenth Amendment as a whole or to the legislative history of the Amendment pertinent to the matter at hand. Stripped of aphorisms, the Court's argument boils down to the assertion that appellees' right to vote has been invidiously "debased" or "diluted" by systems of apportionment which entitle them to vote for fewer legislators than other voters, an assertion which is tied to the Equal Protection Clause only by the constitutionally frail tautology that "equal" means "equal."

Had the Court paused to probe more deeply into the matter, it would have found that the Equal Protection Clause was never intended to inhibit the States in choosing any democratic method they pleased for the apportionment

Supreme Court of the United States, 1963.

of their legislatures. This is shown by the language of the Fourteenth Amendment taken as a whole, by the understanding of those who proposed and ratified it, and by the political practices of the States at the time the Amendment was adopted. It is confirmed by numerous state and congressional actions since the adoption of the Fourteenth Amendment, and by the common understanding of the Amendment as evidenced by subsequent constitutional amendments and decisions of this Court before *Baker v. Carr, supra,* made an abrupt break with the past in 1962.

The failure of the Court to consider any of these matters cannot be excused or explained by any concept of "developing" constitutionalism. It is meaningless to speak of constitutional "development" when both the language and history of the controlling provisions of the Constitution are wholly ignored. Since it can, I think, be shown beyond doubt that state legislative apportionments, as such, are wholly free of constitutional limitations, save such as may be imposed by the Republican Form of Government Clause (Const., Art. IV, § 4), the Court's action now bringing them within the purview of the Fourteenth Amendment amounts to nothing less than an exercise of the amending power by this Court.

So far as the Federal Constitution is concerned, the complaints in these cases should all have been dismissed below for failure to state a cause of action, because what has been alleged or proved shows no violation of any constitutional right. . . .

Thus, it seems abundantly clear that the Court is entirely free to deal with the cases presently before it in light of materials now called to its attention for the first time. To these I now turn.

I

A. The Language of the Fourteenth Amendment

The Court relies exclusively on that portion of § 1 of the Fourteenth Amendment which provides that no State shall "deny to any person within its Jurisdiction the equal protection of the laws," and disregards entirely the significance of § 2, which reads:

> Representatives shall be apportioned among the several States according to their respective numbers, counting the whole number of persons in each State, excluding Indians not taxed. *But when the right to vote at any election for* the choice of electors for President and Vice President of the United States, Representatives in Congress, *the Executive and Judicial officers of a State, or the members of the Legislature thereof, is denied* to any of the male inhabitants of such State, being twenty-one years of age, and citizens of the United States, *or in any way abridged,* except for participation in rebellion, or other crime, the basis of representation therein shall be reduced in the proportion which the number of such male citizens shall bear to the whole number of male citizens twenty-one years of age in such State.

(Emphasis added.)

The Amendment is a single text. It was introduced and discussed as such in the Reconstruction Committee, which reported it to the Congress. It was discussed as a unit in Congress, and proposed as a unit to the States, which ratified it as a unit. A proposal to split up the Amendment and submit each section to the States as a separate amendment was rejected by the Senate. Whatever one might take to be the application to these cases of the Equal Protection Clause if it stood alone, I am unable to understand the Court's utter disregard of the second section, which expressly recognizes the States' power to deny "or in any way" abridge the right of their inhabitants to vote for "the members of the [State] Legislature," and its express provision of a remedy for such denial or abridgment. The comprehensive scope of the second section and its particular reference to the state legislatures preclude the suggestion that the first section was intended to have the result reached by the Court today. If indeed the words of the Fourteenth Amendment speak for themselves, as the majority's disregard of history seems to imply, they speak as clearly as may be against the construction which the majority puts on them. But we are not limited to the language of the Amendment itself.

B. Proposal and Ratification of the Amendment

The history of the adoption of the Fourteenth Amendment provides conclusive evidence that neither those who proposed nor those who ratified the Amendment believed that the Equal Protection Clause limited the power of the States to apportion their legislatures as they saw fit. Moreover, the history demonstrates that the intention to leave this power undisturbed was deliberate, and was widely believed to be essential to the adoption of the Amendment. . . .

The Constitutions of six of the 10 States contained provisions departing substantially from the method of apportionment now held to be required by the Amendment. And, as in the North, the departures were as real, in fact, as in theory. In North Carolina, 90 of the 120 representatives were apportioned among the counties without regard to population, leaving 30 seats to be distributed by numbers. Since there were seven counties with populations under 5,000 and 26 counties with populations over 15,000, the disproportions must have been widespread and substantial. In South Carolina, Charleston, with a population of 88,863, elected two Senators; each of the other counties, with populations ranging from 10,269 to 42,486, elected one Senator. In Florida, each of the 39 counties was entitled to elect one Representative; no county was entitled to more than four. These principles applied to Dade County, with a population of 85, and to Alachua County and Leon County, with populations of 17,328 and 15,236, respectively.

It is incredible that Congress would have exacted ratification of the Fourteenth Amendment as the price of readmission, would have studied the State Constitutions for compliance with the Amendment, and would then have disregarded violations of it.

The facts recited above show beyond any possible doubt:

(1)   that Congress, with full awareness of and attention to the possibility that the States would not afford full equality in voting rights

to all their citizens, nevertheless deliberately chose not to interfere with the States' plenary power in this regard when it proposed the **Fourteenth Amendment;**

(2)   that Congress did not include in the **Fourteenth Amendment** restrictions on the States' power to control voting rights because it believed that, if such restrictions were included, the Amendment would not be adopted; and

(3)   that at least a substantial majority, if not all, of the States which ratified the **Fourteenth Amendment** did not consider that, in so doing, they were accepting limitations on their freedom, never before questioned, to regulate voting rights as they chose.

Even if one were to accept the majority's belief that it is proper entirely to disregard the unmistakable implications of the second section of the Amendment in construing the first section, one is confounded by its disregard of all this history. There is here none of the difficulty which may attend the application of basic principles to situations not contemplated or understood when the principles were framed. The problems which concern the Court now were problems when the Amendment was adopted. By the deliberate choice of those responsible for the Amendment, it left those problems untouched. . . .

D. Today

Since the Court now invalidates the legislative apportionments in six States, and has so far upheld the apportionment in none, it is scarcely necessary to comment on the situation in the States today, which is, of course, as fully contrary to the Court's decision as is the record of every prior period in this Nation's history. As of 1961, the Constitutions of all but 11 States, roughly 20% of the total, recognized bases of apportionment other than geographic spread of population, and to some extent favored sparsely populated areas by a variety of devices, ranging from straight area representation or guaranteed minimum area representation to complicated schemes of the kind exemplified by the provisions of New York's Constitution of 1894, still in effect until struck down by the Court today in No. 20, *post*, p. 633. Since Tennessee, which was the subject of *Baker v. Carr*, and Virginia, scrutinized and disapproved today in No. 69, *post*, p. 678, are among the 11 States whose own Constitutions are sound from the standpoint of the Federal Constitution as construed today, it is evident that the actual practice of the States is even more uniformly than their theory opposed to the Court's view of what is constitutionally permissible. . . .

II

The Court's elaboration of its new "constitutional" doctrine indicates how far—and how unwisely—it has strayed from the appropriate bounds of its authority. The consequence of today's decision is that, in all but the handful of States which may already satisfy the new requirements, the local District Court or, it may be, the state courts, are given blanket authority and the constitutional duty to supervise apportionment of the State Legislatures. It is difficult to imagine a more intolerable and inappropriate interference by the judiciary with the independent legislatures of the States. . . .

Records such as these in the cases decided today are sure to be duplicated in most of the other States if they have not been already. They present a jarring picture of courts threatening to take action in an area which they have no business entering, inevitably on the basis of political judgments which they are incompetent to make. They show legislatures of the States meeting in haste and deliberating and deciding in haste to avoid the threat of judicial interference. So far as I can tell, the Court's only response to this unseemly state of affairs is ponderous insistence that "a denial of constitutionally protected rights demands judicial protection," *ante*, p. 566. By thus refusing to recognize the bearing which a potential for conflict of this kind may have on the question whether the claimed rights are, in fact, constitutionally entitled to judicial protection, the Court assumes, rather than supports, its conclusion.

It should by now be obvious that these cases do not mark the end of reapportionment problems in the courts. Predictions once made that the courts would never have to face the problem of actually working out an apportionment have proved false. This Court, however, continues to avoid the consequences of its decisions, simply assuring us that the lower courts "can and . . . will work out more concrete and specific standards," *ante*, p. 578. Deeming it "expedient" not to spell out "precise constitutional tests," the Court contents itself with stating "only a few rather general considerations." *Ibid.*

Generalities cannot obscure the cold truth that cases of this type are not amenable to the development of judicial standards. No set of standards can guide a court which has to decide how many legislative districts a State shall have, or what the shape of the districts shall be, or where to draw a particular district line. No judicially manageable standard can determine whether a State should have single member districts or multi-member districts or some combination of both. No such standard can control the balance between keeping up with population shifts and having stable districts. In all these respects, the courts will be called upon to make particular decisions with respect to which a principle of equally populated districts will be of no assistance whatsoever. Quite obviously, there are limitless possibilities for districting consistent with such a principle. Nor can these problems be avoided by judicial reliance on legislative judgments so far as possible. Reshaping or combining one or two districts, or modifying just a few district lines, is no less a matter of choosing among many possible solutions, with varying political consequences, than reapportionment broadside.

The Court ignores all this, saying only that "what is marginally permissible in one State may be unsatisfactory in another, depending on the particular circumstances of the case," *ante*, p. 578. It is well to remember that the product of today's decisions will not be readjustment of a few districts in a few States which most glaringly depart from the principle of equally populated districts. It will be a redetermination, extensive in many cases, of legislative districts in all but a few States.

Although the Court—necessarily, as I believe—provides only generalities in elaboration of its main thesis, its opinion nevertheless fully demonstrates how far removed these problems are from fields of judicial competence. Recognizing that "indiscriminate districting" is an invitation to "partisan gerrymandering," *ante* pp. 578–579, the Court nevertheless excludes virtually every basis for the formation of electoral districts other than "indiscriminate districting." In one or another of today's opinions, the Court declares it unconstitutional for a State to give effective consideration to any of the following in establishing legislative districts:

    (1) history;
    (2) "economic or other sorts of group interests";
    (3) area;
    (4) geographical considerations;
    (5) a desire "to insure effective representation for sparsely settled areas";
    (6) "availability of access of citizens to their representatives";
    (7) theories of bicameralism (except those approved by the Court);
    (8) occupation;
    (9) "an attempt to balance urban and rural power."
  (10) the preference of a majority of voters in the state.

So far as presently appears, the *only* factor which a State may consider, apart from numbers, is political subdivisions. But even "a clearly rational state policy" recognizing this factor is unconstitutional if "population is submerged as the controlling consideration. . . ."

I know of no principle of logic or practical or theoretical politics, still less any constitutional principle, which establishes all or any of these exclusions. Certain it is that the Court's opinion does not establish them. So far as the Court says anything at all on this score, it says only that "legislators represent people, not trees or acres," *ante*, p. 662; that "citizens, not history or economic interests, cast votes," *ante*, p. 580; that "people, not land or trees or pastures, vote," *ibid.* All this may be conceded. But it is surely equally obvious, and, in the context of elections, more meaningful, to note that people are not ciphers, and that legislators can represent their electors only by speaking for their interests—economic, social, political—many of which do reflect the place where the electors live. The Court does not establish, or indeed even attempt to make a case for the proposition that conflicting interests within a State can only be adjusted by disregarding them when voters are grouped for purposes of representation.

Conclusion

With these cases, the Court approaches the end of the third round set in motion by the complaint filed in *Baker v. Carr.* What is done today deepens my conviction that judicial entry into this realm is profoundly ill-advised and constitutionally impermissible. As I have said before, *Wesberry v. Sanders, supra,* at 48, I believe that the vitality of our political system, on which, in the last analysis, all else depends, is weakened by reliance on the judiciary for political reform; in time, a complacent body politic may result.

These decisions also cut deeply into the fabric of our federalism. What must follow from them may eventually appear to be the product of state legislatures. Nevertheless, no thinking person can fail to recognize that the aftermath of these cases, however desirable it may be thought in itself, will have been achieved at the cost of a radical alteration in the relationship between the States and the Federal Government, more particularly the Federal Judiciary. Only one who has an overbearing impatience with the federal system and its political processes will believe that cost was not too high, or was inevitable.

Finally, these decisions give support to a current mistaken view of the Constitution and the constitutional function of this Court. This view, in a nutshell, is that every major social ill in this country can find its cure in some constitutional "principle," and that this Court should "take the lead" in promoting reform when other branches of government fail to act. The Constitution is not a panacea for every blot upon the public welfare, nor should this Court, ordained as a judicial body, be thought of as a general haven for reform movements. The Constitution is an instrument of government, fundamental to which is the premise that in a diffusion of governmental authority lies the greatest promise that this Nation will realize liberty for all its citizens. This Court, limited in function in accordance with that premise, does not serve its high purpose when it exceeds its authority, even to satisfy justified impatience with the slow workings of the political process. For when, in the name of constitutional interpretation, the Court adds something to the Constitution that was deliberately excluded from it, the Court, in reality, substitutes its view of what should be so for the amending process.

I dissent in each of these cases, believing that in none of them have the plaintiffs stated a cause of action. To the extent that *Baker v. Carr,* expressly or by implication, went beyond a discussion of jurisdictional doctrines independent of the substantive issues involved here, it should be limited to what it, in fact, was: an experiment in venturesome constitutionalism. I would reverse the judgments of the District Courts in Nos. 23, 27, and 41 (Alabama), No. 69 (Virginia), and No. 307 (Delaware), and remand with directions to dismiss the complaints. I would affirm the judgments of the District Courts in No. 20 (New York), and No. 508 (Colorado), and of the Court of Appeals of Maryland in No. 29. . . .

POSTSCRIPT

Does the Fourteenth Amendment Require the States to Use a "One Person, One Vote" Standard for Apportioning Legislative Districts?

The issues presented in *Reynolds v. Sims* are compelling ones indeed. On one hand, as Justice John M. Harlan inquires, should the judiciary become enmeshed in legislative districting issues, or should they defer to the elected representatives of the people? Or, conversely, was it necessary for the federal courts to give the states another "push" toward racial equality, as it did in *Brown v. Board of Education of Topeka* (1954)? These are controversial issues that implicate the question of the proper role of the judicial branch in our governmental structure as well as the issue of state prerogatives in our democratic republic.

In the years since *Reynolds v. Sims*, it has considered important related issues that help to provide some further guidance in this area of the law. By now, you know that *Reynolds* involved an effort to dilute the voting power of minority voters. Suppose, however, that a state legislature attempted to *increase* the power of a minority voting bloc? Do such policies violate the rights of nonminority voters under the Equal Protection Clause? According to Professors Mason and Stephenson, these so-called "benign race conscious" cases have produced mixed results. In *United Jewish Organizations of Williamsburg, Inc. v. Carey*, 430 U.S. 144 (1977), the Supreme Court used a deferential standard of review and upheld a New York law that had redrawn legislative districts to maintain African American representation in the state legislature in an effort to comply with the Voting Rights Act of 1965. The law had divided a Hasidic Jewish community into different districts. Justice Byron White asserted, "New York was entitled to consider racial factors in redistricting under the Constitution."

Another interesting twist in this area of the law occurred in the aftermath of the 2000 census. *Hunt v. Cromartie*, 532 U.S. 234 (2001), held that if a voting district is created for partisan political reasons, not racial gerrymandering, it will receive greater deference from the courts. As such, it will not be subjected to strict scrutiny. You may recall that when the courts use strict scrutiny to review a challenged law, it is often held unconstitutional.

So, where are we, regarding the issue of reapportionment by state legislatures? Professors Mason and Stephenson have provided an excellent summary of this area of the law:

> It remains to be seen whether the Court's razor-thin majority against most race-based districting holds, and if so, whether states seeking to

enhance minority representation may meet the inevitable challenges by drawing districts with more conventional shapes. It also remains to be seen whether, because African-Americans are among the most reliable Democratic voters, *Cromartie* will now allow *party* to be a proxy for *race* in the effort to increase minority representation.

In concluding our discussion of apportionment and election law issues, one final case that many commentators view as having had highly significant implications for the U.S. electoral system merits consideration. In *Bush v. Gore*, 531 U.S. 98 (2000), the Supreme Court held unconstitutional under the Equal Protection Clause the manual recounts of votes in different Florida districts for the 2000 presidential election. This was the so-called "hanging chads" case because the ballots required voters to perforate a card with a specially designed pen to cast their votes. Unfortunately, some of the voters failed to perforate the ballot completely and thus their votes were unclear. The Supreme Court held that a citizen's "right to vote is protected in more than the initial allocation of the franchise." In a per curiam opinion, the Court continued:

> Equal protection applies as well to the manner of its exercise. Having once granted the right to vote on equal terms, the State may not, by later arbitrary and disparate treatment, value one person's vote over another. [Citations omitted].

Therefore, because the manual recount ordered by the Florida Supreme Court failed to provide a clear standard for evaluating the contested ballots, requiring only that state election authorities try to determine the "intent of the voter," the state had violated the Equal Protection Clause. Moreover, there was significant time pressure in this case. Because time was of the essence (the presidential election hinged on its outcome), the Court's majority ended the recount, essentially declaring George W. Bush the winner of the 2000 presidential election.

It would be difficult to overestimate the amount of controversy generated by this case. Although some have applauded the Supreme Court for moving decisively to end the confusion surrounding the 2000 presidential election, others have criticized it for effectively deciding it in a highly political and partisan manner. Was this a case of a conservative Supreme Court throwing a contentious presidential election to a conservative president? Or, conversely, did it engage in a principled application of Equal Protection Clause analysis? In the end, the debate about *Bush v. Gore* is likely to continue. Moreover, perhaps this case provides an effective illustration of a principle familiar to most American lawyers—"hard cases make bad law."

Fortunately, there are a large number of additional resources to pursue further study in this area, including: Richard C. Cortner, *The Apportionment Cases* (W.W. Norton, 1972); Kathleen M. Sullivan and Gerald Gunther, *Constitutional Law* (Foundation Press, 15th ed., 2004); Laurence H. Tribe, *American Constitutional Law* (Foundation Press, 2nd ed., 1988); Alpheus Thomas Mason and Donald Grier Stephenson, Jr., *American Constitutional Law* (Pearson Prentice Hall, 15th ed., 2009; 14th ed., 2005); Bernard Schwartz, *A History of the Supreme*

Court (Oxford University Press, 1993); Kermit L. Hall, Paul Finkelman, and James Ely, Jr., *American Legal History: Cases and Materials* (Oxford University Press, 3rd ed., 2005); Kermit L. Hall, *The Oxford Companion to the Supreme Court of the United States* (Oxford University Press, 1992); Walter F. Murphy, James E. Fleming, Sotirios A. Barber, and Stephen Macedo, *American Constitutional Interpretation* (Foundation Press, 3rd ed., 2003); David M. O'Brien, *Constitutional Law and Politics: Struggles for Power and Government Accountability* (W.W. Norton, 6th ed., 2005); Craig R. Ducat, *Constitutional Interpretation* (Wadsworth, 9th ed., 2009); John H. Garvey, T. Alexander Aleinikoff, and Daniel A. Farber, *Modern Constitutional Theory: A Reader* (Thompson West, 5th ed., 2004). See also: David G. Oedell, Allen K. Lynch, Sean E. Mulholland, and Neil T. Edwards, "Does the Introduction of Independent Redistricting Reduce Congressional Partisanship?" *Villanova Law Review*, vol. 54, p. 57 (2009); Jocelyn F. Benson, "A Shared Existence: The Current Compatibility of the Equal Protection Clause and Section 5 of the Voting Rights Act," *Nebraska Law Review*, vol. 88, p. 124 (2009); Joshua M. Rosenberg, "Election Law: Defining Population for One Person, One Vote," *Loyola of Los Angeles Law Review*, vol. 42, p. 709 (2009); Laughlin McDonald, "The Looming 2010 Census: A Proposed Judicially Manageable Standard and Other Reform Options for Partisan Gerrymandering," *Harvard Journal on Legislation*, vol. 46, p. 243 (2009); Avram D. Frey, "Manipulated Doctrines, Improper Distinctions, and the Law of Racial Vote Dilution," *New York University Annual Survey of American Law*, vol. 64, p. 343 (2008); Pamela S. Karlan, "Lessons Learned: Voting Rights and the Bush Administration," *Duke Journal of Constitutional Law & Public Policy*, vol. 4, p. 17 (2009).

Internet References . . .

FedWorld

Search and view full text of Supreme Court Decisions.

http://supcourt.ntis.gov/

Supreme Court Hallmarks

List of landmark Supreme Court Decisions

http://library.thinkquest.org/11572/cc/

First Amendment issues and topics

First Amendment Center's Web site, featuring comprehensive research coverage of key First Amendment issues and topics.

http://www.firstamendmentcenter.org/faclibrary/index.aspx

Religious Liberty, Free Speech, and Association

*T*his section focuses on some of the most basic rights we have, those guaranteed by the First Amendment. The fact that the founding fathers enshrined these rights in the "First" Amendment was no accident. The government's role in religious observance and the right to practice religion according to one's personal convictions have been sources of frequent controversy throughout our history. Freedom of speech and the benefits of a free press in a democratic society are critical constitutional safeguards. These are the rights that define what it means to be a citizen of the United States.

- Does a State Law That Requires Public School Teachers to Teach "Creation Science" Whenever They Teach the Theory of Evolution Violate the First Amendment?

- Should Burning an American Flag be a Form of Expression Protected by the First Amendment?

- Does the First Amendment Permit the Government to Censure the Media?

ISSUE 18

Does a State Law That Requires Public School Teachers to Teach "Creation Science" Whenever They Teach the Theory of Evolution Violate the First Amendment?

YES: William J. Brennan, from Majority Opinion, *Edwards v. Aguillard,* 482 U.S. 578 (1987)

NO: Antonin E. Scalia, from Dissenting Opinion, *Edwards v. Aguillard,* 482 U.S. 578 (1987)

ISSUE SUMMARY

YES: Justice William J. Brennan, writing for the U.S. Supreme Court in *Edwards v. Aguillard* (1987), held that the Louisiana law that required public school teachers to teach "creation science" whenever they taught the theory of evolution was a violation of the First Amendment's Establishment Clause because the law lacked a clear secular purpose.

NO: Justice Antonin E. Scalia, dissenting in *Edwards v. Aguillard* (1987), asserted that the Louisiana law had a valid secular purpose—protecting academic freedom and that the statute should therefore be upheld.

The First Amendment to the U.S. Constitution contains some of the most cherished rights that we have as Americans. To use John Locke's terminology, these were many of the rights that the framers considered to be "inalienable." It was therefore no accident that they included these rights in the "First" Amendment as opposed to a later portion of the Bill of Rights. The First Amendment states:

> Congress shall make no law respecting an establishment of religion, or prohibiting the free exercise thereof; or abridging the freedom of speech, or of the press, or the right of the people to peaceably assemble, and to petition the Government for a redress of grievances.

The Amendment contains two religion clauses. First, it states that Congress shall make no law respecting an establishment of religion, the so-called

Establishment Clause. It further states that Congress may not prohibit the free exercise of religion, the *Free Exercise Clause.* You may recall from our previous discussions that these rights have been applied to the states, or *incorporated,* through the Due Process Clause of the Fourteenth Amendment.

The Establishment Clause is designed, according to Thomas Jefferson, to place "a wall of separation between church and state." This means that the government may not develop a state religion, force anyone to participate in religious activities, or punish them for their religious beliefs or lack thereof. In effect, it encompasses the freedom to believe in religion as well as the freedom not to believe, or "freedom from religion."

The Free Exercise Clause, in contrast, prevents the government from placing burdens on the exercise of religious beliefs. These rights are not absolute, however, and the government may develop reasonable laws to satisfy its legitimate objectives. For example, suppose someone's religious beliefs required smoking marijuana at religious rituals. The government would be justified in holding persons responsible for violating its drug laws, even if the conduct was required as part of a religious ceremony.

Likewise, the Supreme Court has upheld state laws against polygamy. In *Reynolds v. United States,* 98 U.S. 145 (1878), the Court held that the Free Exercise Clause did not prevent the states from passing laws that inhibit such practices, even if it is supported by a person's sincere religious belief. In this case, a practicing Morman had argued that it was his religious duty to engage in polygamy.

Unfortunately, the Supreme Court has provided little principled guidance about what governmental actions constitute a violation of the Free Exercise Clause. Therefore, cases presenting these issues are subjected to case-by-case analysis. In effect, the Supreme Court tries to determine if a particular law is supported by a compelling governmental interest and constitutes a good-faith effort to accomplish the objective. For example, suppose a person's religious belief required that they maintain Saturday as a day of rest. This occurred in *Sherbert v. Vermer,* 374 U.S. 398 (1963), when a Seventh-Day Adventist was fired from her job for refusing to work on Saturdays. She was later denied unemployment compensation by the state for her refusal to work. The Supreme Court held that this state law had violated the Free Exercise Clause because the state failed to show that exempting persons who kept the Sabbath on Saturday would prevent it from achieving its goal to assure that only appropriate persons would receive unemployment compensation.

In contrast to cases arising under the Free Exercise Clause, the Supreme Court has provided a better standard for analyzing Establishment Clause cases. This three-part test was developed in the important case of *Lemon v. Kurtzman,* 403 U.S. 602 (1970). The state of Rhode Island had passed a law providing for a 15 percent salary supplement to be paid to teachers in nonpublic schools. Eligible teachers could teach only courses offered in public schools, using only materials used in public schools, and were required to agree not to teach religion. The vast majority of these schools were affiliated with the Catholic Church. In a companion case, a state law in Pennsylvania had authorized authorities to "purchase secular educational services from private schools," directly reimbursing those schools for teachers' salaries, textbooks, and instructional materials. Reimbursement was restricted to courses in secular subjects. Most of the schools impacted by this law were also associated with the Catholic Church. In *Lemon,* the Supreme Court developed a three-part test to determine if state laws violate the Establishment Clause:

1. Does the law have a secular purpose?
2. Does the law's main effect either advance or inhibit religion?
3. Does the law cause an "excessive government entanglement" with religion? According to many commentators, the last part of the *Lemon* test is most critical. If a state's law fosters an "excessive entanglement" with religion, it will be held unconstitutional.

Lynch v. Donnelly, 465 U.S. 668 (1984), illustrates how the Court analyzes these issues. The City of Pawtucket, Rhode Island, had for many years erected a Christmas display as part of its observance of the holiday season. The display included a nativity scene, which was located in a park, owned by a nonprofit organization. The crèche cost the City $1365, and its erection and dismantling cost approximately $20 per year.

The U.S. District Court held that the display violated the Establishment Clause and the U.S. Court of Appeals affirmed. On appeal to the Supreme Court, Chief Justice Warren Burger asserted that "total separation [of church and state] is not possible in an absolute sense. Some relationship between government and religious organizations is inevitable." Observed Chief Justice Burger:

> The line between permissible relationships and those barred by the Clause can no more be straight and unwavering than due process can be defined in a single stroke or phrase or test. The Clause erects a 'blurred, indistinct, and variable barrier depending on all the circumstances of a particular relationship.'

Because the City had a secular purpose for its display of the crèche, to celebrate the holiday season and to depict the origin of that holiday, its purpose was a legitimate one. The Supreme Court held that "notwithstanding the religious significance of the crèche, the City did not violate the Establishment Clause."

The case presented in this section, *Edwards v. Aguillard* (1987), presents an Establishment Clause issue as well. The state of Louisiana's "Creationism Act" prohibited the teaching of the theory of evolution in public elementary and secondary schools unless accompanied by instruction in the theory of "creation science." The Act did not require the teaching of either theory unless the other was taught. It defined the theories as "the scientific evidences for [creation or evolution] and inferences from those scientific evidences." Parents, teachers, and religious leaders challenged the statute's constitutionality in U.S. District Court, which held that the law violated the Establishment Clause and the U.S. Court of Appeals affirmed.

Writing for the U.S. Supreme Court, Justice William J. Brennan posed the issue in this case as follows: "[W]hether Louisiana's 'Balanced Treatment for

Creation-Science in Public School Instruction Act (Creationism Act) is facially as violative of the Establishment Clause of the First Amendment." Stated Justice Brennan:

> [T]he Creationism Act is designed either to promote the theory of creation science which embodies a particular religious tenet by requiring that creation science be taught whenever evolution is taught or to prohibit the teaching of a scientific theory disfavored by certain religious sects by forbidding the teaching of evolution when creation science is not also taught. The Establishment Clause, however, 'forbids alike the preference of a religious doctrine or the prohibition of theory which is deemed antagonistic to a particular dogma.' Because the primary purpose of the Creationism Act is to advance a particular religious belief, the Act endorses religion in violation of the First Amendment.

Justice Antonin E. Scalia, however, disagreed. In a dissenting opinion, Justice Scalia asserted that the Creationism Act had a legitimate secular purpose. He stated:

> [E]ven if one concedes, for the sake of argument, that a majority of the Louisiana Legislature voted for the Balanced Treatment Act partly in order to foster (rather than merely eliminate discrimination against) Christian fundamentalist beliefs, our cases establish that, alone, would not suffice to invalidate the Act, so long as there was a genuine secular purpose as well.

In Your Opinion . . .

- Do you agree with Justice Scalia's position?
- Do you honestly feel that Louisiana's purported secular purpose for this law, eliminating discrimination against fundamentalist Christian beliefs, was a legitimate one?
- Was Justice Brennan correct in asserting that the Creationism Act was little more than a religious dogma, masquerading as a secular law?
- How would you distinguish between *Lynch v. Donnelly* (1984), where the Court permitted a City's religious nativity display, and *Edwards v. Aguillard* (1987), where they held unconstitutional the state's "Creationism Act"?

YES

William J. Brennan

Majority Opinion, *Edwards v. Aguillard*

J USTICE BRENNAN delivered the opinion of the Court.

The question for decision is whether Louisiana's "Balanced Treatment for Creation-Science and Evolution-Science in Public School Instruction" Act (Creationism Act), La.Rev.Stat.Ann. §§ 17:286.1–17:286.7 (West 1982), is facially invalid as violative of the Establishment Clause of the First Amendment.

I

The Creationism Act forbids the teaching of the theory of evolution in public schools unless accompanied by instruction in "creation science." § 17:286.4A. No school is required to teach evolution or creation science. If either is taught, however, the other must also be taught. *Ibid.* The theories of evolution and creation science are statutorily defined as "the scientific evidences for [creation or evolution] and inferences from those scientific evidences." §§ 17.286.3(2) and (3).

Appellees, who include parents of children attending Louisiana public schools, Louisiana teachers, and religious leaders, challenged the constitutionality of the Act in District Court, seeking an injunction and declaratory relief. Appellants, Louisiana officials charged with implementing the Act, defended on the ground that the purpose of the Act is to protect a legitimate secular interest, namely, academic freedom. Appellees attacked the Act as facially invalid because it violated the Establishment Clause and made a motion for summary judgment. The District Court granted the motion. *Aguillard v. Treen,* 634 F.Supp. 426 (ED La.1985). The court held that there can be no valid secular reason for prohibiting the teaching of evolution, a theory historically opposed by some religious denominations. The court further concluded that

> the teaching of "creation-science" and "creationism," as contemplated by the statute, involves teaching "tailored to the principles" of a particular religious sect or group of sects.

Id. at 427 (citing *Epperson v. Arkansas,* 393 U.S. 97, 106 (1968)). The District Court therefore held that the Creationism Act violated the Establishment Clause either because it prohibited the teaching of evolution or because it required the teaching of creation science with the purpose of advancing a particular religious doctrine.

Supreme Court of the United States, 1987.

The Court of Appeals affirmed. 765 F.2d 1251 (CA5 1985). The court observed that the statute's avowed purpose of protecting academic freedom was inconsistent with requiring, upon risk of sanction, the teaching of creation science whenever evolution is taught. *Id.* at 1257. The court found that the Louisiana Legislature's actual intent was "to discredit evolution by counterbalancing its teaching at every turn with the teaching of creationism, a religious belief." *Ibid.* Because the Creationism Act was thus a law furthering a particular religious belief, the Court of Appeals held that the Act violated the Establishment Clause. A suggestion for rehearing en banc was denied over a dissent. 778 F.2d 225 (CA5 1985). We noted probable jurisdiction, 476 U.S. 1103 (1986), and now affirm.

II

The Establishment Clause forbids the enactment of any law "respecting an establishment of religion." The Court has applied a three-pronged test to determine whether legislation comports with the Establishment Clause. First, the legislature must have adopted the law with a secular purpose. Second, the statute's principal or primary effect must be one that neither advances nor inhibits religion. Third, the statute must not result in an excessive entanglement of government with religion. *Lemon v. Kurtzman,* 403 U.S. 602, 612–613 (1971). State action violates the Establishment Clause if it fails to satisfy any of these prongs.

In this case, the Court must determine whether the Establishment Clause was violated in the special context of the public elementary and secondary school system. States and local school boards are generally afforded considerable discretion in operating public schools. *See Bethel School Dist. No. 403 v. Fraser,* 478 U.S. 675, 683 (1986); *id.* at 687 (BRENNAN, J., concurring in judgment); 478 U.S. 675, 683 (1986); *id.* at 687 (BRENNAN, J., concurring in judgment); *Tinker v. Des Moines Independent Community School Dist.,* 393 U.S. 503, 507 (1969).

> At the same time . . . we have necessarily recognized that the discretion of the States and local school boards in matters of education must be exercised in a manner that comports with the transcendent imperatives of the First Amendment.

Board of Education, Island Trees Union Free School Dist. No. 26 v. Pico, 457 U.S. 853, 864 (1982).

The Court has been particularly vigilant in monitoring compliance with the Establishment Clause in elementary and secondary schools. Families entrust public schools with the education of their children, but condition their trust on the understanding that the classroom will not purposely be used to advance religious views that may conflict with the private beliefs of the student and his or her family. Students in such institutions are impressionable, and their attendance is involuntary. *See, e.g., Grand Rapids School Dist. v. Ball,* 473 U.S. 373, 383 (1985); *Wallace v. Jaffree,* 472 U.S. 38, 60, n. 51 (1985);

Meek v. Pittenger, 421 U.S. 349, 369 (1975); *Abington School Dist. v. Schempp,* 374 U.S. 203, 252–253 (1963) (BRENNAN, J., concurring). The State exerts great authority and coercive power through mandatory attendance requirements, and because of the students' emulation of teachers as role models and the children's susceptibility to peer pressure. *See Bethel School Dist. No. 403 v. Fraser, supra,* at 683; *Wallace v. Jaffree, supra,* at 81 (O'CONNOR, J., concurring in judgment). Furthermore,

> [t]he public school is at once the symbol of our democracy and the most pervasive means for promoting our common destiny. In no activity of the State is it more vital to keep out divisive forces than in its schools. . . .

Illinois ex rel. McCollum v. Board of Education, 333 U.S. 203, 231 (1948) (opinion of Frankfurter, J.).

Consequently, the Court has been required often to invalidate statutes which advance religion in public elementary and secondary schools. *See, e.g., Grand Rapids School Dist. v. Ball, supra,* (school district's use of religious school teachers in public schools); *Wallace v. Jaffree, supra,* (Alabama statute authorizing moment of silence for school prayer); *Stone v. Graham,* 449 U.S. 39"]449 U.S. 39 (1980) (posting copy of Ten Commandments on public classroom wall); 449 U.S. 39 (1980) (posting copy of Ten Commandments on public classroom wall); *Epperson v. Arkansas,* 393 U.S. 97"]393 U.S. 97 (1968) (statute forbidding teaching of evolution); *Abington School Dist. v. Schempp, supra,* (daily reading of Bible); 393 U.S. 97 (1968) (statute forbidding teaching of evolution); *Abington School Dist. v. Schempp, supra,* (daily reading of Bible); *Engel v. Vitale,* 370 U.S. 421, 430 (1962) (recitation of "denominationally neutral" prayer).

Therefore, in employing the three-pronged *Lemon* test, we must do so mindful of the particular concerns that arise in the context of public elementary and secondary schools. We now turn to the evaluation of the Act under the *Lemon* test.

III

Lemon's first prong focuses on the purpose that animated adoption of the Act. "The purpose prong of the *Lemon* test asks whether government's actual purpose is to endorse or disapprove of religion." *Lynch v. Donnelly,* 465 U.S. 668, 690 (1984) (O'CONNOR, J., concurring). A governmental intention to promote religion is clear when the State enacts a law to serve a religious purpose. This intention may be evidenced by promotion of religion in general, *see Wallace v. Jaffree, supra,* at 52–53 (Establishment Clause protects individual freedom of conscience "to select any religious faith or none at all"), or by advancement of a particular religious belief, *e.g., Stone v. Graham, supra,* at 41 (invalidating requirement to post Ten Commandments, which are "undeniably a sacred text in the Jewish and Christian faiths") (footnote omitted); *Epperson v. Arkansas, supra,* at 106 (holding that banning the teaching of evolution in public schools violates the First Amendment, since "teaching and learning" must not "be tailored to the principles or prohibitions of any religious sect or dogma"). If the law was enacted for the purpose of endorsing religion, "no consideration of the second or third criteria [of *Lemon*] is necessary." *Wallace v. Jaffree, supra,* at 56. In this case, appellants have identified no clear secular purpose for the Louisiana Act.

True, the Act's stated purpose is to protect academic freedom. *La.Rev. Stat.Ann.* § 17:286.2 (West 1982). This phrase might, in common parlance, be understood as referring to enhancing the freedom of teachers to teach what they will. The Court of Appeals, however, correctly concluded that the Act was not designed to further that goal. We find no merit in the State's argument that the

> legislature may not [have] use[d] the terms "academic freedom" in the correct legal sense. They might have [had] in mind, instead, a basic concept of fairness; teaching all of the evidence.

Tr. of Oral Arg. 60. Even if "academic freedom" is read to mean "teaching all of the evidence" with respect to the origin of human beings, the Act does not further this purpose. The goal of providing a more comprehensive science curriculum is not furthered either by outlawing the teaching of evolution or by requiring the teaching of creation science.

A

While the Court is normally deferential to a State's articulation of a secular purpose, it is required that the statement of such purpose be sincere, and not a sham. *See Wallace v. Jaffree,* 472 U.S. at 64 (POWELL, J., concurring); *Id.* at 75 (O'CONNOR, J., concurring in judgment); *Stone v. Graham, supra,* at 41; *Abington School Dist. v. Schempp,* 374 U.S. at 223–224. As JUSTICE O'CONNOR stated in *Wallace:*

> It is not a trivial matter, however, to require that the legislature mani-fest a secular purpose and omit all sectarian endorsements from its laws. That requirement is precisely tailored to the Establishment Clause's purpose of assuring that Government not intentionally endorse reli-gion or a religious practice.

472 U.S. at 75 (concurring in judgment).

It is clear from the legislative history that the purpose of the legislative sponsor, Senator Bill Keith, was to narrow the science curriculum. During the legislative hearings, Senator Keith stated: "My preference would be that neither [creationism nor evolution] be taught." 2 App. E-621. Such a ban on teaching does not promote—indeed, it undermines—the provision of a comprehensive scientific education.

It is equally clear that requiring schools to teach creation science with evo-lution does not advance academic freedom. The Act does not grant teachers a flexibility that they did not already possess to supplant the present science cur-riculum with the presentation of theories, besides evolution, about the origin of life. Indeed, the Court of Appeals found that no law prohibited Louisiana public school teachers from teaching any scientific theory. 765 F.2d at 1257. As the president of the Louisiana Science Teachers Association testified,

> [a]ny scientific concept that's based on established fact can be included in our curriculum already, and no legislation allowing this is necessary.

2 App. E-616. The Act provides Louisiana schoolteachers with no new authority. Thus, the stated purpose is not furthered by it.

The Alabama statute held unconstitutional in *Wallace v. Jaffree, supra,* is analogous. In *Wallace,* the State characterized its new law as one designed to provide a 1-minute period for meditation. We rejected that stated purpose as insufficient, because a previously adopted Alabama law already provided for such a 1-minute period. Thus, in this case, as in *Wallace,* "[a]ppellants have not identified any secular purpose that was not fully served by [existing state law] before the enactment of [the statute in question]." 472 U.S. at 59.

Furthermore, the goal of basic "fairness" is hardly furthered by the Act's discriminatory preference for the teaching of creation science and against the teaching of evolution. While requiring that curriculum guides be developed for creation science, the Act says nothing of comparable guides for evolution. *La.Rev.Stat.Ann.* § 17:286.7A (West 1982). Similarly, resource services are supplied for creation science, but not for evolution. § 17:286.7B. Only "creation scientists" can serve on the panel that supplies the resource services. *Ibid.* The Act forbids school boards to discriminate against anyone who "chooses to be a creation scientist" or to teach "creationism," but fails to protect those who choose to teach evolution or any other non-creation-science theory, or who refuse to teach creation science. § 17:286.4C.

If the Louisiana Legislature's purpose was solely to maximize the comprehensiveness and effectiveness of science instruction, it would have encouraged the teaching of all scientific theories about the origins of humankind. But under the Act's requirements, teachers who were once free to teach any and all facets of this subject are now unable to do so. Moreover, the Act fails even to ensure that creation science will be taught, but instead requires the teaching of this theory only when the theory of evolution is taught. Thus we agree with the Court of Appeals' conclusion that the Act does not serve to protect academic freedom, but has the distinctly different purpose of discrediting "evolution by counterbalancing its teaching at every turn with the teaching of creationism. . . ." 765 F.2d at 1257.

B

Stone v. Graham invalidated the State's requirement that the Ten Commandments be posted in public classrooms.

> The Ten Commandments are undeniably a sacred text in the Jewish and Christian faiths, and no legislative recitation of a supposed secular purpose can blind us to that fact.

449 U.S. at 41 (footnote omitted). As a result, the contention that the law was designed to provide instruction on a "fundamental legal code" was "not sufficient to avoid conflict with the First Amendment." *Ibid.* Similarly, *Abington School Dist. v. Schempp* held unconstitutional a statute

> requiring the selection and reading at the opening of the school day of verses from the Holy Bible and the recitation of the Lord's Prayer by the students in unison,

despite the proffer of such secular purposes as the

> promotion of moral values, the contradiction to the materialistic trends of our times, the perpetuation of our institutions, and the teaching of literature.

374 U.S. at 223.

As in *Stone and Abington,* we need not be blind in this case to the legislature's preeminent religious purpose in enacting this statute. There is a historic and contemporaneous link between the teachings of certain religious denominations and the teaching of evolution. It was this link that concerned the Court in *Epperson v. Arkansas,* 393 U.S. 97 (1968), which also involved a facial challenge to a statute regulating the teaching of evolution. In that case, the Court reviewed an Arkansas statute that made it unlawful for an instructor to teach evolution or to use a textbook that referred to this scientific theory. Although the Arkansas anti-evolution law did not explicitly state its predominate religious purpose, the Court could not ignore that "[t]he statute was a product of the upsurge of 'fundamentalist' religious fervor" that has long viewed this particular scientific theory as contradicting the literal interpretation of the Bible. *Id.* at 98, 106–107. After reviewing the history of anti-evolution statutes, the Court determined that

> there can be no doubt that the motivation for the [Arkansas] law was the same [as other anti-evolution statutes]: to suppress the teaching of a theory which, it was thought, "denied" the divine creation of man.

Id. at 109. The Court found that there can be no legitimate state interest in protecting particular religions from scientific views "distasteful to them," *id.* at 107 (citation omitted), and concluded

> that the First Amendment does not permit the State to require that teaching and learning must be tailored to the principles or prohibitions of any religious sect or dogma, . . .

id. at 106.

These same historic and contemporaneous antagonisms between the teachings of certain religious denominations and the teaching of evolution are present in this case. The preeminent purpose of the Louisiana Legislature was clearly to advance the religious viewpoint that a supernatural being created humankind. The term "creation science" was defined as embracing this particular religious doctrine by those responsible for the passage of the Creationism Act. Senator Keith's leading expert on creation science, Edward Boudreaux, testified at the legislative hearings that the theory of creation science included belief in the existence of a supernatural creator. *See* 1 App. E-421—E-422 (noting that "creation scientists" point to high probability that life was "created by an intelligent mind"). Senator Keith also cited testimony from other experts to support the creation science view that "a creator [was] responsible for the universe and everything in it." 2 App. E-497. The legislative history therefore reveals that the term "creation science," as contemplated by the legislature that adopted this Act, embodies the religious belief that a supernatural creator was responsible for the creation of humankind.

Furthermore, it is not happenstance that the legislature required the teaching of a theory that coincided with this religious view. The legislative history documents that the Act's primary purpose was to change the science curriculum of public schools in order to provide persuasive advantage to a particular religious doctrine that rejects the factual basis of evolution in its entirety. The sponsor of the Creationism Act, Senator Keith, explained during the legislative hearings that his disdain for the theory of evolution resulted from the support that evolution supplied to views contrary to his own religious beliefs. According to Senator Keith, the theory of evolution was consonant with the "cardinal principle[s] of religious humanism, secular humanism, theological liberalism, aetheistism [*sic*]." 1 App. E-312—E-313; *see also* 2 App. E-499—E-500. The state senator repeatedly stated that scientific evidence supporting his religious views should be included in the public school curriculum to redress the fact that the theory of evolution incidentally coincided with what he characterized as religious beliefs antithetical to his own. The legislation therefore sought to alter the science curriculum to reflect endorsement of a religious view that is antagonistic to the theory of evolution.

In this case, the purpose of the Creationism Act was to restructure the science curriculum to conform with a particular religious viewpoint. Out of many possible science subjects taught in the public schools, the legislature chose to affect the teaching of the one scientific theory that historically has been opposed by certain religious sects. As in *Epperson,* the legislature passed the Act to give preference to those religious groups which have as one of their tenets the creation of humankind by a divine creator. The "overriding fact" that confronted the Court in *Epperson* was

> that Arkansas' law selects from the body of knowledge a particular segment which it proscribes for the sole reason that it is deemed to conflict with . . . a particular interpretation of the Book of Genesis by a particular religious group.

393 U.S. at 103. Similarly, the Creationism Act is designed *either* to promote the theory of creation science which embodies a particular religious tenet by requiring that creation science be taught whenever evolution is taught *or* to prohibit the teaching of a scientific theory disfavored by certain religious

sects by forbidding the teaching of evolution when creation science is not also taught. The Establishment Clause, however, "forbids *alike* the preference of a religious doctrine *or* the prohibition of theory which is deemed antagonistic to a particular dogma." *Id.* at 106–107 (emphasis added). Because the primary purpose of the Creationism Act is to advance a particular religious belief, the Act endorses religion in violation of the First Amendment.

We do not imply that a legislature could never require that scientific critiques of prevailing scientific theories be taught. Indeed, the Court acknowledged in *Stone* that its decision forbidding the posting of the Ten Commandments did not mean that no use could ever be made of the Ten Commandments, or that the Ten Commandments played an exclusively religious role in the history of Western Civilization. 449 U.S. at 42. In a similar way, teaching a variety of scientific theories about the origins of humankind to schoolchildren might be validly done with the clear secular intent of enhancing the effectiveness of science instruction. But because the primary purpose of the Creationism Act is to endorse a particular religious doctrine, the Act furthers religion in violation of the Establishment Clause.

IV

Appellants contend that genuine issues of material fact remain in dispute, and therefore the District Court erred in granting summary judgment. Federal Rule of Civil Procedure 56(c) provides that summary judgment

> shall be rendered forthwith if the pleadings, depositions, answers to interrogatories, and admissions on file, together with the affidavits, if any, show that there is no genuine issue as to any material fact and that the moving party is entitled to a judgment as a matter of law.

A court's finding of improper purpose behind a statute is appropriately determined by the statute on its face, its legislative history, or its interpretation by a responsible administrative agency. *See, e.g., Wallace v. Jaffree,* 472 U.S. at 56–61; *Stone v. Graham,* 449 U.S. at 41–42; *Epperson v. Arkansas,* 393 U.S. at 103–109. The plain meaning of the statute's words, enlightened by their context and the contemporaneous legislative history, can control the determination of legislative purpose. *See Wallace v. Jaffree, supra,* at 74 (O'CONNOR, J., concurring in judgment); *Richards v. United States,* 369 U.S. 1, 9 (1962); *Jay v. Boyd,* 351 U.S. 345, 357 (1956). Moreover, in determining the legislative purpose of a statute, the Court has also considered the historical context of the statute, *e.g., Epperson v. Arkansas, supra,* and the specific sequence of events leading to passage of the statute, *e.g., Arlington Heights v. Metropolitan Housing Dev. Corp.,* 429 U.S. 252 (1977).

In this case, appellees' motion for summary judgment rested on the plain language of the Creationism Act, the legislative history and historical context of the Act, the specific sequence of events leading to the passage of the Act, the State Board's report on a survey of school superintendents, and the correspondence between the Act's legislative sponsor and its key witnesses.

Appellants contend that affidavits made by two scientists, two theologians, and an education administrator raise a genuine issue of material fact, and that summary judgment was therefore barred. The affidavits define creation science as "origin through abrupt appearance in complex form," and allege that such a viewpoint constitutes a true scientific theory. *See* App. to Brief for Appellants A-7 to A-40.

We agree with the lower courts that these affidavits do not raise a genuine issue of material fact. The existence of "uncontroverted affidavits" does not bar summary judgment. Moreover, the postenactment testimony of outside experts is of little use in determining the Louisiana Legislature's purpose in enacting this statute. The Louisiana Legislature did hear and rely on scientific experts in passing the bill, but none of the persons making the affidavits produced by the appellants participated in or contributed to the enactment of the law or its implementation. The District Court, in its discretion, properly concluded that a Monday morning "battle of the experts" over possible technical meanings of terms in the statute would not illuminate the contemporaneous purpose of the Louisiana Legislature when it made the law. We therefore conclude that the District Court did not err in finding that appellants failed to raise a genuine issue of material fact, and in granting summary judgment.

V

The Louisiana Creationism Act advances a religious doctrine by requiring either the banishment of the theory of evolution from public school classrooms or the presentation of a religious viewpoint that rejects evolution in its entirety. The Act violates the Establishment Clause of the First Amendment because it seeks to employ the symbolic and financial support of government to achieve a religious purpose. The judgment of the Court of Appeals therefore is

Affirmed.

Antonin E. Scalia  **NO**

Dissenting Opinion,
Edwards v. Aguillard

JUSTICE SCALIA, with whom THE CHIEF JUSTICE joins, dissenting.

Even if I agreed with the questionable premise that legislation can be invalidated under the Establishment Clause on the basis of its motivation alone, without regard to its effects, I would still find no justification for today's decision. The Louisiana legislators who passed the "Balanced Treatment for Creation-Science and Evolution-Science Act" (Balanced Treatment Act), *La.Rev. Stat.Ann.* §§ 17:286.1–17:286.7 (West 1982), each of whom had sworn to support the Constitution, were well aware of the potential Establishment Clause problems, and considered that aspect of the legislation with great care. After seven hearings and several months of study, resulting in substantial revision of the original proposal, they approved the Act overwhelmingly, and specifically articulated the secular purpose they meant it to serve. Although the record contains abundant evidence of the sincerity of that purpose (the only issue pertinent to this case), the Court today holds, essentially on the basis of "its visceral knowledge regarding what *must* have motivated the legislators," 778 F.2d 225, 227 (CA5 1985) (Gee, J., dissenting) (emphasis added), that the members of the Louisiana Legislature knowingly violated their oaths and then lied about it. I dissent. Had requirements of the Balanced Treatment Act that are not apparent on its face been clarified by an interpretation of the Louisiana Supreme Court, or by the manner of its implementation, the Act might well be found unconstitutional; but the question of its constitutionality cannot rightly be disposed of on the gallop, by impugning the motives of its supporters.

I

This case arrives here in the following posture: the Louisiana Supreme Court has never been given an opportunity to interpret the Balanced Treatment Act, State officials have never attempted to implement it, and it has never been the subject of a full evidentiary hearing. We can only guess at its meaning. We know that it forbids instruction in either "creation science" or "evolution science" without instruction in the other, § 17:286.4A, but the parties are sharply divided over what creation science consists of. Appellants insist that it is a collection of educationally valuable scientific data that has been censored from classrooms by an embarrassed scientific establishment. Appellees insist it is not science at all, but thinly veiled religious doctrine. Both interpretations of

Supreme Court of the United States, 1987.

the intended meaning of that phrase find considerable support in the legislative history.

At least at this stage in the litigation, it is plain to me that we must accept appellants' view of what the statute means. To begin with, the statute itself *defines* "creation science" as "the *scientific evidences* for creation and inferences from those *scientific evidences*." § 17:286.3(2) (emphasis added). If, however, that definition is not thought sufficiently helpful, the means by which the Louisiana Supreme Court will give the term more precise content is quite clear—and again, at this stage in the litigation, favors the appellants' view. "Creation science" is unquestionably a "term of art," *see* Brief for 72 Nobel Laureates *et al.* as *Amici Curiae* 20, and thus, under Louisiana law, is "to be interpreted according to [its] received meaning and acceptation with the learned in the art, trade or profession to which [it] refer[s]." La.Civ.Code Ann., Art. 15 (West 1952). The only evidence in the record of the "received meaning and acceptation" of "creation science" is found in five affidavits filed by appellants. In those affidavits, two scientists, a philosopher, a theologian, and an educator, all of whom claim extensive knowledge of creation science, swear that it is essentially a collection of scientific data supporting the theory that the physical universe and life within it appeared suddenly, and have not changed substantially since appearing. *See* App. to Juris. Statement A-19 (Kenyon); *id.* at A-36 (Morrow); *id.* at A-41 (Miethe). These experts insist that creation science is a strictly scientific concept that can be presented without religious reference. *See id.* at A-19–A-20, A-35 (Kenyon); *Id.* at A-36–A-38 (Morrow); *id.* at A-40, A-41, A-43 (Miethe); *id.* at A-47, A-48 (Most); *id.* at A-49 (Clinkert). At this point, then, we must assume that the Balanced Treatment Act does *not* require the presentation of religious doctrine.

Nothing in today's opinion is plainly to the contrary, but what the statute means and what it requires are of rather little concern to the Court. Like the Court of Appeals, 765 F.2d 1251, 1253, 1254 (CA5 1985), the Court finds it necessary to consider only the motives of the legislators who supported the Balanced Treatment Act, *ante* at 482 U.S. 586"]586, 593–594, 596. After examining the statute, its legislative history, and its historical and social context, the Court holds that the Louisiana Legislature acted without "a secular legislative purpose," and that the Act therefore fails the "purpose" prong of the three-part test set forth in *Lemon v. Kurtzman*, 403 U.S. 602, 612 (1971). As I explain below, *infra* at 636–640, I doubt whether that "purpose" requirement of *Lemon* is a proper interpretation of the Constitution; but even if it were, I could not agree with the Court's assessment that the requirement was not satisfied here.

This Court has said little about the first component of the *Lemon* test. Almost invariably, we have effortlessly discovered a secular purpose for measures challenged under the Establishment Clause, typically devoting no more than a sentence or two to the matter. *See, e.g., Witters v. Washington Dept. of Services for Blind,* 474 U.S. 481, 485–486 (1986); *Grand Rapids School District v. Ball,* 473 U.S. 373, 383 (1985); *Mueller v. Allen,* 463 U.S. 388, 394–395 (1983); *Larkin v. Grende's Den, Inc.,* 459 U.S. 116, 123–124 (1982); *Widmar v. Vincent,* 454 U.S. 263, 271 (1981); *Committee for Public Education & Religious Liberty v. Regan,* 444 U.S. 646, 654, 657 (1980); *Wolman v. Walter,* 433 U.S. 229,

236 (1977) (plurality opinion); *Meek v. Pittenger,* 421 U.S. 349, 363 (1975); *Committee for Public Education & Religious Liberty v. Nyquist,* 413 U.S. 756, 773 (1973); *Levitt v. Committee for Public Education & Religious Liberty,* 413 U.S. 472, 479–480, n. 7 (1973); *Tilton v. Richardson,* 403 U.S. 672, 678–679 (1971) (plurality opinion); *Lemon v. Kurtzman, supra,* at 613. In fact, only once before deciding *Lemon,* and twice since, have we invalidated a law for lack of a secular purpose. See *Wallace v. Jaffree,* 472 U.S. 38 (1985); *Stone v. Graham,* 449 U.S. 39 (1980) (per curiam); *Epperson v. Arkansas,* 393 U.S. 97 (1968).

Nevertheless, a few principles have emerged from our cases, principles which should, but to an unfortunately large extent do not, guide the Court's application of *Lemon* today. It is clear, first of all, that regardless of what "legislative purpose" may mean in other contexts, for the purpose of the *Lemon* test, it means the "actual" motives of those responsible for the challenged action. The Court recognizes this, *see ante* at 585, as it has in the past, *see, e.g., Witters v. Washington Dept. of Services for Blind, supra,* at 486; *Wallace v. Jaffree, supra,* at 56. Thus, if those legislators who supported the Balanced Treatment Act *in fact* acted with a "sincere" secular purpose, *ante* at 587, the Act survives the first component of the *Lemon* test, regardless of whether that purpose is likely to be achieved by the provisions they enacted.

Our cases have also confirmed that, when the *Lemon* Court referred to "a secular . . . purpose," 403 U.S. at 403 U.S. 612"] 612, it meant "*a* secular purpose." The author of *Lemon,* writing for the Court, has said that invalidation under the purpose prong is appropriate when "there [is] *no question* that the statute or activity was motivated *wholly* by religious considerations." 612, it meant "*a* secular purpose." The author of *Lemon,* writing for the Court, has said that invalidation under the purpose prong is appropriate when "there [is] *no question* that the statute or activity was motivated *wholly* by religious considerations." *Lynch v. Donnelly,* 465 U.S. 668, 680 (1984) (Burger, C.J.) (emphasis added); *see also id.* at 681, n. 6; *Wallace v. Jaffree, supra,* at 56 ("[T]he First Amendment requires that a statute must be invalidated if it is *entirely* motivated by a purpose to advance religion") (emphasis added; footnote omitted). In all three cases in which we struck down laws under the Establishment Clause for lack of a secular purpose, we found that the legislature's sole motive was to promote religion. See *Wallace v. Jaffree, supra,* at 56, 57, 60; *Stone v. Graham, supra,* at 41, 43, n. 5; *Epperson v. Arkansas, supra,* at 103, 107–108; *see also Lynch v. Donnelly, supra,* at 680 (describing *Stone* and *Epperson* as cases in which we invalidated laws "motivated wholly by religious considerations"). Thus, the majority's invalidation of the Balanced Treatment Act is defensible only if the record indicates that the Louisiana Legislature had *no* secular purpose.

It is important to stress that the purpose forbidden by *Lemon* is the purpose to "advance religion." 403 U.S. at 613; *accord, ante* at 585 ("promote" religion); *Witters v. Washington Dept. of Services for Blind, supra,* at 486 ("endorse religion"); *Wallace v. Jaffree,* 472 U.S. at 56 ("advance religion"); *ibid.* ("endorse . . . religion"); *Committee for Public Education & Religious Liberty v. Nyquist, supra,* at 788 ("'advancing'. . . religion"); *Levitt v. Committee for Public Education & Religious Liberty, supra,* at 481 ("advancing religion"); *Walz v. Tax*

Comm'n of New York City, 397 U.S. 664, 674 (1970) ("establishing, sponsoring, or supporting religion"); *Board of Education v. Allen,* 392 U.S. 236, 243 (1968) ("'advancement or inhibition of religion'") (quoting *Abington School Dist. v. Schempp,* 374 U.S. 203, 222 (1963)). Our cases in no way imply that the Establishment Clause forbids legislators merely to act upon their religious convictions. We surely would not strike down a law providing money to feed the hungry or shelter the homeless if it could be demonstrated that, but for the religious beliefs of the legislators, the funds would not have been approved. Also, political activism by the religiously motivated is part of our heritage. Notwithstanding the majority's implication to the contrary, *ante* at 589–591, we do not presume that the sole purpose of a law is to advance religion merely because it was supported strongly by organized religions or by adherents of particular faiths. *See Walz v. Tax Comm'n of New York City, supra,* at 670; cf. *Harris v. McRae,* 448 U.S. 297, 319–320 (1980). To do so would deprive religious men and women of their right to participate in the political process. Today's religious activism may give us the Balanced Treatment Act, but yesterday's resulted in the abolition of slavery, and tomorrow's may bring relief for famine victims.

Similarly, we will not presume that a law's purpose is to advance religion merely because it "'happens to coincide or harmonize with the tenets of some or all religions,'" *Harris v. McRae, supra,* at 319 (quoting *McGowan v. Maryland,* 366 U.S. 420, 442 (1961)), or because it benefits religion, even substantially. We have, for example, turned back Establishment Clause challenges to restrictions on abortion funding, *Harris v. McRae, supra,* and to Sunday closing laws, *McGowan v. Maryland, supra,* despite the fact that both "agre[e] with the dictates of [some] Judaeo-Christian religions," *id.* at 442.

> In many instances, the Congress or state legislatures conclude that the general welfare of society, wholly apart from any religious considerations, demands such regulation.

Ibid. On many past occasions, we have had no difficulty finding a secular purpose for governmental action far more likely to advance religion than the Balanced Treatment Act. *See, e.g., Mueller v. Allen,* 463 U.S. at 394–395 (tax deduction for expenses of religious education); *Wolman v. Walter,* 433 U.S. at 236 (plurality opinion) (aid to religious schools); *Meek v. Pittenger,* 421 U.S. at 363 (same); *Committee for Public Education & Religious Liberty v. Nyquist,* 413 U.S. at 773 (same); *Lemon v. Kurtzman,* 403 U.S. at 613 (same); *Walz v. Tax Comm'n of New York City, supra,* at 672 (tax exemption for church property); *Board of Education v. Allen, supra,* at 243 (textbook loans to students in religious schools). Thus, the fact that creation science coincides with the beliefs of certain religions, a fact upon which the majority relies heavily, does not itself justify invalidation of the Act.

Finally, our cases indicate that even certain kinds of governmental actions undertaken with the specific intention of improving the position of religion do not "advance religion" as that term is used in *Lemon.* 403 U.S. at 613. Rather, we have said that, in at least two circumstances, government *must* act to advance religion, and that, in a third, it *may* do so.

First, since we have consistently described the Establishment Clause as forbidding not only state action motivated by the desire to *advance* religion, but also that intended to "disapprove," "inhibit," or evince "hostility" toward religion, *see, e.g., ante* at 585 ("'disapprove'") (quoting *Lynch v. Donnelly, supra,* at 690 (O'CONNOR, J., concurring)); *Lynch v. Donnelly, supra,* at 673 ("hostility"); *Committee for Public Education & Religious Liberty v. Nyquist, supra,* at 788 ("'inhibi[t]'"); and since we have said that governmental "neutrality" toward religion is the preeminent goal of the First Amendment, *see, e.g., Grand Rapids School District v. Ball,* 473 U.S. at 382; *Roemer v. Maryland Public Works Bd.,* 426 U.S. 736, 747 (1976) (plurality opinion); *Committee for Public Education & Religious Liberty v. Nyquist, supra,* at 792–793; a State which discovers that its employees are inhibiting religion must take steps to prevent them from doing so, even though its purpose would clearly be to advance religion. *Cf. Walz v. Tax Comm'n of New York City, supra,* at 673. Thus, if the Louisiana Legislature sincerely believed that the State's science teachers were being hostile to religion, our cases indicate that it could act to eliminate that hostility without running afoul of *Lemon's* purpose test.

Second, we have held that intentional governmental advancement of religion is sometimes required by the Free Exercise Clause. For example, in *Hobble v. Unemployment Appeals Comm'n of Fla.,* 480 U.S. 136 (1987); *Thomas v. Review Bd., Indiana Employment Security Div.,* 450 U.S. 707 (1981); *Wisconsin v. Yoder,* 406 U.S. 205 (1972); and *Sherbert v. Verner,* 374 U.S. 398 (1963), we held that, in some circumstances, States must accommodate the beliefs of religious citizens by exempting them from generally applicable regulations. We have not yet come close to reconciling *Lemon* and our Free Exercise cases, and typically we do not really try. *See, e.g., Hobbie v. Unemployment Appeals Comm'n of Fla., supra,* at 144–145; *Thomas v. Review Bd., Indiana Employment Security Div., supra,* at 719–720. It is clear, however, that members of the Louisiana Legislature were not impermissibly motivated for purposes of the *Lemon* test if they believed that approval of the Balanced Treatment Act was required by the Free Exercise Clause.

We have also held that, in some circumstances, government may act to accommodate religion, even if that action is not required by the First Amendment. *See Hobbie v. Unemployment Appeals Comm'n of Fla., supra,* at 144–145. It is well established that

> [t]he limits of permissible state accommodation to religion are by no means coextensive with the noninterference mandated by the Free Exercise Clause.

Walz v. Tax Comm'n of New York City, supra, at 673; *see also Gillette v. United States,* **401 U.S. 437,** 453 (1971). We have implied that voluntary governmental accommodation of religion is not only permissible, but desirable. *See, e.g., ibid.* Thus, few would contend that Title VII of the Civil Rights Act of 1964, which both forbids religious discrimination by private sector employers, 78 Stat. 255, **42 U.S.C. § 2000e-2**(a)(l), and requires them reasonably to accommodate the religious practices of their employees, § 2000e(j), violates the Establishment Clause, even though its "purpose" is, of course, to advance religion, and even though it is almost certainly not required by the Free Exercise Clause. While we have warned that, at some point, accommodation may devolve into "an unlawful fostering of religion," *Hobbie v. Unemployment Appeals Comm'n of Fla., supra,* at 145, we have not suggested precisely (or even roughly) where that point might be. It is possible, then, that, even if the sole motive of those voting for the Balanced Treatment Act was to advance religion, and its passage was not actually required, or even believed to be required, by either the Free Exercise or Establishment Clauses, the Act would nonetheless survive scrutiny under *Lemon's* purpose test.

One final observation about the application of that test: although the Court's opinion gives no hint of it, in the past we have repeatedly affirmed "our reluctance to attribute unconstitutional motives to the States." *Mueller v. Allen, supra,* at 394; *see also Lynch v. Donnelly,* 465 U.S. at 699 (BRENNAN, J., dissenting). We "presume that legislatures act in a constitutional manner." *Illinois v. Krull,* 480 U.S. 340, 351 (1987); *see also Clements v. Fashing,* 457 U.S. 957, 963 (1982) (plurality opinion); *Rostker v. Goldberg,* 453 U.S. 57, 64 (1981); *McDonald v. Board of Election Comm'rs of Chicago,* 394 U.S. 802, 809 (1969). Whenever we are called upon to judge the constitutionality of an act of a state legislature,

> we must have "due regard to the fact that this Court is not exercising a primary judgment, but is sitting in judgment upon those who also have taken the oath to observe the Constitution and who have the responsibility for carrying on government."

Rostker v. Goldberg, supra, at 64 (quoting *Joint Anti-Fascist Refugee Committee v. McGrath,* 341 U.S. 123, 164 (1951) (Frankfurter, J., concurring)). This is particularly true, we have said, where the legislature has specifically considered the question of a law's constitutionality. *Ibid.*

With the foregoing in mind, I now turn to the purposes underlying adoption of the Balanced Treatment Act.

II

A

We have relatively little information upon which to judge the motives of those who supported the Act. About the only direct evidence is the statute itself and transcripts of the seven committee hearings at which it was considered. Unfortunately, several of those hearings were sparsely attended, and the legislators who were present revealed little about their motives. We have no committee reports, no floor debates, no remarks inserted into the legislative history, no statement from the Governor, and no postenactment statements or testimony from the bill's sponsor or any other legislators. *Cf. Wallace v. Jaffree,* 472 U.S. at 43, 56–57. Nevertheless, there is ample evidence that the majority is wrong in holding that the Balanced Treatment Act is without secular purpose.

At the outset, it is important to note that the Balanced Treatment Act did not fly through the Louisiana Legislature on wings of fundamentalist religious fervor—which would be unlikely, in any event, since only a small minority of the State's citizens belong to fundamentalist religious denominations. *See* B. Quinn, H. Anderson, M. Bradley, P. Goetting, & P. Shriver, Churches and Church Membership in the United States 16 (1982). The Act had its genesis (so to speak) in legislation introduced by Senator Bill Keith in June, 1980. After two hearings before the Senate Committee on Education, Senator Keith asked that his bill be referred to a study commission composed of members of both Houses of the Louisiana Legislature. He expressed hope that the joint committee would give the bill careful consideration and determine whether his arguments were "legitimate." 1 App. E-29–E-30. The committee met twice during the interim, heard testimony (both for and against the bill) from several witnesses, and received staff reports. Senator Keith introduced his bill again when the legislature reconvened. The Senate Committee on Education held two more hearings, and approved the bill after substantially amending it (in part over Senator Keith's objection). After approval by the full Senate, the bill was referred to the House Committee on Education. That committee conducted a lengthy hearing, adopted further amendments, and sent the bill on to the full House, where it received favorable consideration. The Senate concurred in the House amendments, and, on July 20, 1981, the Governor signed the bill into law.

Senator Keith's statements before the various committees that considered the bill hardly reflect the confidence of a man preaching to the converted. He asked his colleagues to "keep an open mind," and not to be "biased" by misleading characterizations of creation science, *id.* at E-33. He also urged them to "look at this subject on its merits, and not on some preconceived idea." *Id.* at E-34; *see also* 2 *id.* at E-491. Senator Keith's reception was not especially warm. Over his strenuous objection, the Senate Committee on Education voted 5-1 to amend his bill to deprive it of any force; as amended, the bill merely gave teachers permission to balance the teaching of creation science or evolution with the other. 1 *id.* at E-442–E-461. The House Committee restored the "mandatory" language to the bill by a vote of only 6-5, 2 *id.* at E-626–E-627, and both the full House (by vote of 52-35), *id.* at E-700–E-706, and full Senate (23-15), *id.* at E-735–E-738, had to repel further efforts to gut the bill.

The legislators understood that Senator Keith's bill involved a "unique" subject, 1 *id.* at E-106 (Rep. M. Thompson), and they were repeatedly made aware of its potential constitutional problems, *see, e.g., id.* at E-26–E-28 (McGehee); *id.* at E-38–E-39 (Sen. Keith); *id.* at E-241–E-242 (Rossman); *id.* at E-257 (Probst); *id.* at E-261 (Beck); *id.* at E-282 (Sen. Keith). Although the Establishment Clause, including its secular purpose requirement, was of substantial concern to the legislators, they eventually voted overwhelmingly in favor of the Balanced Treatment Act: the House approved it 71-19 (with 15 members absent), 2 *id.* at E-716–E-722; the Senate 26-12 (with all members present), *id.* at E-741–E-744. The legislators specifically designated the protection of "academic freedom" as the purpose of the Act. La.Rev.Stat.Ann. § 17:286.2 (West 1982). We cannot accurately assess whether this purpose is a "sham," *ante* at 587, until we first examine the evidence presented to the legislature far more carefully than the Court has done.

Before summarizing the testimony of Senator Keith and his supporters, I wish to make clear that I by no means intend to endorse its accuracy. But my views (and the views of this Court) about creation science and evolution are (or should be) beside the point. Our task is not to judge the debate about teaching the origins of life, but to ascertain what the members of the Louisiana Legislature believed. The vast majority of them voted to approve a bill which explicitly stated a secular purpose; what is crucial is not their *wisdom* in believing that purpose would be achieved by the bill, but their *sincerity* in believing it would be.

Most of the testimony in support of Senator Keith's bill came from the Senator himself, and from scientists and educators he presented, many of whom enjoyed academic credentials that may have been regarded as quite impressive by members of the Louisiana Legislature. To a substantial extent, their testimony was devoted to lengthy, and, to the layman, seemingly expert, scientific expositions on the origin of life. *See, e.g.,* 1 App. E-11–E-18 (Sunderland); *id.* at E-50–E-60 (Boudreaux); *id.* at E-86–E-89 (Ward); *id.* at E-130–E-153 (Boudreaux paper); *id.* at E-321–E-326 (Boudreaux); *id.* at E-423–E-428 (Sen. Keith). These scientific lectures touched upon, *inter alia,* biology, paleontology, genetics, astronomy, astrophysics, probability analysis, and biochemistry. The witnesses repeatedly assured committee members that "hundreds and hundreds" of highly respected, internationally renowned scientists believed in creation science, and would support their testimony. *See, e.g., id.* at E-5 (Sunderland); *id.* at E-76 (Sen. Keith); *id.* at E-100–E-101 (Reiboldt); *id.* at E-327–E-328 (Boudreaux); 2 *id.* at E-503–E-504 (Boudreaux).

Senator Keith and his witnesses testified essentially as set forth in the following numbered paragraphs:

(1) There are two and only two scientific explanations for the beginning of life—evolution and creation science. 1 *id.* at E-6 (Sunderland); *id.* at E-34 (Sen. Keith); *id.* at E-280 (Sen. Keith); *id.* at E-417–E-418 (Sen. Keith). Both are *bona fide* "sciences." *Id.* at E-6–E-7 (Sunderland); *id.* at E-12 (Sunderland); *id.* at E-416 (Sen. Keith); *id.* at E-427 (Sen. Keith); 2 *id.* at E-491–E-492 (Sen. Keith); *id.* at E-497–E-498 (Sen. Keith). Both posit a theory of the origin of life, and subject that theory to empirical testing. Evolution posits that life arose out of inanimate chemical compounds and has gradually evolved over millions of years. Creation science posits that all life forms now on earth appeared suddenly and relatively recently, and have changed little. Since there are only two possible explanations of the origin of life, any evidence that tends to disprove the theory of evolution necessarily tends to prove the theory of creation science, and vice versa. For example, the abrupt appearance in the fossil record of complex life, and the extreme rarity of transitional life forms in that record, are evidence for creation science. 1 *id.* at E-7 (Sunderland); *id.* at E-12–E-18 (Sunderland); *id.* at E-45–E-60 (Boudreaux); *id.* at E-67 (Harlow); *id.* at E-130–E-153 (Boudreaux paper); *id.* at E-423–E-428 (Sen. Keith).

(2) The body of scientific evidence supporting creation science is as strong as that supporting evolution. In fact, it may be stronger. *Id.* at E-214 (Young statement); *id.* at E-310 (Sen. Keith); *id.* at E-416 (Sen. Keith); 2 *Id.* at E-492 (Sen. Keith). The evidence for evolution is far less compelling than we have been led to believe. Evolution is not a scientific "fact," since it cannot actually be observed in a laboratory. Rather, evolution is merely a scientific

theory or "guess." 1 *id.* at E-20–E-21 (Morris); *id.* at E-85 (Ward); *id.* at E-100 (Reiboldt); *id.* at E-328–E-329 (Boudreaux); 2 *id.* at E-506 (Boudreaux). It is a very bad guess at that. The scientific problems with evolution are so serious that it could accurately be termed a "myth." 1 *id.* at E-85 (Ward); *id.* at E-92–E-93 (Kalivoda); *id.* at E-95–E-97 (Sen. Keith); *id.* at E-154 (Boudreaux paper); *id.* at E-329 (Boudreaux); *id.* at E-453 (Sen. Keith); 2 *id.* at E-505–E-506 (Boudreaux); *id.* at E-516 (Young).

(3) Creation science is educationally valuable. Students exposed to it better understand the current state of scientific evidence about the origin of life. 1 *id.* at E-19 (Sunderland); *id.* at E-39 (Sen. Keith); *id.* at E-79 (Kalivoda); *id.* at E-308 (Sen. Keith); 2 *id.* at E-513–E-514 (Morris). Those students even have a better understanding of evolution. 1 *id.* at E-19 (Sunderland). Creation science can and should be presented to children without any religious content. *Id.* at E-12 (Sunderland); *id.* at E-22 (Sanderford); *id.* at E-35–E-36 (Sen. Keith); *id.* at E-101 (Reiboldt); *id.* at E-279–E-280 (Sen. Keith); *id.* at E-282 (Sen. Keith).

(4) Although creation science is educationally valuable and strictly scientific, it is now being censored from or misrepresented in the public schools. *Id.* at E-19 (Sunderland); *id.* at E-21 (Morris); *id.* at E-34 (Sen. Keith); *id.* at E-37 (Sen. Keith); *id.* at E-42 (Sen. Keith); *id.* at E-92 (Kalivoda); *id.* at E-97–E-98 (Reiboldt); *id.* at E-214 (Young statement); *id.* at E-218 (Young statement); *id.* at E-280 (Sen. Keith); *id.* at E-309 (Sen. Keith); 2 *id.* at E-513 (Morris). Evolution, in turn, is misrepresented as an absolute truth. 1 *id.* at E-63 (Harlow); *id.* at E-74 (Sen. Keith); *id.* at E-81 (Kalivoda); *id.* at E-214 (Young statement); 2 *id.* at E-507 (Harlow); *id.* at E-513 (Morris); *id.* at E-516 (Young). Teachers have been brainwashed by an entrenched scientific establishment composed almost exclusively of scientists to whom evolution is like a "religion." These scientists discriminate against creation scientists, so as to prevent evolution's weaknesses from being exposed. 1 *id.* at E-61 (Boudreaux); *id.* at E-63–E-64 (Harlow); *id.* at E-78–E-79 (Kalivoda); *id.* at E-80 (Kalivoda); *id.* at E-95–E-97 (Sen. Keith); *id.* at E-129 (Boudreaux paper); *id.* at E-218 (Young statement); *id.* at E-357 (Sen. Keith); *id.* at E-430 (Boudreaux).

(5) The censorship of creation science has at least two harmful effects. First, it deprives students of knowledge of one of the two scientific explanations for the origin of life, and leads them to believe that evolution is proven fact; thus, their education suffers, and they are wrongly taught that science has proved their religious beliefs false. Second, it violates the Establishment Clause. The United States Supreme Court has held that secular humanism is a religion. *Id.* at E-36 (Sen. Keith) (referring to *Torcaso v. Watkins,* 367 U.S. 488, 495, n. 11 (1961));1 App. E-418 (Sen. Keith); 2 *id.* at E-499 (Sen. Keith). Belief in evolution is a central tenet of that religion. 1 *id.* at E-282 (Sen. Keith); *id.* at E-312–E-313 (Sen. Keith); *id.* at E-317 (Sen. Keith); *id.* at E-418 (Sen. Keith); 2 *id.* at E-499 (Sen. Keith). Thus, by censoring creation science and instructing students that evolution is fact, public school teachers are *now* advancing religion in violation of the Establishment Clause. 1 *id.* at E-2–E-4 (Sen. Keith); *id.* at E-36–E-37, E-39 (Sen. Keith); *id.* at E-154–E-155 (Boudreaux paper); *id.* at E-281–E-282 (Sen. Keith); *id.* at E-313 (Sen. Keith); *id.* at E-315–E-316 (Sen. Keith); *id.* at E-317 (Sen. Keith); 2 *id.* at E-499–E-500 (Sen. Keith).

Senator Keith repeatedly and vehemently denied that his purpose was to advance a particular religious doctrine. At the outset of the first hearing on the legislation, he testified:

> We are not going to say today that you should have some kind of religious instructions in our schools. . . . We are not talking about religion today. . . . I am not proposing that we take the Bible in each science class and read the first chapter of Genesis.

1 *id.* at E-35. At a later hearing, Senator Keith stressed:

> [T]o . . . teach religion and disguise it as creationism . . . is not my intent. My intent is to see to it that our textbooks are not censored.

Id. at E-280. He made many similar statements throughout the hearings. *See, e.g., id.* at E-41; *id.* at E-282; *id.* at E-310; *id.* at E-417; *see also id.* at E-44 (Boudreaux); *id.* at E-80 (Kalivoda).

We have no way of knowing, of course, how many legislators believed the testimony of Senator Keith and his witnesses. But in the absence of evidence to the contrary, we have to assume that many of them did. Given that assumption, the Court today plainly errs in holding that the Louisiana Legislature passed the Balanced Treatment Act for exclusively religious purposes.

B

Even with nothing more than this legislative history to go on, I think it would be extraordinary to invalidate the Balanced Treatment Act for lack of a valid secular purpose. Striking down a law approved by the democratically elected representatives of the people is no minor matter.

> The cardinal principle of statutory construction is to save, and not to destroy. We have repeatedly held that, as between two possible interpretations of a statute, by one of which it would be unconstitutional and by the other valid, our plain duty is to adopt that which will save the act.

NLRB v. Jones & Laushlin Steel Corp., 301 U.S. 1, 30 (1937). So, too, it seems to me, with discerning statutory purpose. Even if the legislative history were silent or ambiguous about the existence of a secular purpose—and here it is not—the statute should survive *Lemon's* purpose test. But even more validation than mere legislative history is present here. The Louisiana Legislature explicitly set forth its secular purpose ("protecting academic freedom") in the very text of the Act. La.Rev.Stat. § 17:286.2 (West 1982). We have in the past repeatedly relied upon or deferred to such expressions, *see, e.g., Committee for Public Education & Religious Liberty v. Regan,* 444 U.S. at 654; *Meek v. Pittenger,* 421 U.S. at 363, 367–368; *Committee for Public Education & Religious Liberty v. Nyquist,* 413 U.S. at 773; *Levitt v. Committee for Public Education & Religious Liberty,* 413 U.S. at 479–480, n. 7; *Tilton v. Richardson,* 403 U.S. at 678–679 (plurality opinion); *Lemon v. Kurtzman,* 403 U.S. at 613; *Board of Education v. Allen,* 392 U.S. at 243.

The Court seeks to evade the force of this expression of purpose by stubbornly misinterpreting it, and then finding that the provisions of the Act do not advance that misinterpreted purpose, thereby showing it to be a sham. The Court first surmises that "academic freedom" means "enhancing the freedom of teachers to teach what they will," *ante* at 586—even though "academic freedom" in that sense has little scope in the structured elementary and secondary curriculums with which the Act is concerned. Alternatively, the Court suggests that it might mean "maximiz[ing] the comprehensiveness and effectiveness of science instruction," *ante* at 588—though that is an exceedingly strange interpretation of the words, and one that is refuted on the very face of the statute. *See* § 17:286.5. Had the Court devoted to this central question of the meaning of the legislatively expressed purpose a small fraction of the research into legislative history that produced its quotations of religiously motivated statements by individual legislators, it would have discerned quite readily what "academic freedom" meant: *students'* freedom from *indoctrination.* The legislature wanted to ensure that students would be free to decide for themselves how life began, based upon a fair and balanced presentation of die scientific evidence—that is, to protect "the right of each [student] voluntarily to determine what to believe (and what not to believe) free of any coercive pressures from the State." *Grand Rapids School District v. Ball,* 473 U.S. at 385. The legislature did not care *whether* the topic of origins was taught; it simply wished to ensure that, *when* the topic was taught, students would receive "'all of the evidence.'" *Ante* at 586 (quoting Tr. of Oral Arg. 60).

As originally introduced, the "purpose" section of the Balanced Treatment Act read:

> This Chapter is enacted for the purposes of protecting academic freedom . . . *of students* . . . and assisting *students* in their search for truth.

1 App. E-292 (emphasis added). Among the proposed findings of fact contained in the original version of the bill was the following:

> Public school instruction in only evolution science . . . *violates the principle of academic freedom because it denies students a choice between scientific models, and instead indoctrinates them in evolution science alone.*

Id. at E-295 (emphasis added). Senator Keith unquestionably understood "academic freedom" to mean "freedom from indoctrination." *See id.* at E-36 (purpose of bill is "to protect academic freedom by providing student choice"); *id.* at E-283 (purpose of bill is to protect "academic freedom" by giving students a "choice," rather than subjecting them to "indoctrination on origins").

If one adopts the obviously intended meaning of the statutory term "academic freedom," there is no basis whatever for concluding that the purpose they express is a "sham." *Ante* at 587. To the contrary, the Act pursues that purpose plainly and consistently. It requires that, whenever the subject of origins is covered, evolution be "taught as a theory, rather than as proven scientific fact," and that scientific evidence inconsistent with the theory of evolution (viz., "creation science") be taught as well. *La.Rev.Stat.Ann.* § 17:286.4A (West 1982). Living up to its title of *"Balanced Treatment* for Creation-Science and Evolution-Science Act," § 17.286.1, it treats the teaching of creation the same way. It does not mandate instruction in creation science, § 17:286.5; forbids teachers to present creation science "as proven scientific fact," § 17:286.4A; and *bans* the teaching of creation science unless the theory is (to use the Court's terminology) "discredit[ed] '. . . at every turn'" with the teaching of evolution. *Ante* at 589 (quoting 765 F.2d at 1257). It surpasses understanding how the Court can see in this a purpose "to restructure the science curriculum to conform with a particular religious viewpoint," *ante* at 593, "to provide a persuasive advantage to a particular religious doctrine," *ante* at 592, "to promote the theory of creation science which embodies a particular religious tenet," *ante* at 593, and "to endorse a particular religious doctrine," *ante* at 594.

The Act's reference to "creation" is not convincing evidence of religious purpose. The Act defines creation science as *"scientific evidenc[e],"* § 17:286.3(2) (emphasis added), and Senator Keith and his witnesses repeatedly stressed that the subject can and should be presented without religious content. *See supra,* at 623. We have no basis on the record to conclude that creation science need be anything other than a collection of scientific data supporting the theory that life abruptly appeared on earth. *See* n. 4, *supra.* Creation science, its proponents insist, no more must explain *whence* life came than evolution must explain whence came the inanimate materials from which it says life evolved. But even if that were not so, to posit a past creator is not to posit the eternal and personal God who is the object of religious veneration. Indeed, it is not even to posit the *"unmoved* mover" hypothesized by Aristotle and other notably nonfundamentalist philosophers. Senator Keith suggested this when he referred to "a creator, *however you define a creator."* 1 App. E-280 (emphasis added).

The Court cites three provisions of the Act which, it argues, demonstrate a "discriminatory preference for the teaching of creation science" and no interest in "academic freedom." *Ante* at 482 U.S. 588"]588. First, the Act prohibits discrimination only against creation scientists and those who teach creation science. § 17:286.4C. Second, the Act requires local school boards to develop and provide to science teachers "a curriculum guide on presentation of creation-science." § 17:286.7A. Finally, the Act requires the Governor to designate seven creation scientists who shall, upon request, assist local school boards in developing the curriculum guides. § 17:286.7B. But none of these provisions casts doubt upon the sincerity of the legislators' articulated purpose of "academic freedom"—unless, of course, one gives that term the obviously erroneous meanings preferred by the Court. The Louisiana legislators had been told repeatedly that creation scientists were scorned by most educators and scientists, who themselves had an almost religious faith in evolution. It is hardly surprising, then, that, in seeking to achieve a balanced, "nonindoctrinating" curriculum, the legislators protected from discrimination only those teachers whom they thought were *suffering* from discrimination. (Also, the legislators were undoubtedly aware of 588). First, the Act prohibits discrimination only against creation scientists and those who teach creation science. § 17:286.4C. Second, the Act requires local school boards to develop and provide to science teachers "a curriculum guide on presentation of creation-science." § 17:286.7A. Finally, the Act requires the Governor to designate seven creation scientists who shall, upon request, assist local school boards in developing the curriculum guides. S 17:286.7B. But none of these provisions casts doubt upon the sincerity of the legislators' articulated purpose of "academic freedom"—unless, of course, one gives that term the obviously erroneous meanings preferred by the Court. The Louisiana legislators had been told repeatedly that creation scientists were scorned by most educators and scientists, who themselves had an almost religious faith in evolution. It is hardly surprising, then, that, in seeking to achieve a balanced, "nonindoctrinating" curriculum, the legislators protected from discrimination only those teachers whom they thought were *suffering* from discrimination. (Also, the legislators were undoubtedly aware of *Epperson v. Arkansas*, 393 U.S. 97 (1968), and thus could quite reasonably have concluded that discrimination against evolutionists was already prohibited.) The two provisions respecting the development of curriculum guides are also consistent with "academic freedom" as the Louisiana Legislature understood the term. Witnesses had informed the legislators that, because of the hostility of most scientists and educators to creation science, the topic had been censored from or badly misrepresented in elementary and secondary school texts. In light of the unavailability of works on creation science suitable for classroom use (a fact appellees concede, *see* Brief for Appellees 27, 40) and the existence of ample materials on evolution, it was entirely reasonable for the legislature to conclude that science teachers attempting to implement the Act would need a curriculum guide on creation science, but not on evolution, and that those charged with developing the guide would need an easily accessible group of creation scientists. Thus, the provisions of the Act of so much concern to the Court *support* the conclusion that the legislature acted to advance "academic freedom."

The legislative history gives ample evidence of the sincerity of the Balanced Treatment Act's articulated purpose. Witness after witness urged the legislators to support the Act so that students would not be "indoctrinated," but would instead be free to decide for themselves, based upon a fair presentation of the scientific evidence, about the origin of life. *See, e.g.,* 1 App. E-18 (Sunderland) ("all that we are advocating" is presenting "scientific data" to students and "letting [them] make up their own mind[s]"); *id.* at E-19–E-20 (Sunderland) (Students are now being "indoctrinated" in evolution through the use of "censored school books. . . . All that we are asking for is [the] open unbiased education in the classroom . . . your students deserve"); *id.* at E-21 (Morris) ("A student cannot [make an intelligent decision about the origin of life] unless he is well informed about both [evolution and creation science]"); *id.* at E-22 (Sanderford) ("We are asking very simply [that] . . . creationism [be presented] alongside . . . evolution, and let people make their own mind[s] up"); *id.* at E-23 (Young) (the bill would require teachers to live up to their "obligation to present all theories," and thereby enable "students to make judgments themselves"); *id.* at E-44 (Boudreaux) ("Our intention is truth, and, as a scientist,

I am interested in truth"); *id.* at E-60–E-61 (Boudreaux) ("[W]e [teachers] are guilty of a lot of brainwashing. . . . We have a duty to . . . [present the] truth" to students "at all levels from grade school on through the college level"); *id.* at E-79 (Kalivoda) ("This [hearing] is being held, I think, to determine whether children will benefit from freedom of information, or if they will be handicapped educationally by having little or no information about creation"); *id.* at E-80 (Kalivoda) ("I am not interested in teaching religion in schools. . . . I am interested in the truth, and [students'] having the opportunity to hear more than one side"); *id.* at E-98 (Reiboldt) ("The students have a right to know there is an alternate creationist point of view. They have a right to know the scientific evidences which suppor[t] that alternative"); *id.* at E-218 (Young statement) (passage of the bill will ensure that "communication of scientific ideas and discoveries may be unhindered"); 2 *id.* at E-514 (Morris) ("[A]re we going to allow [students] to look at evolution, to look at creationism, and to let one or the other stand or fall on its own merits, or will we, by failing to pass this bill, . . . deny students an opportunity to hear another viewpoint?"); *id.* at E-516–E-517 (Young) ("We want to give the children here in this state an equal opportunity to see both sides of the theories"). Senator Keith expressed similar views. *See, e.g.,* 1 *id.* at E-36; *id.* at E-41; *id.* at E-280; *id.* at E-283.

Legislators other than Senator Keith made only a few statements providing insight into their motives, but those statements cast no doubt upon the sincerity of the Act's articulated purpose. The legislators were concerned primarily about the manner in which the subject of origins was presented in Louisiana schools—specifically, about whether scientifically valuable information was being censored, and students misled about evolution. Representatives Cain, Jenkins, and F. Thompson seemed impressed by the scientific evidence presented in support of creation science. *See* 2 *id.* at E-530 (Rep. F. Thompson); *id.* at E-533 (Rep. Cain); *id.* at E-613 (Rep. Jenkins). At the first study commission hearing, Senator Picard and Representative M. Thompson questioned Senator Keith about Louisiana teachers' treatment of evolution and creation science. See 1 *id.* at E-71–E-74. At the close of the hearing, Representative M. Thompson told the audience:

> We, as members of the committee, will also receive from the staff information of what is currently being taught in the Louisiana public schools. We really want to see [it]. I . . . have no idea in what manner [biology] is presented, and in what manner the creationist theories [are] excluded in the public school[s]. We want to look at what the status of the situation is.

Id. at E-104. Legislators made other comments suggesting a concern about censorship and misrepresentation of scientific information. *See, e.g., id.* at E-386 (Sen. McLeod); 2 *id.* at E-527 (Rep. Jenkins); *id.* at E-528 (Rep. M. Thompson); *id.* at E-534 (Rep. Fair).

It is undoubtedly true that what prompted the legislature to direct its attention to the misrepresentation of evolution in the schools (rather than the inaccurate presentation of other topics) was its awareness of the tension between evolution and the religious beliefs of many children. But even appellees concede that a valid secular purpose is not rendered impermissible simply because its pursuit is prompted by concern for religious sensitivities. Tr. of Oral Arg. 43, 56. If a history teacher falsely told her students that the bones of Jesus Christ had been discovered, or a physics teacher that the Shroud of Turin had been conclusively established to be inexplicable on the basis of natural causes, I cannot believe (despite the majority's implication to the contrary, *see ante* at 592–593) that legislators or school board members would be constitutionally prohibited from taking corrective action simply because that action was prompted by concern for the religious beliefs of the misinstructed students.

In sum, even if one concedes, for the sake of argument, that a majority of the Louisiana Legislature voted for the Balanced Treatment Act partly in order to foster (rather than merely eliminate discrimination against) Christian fundamentalist beliefs, our cases establish that that, alone, would not suffice to invalidate the Act, so long as there was a genuine secular purpose as well. We have, moreover, no adequate basis for disbelieving the secular purpose set forth in the Act itself, or for concluding that it is a sham enacted to conceal the legislators' violation of their oaths of office. I am astonished by the Court's unprecedented readiness to reach such a conclusion, which I can only attribute to an intellectual predisposition created by the facts and the legend of *Scopes v. State,* 154 Tenn. 105, 289 S.W. 363 (1927)—an instinctive reaction that any governmentally imposed requirements bearing upon the teaching of evolution must be a manifestation of Christian fundamentalist repression. In this case, however, it seems to me the Court's position is the repressive one. The people of Louisiana, including those who are Christian fundamentalists, are quite entitled, as a secular matter, to have whatever scientific evidence there may be against evolution presented in their schools, just as Mr. Scopes was entitled to present whatever scientific evidence there was for it. Perhaps what the Louisiana Legislature has done is unconstitutional because there is no such evidence, and the scheme they have established will amount to no more than a presentation of the Book of Genesis. But we cannot say that on the evidence before us in this summary judgment context, which includes ample uncontradicted testimony that "creation science" is a body of scientific knowledge, rather than revealed belief. *Infinitely less* can we say (or should we say) that the scientific evidence for evolution is so conclusive that no one could be gullible enough to believe that there is any real scientific evidence to the contrary, so that the legislation's stated purpose must be a lie. Yet that illiberal judgment, that *Scopes*-in-reverse, is ultimately the basis on which the Court's facile rejection of the Louisiana Legislature's purpose must rest.

Since the existence of secular purpose is so entirely clear, and thus dispositive, I will not go on to discuss the fact that, even if the Louisiana Legislature's purpose were exclusively to advance religion, some of the well-established exceptions to the impermissibility of that purpose might be applicable—the validating intent to eliminate a perceived discrimination against a particular religion, to facilitate its free exercise, or to accommodate it. *See supra,* at 617–618. I am not, in any case, enamored of those amorphous exceptions, since I think them no more than unpredictable correctives to what is (as the next Part of this opinion will discuss) a fundamentally unsound rule. It is surprising, however, that the Court does not address these exceptions, since the context of the legislature's action gives some reason to believe they may be applicable.

Because I believe that the Balanced Treatment Act had a secular purpose, which is all the first component of the *Lemon* test requires, I would reverse the judgment of the Court of Appeals and remand for further consideration.

III

I have to this point assumed the validity of the *Lemon* "purpose" test. In fact, however, I think the pessimistic evaluation that THE CHIEF JUSTICE made of the totality of *Lemon* is particularly applicable to the "purpose" prong: it is

> a constitutional theory [that] has no basis in the history of the amendment it seeks to interpret, is difficult to apply, and yields unprincipled results. . . .

Wallace v. Jaffree, 472 U.S. at 112 (REHNQUIST, J., dissenting).

Our cases interpreting and applying the purpose test have made such a maze of the Establishment Clause that even the most conscientious governmental officials can only guess what motives will be held unconstitutional. We have said essentially the following: government may not act with the purpose of advancing religion, except when forced to do so by the Free Exercise Clause (which is now and then); or when eliminating existing governmental hostility to religion (which exists sometimes); or even when merely accommodating governmentally uninhibited religious practices, except that at some point (it is unclear where) intentional accommodation results in the fostering of religion, which is of course unconstitutional. *See supra,* at 614–618.

But the difficulty of knowing what vitiating purpose one is looking for is as nothing compared with the difficulty of knowing how or where to find it. For while it is possible to discern the objective "purpose" of a statute (*i.e.,* the public good at which its provisions appear to be directed), or even the formal motivation for a statute where that is explicitly set forth (as it was, to no avail, here), discerning the subjective motivation of those enacting the statute is, to be honest, almost always an impossible task. The number of possible motivations, to begin with, is not binary, or indeed even finite. In the present case, for example, a particular legislator need not have voted for the Act either because he wanted to foster religion or because he wanted to improve education. He may have thought the bill would provide jobs for his district, or may have wanted to make amends with a faction of his party he had alienated on another vote, or he may have been a close friend of the bill's sponsor, or he may have been repaying a favor he owed the majority leader, or he may have hoped the Governor would appreciate his vote and make a fund-raising appearance for him, or he may have been pressured to vote for a bill he disliked by a wealthy contributor or by a flood of constituent mail, or he may have been seeking favorable publicity, or he may have been reluctant to hurt the feelings of a loyal staff member who worked on the bill, or he may have been settling an old score with a legislator who opposed the bill, or he may have been mad at his wife, who opposed the bill, or he may have been intoxicated and utterly unmotivated when the vote was called, or he may have accidentally voted "yes" instead of "no," or, of course, he may have had (and very likely did have) a combination of some of the above and many other motivations. To look for the sole purpose of even a single legislator is probably to look for something that does not exist.

Putting that problem aside, however, where ought we to look for the individual legislator's purpose? We cannot, of course, assume that every member present (if, as is unlikely, we know who or even how many they were) agreed with the motivation expressed in a particular legislator's preenactment floor or committee statement. Quite obviously, "[w]hat motivates one legislator to make a speech about a statute is not necessarily what motivates scores of others to enact it." *United States v. O'Brien,* 391 U.S. 367, 384 (1968). Can we assume, then, that they all agree with the motivation expressed in the staff-prepared committee reports they might have read—even though we are unwilling to assume that they agreed with the motivation expressed in the very statute that they voted for? Should we consider postenactment floor statements? Or postenactment testimony from legislators, obtained expressly for the lawsuit? Should we consider media reports on the realities of the legislative bargaining? All of these sources, of course, are eminently manipulate. Legislative histories can be contrived and sanitized, favorable media coverage orchestrated, and postenactment recollections conveniently distorted. Perhaps most valuable of all would be more objective indications—for example, evidence regarding the individual legislators' religious affiliations. And if that, why not evidence regarding the fervor or tepidity of their beliefs?

Having achieved, through these simple means, an assessment of what individual legislators intended, we must still confront the question (yet to be addressed in any of our cases) how *many* of them must have the invalidating intent. If a state senate approves a bill by vote of 26 to 25, and only one of the 26 intended solely to advance religion, is the law unconstitutional? What if 13 of the 26 had that intent? What if 3 of the 26 had the impermissible intent, but 3 of the 25 voting against the bill were motivated by religious hostility, or were simply attempting to "balance" the votes of their impermissibly motivated colleagues? Or is it possible that the intent of the bill's sponsor is alone enough to invalidate it—on a theory, perhaps, that even though everyone else's intent was pure, what they produced was the fruit of a forbidden tree?

Because there are no good answers to these questions, tills Court has recognized from Chief Justice Marshall, *see Fletcher v. Peck,* 6 Cranch 87, 130 (1810), to Chief Justice Warren, *United States v. O'Brien, supra,* at 383–384, that determining the subjective intent of legislators is a perilous enterprise. *See also Palmer v. Thompson,* 403 U.S. 217, 224–225 (1971); *Epperson v. Arkansas,* 393 U.S. at 113 (Black, J., concurring). It is perilous, I might note, not just for the judges who will very likely reach the wrong result, but also for the legislators who find that they must assess the validity of proposed legislation—and risk the condemnation of having voted for an unconstitutional measure—not on the basis of what the legislation contains, nor even on the basis of what they themselves intend, but on the basis of what *others* have in mind.

Given the many hazards involved in assessing the subjective intent of governmental decisionmakers, the first prong of *Lemon* is defensible, I think, only if the text of the Establishment Clause demands it. That is surely not the case. The Clause states that "Congress shall make no law respecting an establishment of religion." One could argue, I suppose, that any time Congress acts with the *intent* of advancing religion, it has enacted a "law respecting an establishment of religion"; but, far from being an unavoidable reading, it is quite an unnatural one. I doubt, for example, that the Clayton Act, 38 Stat. 730, as amended, 15 U.S.C. § 12 *et seq.*, could reasonably be described as a "law respecting an establishment of religion" If bizarre new historical evidence revealed that it lacked a secular purpose, even though it has no discernible nonsecular effect. It is, in short, far from an inevitable reading of the Establishment Clause that it forbids all governmental action intended to advance religion; and, if not inevitable, any reading with such untoward consequences must be wrong.

In the past, we have attempted to justify our embarrassing Establishment Clause jurisprudence on the ground that it "sacrifices clarity and predictability for flexibility." *Committee for Public Education & Religious Liberty v. Regan,* 444 U.S. at 662. One commentator has aptly characterized this as "a euphemism . . . for . . . the absence of any principled rationale." Choper, *supra,* n. 7, at 681 I think it time that we sacrifice some "flexibility" for "clarity and predictability." Abandoning *Lemon's* purpose test—a test which exacerbates the tension between the Free Exercise and Establishment Clauses, has no basis in the language or history of the Amendment, and, as today's decision shows, has wonderfully flexible consequences—would be a good place to start.

POSTSCRIPT

Does a State Law That Requires Public School Teachers to Teach "Creation Science" Whenever They Teach the Theory of Evolution Violate the First Amendment?

Cases presenting First Amendment religious issues have been difficult ones for the Supreme Court throughout our history. The result has been a somewhat fragmented body of First Amendment Establishment Clause precedents.

For example, in *McCreary County v. A.C.L.U. of Kentucky,* 545 U.S. 844 (2005), the Supreme Court held unconstitutional a courthouse display that included the Ten Commandments. Later that same day, however, the Court upheld the display of a monument containing the Ten Commandments on the Texas State Capitol grounds, due to its historic significance for Texas's identity, in *Van Orden v. Perry,* 545 U.S. 677 (2005).

In *Grand Rapids School District v. Ball,* 473 U.S. 373 (1985), the Supreme Court banned the use of state and federal funds for public school instructors who taught remedial instruction in religious schools because the program constituted an "excessive entanglement" between church and state. The Court allowed the programs to continue, however, if the classes were moved to off-site public trailers. In *Zobrest v. Catalina Foothills School District,* 509 U.S. 1 (1993), the Court held, however, that a deaf child who attended a private religious school could utilize a sign language interpreter provided and paid for by a public school district. Moreover, in *Agostoni v. Felton,* 521 U.S. 203 (1997), the Supreme Court overruled *Grand Rapids School District v. Ball* (1985) and held that the First Amendment permits both remedial and enrichment instruction by public school teachers in religious schools.

The apparent discontinuity of the above cases lends support to Justice Antonin E. Scalia's characterization of the Court's Establishment Clause precedents in *Edwards v. Aguillard* as "embarassing." Citing Professor Jesse Choper, Justice Scalia further described this jurisprudence as "a euphemism . . . for . . . the absence of any principled rationale."

It is interesting to note as well that there are more recent issues to be addressed under the Establishment Clause of the First Amendment. Apparently, the advocates of religious instruction in public school classrooms are not deterred easily. The new movement involves an effort to infuse the doctrine of "intelligent design" (ID) into public school classrooms as an alternative to Darwin's theory of evolution. ID is defined as "[t]he theory that matter, the various forms of life, and the world were created by a designing intelligence." (http://www.Merriam-Webster.com). *Kitzmiller v. Dover Area School District,* 400 F. Supp. 2d 707 (2005), a case filed in the U.S. District Court for the Middle District of Pennsylvania, challenged a statement mandated by the Dover, Pennsylvania, School Board to be read in all ninth-grade science classes whenever the theory of evolution was taught. The statement was as follows:

> The Pennsylvania Academic Standards require students to learn about Darwin's theory of evolution and eventually to take a standardized test of which evolution is a part.
>
> Because Darwin's Theory is a theory, it is still being tested as new evidence is discovered. The Theory is not a fact. Gaps in the Theory exist for which there is no evidence. A theory is defined as a well-tested explanation that unifies a broad range of observations.
>
> Intelligent design is an explanation of the origin of life that differs from Darwin's view. The reference book *Of Pandas and People* is available for students to see if they would like to explore this view in an effort to gain an understanding of what intelligent design actually involves.
>
> As is true with any theory, students are encouraged to keep an open mind. The school leaves the discussion of the origins of life to individual students and their families. As a standards-driven district, class instruction focuses upon preparing students to achieve proficiency on standards-based assessments.

A majority of the Dover School Board had voted to require public school science teachers to read this statement aloud to their ninth-grade biology classes; three Board members who had voted against it resigned in protest. In addition, the school district's science teachers refused to read the statement. The American Civil Liberties Union (ACLU) filed a lawsuit on behalf of 11 parents of students from the Dover district, and the case was tried by Judge John E. Jones. Stated Judge Jones: "A significant characteristic of the Intelligent Design Movement (IDM) is that . . . it describes ID as a religious argument. In that vein, the writings of leading ID proponents reveal that the designer postulated by their argument is the God of Christianity." Therefore, Judge Jones stated: "ID is not science." He concluded:

> We find that ID fails on three different levels, any one of which is sufficient to preclude a determination that ID is science. They are: (1) ID violates the centuries-old ground rules of science by invoking and permitting supernatural causation; (2) the argument of irreducible complexity, central to ID, employs the same flawed and illogical contrived dualism that doomed creation science in the 1980s; and (3) ID's negative attacks on evolution have been refuted by the scientific community.

Therefore, the Court held that the teaching of ID in public school biology classes violates the Establishment Clause of the First Amendment as well as the Pennsylvania Constitution. In an interesting aside, the Dover School Board members who had voted for the ID statement were all subsequently defeated in the next election, and the members of the new Board declined to appeal Judge Jones's ruling. Although the precedent established in this case is binding throughout the Middle District of Pennsylvania, it would not be binding law in other jurisdictions. It will not be surprising, therefore, to see this issue litigated in future cases in other jurisdictions. Perhaps in the future, the issue of teaching the doctrine of ID in public school classrooms will reach the U.S. Supreme Court. It would be difficult to imagine, however, that the Court would reach a conclusion that differs from Judge Jones's ruling. ID is a theory that emphasizes the role of the supernatural as a key component of creation. It should thus not be considered a "scientific" theory in any objective sense.

There are a large number of additional resources to pursue further study in this area, including: Kathleen M. Sullivan and Gerald Gunther, *Constitutional Law* (Foundation Press, 15th ed., 2004); Laurence H. Tribe, *American Constitutional Law* (Foundation Press, 2nd ed., 1988); Alpheus Thomas Mason and Donald Grier Stephenson, Jr., *American Constitutional Law* (Pearson Prentice Hall, 15th ed., 2009; 14th ed., 2005); Bernard Schwartz, *A History of the Supreme Court* (Oxford University Press, 1993); Kermit L. Hall, Paul Finkelman, and James Ely, Jr., *American Legal History: Cases and Materials* (Oxford University Press, 3rd ed., 2005); Kermit L. Hall, *The Oxford Companion to the Supreme Court of the United States* (Oxford University Press, 1992); Walter F. Murphy, James E. Fleming, Sotirios A. Barber, and Stephen Macedo, *American Constitutional Interpretation* (Foundation Press, 3rd ed., 2003); David M. O'Brien, *Constitutional Law and Politics: Struggles for Power and Government Accountability* (W.W. Norton, 6th ed., 2005); Craig R. Ducat, *Constitutional Interpretation* (Wadsworth, 9th ed., 2009); John H. Garvey, T. Alexander Aleinikoff, and Daniel A. Farber, *Modern Constitutional Theory: A Reader* (Thompson West, 5th ed., (2004). See also: Rupal M. Doshi, "Nonincorporation of the Establishment Clause: Satisfying the Demands of Equality, Pluralism, and Originalism," *Georgetown Law Journal*, vol. 98, p. 459 (2010); Kelly S. Terry, "Shifting Out of Neutral: Intelligent Design and the Road to Nonpreferentialism," *Boston University Public Interest Law Journal*, vol. 18, p. 67 (2008); Andrew Koppelman, "Phony Originalism and the Establishment Clause," *Northwestern University Law Review*, vol. 103, p.727 (2009); Kyle Duncan, "Misunderstanding Freedom from Religion: Two Cents on Madison's Three Pence," *Nevada Law Journal*, vol. 9, p. 32 (2008); Casey Luskin, "Does Challenging Darwin Create Constitutional Jeopardy? A Comprehensive Survey of Case Law Regarding the Teaching of Biological Origins" *Hamline Law Review*, vol. 32, p. 1 (2009); Frank S. Ravitch, "Playing the Proof Game: Intelligent Design and the Law," *Pennsylvania State Law Review*, vol. 113, p. 841 (2009).

ISSUE 19

Should Burning an American Flag Be a Form of Expression Protected by the First Amendment?

YES: William J. Brennan, from Majority Opinion, *Texas v. Johnson*, 491 U.S. 397 (1989)

NO: William H. Rehnquist, from Dissenting Opinion, *Texas v. Johnson*, 491 U.S. 397 (1989)

ISSUE SUMMARY

YES. Justice William J. Brennan, writing for the U.S. Supreme Court in *Texas v. Johnson* (1989), held that the defendant's act of burning an American flag at the Republican National Convention was expressive conduct, protected by the First Amendment. Moreover, the state of Texas could not lawfully prohibit flag desecration as a means of preserving the flag as a symbol of national unity. Furthermore, the statute was not sufficiently narrow to prohibit only those acts that were likely to result in a serious disturbance.

NO: Chief Justice William H. Rehnquist, dissenting in *Texas v. Johnson* (1989), asserted that because the American flag occupies a unique position as the symbol of our nation, the state of Texas is justified in prohibiting flag burning in a case such as this.

Americans can be a surly lot. Protesting against governmental policies seems to be an indelible part of our national character. In fact, many of the events that led directly to the American Revolution were acts of protest by the colonists directed at the British monarchy. One noteworthy incident was the Boston Tea Party in 1773, which had resulted from Parliament's passage of the Townsend Act, a law applied to the colonies that taxed tea, glass, paper, and lead.

More recently, Americans have continued to protest against controversial governmental policies, such as the wars in Iraq, Afghanistan, and Vietnam. Those of us old enough to remember the Vietnam War may recall evening news clips and newspaper photographs of protests at the Lincoln Memorial, Kent State University, Berkeley, California, and in the streets of most major

U.S. cities. As a nation, we tend not to be a complacent people with regard to expressing our opinions about those governmental policies we dislike. Moreover, many would regard the vigorous exchange of different viewpoints to be a wonderful aspect of the American experiment in democratic government. Stated the celebrated British social philosopher John Stuart Mill in 1859:

> But the peculiar evil of silencing the expression of an opinion is that it is robbing the human race, posterity as well as the existing generation— those who dissent from the opinion, still more than those who hold it. If the opinion is right, they are deprived of the opportunity of exchanging error for truth; if wrong, they lose, what is almost as great a benefit, the clearer perception and livelier impression of the truth produced by its collision with error. (*On Liberty*, 1859).

The founding fathers were well aware of the benefits that accompanied the free exchange of ideas. An early attempt by the government to restrict expression was the Sedition Act of 1798. It made it a "high misdemeanor" to "combine or conspire together to oppose any measure of the government of the United States." Moreover, the Act punished "seditious writings." These were defined as follows:

> To write, print, utter or publish, or cause it to be done, or assist in it, any false, scandalous, and malicious writing against the government of the United States, or either House of Congress, or the President, with intent to defame, or bring either into contempt or disrepute, or to excite against either the hatred of the people of the United States, or to stir up sedition, or to excite unlawful combinations against the government, or to resist it, or to aid or encourage hostile designs of foreign nations.

Thomas Jefferson called the Sedition Act an "alarming infraction of the Constitution. As President, he later pardoned those convicted under its provisions.

According to Professor Laurence Tribe, symbolic expression was later given significant protection by the Supreme Court. This protection is not absolute, however, and may be restricted if a sufficiently compelling governmental interest is provided to justify a particular restriction.

For example, in *United States v. O'Brien*, 391 U.S. 367 (1968), David O'Brien and three companions burned their draft cards on the steps of the South Boston Courthouse. The incident was witnessed by a group that included FBI agents. O'Brien and his group were attacked by the crowd following the burning. An FBI agent took O'Brien into the Courthouse, where he told the agent that he had knowingly violated federal law and burned his draft card because of his personal beliefs.

O'Brien was convicted in U.S. District Court, where he admitted that he had burned his draft card. In an argument to the jury, O'Brien told the jury that he had burned the card publicly to influence others to adopt his antiwar beliefs. The law that O'Brien was charged with violating provided that it was a crime "to knowingly destroy" or knowingly "mutilate" a draft card. O'Brien contended that the law was unconstitutional because its purpose was "to suppress freedom of speech." The U.S. Court of Appeals held the statute to be an unconstitutional abridgment of the First Amendment's Freedom of Speech Clause.

On certiorari, the U.S. Supreme Court held that the statute did not violate the First Amendment. Chief Justice Earl H. Warren stated:

> We think it clear that a government regulation is sufficiently justified if it is within the constitutional power of the Government; if it furthers an important or substantial governmental interest; if the governmental interest is unrelated to the suppression of free expression, and if the incidental restriction of alleged First Amendment freedoms is no greater than is essential to the furtherance of that interest. We find that [the statute] meets all of these requirements, and consequently that O'Brien can be constitutionally convicted for violating it.

In 1968, the Supreme Court decided another Vietnam War era case involving symbolic speech as well. In *Tinker v. Des Moines*, 393 U.S. 503 (1968), a group of students decided to publicize their objections to the Vietnam War by wearing black armbands during the holiday season. The Des Moines school authorities learned of the intended plan and adopted a policy that any student wearing an armband to school would be asked to remove it, and, if he refused, he would be suspended until he returned to school without it. The students were aware of the policy, but wore the armbands anyway and were suspended and sent home.

The parents of the students filed suit in U.S. District Court to prohibit the school authorities from enforcing this policy. The District Court dismissed the complaint and the U.S. Court of Appeals affirmed the decision without opinion. The U.S. Supreme Court granted certiorari and held that the school district's policy was unconstitutional. Justice Abe Fortas, writing for the Court, stated:

> The school officials banned and sought to punish [the students] for a silent, passive expression of an opinion, unaccompanied by any disorder or disturbance on the part of [the students]. . . . In order for the State in the person of school officials to justify prohibition of a particular expression of opinion, it must be able to show that its action was caused by something more than a mere desire to avoid the discomfort and unpleasantness that always accompany an unpopular viewpoint. Certainly where there is no finding and no showing that engaging in the forbidden conduct would 'materially and substantially interfere with the requirements of appropriate discipline in the operation of the school,' the prohibition cannot be sustained [citations omitted].

It is interesting to compare the two cases discussed here. *United States v. O'Brien* involved a hostile action directed at a piece of government property, the defendant's draft card. It was therefore an action that the government was empowered to restrict. *Tinker v. Des Moines*, in contrast, involved a much more passive form of expression—wearing an armband in a public setting as a sign of protest. The difference between these cases is a significant one and a reviewing court is much more likely to uphold a free speech claim in the latter type of case.

Another case that will inform our discussion of *Texas v. Johnson* is *Chaplinsky v. New Hampshire*, 315 U.S. 568 (1942), which established the *fighting words doctrine*. Chaplinsky was a Jehovah's Witness who called a city official a "goddammed racketeer" and "a damned facist," and became involved in a fight with him on a public sidewalk. He was convicted under a state law that the New Hampshire Supreme Court interpreted to prohibit speech that was "likely to cause an average person to fight."

The U.S. Supreme Court upheld Chaplinsky's conviction because his words were likely to "inflict injury or tend to incite an immediate breach of the peace." The Court stated further that fighting words have such little expressive value that they are not an "essential part of any exposition of ideas," and that any value they have "is clearly outweighed by the social interest in order and morality."

The case presented in this section, *Texas v. Johnson*, implicates many of the ideas discussed here. It specifically presented the issue of whether a state has the power to prohibit the public desecration of an American flag as a form of symbolic speech and a sign of protest. Writing for the Supreme Court, Justice William J. Brennan stated that the Texas law was unconstitutional:

> Johnson was convicted for engaging in expressive conduct. The State's interest in preventing breaches of the peace does not support his conviction, because Johnson's conduct did not threaten to disturb the peace. Nor does the State's interest in preserving the flag as a symbol of nationhood and national unity justify his criminal conviction for engaging in political expression.

Chief Justice William H. Rehnquist disagreed, however. In a forceful dissenting opinion, Justice Rehnquist stated:

> In holding this Texas statute unconstitutional, the Court ignores Justice Holmes' familiar aphorism that 'a page of history is worth a volume of logic' [citation omitted]. For more than 200 years, the American flag has occupied a unique position as the symbol of our Nation, a uniqueness that justifies a governmental prohibition against flag burning in the way respondent Johnson did here.

In Your Opinion . . .

- Do you agree with Justice Brennan or with Chief Justice Rehnquist?
- Do you feel that "political speech" should ever be regulated under any circumstances?
- Would your position change if burning a flag were likely to cause a riot?
- Try to draft a law that effectively distinguishes between political speech that is permitted and that which is not.

YES

William J. Brennan

Majority Opinion, *Texas v. Johnson*

J USTICE BRENNAN delivered the opinion of the Court.

After publicly burning an American flag as a means of political protest, Gregory Lee Johnson was convicted of desecrating a flag in violation of Texas law. This case presents the question whether his conviction is consistent with the First Amendment. We hold that it is not.

I

While the Republican National Convention was taking place in Dallas in 1984, respondent Johnson participated in a political demonstration dubbed the "Republican War Chest Tour." As explained in literature distributed by the demonstrators and in speeches made by them, the purpose of this event was to protest the policies of the Reagan administration and of certain Dallas-based corporations. The demonstrators marched through the Dallas streets, chanting political slogans and stopping at several corporate locations to stage "die-ins" intended to dramatize the consequences of nuclear war. On several occasions they spray-painted the walls of buildings and overturned potted plants, but Johnson himself took no part in such activities. He did, however, accept an American flag handed to him by a fellow protestor who had taken it from a flagpole outside one of the targeted buildings.

The demonstration ended in front of Dallas City Hall, where Johnson unfurled the American flag, doused it with kerosene, and set it on fire. While the flag burned, the protestors chanted, "America, the red, white, and blue, we spit on you." After the demonstrators dispersed, a witness to the flag burning collected the flag's remains and buried them in his backyard. No one was physically injured or threatened with injury, though several witnesses testified that they had been seriously offended by the flag burning.

Of the approximately 100 demonstrators, Johnson alone was charged with a crime. The only criminal offense with which he was charged was the desecration of a venerated object in violation of Tex.Penal Code Ann. § 42.09(a)(3) (1989). After a trial, he was convicted, sentenced to one year in prison, and fined $2,000. The Court of Appeals for the Fifth District of Texas at Dallas affirmed Johnson's conviction, 706 S.W.2d 120 (1986), but the Texas Court of Criminal Appeals reversed, 755 S.W.2d 92 (1988), holding that the State could not, consistent with the First Amendment, punish Johnson for burning the flag in these circumstances.

Supreme Court of the United States, 1989.

The Court of Criminal Appeals began by recognizing that Johnson's conduct was symbolic speech protected by the First Amendment:

> Given the context of an organized demonstration, speeches, slogans, and the distribution of literature, anyone who observed appellant's act would have understood the message that appellant intended to convey. The act for which appellant was convicted was clearly "speech" contemplated by the **First Amendment**.

Id. at 95. To justify Johnson's conviction for engaging in symbolic speech, the State asserted two interests: preserving the flag as a symbol of national unity and preventing breaches of the peace. The Court of Criminal Appeals held that neither interest supported his conviction.

Acknowledging that this Court had not yet decided whether the Government may criminally sanction flag desecration in order to preserve the flag's symbolic value, the Texas court nevertheless concluded that our decision in *West Virginia Board of Education v. Barnette*, 319 U.S. 624 (1943), suggested that furthering this interest by curtailing speech was impermissible. "Recognizing that the right to differ is the centerpiece of our First Amendment freedoms," the court explained,

> a government cannot mandate by fiat a feeling of unity in its citizens. Therefore, that very same government cannot carve out a symbol of unity and prescribe a set of approved messages to be associated with that symbol when it cannot mandate the status or feeling the symbol purports to represent.

755 S.W.2d at 97. Noting that the State had not shown that the flag was in "grave and immediate danger," *Barnette, supra*, at 639, of being stripped of its symbolic value, the Texas court also decided that the flag's special status was not endangered by Johnson's conduct. 755 S.W.2d at 97.

As to the State's goal of preventing breaches of the peace, the court concluded that the flag desecration statute was not drawn narrowly enough to encompass only those flag burnings that were likely to result in a serious disturbance of the peace. And in fact, the court emphasized, the flag burning in this particular case did not threaten such a reaction. "'Serious offense' occurred," the court admitted,

> but there was no breach of peace, nor does the record reflect that the situation was potentially explosive. One cannot equate "serious offense" with incitement to breach the peace.

Id. at 96. The court also stressed that another Texas statute, Tex.Penal Code Ann. § 42.01 (1989), prohibited breaches of the peace. Citing *Boos v. Barry*, 485 U.S. 312 (1988), the court decided that § 42.01 demonstrated Texas' ability to prevent disturbances of the peace without punishing this flag desecration. 755 S.W.2d at 96.

Because it reversed Johnson's conviction on the ground that § 42.09 was unconstitutional as applied to him, the state court did not address Johnson's argument that the statute was, on its face, unconstitutionally vague and over-broad. We granted certiorari, 488 U.S. 907 (1988), and now affirm.

II

Johnson was convicted of flag desecration for burning the flag, rather than for uttering insulting words. This fact somewhat complicates our consideration of his conviction under the First Amendment. We must first determine whether Johnson's burning of the flag constituted expressive conduct, permitting him to invoke the First Amendment in challenging his conviction. *See, e.g., Spence v. Washington*, 418 U.S. 405, 409–411 (1974). If his conduct was expressive, we next decide whether the State's regulation is related to the suppression of free expression. *See, e.g., United States v. O'Brien*, 391 U.S. 367, 377 (1968); *Spence, supra*, at 414, n. 8. If the State's regulation is not related to expression, then the less stringent standard we announced in *United States v. O'Brien* for regulations of noncommunicative conduct controls. *See O'Brien, supra*, at 377. If it is, then we are outside of *O'Brien's* test, and we must ask whether this interest justifies Johnson's conviction under a more demanding standard. *See Spence, supra*, at 411. A third possibility is that the State's asserted interest is simply not implicated on these facts, and, in that event, the interest drops out of the picture. *See* 118 U.S. at 414, n. 8.

The First Amendment literally forbids the abridgment only of "speech," but we have long recognized that its protection does not end at the spoken or written word. While we have rejected

> the view that an apparently limitless variety of conduct can be labeled "speech" whenever the person engaging in the conduct intends thereby to express an idea,

United States v. O'Brien, supra, at 376, we have acknowledged that conduct may be "sufficiently imbued with elements of communication to fall within the scope of the First and Fourteenth Amendments." *Spence, supra*, at 409.

In deciding whether particular conduct possesses sufficient communicative elements to bring the First Amendment into play, we have asked whether

> [a]n intent to convey a particularized message was present, and [whether] the likelihood was great that the message would be understood by those who viewed it.

418 U.S. at 410–411. Hence, we have recognized the expressive nature of students' wearing of black armbands to protest American military involvement in Vietnam, *Tinker v. Des Moines Independent Community School Dist.*, 393 U.S. 503, 505 (1969); of a sit-in by blacks in a "whites only" area to protest segregation, *Brown v. Louisiana*, 383 U.S. 131, 141–142 (1966); of the wearing of American military uniforms in a dramatic presentation criticizing American involvement in Vietnam, *Schacht v. United States*, 398 U.S. 58 (1970); and of picketing about a wide variety of causes, *see, e.g., Food Employees v. Logan Valley Plaza, Inc.*, 391 U.S. 308, 313–314 (1968); *United States v. Grace*, 461 U.S. 171, 176 (1983).

Especially pertinent to this case are our decisions recognizing the communicative nature of conduct relating to flags. Attaching a peace sign to the flag, *Spence, supra,* at 418 U.S. 409"] 409–410; refusing to salute the flag, *Barnette,* 319 U.S. at 632; and displaying a red flag, 409–410; refusing to salute the flag, *Barnette,* 319 U.S. at 632; and displaying a red flag, *Stromberg v. California,* 283 U.S. 359, 368–369 (1931), we have held, all may find shelter under the First Amendment. *See also Smith v. Goguen,* 415 U.S. 566, 588 (1974) (WHITE, J., concurring in judgment) (treating flag "contemptuously" by wearing pants with small flag sewn into their seat is expressive conduct). That we have had little difficulty identifying an expressive element in conduct relating to flags should not be surprising. The very purpose of a national flag is to serve as a symbol of our country; it is, one might say, "the one visible manifestation of two hundred years of nationhood." *Id.* at 603 (REHNQUIST, J., dissenting). Thus, we have observed:

> [T]he flag salute is a form of utterance. Symbolism is a primitive but effective way of communicating ideas. The use of an emblem or flag to symbolize some system, idea, institution, or personality, is a shortcut from mind to mind. Causes and nations, political parties, lodges and ecclesiastical groups seek to knit the loyalty of their followings to a flag or banner, a color or design.

Barnette, supra, at 632. Pregnant with expressive content, the flag as readily signifies this Nation as does the combination of letters found in "America."

We have not automatically concluded, however, that any action taken with respect to our flag is expressive. Instead, in characterizing such action for First Amendment purposes, we have considered the context in which it occurred. In *Spence,* for example, we emphasized that Spence's taping of a peace sign to his flag was "roughly simultaneous with and concededly triggered by the Cambodian incursion and the Kent State tragedy." 418 U.S. at 410. The State of Washington had conceded, in fact, that Spence's conduct was a form of communication, and we stated that "the State's concession is inevitable on this record." *Id.* at 409.

The State of Texas conceded for purposes of its oral argument in this case that Johnson's conduct was expressive conduct, Tr. of Oral Arg. 4, and this concession seems to us as prudent as was Washington's in *Spence.* Johnson burned an American flag as part—indeed, as the culmination—of a political demonstration that coincided with the convening of the Republican Party and its renomination of Ronald Reagan for President. The expressive, overtly political nature of this conduct was both intentional and overwhelmingly apparent. At his trial, Johnson explained his reasons for burning the flag as follows:

> The American Flag was burned as Ronald Reagan was being renominated as President. And a more powerful statement of symbolic speech, whether you agree with it or not, couldn't have been made at that time. It's quite a just position [juxtaposition]. We had new patriotism and no patriotism.

5 Record 656. In these circumstances, Johnson's burning of the flag was conduct "sufficiently imbued with elements of communication," *Spence*, 418 U.S. at 409, to implicate the First Amendment.

III

The government generally has a freer hand in restricting expressive conduct than it has in restricting the written or spoken word. *See O'Brien*, 391 U.S. at 376–377; *Clark v. Community for Creative Non-Violence*, 468 U.S. 288, 293 (1984); *Dallas v. Stanglin*, 490 U.S. 19, 25 (1989). It may not, however, proscribe particular conduct *because* it has expressive elements.

> [W]hat might be termed the more generalized guarantee of freedom of expression makes the communicative nature of conduct an inadequate basis for singling out that conduct for proscription. A law *directed* at the communicative nature of conduct must, like a law directed at speech itself, be justified by the substantial showing of need that the **First Amendment** requires.

Community for Creative Non-Violence v. Watt, 227 U.S.App.D.C. 19, 55–56, 703 F.2d 586, 622–623 (1983) (Scalia, J., dissenting) (emphasis in original), *rev'd sub nom. Clark v. Community for Creative Non-Violence, supra.* It is, in short, not simply the verbal or nonverbal nature of the expression, but the governmental interest at stake, that helps to determine whether a restriction on that expression is valid.

Thus, although we have recognized that, where

> "speech" and "nonspeech" elements are combined in the same course of conduct, a sufficiently important governmental interest in regulating the nonspeech element can justify incidental limitations on First Amendment freedoms,

O'Brien, supra, at 376, we have limited the applicability of *O'Brien's* relatively lenient standard to those cases in which "the governmental interest is unrelated to the suppression of free expression." *Id.* at 377; *see also Spence*, 418 U.S. at 414, n. 8. In stating, moreover, that *O'Brien's* test "in the last analysis is little, if any, different from the standard applied to time, place, or manner restrictions," *Clark, supra*, at 298, we have highlighted the requirement that the governmental interest in question be unconnected to expression in order to come under *O'Brien's* less demanding rule.

In order to decide whether *O'Brien's* test applies here, therefore, we must decide whether Texas has asserted an interest in support of Johnson's conviction that is unrelated to the suppression of expression. If we find that an interest asserted by the State is simply not implicated on the facts before us, we need not ask whether *O'Brien's* test applies. *See Spence, supra*, at 414, n. 8. The State offers two separate interests to justify this conviction: preventing breaches of the peace and preserving the flag as a symbol of nationhood and national unity. We hold that the first interest is not implicated on this record, and that the second is related to the suppression of expression.

A

Texas claims that its interest in preventing breaches of the peace justifies Johnson's conviction for flag desecration. However, no disturbance of the peace actually occurred or threatened to occur because of Johnson's burning of the flag. Although the State stresses the disruptive behavior of the protestors during their march toward City Hall, Brief for Petitioner 34–36, it admits that "no actual breach of the peace occurred at the time of the flagburning or in response to the flagburning." *Id.* at 34. The State's emphasis on the protestors' disorderly actions prior to arriving at City Hall is not only somewhat surprising, given that no charges were brought on the basis of this conduct, but it also fails to show that a disturbance of the peace was a likely reaction to Johnson's conduct. The only evidence offered by the State at trial to show the reaction to Johnson's actions was the testimony of several persons who had been seriously offended by the flag burning. *Id.* at 6–7.

The State's position, therefore, amounts to a claim that an audience that takes serious offense at particular expression is necessarily likely to disturb the peace, and that the expression may be prohibited on this basis. Our precedents do not countenance such a presumption. On the contrary, they recognize that a principal

> function of free speech under our system of government is to invite dispute. It may indeed best serve its high purpose when it induces a condition of unrest, creates dissatisfaction with conditions as they are, or even stirs people to anger.

Terminiello v. Chicago, 337 U.S. 1, 4 (1949). *See also Cox v. Louisiana,* 379 U.S. 536, 551 (1965); *Tinker v. Des Moines Independent Community School Dist.,* 393 U.S. at 508–509; *Coates v. Cincinnati,* 402 U.S. 611, 615 (1971); *Hustler Magazine, Inc. v. Falwell,* 485 U.S. 46, 55–56 (1988). It would be odd indeed to conclude *both* that "if it is the speaker's opinion that gives offense, that consequence is a reason for according it constitutional protection," *FCC v. Pacifica Foundation,* 438 U.S. 726, 745 (1978) (opinion of STEVENS, J.), *and* that the Government may ban the expression of certain disagreeable ideas on the unsupported presumption that their very disagreeableness will provoke violence.

Thus, we have not permitted the government to assume that every expression of a provocative idea will incite a riot, but have instead required careful consideration of the actual circumstances surrounding such expression, asking whether the expression "is directed to inciting or producing imminent lawless action and is likely to incite or produce such action." *Brandenburg v. Ohio,* 395 U.S. 444, 447 (1969) (reviewing circumstances surrounding rally and speeches by Ku Klux Klan). To accept Texas' arguments that it need only demonstrate "the potential for a breach of the peace," Brief for Petitioner 37, and that every flag burning necessarily possesses that potential, would be to eviscerate our holding in *Brandenburg.* This we decline to do.

Nor does Johnson's expressive conduct fall within that small class of "fighting words" that are "likely to provoke the average person to retaliation, and thereby cause a breach of the peace." *Chaplinsky v. New Hampshire,*

315 U.S. 568, 574 (1942). No reasonable onlooker would have regarded Johnson's generalized expression of dissatisfaction with the policies of the Federal Government as a direct personal insult or an invitation to exchange fisticuffs. *See id.* at 572–573; *Cantwell v. Connecticut,* 310 U.S. 296, 309 (1940); *FCC v. Pacifica Foundation, supra,* at 745 (opinion of STEVENS, J.).

We thus conclude that the State's interest in maintaining order is not implicated on these facts. The State need not worry that our holding will disable it from preserving the peace. We do not suggest that the First Amendment forbids a State to prevent "imminent lawless action." *Brandenburg, supra,* at 447. And, in fact, Texas already has a statute specifically prohibiting breaches of the peace, Tex.Penal Code Ann. § 42.01 (1989), which tends to confirm that Texas need not punish this flag desecration in order to keep the peace. *See Boos v. Barry,* 485 U.S. at 327–329.

B

The State also asserts an interest in preserving the flag as a symbol of nationhood and national unity. In *Spence,* we acknowledged that the government's interest in preserving the flag's special symbolic value "is directly related to expression in the context of activity" such as affixing a peace symbol to a flag. 418 U.3. at 114, n 8 We are equally persuaded that this interest is related to expression in the case of Johnson's burning of the flag. The State, apparently, is concerned that such conduct will lead people to believe either that the flag does not stand for nationhood and national unity, but instead reflects other, less positive concepts, or that the concepts reflected in the flag do not in fact exist, that is, that we do not enjoy unity as a Nation. These concerns blossom only when a person's treatment of the flag communicates some message, and thus are related "to the suppression of free expression" within the meaning of *O'Brien.* We are thus outside of *O'Brien's* test altogether.

IV

It remains to consider whether the State's interest in preserving the flag as a symbol of nationhood and national unity justifies Johnson's conviction.

As in *Spence,* "[w]e are confronted with a case of prosecution for the expression of an idea through activity," and "[a]ccordingly, we must examine with particular care the interests advanced by [petitioner] to support its prosecution." 418 U.S. at 418 U.S. 411"] 411. Johnson was not, we add, prosecuted for the expression of just any idea; he was prosecuted for his expression of dissatisfaction with the policies of this country, expression situated at the core of our First Amendment values. *See, e.g., Boos v. Barry, supra,* at 318; 411. *Frisby v. Schultz,* 487 U.S. 474, 479 (1988).

Moreover, Johnson was prosecuted because he knew that his politically charged expression would cause "serious offense." If he had burned the flag as a means of disposing of it because it was dirty or torn, he would not have been convicted of flag desecration under this Texas law: federal law designates burning as the preferred means of disposing of a flag "when it is in such condition that it is no longer a fitting emblem for display," 36 U.S.C. § 176(k), and Texas has no quarrel with this means of disposal. Brief for Petitioner 45. The Texas law is thus not aimed at protecting the physical integrity of the flag in all circumstances, but is designed instead to protect it only against impairments that would cause serious offense to others. Texas concedes as much:

> Section 42.09(b) reaches only those severe acts of physical abuse of the flag carried out in a way likely to be offensive. The statute mandates intentional or knowing abuse, that is, the kind of mistreatment that is not innocent, but rather is intentionally designed to seriously offend other individuals.

Id. at 44.

Whether Johnson's treatment of the flag violated Texas law thus depended on the likely communicative impact of his expressive conduct. Our decision in *Boos v. Barry, supra,* tells us that this restriction on Johnson's expression is content-based. In *Boos,* we considered the constitutionality of a law prohibiting

> the display of any sign within 500 feet of a foreign embassy if that sign tends to bring that foreign government into "public odium" or "public disrepute."

Id. at 315. Rejecting the argument that the law was content-neutral because it was justified by "our international law obligation to shield diplomats from speech that offends their dignity," *id.* at 320, we held that "[t]he emotive impact of speech on its audience is not a 'secondary effect'" unrelated to the content of the expression itself. *Id.* at 321 (plurality opinion); *see also id.* at 334 (BRENNAN, J., concurring in part and concurring in judgment).

According to the principles announced in *Boos,* Johnson's political expression was restricted because of the content of the message he conveyed. We must therefore subject the State's asserted interest in preserving the special symbolic character of the flag to "the most exacting scrutiny." *Boos v. Barry,* 485 U.S. at 321.

Texas argues that its interest in preserving the flag as a symbol of nationhood and national unity survives this close analysis. Quoting extensively from the writings of this Court chronicling the flag's historic and symbolic role in our society, the State emphasizes the "special place" reserved for the flag in our Nation. Brief for Petitioner 22, quoting *Smith v. Goguen,* 415 U.S. at 601 (REHNQUIST, J., dissenting). The State's argument is not that it has an interest simply in maintaining the flag as a symbol of *something,* no matter what it symbolizes; indeed, if that were the State's position, it would be difficult to see how that interest is endangered by highly symbolic conduct such as Johnson's. Rather, the State's claim is that it has an interest in preserving the flag as a symbol of *nationhood* and *national unity,* a symbol with a determinate range of meanings. Brief for Petitioner 20-24. According to Texas, if one physically treats the flag in a way that would tend to cast doubt on either the idea that nationhood and national unity are the flag's referents or that national unity actually exists, the message conveyed thereby is a harmful one, and therefore may be prohibited.

If there is a bedrock principle underlying the First Amendment, it is that the government may not prohibit the expression of an idea simply because society finds the idea itself offensive or disagreeable. *See, e.g., Hustler Magazine v. Falwell,* 485 U.S. at 55–56; *City Council of Los Angeles v. Taxpayers for Vincent,* 466 U.S. 789, 804 (1984); *Bolger v. Youngs Drug Products Corp.,* 463 U.S. 60, 65, 72 (1983); *Carey v. Brown,* 447 U.S. 455, 462–463 (1980); *FCC v. Pacifica Foundation,* 438 U.S. at 745–746; *Young v. American Mini Theatres, Inc.,* 427 U.S. 50, 63–65, 67–68 (1976) (plurality opinion); *Buckley v. Valeo,* 424 U.S. 1, 16–17 (1976); *Groyned v. Rockford,* 408 U.S. 104, 115 (1972); *Police Dept. of Chicago v. Mosley,* 408 U.S. 92, 95 (1972); *Bachellar v. Maryland,* 397 U.S. 564, 567 (1970); *O'Brien,* 391 U.S. at 382; *Brown v. Louisiana,* 383 U.S. at 142–143; *Stromberg v. California,* 283 U.S. at 368–369.

We have not recognized an exception to this principle even where our flag has been involved. In *Street v. New York,* 394 U.S. 576 (1969), we held that a State may not criminally punish a person for uttering words critical of the flag. Rejecting the argument that the conviction could be sustained on the ground that Street had "failed to show the respect for our national symbol which may properly be demanded of every citizen," we concluded that

> the constitutionally guaranteed "freedom to be intellectually . . . diverse or even contrary," and the "right to differ as to things that touch the heart of the existing order," encompass the freedom to express publicly one's opinions about our flag, including those opinions which are defiant or contemptuous.

Id. at 593, quoting *Barnette,* 319 U.S. at 642. Nor may the government, we have held, compel conduct that would evince respect for the flag.

> To sustain the compulsory flag salute, we are required to say that a Bill of Rights which guards the individual's right to speak his own mind left it open to public authorities to compel him to utter what is not in his mind.

Id. at 634.

In holding in *Barnette* that the Constitution did not leave this course open to the government, Justice Jackson described one of our society's defining principles in words deserving of their frequent repetition:

> If there is any fixed star in our constitutional constellation, it is that no official, high or petty, can prescribe what shall be orthodox in politics, nationalism, religion, or other matters of opinion or force citizens to confess by word or act their faith therein.

Id. at 642. In *Spence*, we held that the same interest asserted by Texas here was insufficient to support a criminal conviction under a flag-misuse statute for the taping of a peace sign to an American flag.

> Given the protected character of [*Spence's*] expression and in light of the fact that no interest the State may have in preserving the physical integrity of a privately owned flag was significantly impaired on these facts,

we held, "the conviction must be invalidated." 418 U.S. at 415. *See also Goguen*, 415 U.S. at 588 (WHITE, J., concurring in judgment) (to convict person who had sewn a flag onto the seat of his pants for "contemptuous" treatment of the flag would be "[t]o convict not to protect the physical integrity or to protect against acts interfering with the proper use of the flag, but to punish for communicating ideas unacceptable to the controlling majority in the legislature").

In short, nothing in our precedents suggests that a State may foster its own view of the flag by prohibiting expressive conduct relating to it. To bring its argument outside our precedents, Texas attempts to convince us that, even if its interest in preserving the flag's symbolic role does not allow it to prohibit words or some expressive conduct critical of the flag, it does permit it to forbid the outright destruction of the flag. The State's argument cannot depend here on the distinction between written or spoken words and nonverbal conduct. That distinction, we have shown, is of no moment where the nonverbal conduct is expressive, as it is here, and where the regulation of that conduct is related to expression, as it is here. *See supra* at 402–403. In addition, both *Barnette* and *Spence* involved expressive conduct, not only verbal communication, and both found that conduct protected.

Texas' focus on the precise nature of Johnson's expression, moreover, misses the point of our prior decisions: their enduring lesson, that the government may not prohibit expression simply because it disagrees with its message, is not dependent on the particular mode in which one chooses to express an idea. If we were to hold that a State may forbid flag burning wherever it is likely to endanger the flag's symbolic role, but allow it wherever burning a flag promotes that role—as where, for example, a person ceremoniously burns a dirty flag—we would be saying that when it comes to impairing the flag's physical integrity, the flag itself may be used as a symbol—as a substitute for the written or spoken word or a "short cut from mind to mind"—only in one direction. We would be permitting a State to "prescribe what shall be orthodox" by saying that one may burn the flag to convey one's attitude toward it and its referents only if one does not endanger the flag's representation of nationhood and national unity.

We never before have held that the Government may ensure that a symbol be used to express only one view of that symbol or its referents. Indeed, in *Schacht v. United States*, we invalidated a federal statute permitting an actor portraying a member of one of our armed forces to "wear the uniform of that armed force if the portrayal does not tend to discredit that armed force." 398 U.S. at 60, quoting 10 U.S.C. § 772(f). This proviso, we held,

> which leaves Americans free to praise the war in Vietnam but can send persons like Schacht to prison for opposing it, cannot survive in a country which has the First Amendment.

Id. at 63.

We perceive no basis on which to hold that the principle underlying our decision in *Schacht* does not apply to this case. To conclude that the government may permit designated symbols to be used to communicate only a limited set of messages would be to enter territory having no discernible or defensible boundaries. Could the government, on this theory, prohibit the burning of state flags? Of copies of the Presidential seal? Of the Constitution? In evaluating these choices under the First Amendment, how would we decide which symbols were sufficiently special to warrant this unique status? To do so, we would be forced to consult our own political preferences, and impose them on the citizenry, in the very way that the First Amendment forbids us to do. *See Carey v. Brown*, 447 U.S. at 466–467.

There is, moreover, no indication—either in the text of the Constitution or in our cases interpreting it—that a separate juridical category exists for the American flag alone. Indeed, we would not be surprised to learn that the persons who framed our Constitution and wrote the Amendment that we now construe were not known for their reverence for the Union Jack. The First Amendment does not guarantee that other concepts virtually sacred to our Nation as a whole—such as the principle that discrimination on the basis of race is odious and destructive—will go unquestioned in the marketplace of ideas. *See Brandenburg v. Ohio*, 395 U.S. 444 (1969). We decline, therefore, to create for the flag an exception to the joust of principles protected by the First Amendment.

It is not the State's ends, but its means, to which we object. It cannot be gainsaid that there is a special place reserved for the flag in this Nation, and thus we do not doubt that the government has a legitimate interest in making efforts to "preserv[e] the national flag as an unalloyed symbol of our country." *Spence*, 418 U.S. at 412. We reject the suggestion, urged at oral argument by counsel for Johnson, that the government lacks "any state interest whatsoever" in regulating the manner in which the flag may be displayed. Tr. of Oral Arg. 38. Congress has, for example, enacted precatory regulations describing the proper treatment of the flag, *see* 36 U.S.C. §§ 173–177, and we cast no doubt on the legitimacy of its interest in making such recommendations. To say that the government has an interest in encouraging proper treatment of the flag, however, is not to say that it may criminally punish a person for burning a flag as a means of political protest.

> National unity as an end which officials may foster by persuasion and example is not in question. The problem is whether, under our Constitution, compulsion as here employed is a permissible means for its achievement.

Barnette, 319 U.S. at 640.

We are fortified in today's conclusion by our conviction that forbidding criminal punishment for conduct such as Johnson's will not endanger the special role played by our flag or the feelings it inspires. To paraphrase Justice Holmes, we submit that nobody can suppose that this one gesture of an unknown man will change our Nation's attitude towards its flag. *See Abrams v. United States*, 250 U.S. 616, 628 (1919) (Holmes, J., dissenting). Indeed, Texas' argument that the burning of an American flag "'is an act having a high likelihood to cause a breach of the peace,'" Brief for Petitioner 31, quoting *Sutherland v. DeWulf*, 323 F.Supp. 740, 745 (SD Ill.1971) (citation omitted), and its statute's implicit assumption that physical mistreatment of the flag will lead to "serious offense," tend to confirm that the flag's special role is not in danger; if it were, no one would riot or take offense because a flag had been burned.

We are tempted to say, in fact, that the flag's deservedly cherished place in our community will be strengthened, not weakened, by our holding today. Our decision is a reaffirmation of the principles of freedom and inclusiveness that the flag best reflects, and of the conviction that our toleration of criticism such as Johnson's is a sign and source of our strength. Indeed, one of the proudest images of our flag, the one immortalized in our own national anthem, is of the bombardment it survived at Fort McHenry. It is the Nation's resilience, not its rigidity, that Texas sees reflected in the flag—and it is that resilience that we reassert today.

The way to preserve the flag's special role is not to punish those who feel differently about these matters. It is to persuade them that they are wrong.

> To courageous, self-reliant men, with confidence in the power of free and fearless reasoning applied through the processes of popular government, no danger flowing from speech can be deemed clear and present unless the incidence of the evil apprehended is so imminent that it may befall before there is opportunity for full discussion. If there be time to expose through discussion the falsehood and fallacies, to avert the evil by the processes of education, the remedy to be applied is more speech, not enforced silence.

Whitney v. California, 274 U.S. 357, 377 (1927) (Brandeis, J., concurring). And, precisely because it is our flag that is involved, one's response to the flag-burner may exploit the uniquely persuasive power of the flag itself. We can imagine no more appropriate response to burning a flag than waving one's own, no better way to counter a flag burner's message than by saluting the flag that burns, no surer means of preserving the dignity even of the flag that burned than by—as one witness here did—according its remains a respectful burial. We do not consecrate the flag by punishing its desecration, for in doing so we dilute the freedom that this cherished emblem represents.

V

Johnson was convicted for engaging in expressive conduct. The State's interest in preventing breaches of the peace does not support his conviction, because Johnson's conduct did not threaten to disturb the peace. Nor does the State's interest in preserving the flag as a symbol of nationhood and national unity justify his criminal conviction for engaging in political expression. The judgment of the Texas Court of Criminal Appeals is therefore

Affirmed.

    1. Tex.Penal Code Ann. § 42.09 (1989) provides in full:
       § 42.09. Desecration of Venerated Object
       (a) A person commits an offense if he intentionally or knowingly desecrates:
       (1) a public monument;
       (2) a place of worship or burial; or
       (3) a state or national flag.
       (b) For purposes of this section, "desecrate" means deface, damage, or otherwise physically mistreat in a way that the actor knows will seriously offend one or more persons likely to observe or discover his action.
       (c) An offense under this section is a Class A misdemeanor. . . .

William H. Rehnquist  **NO**

Dissenting Opinion, *Texas v. Johnson*

CHIEF JUSTICE REHNQUIST, with whom JUSTICE WHITE and JUSTICE O'CONNOR join, dissenting.

In holding this Texas statute unconstitutional, the Court ignores Justice Holmes' familiar aphorism that "a page of history is worth a volume of logic." *New York Trust Co. v. Eisner*, 256 U.S. 345, 349 (1921). For more than 200 years, the American flag has occupied a unique position as the symbol of our Nation, a uniqueness that justifies a governmental prohibition against flag burning in the way respondent Johnson did here.

At the time of the American Revolution, the flag served to unify the Thirteen Colonies at home while obtaining recognition of national sovereignty abroad. Ralph Waldo Emerson's *Concord Hymn* describes the first skirmishes of the Revolutionary War in these lines:

> By the rude bridge that arched the flood
> Their flag to April's breeze unfurled,
> Here once the embattled farmers stood
> And fired the shot heard round the world.

During that time, there were many colonial and regimental flags, adorned with such symbols as pine trees, beavers, anchors, and rattlesnakes, bearing slogans such as "Liberty or Death," "Hope," "An Appeal to Heaven," and "Don't Tread on Me." The first distinctive flag of the Colonies was the "Grand Union Flag"—with 13 stripes and a British flag in the left corner—which was flown for the first time on January 2, 1776, by troops of the Continental Army around Boston. By June 14, 1777, after we declared our independence from England, the Continental Congress resolved:

> That the flag of the thirteen United States be thirteen stripes, alternate red and white: that the union be thirteen stars, white in a blue field, representing a new constellation.

8 Journal of the Continental Congress 1774–1789, p. 464 (W. Ford ed.1907). One immediate result of the flag's adoption was that American vessels harassing British shipping sailed under an authorized national flag. Without such a flag, the British could treat captured seamen as pirates and hang them summarily; with a national flag, such seamen were treated as prisoners of war.

Supreme Court of the United States, 1989.

During the war of 1812, British naval forces sailed up Chesapeake Bay and marched overland to sack and burn the city of Washington. They then sailed up the Patapsco River to invest the city of Baltimore, but to do so it was first necessary to reduce Fort McHenry in Baltimore Harbor. Francis Scott Key, a Washington lawyer, had been granted permission by the British to board one of their warships to negotiate the release of an American who had been taken prisoner. That night, waiting anxiously on the British ship, Key watched the British fleet firing on Fort McHenry. Finally, at daybreak, he saw the fort's American flag still flying; the British attack had failed. Intensely moved, he began to scribble on the back of an envelope the poem that became our national anthem:

> O say can you see by the dawn's early light
> What so proudly we hail'd at the twilight's last gleaming,
> Whose broad stripes & bright stars through the perilous fight
> O'er the ramparts we watch'd, were so gallantly streaming?
> And the rocket's red glare, the bomb bursting in air,
> Gave proof through the night that our flag was still there,
> O say does that star-spangled banner yet wave
> O'er the land of the free & the home of the brave?

The American flag played a central role in our Nation's most tragic conflict, when the North fought against the South. The lowering of the American flag at Fort Sumter was viewed as the start of the war. G. Preble, *History of the Flag of the United States of America* 453 (1880). The Southern States, to formalize their separation from the Union, adopted the "Stars and Bars" of the Confederacy. The Union troops marched to the sound of "Yes We'll Rally Round The Flag Boys, We'll Rally Once Again." President Abraham Lincoln refused proposals to remove from the American flag the stars representing the rebel States, because he considered the conflict not a war between two nations, but an attack by 11 States against the National Government. *Id.* at 411. By war's end, the American flag again flew over "an indestructible union, composed of indestructible states." *Texas v. White*, 7 Wall. 700, 725 (1869).

One of the great stories of the Civil War is told in John Greenleaf Whittier's poem, "Barbara Frietchie":

> Up from the meadows rich with corn,
> Clear in the cool September morn,
> The clustered spires of Frederick stand
> Green-walled by the hills of Maryland.
> Round about them orchards sweep,
> Apple- and peach-tree fruited deep,
> Fair as a garden of the Lord
> To the eyes of the famished rebel horde,
> On that pleasant morn of the early fall
> When Lee marched over the mountain wall,
> —Over the mountains winding down,
> Horse and foot, into Frederick town.
> Forty flags with their silver stars,

Forty flags with their crimson bars,
Flapped in the morning wind: the sun
Of noon looked down, and saw not one.
Up rose old Barbara Frietchie then,
Bowed with her four-score years and ten;
Bravest of all in Frederick town,
She took up the flag the men hauled down;
In her attic-window the staff she set,
To show that one heart was loyal yet.
Up the street came the rebel tread,
Stonewall Jackson riding ahead.
Under his slouched hat left and right
He glanced: the old flag met his sight.
"Halt!"—the dust-brown ranks stood fast.
"Fire!"—out blazed the rifle-blast
It shivered the window, pane and sash;
It rent the banner with seam and gash.
Quick, as it fell, from the broken staff
Dame Barbara snatched the silken scarf;
She leaned far out on the window-sill,
And shook it forth with a royal will.
"Shoot, if you must, this old gray head,
But spare your country's flag," she said.
A shade of sadness, a blush of shame,
Over the face of the leader came;
The nobler nature within him stirred
To life at that woman's deed and word:
"Who touches a hair of yon gray head
Dies like a dog! March on!" he said.
All day long through Frederick street
Sounded the tread of marching feet:
All day long that free flag tost
Over the heads of the rebel host.
Ever its torn folds rose and fell
On the loyal winds that loved it well;
And through the hill-gaps sunset light
Shone over it with a warm good-night.
Barbara Frietchie's work is o'er,
And the Rebel rides on his raids no more.
Honor to her! and let a tear
Fall, for her sake, on Stonewall's bier.
Over Barbara Frietchie's grave,
Flag of Freedom and Union, wave!
Peace and order and beauty draw
Round thy symbol of light and law;
And ever the stars above look down
On thy stars below in Frederick town!

In the First and Second World Wars, thousands of our countrymen died on foreign soil fighting for the American cause. At Iwo Jima in the Second World War, United States Marines fought hand to hand against thousands of

Japanese. By the time the Marines reached the top of Mount Suribachi, they raised a piece of pipe upright and from one end fluttered a flag. That ascent had cost nearly 6,000 American lives. The Iwo Jima Memorial in Arlington National Cemetery memorializes that event. President Franklin Roosevelt authorized the use of the flag on labels, packages, cartons, and containers intended for export as lend-lease aid, in order to inform people in other countries of the United States' assistance. Presidential Proclamation No. 2605, 58 Stat. 1126.

During the Korean War, the successful amphibious landing of American troops at Inchon was marked by the raising of an American flag within an hour of the event. Impetus for the enactment of the Federal Flag Desecration Statute in 1967 came from the impact of flag burnings in the United States on troop morale in Vietnam. Representative L. Mendel Rivers, then Chairman of the House Armed Services Committee, testified that

> The burning of the flag . . . has caused my mail to increase 100 percent from the boys in Vietnam, writing me and asking me what is going on in America.

Desecration of the Flag, Hearings on H.R. 271 before Subcommittee No. 4 of the House Committee on the Judiciary, 90th Cong., 1st Sess., 189 (1967). Representative Charles Wiggins stated:

> The public act of desecration of our flag tends to undermine the morale of American troops. That this finding is true can be attested by many Members who have received correspondence from servicemen express-ing their shock and disgust of such conduct.

113 Cong. Rec. 16459 (1967).

The flag symbolizes the Nation in peace as well as in war. It signifies our national presence on battleships, airplanes, military installations, and public buildings from the United States Capitol to the thousands of county courthouses and city halls throughout the country. Two flags are prominently placed in our courtroom. Countless flags are placed by the graves of loved ones each year on what was first called Decoration Day, and is now called Memorial Day. The flag is traditionally placed on the casket of deceased members of the Armed Forces, and it is later given to the deceased's family. 10 U.S.C. §§ 1481 1482. Congress has provided that the flag be flown at half-staff upon the death of the President, Vice President, and other government officials "as a mark of respect to their memory." 36 U.S.C. § 175(m). The flag identifies United States merchant ships, 22 U.S.C. § 454 and "[t]he laws of the Union protect our com-merce wherever the flag of the country may float." *United States v. Guthrie*, 17 How. 284, 309 (1855).

No other American symbol has been as universally honored as the flag. In 1931, Congress declared "The Star-Spangled Banner" to be our national anthem. 36 U.S.C. § 170. In 1949, Congress declared June 14th to be Flag Day. § 157. In 1987, John Philip Sousa's "The Stars and Stripes Forever" was des-ignated as the national march. Pub.L. 101–186, 101 Stat. 1286. Congress has also established "The Pledge of Allegiance to the Flag" and the manner of its deliverance. 36 U.S.C. § 172. The flag has appeared as the principal symbol on approximately 33 United States postal stamps and in the design of at least 43 more, more times than any other symbol. United States Postal Service, Definitive Mint Set 15 (1988).

Both Congress and the States have enacted numerous laws regulating misuse of the American flag. Until 1967, Congress left the regulation of misuse of the flag up to the States. Now, however, Title 18 U.S.C. § 700(a) provides that:

> Whoever knowingly casts contempt upon any flag of the United States by publicly mutilating, defacing, defiling, burning, or trampling upon it shall be fined not more than $1,000 or imprisoned for not more than one year, or both.

Congress has also prescribed, *inter alia*, detailed rules for the design of the flag, 4 U.S.C. § 1 the time and occasion of flag's display, 36 U.S.C. § 174 the position and manner of its display, § 175, respect for the flag, § 176, and conduct during hoisting, lowering, and passing of the flag, § 177. With the exception of Alaska and Wyoming, all of the States now have statutes prohibiting the burning of the flag. Most of the state statutes are patterned after the Uniform Flag Act of 1917, which in § 3 provides:

> No person shall publicly mutilate, deface, defile, defy, trample upon, or by word or act cast contempt upon any such flag, standard, color, ensign or shield.

Proceedings of National Conference of Commissioners on Uniform State Laws 323–324 (1917). Most were passed by the States at about the time of World War I. Rosenblatt, Flag Desecration Statutes: History and Analysis, 1972 Wash.U.L.Q.193, 197.

The American flag, then, throughout more than 200 years of our history, has come to be the visible symbol embodying our Nation. It does not represent the views of any particular political party, and it does not represent any particular political philosophy. The flag is not simply another "idea" or "point of view" competing for recognition in the marketplace of ideas. Millions and millions of Americans regard it with an almost mystical reverence, regardless of what sort of social, political, or philosophical beliefs they may have. I cannot agree that the First Amendment invalidates the Act of Congress, and the laws of 48 of the 50 States, which make criminal the public burning of the flag.

More than 80 years ago, in *Halter v. Nebraska*, 205 U.S. 34 (1907), this Court upheld the constitutionality of a Nebraska statute that forbade the use of representations of the American flag for advertising purposes upon articles of merchandise. The Court there said:

> For that flag every true American has not simply an appreciation, but a deep affection. . . . Hence, it has often occurred that insults to a flag have been the cause of war, and indignities put upon it, in the presence of those who revere it, have often been resented and sometimes punished on the spot.

Id. at 41.

Only two Terms ago, in *San Francisco Arts & Athletics, Inc. v. United States Olympic Committee*, 483 U.S. 522 (1987), the Court held that Congress could grant exclusive use of the word "Olympic" to the United States Olympic Committee. The Court thought that this

> restrictio[n] on expressive speech properly [was] characterized as incidental to the primary congressional purpose of encouraging and rewarding the USOC's activities.

Id. at 536. As the Court stated,

> when a word [or symbol] acquires value "as the result of organization and the expenditure of labor, skill, and money" by an entity, that entity constitutionally may obtain a limited property right in the word [or symbol].

Id. at 532, quoting *International News Service v. Associated Press*, 248 U.S. 215, 239 (1918). Surely Congress or the States may recognize a similar interest in the flag.

But the Court insists that the Texas statute prohibiting the public burning of the American flag infringes on respondent Johnson's freedom of expression. Such freedom, of course, is not absolute. *See Schenck v. United States*, 249 U.S. 47"] 249 U.S. 47 (1919). In 249 U.S. 47 (1919). In *Chaplinsky v. New Hampshire*, 315 U.S. 568 (1942), a unanimous Court said:

> Allowing the broadest scope to the language and purpose of the Fourteenth Amendment, it is well understood that the right of free speech is not absolute at all times and under all circumstances. There are certain well defined and narrowly limited classes of speech, the prevention and punishment of which have never been thought to raise any Constitutional problem. These include the lewd and obscene, the profane, the libelous, and the insulting or "fighting" words—those which, by their very utterance, inflict injury or tend to incite an immediate breach of the peace. It has been well observed that such utterances are no essential part of any exposition of ideas, and are of such slight social value as a step to truth that any benefit that may be derived from them is clearly outweighed by the social interest in order and morality.

Id. at 571–572 (footnotes omitted). The Court upheld Chaplinsky's conviction under a state statute that made it unlawful to "address any offensive, derisive or annoying word to any person who is lawfully in any street or other public place." *Id.* at 569. Chaplinsky had told a local marshal, "You are a God damned racketeer" and a "damned Fascist and the whole government of Rochester are Fascists or agents of Fascists." *Ibid.*

Here it may equally well be said that the public burning of the American flag by Johnson was no essential part of any exposition of ideas, and at the same time it had a tendency to incite a breach of the peace. Johnson was free to make any verbal denunciation of the flag that he wished; indeed, he

NO / William H. Rehnquist **487**

was free to burn the flag in private. He could publicly burn other symbols of the Government or effigies of political leaders. He did lead a march through the streets of Dallas, and conducted a rally in front of the Dallas City Hall. He engaged in a "die-in" to protest nuclear weapons. He shouted out various slogans during the march, including: "Reagan, Mondale which will it be? Either one means World War III"; "Ronald Reagan, killer of the hour, Perfect example of U.S. power"; and "red, white and blue, we spit on you, you stand for plunder, you will go under." Brief for Respondent 3. For none of these acts was he arrested or prosecuted; it was only when he proceeded to burn publicly an American flag stolen from its rightful owner that he violated the Texas statute.

The Court could not, and did not, say that Chaplinsky's utterances were not expressive phrases—they clearly and succinctly conveyed an extremely low opinion of the addressee. The same may be said of Johnson's public burning of the flag in this case; it obviously did convey Johnson's bitter dislike of his country. But his act, like Chaplinsky's provocative words, conveyed nothing that could not have been conveyed and was not conveyed just as forcefully in a dozen different ways. As with "fighting words," so with flag burning, for purposes of the First Amendment: It is

> no essential part of any exposition of ideas, and [is] of such slight social value as a step to truth that any benefit that may be derived from [it] is clearly outweighed

by the public interest in avoiding a probable breach of the peace. The highest courts of several States have upheld state statutes prohibiting the public burning of the flag on the grounds that it is so inherently inflammatory that it may cause a breach of public order. *See, e.g., State v. Royal*, 113 N. H. 224, 229, 305 A.2d 676, 680 (1973); *State v. Waterman*, 190 N.W.2d 809, 811–812 (Iowa 1971); *see also State v. Mitchell*, 32 Ohio App.2d 16, 30, 288 N.E.2d 216, 226 (1972).

The result of the Texas statute is obviously to deny one in Johnson's frame of mind one of many means of "symbolic speech." Far from being a case of "one picture being worth a thousand words," flag burning is the equivalent of an inarticulate grunt or roar that, it seems fair to say, is most likely to be indulged in not to express any particular idea, but to antagonize others. Only five years ago we said in *City Council of Los Angeles v. Taxpayers for Vincent*, 466 U.S. 789, 812 (1984), that "the First Amendment does not guarantee the right to employ every conceivable method of communication at all times and in all places." The Texas statute deprived Johnson of only one rather inarticulate symbolic form of protest—a form of protest that was profoundly offensive to many—and left him with a full panoply of other symbols and every conceivable form of verbal expression to express his deep disapproval of national policy. Thus, in no way can it be said that Texas is punishing him because his hearers—or any other group of people—were profoundly opposed to the message that he sought to convey. Such opposition is no proper basis for restricting speech or expression under the First Amendment. It was Johnson's use of this particular symbol, and not the idea that he sought to convey by it or by his many other expressions, for which he was punished.

Our prior cases dealing with flag desecration statutes have left open the question that the Court resolves today. In *Street v. New York*, 394 U.S. 576, 579 (1969), the defendant burned a flag in the street, shouting "We don't need no damned flag" and, "[i]f they let that happen to Meredith, we don't need an American flag." The Court ruled that since the defendant might have been convicted solely on the basis of his words, the conviction could not stand, but it expressly reserved the question whether a defendant could constitutionally be convicted for burning the flag. *Id.* at 581.

Chief Justice Warren, in dissent, stated:

> I believe that the States and Federal Government do have the power to protect the flag from acts of desecration and disgrace. . . . [I]t is difficult for me to imagine that, had the Court faced this issue, it would have concluded otherwise.

Id. at 605. Justices Black and Fortas also expressed their personal view that a prohibition on flag burning did not violate the Constitution. *See id.* at 610 (Black, J., dissenting) ("It passes my belief that anything in the Federal Constitution bars a State from making the deliberate burning of the American Flag an offense"); *id.* at 615–617 (Fortas, J., dissenting) ("[T]he States and the Federal Government have the power to protect the flag from acts of desecration committed in public. . . . [T]he flag is a special kind of personality. Its use is traditionally and universally subject to special rules and regulation. . . . A person may 'own' a flag, but ownership is subject to special burdens and responsibilities. A flag may be property, in a sense; but it is property burdened with peculiar obligations and restrictions. Certainly . . . these special conditions are not *per se* arbitrary or beyond governmental power under our Constitution").

In *Spence v. Washington*, 418 U.S. 405 (1974), the Court reversed the conviction of a college student who displayed the flag with a peace symbol affixed to it by means of removable black tape from the window of his apartment. Unlike the instant case, there was no risk of a breach of the peace, no one other than the arresting officers saw the flag, and the defendant owned the flag in question. The Court concluded that the student's conduct was protected under the First Amendment, because

> no interest the State may have in preserving the physical integrity of a privately owned flag was significantly impaired on these facts.

Id. at 415. The Court was careful to note, however, that the defendant "was not charged under the desecration statute, nor did he permanently disfigure the flag or destroy it." *Ibid.*

In another related case, *Smith v. Goguen*, 415 U.S. 566 (1974), the appellee, who wore a small flag on the seat of his trousers, was convicted under a Massachusetts flag misuse statute that subjected to criminal liability anyone who publicly. . . treats contemptuously the flag of the United States." *Id.* at 568–569. The Court affirmed the lower court's reversal of appellee's conviction, because the phrase "treats contemptuously" was unconstitutionally broad and vague. *Id.* at 576. The Court was again careful to point out that

> [c]ertainly nothing prevents a legislature from defining with substantial specificity what constitutes forbidden treatment of United States flags.

Id. at 581–582. *See also id.* at 587 (WHITE, J., concurring in judgment) ("The flag is a national property, and the Nation may regulate those who would make, imitate, sell, possess, or use it. I would not question those statutes which proscribe mutilation, defacement, or burning of the flag or which otherwise protect its physical integrity, without regard to whether such conduct might provoke violence. . . . There would seem to be little question about the power of Congress to forbid the mutilation of the Lincoln Memorial. . . . The flag is itself a monument, subject to similar protection"); *id.* at 591 (BLACKMUN, J., dissenting) ("Goguen's punishment was constitutionally permissible for harming the physical integrity of the flag by wearing it affixed to the seat of his pants").

But the Court today will have none of this. The uniquely deep awe and respect for our flag felt by virtually all of us are bundled off under the rubric of "designated symbols," *ante* at 417, that the First Amendment prohibits the government from "establishing." But the government has not "established" this feeling; 200 years of history have done that. The government is simply recognizing as a fact the profound regard for the American flag created by that history when it enacts statutes prohibiting the disrespectful public burning of the flag.

The Court concludes its opinion with a regrettably patronizing civics lecture, presumably addressed to the Members of both Houses of Congress, the members of the 48 state legislatures that enacted prohibitions against flag burning, and the troops fighting under that flag in Vietnam who objected to its being burned:

> The way to preserve the flag's special role is not to punish those who feel differently about these matters. It is to persuade them that they are wrong.

Ante at 419. The Court's role as the final expositor of the Constitution is well established, but its role as a platonic guardian admonishing those responsible to public opinion as if they were truant schoolchildren has no similar place in our system of government. The cry of "no taxation without representation" animated those who revolted against the English Crown to found our Nation—the idea that those who submitted to government should have some say as to what kind of laws would be passed. Surely one of the high purposes of a democratic society is to legislate against conduct that is regarded as evil and profoundly offensive to the majority of people—whether it be murder, embezzlement, pollution, or flagburning.

Our Constitution wisely places limits on powers of legislative majorities to act, but the declaration of such limits by this Court "is, at all times, a question of much delicacy, which ought seldom, if ever, to be decided in the affirmative, in a doubtful case." *Fletcher v. Peck*, 6 Cranch 87, 128 (1810) (Marshall, C.J.). Uncritical extension of constitutional protection to the burning of the flag risks the frustration of the very purpose for which organized governments are instituted. The Court decides that the American flag is just another symbol, about which not only must opinions pro and con be tolerated, but for which the most minimal public respect may not be enjoined. The government may conscript men into the Armed Forces where they must fight and perhaps die for the flag, but the government may not prohibit the public burning of the banner under which they fight. I would uphold the Texas statute as applied in this case.[1]

> may not satisfy those intent on finding fault at any cost, [it is] set out in terms that the ordinary person exercising ordinary common sense can sufficiently understand and comply with.

CSC Letter Carriers, 413 U.S. 548, 579 (1973). By defining "desecrate" as "deface," "damage" or otherwise "physically mistreat" in a manner that the actor knows will "seriously offend" others, § 42.09 only prohibits flagrant acts of physical abuse and destruction of the flag of the sort at issue here—soaking a flag with lighter fluid and igniting it in public—and not any of the examples of improper flag etiquette cited in respondent's brief.

Note

1. In holding that the Texas statute as applied to Johnson violates the First Amendment, the Court does not consider Johnson's claims that the statute is unconstitutionally vague or overbroad. Brief for Respondent 24-30. I think those claims are without merit. In *New York State Club Assn. v. City of New York*, 487 U.S. 1, 11 (1988), we stated that a facial challenge is only proper under the First Amendment when a statute can never be applied in a permissible manner or when, even if it may be validly applied to a particular defendant, it is so broad as to reach the protected speech of third parties. While Tex.Penal Code Ann. § 42.09 (1989)

POSTSCRIPT

Should Burning an American Flag Be a Form of Expression Protected by the First Amendment?

Flag burning as a form of political expression presents a difficult First Amendment issue. While some would say that political speech and the right to protest the actions of our government are critical, others believe that the ideals and sacrifices symbolized by the American flag are worthy of the most stringent protections. Moreover, the issue of whether the government may suppress an expression if it has the potential to incite violence by an audience is a highly interesting one. It is relatively easy to envision circumstances when someone burning an American flag as a sign of protest might provoke a violent incident. Should the potential for a violent response by onlookers justify suppressing the expression?

Speaking generally, public authorities have a responsibility to control violent reactions to speech if possible. The possibility of a violent reaction by a crowd listening to a speech or witnessing an expression would not be sufficient to constitute fighting words.

For example, in *National Socialist Party of America v. Village of Skokie*, 432 U.S. 43 (1977), a neo-Nazi group had planned to march through Skokie, Illinois. There were many Jewish residents of Skokie, including some who had survived the Nazi Holocaust. The Nazi group had originally planned to march in Marquette Park in Chicago; however, when the Park District demanded a large insurance bond to indemnify them against any possible damage caused by a potentially violent crowd reaction, the Nazis decided to move their march to Skokie.

A trial court issued an injunction prohibiting the Nazis from marching, or displaying the swastika, and from distributing pamphlets or displaying materials inciting or promoting hatred against Jews, or persons of any faith or race. The Illinois Appellate Court denied an application for a stay pending appeal. The Illinois Supreme Court denied the stay as well as a request for an extradited appeal. The Nazis then filed an application for a stay with Supreme Court Justice John Paul Stevens, as Circuit Justice, who referred the matter to the Court.

In a per curiam decision, the U.S. Supreme Court reversed the Illinois Supreme Court's denial of a stay. It held that the state court must permit a stay where procedural safeguards, including immediate appellate review, are not provided, because the injunction against the march would have denied the Nazis' First Amendment rights during the appeal.

The result was that the Nazis held three rallies during that summer, but none in Skokie. There was little attendance at the gatherings. This case demonstrates clearly that the First Amendment protects positive speech, or "speech we like," as well as speech that many persons would consider highly objectionable, or "speech we hate."

What should happen, however, if a speaker advocates violent behavior? May a state criminalize such speech? This question was presented to the U.S. Supreme Court in *Brandenburg v. Ohio*, 395 U.S. 444 (1969). The trial record showed that Brandenburg telephoned an announcer at a Cincinnati television station and invited him to come to a Ku Klux Klan (KKK) rally to be held at a local farm. The reporter attended and filmed the rally, which was later shown on local and national television. Based on the films, Brandenburg, a leader of the KKK group, was convicted under the Ohio Criminal Syndicalism statute for "advocating the duty, necessity, or propriety of crime, sabotage, violence, or unlawful methods of terrorism as a means of accomplish[ing] industrial or political reform" and for "voluntarily assembling with any society, group, or assemblage of persons formed to teach or advocate the doctrines of criminal syndication." At his trial the film was introduced as evidence. It had recorded a speech that Brandenburg had made while wearing Klan robes in which he had stated:

> We're not a revengent [sic] organization, but if our President, our Congress, our Supreme Court, continues to suppress the white, Caucasian race, it's possible that there might have to be some revengence [sic] taken.

Brandenburg was convicted, fined $1,000, and sentenced to 1 to 10 years' imprisonment. The intermediate Ohio Appellate Court affirmed his conviction and the Ohio Supreme Court declined to review it.

The U.S. Supreme Court, in a per curiam opinion, reversed the conviction. It held:

> The [Ohio law] punishes persons who 'advocate or teach the duty, necessity, or propriety' of violence 'as a means of accomplishing industrial or political reform'; or who publish or circulate or display any book or paper containing such advocacy; or who 'justify' the commission of violent acts 'with intent to exemplify, spread or advocate the propriety of the doctrines of criminal syndicalism'; or who 'voluntarily assemble' with a group formed 'to teach or advocate the doctrines of criminal syndicalism.' Neither the indictment nor the trial judge's instructions to the jury in any way refined the statute's bald definition of the crime in terms of mere advocacy not distinguished from *incitement to imminent lawless action* [emphasis added].

Brandenburg v. Ohio, then, emphasizes that in order to criminalize advocacy, the speaker must attempt to incite someone to imminent lawless action and the speech must be likely to produce such action. The connection between the speech and the lawless action must be very close. Theoretical advocacy of lawless action will not satisfy this high standard. Abstract advocacy directed at producing lawless behavior at some future time is insufficient.

For example, if a speaker at your university was to advocate burning the homes of "radical, liberal professors," the speech would not be likely to satisfy the *Brandenburg* free speech test. Therefore, a criminal prosecution of the speaker would be highly unlikely to succeed. Even though the speaker may intend to incite lawless action, the speech is not likely to produce such action in a civilized university community, and the nexus between the speech and the action is not close.

A criminal prosecution might succeed, however, if the speaker directed his speech at a particular professor under circumstances in which violence against the individual is likely to occur. "Let's burn the house of that radical, liberal Professor Jones. Here is a container with two gallons of gas and a pack of matches. This is the map to his home. I have a van ready to go. Let's go now." Under these circumstances, a criminal prosecution of the speaker may succeed. The speaker intends to incite violent lawless action and the nexus between the speech and the lawless action is very close.

After reviewing the myriad of First Amendment precedents considered in this section, what have you concluded about flag burning? Should it be a constitutionally protected form of expression, or should society be able to punish such symbolic speech? This issue is likely to continue to generate considerable controversy well into the future.

For example, a "Flag Desecration" Constitutional Amendment was proposed in Congress in 2006, which stated: "The Congress shall have power to prohibit the physical desecration of the flag of the United States." The amendment would have given the Congress the power to develop statutes to prohibit flag desecration and burning.

Although the amendment was passed by the House of Representatives, it was defeated in the U.S. Senate by a single vote.

As you may have concluded by now, First Amendment cases present U.S. courts with very challenging and interesting issues. Fortunately, there are a large number of additional resources to pursue further study in this area, including: Kathleen M. Sullivan and Gerald Gunther, *Constitutional Law* (Foundation Press, 15th ed., 2004); Laurence H. Tribe, *American Constitutional Law* (Foundation Press, 2nd ed., 1988); Alpheus Thomas Mason and Donald Grier Stephenson, Jr., *American Constitutional Law* (Pearson Prentice Hall, 15th ed., 2009; 14th ed., 2005); Bernard Schwartz, *A History of the Supreme Court* (Oxford University Press, 1993); Kermit L. Hall, Paul Finkelman, and James Ely, Jr., *American Legal History: Cases and Materials* (Oxford University Press, 3rd ed., 2005); Kermit L. Hall, *The Oxford Companion to the Supreme Court of the United States* (Oxford University Press, 1992); Walter F. Murphy, James E. Fleming, Sotirios A. Barber, and Stephen Macedo, *American Constitutional Interpretation* (Foundation Press, 3rd ed., 2003); David M. O'Brien, *Constitutional Law and Politics: Struggles for Power and Government Accountability* (W.W. Norton, 6th ed., 2005); Craig R. Ducat, *Constitutional Interpretation* (Wadsworth, 9th ed., 2009); John H. Garvey, T. Alexander Aleinikoff, and Daniel A. Farber,

Modern Constitutional Theory: A Reader (Thompson West, 5th ed., 2004). See also: James McGoldrick, "Symbolic Speech: A Message from Mind to Mind," *Oklahoma Law Review*, vol. 61, p. 1 (2008); Eugene Volokh, "Symbolic Expression and the Original Meaning of the First Amendment," *The Georgetown Law Journal*, vol. 97, p. 1057 (2009); Allison Barger, "Changing State Laws to Prohibit the Display of Hangman's Nooses: Tightening the Knot Around the First Amendment," *William & Mary Bill of Rights Journal*, vol. 17, p. 263 (2008); Mohammed S. Wattad, "The Meaning of Wrongdoing—A Crime of Disrespecting the Flag: Grounds for Preserving 'National Unity'?," *San Diego International Law Journal*, vol. 10, p.5 (2008); John Greenman, "On Communication," *Michigan Law Review*, vol. 106, p. 1337 (2008); Daniel F. Wachtell, "No Harm, No Foul: Reconceptualizing Free Speech Via Tort Law," *NYU Law Review*, vol. 83, p. 949 (2008).

ISSUE 20

Does the First Amendment Permit the Government to Censure the Media?

YES: Pierce Butler, from Dissenting Opinion, *Near v. Minnesota,*
283 U.S. 697 (1931)

NO: Charles E. Hughes, from Majority Opinion, *Near v. Minnesota,*
283 U.S. 697 (1931)

ISSUE SUMMARY

YES: Justice Pierce Butler, dissenting in *Near v. Minnesota* (1931), asserted that the Court's decision to prevent states from stopping the
publication of malicious, scandalous, and defamatory periodicals
gives to freedom of the press a meaning and a scope not previously
recognized, and construes "liberty" in the Due Process Clause of
the Fourteenth Amendment to restrict the states in a way that is
unprecedented.

NO: Chief Justice Charles E. Hughes, writing for the Court in *Near v.
Minnesota* (1931), held that the Minnesota law, which allowed the
newspaper to be shut down, was the essence of censorship and a
violation of the First Amendment.

$\mathbf{I}$t can be hard to keep people honest. As any parent knows well, one of the best
ways to ensure proper behavior is to keep a vigilant eye on your children. The
same principle seems to apply to our government. Americans believe in open
government. To paraphrase the late Justice William O. Douglas, "sunshine"
may well be the best "disinfectant" for holding our government accountable.

One of the cornerstones of government accountability in the United States
has always been a free and vigilant press. Totalitarian governments are widely
known to use censorship to restrict the flow of information in society. An effective way to do this is with a *prior restraint* on publication. *Black's Law Dictionary*
(1979) defines it as "the imposition of a restraint on a publication before it is
published." One need only look to Google's recent difficulties in the People's
Republic of China for a contemporary example of this type of censorship.

In the U.S. legal system, a prior restraint on a publication bears a heavy presumption against its constitutionality. The founding fathers had a strong distrust of governmental censorship and made great efforts to ensure that we would always have a free and vigorous press. Irresponsible statements, outright falsehoods, invasions of privacy, and defamation may be punished *after the fact*, most often in the civil justice system; however, in the United States it is extremely difficult to restrain a publication *before* it is made. One of the most potent ways to hold persons accountable for what they say or write is a civil tort lawsuit for *defamation*, which *Black's Law Dictionary* (1979) defines as:

> [Using false information to hold up] a person to ridicule, scorn or contempt in a respectable and considerable part of the community; . . . includes both *libel* and *slander*. Defamation is that which tends to injure reputation; to diminish the esteem, respect, goodwill or confidence in which the plaintiff is held, or to excite adverse, derogatory or unpleasant feelings or opinions against him.

Libel is written defamation, whereas *slander* is spoken. The difference is significant because in an action for libel the victim, or plaintiff, need not prove special damages. The best defense to a defamation action is that what the defendant has said is the truth and defamation cases often hinge on this critical issue.

Moreover, because it is so important to encourage the free exchange of ideas in society, it is very difficult for a governmental official, or public figure, to prevail in a libel action against the media. For example, in *New York Times Co. v. Sullivan*, 376 U.S. 254 (1964), the Supreme Court was asked to decide the extent to which the First Amendment's protections for speech and press limit a state's power to award damages in a libel suit brought by a public official against critics of his official conduct. Sullivan was Commissioner of Public Affairs, whose duties included supervising the police department. A full page ad, published on March 29, 1960, titled "Heed Their Rising Voices," stated:

> As the whole world knows by now, thousands of Southern Negro students are engaged in widespread nonviolent demonstrations in positive affirmative of the right to live in human dignity as guaranteed by the U.S. Constitution and the Bill of Rights. In their efforts to uphold these guarantees, they are being met by an unprecedented wave of terror by those who would destroy and negate that document which the whole world looks upon as setting the pattern for modern freedom. . . . In Montgomery, Alabama, after students sang "My Country, Tis of Thee" on the State Capitol steps, their leaders were expelled from school, and truckloads of police armed with shotguns and tear gas ringed the Alabama State College Campus. When the entire student body protested to state authorities by refusing to reregister, their dining hall was padlocked in an attempt to starve them into submission.

Commissioner Sullivan alleged that the above statements had libeled him. At trial in an Alabama court, the jury found that *The New York Times* had committed libel and awarded Sullivan $500,000. Existing Alabama law had imposed *strict liability* for libel. Thus, *The New York Times* could not defend itself by showing that it believed its statements were true. Moreover, even though truth was available as a defense to the libel action, the defendant had the burden to prove it.

The U.S. Supreme Court reversed the judgment. Stated Justice William J. Brennan: "A rule compelling the critic of official conduct to guarantee the truth of all his factual assertions—and to do so on pain of libel judgments virtually unlimited in amount—leads to a . . . 'self-censorship.' Allowance of the defense of truth, with the burden of proving it on the defendant, does not mean that only false speech will be deterred." The Court concluded that the First Amendment will not allow a public official executing his official duties to recover damages for libel unless he or she proves "actual malice." This means that the official would have to prove that the party publishing the defamatory information knew it was false, or acted with reckless disregard of its truth or falsity.

The result of this case is that it is very difficult for a public figure to prevail in a libel action against a media critic acting in good faith. If a plaintiff can meet this high standard, however, he or she may recover damages for libel. Try to remember, however, that there is an important distinction between someone prevailing in an action for defamation *after* it has occurred, as opposed to an effort to prevent the statement from being published in the first place, a prior restraint on publication.

One of the early and important cases involving the latter issue was *Near v. Minnesota*, 283 U.S. 697 (1931), which is considered in this section. A Minnesota statute declared that entities that engage "in the business of regularly and customarily producing [and] publishing . . . a malicious, scandalous and defamatory newspaper, magazine or other periodical," are guilty of a nuisance, and authorize suits, in the name of the state, in which such periodicals could be abated and their publishers enjoined from future violations. In such a suit, malice could be presumed from the fact of the publication. The defendant was permitted to prove that his publications were true and published with good motives and justifiable ends. Disobedience of an injunction was punishable as a contempt of court.

A county attorney in Minnesota brought an action to enjoin the publication of a newspaper known as *The Saturday Press*, published in Minneapolis. The complaint alleged that it had published and circulated editions of that paper that were "largely devoted to malicious, scandalous and defamatory articles," concerning specified public figures. The articles alleged that a Jewish gangster was in control of gambling, bootlegging, and racketeering in the city of Minneapolis and that law enforcement officers and agencies were not energetically performing their duties. The trial court held that *Near*, the owner of the newspaper, "did engage in the business of regularly and customarily producing and circulating a malicious, scandalous and defamatory newspaper." Moreover, it held that *The Saturday Press*, "as a public nuisance . . . is hereby abated," and perpetually enjoined the defendants "from producing, editing, publishing, circulating, having in their possession, selling or giving away any publication whatsoever which is a malicious, scandalous or defamatory newspaper, as defined by law and also "from further conducting said nuisance under the name and title of said *The Saturday Press* or any other name or title." The Minnesota Supreme Court affirmed and the U.S. Supreme Court granted certiorari.

Writing for the Court, Chief Justice Charles E. Hughes held that the Minnesota statute was an "infringement on the liberty of the press guaranteed by the Fourteenth Amendment," because it "imposes an unconstitutional restraint upon publication." Stated Chief Justice Hughes:

> Public officers, whose character and conduct remain upon to debate and free discussion in the press, find their remedies for false accusations in actions under libel laws providing for redress and punishment, and not in proceedings to restrain the publication of newspapers and periodicals.

In a dissenting opinion, Justice Pierce Butler asserted that the majority's holding "gives to freedom of the press a meaning and a scope not heretofore recognized, and construes 'liberty' in the due process clause of the Fourteenth Amendment to put upon the States a federal restriction that is without precedent." Moreover, stated Butler:

> The doctrine that measures such as the [Minnesota statute] are invalid because they operate as previous restraints to infringe freedom of press exposes the peace and good order of every community and the business and private affairs of every individual to the constant and protracted false and malicious assaults of any insolvent publisher who may have purpose and sufficient capacity to contrive and put into effect a scheme or program for oppression, blackmail or extortion.

In Your Opinion . . .

- Why is a prior governmental restraint on publication such a significant issue in the United States?
- If public welfare were at stake, would you approve a prior restraint on publication under those circumstances?

YES

Pierce Butler

Dissenting Opinion,
Near v. Minnesota

MR. JUSTICE BUTLER, dissenting.

The decision of the Court in this case declares Minnesota and every other State powerless to restrain by injunction the business of publishing and circulating among the people malicious, scandalous and defamatory periodicals that in due course of judicial procedure has been adjudged to be a public nuisance. It gives to freedom of the press a meaning and a scope not heretofore recognized, and construes "liberty" in the due process clause of the Fourteenth Amendment to put upon the States a federal restriction that is without precedent.

Confessedly, the Federal Constitution, prior to 1868, when the Fourteenth Amendment was adopted, did not protect the right of free speech or press against state action. *Barron v. Baltimore,* 7 Peters 243, 250. *Fox v. Ohio,* 5 How. 410, 434. *Smith v. Maryland,* 18 How. 71, 76. *Withers v. Buckley,* 20 How. 84, 89–91. Up to that time, the right was safeguarded solely by the constitutions and laws of the States, and, it may be added, they operated adequately to protect it. This Court was not called on until 1925 to decide whether the "liberty" protected by the Fourteenth Amendment includes the right of free speech and press. That question has been finally answered in the affirmative. *Cf. Patterson v. Colorado,* 205 U.S. 454, 462. *Prudential Ins. Co. v. Cheek,* 259 U.S. 530, 538, 543. *See Gitlow v. New York,* 268 U.S. 652. *Fiske v. Kansas,* 274 U.S. 380. *Stromberg v. California, ante,* p. 359.

The record shows, and it is conceded, that defendants' regular business was the publication of malicious, scandalous and defamatory articles concerning the principal public officers, leading newspapers of the city, many private persons and the Jewish race. It also shows that it was their purpose at all hazards to continue to carry on the business. In every edition, slanderous and defamatory matter predominates to the practical exclusion of all else. Many of the statements are so highly improbable as to compel a finding that they are false. The articles themselves show malice.

The defendant here has no standing to assert that the statute is invalid because it might be construed so as to violate the Constitution. His right is limited solely to the inquiry whether, having regard to the point properly raised in his case, the effect of applying the statute is to deprive him of his liberty without due process of law. This Court should not reverse the judgment below upon the ground that, in some other case, the statute may be applied in a way that is repugnant to the freedom of the press protected by the Fourteenth

Supreme Court of the United States, 1931.

Amendment. *Castillo v. McConnico,* 168 U.S. 674, 680. *Williams v. Mississippi,* 170 U.S. 213, 225. *Yazoo & Miss. R. Co. v. Jackson Vinegar Co.,* 226 U.S. 217, 219–220. *Plymouth Coal Co. v. Pennsylvania,* 232 U.S. 531, 544–546.

This record requires the Court to consider the statute as applied to the business of publishing articles that are, in fact, malicious, scandalous and defamatory.

The statute provides that any person who "shall be engaged in the business of regularly or customarily producing, publishing or circulating" a newspaper, magazine or other periodical that is (a) "obscene, lewd and lascivious" or (b) "malicious, scandalous and defamatory" is guilty of a nuisance, and may be enjoined as provided in the Act. It will be observed that the qualifying words are used conjunctively. In actions brought under (b) "there shall be available the defense that the truth was published with good motives and for justifiable ends."

The complaint charges that defendants were engaged in the business of regularly and customarily publishing "malicious, scandalous and defamatory newspapers" known as *The Saturday Press,* and nine editions dated respectively on each Saturday commencing September 25 and ending November 19, 1927, were made a part of the complaint. These are all that were published.

On appeal from the order of the district court overruling defendants' demurrer to the complaint, the state supreme court said (174 Minn. 457, 461, 219 N.W. 770):

> The constituent elements of the declared nuisance are the customary and regular dissemination by means of a newspaper which finds its way into families, reaching the young as well as the mature, of a selection of scandalous and defamatory articles treated in such a way as to excite attention and interest so as to command circulation. . . . The statute is not directed at threatened libel, but at an existing business which, generally speaking, involves more than libel. The distribution of scandalous matter is detrimental to public morals and to the general welfare. It tends to disturb the peace of the community. Being defamatory and malicious, it tends to provoke assaults and the commission of crime. It has no concern with the publication of the truth, with good motives and for justifiable ends. . . . In Minnesota no agency can hush the sincere and honest voice of the press; but our constitution was never intended to protect malice, scandal and defamation when untrue or published with bad motives or without justifiable ends. . . . It was never the intention of the constitution to afford protection to a publication devoted to scandal and defamation. . . . Defendants stand before us upon the record as being regularly and customarily engaged in a business of conducting a newspaper sending to the public malicious, scandalous and defamatory printed matter.

The case was remanded to the district court.

Near's answer made no allegations to excuse or justify the business or the articles complained of. It formally denied that the publications were malicious, scandalous or defamatory, admitted that they were made as alleged, and attacked the statute as unconstitutional. At the trial, the plaintiff introduced evidence unquestionably sufficient to support the complaint. The defendant offered none. The court found the facts as alleged in the complaint, and, specifically, that each edition "was chiefly devoted to malicious, scandalous and defamatory articles" and that the last edition was chiefly devoted to malicious, scandalous and defamatory articles concerning Leach (mayor of Minneapolis), Davis (representative of the law enforcement league of citizens), Brunskill (chief of police), Olson (county attorney), the Jewish race, and members of the grand jury then serving in that court; that defendants, in and through the several publications,

> did thereby engage in the business of regularly and customarily producing, publishing and circulating a malicious, scandalous and defamatory newspaper.

Defendant Near again appealed to the Supreme Court. In its opinion (179 Minn. 40, 228 N.W. 326), the court said:

> No claim is advanced that the method and character of the operation of the newspaper in question was not a nuisance if the statute is constitutional. It was regularly and customarily devoted largely to malicious, scandalous and defamatory matter. . . . The record presents the same questions, upon which we have already passed.

Defendant concedes that the editions of the newspaper complained of are "defamatory *per se*," and he says:

> It has been asserted that the constitution was never intended to be a shield for malice, scandal, and defamation when untrue, or published with bad motives, or for unjustifiable ends. . . . The contrary is true; every person *does* have a constitutional right to publish malicious, scandalous, and defamatory matter though untrue, and with bad motives, and for unjustifiable ends, *in the first Instance,* though he is subject to responsibility therefor *afterwards.*

The record, when the substance of the articles is regarded, requires that concession here. And this Court is required to pass on the validity of the state law on that basis.

No question was raised below, and there is none here, concerning the relevancy or weight of evidence, burden of proof, justification or other matters of defense, the scope of the judgment or proceedings to enforce it, or the character of the publications that may be made notwithstanding the injunction.

There is no basis for the suggestion that defendants may not interpose any defense or introduce any evidence that would be open to them in a libel case, or that malice may not be negatived by showing that the publication was made in good faith in belief of its truth, or that, at the time and under the circumstances, it was justified as a fair comment on public affairs or upon the conduct of public officers in respect of their duties as such. *See* Mason's Minnesota Statutes, §§ 10112, 10113.

The scope of the judgment is not reviewable here. The opinion of the state supreme court shows that it was not reviewable there, because defendants' assignments of error in that court did not go to the form of the judgment, and because the lower court had not been asked to modify the judgment.

The Act was passed in the exertion of the State's power of police, and this court is, by well established rule, required to assume, until the contrary is clearly made to appear, that there exists in Minnesota a state of affairs that justifies this measure for the preservation of the peace and good order of the State. *Lindsley v. Natural Carbonic Gas Co.,* 220 U.S. 61, 79. *Gitlow v. New York, supra.* 668–669. *Corporation Commission v. Lowe,* 281 U.S. 431, 438. *O'Gorman & Young v. Hartford Ins. Co.,* 282 U.S. 251, 257–258.

The publications themselves disclose the need and propriety of the legislation. They show:

In 1913 one Guilford, originally a defendant in this suit, commenced the publication of a scandal sheet called the Twin City Reporter; in 1916, Near joined him in the enterprise, later bought him out and engaged the services of one Bevans. In 1919, Bevans acquired Near's interest, and has since, alone or with others, continued the publication. Defendants admit that they published some reprehensible articles in the Twin City Reporter, deny that they personally used it for blackmailing purposes, admit that, by reason of their connection with the paper their reputation did become tainted, and state that Bevans, while so associated with Near, did use the paper for blackmailing purposes. And Near says it was for that reason he sold his interest to Bevans.

In a number of the editions, defendants charge that, ever since Near sold his interest to Bevans in 1919, the Twin City Reporter has been used for blackmail, to dominate public gambling and other criminal activities, and as well to exert a kind of control over public officers and the government of the city.

The articles in question also state that, when defendants announced their intention to publish *The Saturday Press,* they were threatened, and that, soon after the first publication, Guilford was waylaid and shot down before he could use the firearm which he had at hand for the purpose of defending himself against anticipated assaults. It also appears that Near apprehended violence, and was not unprepared to repel it. There is much more of like significance.

The long criminal career of the Twin City Reporter—if it is, in fact, as described by defendants—and the arming and shooting arising out of the publication of *The Saturday Press,* serve to illustrate the kind of conditions, in respect of the business of publishing malicious, scandalous and defamatory periodicals, by which the state legislature presumably was moved to enact the law in question. It must be deemed appropriate to deal with conditions existing in Minnesota.

It is of the greatest importance that the States shall be untrammeled and free to employ all just and appropriate measures to prevent abuses of the liberty of the press.

In his work on the Constitution (5th ed.), Justice Story, expounding the First Amendment, which declares "Congress shall make no law abridging the freedom of speech or of the press," said (§ 1880):

That this amendment was intended to secure to every citizen an absolute right to speak, or write, or print whatever he might please, without
any responsibility, public or private, therefor is a supposition too wild
to be indulged by any rational man. This would be to allow to every
citizen a right to destroy at his pleasure the reputation, the peace, the
property, and even the personal safety of every other citizen. A man
might, out of mere malice and revenge, accuse another of the most
infamous crimes; might excite against him the indignation of all his
fellow citizens by the most atrocious calumnies; might disturb, nay,
overturn, all his domestic peace, and embitter his parental affections;
might inflict the most distressing punishments upon the weak, the
timid, and the innocent; might prejudice all a man's civil, and political,
and private rights, and might stir up sedition, rebellion, and treason
even against the government itself in the wantonness of his passions
or the corruption of his heart. Civil society could not go on under such
circumstances. Men would then be obliged to resort to private venge-
ance to make up for the deficiencies of the law, and assassination and
savage cruelties would be perpetrated with all the frequency belonging to barbarous and brutal communities. It is plain, then, that the
language of this amendment imports no more than that every man
shall have a right to speak, write, and print his opinions upon any
subject whatsoever, without any prior restraint, so always that he does
not injure any other person in his rights, person, property, or reputation, and so always that he does not thereby disturb the public peace
or attempt to subvert the government. It is neither more nor less than
an expansion of the great doctrine recently brought into operation in
the law of libel, *that every man shall be at liberty to publish what is true,
with good motives and for justifiable ends*. And, with this reasonable limitation, it is not only right in itself, but it is an inestimable privilege in
a free government. Without such a limitation, it might become the
scourge of the republic, first denouncing the principles of liberty and
then, by rendering the most virtuous patriots odious through the ter-
rors of the press, introducing despotism in its worst form. . . .

The Court quotes Blackstone in support of its condemnation of the
statute as imposing a previous restraint upon publication. But the previous
restraints referred to by him subjected the press to the arbitrary will of an
administrative officer. He describes the practice (Book IV, p. 152):

To subject the press to the restrictive power of a licenser, as was formerly done both before and since the revolution [of 1688], is to subject
all freedom of sentiment to the prejudices of one man and make him
the arbitrary and infallible judge of all controverted points in learning,
religion, and government.

Story gives the history alluded to by Blackstone (5 1882):

The art of printing, soon after its introduction, we are told, was looked
upon, as well in England as in other countries, as merely a matter
of state, and subject to the coercion of the crown. It was, therefore,

regulated in England by the king's proclamations, prohibitions, charters of privilege, and licenses, and finally by the decrees of the Court of Star-Chamber, which limited the number of printers and of presses which each should employ, and prohibited new publications unless previously approved by proper licensers. On the demolition of this odious jurisdiction, in 1641, the Long Parliament of Charles the First, after their rupture with that prince, assumed the same powers which the Star-Chamber exercised with respect to licensing books, and during the Commonwealth (such is human frailty and the love of power even in republics), they issued their ordinances for that purpose, founded principally upon a Star-Chamber decree of 1637. After the restoration of Charles the Second, a statute on the same subject was passed, copied, with some few alterations, from the parliamentary ordinances. The act expired in 1679, and was revived and continued for a few years after the revolution of 1688. Many attempts were made by the government to keep it in force, but it was so strongly resisted by Parliament that it expired in 1694, and has never since been revived.

It is plain that Blackstone taught that, under the common law liberty of the press means simply the absence of restraint upon publication in advance as distinguished from liability, civil or criminal, for libelous or improper matter so published. And, as above shown, Story defined freedom of the press guaranteed by the First Amendment to mean that "every man shall be at liberty to publish what is true, with good motives and for justifiable ends." His statement concerned the definite declaration of the First Amendment. It is not suggested that the freedom of press included in the liberty protected by the Fourteenth Amendment, which was adopted after Story's definition, is greater than that protected against congressional action. *And see* 2 Cooley's Constitutional Limitations, 8th ed., p. 886. 2 Kent's Commentaries (14th ed.) Lect. XXIV, p. 17.

The Minnesota statute does not operate as a *previous* restraint on publication within the proper meaning of that phrase. It does not authorize administrative control in advance such as was formerly exercised by the licensers and censors but prescribes a remedy to be enforced by a suit in equity. In this case, there was previous publication made in the course of the business of regularly producing malicious, scandalous and defamatory periodicals. The business and publications unquestionably constitute an abuse of the right of free press. The statute denounces the things done as a nuisance on the ground, as stated by the state Supreme Court, that they threaten morals, peace and good order. There is no question of the power of the State to denounce such transgressions. The restraint authorized is only in respect of continuing to do what has been duly adjudged to constitute a nuisance. The controlling words are

All persons guilty of such nuisance may be enjoined, as hereinafter provided. . . . Whenever any such nuisance is committed . . . , an action in the name of the State

may be brought

to perpetually enjoin the person or persons committing, conducting or maintaining any such nuisance, *from further committing, conducting or maintaining any such nuisance. . . .* The court may make its order and judgment permanently enjoining . . . defendants found guilty . . . from committing or continuing the acts prohibited hereby, and in and by such judgment, such nuisance may be wholly abated. . . .

There is nothing in the statute purporting to prohibit publications that have not been adjudged to constitute a nuisance. It is fanciful to suggest similarity between the granting or enforcement of the decree authorized by this statute to prevent *further* publication of malicious, scandalous and defamatory articles and the *previous* restraint upon the press by licensers as referred to by Blackstone and described in the history of the times to which he alludes.

The opinion seems to concede that, under clause (a) of the Minnesota law, the business of regularly publishing and circulating an obscene periodical may be enjoined as a nuisance. It is difficult to perceive any distinction, having any relation to constitutionality, between clause (a) and clause (b) under which this action was brought. Both nuisances are offensive to morals, order and good government. As that resulting from lewd publications constitutionally may be enjoined, it is hard to understand why the one resulting from a regular business of malicious defamation may not.

It is well known, as found by the state Supreme Court, that existing libel laws are inadequate effectively to suppress evils resulting from the kind of business and publications that are shown in this case. The doctrine that measures such as the one before us are invalid because they operate as previous restraints to infringe freedom of press exposes the peace and good order of every community and the business and private affairs of every individual to the constant and protracted false and malicious assaults of any insolvent publisher who may have purpose and sufficient capacity to contrive and put into effect a scheme or program for oppression, blackmail or extortion. The judgment should be affirmed.

MR. JUSTICE VAN DEVANTER, MR. JUSTICE McREYNOLDS, and MR. JUSTICE SUTHERLAND concur in this opinion.

Majority Opinion, *Near v. Minnesota*

MR. CHIEF JUSTICE HUGHES delivered the opinion of the Court.

Chapter 285 of the Session Laws of Minnesota for the year 1925 provides for the abatement, as a public nuisance, of a "malicious, scandalous and defamatory newspaper, magazine or other periodical." Section one of the Act is as follows:

> Section 1. Any person who, as an individual, or as a member or employee of a firm, or association or organization, or as an officer, director, member or employee of a corporation, shall be engaged in the business of regularly or customarily producing, publishing or circulating, having in possession, selling or giving away
>
> (a) an obscene, lewd and lascivious newspaper, magazine, or other periodical, or
> (b) a malicious, scandalous and defamatory newspaper, magazine or other periodical,

is guilty of a nuisance, and all persons guilty of such nuisance may be enjoined, as hereinafter provided.

> Participation in such business shall constitute a commission of such nuisance and render the participant liable and subject to the proceedings, orders and judgments provided for in this Act. Ownership, in whole or in part, directly or indirectly, of any such periodical, or of any stock or interest in any corporation or organization which owns the same in whole or in part, or which publishes the same, shall constitute such participation.
>
> In actions brought under (b) above, there shall be available the defense that the truth was published with good motives and for justifiable ends and in such actions the plaintiff shall not have the right to report (*sic*) to issues or editions of periodicals taking place more than three months before the commencement of the action.

Section two provides that, whenever any such nuisance is committed or exists, the County Attorney of any county where any such periodical is published or circulated, or, in case of his failure or refusal to proceed upon written request in good faith of a reputable citizen, the Attorney General, or, upon like failure or refusal of the latter, any citizen of the county may maintain an

Supreme Court of the United States, 1931.

action in the district court of the county in the name of the State to enjoin perpetually the persons committing or maintaining any such nuisance from further committing or maintaining it. Upon such evidence as the court shall deem sufficient, a temporary injunction may be granted. The defendants have the right to plead by demurrer or answer, and the plaintiff may demur or reply as in other cases.

The action, by section three, is to be "governed by the practice and procedure applicable to civil actions for injunctions," and, after trial, the court may enter judgment permanently enjoining the defendants found guilty of violating the Act from continuing the violation, and, "in and by such judgment, such nuisance may be wholly abated." The court is empowered, as in other cases of contempt, to punish disobedience to a temporary or permanent injunction by fine of not more than $1,000 or by imprisonment in the county jail for not more than twelve months.

Under this statute, clause (b), the County Attorney of Hennepin County brought this action to enjoin the publication of what was described as a "malicious, scandalous and defamatory newspaper, magazine and periodical" known as *"The Saturday Press,"* published by the defendants in the city of Minneapolis. The complaint alleged that the defendants, on September 24, 1927, and on eight subsequent dates in October and November, 1927, published and circulated editions of that periodical which were "largely devoted to malicious, scandalous and defamatory articles" concerning Charles G. Davis, Frank W. Brunskill, *The Minneapolis Tribune, The Minneapolis Journal,* Melvin C. Passolt, George E. Leach, the Jewish Race, the members of the Grand Jury of Hennepin County impaneled in November, 1927, and then holding office, and other persons, as more fully appeared in exhibits annexed to the complaint, consisting of copies of the articles described and constituting 327 pages of the record. While the complaint did not so allege, it appears from the briefs of both parties that Charles G. Davis was a special law enforcement officer employed by a civic organization, that George E. Leach was Mayor of Minneapolis, that Frank W. Brunskill was its Chief of Police, and that Floyd B. Olson (the relator in this action) was County Attorney.

Without attempting to summarize the contents of the voluminous exhibits attached to the complaint, we deem it sufficient to say that the articles charged in substance that a Jewish gangster was in control of gambling, bootlegging and racketeering in Minneapolis, and that law enforcing officers and agencies were not energetically performing their duties. Most of the charges were directed against the Chief of Police; he was charged with gross neglect of duty, illicit relations with gangsters, and with participation in graft. The County Attorney was charged with knowing the existing conditions and with failure to take adequate measures to remedy them. The Mayor was accused of inefficiency and dereliction. One member of the grand jury was stated to be in sympathy with the gangsters. A special grand jury and a special prosecutor were demanded to deal with the situation in general, and, in particular, to investigate an attempt to assassinate one Guilford, one of the original defendants, who, it appears from the articles, was shot by gangsters after the first issue of the periodical had been published. There is no question but that the articles made serious accusations against the public officers named and others in connection with the prevalence of crimes and the failure to expose and punish them.

At the beginning of the action, on November 22, 1927, and upon the verified complaint, an order was made directing the defendants to show cause why a temporary injunction should not issue and meanwhile forbidding the defendants to publish, circulate or have in their possession any editions of the periodical from September 24, 1927, to November 19, 1927, inclusive, and from publishing, circulating, or having in their possession, "any future editions of said *The Saturday Press*" and

> any publication, known by any other name whatsoever containing malicious, scandalous and defamatory matter of the kind alleged in plaintiff's complaint herein or otherwise.

The defendants demurred to the complaint upon the ground that it did not state facts sufficient to constitute a cause of action, and on this demurrer challenged the constitutionality of the statute. The District Court overruled the demurrer and certified the question of constitutionality to the Supreme Court of the State. The Supreme Court sustained the statute (174 Minn. 457, 219 N.W. 770), and it is conceded by the appellee that the Act was thus held to be valid over the objection that it violated not only the state constitution, but also the Fourteenth Amendment of the Constitution of the United States.

Thereupon, the defendant Near, the present appellant, answered the complaint. He averred that he was the sole owner and proprietor of the publication in question. He admitted the publication of the articles in the issues described in the complaint, but denied that they were malicious, scandalous or defamatory as alleged. He expressly invoked the protection of the due process clause of the Fourteenth Amendment. The case then came on for trial. The plaintiff offered in evidence the verified complaint, together with the issues of the publication in question, which were attached to the complaint as exhibits. The defendant objected to the introduction of the evidence, invoking the constitutional provisions to which his answer referred. The objection was overruled, no further evidence was presented, and the plaintiff rested. The defendant then rested without offering evidence. The plaintiff moved that the court direct the issue of a permanent injunction, and this was done.

The District Court made findings of fact which followed the allegations of the complaint and found in general terms that the editions in question were "chiefly devoted to malicious, scandalous and defamatory articles" concerning the individuals named. The court further found that the defendants, through these publications,

> did engage in the business of regularly and customarily producing, publishing and circulating a malicious, scandalous and defamatory newspaper,

and that "the said publication" "under said name of *The Saturday Press,* or any other name, constitutes a public nuisance under the laws of the State."

Judgment was thereupon entered adjudging that "the newspaper, magazine and periodical known as *The Saturday Press*," as a public nuisance, "be and is hereby abated." The Judgment perpetually enjoined the defendants

> from producing, editing, publishing, circulating, having in their pos-
> session, selling or giving away any publication whatsoever which is a
> malicious, scandalous or defamatory newspaper, as defined by law, and
> also "from further conducting said nuisance under the name and title
> of said *The Saturday Press* or any other name or title."

The defendant Near appealed from this judgment to the Supreme Court of the State, again asserting his right under the Federal Constitution, and the judgment was affirmed upon the authority of the former decision. 179 Minn. 40, 228 N.W. 326. With respect to the contention that the judgment went too far, and prevented the defendants from publishing any kind of a newspaper, the court observed that the assignments of error did not go to the form of the judgment, and that the Lower court had not been asked to modify it. The court added that it saw no reason

> for defendants to construe the judgment as restraining them from oper-
> ating a newspaper in harmony with the public welfare, to which all
> must yield,

that the allegations of the complaint had been found to be true, and, though this was an equitable action, defendants had not indicated a desire "to con-duct their business in the usual and legitimate manner."

From the judgment as thus affirmed, the defendant Near appeals to this Court.

This statute, for the suppression as a public nuisance of a newspaper or periodical, is unusual, if not unique, and raises questions of grave importance transcending the local interests involved in the particular action. It is no longer open to doubt that the liberty of the press, and of speech, is within the liberty safeguarded by the due process clause of the Fourteenth Amendment from invasion by state action. It was found impossible to conclude that this essen-tial personal liberty of the citizen was left unprotected by the general guaranty of fundamental rights of person and property. *Gitlow v. New York*, 268 U.S. 652, 666; *Whitney v. California*, 274 U.S. 357, 362, 373; *Fiske v. Kansas*, 274 U.S. 380, 382; *Stromberg v. California, ante*, p. 359. In maintaining this guaranty, the authority of the State to enact laws to promote the health, safety, morals and general welfare of its people is necessarily admitted. The limits of this sover-eign power must always be determined with appropriate regard to the particu-lar subject of its exercise. Thus, while recognizing the broad discretion of the legislature in fixing rates to be charged by those undertaking a public service, this Court has decided that the owner cannot constitutionally be deprived of his right to a fair return, because that is deemed to be of the essence of owner-ship. *Railroad Commission Cases*, 116 U.S. 307, 331; *Northern Pacific Ry. Co. v. North Dakota*, 236 U.S. 585, 596. So, while liberty of contract is not an absolute right, and the wide field of activity in the making of contracts is subject to legislative supervision *(Frisbie v. United States,* 157 U.S. 161, 165), this Court has held that the power of the State stops short of interference with what are deemed to be certain indispensable requirements of the liberty assured, notably with respect to the fixing of prices and wages. *Tyson Bros. v. Banton,* 273 U.S. 418; *Ribnik v. McBride,* 277 U.S. 350; *Adkins v. Children's Hospital,* 261 U.S. 525, 560, 561. Liberty of speech, and of the press, is also not an absolute right, and the State may punish its abuse. *Whitney v. California, supra; Stromberg v. California, supra.* Liberty, in each of its phases, has its history and connotation, and, in the present instance, the inquiry is as to the historic conception of the liberty of the press and whether the statute under review violates the essential attributes of that liberty.

The appellee insists that the questions of the application of the statute to appellant's periodical, and of the construction of the judgment of the trial court, are not presented for review; that appellant's sole attack was upon the constitutionality of the statute, however it might be applied. The appellee contends that no question either of motive in the publication, or whether the decree goes beyond the direction of the statute, is before us. The appellant replies that, in his view, the plain terms of the statute were not departed from in this case, and that, even if they were, the statute is nevertheless unconstitutional under any reasonable construction of its terms. The appellant states that he has not argued that the temporary and permanent injunctions were broader than were warranted by the statute; he insists that what was done was properly done if the statute is valid, and that the action taken under the statute is a fair indication of its scope.

With respect to these contentions, it is enough to say that, in passing upon constitutional questions, the court has regard to substance, and not to mere matters of form, and that, in accordance with familiar principles, the statute must be tested by its operation and effect. *Henderson v. Mayor,* 92 U.S. 259, 268; *Bailey v. Alabama,* 219 U.S. 219, 244; *United States v. Reynolds,* 235 U.S. 133, 148, 149; *St. Louis Southwestern R. Co. v. Arkansas,* 235 U.S. 350, 362; *Mountain Timber Co. v. Washington,* 243 U.S. 219, 237. That operation and effect we think is clearly shown by the record in this case. We are not concerned with mere errors of the trial court, if there be such, in going beyond the direction of the statute as construed by the Supreme Court of the State. It is thus important to note precisely the purpose and effect of the statute as the state court has construed it.

First. The statute is not aimed at the redress of individual or private wrongs. Remedies for libel remain available and unaffected. The statute, said the state court, "is not directed at threatened libel, but at an existing business which, generally speaking, involves more than libel." It is aimed at the distribution of scandalous matter as "detrimental to public morals and to the general welfare," tending "to disturb the peace of the community" and "to provoke assaults and the commission of crime." In order to obtain an injunction to suppress the future publication of the newspaper or periodical, it is not necessary to prove the falsity of the charges that have been made in the publication condemned. In the present action, there was no allegation that the matter published was not true. It is alleged, and the statute requires the allegation, that the publication was "malicious." But, as in prosecutions for libel, there is no requirement of proof by the State of malice in fact, as distinguished from malice inferred from the mere publication of the defamatory matter. The judgment in this case proceeded upon the mere proof of publication. The statute permits the defense not of the truth alone, but only that the truth was published with good motives and for justifiable ends. It is apparent that, under the statute, the publication is to be regarded as defamatory if it injures reputation, and that it is scandalous if it circulates charges of reprehensible conduct, whether criminal or otherwise, and the publication is thus deemed to invite public reprobation and to constitute a public scandal. The court sharply defined the purpose of the statute, bringing out the precise point, in these words:

> There is no constitutional right to publish a fact merely because it is true. It is a matter of common knowledge that prosecutions under the criminal libel statutes do not result in efficient repression or suppression of the evils of scandal. Men who are the victims of such assaults seldom resort to the courts. This is especially true if their sins are exposed and the only question relates to whether it was done with good motives and for justifiable ends. This law is not for the protection of the person attacked, nor to punish the wrongdoer. It is for the protection of the pubic welfare.

Second. The statute is directed not simply at the circulation of scandalous and defamatory statements with regard to private citizens, but at the continued publication by newspapers and periodicals of charges against public officers of corruption, malfeasance in office, or serious neglect of duty. Such charges, by their very nature, create a public scandal. They are scandalous and defamatory within the meaning of the statute, which has its normal operation in relation to publications dealing prominently and chiefly with the alleged derelictions of public officers.

Third. The object of the statute is not punishment, in the ordinary sense, but suppression of the offending newspaper or periodical. The reason for the enactment, as the state court has said, is that prosecutions to enforce penal statutes for libel do not result in "efficient repression or suppression of the evils of scandal." Describing the business of publication as a public nuisance does not obscure the substance of the proceeding which the statute authorizes. It is the continued publication of scandalous and defamatory matter that constitutes the business and the declared nuisance. In the case of public officers, it is the reiteration of charges of official misconduct, and the fact that the newspaper or periodical is principally devoted to that purpose, that exposes it to suppression. In the present instance, the proof was that nine editions of the newspaper or periodical in question were published on successive dates, and that they were chiefly devoted to charges against public officers and in relation to the prevalence and protection of crime. In such a case, these officers are not left to their ordinary remedy in a suit for libel, or the authorities to a prosecution for criminal libel. Under this statute, a publisher of a newspaper or periodical, undertaking to conduct a campaign to expose and to censure official derelictions, and devoting his publication principally to that purpose, must face not simply the possibility of a verdict against him in a suit or prosecution for libel, but a determination that his newspaper or periodical is a public nuisance to be abated, and that this abatement and suppression will follow unless he is prepared with legal evidence to prove the truth of the charges and also to satisfy the court that, in addition to being true, the matter was published with good motives and for justifiable ends.

This suppression is accomplished by enjoining publication, and that restraint is the object and effect of the statute.

Fourth. The statute not only operates to suppress the offending newspaper or periodical, but to put the publisher under an effective censorship. When a newspaper or periodical is found to be "malicious, scandalous, and defamatory," and is suppressed as such, resumption of publication is punishable as a contempt of court by fine or imprisonment. Thus, where a newspaper or periodical has been suppressed because of the circulation of charges against public officers of official misconduct, it would seem to be clear that the renewal of the publication of such charges would constitute a contempt, and that the judgment would lay a permanent restraint upon the publisher, to escape which he must satisfy the court as to the character of a new publication. Whether he would be permitted again to publish matter deemed to be derogatory to the same or other public officers would depend upon the court's ruling. In the present instance, the judgment restrained the defendants from

> publishing, circulating, having in their possession, selling or giving away any publication whatsoever which is a malicious, scandalous or defamatory newspaper, as defined by law.

The law gives no definition except that covered by the words "scandalous and defamatory," and publications charging official misconduct are of that class. While the court, answering the objection that the judgment was too broad, saw no reason for construing it as restraining the defendants "from operating a newspaper in harmony with the public welfare to which all must yield," and said that the defendants had not indicated "any desire to conduct their business in the usual and legitimate manner," the manifest inference is that, at least with respect to a new publication directed against official misconduct, the defendant would be held, under penalty of punishment for contempt as provided in the statute, to a manner of publication which the court considered to be "usual and legitimate" and consistent with the public welfare.

If we cut through mere details of procedure, the operation and effect of the statute, in substance, is that public authorities may bring the owner or publisher of a newspaper or periodical before a judge upon a charge of conducting a business of publishing scandalous and defamatory matter—in particular, that the matter consists of charges against public officers of official dereliction—and, unless the owner or publisher is able and disposed to bring competent evidence to satisfy the judge that the charges are true and are published with good motives and for justifiable ends, his newspaper or periodical is suppressed and further publication is made punishable as a contempt. This is of the essence of censorship.

The question is whether a statute authorizing such proceedings in restraint of publication is consistent with the conception of the liberty of the press as historically conceived and guaranteed. In determining the extent of the constitutional protection, it has been generally, if not universally, considered that it is the chief purpose of the guaranty to prevent previous restraints upon publication. The struggle in England, directed against the legislative power of the licenser, resulted in renunciation of the censorship of the press. The liberty deemed to be established was thus described by Blackstone:

> The liberty of the press is indeed essential to the nature of a free state; but this consists in laying no *previous* restraints upon publications, and not in freedom from censure for criminal matter when published. Every freeman has an undoubted right to lay what sentiments he pleases before the public; to forbid this is to destroy the freedom of the press; but if he publishes what is improper, mischievous or illegal, he must take the consequence of his own temerity.

4 Bl.Com. 151, 152; *see* Story on the Constitution, §§ 1884, 1889. The distinction was early pointed out between the extent of the freedom with respect to censorship under our constitutional system and that enjoyed in England. Here, as Madison said,

> the great and essential rights of the people are secured against legislative as well as against executive ambition. They are secured not by laws paramount to prerogative, but by constitutions paramount to laws. This security of the freedom of the press requires that it should be exempt not only from previous restraint by the Executive, as in Great Britain, but from legislative restraint also.

Report on the Virginia Resolutions, Madison's Works, vol. IV, p. 543. This Court said, in *Patterson v. Colorado,* 205 U.S. 454, 462:

> In the first place, the main purpose of such constitutional provisions is "to prevent all such previous restraints upon publications as had been practiced by other governments," and they do not prevent the subsequent punishment of such as may be deemed contrary to the public welfare. *Commonwealth v. Blanding,* 3 Pick. 304, 313, 314; *Respublica v. Oswald,* 1 Dallas 319, 325. The preliminary freedom extends as well to the false as to the true; the subsequent punishment may extend as well to the true as to the false. This was the law of criminal libel apart from statute in most cases, if not in all. *Commonwealth v. Blanding, ubi sup.;* 4 Bl.Com. 150.

The criticism upon Blackstone's statement has not been because immunity from previous restraint upon publication has not been regarded as deserving of special emphasis, but chiefly because that immunity cannot be deemed to exhaust the conception of the liberty guaranteed by state and federal constitutions. The point of criticism has been "that the mere exemption from previous restraints cannot be all that is secured by the constitutional provisions," and that

> the liberty of the press might be rendered a mockery and a delusion, and the phrase itself a byword, if, while every man was at liberty to publish what he pleased, the public authorities might nevertheless punish him for harmless publications.

2 Cooley, Const.Lim., 8th ed., p. 885. But it is recognized that punishment for the abuse of the liberty accorded to the press is essential to the protection of the public, and that the common law rules that subject the libeler to responsibility for the public offense, as well as for the private injury, are not abolished by the protection extended in our constitutions. *Id.,* pp. 883, 884. The law of criminal libel rests upon that secure foundation. There is also the conceded authority of courts to punish for contempt when publications directly tend to prevent the proper discharge of judicial functions. *Patterson v. Colorado, supra; Toledo Newspaper Co. v. United States,* 247 U.S. 402, 419. In the present case, we have no occasion to inquire as to the permissible scope of subsequent punishment. For whatever wrong the appellant has committed or may commit by his publications the State appropriately affords both public and private redress by its libel laws. As has been noted, the statute in question does not deal with punishments; it provides for no punishment, except in case of contempt for violation of the court's order, but for suppression and injunction, that is, for restraint upon publication.

The objection has also been made that the principle as to immunity from previous restraint is stated too broadly, if every such restraint is deemed to be prohibited. That is undoubtedly true; the protection even as to previous restraint is not absolutely unlimited. But the limitation has been recognized only in exceptional cases:

> When a nation is at war, many things that might be said in time of peace are such a hindrance to its effort that their utterance will not be endured so long as men fight, and that no Court could regard them as protected by any constitutional right.

Schenck v. United States, 249 U.S. 47, 52. No one would question but that a government might prevent actual obstruction to its recruiting service or the publication of the sailing dates of transports or the number and location of troops. On similar grounds, the primary requirements of decency may be enforced against obscene publications. The security of the community life may be protected against incitements to acts of violence and the overthrow by force of orderly government. The constitutional guaranty of free speech does not

> protect a man from an injunction against uttering words that may have all the effect of force. *Gompers v. Buck Stove & Range Co.,* 221 U.S. 418, 439.

Schenck v. United States, supra. These limitations are not applicable here. Nor are we now concerned with questions as to the extent of authority to prevent publications in order to protect private rights according to the principles governing the exercise of the jurisdiction of courts of equity.

The exceptional nature of its limitations places in a strong light the general conception that liberty of the press, historically considered and taken up by the Federal Constitution, has meant, principally, although not exclusively, immunity from previous restraints or censorship. The conception of the liberty of the press in this country had broadened with the exigencies of the colonial period and with the efforts to secure freedom from oppressive administration. That liberty was especially cherished for the immunity it afforded from previous restraint of the publication of censure of public officers and charges of official misconduct. As was said by Chief Justice Parker, in *Commonwealth v. Blanding,* 3 Pick. 304, 313, with respect to the constitution of Massachusetts:

> Besides, it is well understood, and received as a commentary on this provision for the liberty of the press, that it was intended to prevent all such *previous restraints* upon publications as had been practiced by other governments, and in early times here, to stifle the efforts of patriots towards enlightening their fellow subjects upon their rights and the duties of rulers. The liberty of the press was to be unrestrained, but he who used it was to be responsible in case of its abuse.

In the letter sent by the Continental Congress (October 26, 1774) to the Inhabitants of Quebec, referring to the "five great rights," it was said:

> The last right we shall mention regards the freedom of the press. The importance of this consists, besides the advancement of truth, science, morality, and arts in general, in its diffusion of liberal sentiments on the administration of Government, its ready communication of thoughts between subjects, and its consequential promotion of union among them whereby oppressive officers are shamed or intimidated into more honourable and just modes of conducting affairs.

Madison, who was the leading spirit in the preparation of the First Amendment of the Federal Constitution, thus described the practice and sentiment which led to the guaranties of liberty of the press in state constitutions:

> In every State, probably, in the Union, the press has exerted a freedom in canvassing the merits and measures of public men of every description which has not been confined to the strict limits of the common law. On this footing the freedom of the press has stood; on this footing it yet stands. . . . Some degree of abuse is inseparable from the proper use of everything, and in no instance is this more true than in that of the press. It has accordingly been decided by the practice of the States that it is better to leave a few of its noxious branches to their luxuriant growth than, by pruning them away, to injure the vigour of those yielding the proper fruits. And can the wisdom of this policy be doubted by

any who reflect that to the press alone, chequered as it is with abuses, the world is indebted for all the triumphs which have been gained by reason and humanity over error and oppression; who reflect that to the same beneficent source the United States owe much of the lights which conducted them to the ranks of a free and independent nation, and which have improved their political system into a shape so auspicious to their happiness? Had "Sedition Acts," forbidding every publication that might bring the constituted agents into contempt or disrepute, or that might excite the hatred of the people against the authors of unjust or pernicious measures, been uniformly enforced against the press, might not the United States have been languishing at this day under the infirmities of a sickly Confederation? Might they not, possibly, be miserable colonies, groaning under a foreign yoke?

The fact that, for approximately one hundred and fifty years, there has been almost an entire absence of attempts to impose previous restraints upon publications relating to the malfeasance of public officers is significant of the deep-seated conviction that such restraints would violate constitutional right. Public officers, whose character and conduct remain open to debate and free discussion in the press, find their remedies for false accusations in actions under libel laws providing for redress and punishment, and not in proceedings to restrain the publication of newspapers and periodicals. The general principle that the constitutional guaranty of the liberty of the press gives immunity from previous restraints has been approved in many decisions under the provisions of state constitutions.

The importance of this immunity has not lessened. While reckless assaults upon public men, and efforts to bring obloquy upon those who are endeavoring faithfully to discharge official duties, exert a baleful influence and deserve the severest condemnation in public opinion, it cannot be said that this abuse is greater, and it is believed to be less, than that which characterized the period in which our institutions took shape. Meanwhile, the administration of government has become more complex, the opportunities for malfeasance and corruption have multiplied, crime has grown to most serious proportions, and the danger of its protection by unfaithful officials and of the impairment of the fundamental security of life and property by criminal alliances and official neglect, emphasizes the primary need of a vigilant and courageous press, especially in great cities. The fact that the liberty of the press may be abused by miscreant purveyors of scandal does not make any the less necessary the immunity of the press from previous restraint in dealing with official misconduct. Subsequent punishment for such abuses as may exist is the appropriate remedy consistent with constitutional privilege.

In attempted justification of the statute, it is said that it deals not with publication *per se*, but with the "business" of publishing defamation. If, however, the publisher has a constitutional right to publish, without previous restraint, an edition of his newspaper charging official derelictions, it cannot be denied that he may publish subsequent editions for the same purpose. He does not lose his right by exercising it. If his right exists, it may be exercised in publishing nine editions, as in this case, as well as in one edition. If previous restraint is permissible, it may be imposed at once; indeed, the wrong may be as serious in one publication as in several. Characterizing the publication as a business, and the business as a nuisance, does not permit an invasion of the constitutional immunity against restraint. Similarly, it does not matter that the newspaper or periodical is found to be "largely" or "chiefly" devoted to the publication of such derelictions. If the publisher has a right, without previous restraint, to publish them, his right cannot be deemed to be dependent upon his publishing something else, more or less, with the matter to which objection is made.

Nor can it be said that the constitutional freedom from previous restraint is lost because charges are made of derelictions which constitute crimes. With the multiplying provisions of penal codes, and of municipal charters and ordinances carrying penal sanctions, the conduct of public officers is very largely within the purview of criminal statutes. The freedom of the press from previous restraint has never been regarded as limited to such animadversions as lay outside the range of penal enactments. Historically, there is no such limitation; it is inconsistent with the reason which underlies the privilege, as the privilege so limited would be of slight value for the purposes for which it came to be established.

The statute in question cannot be justified by reason of the fact that the publisher is permitted to show, before injunction issues, that the matter published is true and is published with good motives and for justifiable ends. If such a statute, authorizing suppression and injunction on such a basis, is constitutionally valid, it would be equally permissible for the legislature to provide that at any time the publisher of any newspaper could be brought before a court, or even an administrative officer (as the constitutional protection may not be regarded as resting on mere procedural details) and required to produce proof of the truth of his publication, or of what he intended to publish, and of his motives, or stand enjoined. If this can be done, the legislature may provide machinery for determining in the complete exercise of its discretion what are justifiable ends, and restrain publication accordingly. And it would be but a step to a complete system of censorship. The recognition of authority to impose previous restraint upon publication in order to protect the community against the circulation of charges of misconduct, and especially of official misconduct, necessarily would carry with it the admission of the authority of the censor against which the constitutional barrier was erected. The preliminary freedom, by virtue of the very reason for its existence, does not depend, as this Court has said, on proof of truth. *Patterson v. Colorado, supra.*

Equally unavailing is the insistence that the statute is designed to prevent the circulation of scandal which tends to disturb the public peace and to provoke assaults and the commission of crime. Charges of reprehensible conduct, and in particular of official malfeasance, unquestionably create a public scandal, but the theory of the constitutional guaranty is that even a more serious public evil would be caused by authority to prevent publication.

To prohibit the intent to excite those unfavorable sentiments against those who administer the Government is equivalent to a prohibition of the actual excitement of them, and to prohibit the actual excitement of them is equivalent to a prohibition of discussions having that tendency and effect, which, again, is equivalent to a protection of those who administer the Government, if they should at any time deserve the contempt or hatred of the people, against being exposed to it by free animadversions on their characters and conduct.

There is nothing new in the fact that charges of reprehensible conduct may create resentment and the disposition to resort to violent means of redress, but this well understood tendency did not alter the determination to protect the press against censorship and restraint upon publication. As was said in *New Yorker Staats-Zeitung v. Nolan*, 89 N.J. Eq. 387, 388, 105 Atl. 72:

> If the township may prevent the circulation of a newspaper for no rea-
> son other than that some of its inhabitants may violently disagree with
> it, and resent its circulation by resorting to physical violence, there is
> no limit to what may be prohibited.

The danger of violent reactions becomes greater with effective organiza-
tion of defiant groups resenting exposure, and if this consideration warranted legislative interference with the initial freedom of publication, the constitutional protection would be reduced to a mere form of words.

For these reasons we hold the statute, so far as it authorized the proceed-
ings in this action under clause (b) of section one, to be an infringement of the liberty of the press guaranteed by the Fourteenth Amendment. We should add that this decision rests upon the operation and effect of the statute, without regard to the question of the truth of the charges contained in the particular periodical. The fact that the public officers named in this case, and those associated with the charges of official dereliction, may be deemed to be impecca-
ble cannot affect the conclusion that the statute imposes an unconstitutional restraint upon publication.

Judgment reversed.

POSTSCRIPT

Does the First Amendment Permit the Government to Censure the Media?

At the conclusion of the introduction to this issue, we posed the question of whether you would permit a prior restraint by the government if the publication might somehow compromise public welfare. Approximately 40 years after *Near v. Minnesota* (1931), the Supreme Court was presented with this issue in the famous "Pentagon Papers" case, *New York Times Co. v. United States*, 403 U.S. 713 (1971). *The New York Times* and *The Washington Post* started to publish parts of a secret Defense Department study on U.S. policy in Vietnam. The government sought to enjoin further publication of the study that it conceded contained only historical events. It asserted, however, that further publication would harm its diplomatic efforts and prolong the war.

The issue in this case was whether the government, which was seeking to restrain the newspapers from publishing the classified material, had met its "heavy burden of showing justification for the enforcement of such a [prior] restraint." Each of the justices wrote separate opinions and in a per curiam decision held that the government was not entitled to an injunction to restrain the publication of additional materials.

Justice Hugo L. Black, in a concurring opinion, asserted that "the Executive Branch seems to have forgotten the essential purpose and history of the First Amendment." Stated Justice Black in a now famous passage:

> In the First Amendment, the Founding Fathers gave the free press the protection it must have to fulfill its essential role in our democracy. The press was to serve the governed, not the governors. The Government's power to censor the press was abolished so that the press would remain forever free to censure the Government. The press was protected so that it could bare the secrets of government and inform the people. Only a free and unrestrained press can effectively expose deception in government. And paramount among the responsibilities of a free press is the duty to prevent any part of the government from deceiving the people and sending them off to distant lands to die of foreign fevers and foreign shot and shell. In my view, far from deserving condemnation for their courageous reporting, *The New York Times*, *The Washington Post*, and other newspapers should be commended for serving the purpose that the Founding Fathers say so clearly. In revealing the workings of government that led to the Vietnam War, the newspapers nobly did precisely that which the Founders hoped and trusted they would do.

Chief Justice Warren E. Burger, dissenting, saw the issue differently, however. He observed: "In these cases, the imperative of a free and unfettered press comes into collision with another imperative, the effective functioning of a complex modern government . . . and the effective exercise of certain . . . powers by the Executive."

After reading these excerpts from *New York Times Co. v. United States*, and having considered the arguments for and against prior restraint of publication developed in *Near v. Minnesota*, which position do you feel is the more compelling one? The debate in many important respects focuses on the issue of the proper role of the press in a democratic society. Should the media serve as a watchdog holding the government accountable for its policies and actions, or should its central function be to support governmental policies?

Moreover, the issue of the actual extent of the damage that could have resulted to national security from the publication of the *Pentagon Papers* appears to have been a significant one. Essentially, the documents contained historical information. They did not contain information that would have posed an immediate threat to our military personnel. Under those circumstances, the case may well have had a different outcome. While Justice Black would appear to have endorsed a ban on prior restraints in all circumstances, other members of the Court appeared more willing to consider a restraint if it were shown that disclosure would cause an immediate threat to our nation.

Moreover, according to Professors Sullivan and Gunther, the Supreme Court in *Near v. Minnesota* had expressly considered this contingency. It stated:

> No one would question but that a government might prevent actual obstruction to its recruiting service or the publication of the sailing dates of transports or the number and location of troops.

What appears to emerge from this discussion is an effective rule regarding prior restraint: There is a very heavy presumption against any prior restraint on a publication by the government. As Justice Potter Steward recognized, however, in *New York Times Co. v. United States*, if the government is able to demonstrate that it is highly probable that a disclosure will result in "direct, immediate and irreparable damage" to the national interest, it may satisfy this heavy burden.

The Supreme Court has also extended the principles established in these cases even to situations that implicate a defendant's interest in obtaining an unbiased jury and a fair criminal trial. In *Nebraska Press Ass'n v. Stuart*, 427 U.S. 539 (1976), a trial court had issued a "gag order" prior to a mass murder case. The court order mandated that the defendant's statements and confessions not be published in the media in order to preserve his right to a fair trial. Chief Justice Burger held that the circumstances of this case did not warrant the prior restraint. The Court also noted that possible alternatives to a prior restraint on publication included a change of venue, postponement of the trial, and orders to the attorneys to restrict public statements about the case. Moreover, in a noteworthy concurring opinion, Justice William J. Brennan asserted that a prior restraint on publication is never permissible to support a defendant's right to a fair trial.

Another significant aspect of the Supreme Court's decision in *Near v. Minnesota* is that it was one of the first cases to use the doctrine of *selective incorporation* to apply a provision in the Bill of Rights to the states through the Due Process Clause of the Fourteenth Amendment. You may recall from our earlier discussions that selective incorporation involves applying those rights in the federal Bill of Rights that, to paraphrase Justice Benjamin Cardozo's words, "are implicit in a concept of ordered liberty," and therefore fundamental to state proceedings. It was no accident that cases asserting rights arising under the First Amendment were the earliest ones to be so applied.

After reading the excerpts from the cases discussed in this section, what is your position on the government's use of a prior restraint on publication? Certainly, the question is not an easy one, especially in a case that would truly implicate national security concerns. As you may have concluded by now, these cases can be difficult ones. Fortunately, there are a large number of additional resources to pursue further study in this area, including: Kathleen M. Sullivan and Gerald Gunther, *Constitutional Law* (Foundation Press, 15th ed., 2004); Laurence H. Tribe, *American Constitutional Law* (Foundation Press, 2nd ed., 1988); Alpheus Thomas Mason and Donald Grier Stephenson, Jr., *American Constitutional Law* (Pearson Prentice Hall, 15th ed., 2009; 14th ed., 2005); Bernard Schwartz, *A History of the Supreme Court* (Oxford University Press, 1993); Kermit L. Hall, Paul Finkelman, and James Ely, Jr., *American Legal History: Cases and Materials* (Oxford University Press, 3rd ed., 2005); Kermit L. Hall, *The Oxford Companion to the Supreme Court of the United States* (Oxford University Press, 1992); Walter F. Murphy, James E. Fleming, Sotirios A. Barber, and Stephen Macedo, *American Constitutional Interpretation* (Foundation Press, 3rd ed., 2003); David M. O'Brien, *Constitutional Law and Politics: Struggles for Power and Government Accountability* (W.W. Norton, 6th ed., 2005); Craig R. Ducat, *Constitutional Interpretation* (Wadsworth, 9th ed., 2009); John H. Garvey, T. Alexander Aleinikoff, and Daniel A. Farber, *Modern Constitutional Theory: A Reader* (Thompson West, 5th ed., 2004). See also: Doug Meier, "Changing With the Times: How the Government Must Adapt to Prevent the Publication of Its Secrets," *Review of Litigation*, vol. 28, p. 203 (2008); Note, "Media Incentives and National Security Secrets," *Harvard Law Review*, vol. 122, p. 2228 (2009); Michelle Ward Ghetti, "The Terrorist is a Star!: Regulating Media Coverage of Publicity-Seeking Crimes," *Federal Communications Law Journal*, vol. 60, p. 481 (2008); Arlen Pyenson, "Criminal Manifestos and the Media: Revisiting Son of Sam Laws in Response to the Media's Branding of the Virginia Tech Massacre," *The Cardozo Arts & Entertainment Law Journal*, vol. 26, p. 509 (2008); Heidi Kitrosser, "Classified Information Leaks and Free Speech," *Illinois Law Review*, vol. 2008, p. 881 (2008); Susan H. Duncan, "Pretrial Publicity in High Profile Trials: An Integrated Approach to Protecting the Right to a Fair Trial and the Right to Privacy," *Ohio Northern University Law Review*, vol. 34, p. 755 (2008).

Contributors to This Volume

EDITOR

THOMAS J. HICKEY is the dean of the School of Liberal Arts and Sciences and a professor of government at the State University of New York (SUNY Cobleskill). He received his bachelor's degree from Providence College, M.A. and Ph.D. degrees from Sam Houston State University, and a law degree from the University of Oregon, School of Law. His areas of expertise include criminology and law and he is the author of two books, *Criminal Procedure* (McGraw-Hill, Inc., 2001, 1998) and *Stand: Legal Issues* (Coursewise, 1999) as well as many journal articles. He is a licensed attorney who specializes in the areas of labor law and tort litigation. Professor Hickey may be reached by e-mail at hickeytj@cobleskill.edu.

AUTHORS

AKHIL REED AMAR is the Southmayd Professor of Law at Yale Law School where he teaches constitutional law, criminal procedure, federal jurisdiction, and American legal history. He is a prolific author who has published numerous books and academic articles, including *Processes of Constitutional Decisionmaking: Cases and Materials* (ed., with Paul Breas, Sanford Levinson, and J.M. Balkin).

HUGO L. BLACK was nominated to the Supreme Court by President Franklin D. Roosevelt and confirmed by the Senate by a vote of 63 to 13. Black is widely regarded as one of the most influential Supreme Court justices in the twentieth century.

HARRY A. BLACKMUN was an Associate Justice of the Supreme Court of the United States from 1970 until 1994. He is best known as the author of *Roe v. Wade.*

WILLIAM J. BRENNAN served as an Associate Justice of the Supreme Court from 1956 to 1990. He was known for his outspoken progressive views, including opposition to the death penalty and support for abortion rights. He authored several landmark case opinions, including *Baker v. Carr*, establishing the "one person, one vote" principle, and *New York Times Co. v. Sullivan*, which required "actual malice" in a libel suit against those deemed "public figures."

STEPHEN BREYER is an Associate Justice of the U.S. Supreme Court. He received an A.B. from Stanford University, a B.A. from Magdalen College, Oxford, and an LL.B. from Harvard Law School. He served as a law clerk to Justice Arthur Goldberg of the Supreme Court of the United States during the 1964 term. Prior to being appointed as a judge of the U.S. Court of Appeals for the First Circuit, he was a professor at Harvard Law School. From 1990 to 1994, he served as Chief Judge for the First Circuit Court of Appeals. President Bill Clinton nominated him as an Associate Justice of the Supreme Court in 1994.

HENRY B. BROWN was an associate justice of the Supreme Court of the United States from January 5, 1891 to May 28, 1906. He was the author of the opinion for the Court in *Plessy v. Ferguson*, a decision that upheld the legality of racial segregation in public transportation.

BENJAMIN N. CARDOZO was a well-known American lawyer and associate Supreme Court justice. Cardozo is remembered for his significant influence on the development of American common law in the twentieth century, in addition to his modesty, philosophy, and vivid prose style. Although Cardozo only served on the Supreme Court from 1932 until his death six years later, the majority of his landmark decisions were delivered during his 18-year tenure on the New York Court of Appeals, the highest court of that state.

WILLIAM O. DOUGLAS was a U.S. Supreme Court associate justice. With a term lasting 36 years and 209 days, he is the longest-serving justice in the history of the Supreme Court. On the bench Douglas became known as a strong advocate of First Amendment rights. With fellow Justice Hugo Black, Douglas argued for a "literalist" interpretation of the First Amendment, insisting that the First Amendment's command that "no law" shall restrict freedom of speech should be interpreted literally.

JOHN B. GIBSON served in the state legislature of Pennsylvania from 1810 to 1812. Gibson was named president judge of the newly organized 11th judicial district of the court of common pleas in 1813. He was promoted to Associate Justice of the Pennsylvania Supreme Court in 1816 and served in that capacity until he was appointed chief justice in 1827. Gibson served in that capacity until 1851, and he stayed on the Court for two more years as associate justice until his death in Philadelphia on May 3, 1853. Gibson's range of knowledge was remarkable. He was known as a profound student of Shakespeare. He read French and Italian literature. He knew medicine and the fine arts.

ROBERT H. JACKSON was U.S. attorney general (1940–1941) and an associate justice of the U.S. Supreme Court (1941–1954). He was also the chief U.S. prosecutor at the Nuremberg Trials. He remains the last Supreme Court justice appointed who did not graduate from any law school.

YALE KAMISAR is the Clarence Darrow Distinguished University Professor of Law Emeritus at the University of Michigan School of Law. He is an internationally recognized authority of constitutional law and criminal procedure. A graduate of New York University and Columbia Law School, he has written extensively on criminal law, the administration of criminal justice, and the "politics of crime."

ANTHONY M. KENNEDY is an associate justice of the U.S. Supreme Court. He received his LL.B. from Harvard Law School in 1961 and worked for law firms in San Francisco and Sacramento, California, until he was nominated by President Gerald Ford to the U.S. Court of Appeals for the Ninth Circuit in 1975. He was nominated by President Ronald Reagan to the Supreme Court in 1988.

JOHN MARSHALL was chief justice of the U.S. Supreme Court, serving from January 31, 1801, until his death in 1835. He served in the U.S. House of Representatives from March 4, 1799, to June 7, 1800, and was Secretary of State under President John Adams from June 6, 1800, to March 4, 1801. Marshall was from the Commonwealth of Virginia and a leader of the Federalist Party.

EDWIN MEESE III is an attorney, law professor, and author who served in official capacities within the Ronald Reagan Gubernatorial Administration (1967–1974), the Reagan Presidential Transition Team (1980), and the Reagan White House (1981–1985), eventually rising to hold the position of the 75th Attorney General of the United States (1985–1988). He currently holds fellowships and chairmanships with several public policy councils and think tanks, including the Constitution Project and the Heritage Foundation.

SANDRA D. O'CONNOR was an associate justice of the U.S. Supreme Court. She worked in various legal capacities both in the United States and in Germany until she was appointed to the Arizona State Senate in 1969. She served as a state senator for four years and served in the Arizona judiciary for six years before she was nominated to the Supreme Court by President Ronald Reagan in 1981.

WILLIAM H. REHNQUIST (1924–2005) became the 16th chief justice of the U.S. Supreme Court in 1986. He engaged in a general practice of law with primary emphasis on civil litigation for 16 years before being appointed Assistant Attorney General, Office of Legal Counsel, by President Richard Nixon in 1969. He was nominated by Nixon to the Supreme Court in 1972.

ANTONIN E. SCALIA is an associate justice of the U.S. Supreme Court. He taught law at the University of Virginia, the American Enterprise Institute, Georgetown University, and the University of Chicago before being nominated to the U.S. Court of Appeals by President Ronald Reagan in 1982. He served in that capacity until he was nominated by Reagan to the Supreme Court in 1986.

JOHN PAUL STEVENS is an associate justice of the U.S. Supreme Court. He worked in law firms in Chicago, Illinois, for 20 years before being nominated by President Richard Nixon to the U.S. Court of Appeals in 1970. He served in that capacity until he was nominated to the Supreme Court by President Gerald Ford in 1975.

CLARENCE THOMAS is an associate justice of the U.S. Supreme Court. A former judge on the U.S. Court of Appeals for the District of Columbia, he was nominated by President George Bush to the Supreme Court in 1991. He received his J.D. from the Yale University School of Law in 1974.

FRED M. VINSON served the United States in all three branches of government and was the most prominent member of the Vinson political family. In the legislative branch, he was an elected member of the U.S. House of Representatives from Louisa, Kentucky, for 12 years. In the executive branch, he was the Secretary of Treasury under President Harry S. Truman and in the judicial branch, he was the 13th chief justice of the United States, appointed by President Truman.

EARL WARREN was the 14th chief justice of the United States and the only person elected governor of California three times. Before holding these positions, Warren served as a district attorney for Alameda County, California, and attorney general of California. He is best known for the sweeping liberal decisions of the Warren Court, which ended school segregation and transformed many areas of American law, especially regarding the rights of the accused, ending school prayer, and requiring "one-man-one vote" rules of apportionment. He made the Court a power center on a more even base with Congress and the presidency especially through four landmark decisions: *Brown v. Board of Education* (1954), *Gideon v. Wainwright* (1963), *Reynolds v. Sims* (1964), and *Miranda v. Arizona* (1966).